CRIMINOLOGY

A BOOK OF READINGS

THE DRYDEN PRESS · NEW YORK

PREFACE

THE CHIEF AIM of the present volume is to provide students in criminology courses with a book of readings which give them at first hand the original research contributions of criminologists responsible for creating or expanding the knowledge in the field. The book is so designed that it can be used as either a basic textbook or for required outside reading in conjunction with another text.

Topically and organizationally this book follows closely the most widely used basic textbooks. The authors included are those repeatedly cited in the texts; here, however, they speak for themselves instead of through another's interpretation or synopsis. The book lends itself, therefore, to use as a basic textbook by those instructors who prefer sending their students to original materials and who, through lectures and classroom discussion, elaborate and integrate the reading materials.

On the other hand, where the use of a basic textbook is deemed desirable, this volume obviates the necessity for compiling lists of assignments for outside readings and simplifies the students' task of fulfilling these assignments—especially where library facilities are limited or course enrollments very large. For the convenience of both instructor and student, suggestions are given on pp. vii-xiv correlating the selections in this volume with the chapters in a number of popular textbooks. These are suggested correlations only; the instructor may wish to follow a pattern of reading assignments of his own making.

The criteria used in choosing materials may be of interest. Primarily, we have sought for authoritativeness coupled with readability. From the vast literature of original research or observation by competent scientists and scholars or by persons connected with a penal institution or agency, we have attempted to choose materials clearly relevant both to the various approaches to the study of crime and to the topics usually covered in textbooks of criminology. We have kept fragmentary excerpts to a minimum and chosen, instead, complete articles that stand by themselves as independent pieces of research or study.

No book of readings, of course, can possibly include contributions by every recognized authority in the field. In order to achieve our objectives within the practical limitations of space, it was necessary, moreover, to omit from some of the selections passages of subordinate importance, footnotes, and tabular matter. Extreme care was taken to indicate such deletions and to avoid any distortion of the original thesis of the author.

Although they are of little more than historical significance at present, we have included the theories of some of the outstanding pioneers in criminology—Lombroso, Ferri, Tarde, and Bonger. These investigators are, of course, outmoded in most respects, and yet they represent a significant period in the development of criminological thought and in the struggle of criminologists to achieve an understanding of the nature of crime and the criminal. With these, we believe, the student should become acquainted—preferably by reading their own words instead of hearing at second or even third hand about their theories.

In a few sections of the book, good popular accounts by journalists or "lay criminologists" have been included for the insight they afford into a specific problem—insight of a kind that many a strictly scientific article fails to provide.

The editors are deeply grateful to all the authors and publishers who have granted permission to reproduce their materials. Needless to say, the strength of the book is due to the work of the various authors; its weaknesses must be shouldered by the editors alone.

University of Florida   Clyde B. Vedder
Brooklyn College   Samuel Koenig
Pennsylvania State College   Robert E. Clark
February 16, 1953

SUGGESTED READING ASSIGNMENTS

Edwin H. Sutherland: PRINCIPLES OF CRIMINOLOGY
(Lippincott, 4th ed., 1947)

Textbook Chapter	Reading Assignment
1	33
2	3, 11-13
3	5, 14, 15, 48
4	1, 2, 4, 8-10, 16
5	6, 18, 25, 26, 28, 52
6	17
7	7, 20-22, 24, 37-40
8	31, 32
9	27, 29, 30
10	23, 36, 51, 53
11	19, 49, 50
12	34, 35
13	41-47
14	55, 56, 60
15	72
16	57-59, 61
17	54
18	62-64, 67
20	74-77
22	65, 68-71, 73
25	81
26	78-80, 82
27	66
29	83-86

John Lewis Gillin: CRIMINOLOGY AND PENOLOGY
(Appleton-Century, 3d ed., 1945)

Textbook Chapter	Reading Assignment
1	3, 5, 11, 12
2	14, 15
3	1, 8, 27, 29-31
6	16
8	7, 20-22, 24, 51
10	19, 41-48
11	6, 18, 23, 32, 36, 53
12	10, 26, 28, 34, 35, 37-40, 49, 50, 52
13	9, 62, 63
14	17
15	2, 4, 25, 33
16	55, 56, 60
17	13, 57-59, 61
18	54
19	74-77
20	64, 65, 67
21	66
26	70
27	68, 69, 71
28	73
29	72
33	78-80, 82
34	81
35	83-86

Walter C. Reckless: THE CRIME PROBLEM
(Appleton-Century-Crofts, 1950)

Textbook Chapter	Reading Assignment
1	3, 5, 9, 11, 12, 14, 15, 25, 49
2	1, 2, 4, 6, 8, 10, 13, 19-22, 24, 26, 50, 63
3	7, 16, 17, 23, 31, 32
4	27, 30
5	18, 33
6	73
7	44-47
8	48
9	51-54
10	34-36
11	37, 38
12	39, 40
13	41-43
15	55-62, 64, 66, 67
16	72
17	74-77
19	65, 68-71
20	78-82
21	83-86

Donald R. Taft: CRIMINOLOGY: A CULTURAL
INTERPRETATION
(*Macmillan*, 1950)

Textbook Chapter	Reading Assignment
1	5, 9
2	14, 15
3	1, 2, 4, 16-18
4	8, 10, 25
5	7, 20-22, 24, 51
6	31
7	32
8	19
9	23, 36
10	27, 29, 30
11	6
12	41-47
15	26, 28, 33, 48-50
16	37-40
17	34, 35
18	62
19	64, 66, 73, 84-86
20	3, 11-13
21	55, 56
22	22
23	57-61, 63
25	70
28	83
30	65, 68, 69, 71
31	78-82
33	54
34	74-77
37	53
38	52
39	67

H. E. Barnes and N. K. Teeters: NEW HORIZONS IN
CRIMINOLOGY
(Prentice-Hall, 2nd ed., 1951)

Textbook Chapter	Reading Assignment
1	5, 33, 41-50
2	3, 12, 14, 15
3	34, 35, 37-40
4	1, 2, 10, 25
5	27, 29-31
6	16-17
7	32
8	19
9	4, 6, 18, 26, 28, 52
10	23, 36, 53
11	7, 13, 20-22, 24, 51, 61
12	55, 56, 60
13	57-59, 63, 67
15	54
16	64
17	66
19	62
22	8, 65, 68-71, 73
23	72
36	74-77
37	78-82
39	9
40	83-86

Ruth Shonle Cavan: CRIMINOLOGY
(Crowell, 1948)

Textbook Chapter	Reading Assignment
1	2-5, 12, 25, 28
2	14, 15
3	6, 26, 29, 30
4	23, 36, 51, 53
5	52
6	41-47
7	10, 48-50
8	34, 37-40
9	13, 20, 21, 24, 35
10	27
11	7, 9, 31, 32
12	1, 16-19, 33
13	83-86
14	54, 67
15	55, 56, 60
16	11, 57-59, 61-63
17	66, 72
18	74, 70
19	8, 65, 68, 69, 71, 73
20	74-77
21	78-82

Mabel A. Elliott: CRIME IN MODERN SOCIETY
(Harper, 1952)

Textbook Chapter	Reading Assignment
1	1
2	3, 8, 11, 12
3	14, 15, 48, 49
4	5, 29, 30, 67
5	16, 36, 37, 50
6	41-45, 47
7	10, 37-40
9	34
10	6, 9, 18, 26-28, 33
11	31, 32
12	7, 17, 20-22, 24, 51
13	4, 19, 23, 52, 53
14	2, 13, 25, 61-63
15	64, 66, 68, 69, 71, 73
16	65
17	46, 55, 56, 60
18	72
19	54, 57, 59
21	74-77
23	70
27	78-82
29	83-86

Hans von Hentig: CRIME: CAUSES AND CONDITIONS
(*McGraw-Hill, 1947*)

Textbook Chapter	Reading Assignment
1	1, 2, 4
2	2
3	3, 5, 6
5	9, 10
6	14
7	8
8	6
9	8
10	8, 14
11	7, 8, 14
12	8, 12, 13
14	21

CONTENTS

PART ONE

Criminology, Crime, and the Criminal

PART TWO

Factors in Criminality

VIII · Social and Cultural Factors in Crime

PART THREE

Types of Criminality

IX · Sex Delinquency

XIV · Juvenile Delinquency

PART FOUR

Treatment of the Criminal

XV · The Police

XVI · Legal Procedure and the Courts

XVII · Punishment

XVIII · The Prison and Its Inmates

XIX · Probation

XX · Parole

XXI · Crime Prevention

Part One

CRIMINOLOGY, CRIME, AND

THE CRIMINAL

CHAPTER ONE

What Is Criminology?

Part One

CRIMINOLOGY · CRIME AND

THE CRIMINAL

1 · The Emergence of Criminology

by J. P. SHALLOO

Like other disciplines, criminology has gone through periods during which it was studied largely by speculation and by spurious methods of observation and investigation. The scientific study of crime and the criminal is of comparatively recent origin. In the following article, J. P. Shalloo, professor of sociology, of the University of Pennsylvania, summarizes the past and present theories of crime causation. ["Trends in Criminological Research," by J. P. Shalloo, *Federal Probation*, Vol. VI, Oct.-Dec. 1942, pp. 21-24. Reprinted by permission. Footnotes omitted.]

RESEARCH INTO the causes of crime is comparatively recent. Attempts to discover causes or *the* cause of criminal conduct by means of scientific procedures are less than a century old. The theoretical explanations of the Middle Ages stemming from and ending in theological, metaphysical, and philosophic speculations about the nature of the will and its relation to sin probably set back our understanding of human conduct at least 500 years as the doctrine of moral defect overwhelmed scholars of the sixteenth, seventeenth, and eighteenth centuries. The insistence of moral philosophers, even of the nineteenth century, that crime was directly traceable to perversity of the individual practically prevented the scientific or objective examination of the reasons for criminal conduct until the world-shaking impact of Darwinian biology, with its emphasis upon the long history of man and the importance of heredity for a clear understanding of man's biological constitution and its relation to his behavior.

The doctrine of evolutionary biology, the scientific discoveries of man's greatest century—the seventeenth—the work of Lyell in geology, the gradual crumbling of self-willed behavior as theology and philosophy were undermined by the new orientation of determinism, and the wider knowledge of the physical, political, economic, social, and ethnographic universe threw doubt upon the finality of the pronouncements of the earlier writers and the acute generalizations of speculative philosophy. By the end of the eighteenth century the intellectual history of the Western World revealed for the most part an untiring effort to retain and defend the dogmas and doctrines of the past. Reformers who were not in the least motivated beyond superficial legal change in the direction of what they regarded as greater freedom, particularly for the rising *bourgeoisie*, never seriously disturbed the common belief that man's destiny was in the hand of God and man's conduct was wholly and exclusively determined by his free moral agency. No one need be a felon. Only the morally defective were criminals. Those who became criminals freely chose the path of evil and freely chose the risks of punishment, and, even as implied in contemporary penal codes, freely chose the penalty for their voluntary disregard for the law of man which was also the law of God.

BIOLOGICAL AND ENVIRONMENTAL THEORIES OF CRIME

Sin was the preoccupation of even the best minds of the eighteenth and early nineteenth century when causes were assigned for man's antisocial conduct; although the terminology differed from the earlier medieval explanations, the fundamental conclusions remained the same. The criminal was a bad man. Why he found it impossible to conform to the moral and legal norms had already been determined. Constant repetition of theological definitions became tested truth. This general reliance upon an extraterrestrial philosophy of conduct received its most devastating blow from the Italian criminologist, Cesare Lombroso, in a pamphlet wherein he pointed out that it was more than probable that the biological constitution of the criminal had more control over his behavior than inherited sin which informed his nature because Adam and Eve had bequeathed him their defects. Since the criminal is so constituted biologically as to make crime his normal condition, all schemes of punishment were not only unjust but futile. The only procedure to be followed was to study the individual himself.

Lombroso's outstanding contribution to criminological research reaches monumental stature, not because his born criminal provided the answer to crime causation, but because he recognized the utter inadequacy of methods in vogue to discover the causes of criminal conduct. In every age of recorded history the dominant intellectual interests of man have determined to a large degree the methods which he will employ to seek answers to why we behave as human beings; and the criminal is a human being, but unfortunately for him, only more so. It may be noted briefly that there had been other physiologists and phrenologists who preceded Lombroso and anticipated and contributed to his general findings, but for our purposes they are only of archeological interest.

A counter trend soon developed to challenge Lombroso's sweeping explanation with emphasis upon the environment. Criminals are not born, criminals are made. Biology does not produce criminals. They are an inevitable result of social conditions such as poverty, alcohol, lack of moral guidance, unemployment, and all the other complex factors of a highly dynamic social development which result in frustration, maladjustment, and revolt. To this were added the psychosocial motivations inhering in imitation, competition, invention, and definitional relativity. Thus the biological, in its cruder aspects, recedes only to reappear at the turn of the century in the doctrine of the feeble-minded criminal. The social factors became more and more sociopsychological until the explanation of delinquency depended on mental conflict and was later explained by the concept of culture conflict.

MENTALITY AND CRIME

The intensive studies of dysgenic families and their unlovely progeny gave emphasis to feeble-mindedness as a cause for crime that is still with us, albeit we are now more precise and quantitative as we speak of the psychometrically deficient. The intelligence inventory of 1917 gave sound reasons for the most criminal nation on earth but in a few years the psychologists finally studied the prisoners and learned that they had been wrong. While low mentality may have been or may be important in a given case, it is unimportant statistically. And so the Jukes, Kallikaks, and the mentally subnormal joined the growing ranks of discarded theories to take their places beside the demons of Augustine, the humors of the Middle Ages, and the free will of the speculative philosophers.

MENTAL CONFLICT AND CRIME

In the meantime the doctrine of mental conflict made its bid as the final answer in a long series of guesses. Research was coming of age. Human behavior depended no longer on biological determinants, nor upon kind of mentality, but rather upon mental content and how this content was organized and integrated in relation to life situations faced by the individuals. Crime at last could be defined as an escape from an intolerable situation wherein the human mind resolved the conflict by attempting to maintain its equilibrium and achieving such balance through criminal conduct.

CRIME IN RELATION TO THE PERSON'S
DEFINITION OF THE SITUATION

At this time there were added to the repertory of causation concepts the invaluable methodological ideas of attitudes and values, and the definition of the situation. Not only could criminal behavior be given a valid scientific explanation but so could any type of human conduct. Thus an attitude, or tendency to act or react, involved a value or object which was acted upon or reacted to. For example, honesty is a value and one's reaction to it will be determined by his attitude toward it, which in turn will be determined by his life conditioning. His solution to this problem may be conformity, criminal conduct, or even insanity; but whatever the final product of the interaction of the attitude and value, it becomes that person's definition of the situation. This, methodologically, merged behaviorism with social psychology and probably threw more theoretical light upon the basic patterns of conduct causation than any other theory yet formulated. In varying forms and terminology this theoretical explanation of human motivation is still the dominant theme among American sociologists.

CRIME AS EMANATING FROM EMOTIONAL
INSECURITY AND INADEQUACY

In line with this general theory of human conduct and probably strongly influenced by it is the current analysis of delinquency in terms of emotional distress or discomfort. The person aware of emotional insecurity or inadequacy in his relation to other persons, notably members of the family, seeks emotional satisfaction and security in the mental hygiene he finds in delinquency. Thus the attitudes of the individual toward or with respect to certain values leave much to be desired, so this much is sought by removing the inadequacy by an emotionally satisfying definition of the situation; in other words, by the substitute behavior—delinquency.

POINT OF VIEW OF PSYCHOANALYSIS

In this country during the past 20 years we have witnessed a proliferation of specialized fields, each intent upon pursuing the will-o'-the-wisp which constantly beckons its workers onward by revealing its label intermittently. Thus we have the immense vogue of this century's greatest innovation, and in many respects its most challenging point of view— psychoanalysis. The 1920's found an increasing number of investigators striving to find the roots of human motivations in a whole host of terms and concepts whose illumination clearly revealed nothing more clarifying than the entelechy of Aristotle or the dialectic of Hegel as scholars struggled with the influence of the unconscious upon human conduct. Nevertheless, psychoanalysis, maturing under the patient manipulation of the psychiatrists at the present time, is of immense diagnostic value in seeking out and finding the basic motivations of both criminal and noncriminal conduct. Formal psychiatry which concerned itself primarily with the mentally unhinged further proliferated into orthopsychiatry, which attempts to understand the forces which shape and determine all conduct, while psychoanalysis, together with these two types of psychiatry, has gradually inquired into the changing and varihued culture configurations through which and by means of which human personality emerges, bearing its memories of things past and its distortions of things present.

Child guidance clinics, less than 30 years old in this country, have applied the methods and philosophy of the mental-conflict school and by means of play analysis, psychodramatic techniques, and psychodiagnostic methods such as developed by Rorschach, have made commendable contributions to the understanding of behavior problems in children, who, if everything went according to schedule, would undoubtedly one day increase the volume of criminal statistics. The integration of the findings of the sociologist with the psychiatrists into a general sociopsychiatric approach is one of the more hopeful trends at the present time in the baffling quest for human motivations.

CULTURE CONFLICT AND CRIME

Quite recently, growing partly out of the work of the human ecologists, there has been a growing emphasis upon culture conflict. The handiest guinea pigs for these research workers have been the children of the foreign-born in this country. At this time it is too early to state definitely how valuable their discoveries will be, but as far as their methodology is concerned I feel quite sure that culture conflict is not even central to the problem of delinquency among the children of the foreign-born.

Although of honorable age at the time of its birth in this country, the ecological school of delinquency has provided many suggestions which may have theoretical value for the student of crime causation. While it is entirely possible to dismiss the whole field as essentially descriptive, it is also possible that the implications of the ecologists may be well worth understanding and developing. The best example to date of this type of research remains Volume II of the *Wickersham Report on the Causes of Crime*, published in 1931. The fundamental doctrine of the ecologist appears to be that in the unplanned evolution of the city certain types of areas emerge, each with its identifying characteristics. Among these areas is the so-called delinquency area, which is an interstitial zone or zone in transition. The peculiar sociological characteristic of the delinquency area is its basic disorganization. Working on the hypothesis that disorganized areas attract disorganized personalities, or have a disorganizing effect upon personality, we arrive at the thesis that delinquency has a higher numerical frequency in zones which lack stability in terms of acceptable legal and moral norms. In other words, there is a selective factor which tends to draw unstable, disorganized persons into unstable, disorganized areas, where social control is ineffective. This process tends to identify certain regions as criminal and the regions tend to stabilize at the criminal level.

There can be no doubt that neighborhood characteristics are important for understanding the high delinquency rates of slum areas, but whether there is a causal relationship between these characteristics and delinquency remains as uncertain and vague as does culture conflict as a causal motivation for delinquency among the children of the foreign-born. Too many undiscovered and undiscoverable variables leave the methodology of the ecologist open to serious question from the standpoint of its scientific adequacy. Nonetheless, their researches have a dramatic and effective appeal, particularly for those interested in social reform.

Merely for the record, it should be noted that recently an attempt to revive the biological thesis that crime is a result of degeneration, deterioration, or biological inferiority was presented exhaustively to the American criminologists, only to call forth jeers and cries of despair that with so many people in need of funds so much money should have been wasted to produce nothing more than a dreadful bang of failure and arrant nonsense.

GLANDULAR DYSFUNCTION AND CRIME

With respect to concrete results not much more can be said of the neo-Lombrosians who thought they had discovered the causation alkahest in glandular dysfunction. That endocrinology may eventually prove one of the most useful fields of research into conduct disorders. cannot be doubted. At the present time, however, such data as are available for understanding crime causation are vague and none too well founded. Nevertheless, hormone research, which at present is being carried on, offers remarkable possibilities for understanding personality changes and concomitant conduct difficulties.

What has thus far been written must be viewed as groundwork for what is at the present time regarded as the most effective method for analyzing the basic factors which produce criminal conduct. No single answer is possible. Personality is too highly complex a product of too many unknown variables whose presence or absence cannot always be detected even by the shrewdest research mind. Only cooperative study yielding tentative conclusions can furnish us with clues and insights which may suggest the next step. Man—and criminals are men—is a physiological, neurological, endocrinological, intellectual, emotional, and sentient animal upon whom many influences play, varying in intensity from revery to bereavement, with meanings peculiar to each individual. Since this is all too true, the complete examination of all phases of personality organization, origin, development, and present manifestations and characteristics must be the concern of many specialized disciplines. The real problem is not how we may understand the separate aspects of personality and their adaptive problems, but rather how we may take the findings of the specialists, give due and proper weight to their suggestions, and finally integrate the suggestions and findings of all the specialists, so that eventually we behold the total picture devoid of shadows of bias. I think we are moving in that direction.

The life-history method, which must include the medical history of the person, has been one of the more frequently employed techniques in attempts to discover factor relationships in the apperceptive background of the criminal. The emergence of depth psychology, with emphasis upon the cultural milieu, is a good example of what I have suggested as to the necessity for co-operation and collaboration among and between students trained and skilled in recognizing clues and insights which suggest next steps. We see a partial application of this procedure in contemporary clinical studies of behavior problems.

CONCEPT OF DIFFERENTIAL ASSOCIATION

The most recent theory of crime causation, which, incidentally, is also a theory of behavior, has been advanced under the general concept of differential association. Precisely what specific role such all-embracing theoretical explanations will play in the maturing synthetic theory of crime causation, I am unable to say. But this much is true, the general trend in criminological research is toward, and has been, an eclectic theory—a processual analysis, if you will—which is the only sound approach to a defiant puzzle like crime causation.

2 · Criminology as a Field in American Sociology

by MARSHALL B. CLINARD

The systematic study of crime and the criminal has engaged scholars and scientists in a number of fields and in many lands, notably England, France, Italy, and Germany. In Europe, students of the problem have been drawn primarily from among jurists, psychologists, and physicians. In the United States, on the other hand, criminology has been developing chiefly as a sociological field of investigation, occupying mainly the attention of sociologists, and is taught in colleges and universities in departments of sociology. Crime and the criminal are studied at present to a much greater extent in colleges in this country than in any other. Marshall B. Clinard, a University of Wisconsin professor of sociology who specializes in the field of criminology and social disorganization, presents here an account of the nature of American criminology and its contribution to an understanding of the phenomenon of crime. ["Sociologists and American Criminology," *Journal of Criminal Law and Criminology*, Vol. 41, Jan.-Feb. 1951, pp. 549-577. Abridgement of pp. 549-560. Reprinted by permission. Footnotes omitted.]

THE CONTROL of any social problem begins with an awareness of it. The next step is to collect facts about crime, and to discover those processe which have an etiological relationship to criminal behavior. It is fortu nate that in the United States, where the incidence of crime is one o the highest in the world, there has been an awareness of the seriousnes of the problem, as well as the development of a substantial body o theory and empirical scientific data in the field of criminology withir the past twenty-five years. Other countries with less crime, but, on the other hand, little awareness or scientific research, are in a position where they not only cannot adopt measures of control but also probably are not able to check an increase in crime.

Translations of the works of such European pioneers in criminology as Lombroso, Ferri, Garofalo, and Tarde, the publication of *The Indi vidual Delinquent* (1915) by William Healy, Thomas and Znaniecki': monumental volume *The Polish Peasant in Europe and America* (1918-21), and the development in the 1920's of urban sociologica studies in Chicago by students of Robert E. Park and Ernest W. Bur gess served as the chief stimuli in the development of American socio logical interest in criminology. The early writings of Henderson and the first comprehensive American textbooks in this field by Parmelee, 1918, Sutherland, 1924, and Gillin in 1926 aided this development. Today practically all American universities have a sociology department, and criminology is a standard course attracting large numbers of students. All widely used textbooks in criminology today were written by sociolo gists, including those by Sutherland, Taft, Reckless, Gillin, Barnes and Teeters, Cavan, Wood, Morris, Haynes, Cantor and Von Hentig. Soci ologists have also written textbooks in the field of juvenile delinquency, such as Reckless and Smith (1932) and two recent books by Neumeyer and Tappan. The sociology departments of many universities offer grad uate work leading to teaching and research in criminology. The most extensive training is now offered by Chicago, Wisconsin, Ohio State, Pennsylvania, Minnesota, Illinois, Michigan, Indiana, Maryland, and New York University, the largest number of these universities being located in the Middle West.

In addition to their teaching function, many sociologists are doing research in criminology and many also serve as consultants to public or private agencies. A recent incomplete census listed thirty-seven crim inological research projects underway by members of the American Sociological Society. While on the whole sociologists have done little clinical work, a research center from which has emanated much research by sociologists under the leadership of Shaw and McKay is an agency of the state of Illinois: the Institute for Juvenile Research in Chicago.

Most sociological publications in criminology appear in the *American Sociological Review*, *American Journal of Sociology*, the *Journal of Criminal Law and Criminology* and *Federal Probation*.

Since the bulk of the literature in American criminology is by sociologists it goes without saying that American criminology and sociology have developed together. As sociology has become more systematic so has criminology, and new research methods have been developed in criminology which have been later applied to other fields of sociology. The eclectic approach which formerly tended to characterize sociology in general and criminology in particular, combining constitutional, psychological, economic, and sociological factors into one great confusing "hodge podge," is giving way gradually to a more rigorous interest in a specific social psychological approach to human behavior, criminal and non-criminal alike. Such disagreements as exist among writers in the field of criminology are but reflections of the confusion in sociological theory and research. Many American sociologists interested in criminology, for example, still have not sufficiently recognized the implications for criminology of many findings about social processes and personality development in general. An adequate research program in criminology inevitably will reflect developments in general sociology and social psychology.

CRIME EXPLAINED PRIMARILY BY GROUP FACTORS

The work of American sociologists reveals a number of points of emerging emphasis both in theory and research methods although by no means complete agreement. Most sociologists believe that there is a preponderance of evidence to indicate that crime is a product of definitions of situations acquired in life experience. They are generally skeptical of individualistic explanations of criminal behavior in terms of constitutional and abnormal personality patterns. Rather, the origin of crime must be sought in definitions which are present in the culture in the form of competing value systems or culture conflict. These competing value systems arise out of disorganization in social institutions and community situations.

Burgess pointed out, some twenty-five years ago in a significant paper on "The Study of the Delinquent as a Person," that the group, rather than the individual, is the source of deviant behavior. Sociologists have continued this emphasis on the group and culture in their studies of criminal behavior. They are increasingly interested in the conflicting values present in our culture, in the extent of a criminal's membership in social groups with deviant values, the role the person plays in such deviant groups, his conception of himself arising out of such group participation, the conduct norms in the neighborhood from which he comes, the extent of his mobility and association with other deviant norms, his attitude toward law and society, and his degree of criminal association. In explaining deviant behavior the sociologist feels it is necessary to study the associates of the deviant, his family, neighborhood agencies, the school, the effect of law enforcement agencies such as the police and prisons, and various other social institutions, as well as secondary influences including motion pictures, the radio, newspapers, and "comic books."

Some European social scientists, notably Kinberg, have tended to regard this American emphasis on culture conflict as unique to our culture, being related notably to a more recent cultural development, immigration of diverse peoples, and extensive mobility. Factors explaining crime, however, should apply to all societies, and the findings of American sociologists in this regard cannot be assumed to be unique but rather part of the general social process. It is likely that the extensive criminality and some of the extreme social conditions in the American social scene make it possible to see some of these processes more clearly than in older and more stable cultures. The fact that they may have not been found in other cultures may be purely a matter of not looking for them.

According to the view of most sociologists, participation in deviant norms, particularly through the tutelage of others, is the basic situation out of which most crimes and delinquency arise. Supporting evidence may be found in numerous studies of ordinary delinquents, petty thieves, the highly organized profession of professional theft, organized crime, and crime among business men. Studies which have indicated that the origin of crime can be looked for chiefly in participation in group norms include Thrasher's *The Gang* (1927), a study of 1313 boys' gangs in Chicago, the various volumes by Shaw and McKay such as the study of the group factors in *Delinquency Areas* (1929), *The Jack-Roller* (1930), *The Natural History of a Delinquent Career* (1931), *Social Factors in Juvenile Delinquency* (1931), *Brothers in Crime* (1938), and *Juvenile Delinquency and Urban Areas* (1942). More recently Sutherland's *The Professional Thief* (1937) and *White Collar Crime* (1949) have shown how crime must primarily be looked for in participation in deviant group norms. Shaw and McKay have presented evidence from studies of thousands of delinquents, that delinquency is a product of social and cultural forces and represents a reaction of the individual in the social group. Their studies have indicated that certain areas of the city are characterized by uniform attitudes of "stimulation and excitement in delinquency situations, security in the gang, opposition to authority, contempt for the traitor, recognition and prestige through delinquency, hero-worship, stigma of petty stealing, and control of the gang over behavior of its members." One study by Shaw and McKay has shown that over 85 percent of boys arrested in Chicago had companions and that of the remainder it may be assumed that most of them did on the first offense. If thefts alone are considered, 93.1 percent of the boys had at least one companion.

Professional theft, such as pickpocketing, has been likened to any other profession. One not only enters the profession through tutelage on the part of others but maintains membership through group acceptance. The essential characteristics of professional theft, as of any other profession, are technical skill, status, consensus, differential association, and organization, all of which are acquired by association. Crime among business men, professional men, and politicians (white collar crime), has been suggested by Sutherland and Clinard to be a product of subcultural definitions of behavior acquired from associates, much of this diffusion of illegal practices being organized activity.

This approach to crime has not only been supported by a considerable, although still insufficient, number of studies of criminals and delinquents, but other support has come from the field of social psychology and comparative cultures. It is clear that since a criminal is a human being and criminal behavior is human behavior, the fundamental processes of personality development explaining non-criminal behavior also must explain criminal behavior. From an abstract point of view human behavior may be thought of as consisting of (1) sociogenic traits (attitudes) derived from the definitions of situations furnished by the culture or subcultures to which a person belongs, and (2) psychogenic traits or general reaction patterns which are often referred to as basic personality traits. From present evidence both sociogenic and psychogenic traits are acquired through association with others. Attitudes toward law and property are examples of sociogenic traits, while feelings of emotional security or insecurity, in gradations, of course, or feelings of adequacy or inadequacy, might be examples of psychogenic traits. If there is criminal or non-criminal behavior it must be explained in terms of not one aspect but both attitudes and personality traits. Criminals and delinquents, like all human beings, started life without attitudes and in the same fashion as non-delinquents and non-criminals, the meanings of the world and the definitions of situations being acquired through association. Criminals and delinquents are persons who not only have turned away from the conventional conduct norms of society but have established their own. Attitudes toward property, the law, sexual conduct, or the rights of others are socially defined. Not only is a delinquent or criminal philosophy, with all its rationalizations, learned, but the techniques of committing a crime likewise are learned, as for example knowledge of how to "wire" and dispose of a car to a "fence," or to commit acts of vandalism. In fact, one learns not only criminal and delinquent attitudes but one learns to be a psychiatrist or sociologist, a business man, or a mechanic by association with others. To explain why a person is not criminal we must look chiefly to the lack of those associations that caused the criminality in another person.

Other evidence for the sociological view comes from studies of various societies, folk, provincial, rural and urban, which have indicated that criminality on the whole varies not according to the biological structure or personality patterns of the people but according to the presence of what might be termed characteristics of urbanization. These characteristics appear primarily to be culture conflict, individualism, mobility, impersonal relationships, and materialism. The migration of peoples or the acquisition of an urbanized pattern by a society, without migration, appears to increase crime. While we need much more evidence on this score, many American criminologists to some degree use this frame of reference in their analysis and recognize that since types of cultures may produce greatly different behavior it is likely that subcultures could produce deviant behavior within a culture. Clinard in an analysis of farm, village, and urban criminal offenders has shown that offenders from these areas vary in the degree of urban characteristics. Wood has pointed out that minority group criminality, as well as the crime rates of small communities, are related to cultural integration, and Angell has tried to show that variations in the crime rates of large American cities are closely tied to the degree of social integration.

DISAGREEMENTS AS TO IMPORTANCE OF
PERSONALITY PATTERN

There is general agreement among American sociologists about the primary importance in criminality of acquired attitudes derived from social experience. There is disagreement, however, as to the extent and nature of this emphasis, particularly as to whether the personality pattern (psychogenic traits) should also enter into the explanation. Sutherland is an advocate of the extreme position that "differential association" alone appears to be the explanation of criminal behavior, although there is some question as to whether he would apply his frame of reference to personal crimes as well. Earlier he had even limited such an explanation to "systematic" criminal careers of property offenders. According to him, crime is learned behavior, both in techniques, motives, drives, rationalizations, and attitudes growing out of intimate personal associations with a series of pushes towards and pulls away from criminal norms. The variable of why one person participates in crime cannot be attributed to constitutional or personality factors but rather to the frequency, duration, priority, and intensity of such criminal association as opposed to non-criminal. On the surface this process resembles the theory of Tarde, but there are great differences and Sutherland, of course, does not make the mistake of attributing it to imitation.

*   *   *

This theory, in which the details are still largely untested, is based on the learning process operating within the framework of an organized society which has, by processes of urbanization and the presence of conflicting conduct norms, reached a stage of partial disorganization great enough to permit the existence of groups maintaining anti-legal motives and attitudes. In his theoretical analysis of criminal behavior, Sutherland has stated that the life history of the criminal, his interaction with the public, and with other criminals reveals the processes seen in all social life. These processes include maturation, segregation, conflict, and the competitive development of techniques of crime and protection against crime. Fashions in crimes, organization, and professionalization are other important processes in social interaction among criminals.

A broader and less specific approach to criminal behavior has been adopted by Taft who has attributed it to certain characteristics of American culture. In a sense this explanation is closely associated with those who feel that social problems in general, and crime in particular, are an outgrowth of processes of urbanization. According to Taft, the many conflicts in our society, its excessive competition, and exploitation are basic factors in our high crime rate. While Taft acknowledges that his explanation is based chiefly on the United States and there is need for an analysis of the relation of culture to crime in European countries, he feels that crime grows out of a materialistically minded society with its constant striving for prestige and wealth. Taft recognizes, moreover, that biological and psychological factors must be taken into account because they contribute to an analysis of any situation.

Some sociologists, notably Reckless, Sellin, Clinard, and Cavan have felt that the culture conflict theory by itself is inadequate and that the differential response patterns of individuals must also be taken into account. None of them, however, would discount the primary importance of culture conflict in the explanation of crime. Sellin believes that we should not only study deviant norms but also the incorporation of these norms in the personalities of members of the group. Criminological research must isolate the personality elements which differentiate the conformist from the non-conformist and seek to define types of personality based on these elements.

*   *   *

Reckless has suggested that criminologists concentrate on the study of categoric risks and discover what class of individuals are most likely to engage in crime, become arrested, or admitted to institutions. From a computation of the categoric risks of being involved in judicial action one can devise hypotheses to explain why sex, age, occupation, nativity, race, and other factors operate as they do. In fact, he would go so far as to limit the efforts of sociologists primarily to "actuarial sociology" or efforts to compute these actual differential risks rather than seeking any universal propositions about crime based on cultural variables alone.

Clinard has pointed out that a theory of "differential association" as stated by Sutherland entirely neglects the psychogenic trait component of personality and, in attributing all crime to a mathematical ratio of exposure to criminal norms, makes it often difficult to explain why some engage in crime while others do not. An explanation of all crime in terms of calculating a balance of pushes and pulls in the life history of a given criminal offender appears extremely difficult. In some, but not all, cases the differential response of certain psychogenic traits and identification with deviant norms must also be considered. Cavan feels that one type of criminal consists of mentally abnormal personalities and that explanations of crime should include this group.

SOME RESEARCH FINDINGS

Research by sociologists has been instrumental in pointing out fallacies in a number of contentions about crime; they also have made analyses of the research findings of others and pointed out flaws in reasoning. Sutherland and Zeleny have shown by a shrewd analysis of various reports on the general feeblemindedness of criminals that this belief is not substantiated by the evidence. Claims by the physical anthropologist Hooton that crime is correlated with certain biological types and a more recent claim by Sheldon that delinquency is similarly correlated have been shown by a number of sociologists to represent fallacious reasoning, unrepresentative sampling, and errors in interpreting statistical findings. Efforts of some sociologists to show a significant correlation between the economic cycle and crime have not resulted in any definite conclusion that such a correlation exists. In fact, studies of criminality among the upper socio-economic groups have also helped to eliminate the idea that crime is a product of poverty. A few studies have indicated that broken families not only cannot be regarded as a direct cause of crime and delinquency but that the incidence of such situations among deviants may not be much higher than among non-deviants. Studies of neighborhood influences have also made sociologists extremely skeptical of the family as the chief source of patterns of delinquency and crime. Moreover, there is at present no knowledge of how many non-delinquents come from families with poor moral backgrounds.

Companions have been found to be definitely correlated with crime in the "causation of initial delinquency, continuation in a criminal career, and association in the delinquent act or on the criminal job." Studies by Clemmer, Shaw and McKay, as well as the autobiographies of many criminals, have indicated that most so-called "correctional institutions" as now constituted, furnish not rehabilitation but actual training in criminal techniques and can thus be regarded as a further cause of crime. Community disorganization has been shown to be an important factor in the cause of crime. Von Hentig has indicated that the role the victim plays should be considered in the causal explanation of any crime.

In presenting some of these conclusions it is not implied that they are final or that much more research does not still need to be done to gain further insights. What is particularly needed is more precise knowledge of the differential effect of criminal norms on individuals as well as comparisons with control groups of non-criminals. Some areas of research have hardly been touched. One of these is the area of secondary influences such as the effect of motion pictures, radio and television, newspapers, "comic books," and such "agencies of moral risk" as taverns, poolrooms, and cheap dance halls. Considering the seriousness of the problem of crime and delinquency, the amount of largely scientifically unsupported discussion of the relation of secondary controls and the large financial investment in such media as the motion pictures and the radio, it is surprising that there is not more valid evidence of the relationship today. Extensive legislation has been passed against taverns and so-called "comic books" with, to date, no rigorous scientific study of their influence on delinquency and crime.

*　　*　　*

RELATION OF SOCIOLOGICAL AND
PSYCHIATRIC APPROACHES

Some psychologists and psychiatrists object strongly to the culture conflict theory on the grounds that some psychogenic factors, such as emotional insecurity, must account in all cases for participation in deviant norms. Part of this difficulty will undoubtedly be overcome as sociology and psychiatry recognize that they represent mutual and not conflicting approaches to human behavior as is indicated by the recent development of the field of social psychiatry. Psychiatrists are recognizing the importance of group factors and culture, while sociologists are admitting that some crimes involve psychogenic factors. Part of the misunderstanding arises from a rather loose use of the term "crime" rather than types of crime. Sociologists have, for the most part, studied only property offenses which in America constitute over 94 percent of all felonies, while psychiatrists have been chiefly concerned with personal crimes or rather abnormal property offenders. As Dunham and Lindesmith have pointed out, sociologists have consequently found that sociogenic traits (attitude-values) are the most important factors and that these are derived chiefly from group and cultural factors, while psychiatrists studying chiefly personal crimes have found crime to be more individualistic and related to psychogenic traits. Each discipline has often used their studies to generalize about all crime. It is possible, of course, that the explanation of personal crimes may turn out on closer study to have group and cultural factors involved and be more the concern of sociologists than is indicated at present.

Most sociologists are familiar with a large part of the research on crime done by psychiatrists. Their objections to the extreme psychiatric emphasis on the emotional structure of the offender and other psychogenic traits, including the term "psychopathic personality," are as follows. (1) Such patterns, with few exceptions, appear to be largely meaningless without interaction with the culture or sub-culture. (2) Many of the studies which have attempted to establish a universal relation between personality deviation and crime have failed to raise the question of association with deviant norms or failed to eliminate it as the chief variable involved in the explanation. (3) Many who advocate this explanation have failed to reconcile their position with reports of the widespread evidence of such unprecise concepts as "emotional immaturity," "inadequate personality," and "insecurity feelings" among the so-called non-criminal and non-delinquent population. Even to indicate a higher percentage does not answer the problem because one must still explain the presence of the trait structure among the non-deviant. (4)

Many delinquents and criminals are not found to be neurotic. (5) Judicial experience and imprisonment may have affected the individual's emotional stability even though not present before. Two sociologists, Schuessler and Cressey, recently examined some 113 previous studies which tested the personality traits of delinquents and criminals as compared with groups of non-delinquents and non-criminals. They conclude that while 42 percent of the studies showed differences in favor of the non-criminals the rest were indeterminate. "The doubtful validity of many of the obtained differences as well as the lack of consistency in the combined results makes it impossible to conclude from these data that criminality and personality elements are associated."

CHAPTER TWO

The Phenomenon of Crime

3 · The Concept of Crime

by ALBERT MORRIS

It is society that determines what is right and what is wrong and what particular act constitutes a crime. Since societies themselves differ in their conception of what is right and wrong, and since, in the course of time, any given society changes its values and attitudes, it follows that "crime" is relative to society as well as to time. What is considered as a crime in one society may not be so considered in another, and what is looked upon or defined in a specific society as a crime today may not have been regarded as such yesterday and *vice versa*. The seriousness with which any criminal act is regarded will also vary with the society and, in any given society, with the time. Finally, since change, particularly of a technological nature, necessitates the imposition of new regulations by a society upon its members, it opens up new, heretofore nonexisting, possibilities for violating those regulations—hence of new forms of crime.

Thus, acts—including criminal acts—virtually impossible of commission yesterday become possible today. Stealing an automobile—to take an obvious example—requires the existence of an automobile. In the article that follows, Professor Albert Morris, of Boston University, a sociologist specializing in the field of criminology, writes of the changes in the concepts of crime relative to time and society, tracing particularly the changes that have occurred in the Western world. ["Changing Concepts of Crime," *Encyclopedia of Crime*, V. C. Branham and S. B. Kutash, Eds., The Philosophical Library, 1949, pp. 47-55. Reprinted by permission.]

"CRIME" IS a broad term of variable and often uncritical usage. Its definition may be approached at several semantic levels.

All societies recognize and distinguish between behavior believed to be harmful to the group and behavior believed to be beneficial and respond emotionally with blame or approval proportioned to the assumed importance of the behavior. The acceptance and evaluation of any particular behavior as harmful is dependent upon the total organization and culture of the group.

The line between crimes, defined as public wrongs, and other wrong doing cannot be sharply drawn. Probably no harmful act, whether directed towards another individual as a tort, or towards a deity as a sin, or towards the individual himself as a vice, is without some unfortunate effect upon the group as a whole. Conversely, whatever harms the group inevitably harms each individual member of it. In principle, crimes are acts that are considered by those in authority to be sufficiently inimical to the general welfare as to warrant official interdiction and punishment.

In small, homogeneous, culturally isolated societies where a common store of knowledge and belief and similar problems of survival support generally accepted customs, crimes may be defined by consensus. In populous and complex societies, in which the social consequences of behavior are more difficult to assess and the state of public opinion more difficult to determine, and where political authority is delegated to or assumed by a socially remote minority, the definition of crime may not in the same measure reflect the protective emotional response and the moral disapproval of the total group.

The law of custom, strong in more stable and simple societies, has inherently a measure of flexibility that permits its modification to deal with the unique circumstances of each individual case. Statutory law, made necessary by the rapidity of social change and the need for predictability under conditions where custom has not matured, is inherently rigid and may offend the public sense of justice in particular cases. Furthermore, it is not self-defining. There is therefore need and pressure to define the statutory criminal law to conform to strong currents of public opinion, and the tendency of the courts to so define the law permits the interpretation to reflect the conscious or unconscious bias of the interpreter.

This being so, the authority which defines and punishes crime may reflect only the judgment of a segment of the population (a majority in a democracy, a handful in a dictatorship), as to what behavior is socially harmful. Harmful might, under some circumstances, mean contrary economic or political views, or it might even include any behavior in opposition to the interest of those in power however publicly beneficial. From the standpoint of the lawbreaker, then, his crime could appear as socially desirable conduct while official behavior might appear to him morally wrong if not technically criminal.

The common denominator of crime is recognition by those in political authority that an act is of such a nature and is sufficiently dangerous to the solidarity of the group as to warrant interdiction and punishment. Whether an act will seem to threaten group survival will depend upon the cultural-evaluative frame of reference within which it has its setting.

There is probably no type of specific act which has not under certain circumstances been given official approval. Deliberate killing is not always murder; sexual intercourse by force and without the victim's consent is not always rape; the taking of another's property without his consent is not always theft; as witness the legally justifiable killing of a condemned criminal by an executioner, the exposure of Australian aboriginal women to sexual attack for violation of the sexual code, or the seizure of an allegedly immoral book by a customs officer.

The assumed mental state of the actor and his alleged purpose may therefore be quite as essential as the act itself in the determination of whether in any specific circumstance an act is a crime. Modern criminal law generally recognizes that a guilty mind intending to commit an act that is criminal is essential to conviction. However, since under the criminal law legally responsible adults are held to the standard of a "reasonable" man, it is quite possible for the individual to have a legal criminal intent while being entirely clean of conscience. In primitive societies, however, the element of intent as a factor in crime may be entirely absent.

Necessarily, therefore, the acts that have at some time been recognized as crimes are numerous and varied, and the content of the criminal code in the form of specific acts tends to change roughly in proportion to the rapidity and extent of cultural change in general, although with something of a lag.

Many of the simpler and more primitive societies handled theft, rape, arson, murder and other secular offenses, not as crimes, but as private wrongs to be settled by the direct action of families or clans rather than by tribal authority. Crime was more nearly synonymous with sin and consisted of acts considered offensive to the spirit world and dangerous to the entire group because they invited punishment by supernatural powers. In Ashanti the historian who made an error in the ceremonial recitation of the titles of the great ancestral spirits would have been executed. In Polynesia the violation of a tabu might be punished by the community if not directly by the gods. Among Eskimos the eating of seal and caribou at the same meal is an offense to the supernatural and is regarded as a crime. Among the Ifugao one who breaks the tabu on asking the relative of a dead man if he is dead would be fined.

In the Western world the centralization of authority in the kingship was accompanied by the extension of the king's protection beyond the limits of his immediate household to the entire kingdom. As a result, many acts that had been private wrongs became violations of the king's peace to be dealt with by the state as crimes.

The persisting idea of divinity associated with the kingship and the existence of theocratic states continued to give to violations of the king's peace the connotation of an affront to the supernatural and hence of something more than a breach of public order. As a consequence of the dominance of a theological interpretation of the universe and the limitations of scientific knowledge, witchcraft, sorcery, sacrilege, heresy and blasphemy were serious crimes frequently punishable by death. In England the offense of witchcraft, punishable by death, was not repealed until 1736. Blasphemy is still forbidden both at common law and by statutes in many states of the United States and in several foreign countries.

In England, and in Pennsylvania, New York, Connecticut, Delaware and Massachusetts, Christianity has been judicially declared to be part of the law of the land. The crime of perjury involves the wilful giving under oath of false testimony material to the issue at hand. The common requirement that testimony be given under oath has been defined as "a religious act by which the party invokes God not only to witness the truth and sincerity of his promise but also to avenge his imposture or violated faith, or, in other words, to punish his perjury if he be guilty of it." (Bouvier.)

Since the Renaissance, the extension and secularization of knowledge and belief about man and the universe, and the attendant development of technology, have necessarily affected the social consequences and the related evaluation of behavior. The relations of men to one another were altered and new political, economic, and social organizations and interests required support and protection. The spread of rationalistic philosophy was accompanied by a decline in the scope and prosecution of religious offenses.

The decline of a feudal caste system led to a limitation of the crime of treason. The English Statute of Treasons in 1351 defined petit treason as the killing of a master by his servant, of a husband by his wife, or of a prelate by a priest owing him obedience. In 1828 these acts were made simple murders and the crime of petit treason vanished. High treason, of which there were seven forms in 1351, has been much restricted, and in the United States includes only two acts: levying war against them, or adhering to their enemies giving them aid and comfort.

The rise of towns and cities brought new problems of sanitation, housing and transportation. Mumford notes that "in France the stage-coach introduced in the seventeenth century killed more people annually than the railroad that followed." Official notice was taken of the increased dangers of pestilence and riot. Laws with reference to the disposal of refuse, the keeping of livestock, the quarantine of strangers, and the use of streets, and the construction of buildings reflected these public dangers.

The displacement of populations attendant upon the breakdown of the feudal system left multitudes of people in poverty and resulted in hordes of wandering vagrants and beggars. With feudalism had gone a measure of responsibility of the lords for their serfs, but no well-established system of social responsibilities accompanied the rise of the newly rich, and the gap between wealth and power on the one hand and poverty and weakness on the other was great.

In 1552 a group of prominent London citizens besought the Privy Council to help them control the troublesome poor and the multitudes of petty thieves, gypsies, beggars and vagabonds. The countries of the continent faced a similar problem. Paris, alone, in the late seventeenth century had in the neighborhood of 50,000 beggars.

The great social gap between the powerful privileged few and the common man encouraged petty crime and general maladjustment among the dispossessed and politically helpless masses. Crime, as an expression of mass misery, consisted predominantly of behavior disturbing to those in authority. Houses of correction during the sixteenth to the eighteenth centuries were filled with unlicensed beggars and peddlers, lazy and disobedient children, refractory apprentices, and idle, frivolous and insolent men, while thousands of petty thieves and vagabonds were exiled or executed. In England during the reign of Henry VIII alone some 72,000 offenders were executed.

It is during periods of rapid social change that the gap between the legal and the popular conception of crime is apt to be greatest. Since the law finds its ultimate support in public attitudes, these exert a pressure leading to the definition of new crimes or the redefinition of old ones where new public interests are inadequately protected, and to the modification by direct or indirect means of old laws that seem, under new conditions, to work with undue severity.

The great changes in finance, industry and transportation that accompanied the development of foreign colonies and the invention and utilization of power machinery profoundly affected the structure of Western society and created extensive new interests to be protected, and so new crimes. As Jerome Hall demonstrates (*Theft, Law and Society*), the law of theft is largely a development of the eighteenth century and an accompaniment of the rise of the factory system, mass production, distant bulk shipments, more complex business organizations, and new impersonal trade relations.

The establishment of the Bank of England in 1694 followed slowly by the organization of provincial banks led to the embezzlement acts of 1742, 1751, 1763 and 1799, which first recognized and defined embezzlement in the modern sense. Public disturbances over losses suffered through investment in joint stock companies led to a demand for protection against misrepresentation. The Anglo-Saxon concept of property, as consisting of movable goods, sufficient when cattle were the chief objects of larceny, became inadequate with the possibility of appropriating such items as electricity, gas, news, trademarks, patents, copyrights, or the use of labor and machinery. In some instances the courts have extended the concept of property to include gas and electricity as subject to larceny. By statutes the wilful infringement of trademarks, patents, and copyrights has been made a criminal offense. A systematic revision of the criminal law with reference to the subject matter of larceny under modern conditions has not yet, however, been brought to fruition.

That the concepts of crime and punishment reflect the nature of the societal structure is seen in the former practice of excusing ecclesiastics from liability under the secular law, permitting even murder with no more serious penalty than thumb branding until 1547. The so-called benefit of clergy was extended in 1350, by statute and judicial interpretation to all who could read, and in 1706 to everyone, regardless of literacy. What had formerly been a class privilege, extended in varying degrees to the clergy, peers and peeresses and male commoners (women commoners having no benefit of clergy), was made available to the masses. However, an accompaniment of this democratization of procedure was an increase in the number of offenses excluded from benefit of clergy so that, in spite of it, during the sixteenth and seventeenth centuries England experienced its greatest severity of punishment.

The four-fold increase in the volume of criminal laws attendant upon the industrial changes of the eighteenth century was not based upon any careful analysis and classification of offenses and their social sources and effects but was simply a patch-work extension of the law to cover new types of behavior. The lack of discrimination in the law which assessed capital punishment alike for poaching, simple theft, and a wide range of petty offenses, as well as for murder and other crimes of violence, was contrary to the evolving public sense of fitness.

As the humanitarian movement of the eighteenth century developed, it affected the practices of the courts, which, in the absence of adequate legislative revisions, brought the practice of the law more nearly into line with public sentiment by evasive judicial technicalities and by jury findings that in thousands of cases obviously avoided the facts by what Blackstone called "a kind of pious perjury" in order to avoid capital punishment for offenses committed without violence. Modifications in the severity of punishment more formally introduced into the criminal law by nineteenth century legislation represented primarily a more precise formulation of what the courts had long been accomplishing by administrative practice.

The transformation of modern Western society is a consequence of an intricate interplay of many factors among which the successful application of science to the understanding of the physical world and the resulting changes in technology are merely the most concrete and obvious. The tremendous increase in population during the nineteenth century, the rise of vast urban agglomerations, the economic interdependency of individuals, the decline in family size and authority, the mobility of population, the factory system and mass production for distant markets, and the emphasis on money and credit, are aspects of the great social changes associated with the final displacement of the landed aristocracy by the capitalistic bourgeoisie.

The need and opportunities for large concentrations of capital, and for the sharing of risks, favored corporate organization for business purposes and led to increasing concentration of economic, and related political, power in the managers of capitalistic enterprises. The development of effective mass communication and control of the media of communication by those possessing the necessary wealth helped them to build an ideology favorable to the principles and practices associated with wealth getting. The resulting emphasis upon secular and sensate values, supported in part by the ethos of Protestantism and, in turn, permeating even the church itself, has given rise to a new hedonistic morality.

The increased variety and impersonality of human interrelations in an aggressive competitive society is associated with selfishness and a minimum degree of social morality. The effects of conduct are diffused and concealed. Impersonality in business relations tends to acceptance of the letter of agreements, rather than the spirit. The power of organization is often used to achieve desired ends with little regard for the general welfare. Associations whose activities are socially acceptable seek to obtain privileges from the state which they may, in some instances, rival in power.

Wage earners reacted to the weakness of their economic bargaining position in the new industrial society by attempts at organization also, and these have become increasingly successful under the pressure of industry-created wants. The democratization of education, the pooling of financial resources, and the utilization of effective techniques for exploiting the economic power of the strike and the political power of the vote have contributed to that success.

Inevitably in a society undergoing profound technical, organizational and ideological changes, moral codes established under simpler and more stable conditions are inadequate as guides to conduct. The difficulty of assessing the social consequences of much of contemporary behavior contributes to a lack of moral consensus and to a weakening of social controls over behavior.

Many traditional crimes such as unorganized murder, rape, robbery, burglary, arson, and larceny, in its more direct and obvious forms, are clearly disapproved. Organized crime, however, while not new, as witness the early and continued group activities of bandits, brigands, pirates and smugglers, or the organizational activities of such men as the notorious eighteenth century Jonathan Wild, has developed a new dimension through the application of modern organizational techniques to criminal enterprises.

Modern rapid bulk transportation facilitates the wholesale theft of furs, silks, cigarettes, liquor and other merchandise from warehouses, freight cars and trucks in amounts of many millions of dollars annually. As early as the International Congress on the Prevention and Repression of Crime held at London in 1872, Edwin C. Hill read a paper on "Criminal Capitalists," which, though limited in conception, indicated the growing significance of crime as an organized business requiring the cooperation of real estate owners, investors and manufacturers of the implements used by criminals and other "honest" people.

The mobility and concentration of urban populations under conditions of relative anonymity and freedom from social control are favorable to a ready market for opportunities for gambling, prostitution and the consumption of alcoholic beverages. Lack of agreement as to the social consequences and the morality of this demand is reflected in the sporadic prohibition or legalization of gambling, prostitution and the sale of alcoholic liquor or the frequent non-enforcement of criminal laws forbidding these activities. The demand for illegal services in connection with vice is not limited to criminals by vocation but comes from the general population and is extensive enough to require and to support major organizations which rely upon corruption of law enforcement authorities, and upon public ignorance and apathy, for the continuance of operations not subject to concealment.

*　　*　　*

The maturing of sociology brought an increasing measure of objectivity to the analysis of the contemporary social structure that has been reflected in a new valuation of the relative consequences and importance of specific patterns of behavior upon the social welfare. The economic depression of the 1930's dramatized in concrete fashion the effects of a socially inadequate economic philosophy. The attendant revelations of criminal behavior among those engaged in occupations, in themselves legitimate, made almost inevitable the crystallization of such concepts as that of "upperworld crime," suggested by Morris (*Criminology*, 1934), and of "white-collar crime," suggested by Sutherland (*American Sociological Review*, February, 1940), to refer to criminal behavior among respected, socially accepted and trusted members of society. These terms helped to bring into focus a grist of earlier and later writings which gave evidence of extensive violations of the criminal law by those whose social authority and position has largely protected them from exposure, prosecution, or conviction.

*　　*　　*

The concept of upperworld crime, as applied either to the more or less frequent or habitual violations of the criminal codes of a nation or to violations of an embryonic international criminal code, has seemingly not been well assimilated by the public. In part, this may be due to the fact that many upperworld crimes, usually non-violent and non-frightening, are but elaborations of offenses of which, at a petty level, probably all adults are occasionally guilty. The inclusion of them in the criminal code, to cope with the more extreme instances of injurious behavior, may represent a public ideal rather than a workable standard.

The psycho-somatic-sociological approach to the study of man, as distinct from the pre-scientific or theological, tends to view the interacting factors in human behavior, including the role of the individual organism, in an impersonal and non-moralistic manner. This does not preclude recognition of the fact that the personality is, itself, a vital factor in interaction. It does, however, tend to minimize concern with the guilt or moral responsibility of the individual and to emphasize, instead, the personal and social consequences of behavior evaluated in the light of what seem to be currently accepted or desirable human values. The objective of treatment would then be social protection and the social readjustment of the offender, rather than punishment.

This tendency may lead towards a reduction in the use of the generalized, omnibus, changing, concept "crime" as unserviceable for the purpose of scientific research and to a concern with the more precise analysis and definition of the nature and social consequences of specific types of socially injurious behavior.

4 · The Sociological Approach to the Study of Crime

by WALTER C. RECKLESS

Criminologists, particularly those in the United States, have, for the most part, been inclined to look for the causes of criminal behavior in the social and cultural environment rather than in the biological or psychological make-up of criminals, although the latter is not excluded as a factor in certain types of criminals and crimes. In the article that follows, Walter C. Reckless, a professor of criminology at Ohio State University and director of a training program in penology at that institution, critically examines the social factors which criminologists have found to play an important role in inducing crime and delinquency. ["The Sociologist Looks at Crime," *The Annals of the American Academy of Political and Social Science*, Vol. 217, Sept. 1941, pp. 76-83. Reprinted by permission. Footnotes omitted.]

IT IS now pretty generally recognized among sociologists that crime and delinquency are violations of a behavior code of a state and are not fundamentally different from violations of behavior codes of other social groups, as for example the church, the school, the family, the lodge, the labor union. Some of the violations of the latter codes overlap the violations of the criminal code and are covered by the criminal code.

VOLUME OF CRIME

The volume of violations of the criminal code is therefore only a small part of the total volume of violations of all behavior codes in a modern, complex society. Only a small part of the violations of the criminal code become officially known, whereas varying proportions of crimes known to the police actually lead to arrest. From arrest on through execution of sentence, there are drastic drop-outs of cases, i.e., great mortality of cases.

Such considerations apply also to the volume of juvenile delinquency. The juvenile delinquent is the misbehaving youth who gets acted upon officially—the one who gets caught. But the volume of known cases is just a small fraction of the total volume of violation of the junior criminal code and a still smaller fraction of the total volume of violations of all behavior codes applying to children.

In both adult crime and juvenile delinquency, there are several extraneous social and administrative considerations, other than the particular nature of the behavior, which determine what violation is going to become known and acted upon officially.

DEFINITIONS OF CRIMES VARY

There is still another salient fact about criminal and delinquent behavior which has gained wide recognition. It is that the definitions of what is criminal and delinquent vary in time and place. Sociologists have discovered that the definition of what is a violation is contained in the behavior codes or conduct norms of a society, which include a recognizable rating of behavior along a scale of approval-disapproval. Behind the specific conduct norms is a set of social values which the society or the dominant elements in it are seeking to perpetuate and to protect. Hence, rape does not fall at the same point of the scale in several different societies, due to the existence of differing sets of social values which give significance and point to behavior.

In view of these prefacing remarks, it is understandable why the sociologist rejects the idea that crimes are natural and universal, and why he is skeptical of claims for the existence of a criminal constitution which is prepotently prepared to violate rules of behavior. It is understandable also why the sociologist looks at criminal behavior pretty much as other kinds of violating behavior, and views criminals and delinquents pretty much as violators of behavior codes who are not caught, and not as a special constitutional order of human creature.

When violation depends upon so many variables in the social matrix and is not dependent primarily upon the nature of the behavior and the nature of the violator, one also realizes that it is difficult to work out the causes of a phenomenon such as crime and delinquency. Nevertheless, valiant efforts have been made to determine the causes. Sociologists, quite naturally, have been principally interested in the environmental influences, and have made about as good progress in etiological studies as have the representatives of other fields; which is not saying much, because progress in isolating causes has been beset with grave difficulties. In some areas of scientific research, the notion of causation has been abandoned.

RECONSIDERATION OF ENVIRONMENT

In the classical age of criminology, criminal sociology was identified with one and all environmental influences on crime. American sociologists soon dropped consideration of the physical and paid attention more strictly to the social aspects of environment. Still later, after analysis of causative factors from case studies came into vogue, the social environment was reduced still farther to those social conditions which could be shown to have a reasonably direct effect on conduct. Later still, when case studies included the person's own story, the environment became not the conditions around the person but rather the particular set of objects and individuals to which he responded.

Just about the time that this individualized conception of environment was dawning, sociologists, psychologists, and other students of behavior problems began emphasizing the importance of the social situation in the determination of behavior. The total situation was conceived to be the person interacting in his life situations. The total situation and the social world of the person became heirs in sociological thinking to the old conception of environment.

Looking at the immediate environment rather than at the larger one led American sociologists to narrow their coverage on causative factors considerably. Certain family, community, and companionship factors received special attention.

FAMILY FACTOR IN DELINQUENCY

Workers in the field have been impressed with the frequency with which delinquents and criminals come from broken homes. But it soon became apparent to critical observers that nondelinquents and noncriminals might come from broken homes quite as frequently as court cases. Shideler estimated, probably without justification, that the proportion of broken homes among correctional school populations is almost twice as high as that among the general population. Slawson found that the proportion of correctional school boys from New York City was over twice as high as the proportion among children in three New York public schools. It has been claimed that this was not a fair comparison. The Gluecks likewise found that the percentage of Massachusetts young adult male and female reformatory cases coming from broken homes was several times higher than an estimated proportion of one out of seven broken homes in the family population of Chicago.

Shaw and McKay, by more scientifically justifiable methods, discovered that the percentage of broken homes among male juvenile court cases in Chicago stood to the percentage of broken homes among the male school population of comparable age and comparable district as 1.18 to 1. They discovered also that there was no tendency for juvenile delinquency rates in local areas to increase as the percentage of broken homes among the school boys increased. It was found, too, that the ratio of broken homes among the delinquents to that of the school population was greatest for the youngest ages and decreased markedly as age increased. Shaw and McKay concluded that it is not so much the formal break in the family as the cumulative discord between family members that operates as a causative factor in delinquent behavior.

More recently, Weeks, using Spokane data, indicated that the broken home factor is connected much more frequently with juvenile delinquency cases charged with ungovernability, running away, and truancy than with cases charged with property offenses, traffic violations, and misdemeanors. The former are offenses in which girls are much more involved than boys, and the latter are offenses in which boys are much more involved than girls. The latter type of offenses are those referred to court mainly by the police, while the former are referred to court principally by sources other than police, such as parents, relatives, neighbors, and school. Hence, the proportion of broken homes among delinquents is acted on selectively by sex, type of offense, and source of referral. Such a discovery signifies that the broken home is more important as a risk factor in referral than a causative factor of behavior problems.

Unsatisfactory member-to-member relationships in the family, including parent-child relationships, have been suspected of having a direct bearing on misconduct and delinquency. The assumption is that the individual falls into delinquent activity as an escape from discomfort and unpleasantness. This is the family tension or family discord factor in behavior. One finds much evidence for the operation of it in individual cases of both delinquents and criminals. Healy and Bronner found that unhappiness and emotional disturbances, resulting from jangled family relationships, were present in 92 per cent of a sample of cases undertaken for treatment. The belief is that family tensions are more prevalent in the family relationships of delinquents than those of nondelinquents, but this point has not been proven.

The presence of demoralizing conditions or demoralized persons in the home has been cited as an important causative factor in the breeding of delinquents and criminals. It is realized that an immoral mother or a drunken father may produce intolerance of vice and alcohol in offspring. But it is also realized that children exposed to lewdness, immorality, criminality, gambling, and drunkenness in the home have a good chance of becoming infected by such social viruses. Studies of delinquent and criminal samples indicate the frequent presence of one or more vicious and criminal persons in the family situation prior to arrest or incarceration of the subjects. One imagines that, if the coverage on the gross moral faults of family members of delinquent and criminal cases was more adequate in investigations, the percentage of inimical home environments would be even greater than is now indicated. But we do not know the extent to which comparable groups of nonoffenders have family members who are lewd, alcoholic, immoral, and criminal, and we cannot tell at present how much more, if at all, we should expect delinquents than nondelinquents to issue from such circumstances.

THE COMPANIONSHIP FACTOR

The role of accomplices and associates in criminal activity has been recognized from time immemorial. In recent years notice has been taken of the occurrence of associated crime and lone-wolf offenses, particularly at the juvenile level. We are justified in saying that companionate crimes among juvenile offenders in American cities should be expected to outweigh the lone-wolf offenses two to one and better. The proportion of companionate crime among boys is expected to be much higher than among girls. It is expected also that the property crimes will show a higher amount of companionate activity than will other crimes.

The sex differential in regard to companionate crime might be explained in terms of greater gregariousness in street play and roving activities among boys than girls—a fact which in turn reflects the influence of custom on activity. The preponderance of companionate delinquency among boys in American cities gives rise to the thought that delinquency might be in large measure group activity and that one is unable to tell where group play ends and delinquency begins. Thrasher discovered that gang life of American city boys veered easily toward delinquency and crime.

When various samples of delinquents have been studied by the case study method, the companionship factor has stood out as important. Even in Healy's pioneer work on the individual delinquent, bad companions were found to have been a causative factor in 34 per cent of the cases. But from such simple enumerations as this, one cannot tell whether bad companions are more characteristic of the associative life of delinquents than of nondelinquents. One might think so, but we do not actually know.

There are indications that delinquents are more active in social participation and more gregarious in play than nondelinquents. Atwood and Shideler found that a small sample of Indiana reformatory boys had a greater degree of group participation than a matched group of nondelinquent boys. The inference is that the delinquents, by having more contacts than nondelinquents, are in a better position to get into trouble and to get caught. The inference is, also, that delinquents are thereby more likely to get exposed to criminal patterns of behavior.

Further evidence along the same line comes from Healy and Bronner's comparison of 105 delinquents with 105 nondelinquent siblings of the same sex and nearest age. Only 16 of the delinquents were fairly solitary in interests, while only 11 of the nondelinquents participated in gang activities. Twenty-three of the nondelinquents avoided companionship as a way of keeping out of trouble, while many of them busied themselves with activities at home which removed them from association on the streets.

Tracing the companionship affiliations in acts of delinquency through the records of five brothers as a starting point, Shaw discovered that there seemed to be carriers of delinquent behavior patterns from one companionship association over to another. The carriers, so to speak, had been infected by the virus of crime in previous delinquency situations and were in turn infecting their associates in current situations. If a boy was exposed to a carrier he usually succumbed, that is, became implicated in delinquency, almost regardless of personality and background factors. Such a conclusion implies either that infection is virile or that the companionship situation weakens resistance, both of which could be true. It also implies that the personality and social background factors prepare the way for the exposure but do not explain the infection.

The jail, reformatory, or prison situation provides the means for contact of the less with the more criminally sophisticated inmates and hence gives the opportunity for passing along criminal ideas, attitudes, and skills. In spite of the development of institutional programs which are aimed in part at the prevention of contamination, the penal institutions are still schools for crime for a large proportion of inmates—how large, no one knows. On the outside, there is the job affiliation of former cell mates or prison mates. It has been observed many times that one of the great stumbling blocks in reformation is the meeting up with ex-convicts. Exposure to criminal sophistication in the institution and association with ex-inmates on release are factors which do not explain initial delinquency, but they do help to explain continuation in crime and the furtherance of a criminal career.

COMMUNITY FACTORS

Community disorganization has been found to be related to several social problems, including crime and delinquency. However, it has been impossible to show that there is a one-to-one connection between personal and social disorganization. Many, perhaps most, individuals in a disorganized community may not be delinquent, whereas some persons, not very many, will be violators even in a well-organized social environment. Reckless has suggested that, while no direct causality between social disorganization and criminal behavior can be established, there is more opportunity to become a violator in a disorganized than in an organized environment.

The same line of argument must be used in the evaluation of the studies which have uncovered the tendency for crime and delinquency to decrease in rate with the distance from the center of the city. Such gradient tendency has been demonstrated for several cities of the United States. It was found to exist for concentric zones in the metropolitan area of Detroit, and even for counties of Kansas arranged on a tier basis according to size of the largest city or town. The reputed greater per capita volume of crime in cities as compared with rural areas is also in line with the general gradient tendency. The point is that there are more opportunities to commit crimes, to get demoralized, to pursue criminal careers, and to get caught in the areas of highest delinquency and crime rates. The gradient indicates spatial risks rather than causality.

The areas of highest crime and delinquency rates in American cities, namely, those around the center, are likewise areas of the greatest amount of disorganization as is indicated by the encroachment of business and industry on former residential neighborhoods, by the physical deterioration of residential property, by the declining population, and by the heavy concentration of other social problems. As we proceed outward from the center, we move more and more away from disorder and more and more toward order in American cities. But this means that we are moving away from greater to fewer opportunities for resident and nonresident individuals to become delinquent and criminal.

Special community institutions or enterprises have been singled out for their delinquency and crime-producing potency, such as saloons, poolrooms, criminal fences, junk yards, cheap dance halls, dens of vice and gambling, and so forth. These agencies of moral risk present opportunities to be exposed to delinquent and criminal patterns of behavior or to pursue a criminal career. Some of them are even the locus for carriers of criminal virus.

As in the case of the companionship or gang infection, these agencies of moral risk do not constitute a great risk for everyone, but they do constitute a risk for those whose personality and background factors have paved the way for individuals to respond to their wares.

The movies, the newspapers, magazines, the radio, and other agencies of mass impression have been suspected of infecting some individuals with criminal virus. In routine clinical case studies of delinquents, this factor has not assumed a position of grave importance. On the other hand, when delinquents are asked to indicate whether or not movies had any direct effect on misconduct, it appears that the movies play a more important role—more so for girls than for boys. It is safe to say that the significant patterns of behavior conveyed by movies, press, or radio must fall on prepared ground, that is, must reach individuals whose behavior resistance is low, in order to be influential, much the same as propaganda needs prepared soil upon which to work most effectively.

OPERATION OF SOCIOLOGICAL FACTORS

One can readily surmise that there is really nothing positive which can be said about the workings of the sociological factors in crime and delinquency. In making this confession, we should hasten to say that this status of affairs applies to the workings of biological and mental factors also. Causation is difficult to work out for behavior which must be socially defined in the first place and acted on officially in the second place.

Nevertheless, it may not be too unwarranted to point out that there seem to be two very important ways in which sociological factors in causation operate to produce delinquent and criminal behavior. The first is that the pressure of an unsatisfactory and discordant set of social relationships often forces some persons—we do not know exactly what sorts as yet—into delinquency as an out, just as they force persons into other behaviors of social escape such as desertion, vagrancy, and drink.

The relation of an unhappy set of human relationships to deviant behavior must be considered in connection with wish blockage and frustration. But we do not know which comes first or which is the more important: unbearable relationships or emotional distress.

The second, and perhaps the more, important relationship of sociological factors to delinquent and criminal behavior applies equally as well in cases where frustration is indicated as in those where it is not indicated. Reference is made to actual inculcation or transmission of delinquent and criminal behavior patterns in the companionship situation, in families with criminal or delinquent members, at agencies of moral risk in the community, and by agencies of mass impression—all of which contain carriers of infectious patterns. Here, again, we do not know just what sorts of persons adopt the available patterns of deviation. The theory of a special trait of suggestibility to account for unresisted takeover is not particularly satisfactory. All we know is that some individuals readily adopt the delinquent and criminal patterns available to them.

SOCIALLY PROCESSED CAREERS

Sometimes the confronting patterns of deviant behavior merely take the form of ordinary delinquency and crime. Other times they take the form of definite criminal skills and attitudes as may be found in professional and organized crime.

The acquisition of criminal patterns of behavior is most clearly shown in the development of individuals with criminal careers, because the acquisition is visibly cumulative and progressive. Habitual and professional offenders are verily socially processed products, although the former may take the low road in crime (the way of the derelict and the bum) and the latter, the high road (the way of the successful operators).

The processing of careers in crime is essentially no different sociologically than the processing which turns out surgeons, ministers, newspaper reporters, longshoremen, professional baseball players, and so on. The prostitute, the safecracker, the bookie, the peddler, each in his own way, has acquired progressively the skills, the attitudes, and the philosophy of life of his peculiar milieu, in spite of differences in personality and background of the individuals in any one career.

If, in the future, students of behavior finally give up the study of causation of crime as too unyielding a job, they can certainly study the behavior patterning or behavior processing which comes off the social assembly line. Sociologists might never be able to tell why a person committed his initial delinquencies, but they may be able to tell how far he has been steeped in crime. And for what purpose, one might ask. Possibly to indicate in advance of treatment an adequate prognosis of the degree of unimprovability.

SUMMARY

The sociologist looking at crime has called attention to four important points: (1) Crime is a violation of the criminal code which is just one type of behavior code, and hence it is unreasonable to expect criminals to be essentially different from violators of other behavior codes. (2) As a form of deviating behavior, crime and delinquency have a rather small liability of being acted upon officially, that is, becoming known and the violator caught. (3) The pressure of unbearable social relationships forces some persons into delinquency as an out for themselves. (4) The impact of confronting delinquent and criminal patterns of behavior may account for much of ordinary delinquency and crime and still more for criminal careers, which are socially processed products.

Society, in setting up the norms for deviating behavior and in developing informal or formal machinery to bring deviations to light, thereby subjects the various categories of people to differential criminal liability, according to their age, sex, class, and spatial position in the social order. Individuals falling within various combinations of these sociological categories are a greater or lesser risk for becoming violators and for getting caught. By their circumscribed social position, they are more or less exposed to unsatisfactory relationships, confronting patterns of delinquency and crime, and to official police action. The chances of a middle-aged widow, living in a fashionable hotel, to commit a crime and to be acted on officially are pretty slim indeed. But the chances of a nineteen-year-old boy, living in an area of high delinquency in American cities, would be very, very much greater.

With better and more adequate reporting of information on the records of offenders acted upon officially, it should be possible to compute the categoric crime risks for any area of consistent and uniform coverage. If causative studies cannot solve the riddle of why people become violators, actuarial methods should at least be able to predict what categories of people are a high or low risk for getting involved in crime.

CHAPTER THREE

The Criminal

5 · Who Is the Criminal?

by PAUL W. TAPPAN

Among the unsettled problems in scientific criminology is
that of defining a "criminal," of distinguishing the criminal
from the noncriminal. The traditional, legal definition that
a criminal is one who violates a law and is adjudicated as
such by the court is thought to be inadequate from the
sociological point of view, which inclines to conceive of the
criminal as one who commits an act believed to be injurious
to society, regardless of whether it is designated by law as a
crime or not. Although this concept suffers from a lack of
precision, it is sociologically more meaningful than the legal
definition. In the following selection, Paul Tappan, a legally
trained and oriented sociologist of New York University,
critically examines the legal and the sociological points of
view. [From the *American Sociological Review*, Vol. 12,
No. 1, pp. 96-102. Reprinted by permission. Footnotes
omitted.]

WHAT IS crime? As a lawyer-sociologist, the writer finds perturbing the
current confusion on this important issue. Important because it delimits
the subject matter of criminological investigation. A criminologist who
strives to aid in formulating the beginnings of a science finds himself

in an increasingly equivocal position. He studies the criminals convicted by the courts and is then confounded by the growing clamor that he is not studying the real criminal at all, but an insignificant proportion of non-representative and stupid unfortunates who happened to have become enmeshed in technical legal difficulties. It has become a fashion to maintain that the convicted population is no proper category for the empirical research of the criminologist. Ergo, the many studies of convicts which have been conducted by the orthodox, now presumably outmoded criminologists, have no real meaning for either descriptive or scientific purposes. Off with the old criminologies, on with the new orientations, the new horizons!

This position reflects in part at least the familiar suspicion and misunderstanding held by the layman sociologist toward the law. To a large extent it reveals the feeling among social scientists that not all antisocial conduct is proscribed by law (which is probably true), that not all conduct violative of the criminal code is truly anti-social, or is not so to any significant extent (which is also undoubtedly true). Among some students the opposition to the traditional definition of crime as law violation arises from their desire to discover and study wrongs which are absolute and eternal rather than mere violations of a statutory and case law system which vary in time and place; this is essentially the old metaphysical search for the law of nature. They consider the dynamic and relativistic nature of law to be a barrier to the growth of a scientific system of hypotheses possessing universal validity.

Recent protestants against the orthodox conceptions of crime and criminal are diverse in their views: They unite only in their denial of the allegedly legalistic and arbitrary doctrine that those convicted under the criminal law are the criminals of our society and in promoting the confusion as to the proper province of criminology. It is enough here to examine briefly a few of the current schisms with a view to the difficulties at which they arrive.

I

A number of criminologists today maintain that mere violation of the criminal law is an artificial criterion of criminality, that categories set up by the law do not meet the demands of scientists because they are of a "fortuitous nature" and do not "arise intrinsically from the nature of the subject matter." The validity of this contention must depend, of course, upon what the nature of the subject matter is. These scholars suggest that, as a part of the general study of human behavior, criminology should concern itself broadly with all anti-social conduct, behavior injurious to society. We take it that anti-social conduct is essentially any sort of behavior which violates some social interest. What are these social interests? Which are weighty enough to merit the concern of the sociologist, to bear the odium of crime? What shall constitute a violation of them?—particularly where, as is so commonly true in our complicated and unintegrated society, these interests are themselves in conflict? Roscoe Pound's suggestive classification of the social interests served by law is valuable in a juristic framework, but it solves no problems for the sociologist who seeks to depart from legal standards in search of all manner of anti-social behavior.

However desirable may be the concept of socially injurious conduct for purposes of general normation or abstract description, it does not define what is injurious. It sets no standard. It does not discriminate cases, but merely invites the subjective value-judgments of the investigator. Until it is structurally embodied with distinct criteria or norms—as is now the case in the legal system—the notion of anti-social conduct is useless for purposes of research, even for the rawest empiricism. The emancipated criminologist reasons himself into a cul-de-sac: having decided that it is footless to study convicted offenders on the ground that this is an artificial category—though its membership is quite precisely ascertainable, he must now conclude that, in his lack of standards to determine anti-sociality, though this may be what he considers a real scientific category, its membership and its characteristics are unascertainable. Failing to define anti-social behavior in any fashion suitable to research, the criminologist may be deluded further into assuming that there is an absoluteness and permanence in this undefined category, lacking in the law. It is unwise for the social scientist ever to forget that all standards of social normation are relative, impermanent, variable. And that they do not, certainly the law does not, arise out of mere fortuity or artifice.

II

In a differing approach certain other criminologists suggest that "conduct norms" rather than either crime or anti-social conduct should be studied. There is an unquestionable need to pursue the investigation of general conduct norms and their violation. It is desirable to segregate the various classes of such norms, to determine relationships between them, to understand similarities and differences between them as to the norms themselves, their sources, methods of imposition of control, and their consequences. The subject matter of this field of social control is in a regrettably primitive state. It will be important to discover the individuals who belong within the several categories of norm violators established and to determine then what motivations operate to promote conformity or breach. So far as it may be determinable, we shall wish to know in what way these motivations may serve to insure conformity to different sets of conduct norms, how they may overlap and reinforce the norms or conflict and weaken the effectiveness of the norms.

We concur in the importance of the study of conduct norms and their violation and, more particularly, if we are to develop a science of human behavior, in the need for careful researches to determine the psychological and environmental variables which are associated etiologically with non-conformity to these norms. However, the importance of the more general subject matter of social control or "ethology" does not mean that the more specific study of the law-violator is non-significant. Indeed, the direction of progress in the field of social control seems to lie largely in the observation and analysis of more specific types of nonconformity to particular, specialized standards. We shall learn more by attempting to determine why some individuals take human life deliberately and with premeditation, why some take property by force and others by trick, than we shall in seeking at the start a universal formula to account for any and all behavior in breach of social interests. This broader knowledge of conduct norms may conceivably develop through induction, in its inevitably very generic terms, from the empirical data derived in the study of particular sorts of violations. Too, our more specific information about the factors which lie behind violations of precisely defined norms will be more useful in the technology of social control. Where legal standards require change to keep step with the changing requirements of a dynamic society, the sociologist may advocate—even as the legal profession does—the necessary statutory modifications, rather than assume that for sociological purposes the conduct he disapproves is already criminal, without legislative, political, or judicial intervention.

III

Another increasingly widespread and seductive movement to revolutionize the concepts of crime and criminal has developed around the currently fashionable dogma of "white collar crime." This is actually a particular school among those who contend that the criminologist should study anti-social behavior rather than the law violation. The dominant contention of the group appears to be that the convict classes are merely our "petty" criminals, the few whose depredations against society have been on a small scale, who have blundered into difficulties with the police and courts through their ignorance and stupidity. The important criminals, those who do irreparable damage with impunity, deftly evade the machinery of justice, either by remaining "technically" within the law or by exercising their intelligence, financial prowess, or political connections in its violation. We seek a definition of the white collar criminal and find an amazing diversity, even among those flowing from the same pen, and observe that characteristically they are loose, doctrinaire, and invective. When Professor Sutherland launched the term, it was applied to those individuals of upper socio-economic class who violate the criminal law, usually by breach of trust, in the ordinary course of their business activities. This original usage accords with legal ideas of crime and points moreover to the significant and difficult problems of enforcement in the areas of business crimes, particularly where those violations are made criminal by recent statutory enactment. From this fruitful beginning the term has spread into vacuity, wide and handsome. We learn that the white collar criminal, may be the suave and deceptive merchant prince or "robber baron," that the existence of such crime may be determined readily "in casual conversation with a representative of an occupation by asking him, 'What crooked practices are found in your occupation?'"

Confusion grows as we learn from another proponent of this concept that, "There are various phases of white-collar criminality that touch the lives of the common man almost daily. The large majority of them are operating within the letter and spirit of the law. . . ." and that "In short, greed, not need, lies at the basis of white-collar crime." Apparently the criminal may be law obedient but greedy; the specific quality of his crimes is far from clear.

Another avenue is taken in Professor Sutherland's more recent definition of crime as a "legal description of an act as socially injurious and legal provision of penalty for the act." Here he has deemed the connotation of his term too narrow if confined to violations of the criminal code; he includes by a slight modification conduct violative of any law, civil or criminal, when it is "socially injurious."

In light of these definitions, the normative issue is pointed. Who should be considered the white collar criminal? Is it the merchant who, out of greed, business acumen, or competitive motivations, breaches a trust with his consumer by "puffing his wares" beyond their merits, by pricing them beyond their value, or by ordinary advertising? Is it he who breaks trust with his employees in order to keep wages down, refusing to permit labor organization or to bargain collectively, and who is found guilty by a labor relations board of an unfair labor practice? May it be the white collar worker who breaches trust with his employers by inefficient performance at work, by sympathetic strike or secondary boycott? Or is it the merchandiser who violates ethics by under-cutting the prices of his fellow merchants? In general these acts do not violate the criminal law. All in some manner breach a trust for motives which a criminologist may (or may not) disapprove for one reason or another. All are within the framework of the norms of ordinary business practice. One seeks in vain for criteria to determine this white collar criminality. It is the conduct of one who wears a white collar and who indulges in occupational behavior to which some particular criminologist takes exception. It may easily be a term of propaganda. For purposes of empirical research or objective description, what is it?

Whether criminology aspires one day to become a science or a repository of reasonably accurate descriptive information, it cannot tolerate a nomenclature of such loose and variable usage. A special hazard exists in the employment of the term, "white collar criminal," in that it invites individual systems of private values to run riot in an area (economic ethics) where gross variation exists among criminologists as well as others. The rebel may enjoy a veritable orgy of delight in damning as criminal most anyone he pleases; one imagines that some experts would thus consign to the criminal classes any successful capitalistic business man; the reactionary or conservative, complacently viewing the occupational practices of the business world might find all in perfect order in this best of all possible worlds. The result may be fine indoctrination or catharsis achieved through blustering broadsides against the "existing system." It is not criminology. It is not social science. The terms "unfair," "infringement," "discrimination," "injury to society," and so on, employed by the white collar criminologists cannot, taken alone, differentiate criminal and non-criminal. Until refined to mean certain specific actions, they are merely epithets.

Vague, omnibus concepts defining crime are a blight upon either a legal system or a system of sociology that strives to be objective. They allow judge, administrator, or—conceivably—sociologist, in an undirected, freely operating discretion, to attribute the status "criminal" to any individual or class which he conceives nefarious. This can accomplish no desirable objective, either politically or sociologically.

Worse than futile, it is courting disaster, political, economic, and social, to promulgate a system of justice in which the individual may be held criminal without having committed a crime, defined with some precision by statute and case law. To describe crime the sociologist, like the lawyer-legislator, must do more than condemn conduct deviation in the abstract. He must avoid definitions predicated simply upon state of mind or social injury and determine what particular types of deviation, in what directions, and to what degree, shall be considered criminal. This is exactly what the criminal code today attempts to do, though imperfectly of course. More slowly and conservatively than many of us would wish: that is in the nature of legal institutions as well. But law has defined with greater clarity and precision the conduct which is criminal than our anti-legalistic criminologists promise to do; it has moreover promoted a stability, a security and dependability of justice through its exactness, its so-called technicalities, and its moderation in inspecting proposals for change.

IV

Having considered the conceptions of an innovating sociology in ascribing the terms "crime" and "criminal," let us state here the juristic view: Only those are criminals who have been adjudicated as such by the courts. Crime is an intentional act in violation of the criminal law (statutory and case law), committed without defense or excuse, and penalized by the state as a felony or misdemeanor. In studying the offender there can be no presumption that arrested, arraigned, indicted, or prosecuted persons are criminals unless they also be held guilty beyond a reasonable doubt of a particular offense. Even less than the unconvicted suspect can those individuals be considered criminal who have violated no law. Only those are criminals who have been selected by a clear substantive and a careful adjective law, such as obtains in our courts. The unconvicted offenders of whom the criminologist may wish to take cognizance are an important but unselected group; it has no specific membership presently ascertainable. Sociologists may strive, as does the legal profession, to perfect measures for more complete and accurate ascertainment of offenders, but it is futile simply to rail against a machinery of justice which is, and to a large extent must inevitably remain, something less than entirely accurate or efficient.

Criminal behavior as here defined fits very nicely into the sociologists' formulations of social control. Here we find *norms* of conduct, comparable to the mores, but considerably more distinct, precise, and detailed, as they are fashioned through statutory and case law. The *agencies* of this control, like the norms themselves, are more formal than is true in other types of control: the law depends for its instrumentation chiefly upon police, prosecutors, judges, juries, and the support of a favorable public opinion. The law has for its *sanctions* the specifically enumerated punitive measures set up by the state for breach, penalties which are additional to any of the sanctions which society exerts informally against the violator of norms which may overlap with laws. *Crime* is itself simply the breach of the legal norm, a violation within this particular category of social control; the criminal is, of course, the individual who has committed such acts of breach.

Much ink has been spilled on the extent of deterrent efficacy of the criminal law in social control. This is a matter which is not subject to demonstration in any exact and measurable fashion, any more than one can conclusively demonstrate the efficiency of a moral norm. Certainly the degree of success in asserting a control, legal or moral, will vary with the particular norm itself, its instrumentation, the subject individuals, the time, the place, and the sanctions. The efficiency of legal control is sometimes confused by the fact that, in the common overlapping of crimes (particularly those *mala in se*) with moral standards, the norms and sanctions of each may operate in mutual support to produce conformity. Moreover, mere breach of norm is no evidence of the general failure of a social control system, but indication rather of the need for control. Thus the occurrence of theft and homicide does not mean that the law is ineffective, for one cannot tell how frequently such acts might occur in the absence of law and penal sanction. Where such acts are avoided, one may not appraise the relative efficacy of law and mores in prevention. When they occur, one cannot apportion blame, either in the individual case or in general, to failures of the legal and moral systems. The individual in society does undoubtedly conduct himself in reference to legal requirements. Living "beyond the law" has a quality independent of being nonconventional, immoral, sinful. Mr. Justice Holmes has shown that the "bad men of the law"—those who become our criminals —are motivated in part by disrespect for the law or, at the least, are inadequately restrained by its taboos.

From introspection and from objective analysis of criminal histories one can not but accept as axiomatic the thesis that the norms of criminal law and its sanctions do exert some measure of effective control over human behavior; that this control is increased by moral, conventional, and traditional norms; and that the effectiveness of control norms is variable. It seems a fair inference from urban investigations that in our contemporary mass society, the legal system is becoming increasingly important in constraining behavior as primary group norms and sanctions deteriorate. Criminal law, crime, and the criminal become more significant subjects of sociological inquiry, therefore, as we strive to describe, understand, and control the uniformities and variability in culture.

We consider that the "white collar criminal," the violator of conduct norms, and the anti-social personality are not criminal in any sense meaningful to the social scientist unless he has violated a criminal statute. We cannot know him as such unless he has been properly convicted. He may be a boor, a sinner, a moral leper, or the devil incarnate, but he does not become a criminal through sociological name-calling unless politically constituted authority says he is. It is footless for the sociologist to confuse issues of definition, normation, etiology, sanction, agency and social effects by saying one thing and meaning another.

V

To conclude, we reiterate and defend the contention that crime, as legally defined, is a sociologically significant province of study. The view that it is not appears to be based upon either of two premises: 1. that offenders convicted under the criminal law are not representative of all criminals and 2. that criminal law violation (and, therefore, the criminal himself) is not significant to the sociologist because it is composed of a set of legal, non-sociological categories irrelevant to the understanding of group behavior and/or social control. Through these contentions to invalidate the traditional and legal frame of reference adopted by the criminologist, several considerations, briefly enumerated below, must be met.

1. Convicted criminals as a sample of law violators:

a. Adjudicated offenders represent the closest possible approximation to those who have in fact violated the law, carefully selected by the sieving of the due process of law; no other province of social control attempts to ascertain the breach of norms with such rigor and precision.

b. It is as futile to contend that this group should not be studied on the grounds that it is incomplete or non-representative as it would be to maintain that psychology should terminate its description, analysis, diagnosis, and treatment of deviants who cannot be completely representative as selected. Convicted persons are nearly all criminals. They offer large and varied samples of all types; their origins, traits, dynamics of development, and treatment influences can be studied profitably for purposes of description, understanding, and control. To be sure, they are not necessarily representative of all offenders; if characteristics observed among them are imputed to law violators generally, it must be with the qualification implied by the selective processes of discovery and adjudication.

c. Convicted criminals are important as a sociological category, furthermore, in that they have been exposed and respond to the influences of court contact, official punitive treatment, and public stigma as convicts.

2. The relevance of violation of the criminal law:

a. The criminal law establishes substantive norms of behavior, standards more clear cut, specific, and detailed than the norms in any other category of social controls.

b. The behavior prohibited has been considered significantly in derogation of group welfare by deliberative and representative assembly, formally constituted for the purpose of establishing such norms; nowhere else in the field of social control is there directed a comparable rational effort to elaborate standards conforming to the predominant needs, desires, and interests of the community.

c. There are legislative and juridical lags which reduce the social value of the legal norms; as an important characteristic of law, such lag does not reduce the relevance of law as a province of sociological inquiry. From a detached sociological view, the significant thing is not the absolute goodness or badness of the norms but the fact that these norms do control behavior. The sociologist is interested in the results of such control, the correlates of violation, and in the lags themselves.

d. Upon breach of these legal (and social) norms, the refractory are treated officially in punitive and/or rehabilitative ways, not for being generally anti-social, immoral, unconventional, or bad, but for violation of the specific legal norms of control.

e. Law becomes the peculiarly important and ultimate pressure toward conformity to minimum standards of conduct deemed essential to group welfare as other systems of norms and mechanics of control deteriorate.

f. Criminals, therefore, are a sociologically distinct group of violators of specific legal norms, subjected to official state treatment. They and the non-criminals respond, though differentially of course, to the standards, threats, and correctional devices established in this system of social control.

g. The norms, their violation, the mechanics of dealing with breaches constitute major provinces of legal sociology. They are basic to the theoretical framework of sociological criminology.

6 · The Criminal Personality

by WALTER COUTU

> Criminologists tend more and more to view the criminal as a product of the environment in which he lives and as a result of his responses to its stimuli. Hence, his behavior is "natural" and "normal" to him. Accordingly, to understand the behavior of the criminal one must understand his social milieu—*i.e.*, his ethnic group, his family, his playmates, his economic situation, and his response to it. In the article that follows, Walter Coutu, a professor of social psychology of the University of Texas, upholds this view and explains why it should be accepted as valid. [From *Federal Probation*, Vol. VI, Oct.-Dec. 1942, pp. 25-30. Reprinted by permission.]

BEFORE we get into this discussion let us be sure we are discussing the same thing. What I mean by *criminal personality* is something very specific. If a man is convicted of one crime he is referred to as a criminal, even though this was his only crime. Other men who have been convicted of several crimes also are called criminals, even though these acts could not be said to be "characteristic" of their behavior. The word personality as used in this paper refers to one's *characteristic pattern* of behavior. The criminal personality, then, is one whose characteristic pattern of behavior is composed of criminal acts. Such people we refer to as the professional, the habitual, the systematic criminal.

I. CRIME AS NORMAL BEHAVIOR

The problem set for this discussion is not to describe the criminal personality, but to account for it. Why is the life pattern of some people's behavior characteristically criminal? Any pattern of behavior that is *characteristic* of a person is *normal* for that person. The thesis here maintained is that *all behavior, criminal or otherwise, is normal for the conditions under which it occurs.* If you ask me why such men commit crime, I may properly ask you why men do anything. They do it for the same reason we do what we do—for the same reason we go to bed, or pay our taxes, or go to church, or stop at a traffic light. They do it because they feel a need to do it.

This is an accurate statement, but it calls for explanation. Why don't we commit crimes? Perhaps I should say, why don't we feel the need to do the sort of things which the courts define as criminal? Why is it that some of us don't feel the need to do such things whereas others do?

Some Important Needs. The sociologist is interested in the needs which men feel because he knows that most of the important needs are *products* of the groups in which these men have lived. Among the important needs arising out of group life in our culture are four: (1) the need to feel secure, both economically and emotionally; (2) the need for personal recognition by our fellows; (3) the need for dependable affectional response from those of our groups for whom we care, from those whose opinions we value; and (4) the need for some new experience now and then—some adventure, excitement, or just plain fun.

Take the first one—the need for security. In all countries of the world, races, age groups, and classes reveal this need in differing degrees. In a highly competitive socio-economic system like ours the need for security is probably the most powerful drive to human behavior. Everyone must compete for the things he wants, the things he has been taught are desirable; we are under a constant nervous strain not only to get them but to keep from losing them once we get them. Throughout this discussion let us use ourselves as one example, and for comparison, a fellow—say Skinny Dugan—born and reared in a slum area of a large city.

Skinny Dugan Finds Security. How do we satisfy our need for security? We do it primarily through our jobs. From the time we learned to talk, the idea "life work" has been drilled into us by members of our families, relatives, friends, teachers. The idea of vocation was developed in us as one of our ambitions. So powerful has this expectancy been in us that if we were denied the opportunity for some significant life work, we would feel unjustly treated. We want to work; and the satisfaction of this need gives us both economic and emotional security.

But from the time Skinny Dugan learned to talk it was impressed upon him, by members of his family, relatives, friends, gang leaders, and big shots, that only "saps" work. Consequently, work will not be involved in the satisfaction of Skinny Dugan's need for security. He will find security, just as we do, by doing what is expected of him by those whose opinions he values. He will get security primarily by fighting and stealing. The more clever and daring he is at stealing and fighting, the more he will have of those things and relationships which his group has led him to believe are desirable.

Skinny Dugan Gets Recognition. All of us need recognition. We need to feel that our lives are significant, in our own eyes as well as in the eyes of those we admire. How do we satisfy this need? We do it primarily through our occupation and social status, that is our position in our group. We have received recognition all our lives from our families, relatives, friends, play groups—in fact, from everyone we hold important —whenever we have done well those things we were expected to do. We were expected to play fair, to be honest, thoughtful, and kind to others, to go to school and to church, to join clubs and organizations, to own property and pay taxes, to marry and to have children. Whenever we did any of these things well, our people praised us, said pleasant things; we were pleased; we received recognition from those who were important to us.

Skinny Dugan gets recognition in exactly the same way, by excelling in those things that are expected of him at the various stages of his growth from child to man. He must learn to fight hard and skillfully, to swear, to steal, to be hard-boiled, to put something over. If he does these things well, people (his people) say nice things about him (nice to him), they praise and envy him, and he feels good inside himself; he is satisfying his need for recognition in the only way he knows how, in the way which is normal for him, for his people, for his situation.

Skinny Dugan Finds Affection. Skinny Dugan needs affectional response; so do we. How do we satisfy this need? When we were children we had affectionate parents whose manners toward each other were friendly. They held us in line, but they were kind. There were birthday and Christmas celebrations; they bought us clothes and playthings and gave us spending money; home was a cozy place, full of the warmth of the more tender human emotions. We had sisters and aunts with good manners, and they liked us. Our teachers were friendly, and even the grocer gave us a cookie now and then. Then there were girls—lovely girls, pretty girls. In a pleasant way, which we liked, older people chided us about girls. People invited us to parties; mother helped us to get ready, gave us a quarter, saying, "Next time you can give the party at *our* home." The luncheon clubs and American Legion, Y.M.C.A. and Scouts —they were all friendly. Life was good, friendly, kind; we felt warm inside, and it was fine.

Skinny Dugan appeared at the gang headquarters laughing at the top of his voice. "Boy," he says, "did my old man sock the old woman this afternoon! He hit her with a beer bottle. But she had it coming; she's always telling us what to do. She tries to tell me too, and I tell her to go to hell."

People watch Skinny Dugan when he goes into a store. "People are always so damned suspicious. The coppers watch me till I get around the corner. Those sissy-britches at the Y.M.C.A. are just as disgusting as those mama's darlings who dress in those crazy scout uniforms. The lousy politicians always see to it that playgrounds are built in those parts of town where the sissies live. To hell with 'em; we can take care of ourselves." And Skinny Dugan does take care of himself; he is tough, he is hard-boiled, he "don't want none of that soft stuff."

Skinny is building the groundwork for a criminal personality. Perhaps the most noticeable trait of practically all professional criminals is this hardness which many people interpret as meanness. This is the normal result of failure to satisfy the need for affectional response in the "normal" way, which means, of course, our way. Overt expressions of affection, tenderness, kindness are prohibited by Skinny's folkways because such behavior patterns are interpreted by his group as forms of weakness. Skinny, like the rest of us, needs this kind of response, but he dares not admit the need, even to himself, for to do so would result in ridicule and loss of status in his group. His ever-present fear that he might, in an off moment, reveal this need, leads Skinny (and his pals) to over-assert this hardness in a braggadocio, defiant spirit. This is normal for Skinny and his kind.

Skinny Dugan Gets New Experience. Skinny Dugan may not satisfy the great human need for affection, but he knows his way around when it comes to new experience. How do we satisfy our need for new experience? We go fishing, play golf, go on picnics, travel, go to night clubs, art galleries, operas, theatres, read good books, attend concerts and lectures. Skinny Dugan gets his new experience, excitement, and stimulation, by raiding freight cars and being "chased by the bulls"; he steals from department stores when the clerks are not looking; he strips cars and raids empty houses for plumbing fixtures; he stops in to "gas" with the neighborhood "fence"; he "rolls a drunk," "pulls a stickup," "cracks a safe." Life is exciting, full of new experience. That's how he gets it; that is normal for him, for his kind, for his situation.

Some people have trouble with the generalization that *all behavior is normal for the conditions under which it occurs.* Everybody knows what is normal. Or do they? Errors have crept into our popular thinking habits, and one of the errors concerns the concept "normal." Most people, when they hear the term "criminal personality," conjure up all sorts of ideas about strange, mysterious, psychological mechanisms. They think of the criminal as a person different from "normal" people. The assumption is, no doubt, that there is a special kind of psychology to explain and describe this different kind of being. Perhaps he was born queer; perhaps he lacks something that "normal" men have, or maybe he has something in him which other men do not have. To them the criminal is not a man; he is—well—a criminal. Somehow, apparently, he is not the product of his group, as other men are.

II. CRIME AS A GROUP PRODUCT

This brings us to our second generalization, one that concerns the group: *A person's behavior is determined by the group with which he is most closely identified.*

In a general way we recognize that this second generalization is true. Germans act like Germans; Frenchmen, like Frenchmen; Americans, like Americans. But what has this to do with criminal behavior? These criminals are in America, aren't they? Well, then, why don't they act like Americans? The fact is, they do; they act exactly like Americans. An error in popular thinking is that people assume that the word "American" describes a specific group. We say we live in America, but do we, really? What is living? Living is behaving, responding to stimuli according to the meanings we have learned. We learn these meanings from relatively small groups. We "live" in relatively small and restricted groups, and we respond hour by hour in accordance with the meanings established by these groups. But very few of us respond to meanings which are as broad as "America."

Take the meaning "Democracy." In a city controlled by a corrupt political machine this meaning or stimulus is quite different from what it is in a small town or on Park Avenue. Indeed the meaning "Democracy" may indicate several things, depending on what State we live in; or our race, social class, age group, sex; whether we are a manufacturer or a worker, a policeman or soldier, a Roosevelt or a Skinny Dugan.

The Boundaries of Our Lives.   People learn their meanings from the groups in which they live. The groups in which people live differ in size —States, counties, cities, towns, neighborhoods, families. They differ in other important respects too—white, black; rich, poor; old, young. No one lives in all of these groups, and he would be an amazing person who could say that he lives in a group as big as America. The groups with which we identify ourselves form the boundaries of our lives.

From Whence Do Standards Come?   Every group sets up for its members fairly well-recognized norms or standards of behavior. These standards differ tremendously as between the groups mentioned above. Behavior that may be proper for a Negro may not be proper for a white man. Socially approved behavior in a boy may not be socially approved in a girl. Behavior approved south of the railroad tracks (where Skinny Dugan lives) may not be socially approved north of the tracks.

As we have seen in the first part of this paper, a man's behavior is the result of the needs he feels. The main job of living is to satisfy the four great needs already mentioned—the need to feel secure, the need for recognition, the need for affectional response, and the need for new experience. But all of us do not satisfy these same needs in the same way. We satisfy them in the only way we can; that is, by the devices, patterns, standards with which our group provides us. The normal way in the slum is not the normal way on Park Avenue, but Skinny Dugan's way is normal for him. Our group determines what is normal; our group determines and controls our behavior.

It is the function of the adults of a group to teach, and of the children of a group to learn, these approved standards of behavior. It is expected that all members of the group will abide by these standards; and we usually do what is expected of us—by our group.

Conflicting Ways of Doing Things. When the standards of two or more groups or levels of society conflict with each other, the sociologist refers to the situation as a conflict of culture patterns, or as a culture conflict. Such conflicts are rather frequent in an urban-industrial society like ours with different races, nationalities, and competing socio-economic classes. Because of these conflicting group-standards, and for other reasons, the larger or dominant groups have established agencies of social control, among which are the laws and the courts which interpret them. But the group standards represented by the laws and courts are always the standards of the larger group.

A man of a smaller group may behave in a manner quite in keeping with the standards of his group; but since these standards are not the same as those of the larger group, the control agencies of the larger group will not consider his behavior "normal," and he will be expected to suffer the penalties of his "abnormal" behavior. We have here the phenomenon of the larger group holding a member of the smaller group liable for the standards of the larger group even though the behavior pattern of this person was learned, not in the larger group, but in the smaller one, and even though he is not "accepted" in the larger group and has never received its benefits. It is like taxation without representation. It is the kind of thing that makes men fight.

We Always Learn From Somebody. The greater part of our personality is learned while we are still children. Children must learn from those about them—their parents and their playmates primarily. These are the people who furnish them their stimuli; that is, their life goals, their ideals, their hopes, fears, attitudes, values, and prejudices. If a child grows up in a relatively small group—say a city neighborhood—where stealing, cheating, fighting, and swearing are the normal everyday behavior for children, we must expect that the child will consider these things normal. Children have the same basic needs which adults have. Most of these needs are learned in the competitive life of childhood activities. They want to be thought well of by those for whom they care. They want to feel secure; they want to feel that they belong. They want recognition in order that they may feel that their lives are significant. These are powerful stimuli.

How the Group Determines Behavior. The means by which one can satisfy these needs are limited to the response patterns which are characteristic of the group in which one lives. If the child wants status, recognition, and prestige, he can get them only from his group. If, in his group, these values are gained by stealing, fighting, and truancy, he will steal, fight, and play truant. If he wants a feeling of belonging, he will make the responses necessary to gain that value in his group, which usually means, for Skinny Dugan, becoming a member of a gang. If he wants a sense of security, he satisfies this need in the manner which his group provides, which is primarily stealing. If he wants new experience, thrill, adventure, he gets them by responding as his group does, primarily by running away from home, exploring the city, worrying the police.

The Importance of Meanings. These powerful needs are not different from those which push you and me; but the responses you and I make to satisfy them are quite different because our groups provide different methods for satisfying them. And what we frequently overlook in "delinquent" children is that the *responses* which they learn in their groups soon provide the children with new *stimuli* which are not at all the same as ours. Since they gradually build up patterns of stealing, almost all property they see comes to offer them the stimulus "steal"; almost every new person they meet becomes the stimulus "fight"; almost every command from authority—parents, truant officers, police—becomes the stimulus "rebellion." The sense of belonging, derived from loyalty to the gang or their total group, becomes the stimulus to see the larger group and its authorities as enemies.

Ideas are among the most powerful stimuli in the behavior of man. Every group develops its own characteristic ideals and ideologies. Some of those in the larger society which gave us our meanings are democracy, home, family, church, school, property, consideration for others, honesty, cleanliness, law and order. The members of Skinny's group hear about these ideas, institutions and values; but the *meanings* they learn are different. Church and school are places for sissies; home and family are places of frustration and unhappiness; honesty is a form of weakness, except, perhaps, toward the gang; cleanliness is a mark of the hated larger group; law and order is the rule of the police; democracy is rule by and for corrupt politicians.

The criminal personality does not appear full grown, as an adult personality. It develops out of the "delinquent" child and the "delinquent" child is one who has learned behavior patterns which the larger group, but not his own, has defined as "delinquent." His behavior is defined as aggressive and is met by the police and the courts with aggression. When aggression is met with aggression, aggression is multiplied on both sides, and the result is a stimulus to vengeance on both sides.

It frequently happens that a member of the smaller group would like to "belong" to the larger group; that is, he would like to be "normal" in the eyes of the larger society, but he finds that such an attempt is blocked by both groups. He is rejected by the larger group and ridiculed by his own. This blocking leads to a sense of frustration which only enhances his aggressiveness and embitters his whole outlook on life. He is then graduated from the school of delinquency into the school of crime; he has become a criminal personality.

III. BEHAVIOR IS ALWAYS CAUSED

So we arrive at the third and last generalization: *All behavior is the result of stimuli; if you would understand man's behavior, investigate the stimuli which produce it.* It is a bit startling to realize that we could not have an idea, a hope, a fear, a desire, we could not get hungry, thirsty, angry, happy, or go fishing, or steal a watch unless we received a push or stimulus to do such things.

Stimuli Are Meanings: Meanings Are Stimuli. What, then, is a stimulus? We say that men make responses to their experiences in life; we say that men respond to other people or to things or to needs. But we run into error when we talk like this, for strictly speaking, we do not respond to people and objects. Whenever we receive a sensation or stimulus we immediately convert it into meaning, and then we respond to that meaning. If I meet a man on the street and he raises his hand, the first thing that I do is try to interpret what he means by this act. He may intend to shake hands or strike me, or he may mean to point out something to me. In any case, I immediately give his act a meaning and then I respond to that meaning. If you are walking with me, you may give this man's act a different meaning, and you will respond to that meaning. We both see the man raise his hand, but we may respond differently. Presumably we are responding to the same act, but we do not respond to the observed act at all; each of us responds to the meaning which he has put on this act. So, I define stimuli in terms of meaning. Likewise, I define environment in terms of stimuli, not in terms of objects, things, people. The environment, which has so much to do with our behavior, consists of thousands of stimuli of different kinds; and since we define stimuli in terms of meaning, we may say that our environment consists of thousands of meanings to which we are constantly responding.

But our environment is not all on the outside of us; some of the most important elements of our environment are inside of us. We are constantly receiving stimuli from the inner man, and we lose no time in giving meaning to these stimuli so that we can respond to them promptly and intelligently.

Behavior—Learned and Unlearned. Men always have been interested in these two sets of stimuli—those from within and those from without. Roughly speaking, those from within usually are thought of as due to heredity, and those from without as due to environment. Men have argued for centuries about whether heredity or environment is the more important in accounting for personality. We are now able to bury the hatchet for we recognize that whether we like it or not, both heredity and environment are with us forever, and both are working on us all the time. The point of view presented in this paper makes it easier for us to abandon the argument, for whether the stimuli are due to hereditary or environmental factors, whether they are learned or unlearned, we don't respond to them until we first give them a meaning.

It appears obvious that meanings are learned, but very few of them are learned from books. They are learned from the people with whom we live. The policeman is not primarily interested in such facts; the policeman is vitally interested in what men do, not why they do it. He is interested in the pickpocket's response, not his stimulus.

The sociologist, however, is primarily interested in the pickpocket's stimulus. We, of course, are interested in what men do, but we want to know why they do one thing rather than another. Investigation of the behavior of all sorts and conditions of men has demonstrated that when a man does something there is a reason for it. In fact, we have learned that every act of a man is a part of a pattern of behavior—his pattern. Every man has a characteristic pattern of behavior, and this pattern we call his personality. He may have a criminal personality.

Personality is a Product. It was stated above that the meanings to which we respond are learned from the people with whom we live. The people with whom we live largely determine the kind of stimuli that come to us. Both the stimuli and the socially approved meanings which come to Skinny Dugan are quite different from those which come to a boy who lives in the better neighborhoods near the outskirts of the city. This same differential in type of stimuli or meanings exists also between people of different races, social classes, occupations, ages, sexes, religions, and even different regions of the country.

We have grown up with the idea that all men are created equal, and that if they don't grow up to be nice people like us, it is their own fault. The assumption is that we are all presented with a choice of two alternatives—of being good, or bad—and that we deliberately make our choice. We have grown up also with another idea which is in direct conflict with this; that is, that we good people are born of superior biological stock and that the bad people are born of inferior biological stock.

Apparently it is difficult in our culture for people to understand that our personality is the product of the groups in which we live; that we see others not as they are, but as we are; that whatever status we have has been given us by our group; that our concept of ourself is a gift of our group; that we are not born with social values but have to learn our ideals, hopes, fears, ambitions, prejudices, hates, loves, tastes, patience, aggressiveness, bravery, cowardice, and practically everything else that characterizes the behavior of man.

We are born into this world as a bundle of potentialities and whether or not these potentialities are ever realized depends on our experiences with the people with whom we live. What potentialities are going to be fulfilled is pretty much determined by what stimuli we receive in our group during the first 5 years of life.

Scholars for ages have attempted to describe the differences in men by classifying them into types, but science has not yet demonstrated that men's behavior patterns, criminal or otherwise, are determined by any single type of phenomenon—biological, psychological, or sociological. There are some bright criminals; some dull. They are short, tall; fat, thin; light, dark; old, young; male, female; rich, and poor.

What men do depends on the stimuli they receive, and the stimuli they receive are determined largely by the group with which they are identified. All these stimuli are not conscious, but they determine behavior just the same.

When the prison warden shakes his head and says, "Why do they do it, why do they do it?" his amazement is not due to a rediscovery of the "mystery" of the criminal personality; it is more likely due to the recognition of the relatively simple truth that although personality is the product of the group, the group is still content to produce "bad" as well as "good" personalities.

7 · Personality Characteristics of Criminals

by KARL F. SCHUESSLER and DONALD R. CRESSEY

Does the criminal differ in his personality from the non-criminal? Various studies have attempted to answer this question by subjecting prisoners to various personality tests and comparing the results with those obtained from control groups of the general population. Here two sociologists examine the techniques and results of such tests administered over a number of years by several psychologists with the objective of determining their validity and of discovering the extent, if any, to which one is justified in speaking of a distinct criminal personality. [From the *American Journal of Sociology*, Vol. LV, No. 5, March 1950, pp. 476-484. Reprinted by permission. Footnotes and table omitted.]

STUDENTS of criminal behavior have always wondered whether criminals are psychologically different from the general population. During the last twenty-five years this problem has been investigated many times by means of personality tests. It is timely to evaluate the contribution of this research to criminological theory. In this paper an evaluation is made of all material published in this country on the subject of personality differences between criminals and non-criminals as determined by objective tests of personality.

In general the studies examined are characterized by a tendency merely to apply a personality test without reference to a hypothesis about personality elements and criminal behavior. Some testing was done primarily for screening purposes and only incidentally as a way of contrasting criminals and noncriminals, but even these comparisons generally involved the assumption, expressed or implied, that personality differences between criminals and noncriminals exist. The usual procedure has been to compare a group of prisoners with a control group specially selected for that purpose or with a test norm for the general population. As a rule, delinquent and control subjects were not carefully matched, but an attempt was made to obtain equal averages and variability on such factors as age and intelligence. The common practice of comparing the average of a group of prisoners with a norm which is supposed to estimate the population average is obviously a questionable one.

An appraisal of the relative adequacy of the personality tests used in this kind of work does not come within the scope of this paper, although the general opinion as to a test's value is given whenever possible. Personality tests are usually considered to be less reliable and less valid than intelligence tests. The well-known inadequacies of the objective tests of personality are doubtless related to the vagueness of the concept "personality" and to the uncertainty and confusion which exists over the existence, nature, and number of personality traits. Because of this the term "personality" is used simply to refer to whatever it is that a given test of personality claims to measure.

The material is . . . discussed under five main headings: emotions, temperament, character, total personality, and miscellaneous. This classification, although somewhat arbitrary, is useful in determining whether these data establish personality differences between criminals and the general population. The results might have been grouped by type of test —pencil-and-paper, performance, and projective—but that would have obscured the agreement and conflict in the evidence produced by different kinds of tests which purport to measure the same thing. Not every study is reviewed in detail: a few studies are briefly described in order to illustrate summarizing statements about the findings.

EMOTIONALITY

Emotional stability. The question of whether criminals are emotionally less stable than noncriminals has been studied many times by means of personality questionnaires such as the Woodworth, the Bernreuter, and the Thurstone, but the combined results of these studies fail to provide a definite answer. The Woodworth test has been used at least nineteen times with various groups of criminals, but a general conclusion on criminal emotional stability cannot be drawn from these findings for the following reasons: First, this questionnaire has been given only a few times to adult offenders, conclusions being limited to delinquent children. Second, it fails to differentiate consistently between groups of criminals and noncriminals, only nine comparisons yielding substantial differences between groups. The test differentiated delinquent and nondelinquent girls more consistently than it did delinquent and nondelinquent boys. Third, the average scores among groups of delinquents showed considerable variation. For example, Daniel and Watts tested delinquent Negro boys of the same age and intelligence, but the group medians differed by 6.3, a difference larger than many of the differences between delinquent and controls. Fourth, the failure in many studies to control such variables as educational level and socioeconomic background limits any conclusion based on these findings. . . .

Like the Woodworth comparisons, those made by means of the Bernreuter neurotic score did not consistently favor the controls. A study by

Horch and Davis revealed that the average scores for industrial school boys and penitentiary inmates deviated from the population norms in the expected direction, but the reformatory group proved to be more stable emotionally than Bernreuter's sample of college men. The opposition between Hargan's results and Corsini's may be cited as another example. Hargan's study of 100 prisoners indicated that "the convict is not as likely to show great emotional instability or neurotic tendency as the average adult," while Corsini's 50 prisoners of superior mental ability were "more unstable than normal men." Another feature of the Bernreuter evidence is that practically all the differences which did support the view that criminals are more unstable than are noncriminals lacked statistical significance.

The Thurstone, Brown, and California personality schedules have also been used occasionally for the purpose of distinguishing criminals from noncriminals in terms of emotional stability. In general, the results resemble those obtained by means of the Woodworth and the Bernreuter tests. An application of the California schedule by Freeman is worth mentioning, since he compared delinquent and nondelinquent brothers. These groups did not differ in their emotional behavior, and the proportion of severe personality disorders was as high among the nondelinquent as among the delinquent boys. Brown's finding that personality tests in part gauge variation in socioeconomic background is also noteworthy because most institutionalized offenders come from the lower class.

It is obvious that the question of whether criminals are emotionally less stable than noncriminals cannot be answered by the results of the pencil-and-paper personality questionnaires. These inventories have been applied many times to groups of criminals, but the findings, as has been shown, are not at all consistent. The position might be taken that the inconsistency in the evidence is a function of the low validity of these tests. Such a position is taken by Ellis, who uses the ability of personality questionnaires to discriminate between delinquent and nondelinquent children as one criterion of questionnaire validity. This criterion is wholly indefensible, however, since it is necessary to assume in advance precisely what the criminologist questions, namely, that delinquents are inferior in emotional stability to the general population. An alternative hypothesis is that criminals are not different from the general population with respect to this trait; differences obtained between groups when compared by personality schedules are the result of sampling errors and/or faulty experimental controls.

Emotional maturity. A small number of studies bear on the question of whether criminals differ from the general population in emotional maturity. Durea used the Pressey test in a series of studies made between 1937 and 1941 and reported that delinquent children were emotionally retarded and that delinquent girls were more retarded than delinquent boys. Odoroff and Harris sought to verify Durea's conclusion by testing delinquents and nondelinquents of similar intelligence and socioeconomic background. When the two groups were matched for intelligence, the nondelinquents were more retarded than were the delinquents in all mental ages below fifteen, leading the authors to conclude that "there appears to be a sufficient correlation of Pressey test score with mental ability to account for some, if not all, of the delinquents' emotional retardation." Banay regarded the deviation between the average score made by 100 prisoners on the Kent-Rosanoff word list and the test norm as evidence of emotional immaturity, but Houtchens found that the Kent-Rosanoff list, augmented by twenty-five words selected by himself, failed to differentiate delinquent and nondelinquent boys. Contradictions of this sort make it impossible to conclude from these data that criminals are emotionally immature.

Emotional disturbance.   Studies with Minnesota Multiphasic Personality Inventory are discussed here since the norms are the average scores of persons clinically diagnosed as suffering from the several categories of emotional disturbance. This questionnaire has been given only several times to delinquents, but its adequacy as a device for discriminating between delinquents and nondelinquents is certain to be explored. Capwell gave this inventory twice to the same groups of girls and found that, with the exception of the lie and hysteria scores on the first testing and the hysteria score on the retest, the delinquents' scores were closer to the norms than were the nondelinquents'. When 52 pairs were matched for intelligence, the inventory continued to differentiate significantly in all but the hypochondriasis score. In a later study Monachesi compared delinquent and nondelinquent girls, and delinquent and nondelinquent boys. Although the critical ratios were not so large, the differences between the two groups of girls closely resembled those obtained by Capwell. However, the delinquent boys were not consistently differentiated, as shown by the fact that on five of the nine personality characteristics the nondelinquent boys were closer to the norms. The difference between delinquent boys and girls in emotionality as measured by the Minnesota test (or any other personality questionnaire) may be due to a difference in the types of offense committed by boys and girls. It is possible that for the same type of offense (e.g., ungovernability) the average scores for delinquent boys and for delinquent girls would not differ a great deal. This hypothesis is at least worth testing.

The results of the Minnesota test cannot be evaluated at this time simply because the sampling has been too limited. Criminologists, however, are sure to consider carefully the results of this inventory, since such data relate to the hypothesis, favored by the psychiatrists, that criminal behavior is caused by an emotional disturbance.

*   *   *

TEMPERAMENT

Few, if any, of the studies using temperament tests have sought to establish the criminal as a distinct temperamental type but rather seem to have been undertaken mainly to find out whether certain tests differentiated criminals from noncriminals. It should perhaps be noted again that the absence of a well-defined theoretical problem characterized most of the studies covered in this review.

On the basis of various studies with the maze test, Porteus makes the claim that there are "delinquent traits of temperament." In his most recent studies various groups of Hawaiian delinquents and nondelinquents were contrasted by means of an index of qualitative performance on the maze, designed to measure such traits as carelessness and dependability. Because qualitative performance may be difficult to judge accurately and consistently, the bias of the observer may easily affect the reliability of the findings. Therefore, in order to determine the effect of observer bias, this test should be applied by someone not committed to the view that there are delinquent traits of temperament. Studies might also be made with various experimental groups in this country. Such studies, if properly designed, would (a) serve to check both the reliability and the validity of this method, (b) indicate the effect of sampling on previous findings, and (c) touch on the problem of whether criminal causation varies with the culture setting.

Very little importance can be attached to the results obtained with other temperament tests. . . .

*   *   *

. . . All that can be said about these temperament data is that they neither establish the criminals as a temperamental type nor demonstrate an invariant relationship between any certain aspect of temperament and criminal behavior.

CHARACTER

The possibility of using character tests to differentiate delinquents and nondelinquents was rather thoroughly explored between 1925 and 1935. The notion that criminals have poor character is not borne out by these studies, as shown by the following material: Raubenheimer administered a battery of specially constructed character tests to public school, parental school, and training school boys. As expected on the assumption that criminals have inferior character, the differences between the public school and the parental school boys favored the former, while, contrary to expectation, the differences between the parental school and the training school boys were in favor of the latter. Casselberry assigned each delinquent and nondelinquent a "character index" on the basis of his Raubenheimer scores; a comparison of the distributions disclosed that about one-third of the delinquents were separated from most of the nondelinquents but that only 7 per cent of the delinquents fell outside the range of nondelinquent scores. Courthial compared 78 delinquent and nondelinquent white girls, carefully matched as to age, intelligence, social class, and occupational level, by means of several moral-knowledge tests taken from a battery prepared by Hartshorne and May, and a cheating test devised by the same authors. The delinquent girls did not differ much from the control group in moral knowledge but cheated more on the honesty test than the controls. Daniel gave a moral-knowledge test and a test of honesty, both prepared by Maller, to three groups of Negro boys, selected to represent different parts of a delinquency continuum. These groups did not differ in moral knowledge, but the delinquent boys were more honest than the public school boys who were considered by their teachers to be behavior problems, and less honest than those boys whose behavior was considered satisfactory.

The foregoing material is typical of the findings of the character-test studies. These findings, considered together, can be summarized by two fairly definite statements: (1) delinquents are not inferior to nondelinquents in moral knowledge as measured by pencil-and-paper tests, and (2) most delinquent boys and girls did not cheat on honesty tests, although a larger proportion of delinquent than of nondelinquent children cheated.

TOTAL PERSONALITY

The Rorschach test, in contrast with practically all pencil-and-paper personality schedules, purports to represent the total personality rather than to measure one or more personality traits. The results of this method, then, might be expected to indicate whether the criminal is a distinct personality type. Because of the small number of studies expressly designed to determine differences between criminals and noncriminals, the Rorschach results as yet throw very little light on the relationship between personality and criminal behavior.

As far as can be ascertained, only two studies have been undertaken primarily to compare criminals with the general population. Endacott gave the Rorschach to 100 industrial school boys and compared his results with those obtained by three European investigators, Behn-Eschenburg, Loosli-Ustern and Lopfe, and one American, Hertz. On the basis of this comparison, he concludes that delinquents show a "tendency for the inhibition of all segments of the personality while at the same time retaining good intellectual control and an almost pedantic regard for form." Boynton and Walsworth scored the Rorschach responses in such a way that delinquent and nondelinquent girls could be compared with respect to intellectual development, instability, impulsiveness, excitability, and adaptability. The two groups differed in that the public school girls showed greater intellectual development and more impulsiveness. These investigators conclude that "in so far as emotionality or personality measurement per se is concerned the Rorschach test as here scored is of little assistance in differentiating between the two groups." In a study of the reliability of the group method, Harrower-Erickson gave the Rorschach to 33 superior adults, 31 unselected adults, 48 student nurses, 217 women in the service, 229 male prisoners, and 173 mental patients. Her findings revealed that the prisoners "are much closer to the normal distribution than . . . the psychiatric patients, but at the same time they have a smaller percentage of persons with outstandingly good records when compared with superior adults, the women in service, and the student nurses."

It may be that the Rorschach method, considered by many clinical psychologists to be the best available, will eventually help to settle some of the questions about personality and criminal behavior. If the results are to be at all convincing, however, investigators using it will have to design their experiments with as much care as possible. Two of the Rorschach studies described in this paper failed to satisfy the requirement that experimental and control groups be equated with respect to those factors usually considered to be associated with difference in test performance, while in the third the girls were purposely chosen to represent different social classes.

MISCELLANEOUS

Adjustment. The results obtained with adjustment questionnaires indicate that delinquent children are very similar to the general population in their personal and social adjustments. At least these results do not confirm the popular impression that the typical delinquent child is poorly adjusted. Only four out of nine studies of this type revealed some difference in adjustment. In three of these cases the groups compared were similar in all aspects of adjustment but one, and in the fourth the observed difference lost statistical significance (c.r. = .38) when intelligence was held constant.

Introversion-Extroversion. Studies with the Bernreuter and Neymann-Kohlstedt touch on the problem of whether the criminal is more introverted than the average person is. These studies are about evenly divided on this question, that is, about one-half showed the delinquents to be slightly more introverted on the average than the controls are. It should be noted that none of the Bernreuter differences favoring the controls were statistically significant, and in the three Neymann-Kohlstedt studies test scores were merely compared with the score distribution obtained by the authors of the test.

Maturity. The findings obtained with questionnaires which measure various aspects of maturity (e.g., Vineland Social Maturity Scale) follow the general pattern: the findings are not consistent among themselves, and the sampling is too restricted to permit a generalization about the criminal population or even a part of it.

Self-feelings. The Sweet Personal Attitudes Test was used several times to determine whether delinquent children have the same self-feelings as other children have. Two studies revealed the delinquent children as feeling more critical of, more different from, and more superior to, the average child; while three studies showed no essential differences. If delinquent children have self-feelings which set them off from everyone else, such feelings will probably have to be identified by some other technique.

CONCLUSIONS

1. Research in the criminal personality has enjoyed a steady popularity during the last twenty-five years, although no single test has been used continuously throughout this period. Its popularity seems to be due mainly to the availability of personality tests and to the repudiation of the view that criminals are inferior in intelligence to the general population.

2. When the results are considered chronologically, there is nothing to indicate that the personality components of criminal behavior are being established by this method. On the contrary, as often as not the evidence favored the view that personality traits are distributed in the criminal population in about the same way as in the general population. . . . Moreover, the statistical evidence opposed to the null hypothesis is equivocal because of the overlap between distributions whose means

did differ by a significant amount. It may be remarked parenthetically that this overlap makes it practically impossible to predict individual delinquent behavior from an individual test score.

3. The results of this method do not indicate whether criminal behavior is the result of a certain personality trait or whether the trait is the result of criminal experiences. In other words, whether a given trait was present at the onset of a delinquent career or whether the trait developed during that career is not shown. Conceivably, personality factors and criminal behavior are merely correlates, both being the function of a third condition or set of conditions. The fact that many differences between criminal and control groups decreased sharply when factors affecting the individual's participation in a culture, such as age and socioeconomic position, were controlled, confirms this idea.

4. Practically all criminal samples were drawn from prison population. Conclusions based on samples of prisoners cannot be extended to the criminal population for the following reasons: (a) Samples of prisoners are generally regarded as not being representative of the criminal population; (b) the answers given by prisoners to personality questionnaires may be unreliable because of the prison situation; and (c) the prison experience may produce changes in the personality.

5. The results of these studies cannot be grouped together for the purpose of establishing generalizations about criminal behavior and personality, because they are not equally valid. Few experiments were designed in such a way that comparisons could be drawn between criminals and noncriminals similar in regard to age, intelligence, and cultural background. In many studies control groups were not used at all, but, rather, the average score for the experimental group was compared with a test norm, a procedure which may be considered defective unless the experimental group and the standard population are alike in all significant respects.

6. Most studies proceeded as if the criminal population is homogeneous, since they grouped all types of offenders together. Future studies of this type should at least classify individuals by type of offense in order to determine whether differences between different classes of offenders exist.

7. At present, personality tests seem to be useful chiefly as diagnostic aids in penal institutions rather than as a technique of criminological research. The Guttman technique offers another approach to the problem of whether criminals are psychologically different from noncriminals. Working from the usual sociological view that criminals possess distinct attitudes, an attempt can be made to establish a cutting point on the

attitude scale which will completely separate criminals and noncriminals. Work on this problem is now in progress.

8 · As the Criminal Sees Himself

by ALBERT MORRIS

How do criminals explain their criminal behavior? To what extent do their explanations of what caused them to commit crimes correspond with reality? Professor Albert Morris attempted to answer these questions by means of interviews with, and authoritative data collected about, criminals of various kinds. He succeeded in obtaining information not only about prisoners serving sentence both as first offenders and as repeaters, or recidivists, but also—an obviously difficult task—about unconvicted white-collar criminals. The following article presents the results of the study and the conclusions to be drawn from it. ["Criminals' Views on Crime Causation," *The Annals*, Vol. 217, Sept. 1941, pp. 138-144. Reprinted by permission. Footnotes omitted.]

CRIMINAL OCCUPATIONS, like others, are both selective of those who enter them and to some extent determinative of the bias of their opinions. Conventional police methods are much better adapted to the detection of criminals who commit crimes which have what might be called a high social visibility than they are to the discovery of those committing concealed and devious offenses involving fraud, bribery, or complex accounting and financial manipulations. For this reason, criminal vocations and avocations are not represented in their proper proportions among convicted offenders. This condition is well recognized by convicted offenders, at least, and is often the basis of cynical comparisons whose tone is suggested by a frank, if halting, bit of poetry written by an inmate of the Massachusetts Reformatory for Women, beginning:

> I'm walking about a prison,
>   What do you think I see?
> A lot of dumb-bells doing time,
>   While all the crooks go free.

The data to be considered in an adequate survey of criminals' views on crime causation ought therefore to come both from upperworld or white-collar criminals and from underworld or traditional criminals.

DIFFICULTY OF SECURING VIEWS

Unfortunately, lawbreakers who have been so fortunate as to escape conviction for their criminal offenses are not readily identified except by their intimates, and they are not likely to feel any great impulse to discuss, even with their friends, much less with others, the origins of their misbehavior. Data from the upperworld group are therefore disproportionately limited and derived chiefly, though not entirely, from a few convicted upperworld offenders without previous police records. The greater part of the materials available have come from the convicted recidivist group.

Men undergoing punishment for their crimes may more or less willingly answer direct oral inquiries by staff members about their lives, but in so doing they are apt to have always the feeling that whatever they say goes into the record and may have an important bearing upon the comfort with which they can live in prison among their fellow inmates or with the prison staff, and upon their chances of early release. Even when the inquiry is made in confidence after friendly relations have been established, by one not having any official relation to the institution, complete frankness may be lacking, for it is difficult for the prisoner to dissociate himself from the general attitude of the prison community toward outsiders even under such circumstances.

Such expressions of views on crime causation as can be obtained from criminals are nevertheless of some worth. Even when they are lacking in penetration or sincerity, the verbalizations of criminals may have a diagnostic value as great as other overt behavior.

Occasionally the most ordinary person may, under circumstances of great emotional stress or relief, throw new light upon the dynamics of his and others' behavior by a casual but penetrating remark. Fortunately, also, there are a few criminals of rare insight and objectivity, whose comments on crime causation may be particularly valuable in helping us to understand their mental dynamics. This is a useful result, because the factors, both causative and curative, of criminal behavior operate only as they are brought to a focus in the human mind with a resulting interpretation of them and a correlated initiation of response. Perhaps the more general usefulness of obtaining the views of criminals, however, is in the suggestions they may embody for programs of crime prevention and treatment. What a man needs and will accept is to some extent correlated with his own judgment of his present condition and how he got into it.

THE UNCONVICTED OFFENDER

In general, it would seem that the unconvicted upperworld criminals (excluding those who are unconvicted because they are new offenders or too petty to attract official notice) are above the average of prisoners in their intellectual powers as well as in social and economic status. Data obtained from men who have most probably been engaged, though undetected, in serious violations of the criminal law, though not extensive, suggest that such offenders more generally analyze their conduct with understanding and objectivity than do run-of-the-mill prisoners.

One intelligent unconvicted offender, married but without children or near relatives, explained his behavior in defrauding the company for which he worked by saying:

My wife knew perfectly well what I was about, but we had no one to worry over. We liked to do things that we couldn't afford on my salary, and this seemed like a good risk. The loss was spread out so that nobody suffered, or I wouldn't have done it. I more or less expected to get caught ultimately, but not until I had what I wanted, and they would only have discharged me then, for it would not have helped their business to do otherwise.

Then in answer to further questioning:

Certainly I believe it was wrong, but *chiefly because you can't have everybody doing what I did*. I didn't get much satisfaction out of my work, and my business relations were impersonal. There was no one to get hurt but ourselves.

FIRST OFFENDERS

Men serving their first prison term seem to belong chiefly to the group in which a socioeconomic situation is an obvious causative factor, and secondarily to the medical and personality defect groups. The situational group of first convictions includes upperworld or white-collar criminals guilty of such crimes as embezzlement and fraud, and those among our Federal prisoners who have violated securities or income tax laws or other legislation, much of which is of recent passage.

These situational offenders are allied to the unconvicted group in their relatively high economic, social, and intellectual levels. Though individual differences are obvious, they have been exposed to conventional ethical training, and tend, as a group, to recognize rather clearly the general nature of their own problems, and are willing to accept a fair measure of responsibility for them. They know that they and their families have lacked the self-control to live within their means in a highly competitive acquisitive society. Creatures of a sensate culture, they are without the sustaining framework of substantial inner resources, and hence without the moral stamina to resist temptation when deprived of the things of the flesh.

One prisoner, without previous record, serving a term of two to four years for Second Degree Grand Larceny, expresses himself in a manner similar to that of a number of first offenders of substantial education and reputation who, for one reason or another, have come to bet on horse races:

My wife joined a bridge club. She began to gamble and lost heavily. We were behind in our bills. I borrowed some money from my employer's funds that I intended to return. Finally, I tried to get even by betting on the horses and just kept getting into debt heavier. I kept borrowing more money from the fund. When the auditors came I just gave up the cause, because I was $23,000 in arrears. My wrong was an attempt to make my wife's wrong a right, but it was poor judgment on my part primarily that finds me in prison.

A sixty-year-old former department-store executive, convicted of his first offense in devising a fraudulent scheme which mulcted the business of several thousands of dollars, attributes his criminality to a desire for revenge upon the store because he was not given promotions promised by the store owner.

A thirty-eight-year-old auditor whose wages were insufficient to meet his expenses stole from his employer in the belief that he could build up a profitable chicken farm with it and return the original investment to its owner's account without discovery.

Some men, caught in a hopeless tangle, are relieved that the strain is over and that a new sense of perspective has been gained; others are disgruntled at an economic order that limits their opportunities. But by no means are all of those serving their first sentences able to review the factors involved in their misbehavior so rationally. Some are unstable individuals who have committed casual or impulsive crimes of a serious nature, unplanned and often pointless, and frequently involving attacks upon the person. These various cases in which medico-psychological factors are most obvious include both organic and functional disorders ranging in a few instances into the area of definite psychotic conditions. Occasionally such offenders discuss the sources of their misbehavior with some insight, as did a twenty-two-year-old college student with a marked deformity of face and chest, who felt that he would not have attempted a felonious assault if his parents had taken him to a plastic surgeon to have his physical deformities corrected. But more often the prisoner, seemingly more surprised than anyone else, exclaims, "I don't know what made me do it."

RECIDIVISTS

First offenders, however, constitute a minority of penitentiary inmates. Probably three-fifths or more of penitentiary prisoners are those who have previous records of criminal activity. Among them is found no consensus of opinion as to why they or other men commit crimes. Their views range all the way from a denial of their own guilt (a common attitude of sex offenders, who look upon fellow prisoners convicted of crimes against property with all the naïveté of the prison visitor) to those who discuss crime causation in the jargon of academic criminologists, with whose writings they have some acquaintance and whose views on the interrelationship of multiple causative factors they expound with conviction. In between falls a large group of those who associate their criminality superficially with some one obvious factor, usually of a socioeconomic nature. Typical of this type are the alcoholic offenders, who without hesitancy point to drinking as the cause of all their troubles, but who seem never to wonder what factors may underlie their alcoholism.

Every time I get drunk and need money, I write "phoney" checks. After I am in jail I realize that it was wrong, but I just cannot help myself. Drink is the real reason for me being a convicted man.

Bad companions, difficulties with parents or wife, lack of employment or money, are common socioeconomic sources indicated more or less sincerely as the single cause of their crimes by a considerable number of prisoners.

"I stole because I was nearly starving and needed the money."

"The whole cause of my trouble is my father."

"My mother is the cause of my delinquencies. When I was a child she used to punish me by cutting my hands with a knife."

"I was drinking with some fellows and they suggested that we could make some easy money. I didn't know what they intended to do."

"My father threw me out when I was eighteen because I couldn't get along with my stepmother."

In a summary of statements made during a careful psychiatric study of 250 recent admissions to Sing Sing Prison and compiled for the writer by Dr. Ralph S. Banay, Senior Clinic Psychiatrist, the following answers were given, listed in order of their frequency:

Needed money	43
Intoxication	40
Denies guilt	37
Can't explain	26
Fight	17
Marital troubles	13
Bad association	9
Lost head	8
Business difficulties	7
Accident	7
Sexual difficulties	7
Miscellaneous	36
Total	250

A somewhat smaller group includes recidivists who have accepted organized crime or some specific criminal trade or profession as their proper way of life, and who, though reluctant to discuss it, are apt to give straight, if not extended, answers when they do.

Distinctive among the alleged causes of crime are the statements made by some intelligent habitual offenders that their way of life offers them freedom ("I'd rather die than be a wage-slave") and adventure which they cannot find in legitimate pursuits and which are essential to a tolerably satisfying existence for them. Such a viewpoint is common among professional criminals who rely upon technical skill and their wits rather than upon force, and who are likely to look upon violence as stupid. Forgers and confidence men frequently express such views, and burglars have been known to. One able second-story worker who has never owned a gun has for more than twenty years wintered in Florida and spent his summers in New England, carefully planning a limited number of profitable jobs just before each seasonal migration.

Such criminal businessmen regard imprisonment as one of the risks of their trade, and accept it without bitterness, as an undesirable but inevitable occasional interruption roughly comparable to hospitalization for a businessman who has become ill.

The thrill motive in less mature guise is also found among many youthful delinquents, particularly auto thieves, who take cars primarily for the sake of joy riding, but who may sell them to junk dealers for profit if they are not caught.

Another causative force recognized by some recidivists might be described as a sort of cultural compulsion. Without resorting to claims of special advantages for their "businesses," professional offenders may make no moral distinction between their methods and those of other so-called "legitimate" businessmen. Although they know that their acts are considered wrong, they do not regard themselves as criminals. Every one has a racket; theirs suits them, and beyond that they do not go except to venture a slight feeling of contempt for the hypocrites who assume a holier-than-thou pose because they seem to keep within the law.

One unusually intelligent inmate maintained to Dr. Glenn Kendall that there is a definite hoodlum culture, and that boys who grow up in areas where it prevails come naturally by it, accepting its code of behavior even to their manner of dressing, its heroes, and its contemptuous attitude toward "working stiffs."

Another example of cultural compulsion is represented among Federal offenders by the southern hillbilly moonshiners, who follow the ways of their fathers without consciousness of moral guilt, and who, according to Dr. Lindner, are often painfully honest outside of their distilling activities.

THE PSYCHOPATHS

Perhaps the most annoying and hopeless offenders that treatment agencies deal with are the psychopaths of good intelligence, who often know what they have done, appear genuinely sorry for it, verbally assume their responsibilities manfully, and promise with utter sincerity to keep out of trouble hereafter, only to give way almost as soon as they are released, to emotional impulses which they have never managed to bring into harmony with their knowledge.

*　　*　　*

MAJOR GROUPS OF CRIMINALS: A HYPOTHESIS

The views of criminals on crime causation, whether accepted at their face value or critically analyzed and compared with verified case records, make it quite clear that the stereotype "criminal" does not exist except as a handy literary figure. Nevertheless, from the standpoint of their views on crime causation, the hypothesis may be advanced that four major, if somewhat indefinitely bounded, divisions appear:

First, unconvicted and once convicted upperworld criminals of normal to superior intelligence and social opportunities who have failed to comport themselves acceptably under great socioeconomic pressure, and who understand as well as most persons the roots of their difficulties. Their views on causation as applied to themselves are likely to be sincerely expressed, often in great detail, within a normal range of human bias and rationalization.

Second, a major group of recidivists within the prison population, or normal to dull intelligence and from average to marginal social and economic levels, beset with medico-psychological weaknesses and hence incapable of living acceptably in their difficult world without help. Such offenders may or may not intend to express honestly their understanding of how they came to behave criminally, but in either event, they generally point with assurance to one particular factor, with little apparent comprehension of the complexity of their own motivation.

A third group, recidivists, not too numerous, ranging from normal to dull intelligence, have departed from the accepted limits of legal behavior because of the overwhelming strength of the culture that immediately touches the offender, or because of a choice made gradually but more or less consciously in favor of a way of life, criminal primarily in its economic aspect, because of a preference for its apparently greater satisfactions in terms of freedom and variety. Such criminals can rarely be induced to comment on causation in their own lives, but seem likely to answer intelligently, though laconically and with what seems to those outside of that group to be a biased dogmatism, when they speak at all.

Finally, there seems to be a group of recidivists of average or higher intelligence who comprise the vaguely defined unstable group of psychopaths whose intriguing discussions of causation in their own lives, though often readily obtained and convincingly given, are entirely unreliable because the offender fails to recognize or at least to face the basic constitutional limitation for which his criminal attack upon society seems attempted compensation.

HOPE FOR REFORMATION

There is little support in these suggestions for either extreme environmentalist or neo-Lombrosian biological interpretations of crime causation. The general pattern of culture, though important, is not always a predominant factor. The offender may be insulated from much of it, so that even as one factor it is only the part that touches the offender that may be demonstrably operative. In any event, the range of causative factors is great, their functions relative, their combinations varied and unique in each instance.

If genuine reformation be thought of as a sincere acceptance by a criminal of a legally approved pattern of behavior, and the development of his capacity to live in accordance with it, then the chances of bringing an offender to that desirable state would seem to bear some direct relation to his views on the causes of his criminality. There seems little likelihood that the criminal who is contented with his choice can be converted by any consciously designed treatment now available. Only slightly more hopeful are the psychopathic recidivists whose cure, if it comes at all, will require extended and competent psychiatric care—a point that might well be considered by those sincere friends of prisoners who are led by the convincing rationalizations and earnest professions of good intentions of this type to spend so much time, effort, and money attempting with little success to restore them to the good life.

From the situational group of first offenders may come a considerable proportion of successful releases. These are the most hopeful cases; among them are fortunate outcomes to which formal treatment beyond the shock of detection and conviction has contributed little or nothing, and which we may some day find the means of treating with necessary deference to society's demand for expiation but in a more economical fashion than is now customary.

The large group of socially and biologically inadequate offenders offers perhaps the greatest variety of possibilities for treatment, and invites the widest range of approaches. It continues to challenge an unimaginative and conservative public opinion to support for an indefinite period of time an array of honestly and ably conceived experimental treatment programs.

9 · The Victim and the Criminal

by HANS VON HENTIG

Criminology is concerned with the study of crime and the criminal. It pays little, if any, attention, therefore, to the victim, although he plays an essential, and often an active, part in many types of crime. What is the role of the victim in the crime perpetrated against him? To what extent is he responsible for it? Hans von Hentig, professor of criminology at the University of Kansas City, attempts to answer these questions in the selection that follows. [From *The Criminal and His Victim*, Yale University Press, 1948, pp. 383-389. Reprinted by permission. Footnotes omitted.]

CRIME, for the most part, is injury inflicted on another person. Setting aside felonies directed against fictitious victims, the state, order, health, and so forth, there are always two partners: the perpetrator and the victim.

This doer-sufferer relation is put by our codes in mechanical terms. A purse is snatched, bodily harm is done. The sexual self-determination of a woman is violated. Mental factors are, of course, taken into account. So is felonious intent or malice aforethought. The "consent" of an adult woman changes the otherwise criminal act of rape into a lawful occurrence, or at least a happening in which the law is not very much interested. *Volenti non fit iniuria.* No one can complain of injury to which he has submitted willingly. In many other instances consent changes the legal aspect while the factual situation remains unaltered. By his or her decision the victim can, in spite of loss and pain endured, turn factual crime into a situation devoid of legal significance. Noncomplaint after the event practically stands on a par with consent.

Yet experience tells us that this is not all, that the relationships between perpetrator and victim are much more intricate than the rough distinctions of criminal law. Here are two human beings. As soon as they draw near to one another male or female, young or old, rich or poor, ugly or attractive—a wide range of interactions, repulsions as well as attractions, is set in motion. What the law does is to watch the one who acts and the one who is acted upon. By this external criterion a subject and object, a perpetrator and a victim are distinguished. In sociological and psychological quality the situation may be completely different. It may happen that the two distinct categories merge. There are cases in which they are reversed and in the long chain of causative forces the victim assumes the role of a determinant.

We are wont to say and to think that the criminal act is symptomatic for the lawbreaker, as a suicide would be, or a red rash on the skin. We have gone to great lengths, in studying our society, to classify and reclassify groups. Among common situations usually enumerated, however, we do not find the evildoer-evil-sufferer group. It is not always true that common interests give rise to a group; the problem presents many more depths. I maintain that many criminal deeds are more indicative of a subject-object relation than of the perpetrator alone. There is a definite mutuality of some sort. The mechanical outcome may be profit to one party, harm to another, yet the psychological interaction, carefully observed, will not submit to this kindergarten label. In the long process leading gradually to the unlawful result, credit and debit are not infrequently indistinguishable.

In a sense the victim shapes and moulds the criminal. The poor and ignorant immigrant has bred a peculiar kind of fraud. Depressions and wars are responsible for new forms of crimes because new types of potential victims are brought into being. It would not be correct nor complete to speak of a carnivorous animal, its habits and characteristics, without looking at the prey on which it lives. In a certain sense the animals which devour and those that are devoured complement each other. Although it looks one-sided as far as the final outcome goes, it is not a totally unilateral form of relationship. They work upon each other profoundly and continually, even before the moment of disaster. To know one we must be acquainted with the complementary partner.

Often victims seem to be born. Often they are society-made. Sometimes the most valuable qualities render us easy victims. As always, mere chance, blind and senseless, is liable for what befalls us.

Some articles of criminal law determine the age level or the sex of the victim. Rape can only be committed against a female, mostly up to 18 years; as also abduction. Abandonment of wife, selling liquor or tobacco to children, can only be directed against these limited groups. Among the breaches of trust we find the "dishonest friend," dishonest servant, employee, trustee, bailee, attorney, and so on. Among the types of larceny there is that from intoxicated or sleeping persons.

Some crimes require personal contact, first for the approach and preparatory moves, then for the execution. The confidence man must establish personal relations: that is his medium. This approach may take the form of a connection by writing, telephone, or telegraph. In other felonies this direct and personal touch is avoided, since it would provoke defensive and obstructing reactions. In a burglary personal contact with the houseowner is not desired, and this holds true for most forms of larceny.

In felonies, such as robbery, the victim is met. In this case, however, the role of the victim is regularly a passive one. The instances in which resistance is offered and the victim assumes an active part are not frequent.

Even violence can only be exerted after the victim has been isolated or led away from the protective devices of nature or society. In Germany more than 35% of all murders committed in the country were executed in the woods. How were the victims prevailed upon to enter the forest? The term "out of the woods," meaning out of anxiety or peril, is certainly not out of place here.

The victim is the injured party, and because he has been despoiled or harmed he is at the same time a claimant for punishment, for harm to be inflicted on the injurer. It is therefore of the utmost importance to the perpetrator that this capacity to be an informant and prosecutor should be eliminated or reduced. The criminal accordingly prefers victims who, for peculiar reasons, after suffering damage cannot breathe a word of it. Why should any victim set silence above retaliation? Criminal prosecution entails publicity. This publicity may be unwelcome for two reasons. Either it would do harm to the social status, marital security, or other vital condition of the victim, or the victim is a criminal or a delinquent himself and thus unable to set the mechanisms of the state in operation without himself coming too close to the crime-repressing agencies.

All these groups of criminally active persons would be a much vaster problem if the criminal who can be victimized in one way or another had not developed an *ersatz* law enforcement. Cut off from the protection of society, the criminal has developed most energetic patterns of intertribal morals, rules of conduct, and defensive taboos. He has strengthened the elaborate system of criminal ethics by the only mode of enforcement left to him: strong-arm methods.

Since it would be hard and wearisome to wait for situations in which the victim is practically defenseless, many criminal games aim at giving the prospect a lift. The wanted combination of circumstances is brought about. Some sort of temptation is dangled before the strongest human urges; the victim takes the bait and the crime is committed in the ensuing discrediting situation.

The number of victims, for obvious reasons, surpasses that of perpetrators. This is precisely the meaning of the term and phenomenon of "mass murder." Yet the number of people killed cannot compare with those robbed or harmed by mass burglars, mass swindlers, and mass rapers. If a study were to be made of a majority of persons victimized by the same criminal, using the same method, in the same circumstances, science would gain a more comprehensive picture of this subject-object relationship, which has not only theoretical but practical significance.

Most crimes leave us with an unknown lawbreaker and a known victim. A thorough knowledge of all possible and typical relationships between the one who injures and the one who is injured presents the investigator with valuable clues, as do the mode of execution, the locality of the crime, and the time it was committed. Through this type of knowledge we would learn a lot, too, in the realm of prevention; recognizing potential victims, potential injurious situations, and such material as would tend to complement the dangerous perpetrator-victim relationship. However, we are only at the beginning of the task and still fighting for mere recognition of the grave problem.

That the ideas of the criminal center on the victim, his assailable qualities, his appetites and foibles is not surprising. This continual preoccupation is reflected by his lingo. The terms "mark," "chump," or "clown" only designate the aim of the attack or the inferiority of the attacked. In contrast, the word "prospect" seems to indicate a relationship: the victim is considered as a prospective and ill-fated business partner. He is the object of a "prospector." Whether Webster's interpretation of the term "sucker" as one "who is sucked or bled, hence one easily duped or gulled" is correct I do not venture to decide. It could be that the original meaning was a victim who is easy to deceive, or one who could be made to suck. It is certainly not without psychological significance that "sucker" means both the sucking individual and the sucked, and that "gull" embraces both cheater and cheated. It is the linguistic expression of an intimate doer-sufferer relation which consists of a series of changing situations. Criminal law looks at the latter phase and distinguishes roughly between the active and the passive partners of the game.

Many terms of jargon describe vividly the stages in this tightening and then again dissolving partnership between the swindler and the victim of a confidence game. This term itself indicates a contest between two or more, and finally takes on the connotation of an animal under pursuit, an object of chase.

Professional thieves hold that most law-abiding people would willingly be dishonest if certain to remain undetected and unpunished. A thief, we are told, "contacted a bank employee in the can (lockup) where the employee was held on a domestic court case of some kind. The thief asked the teller if bank employees ever thought of stealing the bank's money which they handled daily. The reply was: 'Everyone of them in every bank every hour thinks of stealing money but does not know how.'"

Regardless of whether this is a warranted generalization, it appears true that confidence men and card cheats very often encounter people who are themselves determined to make money in a dishonest way. The knowledge that he has to deal with a partner who has larceny in his heart or in his fingers does not operate as an inhibition to predatory instincts. A philosophy of "he asked for it" or "it serves him right" comes into play. The moral inferiority of the victim bestows not only practical but moral immunity, especially when the victim is well to do and the offender hard up.

Will Irwin, the card cheat, reports himself as addressing the district attorney in these words:

See here. As far as this complaint goes, you've got me to rights. It don't go far enough—that's all. That fellow did go up against me in three-card monte, and I did skin him out of his roll. But he ain't telling the rest. I knew he was a city man of easy means; he thought I was a poor granger from Texas who had sold my farm and was bringing the money East to put my wife into a sanatarium. Believing that, he put his roll up against mine under the impression that I would be easy. Now who's the worst of us two, that drummer or me?

If the district attorney really let him go he was acknowledging a new causative factor: the large amount of latent dishonesty in law-abiding mankind.

10 · Classification of Criminals

by ALFRED R. LINDESMITH and H. WARREN DUNHAM

A recurrent problem in criminology is the classification of criminals into categories, as it is quite obvious that criminals differ widely from one another as to their motivation and the form, seriousness, frequency, etc. of crime committed. The legal classifications of felon and misdemeanant and their various subgroups, or the classification of criminals according to type of crime, such as murder, theft, and burglary, have been found to be inadequate and unsatisfactory to the student of crime. Various attempts have therefore been made by criminologists to offer a classification that would meet the needs of a discipline that seeks to establish a scientific understanding of the criminal. Alfred R. Lindesmith and H. Warren Dunham, professors of sociology at Indiana University and Wayne University, respectively, here examine these attempts and suggest a system of classification which they believe is scientifically sounder than those offered previously. ["Some Principles of Criminal Typology," *Social Forces*, Vol. 19, No. 3, March 1941, pp. 307-314. Reprinted by permission. Footnotes omitted.]

ONE OF THE difficult problems which has faced criminologists has been that of giving precise meaning to the term "criminal." For practical purposes the criminal has been defined as one who violates the criminal law, but because laws change and multiply in the course of time, and vary from one locality to another, and are sometimes arbitrary, the legal definition has not provided a satisfactory category for purposes of scientific analysis. The recent inclusion of the white collar criminal in the field of criminology has emphasized the difficulty by making more extensive the meaning of a word which was already very extensive. One way of avoiding the difficulties in the too comprehensive meaning attached to the word "criminal" is to classify law violators, in general, into subtypes. Such a classification, if carried out according to consistent principles provides the possibility of concentrating attention upon problems of limited scope and of dealing with manageable groups presenting relatively homogeneous behavior. As now used, the term "criminal" refers to such heterogeneous behavior that the possibility of constructing theories of crime causation, excepting in extremely general terms, is excluded. It is, therefore, necessary to develop some consistent general principle for the classification of criminals into homogeneous subgroups.

The difficulties involved in an attempt to classify all law violators into a fixed number of rigid and mutually exclusive categories are, of course, very great, particularly in as complex a society as ours with its multiplicity of changing laws. There are numerous and transitional types, and very often essential information about the law violator which is necessary for the purpose of classification is lacking. Also, it is to be expected that many personalities will reflect the disunity of our culture by displaying conflicting behavior tendencies. However, it is not the purpose of this article to propose a final airtight system of classification but rather to discuss some of the basic principles underlying classification and to sketch the tentative outlines of a broad classificatory scheme. It is from reflection on matters of this kind that the framework, within which criminological research will assume a systematic character, will emerge.

Most past attempts to classify criminals take their cue from the kind of scheme proposed by Lombroso, who divided them into the following five classes: the born criminal, the insane criminal, the criminal by passion, the habitual criminal, and the occasional criminal. Ferri's scheme was similar. Garofalo, another member of the Lombrosian school, classified them as murderers (all altruism lacking), violent criminals, criminals lacking in probity, and lascivious criminals. Parmelee gives an excellent criticism of these systems and then gives his own which is much like them. These attempts may be taken as representative of other efforts to develop some adequate system for classifying criminals. The chief difficulty with these classifications is the absence of any principle guiding them and usually there is no analysis of the classification in terms of the theoretical base upon which it is supposed to depend. As a matter of fact, these schemes are largely either empirical in character or based upon conventional legal categories, as, for example, the current notions of the "defective delinquent," the first offender, and the recidivist. Sometimes, categories are established upon the basis of theories which have been discarded. Thus, Lombroso had as one type the "born criminal," and later writers spoke of the "instinctive criminal." In general, no classification of this general type has proved to be particularly valuable as a research instrument.

Another approach to the problem of classification of criminals which, in our opinion, has not been sufficiently elaborated or given the attention that it deserves is represented in such schemes as those proposed by Mayhew and Moreau. Mayhew, on the basis of extensive knowledge of criminals, divided them into two main categories, the "professional," who indulges in dishonest practices as a means of livelihood, and "casual," who is dishonest from some accidental cause. Moreau in a similar manner suggested three types, the "accidental," the "habitual," and the "professional." The accidental was thought of as a person who under the pressure of unusual circumstances commits a crime which he is unlikely to repeat and which is not in harmony with his general character. The habitual criminal repeatedly yields to the influence of circumstances and, so to speak, forms a habit of so doing. In this class would be included the man who repeatedly loses his temper and commits acts of violence at such times and the man who commits a crime when intoxicated. The professional criminal, on the other hand, deliberately commits himself to a life of crime and develops a philosophy of crime. The crimes of these three types are different and involve differential risks. Crimes against the person appear in classes one and two but are proportionately insignificant in class three where the crime is ordinarily committed for economic gain. The accidental criminal is easily apprehended and sentenced for his offenses. The habitual likewise is rather easily apprehended, but the professional by virtue of the very fact that he is a professional is difficult to catch and convict.

The principle implicit in the schemes of Mayhew and Moreau is that, since crime is a social phenomenon, criminals must be classified in accordance with their social orientation and in accordance with the values and cultural definitions in the social world in which they live. This principle is already implicitly recognized by the general public and definitely taken account of in the law when we refuse to hold an insane person responsible for his criminal acts, or when we give juvenile delinquents special treatment in the courts because they "do not understand right and wrong" or because they "do not understand the criminal character of their acts." This means that persons who, either because of youth or of mental disturbances, have not incorporated certain mores into their personalities are not held responsible for acts with reference to these mores. Responsibility, therefore, depends upon socialization.

In accordance with the principle that criminals should be grouped according to the degree and manner in which their crimes are related to or spring from cultural definitions, they may be thought of in terms of polar points of reference. At one end of this polarity there is a general category which we will call the "social criminal." The crimes of this type are supported and prescribed by a culture, and the person committing such crimes achieves status and recognition within a certain minority group by skillfully and daringly carrying out the criminal activity which, in that group, is customary and definitely designated. This type of criminal acts in close collaboration with other persons without whose direct or indirect cooperation his career would be virtually impossible. By means which are generally regarded as illegitimate he seeks ends which are socially accepted in the broader cultural milieu. Thus, the thief steals for economic gain and security.

At the opposite pole there is another general category which we may designate as the "individualized criminal." His crimes are not prescribed forms of behavior in his cultural milieu nor does he gain prestige or recognition in his social world by committing them. They are committed for diverse ends which are personal and private rather than common and socially accepted. That is why the layman finds it difficult to understand the kleptomaniac, and consequently why it is almost impossible to take account of this type in the legal framework of society. The crimes of the "individualized criminal" are, in short, not supported by a culture which prescribes them. Neither do they take on the character of an occupation with developed techniques and devices for evading conviction. The "individualized criminal" commits his crimes alone, and, ideally conceived, is a stranger to others who commit similar crimes.

The clearest example of the first polar type described is obviously the professional criminal who pursues crime, deliberately and voluntarily, as an occupation which he shares with other persons. Criminal techniques are developed and handed down from one generation to the next, a special language or argot develops out of the common social life in which these persons are implicated, and a definite criminal philosophy tends to emerge. There is a similar specialization, organization, and a division of labor as seen in the economic life of the larger society.

The "individualized criminal" is epitomized by the criminal insane. The crime of such a person is essentially accidental and symptomatic of an underlying physiological or personality disturbance and has no current rational meaning except as a symptom of the mental derangement. Whereas there is no question about the responsibility of the professional criminal for his crimes, there is no question about the lack of responsibility of the insane person provided the mental disease is unequivocal. In this sense the insane person is incapable of crime, sometimes probably because the "sense of right and wrong" which depends upon the mores of a group is not there by reason of the fact that the insane man is, in large part, isolated from other men and has not sufficiently experienced normal group life, and sometimes probably because the mentally deranged person, while he intellectually recognizes "right from wrong," is unable to control his behavior. His crime may be similar to the crimes of others but this uniformity is not culturally imposed as in the case of the professional criminal.

It thus seems that the criminal insane is criminal only in the formal sense that he has committed an act ordinarily regarded as criminal. Actually there are so few points of similarity between this type and the professional criminal that the two must be regarded as categorically different phenomena arising from different types of causes. In so far as a man is insane he cannot be criminal in the professional sense and in so far as he is criminal he cannot be insane. Crime and insanity are incompatible contrasting phenomena. Insanity is not a cause of crime but rather provides immunity to crime.

In order to satisfactorily clarify the typological principles which we are suggesting it is necessary to distinguish between vice and crime. August Vollmer, a police administrator, without specifically defining vice includes within it prostitution, gambling, and illegal sale and/or use of liquor and narcotics. To this list there might be added homosexuality, adultery, fornication with consent, and perhaps some other sex offenses. Vollmer bases his distinction on the grounds that vice involves questions of private morality rather than of criminality and that penal sanctions cannot control it. The attempt to suppress vice leads, according to him, to corruption and demoralization of police and officials, and usually to the perpetuation of the vice in underground ways and through the payment of protection money. The difficulty in attempting to use the police force to suppress these activities, says Vollmer, is that public sentiment is by no means united in regarding them as serious and eradicable evils. There are, therefore, reasonable grounds for asserting that, even though some forms of vice are treated as crimes in our legal codes, we should not confuse vice with crime nor discuss the vice law violator in the same terms as we do the criminal. We feel that if future thinking can more adequately clarify the conditions under which this distinction between vice and crime can be established, a firmer foundation will be laid for criminological research to assume a more systematic character.

Between the polarity which we have described there are a number of other types leaning in the direction of one pole or the other. The individualized type is represented by the man who under the influence of alcohol commits a crime which is quite out of line with his usual character. Other similar instances: the crime of passion (as, for example, the husband's killing of his wife's lover), the commission of theft under the stress of dire economic need by an individual who is not otherwise inclined toward theft, and other crimes produced by crisis situations. The characteristics of criminal behavior of this general category are, that it has an accidental character in the sense that the acts committed do not represent the settled character of the individual who commits them, and that the criminal act is not a prescribed form of behavior in the social world of the guilty person. Criminals of this type do not form groups made up of persons who are inclined toward the same crimes but are rather found scattered throughout respectable society, though more frequently in certain classes than in others. It may be said of this sort of behavior that it involves criminality to a slight degree. It is the kind of behavior that any respectable person might conceivably commit under the pressure of circumstances. Although this behavior is not definitely prescribed by the mores it may and usually is encouraged or facilitated by prevailing ideas of conduct. Thus, in a country where honor killings are numerous, people in general do not believe in murder but they do hold ideas concerning certain situations which makes murder an understandable, excusable, and even probable outcome in certain cases.

There are other types of criminal activity which more nearly resemble those of the professional and which consequently lean in the direction of the opposite pole. These are represented by political crime, white collar crime, some juvenile delinquency, and what we may call "habitual crime" of certain kinds. The political criminal frequently belongs to a group in which criminal behavior is required, as for example, when a terrorist organization assigns an assassination by lot to one of its members. Unlike the case of the professional criminal, however, the political criminal does not accept the general public definition of his act as criminal, but regards it as meritorious and justified by the ends which it subserves. The crime is also usually not committed for gain but rather involves self-sacrifice for the sake of ideals or for the sake of political reconstruction which is regarded as desirable. These political criminals, actual and potential, become public heroes or martyrs if the revolution succeeds. They are not simply predatory.

The white collar criminal, so-called, is both similar to and different from the professional, although the differences are more marked than the similarities. He is similar in the sense that he has to learn through contact with his business associates and others the ways for violating the law with a minimum of risk. He is different by reason of the fact that his crimes are usually furtive and secret, and while the financial gain obtained may give him prestige in the respectable society in which he moves or seeks to move, his crimes as such, when discovered lead to disgrace. The criminal activity in which he indulges may also be practiced by others in the same occupation and be officially winked at, but it is not a prescribed or required form of behavior and the group is not definitely organized around it. Bankers are not required to become embezzlers and they are, in fact, expected not to, but, no doubt, there are a number of aspects of the profession which make it relatively easy for them to succumb. Embezzling is usually not a career nor are embezzlers united in a single social group. It has often been noted that they do not "belong to what is ordinarily called 'the criminal classes.'"

In the case of criminals of the white collar and the political variety the criminal intent of the act is frequently very much in doubt precisely because of the particular grounds from which these acts proceed and also because the persons involved belong to the respectable classes of society. Because these acts do not have a definite supporting culture which is definitely and self-consciously predatory their criminality is often in doubt. Samuel Insull has been spoken of as a white collar criminal, but he was found innocent by a jury.

We should again like to emphasize that while from the legal point of view all of these persons are law violators, from the sociological viewpoint they constitute divergent and probably essentially dissimilar types. Their attitudes toward their crimes, the public interpretation of their acts, the various means which they employ, and their class affiliations separate them sharply and radically from professional criminals. The ways in which they become involved in crime, or in other words the causation of their behavior, is also probably different, though there may be some general points of resemblance.

Another type of crime which should be mentioned is what we will call "habitual." It does not constitute a very sharp category and is often simply incipient professional crime. We are thinking here of the type of crime that flourishes in slums and of much juvenile delinquency. In contrast to the accidental type of crime, which we first discussed, the crimes committed here are more or less in harmony with the habitual character of the persons guilty of them. These persons live in areas characterized by poverty, crowding, low rents, prevalence of vice, drinking, irregular sex activity, and violence. In contrast to the crime of the respectable business man with too many cocktails under his belt, the drunkard of the slum is often of the type who is constantly in trouble and in his cups. His crime reflects the lack of constructive influences and the chaos of his social environment. Persons reared in such a community may become professional if they are thrown into direct contact with the positive criminal culture of the professional, they may reform if they come into contact with the standards of outside respectable society, or they may simply continue a slap-dash, irresponsible, indigent, derelict existence. While the slum is primarily instrumental in producing the "habitual" type, it, by no means, tells the whole story of the professional criminal. Many rural or small town slums have almost no connection with professional crime and many professional criminals are not recruited from either small town, rural or city slums. Slum conditions alone do not produce serious or professional crime. What is required in addition, as Sutherland has indicated, is the positive influence of the presence of an already developed criminal culture and an active criminal class.

In terms of the classification proposed a number of general observations may be made concerning the significance of the various types. Individualized criminals do not constitute social groups and they are therefore extremely heterogeneous in character. The principal methodological implication of this category in our classification is that the study of the types of behavior included under it must proceed in a different manner from the study of professional crime, since the entire cultural orientation is different.

The social criminal and the related types considered constitute a number of relatively homogeneous groups because of the fact that the cultures which support their criminal activity impose certain uniformities upon them. The student of culture would probably therefore find the search for "behavior systems" of a definable and delimitable character most fruitful at this pole. The interpretations of Tannenbaum and Sutherland in fact already imply some such division as suggested.

In terms of general social significance the social criminal is most important in the sense that the overwhelming proportion of felonies committed are violations of property rights and are either professional in character or closely related. Vollmer regards professional crime as the main consideration of the police. It is with respect to the professional also that there is the greatest difficulty in apprehension and conviction. The emphasis placed upon the study of abnormal criminal types by some schools of thought is a mistake in the sense that it places the emphasis upon an exceedingly small minority of law breakers. The social criminal is definitely an urban type since it is only in the city that full fledged criminal cultures can flourish. The individualized criminal, on the other hand, is neither an urban or rural type. He is disproportionately represented in prison because he is easily caught and convicted. Individualized crime is an index of disorganization within respectable society, whereas professional crime represents the existence of a culture within a culture and is not so much disorganization as organization for ends which are socially approved in the larger society but by means which are not socially approved.

The research problem suggested by the above classification is that of breaking up the general category, law violator, into a number of homogeneous types which are homogeneous according to a consistent and significant principle. We have already indicated that the principle suggested correlates with the postulations of responsibility and of criminal intent. Cultural influences, no doubt, are at work in reference to all criminal types which have been described, but the research worker must determine the different kinds and degrees of cultural influences, and the specific character of these influences in the production of the various types. In the literature on crime, sociologists have traditionally concerned themselves mainly with the "social criminal" and psychiatrists with the "individualized criminal," but neither group of specialists has been altogether clear about this fact and each has attempted to appropriate to himself the entire field and to extend to all types the theories evolved with respect to one. Such procedure ignores the possibility, which seems very strong, that the term "criminal" refers to many different kinds of individuals whose behavior may have developed in totally different ways. The attempt to develop unitary theories of crime causation in general may be futile, as Reckless suggests, but the attempt to develop similar theories for restricted portions of the total crime problem may not be.

CHAPTER FOUR

Crime and the Law

11 · Defects in Our Criminal Law

by HARRY ELMER BARNES and NEGLEY K. TEETERS

Although the volume of crime depends on a number of factors not yet clearly defined by criminologists, there can be little doubt that the way in which a society's socio-legal machinery is set up and operates and the extent to which its legal system meets its changing needs have much to do with the frequency of crime among its members. In this selection two well-known criminologists, Harry Elmer Barnes and Negley K. Teeters, point out some of the defects in our legal system which, according to them, chiefly account for the frequency of certain types of crime. [From *New Horizons in Criminology* (2d ed.), Prentice-Hall, 1951, pp. 75-78. Reprinted by permission. Footnotes omitted.]

THERE IS no real solution for crime. No doubt much of it can be eliminated—especially that portion due to economic causes and arising from the gross inequalities inherent in our social system. But the extent of petty crime depends largely on the number and tyranny of our laws. Each year finds thousands of new laws and ordinances added to our tatute books, which are already cluttered with outgrown or unnecessary laws. Much of the time of police officers is absorbed by snooping into matters that should be left to the control of public opinion and common decency. Jails and prisons are clogged with men who are in no serious way a menace to society.

Railroading of inconspicuous and friendless persons is especially glaring in our large cities in connection with members of minority nationalities or races. Negroes and Mexicans are discriminated against in some sections of the country and the foreign-born in others, so that certain statistical studies often give the impression that these groups are more criminal than the native-born white American. We must be cautious in interpreting such statistics and statements because there is little reason for accepting the thesis that racial or national groups vary in the extent of innate criminality.

Many of the laws still on the statute books of some of our states reflect ideas and conditions of long ago. Some years ago the state of Delaware invoked the notorious "blue laws" of colonial days. Hundreds of citizens were prevented from engaging in business on Sunday, others were denied the twentieth-century privilege of going for a Sunday afternoon automobile ride. The Attorney General, in an attempt to have these absurd laws repealed, maintained he would be obliged to enforce them to the letter of the law, so that Delaware citizens would understand what an obsolete set of laws really meant. Accordingly, some five hundred citizens were arrested. Persons engaged in "worldly employment" on Sunday, including filling station proprietors, druggists (to fill a prescription, perhaps badly needed for a sick person), milkmen, and news-dealers were arrested, and many were fined.

The municipal judge, in fining the blue law violators in Wilmington, was guided by what he interpreted as "necessary" work. For example, storekeepers were penalized if they were open to do a "general business," but they were not fined if their services were indispensable. The judge added: "There is no more pleasant recreation than an auto drive on Sunday, but the Lord's Day must be preserved." The "blue laws" are only a part of the archaic legal picture confronting modern citizens of America. In one Southern state, a third successive failure to attend church is still a capital crime. Laws against blasphemy and witchcraft abound. In one state it is against the law to ride a jackass more than six miles an hour. In another state it is robbery to loot a building, but not robbery to loot a railway car, since the car is not a building. The height of absurdity is a state law in which a child may not pass from the seventh grade to the eighth unless he can recite the words of *The Star-Spangled Banner*. Recently it was disclosed that three Indians were sentenced to 18 years in

the Idaho state prison for stealing sheep. They had broken a law enacte
in 1864 to protect settlers from having their stock stolen—at a time whe
this was a serious loss. Conviction of these men made it mandatory f
the judge to invoke this extreme penalty. To make matters even mo
serious for these lawbreakers, they were not given the benefit of couns
and were urged to plead guilty.

Another offense that causes much concern of the federal governmei
is the illicit manufacture and sale of liquor—moonshining—primarily i
the southern mountains. For a century or more the people living in thes
isolated areas have made "moonshine" for sale, without paying the excis
tax. The Treasury Department points out that this illegal business
again on the increase, approaching a "multi-million dollar industry.
Agents of the Alcohol Tax Unit seized 8,649 distilleries during 1948 an
arrested 9,498 persons. Of this number, 4,746 were convicted. Little co
structive work has been done to offset the prevailing mores of thes
mountain folk; thus they will persist in their occupation and we sha
continue to use punitive methods for behavior, illegal though it is, tha
is understandable to social scientists.

At the same time, we are unduly hasty in creating new crimes b
statute. In 1931, 76 per cent of all the inmates of federal and stat
prisons had been incarcerated for committing acts that had not bee
crimes 15 years earlier. Since 1900 some 500,000 new state laws hav
been enacted. Our state penal codes are antiquated, often absurd, an
in disagreement one with another. A felony in one state is a misdemeanc
in another. A crime punishable by life imprisonment in one state call
for only a few years' sentence in another. Grand larceny is interprete
to mean theft of as little as $15 in one state; in another it involve
amounts of over $200.

Out of this welter of antiquarianism and confusion, a rational, moc
ernized, and integrated system of criminal jurisprudence must emerge i
we are to make any progress in dealing with criminals. A real effort a
legal uniformity throughout the country should be attempted, so tha
serious forms of antisocial conduct are listed as crimes, and all acts tha
are not a challenge to social well-being are expunged. Especially shoul
we remove from the statute books acts that are purely a matter of tast
or private morals.

The inept offender is not familiar with this maze of law. The mo
expert criminal is well acquainted with the various penal codes and cor
forms his professional acts to their provisions. Judges sentence th
offender according to the provisions of the penal code, so we find tha
those convicted are often the "small fry," who either are unfamiliar wit
the law or do not have the proper legal connections. There is a genera

practice by which an offender may plead guilty to a lesser offense and thus save time and expense to all concerned. The well-informed professional criminal frequently saves himself a long prison sentence by taking advantage of this practice.

It would not be an exaggeration to state that 50 to 75 per cent of those actually convicted and sent to prison are either ignorant violators of the law or those who do not have the financial resources to fight their cases. The professional criminal is protected by the "war-chest" accumulated by his gang over a period of years; he or his bosses employ the best available lawyers, who usually see to it that he escapes a prison sentence completely or is sentenced to a nominal term with a more or less speedy discharge. As Professor Frank Tannenbaum says: "If we may generalize from these eight cases [representing a study of offenders in Massachusetts in 1933], a persistent offender has almost seven chances in ten of escaping any effective penalty when charged with a serious crime."

No significant change in the philosophy of penal treatment can be consummated until our penal codes are drastically amended and a national system of criminal procedure developed. This radical suggestion is not made by dreamers or sentimentalists. Insistence upon a repressive philosophy is outmoded. Penal history has shown that where punishments are severe and prison sentences are long, crime increases. The more progressive jurists are unanimous in their conviction that a new order must be ushered into our legal and penal philosophy if we are to cope with the serious problem that confronts this country. Instead of dealing with crime as we have in the past, there must be brought to each trial a complete knowledge of the criminal, including his background, his potentialities, his habits, and his modes of social thinking. The disposition of his case must be determined in the light of these data.

12 · Morals and the Criminal Law

by RICHARD C. FULLER

What is the relationship between criminal law and the moral code, or between criminality and immorality? Although nonliterate, or primitive, societies make virtually no distinction, civilized—especially modern, technologically advanced—societies make definite distinctions between the two. Immorality, or vice, and crime do not always correspond in our society. Why and to what extent are immoral acts differentiated from criminal ones? What

effect does this have on law enforcement? How can the tw
be brought into closer harmony? These are some of th
questions which Richard C. Fuller, professor of sociolog
at the University of Michigan, attempts to answer in th
article that follows. [From the *Journal of Criminal La
and Criminology*, Vol. XXXII, Mar.-Apr. 1942, pp. 62.
630. Reprinted by permission. Footnotes omitted.]

LEGAL CONCEPTION OF CRIME

A CRIME, considered as a legal category, is an act punishable by the stat
For conduct to be considered criminal in this legal sense, it must k
something more than the violation of group morality or custom. A pe
son's conduct may deviate from some social norm and be regarded :
eccentric, bad manners, highly improper, or even downright immora
but it is not criminal conduct in the legal aspect unless it is also
deviation from the criminal code established and enforceable by th
state.

This juridical conception of crime has its logic in expediency, rathe
than in sociological realism. It conveniently delimits misconduct whic
is the domain of police, prosecutor and judge from misconduct whic
must be regulated exclusively by the pressures of public opinion. Soci
logically speaking, however, a criminal statute is simply the formal en
bodiment of someone's moral values (usually the group dominant i
political authority) in an official edict, reinforced with an official pen;
sanction. Moreover, the mere fact that a given act is made punishab
by law does not settle the question of the immorality of the prohibite
conduct; it does not preclude people from passing moral judgments o
the rightfulness or wrongfulness of the behavior. The dominant grou
whose values are expressed in the law is only one of many groups whic
are integrated in the moral and political fabric of the community. Whe
the moral values of one or more of these other groups are not in accor
with the moral values of the dominant group we are likely to have
persistent problem of law enforcement. Thus viewed, the problem c
the criminal law in action reduces to the problem of conflicting mor;
values held by different groups and classes in the community.

"CRIMINAL" AND "IMMORAL" NOT ALWAYS SYNONYMOUS

If we are to study crime in its widest social setting, we will find
variety of conduct which, although criminal in the legal sense, is nc
offensive to the moral conscience of a considerable number of person
Traffic violations do not often brand the offender as guilty of mor;

turpitude. In fact, the recipient of a traffic ticket is usually simply the butt of some good-natured joking by his friends. Newspapers in reporting chronic traffic violators who come before the courts are prone to play up the humorous rather than the ominous side of such incidents. Although there may be indignation among certain groups of citizens against gambling and liquor law violations, these activities are often tolerated if not openly supported by numerous residents of the community. Indeed, certain church groups and service clubs regularly conduct gambling games and lotteries for the purpose of raising funds. Professional gamblers rationalize that there cannot be anything very unethical about their games when "legitimate" groups are in the same business. With social drinking now morally acceptable in most communities, the operation of drinking emporiums during prohibited hours, the sale of liquor to minors, and many other infractions of local liquor laws are regarded by many with apathy, if not approval. Some communities tolerate such conditions in order to profit from the license fees paid by those who operate such dispensaries. Even brothels, which normally carry a stigma of disrepute, are in some of our municipalities accepted with a shrug by citizens who are inclined to view them as inevitable appurtenances of the community. The thousand and one forms of political graft and corruption which infest our urban centers only sporadically excite public condemnation and official action.

ROLE OF PUBLIC OPINION

There are several reasons why the criminal behavior in the examples cited is not regarded as immoral by general community consensus. Such deviations simply do not carry the same opprobrium of vicious immorality as do other offenses such as murder, kidnapping, rape, arson, and robbery. They do not threaten our physical and pecuniary survival in the same way as do the more heinous offenses against person and property. Even more significant is the fact that such violations are essential to the normal conduct of business of persons engaged in liquor, gambling, and vice enterprises. Moreover, the direct pecuniary interest of these entrepreneurs is shared indirectly by innumerable public officials and plain citizens whose bread and butter are dependent upon the continued operation of such commercial activities. Finally, the survival of these forms of crime is made possible by the patronage of a public whose personal tastes and morals diverge from the values expressed in the criminal law.

So far as the support of public opinion is concerned, the situation is much the same in a relatively new sphere of criminal definitions—that

of business and industrial relations. Offenses of this character includ
violations of laws pertaining to trusts and combines, insurance, market
ing of securities, traffic in food and drugs, the employment of children
collective bargaining, and wage and hour standards. The broker wh
profits from an illegal stock or insurance transaction, the employer c
child labor contrary to government codes, the anti-union boss wh
flaunts the National Labor Relations Act, the manufacturer who d
fiantly violates wage and hour legislation—all are engaging in crimina
behavior in the legal sense. But are these persons regarded as immora
or anti-social in their conduct by the community in general?

With respect to these white-collar crimes of businessmen, there i
usually no militant and community-wide public opinion which will reir
force the legal sanction and put down the legally wrongful behavio
The social philosophy underlying recent governmental regulations c
employer-employee and buyer-seller relations is not yet understoo
much less accepted by the general public. Indeed, as regards conduct i
business, there is a "live and let live" attitude abroad in the communit
Business relations have traditionally been left to individual enterpris
and there are a great many who feel that if business is to prosper pe
sonal conscience rather than public conscience should be the arbiter i
these matters.

The degree to which the sphere of conduct defined as criminal coi
cides with the sphere defined as immoral depends upon the relativ
homogeneity of moral values within the society represented in an
political jurisdiction. Theoretically, in a primitive society where ther
is almost complete agreement on moral values the public opinion er
forced mores for all practical purposes comprise the unwritten crimina
code of the tribe. What is immoral is by hypothesis criminal. In societie
other than the primitive where there is little social change, such as th
small rural communities of early nineteenth century America, ther
would likewise be a very small area of criminal conduct not defined a
immoral. In advanced, industrialized societies, characterized by urba
ization, where there is only a small core of common values, surrounde
by numerous conflicting codes of behavior, the sphere of conduct ger
erally agreed upon as wrongful grows smaller as the segmentation an
differentiation of the society continues. Yet the number of crimina
laws rapidly increases.

NO COHESIVE OPINION—MANY LAWS

As societies become more differentiated and complex, opinion er
forced mores no longer suffice to guarantee uniform norms of conduc

With the increasing disparity in values some common denominator for conduct is needed and hence resort is made to the codes of the criminal law which apply to everyone within the same political jurisdiction. Not only are the older and generally accepted mores which punish such offenses as murder, rape, and robbery perpetuated in the criminal code, but a host of new laws spring up which seek to define new areas of behavior where conduct is impinging on the values held by the group in dominant political authority. Sutherland and Gehlke, examining the essential trends in the criminal laws of the United States between 1900 and 1930, discovered very little increase in criminal laws dealing with the "bolder offenses"—the felonies such as murder, robbery, rape, assault, and arson upon which there is very general agreement in any community that they are threats to the general welfare. The large increase in criminal laws has come precisely in an area of behavior where there is no cohesive public opinion branding the conduct as immoral. It is an area of disparate and conflicting values such as public morals, business ethics, and standards of health and public safety. Even more recently the great depression facilitated new definitions of offenses in tax and banking laws, social insurance legislation, and collective bargaining regulations. Such social legislation, perhaps acquiesced to in principle by the masses, opposed in principle by powerful business groups, and often militantly supported only by a vigorous minority of socially conscious individuals, gives rise to an entirely new sphere of criminal behavior.

ORIGIN OF PRESSURE GROUPS

This trend toward new criminal definitions presents a neat dilemma so far as law enforcement is concerned. When a modern community is faced with new conditions such as traffic hazards, liquor and gambling institutions open to all ages and classes of the population, consumer exploitation by business interests, cut-throat business competition, oppression of wage labor by employers, those whose values are shocked by such conditions feel that they cannot wait until there is a spontaneous ground-swell of community indignation. Indeed, if all groups in the population frowned on such practices there would be little need of any criminal legislation to suppress them. So the socially minded reformers, or special groups whose interests are being hurt, although often numerically in the minority, put pressure on the legislatures to outlaw the disapproved behavior. Our parliamentary democracy is so constituted that much of our legislation is, in fact, the legislation of well-organized, articulate, and powerful minorities.

Such minorities, in effect, become the dominant groups in casting the

new moral molds of the criminal law. The notion that legislatures, in
enacting new criminal legislation, are intervening for the "common
good" or "general welfare" cannot be reconciled with the harsh realism
of our politics. Such intervention is usually simply the result of effective
pressure exerted by some group with important political influence. Yet
without general community support for the moral values expressed in
these laws, enforcement proves a troublesome problem and the criminal
definition may prove to be nothing more than a paper law, not a law in
action.

"MORAL" AND "AMELIORATIVE" PROBLEMS

It is probably true that our criminal codes do contain the *moral minimum* of our day and age. That is to say, those values which we hold
most sacred and least dispensable are elevated by public opinion to the
status of protection by the criminal law. Thus, many of the statutory
enactments of our modern criminal codes merely redefine as criminal
certain behavior which for many generations has been outlawed by the
unwritten mores of our ancestors. These moral minima are found in the
many criminal laws which punish offenses against property, such as
burglary and robbery; against the person, such as murder, assault, and
rape; against the marriage institution, such as incest and bigamy; against
public order and decency, such as disturbing the peace and public immorality; against the state, such as insurrection and treason. All these
instances represent behavior which the vast majority of the community
deems to be injurious to its best interests, welfare, and survival. No
matter what an individual's age, sex, race, nationality, religion, or income, he will likely subscribe to the moral values protected by such laws.
Offenses of this type are condemned by all "respectable" and "right
thinking" citizens, and even abhorred by criminals themselves when
committed against members of their ingroup. There are no well-organized pressure groups contending openly in community forum for legal
approval of such conduct. Rather, the conduct is not only criminal by
legal definition but also by the common moral definition of the community. The "social problem" involved in crimes of this type is *ameliorative* rather than moral in nature. That is to say, the problem is not one
of convincing the community that such behavior is wrongful and that
it should be put down. Rather, the essential difficulty is one of amelioration, of working out solutions and getting people to agree upon programs of prevention and penology.

On the other hand, contemporary criminal codes go far beyond the
moral minimum in prohibiting various forms of conduct which are not

iewed as wrongful by important groups and classes in the community. Violations of such laws constitute a second type of offenses which exploit a high threshold of community tolerance or endorsement. Crimes of this category are exemplified by circumvention of new social legislation, bribery of public officials to secure favorable contracts and legislation, fraud and misrepresentation in the financial statements of corporations, manipulations on the stock exchange, embezzlement and misapplication of funds, illegal transactions of public utility companies, gambling syndicates, liquor law violations, and commercialized vice. These crimes are committed either by white-collar upper-class businessmen who have the respect of most of the community, or by organized criminal rings which have the support and patronage of a sizable segment of the citizenry. White-collar crime and organized racketeering are not in the first instance ameliorative problems. Rather they are *moral problems*, because the fundamental issue is the moral unwillingness of the community as a whole to organize to put down wrong. No questions of prevention or punishment can arise until there has been effective action by law enforcement officials backed by an indignant community opinion. Crimes in this moral category persist because the violations themselves are an integral part of the community pattern of living. "Good" citizens may abhor the corruption of their public officials, protest the illegal practices of bankers, doctors and business executives, and they are even more likely to rise against organized gambling and vice. The fact remains that these practices and practitioners are woven into the economic and moral fabric of the community as an established part of "business as usual," and because of this people cannot agree on the basic moral question of whether or not such conduct should be tolerated.

So it is that in contemporary society behavior often comes to be defined as criminal where the opinion of many individuals and groups is not in support of the definition. This is perhaps inevitable in any culture which is split into so many diversified groups having so very little in common, but it is manifest that legal controls alone will not suffice to guarantee the high standards of moral behavior desired by those who support a given law. If the criminal definitions are to become incorporated into our central core of moral sanctions, many more people, representative of the community as a whole, must be won over to their support.

ADMINISTRATION AN EDUCATIONAL TECHNIQUE

It is not that the law must in all instances wait for widespread moral support. It is possible that the very administration of the law itself, if

wisely undertaken, may serve as a technique of popular educatic
through which to mold opinion in its favor. The enforcement of a la
inevitably awakens popular discussion as to its merits. This is the ca
with some of the recent social legislation such as the Securities and E
change Act regulating transactions on the stock exchange. Moreove
even in the instance of a very unpopular law, people are likely to obser
it for some time after its passage simply because it is the law of the lan
We have respect for *the law*, as an institution, even though we may ha
little or no respect for a specific legal measure. There were instanc
where even the much despised Prohibition Act was obeyed in letter an
in spirit by socially responsible citizens whose sentiments were not in a
cord with the law itself. But we cannot depend upon the habit of la
obedience exclusively. Ultimately the problem is one of supplementir
the political sanctions of the law, which operate through threat of pur
ishment more or less externally on individuals, with spontaneous mor
sanctions which operate on the habits, attitudes, and conscience of ind
viduals. Moral sanctions rarely originate in legislature, but rather in tl
more primary social groupings of the family, neighborhood discussio
groups, school and church. Even where the law is so technical or specia
ized in subject matter that it must necessarily come in advance of a
enlightened public opinion, as in the case of public health measures an
conservation of game statutes, it has little chance of permanent succe
so long as its social objectives remain unintelligible to the general publi

EDUCATION VERSUS THE "BIG STICK"

Should we not rely less on the "big stick" of the law and more on tecl
niques of popular education to the values implicit in the law? There ar
significant instances where the dominant group has not stopped wit
control by legal fiat, but has sought by other methods to educate pe
sistent offenders to its way of thinking. Witness traffic schools for adul
and programs of safety instruction for child pedestrians; temperanc
movements supplementing legal restrictions on the liquor business; co
servation films and lectures explaining the objectives of new fishing an
hunting regulations; and the intensive educational programs of the Fee
eral government relative to new social insurance, wage and hour, an
collective bargaining laws. These appeals are directed to the self-intere
of individuals as well as to their social conscience, but in any case the
seek to lighten the burdensome problem of law enforcement by chan
ing obstructive attitudes and values. Many more experiments in this d
rection will likely replace the "crack down and educate later" techniqu

which has too often characterized our passion for legislating against things which we do not like.

CONCLUSION

Sociologists interested in the problem of crime in contemporary America should further explore the implications of this relationship between moral and legal patterns. We have been prone to think of crime too much in terms of its legalistic aspects, and too little in terms of its community or cultural sources. The behavior of a criminal is always abnormal or atypical in the restricted sense that it is a deviation from some social norm established in the criminal law, but it is perfectly normal and typical when it subscribes to some cultural conduct norm other than that implicit in the law. If we are to do away with the forms of crime which are supported by the cultural values of the community, we must change these values. The failure of legal controls to eradicate such behavior is merely symptomatic of our failure to alter fundamentally the real source of the conduct which we condemn.

3 · Law and Psychiatry

by BENJAMIN KARPMAN

The law is primarily interested in the criminal deed rather than in the doer, in the immediate causes rather than the real motives, which almost invariably are remote and hidden. This practice is presumably based on the principle that what matters is the damage inflicted by the criminal upon the victim. Yet it is claimed that if our legal system is to be just with the perpetrator of a crime and is interested in finding effective ways of combatting criminality, both of which it proclaims as goals, it must go beyond a mere concern with the criminal act and the superficial reasons leading to it, and consider the criminal himself and his deeper motivations. Benjamin Karpman, a well-known psychiatrist of many years' experience, deals with this problem in the following selection. ["An Attempt at Re-Evaluation of Some Concepts of Law and Psychiatry," *Journal of Criminal Law and Criminology*, Vol. 38, Sept.-Oct. 1947, pp. 206-217. Reprinted by permission.]

MAN'S MIND is incurably a compulsive mind. It is a restless mind, alway asking questions, seeking problems, and craving answers; confronte with a fact, it looks for a cause. Hence religion which attempts to giv us something definitive about that which is basically infinite; henc science which attempts to satisfy a curiosity that is forever insatiabl hence medicine and medical research which seek a cure on a basis of known causes.

Withal, the human mind is equally limited and, for the most pa perhaps, superficial. All too often, as soon as an answer to the questio is given, it ceases searching for further answers. If a fact is explained i terms of an immediate cause, it ceases to search for deeper causation Yet the history of mankind has long taught us that behind an immediat cause there is universally a preceding cause, behind which there is a sti deeper cause; perhaps there are many deeper causes. In particular, w often fail to recognize the fact that a phenomenon may not have a immediate, clearly demonstrable cause, but may be the result of mar little causes, each in itself not significant as a direct determining facte in the final phenomenon, yet all these causes, in totality, providing th large background from which the phenomenon has emerged. And so happens, for instance, in our political or international life, that a wa may start seemingly from very trivial causes, yet in historical perspectiv it becomes clearly evident that these trivial causes were only curtai phenomena, and that back of these there have been many contributir factors going deeply and remotely into the national and political life of the belligerent nations, which explain more fully and adequately th phenomenon of war. Likewise in medicine where some diseases are u. questionably due to major cause; yet here, too, we are often confronte with diseases which start from an insignificant agent or no ascertainab cause at all, yet may lead to profound bodily disturbances.

Now, this is the situation with criminality, as it is quite universal with other human phenomena. An individual commits a crime, seen ingly for a very simple reason. He stole money because he needed it; of he killed a rival for the affection of a loved woman; or he violated or moral sense because perversely he wished to indulge in sexual behavio which is regarded as immoral and abnormal. These would seem to k the immediate motives, if motives they can be called. And yet, if one not satisfied with a mere cross-section but attempts to look deeper int the causation, he may discover, as he goes further, a great multiplici of factors streaming from different directions, all having combined t emerge through one particular act which in itself is insignificant excep in a symbolic sense, as an indicator of underlying problems.

It is a frequent observation that two disciplines dealing with the san material, but from different angles, often develop not only different approaches but even different technical languages as well, so that in time they come not even to understand each other. It is just such a situation which appears to have developed between law and psychiatry in dealing with crime. No clear understanding will ever come between the two unless they are interpreted to each other; just as one translates one language into another. It is in the hope of contributing somewhat to a better rapprochement between the two disciplines that the following considerations are offered.

THE DEED VS./AND/OR THE DOER

One of the severest limitations that still exist in modern law is the concept that so rigidly separates the *deed* from the *doer*; more specifically, the crime from the criminal. We pay but little attention to the criminal as an individual. This is even noticeable in criminal semantics. We speak of petty and grand larceny, or of mayhem but we do not have a corresponding noun for these, such as grand larcenist or mayhemist. The word murder includes all degrees and types; murder, homicide, second degree murder, manslaughter, etc. but there are no corresponding nouns for the various degrees. This situation often develops absurdities. A man steals a case of whiskey with a retail value of $65.00 and is charged with grand larceny, which is a felony. The defense lawyer, however, contends that the wholesale price of the goods is only $48.00, which brings the crime within the range of petty larceny, which is a misdemeanor. The argument is unanswerable and the original indictment can not be sustained. Nothing, however, is said of the thief himself. When committing the crime, he did not, it seems, consider that he was committing grand or petty larceny; he was committing larceny. His intent was to get the case of whiskey, be it grand or petty larceny. Intent gets closer to motivation than the mere size of the loot; but though it is recognized in both cases, it is not differential. In all reason he should be charged on the basis of the executed criminal intent rather than on the size of the crime. The law, however, emphasizes the result of crime rather than degree of intent. But in any criminal indictment, while intent is recognized, degrees of intent are less emphasized than degrees and gradations of crime.

Or let us take the instance of John A., who fires several shots at William B. with the obvious intention of killing him. He only succeeded, however, in injuring him, and he is charged with aggravated assault, for which he gets a sentence of, say, five years. Had he succeeded in his original aim, he would have been charged with first degree murder and punished accordingly. In either situation, however, his full intent was to kill; he was a murderer in every sense of the word; it was by sheer accident that he failed of his purpose. Yet the punishment is neatly differentiated on the basis of results rather than intent.

But why should we be at all concerned with the doer instead of merely taking care of the deed at its face value? After all, so it is maintained society's prime concern is with results, with acts as they affect the life of the community, and the effect is the same whatever causes may be back of the act. What indeed is the relationship, if there be any, between the deed and the doer? It is our contention that, be it a social deed or only a personal reaction, it is no more possible to treat satisfactorily the deed without considering the doer, than it is possible to treat a symptom without considering the disease that produced it. To a physician the deed has the same relationship to the doer as a symptom of a disease has to the disease as such. In early days, medicine was obliged to treat disease by symptoms only, for it did not know the pathology back of it. Modern medicine, however, is not satisfied with the treatment of symptoms as such, but instead attempts to treat the disease that is responsible for it. For, from its point of view, the symptom is merely the particular point at which a great many factors streaming from different directions each one having an origin and significance of its own, become confluent. Obviously, in order to do away with an annoying symptom, one must take into consideration all factors that have gone into its making. Thus, 100 years ago, we used to treat headache by a few established home remedies (and we do to a large extent even today). It was a blind treatment, a stab in the dark, as it were, and sometimes it worked and then again it did not. By this time, however, we know what a complicated symptom headache may be. It may be entirely an expression of some inflammation of the coverings of the brain. It may be due to some disease of the internal matter of the brain itself or its blood vessels, or it may be due to an expression of some particular psychological difficulties when the head aches with conflicts. Obviously, to treat all these headaches in the same manner would be fallacious, for while the remedy may reach one kind of headache it cannot possibly, by reason of the different pathology present, reach another type of headache. We therefore make a differential diagnosis and try to figure out the nature of the headache, and the type of remedy suitable for it.

Or let us say there is a skin eruption. One can of course scrape it off or put a salve on it. The salve may clear up the eruption, but as soon as the application of salve is removed, the eruption comes back. This is due to the fact that, although the skin eruption is on the surface of the body, its basic cause is entirely internal, a product of disturbed metabolism and not until the physician learns, by various tests at his disposal, the internal cause of the skin condition will he ever be able to do away with it.

Too, it must be remembered that treatment of a headache, skin eruption or any other symptom, symptomatically can at best be only palliative. As often as headache recurs, the particular medicine must be taken which only temporarily relieves the headache, but does not reach the basic source of it. It is, therefore, an endless proposition, whereas, on the other hand, if we know the basic cause of it, we can by radical treatment cure it and thus stop the headache altogether.

In like manner we view the deed. It is, as we see it, the surface expression of a large number of factors, some external to the individual, but for the most part entirely internal and having a long history. No deed can be understood unless the psychology of the doer is understood. And society, which is concerned with the abolition of deeds, will never accomplish that as long as it deals with the deed only. Hence, because of the system of punishing the deed and not the doer, crime has never abated and goes on from year to year, increasing in severity. A most radical change is needed; one must reach the deed through the doer.

CAUSATION VS./AND/OR MOTIVATION

Just as in criminal law the deed is regarded as being more important than the doer, so is causation considered more important than motivation. Causation refers chiefly to factors external to the individual responsible for the effect produced. Thus we speak of the effect of physical, economic, and general factors as causative factors in crime. Motivation, on the other hand, refers to factors which spring from the inner life of the individual, stimulating him to act in a particular way; it refers chiefly to inner psychological mainsprings in human behavior. The consideration of causative factors does not give us a clue as to why one of two men living in the same community and under apparently identical social conditions, becomes a habitual criminal while the other develops into an upright citizen and much respected member of the community. Only a study of their inner lives could reveal to us the true personal reasons for the difference in their behavior; only this knowledge can help us to understand the meaning of the crime for the criminal and the community, and how to dispose of it. And in any event, be it a question of causation or motivation, little more is sought in any criminal trial than the most immediate causation or motive. It is recognized as an established principle in law that motive does not enter into any crime as an essential ingredient, though it may be inquired into. Neither the failure

to prove any motive, nor even furnishing proof of a good motive, wil
prevent conviction. In the case of a man charged with the murder o
his wife or of the other man because of jealousy, he may be freed er
tirely if the unwritten law is invoked, or he may be charged with secon
degree murder and get from 20 years to life. In no instance, howeve:
does the motivation go beyond the statement of jealousy which ma
mean any number of things. Yet in terms of deeper motivations, unde
standable only in the light of the man's developmental psychology, ar
other man may have had far greater justification for committing murde
than did this one who did the killing in a more premeditated way an
in the belief that the unwritten law will free him, which in fact it di

THE SETTING

Another consideration is that extremely little attention is given t
the best indicator of criminal dynamics, namely the setting in which th
crime has been committed, and more particularly the basic origins fror
which criminal behavior is derived. While the search for motives is, a
a rule, neglected when a cause of crime is looked for, the emphasis is o
immediate rather than remote motivation and a specific individual mc
tivation at that, disregarding the multitude of circumstances that pr
ceded it and went directly into its making. Yet it is a fact that very ofte
single, definite, specific motivations in criminal behavior cannot b
found, but rather an accumulation of many minute influences whicl
in totality, produce the effects noted. In the words of many of my p:
tients, the influence is not specific but general and "atmospheric." Th
indeed is also true of many cases of neuroses in which no specific traum
can be pointed to as the cause of the neurosis, but the etiology must b
sought in the many varied minute influences that finally bring about th
neurosis. It is true for that matter of normal people when the develoj
ment of the personality make-up and traits of the individual can not b
traced to any specific environmental situations and effects but rather t
subtle but continuous influences that pervaded and permeated one
environment and development.

RIGHT AND WRONG: RESPONSIBILITY

But why need we be concerned at all with the motivations behin
the crime and the setting in which it has been committed? Because the
have an important bearing in the consideration of right and wrong, an
the problem of responsibility, both being essential in determining th
legal and social disposition of the case. For neither the knowledge (

ight or wrong, nor the feeling of responsibility, are abstract terms that appear in a vacuum. Nor yet are they immediate and spontaneous reactions that suddenly appear on the scene in response to a definite situation. On the contrary, they are human expressions that have a long history and evolution, a history as long as the development of the individual himself. From our point of view, it is not sufficient to say that the defendant knows or does not know the difference between right and wrong (and in some jurisdictions, whether he can adhere to it), or that he is guilty or not guilty, partly responsible or not at all responsible, but whether he can choose emotionally right from wrong; why, and to what extent he is guilty and why and to what extent he is responsible. An individual, and presumably a sane individual, may indeed know intellectually the difference between right and wrong, yet be wholly unable to choose emotionally the right, the emotional forces within him driving him irresistibly toward the wrong.

Total or even partial guilt and responsibility as viewed by law can not be determined by the consideration of the external factors of the case but only in the light of the individual defendant's own history and development. The individual must be considered first and not his crime, which is only a pale symbol of him. That is to say, regardless of what his present knowledge of right and wrong may be, what his guilt or responsibility may appear in the present cross section when charged with crime, we must go back to his life history—what sort of guilt feelings and sense of responsibility did he have long before the commission of the crime, and what were the forces that controlled their expression, blocking at times the operation of his conscience and guilt sense and allowing the commission of the crime. When we have a knowledge of all these situations, our entire treatment of the criminal will change. From the time of Beccaria and Bentham, we have been guided by the principle of "let the punishment fit the crime." Because of the universality of these concepts, which at the same time are obviously antiquated, it becomes important to investigate these more closely. We submit as a more correct formulation, "let the punishment fit the criminal" or even "let the treatment fit the criminal," for punishment is only one of the many treatments possible, and by no means the most effective or deterrent. And to paraphrase that great lawyer and humanitarian, Clarence Darrow, "I hate crime, but never the criminal."

INTELLECTUAL VS. EMOTIONAL KNOWLEDGE

In all discussion of right and wrong, and responsibility, the tacit underlying assumption is that we are dealing entirely with motives at the intellectual level, that every member of the community, unless he be definitely insane or feebleminded, has a perfect and clear-cut knowledge of right and wrong, and responsibility. This conception has been challenged by modern psychiatry. On the basis of undeniable and over whelming clinical evidence, it has been proven that human behavior is basically emotionally conditioned and that intellectual activities are emotionally determined. We are basically emotional, not reasoning beings. A man born and raised in the South, in a family atmosphere steeped in the traditions of the Democratic party, will have no difficulty in furnishing any number of valid intellectual reasons why democratic principles are superior to those of any other party. Likewise, an individ ual born and raised in Maine or Vermont in the best Republican tradi tions can offer equally cogent arguments proving what to him is beyond any peradventure of doubt, that the Republican party is the mainstay of our country.

Yet can any dispassionate and objective observer doubt for a moment that in both these gentlemen the intelligence is merely a tool and a vehicle through which is expressed the language of the underlying emo tions. Could they speak any other language, could they escape the emo tional influence of their early environment which began to work on their little minds when they could offer no resistance but all they could do was to absorb influences? The pre-war Japanese was convinced against all reason that the Emperor was divine, a proposition which to him was axiomatic and admitted of no doubt or argument. This was because from the earliest childhood he was emotionally influenced to think that way when his reason had not yet developed to a point that he could see the unreasonableness of it and contradict it. And that which is trained in us from childhood becomes emotionally fixed, solidified, structural- ized; and it is virtually impossible to change such an influence except perhaps through some other set of powerful emotional influences. Thus as Japan lost the war, it shook to its foundations the belief of the Jap anese in the divine power of the Emperor. It made them feel very in secure—and insecurity is a powerful emotional reaction—and now they look to America as a symbol of security. Hence, pictures of Hirohito disappear from their newspapers and in their place we have pictures of General MacArthur and other Americans. Who then can doubt that our intelligence is basically influenced by underlying emotions?

TWO CHIEF TYPES OF CRIMINALS

If there be, therefore, any validity in our contention that the con- sideration of the doer is more important than the consideration of the deed, then we disregard the technical legal considerations of crime, but instead view crime from the standpoint of the types of personalities involved. Thus, surveying crime as a whole, not from its surface behavior, but from its deeper motivations, especially against its background and setting, two clearly defined types of crime seem to emerge. One would appear to be committed on a purely mercenary, predatory basis. Take if you will, the immediate causations, or if you choose, go as far back as you can into the life of such a criminal and the most you can uncover is a life of predation and parasitism. We may call this the psychopathic type of criminal. And there is another type of criminal, who in terms of crime as such, may have committed the same crime, yet even a brief search may reveal definite psychological reasons that often are deeply tied with the emotional life of the individual. This is the psychogenic type of criminal. Superficially, the two types may seem very much alike. One might say: "If I am robbed, hurt or killed, it makes little difference to me, in terms of its ultimate effect on me, as to the particular motive the offender may have had in committing the crime." This indeed is true. But the offender is also a member of the community and as such has certain rights and privileges which he cannot be denied. In a large sense, society has produced him and is therefore in a sense responsible for him. Yet society may even have interests in the situation that go beyond the immediate interests of the victim and/or the criminal as individual members of the community; it must consider the larger needs of the community as such. There is foremost here the problem of disposition of the case. Punishment is not enough! Punishment will not restore stolen property, nor return to wife and children a man who has been killed, nor yet re-establish in the woman victim of rape the consciousness of unviolated chastity. It is even doubtful whether it acts as a deterrent as seen from the rising rate of crime. But to know how to dispose of a case, more than mere knowledge of the man's surface behavior is needed. We need to know all we can about him: the type of family he was born in, for that, no doubt, influences his subsequent behavior; his development at a period of life when he could have no control over his developing moral sense and his emotional make-up. For, as Wordsworth truly said, "the child is the father of the man." And can a child be held responsible for having been influenced in the way he was influenced at a highly impressionable age when he could neither choose his influences nor control their effect on him?

Supposing then that we tentatively divide criminality and criminals into two main groups: psychopathic and psychogenic. It isn't difficult to cite instances from actual experiences indicating the chief differences between the two types. Here is a man who is engaged in stealing. He prizes his theft in proportion to the value of the loot obtained; that and no more. He has no relation whatever to the victim. He has neither pity nor hate for the victim. Though the victim may suffer privation because of the theft, the thief never stopped to reflect on that, let alone identifying himself with the victim, whom he does not even regard in the light of a victim, if he regards him at all. This is how he acted and behaved all his life; this is the psychopathic thief and robber.

In contrast to him, is another man who, too, steals. He happens to concentrate his thefts on jewelry to the exclusion of everything else. Does he dispose of his jewelry and convert it into cash? Not at all! He keeps it at home where he has by now a large accumulation of gems. Every now and then, in the manner of the proverbial miser, he takes out his jewelry and stares at it for long periods of time as if enchanted or intoxicated. Dispose of it! Never! These gems have a strong emotional value to him. They take him back emotionally to the time of his early childhood when he saw his mother carefully putting away her jewels lest someone steal them. Symbolically, he steals his mother's jewelry and thus shares with her things that are most precious to her. In this way he feels he gets closer to her and re-animates the old memories of her. This is the psychogenic criminal.

Contrast a man who will set fire to his establishment because he expects to collect insurance money which he needs so badly—the motive here would seem to be psychopathic—with another individual who will set fire to house after house, out of revenge for betrayal, or as a form of protest against particular iniquities—that is the psychogenic. So it is also in the case of murder. One man will kill for money while one will kill because of unrequited love or undischarged hate. Likewise, too, are the cases of white slavery wherein we find individuals who engage in it solely for the profit in it, as against those who will resort to it for any emotional reasons they may have at the time. It is conceivable that, as time goes on and we search deeper and deeper into the basic motivations of criminal behavior, the differences separating these two types may become more obvious.

A PLEA FOR DIFFERENTIAL TREATMENT OF CRIMINALS

In any event, can society treat these two types of criminals alike? Certainly not! The psychogenic cases should be treated, for they can be cured, as many have been. The psychopathic cases, however, at least in the present state of our knowledge, are not approachable by psychotherapy or some other form of dealing or treatment; these must be devised. It is primarily in the interest of society much more than in the interest of the individual that before any decision be made as to disposition, a more careful and thorough study be made of the entire situation. This is the method of medicine as a profession, the scientific approach, in the long run the only approach that can truly solve the problem of crime.

IN SUMMARY

It is essential that law dealing with the more formal social aspects of crime, and psychiatry dealing with the human motives behind criminal behavior, pool their respective resources and approaches, so that out of this there may develop superior methods of dealing with the problem. For in spite of all measures and methods heretofore and presently used, crime seems to show no signs of abatement, but, on the contrary, grows more acutely every day. Dynamic psychiatry therefore offers the following considerations:

1. Emphasis should be laid primarily on the *doer* and not on the *deed*.

2. Prime consideration should be given to deeper emotional *motivations* behind the crime, and assign immediate *causation* a secondary importance.

3. The setting in which the crime has been committed is important, but more important yet is the *environmental setting* in which the criminal was brought up and developed as a child and/or an individual.

4. It is fallacious to assume that everybody knows exactly what is right and what is wrong, and thus charge everyone with full and equal responsibility. It is submitted here that due consideration must be given to the origin and life-time development of the *right* and *wrong* attitudes in each accused individual on the basis of which the degree of guilt and responsibility may be more correctly evaluated.

5. In the light of advanced psychiatric knowledge, our behavior and our knowledge are determined basically more by *emotional* than *intellectual* considerations.

6. Rather than to treat and charge individuals with this or that type of crime, it is more correct to view criminals in terms of the type of personalities involved. On this basis, criminals may be divided into two main classes: The psychogenic and psychopathic, respectively.

a) To the *psychogenic* group belong those cases in which definite emotional motivations may be found back of the criminal behavior. For the most part they may be reached psychotherapeutically, sometimes with but little difficulty. Many are therefore redeemable. This group contributes the larger percentage of habitual criminals.

b) The other group, the *psychopathic*, fails to reveal the presenc of psychogenic motivations and therefore can be but little influence psychotherapeutically. Instead of giving them a definite sentence, the should be segregated and confined for an indefinite period of time.

The basic tenet of this contribution is that if criminals are to b treated effectively, they must be treated differentially on the basis c their personality as a whole.

CHAPTER FIVE

Criminal Statistics

=====================================

14 · Statistics in the Analysis of
Social Problems

by FREDERICK A. CONRAD

That statistics are popularly considered the most reliable
type of proof of a contention is indicated by the widely
held notion that "figures don't lie." Scholars and scientists
as well as laymen often accept uncritically figures compiled
by their colleagues or even obtained by them at second
hand and build upon them their own theories and claims.
This occurs in spite of the fact that there exists a contrary
belief, also widespread, that "statistics can prove anything."
In criminology, where wide use is made of statistics, a critical attitude toward them is especially important. It is for
this reason that a general discussion, by a University of
Arizona sociologist, on the pitfalls in the use of statistics,
is presented here. [From *Sociology and Social Research*,
Vol. XXVI, No. 6, July-Aug. 1942, pp. 538-549. Reprinted
by permission. Footnotes omitted.]

THE USE of statistics for purposes of propaganda is widespread. Figures
are used to prove anything from the most popular brand of cigarettes

to the best form of patriotism. Such statements as "figures do not lie" and "statistics can be used to prove anything" indicate a flexibility in the use of statistics which enables the skillful propagandist to make white appear black or vice versa. Many a doubting Thomas has been pulled into line by the simple assertion, "The figures speak for themselves." However, the inferences to be drawn from the figures have been subtly suggested by the propagandist, and fallacies often can be detected only by careful analysis. The unsuspecting person can thus be easily overwhelmed by a barrage of figures when he lacks the critical weapons to make a statistical counterattack.

Social scientists are not always above criticism in their use of statistical data. The uncritical use of figures to impress on the public the seriousness of its problems is a common practice which often tends to mislead, if not to deceive, the public. The desire to make a problem "obvious" and an argument convincing frequently leads, perhaps unintentionally, to the acceptance of statistics which support the viewpoint of the writer or make his analysis impressive. "Sticking to the facts" means hard work and patient research. Writers find it much more convenient to use the evidence submitted by other scholars who, presumably, have checked the facts. Figures may thus be used, with the sanction of numerous scholars, without a critical analysis of how the figures were compiled or the theoretical assumptions upon which they are based. Inasmuch as the reader is not, as a rule, in a position to evaluate the methodology of the social sciences, the responsibility rests on the social scientist to examine his data and his assumptions thoroughly. A little more realism and caution in the use of statistical material would go a long way toward removing some of our social science literature from the realm of propaganda and wishful thinking.

Textbooks in the field of social problems are particularly subject to the above criticisms. Figures are freely quoted to stress the magnitude of given problems. Monetary standards of measurement are frequently used to inform the pecuniary-minded reader of the financial losses to the nation of its social maladjustments, wastes, and inefficiency. Students, as a rule, have little comprehension of the problems involved in using a monetary standard of measurement and are therefore susceptible to the suggestions of the writer. In formulating the student's conception of social problems, much depends, therefore, upon the care with which financial statistics are presented.

A comparison of a number of texts which submit estimates of the costs of particular social problems shows considerable variation in the degrees of regard or disregard for the problems involved in determining such costs and offers *prima facie* evidence of the confusion which may arise when social problems are reduced to a dollar-and-cents basis. Categories are not clearly defined; distinctions between real and hypothetical costs are not always made clear; private and public losses are added together to swell the total "social costs" to the nation; and little, if any, consideration is given to fluctuating market values and business cycles which, in time, invalidate any estimates not readjusted to changes in the value of money. Estimates on the costs of crime and health will serve to illustrate the difficulties confronting a student consulting different texts in the hope of finding reliable objective data on the costs of a given problem.

Estimates on the annual cost of crime vary from 1 to 18 billion dollars. There is no agreement as to what items should be included in the estimates or what the actual or hypothetical costs are. One text considers estimates of 10 billion dollars as "extravagant" because they include "many nebulous and mythical costs"; another concludes that 15 billion dollars is "quite possibly an underestimate"; while a third concludes that the cost is probably somewhere between 10 and 18 billion dollars. This allows plenty of latitude to discuss "the gigantic annual crime bill."

The large element of guesswork in these figures is readily apparent. The estimates, as Professor Sutherland points out, are based mainly upon unwarranted assumptions. "They start with the question, 'How much would be saved if no crimes were committed and no precautions had to be taken against future crimes?' " How much, for example, would the nation save if there were no gambling? The assumed answer is 6 billion dollars. However, inasmuch as this sum represents a transfer of private funds from one person to another, by more or less mutual consent, what one person loses, another gains; and the nation has lost nothing directly except the cost of enforcing the laws against gambling. Likewise, racketeering, robberies, thefts, embezzlements, forgeries, commercial frauds, organized extortions, et cetera, which constitute a large proportion of the total costs of crime, represent primarily losses to private citizens except insofar as the government itself has been robbed and defrauded or has made expenditures for law enforcement. When a bank is robbed, the bankers suffer a loss which is not shared directly by the community as a whole. The main difference as far as the community is concerned, except insofar as essential services are impaired, is that the robbers are spending money which otherwise would have been spent by bankers. If the robbers burn down the bank building and destroy other property in the course of their activities, the community as well as the private owners suffers an economic loss in the sense that useful wealth has been destroyed. In the illegal transfer of wealth, its use in the community continues; by destruction, however, its use ceases. The failure to differentiate properly between the categories of private and community losses ends in confusion when these different classes of costs are added together in the estimates for the nation.

In computing the costs of law enforcement, a distinction must also be made between civil and criminal cases. Courts and police forces must be maintained, whether we have much or little crime, because precaution is always necessary and these agencies perform many civil functions not directly related to crime. Penal institutions could not be dispensed with even if there were only a few criminals. How much the nation could save annually in the costs of its courts, police, and penal and correctional institutions if there were no crime is uncertain because there is no way of knowing how much protection is necessary as a precautionary measure or what share of the costs should be attributed specifically to the commission of crime.

The indirect costs of crime are still more difficult to determine because they involve a hypothetical question as to what the criminal class would add to the national income if it engaged in productive labor. This is pretty much like an inquiry into what differences in our national history would have resulted if Washington instead of Cornwallis had surrendered at Yorktown. There can be only hypothetical answers to hypothetical questions. An aggregate figure on the cost of crime compiled out of such data can have little, if any, accuracy. The National Commission on Law Enforcement and Observance, which attempted the first comprehensive study of the cost of crime, concludes:

We are of the opinion that no such aggregate figure can be worked out with even approximate accuracy and are unwilling to indulge in vague estimates which could, at best, be no more than guesses.

If it is, however, considered valid to add the imputed value of the productive labor of the criminal class to the total cost of crime, it becomes necessary, in the interests of accuracy, to deduct the cost of eliminating crime before any estimate of the net addition to the national income can be made. The cost of eliminating crime and of rehabilitating the criminal class would be enormous. Inasmuch as no data exist to form actual estimates on either proposition, it would be just as valid, hypothetically, to assume that the costs of eliminating crime would exceed any probable gains in the national income as vice versa.

The lack of a strictly objective approach in dealing with the cost of crime is apparent in some of the texts under consideration. The difficulties involved in making reliable estimates are ignored or minimized, and estimates of doubtful value are accepted for purposes of hypothetical discussions in order to impress the student with the magnitude of the problem. Costs of crime are referred to in superlative terms as "enormous," "gigantic," "terrifying," and "appalling." What is "appalling" depends on both the estimate considered valid and what appalls a given person. Obviously one billion dollars is not so appalling as 18 billion dollars.

Such phraseology represents an evaluation which is highly suggestive and has good propaganda value. To suggest on "competent" authority that crime and rackets cost the nation 18 billion dollars annually is not only impressive—it is startling. It has news value and is a concise estimate of the problem which the reader can easily remember. Such a figure, if true, is a revelation and a challenge. To allow criminals, for example, to get away with approximately twice as much annually as the value produced by the entire farm population should arouse every honest citizen to action. Instructors may also find the average student more interested in a vivid portrayal of the evils of society than in a matter-of-fact analysis of the fallacies in criminal statistics. This makes the course interesting, but it does not make it scientific.

Estimates on the annual costs of sickness show a variation from 3½ to 10½ billion dollars. This variation is due to a difference of opinion as to whether the indirect costs of sickness constitute valid data to be included in the estimates. One text concludes that the indirect costs attributed to the loss of wages and preventable deaths cannot be reliably calculated and should not, therefore, be included in the nation's health bill, whereas other texts take the opposite view and include the indirect costs.

A decision as to which of these views is scientifically valid cannot be expected from the beginning student. It involves an examination of the statistical procedure used in calculating the economic value of health and the cost of preventable deaths. The studies originally made by Dublin are generally used in this connection. By a number of hypothetical calculations based on assumptions which events have later proved to be untenable, Dublin concluded that the net economic value of a man at the age of 18 is $29,000, and the corresponding value of a woman is half of that sum. From this he calculated the losses due to preventable deaths and the value of the nation's health. Dublin thus formulated a financial index of health and concluded that "the total vital assets" of the nation are over 1,500 billion dollars, whereas its material assets in 1922 were only 321 billion dollars, a ratio of approximately 5:1.

In several texts, Dublin's figures, which are purely hypothetical, are submitted as factual evidence without regard to the validity of his original assumptions or without considering the effect of the depression and changes in the value of money upon his calculations. With fifteen million unemployed laborers on the streets during the dark days of the depression and over twenty-one million persons still dependent on government assistance in 1936, after considerable recovery of business, it is an error of the first magnitude to assume that the average man's net worth remained on the level of the boom period of the late twenties. Presumably, if we use a monetary measure, his value tumbled in the crash of 1929, just as the value of securities, real estate, or commodities.

Furthermore, to assume at a given time that the vital assets of the nation can have five times as much value as its material assets is a confusion of terms. In the terminology of the market, when a corporation fixes its capitalization at a figure above the value of its real assets, it is accused of "watering its stock." One of the old problems in dealing with railroads and public utilities has been to "squeeze the water out of their stock" until their capitalization represents their real value. Similarly, if the capitalization of the nation's health is made to conform to real values, we should "squeeze" 1,179 billion dollars out of Dublin's original figures without allowing for the decline of values after 1929.

Stated in other terms, Dublin's contention was that the nation's wealth could be increased five times if the potential energies of its people were fully utilized. As long as this is conceived in terms of goods, there may be some justification for the argument. Waste of the nation's vital energies is obvious enough, although the degree of efficiency expected in Dublin's figures may be properly questioned. However, as soon as the proposition is transferred to a monetary basis, the validity of his ratios is destroyed. Only by a process of statistical jugglery can the conclusion be made that five times as many goods offered on the market, where values are determined, would have five times as much value. Other things being equal, the same dollar would merely buy five times as many goods and the hypothetical value of the average man would be reduced five times.

The addition of 8 billion dollars to the nation's health bill by such a method of calculating the indirect costs of illness and preventable deaths gives us an impressive total. It departs from strictly objective procedure, however, and introduces a number of assumptions which must be explained and interpreted. In the end, the acceptance or rejection of the figures becomes a matter of personal opinion in which the suggestions of an instructor and the suggestibility of the student may be deciding factors.

In view of the hypothetical character of the suggested costs of various social problems, another difficulty occurs when the figures are totaled and checked against the national income. The following estimates taken from a single text serve to illustrate the difficulty.

Gambling	6.0	(billion dollars)
"Sin" (chiefly drink, tobacco, commercialized recreation, and vice)	13.5- 40.0	" "
Luxuries (mostly wasteful consumption)	22.7	" "
Preventable disease, accidents, and death	5.0- 15.0	" "
Medical costs	3.6	" "
Crime and rackets	12.0- 18.0	" "
War	2.7	" "
Totals	65.5-108.0	" "

Estimates of the losses of farm products due to insects, rodents, and weeds; the loss and waste of forest, minerals, and soil resources; losses due to the destruction of property by floods, fires, and other national catastrophes; the costs of strikes, unemployment, relief; and, in general, the maintenance of the socially inadequate classes should be added to get a more complete aggregate of the nation's annual losses. By the same methods of calculation these items would probably add 10 to 20 billion dollars to the above totals.

The attempt to catalogue losses and waste involves the initial difficulty of defining the specific classes of costs to be added in the aggregate. Good statistical procedure requires the use of quantitative units capable of exact measurement or enumeration. The categories of costs used above are ambiguous, qualitative, and only vaguely indicative of the thing to be measured. By what standard, for example, is the use of tobacco to be regarded as "sin" or the purchase of the latest design of an automobile a wasteful superluxury? Unless we accept some absolute Puritanical standard of consumption, such a classification of wastes is untenable. Automobiles, which were a luxury in the horse-and-buggy days, have become a necessity in the automotive age. The same automobile may be subjected to different uses, necessary or otherwise. Discarding last year's model to secure the latest streamlined car does not imply the waste of useful goods. In fact, the used car market enables people of low incomes to purchase and utilize older models indefinitely. The transfer of goods between different classes of users may thus represent an actual gain to society by assuring their maximum use. Until such categories as "sin" and wasteful consumption are, therefore, clearly defined, there can be no accurate basis of measurement.

There is, no doubt, a great deal of overlapping in the figures given above, but the text does not indicate the extent of such overlapping, and the reader is at liberty to take the estimates at their face value. The figures are astonishing because they suggest the enormity of our wastes, which was, perhaps, the purpose of the author. A difference of 42.5 billion dollars between the higher and lower estimates does not, however, inspire much confidence in the accuracy of the data.

When these figures are compared with the total national income, which is quoted at $43,625,000,000, the probable error becomes more apparent. The logical inference which may be drawn from these comparisons is that the nation normally loses or wastes a sum far in excess of its income before there is allowance made for the normal expenditures for necessities, capital expansion, and capital replacements. A nation given to such extravagance when its income is low would probably become more wasteful when its income is high. Thus, "it is probably not going too far to hold that we spend a sum pretty close to half of our total national income each year on wasteful and needless forms of consumption." This item should thus exceed 40 billion dollars in 1941. If the losses due to gambling, "sin," crime, disease, war, relief, rackets, et cetera, remain fairly constant, the problem presented by these figures, in 1941 as in 1935, is how the nation can meet the normal requirements for its existence and development. If the estimated losses and waste quoted above are accurate, they are a terrible indictment of our national economy; if they are not accurate, they are, at best, a reflection upon the statistical methods used in attempting to measure social problems by monetary standards. A more factual approach is necessary to avoid the confusion which is bound to arise when students attempt to find the total losses and waste which may be actually charged against the national income.

Illustrations need not be multiplied further. Several conclusions seem to be justified.

1. Data on the costs of social maladjustments used in text books on social problems are, in the main, objectionable because they attempt the measurement of social problems by a variable yardstick—the dollar. The difficulties of measuring variable problems by a variable standard are too largely ignored, and questionable data are used to emphasize the magnitude of given social problems.

2. Much research is necessary before the costs of our major social problems can be confidently stated in items of dollars and cents. This is true, for the most part, of the direct costs, but it applies particularly to estimates of the indirect costs of social problems.

3. In the interests of clarity in presenting such cost data as are now available, more attention should be given to the methods used in determining such costs. Discrepancies, inaccuracies, duplications, and assumptions in the figures need to be pointed out to avoid misconceptions as to

the nature and importance of particular social problems. This necessarily implies considerable diversion from the analysis of social problems to a consideration of the validity of the financial rating given them.

4. In view of the difficulties involved in attempting to measure social problems by monetary standards, the elimination of cost data should be considered and attention given to other methods of approach. The development of a valid frame of reference which will serve the beginner as a basis of interpretation seems preferable to a compilation of statistics and information which supply the student with a lot of opinions and impressions but leave him without a consistent basis for his analysis of social problems.

15 · The Need for Uniformity in Criminal Statistics

by THORSTEN SELLIN

Crime statistics, essential in criminology, have been considered by criminologists as faulty, unreliable, and, for scientific purposes, of very limited use. Although the gathering of reliable data is beset with great difficulties, effort and willingness on the part of municipalities, counties, states, and the federal government can overcome most of the obstacles. In the United States, where there are wide differences among legal systems, procedures, and administrative methods, one of the greatest needs is to bring about uniformity in the recording of criminal data in the various jurisdictional divisions, so that the statistics published are more reliable. Professor Thorsten Sellin, of the University of Pennsylvania, an authority on criminal statistics, presents here the reasons for the need for a uniform system of recording criminal data and tells of the efforts made in this direction. ["The Uniform Criminal Statistics Act," *Journal of Criminal Law and Criminology*, Vol. 40, Mar.-Apr. 1950, pp. 679-700. Reprinted by permission. Abridged and footnotes omitted.]

OUR HIGH RATES of criminality present a constant challenge to the legislator and others interested in remedial social action. Such action must be founded, however, on an understanding of the problems involved and of the value or efficacy of possible solutions. In either case, an indispensa-

ble tool and source for information is to be found in what is commonly
called *criminal statistics*.

WHAT CAN WE LEARN FROM CRIMINAL STATISTICS?

1. It would be impossible to form any valid opinion about the amount
of criminality in a given jurisdiction nor could we know how criminality
changes over a period of time or how its component parts vary, were it
not for the fact that information in the possession of police and other
agencies can be tabulated and analyzed. The importance of such knowledge is obvious; it provides a necessary basis for administrative and legislative action, as well as a check on the efficiency of remedial or preventive
measures or programs.

2. It is essential that we should know as much as possible about those
who offend against the law. Who are they? From what racial, sex, age,
nativity, or regional groups do they come? What are their previous records of delinquency, their mental and physical state, their educational
and vocational history? Answers to these and other questions concerning
the offender in the mass should at all times be available so that we may
be wholly aware of conditions or changes pointing to the need for remedial or preventive measures. This does not mean that criminal statistics
can be used to discover the roots of the individual offender's conduct,
for this demands other and finer diagnostic instruments. Nevertheless,
statistical study of the offender in the mass has obvious social utility.

3. We have created a vast network of official agencies to bring offenders to justice to determine their guilt, to impose penalties, and to administer penal or correctional treatment. The operation of these agencies,
the manner in which they apply policies dictated by law, and their relations to offenders in their charge are phenomena concerning which we
are poorly informed. Some of the problems involved have been laid bare
by various local and state surveys of criminal justice or by piecemeal
research, but what is needed as a basis for administrative improvements
is a permanent system of social accounting in this field. The statistical
analysis of administrative processes offers the soundest basis for administrative reform. Archaic and ineffective methods of dealing with offenders
would have less chance of survival in law and practice had their nature
and operation been the object of continuous statistical scrutiny.

The truth of the above assertions has long been recognized, but the
steps taken to develop criminal statistics of a quality or scope designed
to bring out their full value have been sporadic and uneven. Nowhere
in the United States today is it possible to find a well integrated and
reasonably adequate system of criminal statistics, either on the local,

state, federal, or national basis, in spite of the fact that we have long been deeply concerned with the serious character of our crime problem. We should no longer ignore one of the most necessary instruments available to us in our efforts to cope with criminality.

THE NEED FOR CENTRALIZATION

Criminal statistics are constructed from items of information recorded by the different agencies that have contact with offenders and offenses. While some of these agencies are operated by the state, such as penitentiaries, most of them are local in character. In the enforcement of the criminal law, the municipality or the county plays a dominant role. Inferior and trial courts are local institutions and so are nearly all juvenile courts. Persons held for trial or serving short sentences are found in local jails or workhouses. Most of the data for criminal statistics are therefore contained in municipal or county records.

One of the effects of the condition referred to above is a lack of uniformity in the extent and the manner of recording information. In the absence of any superior directive or coordinating agency each institution or office tends to develop its own record system with a result that data recorded by one agency may not be recorded at all by another, or insufficiently recorded, precluding comparison. The conclusion is inescapable that adequacy and uniformity can be achieved only by some superior central agency which has the power to require local or state officials to maintain uniform and comparable record systems.

These considerations have prompted the drafting of the Uniform Criminal Statistics Act approved by the National Conference of Commissioners on Uniform State Laws and the American Bar Association in 1946. The adoption of this act by a state, the selection of competent persons to administer it, and the appropriation of sufficient funds for their work would ultimately give to such a state a good system of criminal statistics yielding the benefits already discussed. When this has been achieved in a considerable number of states, the groundwork will be laid for good national criminal statistics, assembled by some federal agency from the various state bureaus. For in spite of the worthwhile attempts made by different federal bureaus to compile national data, the next forward steps of any importance in this direction will be impossible without the improvements of state statistics and the assistance of state bureaus created for their collection.

The struggle to develop national criminal statistics in the United States has been going on for a long period. By national criminal statistics we mean statistics of crimes and of delinquents and criminals regardless of whether state or federal laws have been violated and so inclusive that they permit us to make inferences concerning the problems faced by the nation as a whole, as well as by its component regions and states. It has been well understood that such a task could only be undertaken by one or more federal agencies, since such agencies alone would possess the prestige that would invite the cooperation of state and local reporting agencies, for in the absence of federal power compelling the latter to submit reports, national criminal statistics must rest entirely on voluntary cooperation by state, county, and municipal agencies.

The story of national efforts is soon told. Prior to 1930 the only statistics of national scope were found in the decennial census of prisoners in or admitted to penal institutions and in the annual reports on prisoners committed to federal and state prisons and reformatories (beginning with 1926) issued by the Bureau of the Census. Beginning with the year 1927, the Children's Bureau initiated a statistical report on children in juvenile proceedings. In 1930 the Federal Bureau of Investigation assumed the responsibility for compiling and publishing *Uniform Crime Reports* from police agencies and in 1932, the Bureau of the Census launched a series of judicial criminal statistics secured from the states.

Only the decennial census of penal institutions, last made in 1933, could lay claim to a national coverage. The annual reports on prisoners ignored county and local institutions and were in no year complete, since two or three states refused regularly to cooperate with the bureau. The juvenile court statistics have been increasing the area of reporting but are still far from being nation-wide. The judicial criminal statistics covered as few as six states one year and a maximum of 30 states when they reached their height. The *Uniform Crime Reports* cover chiefly urban areas containing about half of the population of the nation.

The efforts made by organizations and private individuals to secure the initiation of the above services in the 1920's and the early 1930's were based on a conviction that they were essential tools in the struggle for crime prevention and better methods of dealing with offenders. This conviction has surely not grown weaker. Nevertheless, in the preoccupation of the nation with war and the stabilization of peace, the work of securing increasingly better national criminal statistics has suffered, so much, indeed, that we can now record a definite setback. As a result of reorganization, the Bureau of the Census abandoned both its annual reports on prisoners and its judicial criminal statistics in 1946. This leaves for the present only the two other series mentioned to represent our national endeavors in this field. The action of the Bureau of the Census was not intended to bury both of its series. It was expected that at least the annual report on prisoners would be carried on by the Federal Bureau of Prisons. So far, however, the latter bureau has been unable to secure the modest appropriation from Congress which is necessary. The judicial criminal statistics series was presumably to be continued by the Department of Justice, but so far there is no indication that this will happen. While it is clear that the last mentioned statistics were of very limited use, this was in part due to the lack of any real effort to improve them. The prison statistics, on the other hand, were of superior quality, and their disappearance would be a great loss. Even the loss of the judicial statistics is important because they afforded the agency collecting them a foothold which could have been utilized to bring gradual improvement in the reporting of data by courts.

In the light of the developments mentioned, we should perhaps reconsider the problem. It is likely that those working for better national criminal statistics have put the cart before the horse. It is more than likely that we can never hope for further *fundamental* improvement in the structure of a system of national statistics *based on voluntary cooperation* until we have strengthened the foundation. That foundation must be laid in the individual states.

In a country made up of states with widely different laws, procedures, and administrative methods and techniques, it is not easy to secure uniform national data. This is a problem typical of federated states. The same situation existed in Switzerland, which went a long way toward solving it when it adopted a uniform penal code just before the last world war. Lacking such a code, systems of good state statistics are not enough; these systems must also allow for enough uniformity so as to be able to supply uniform data for a national report. This is the reason why the National Commission of Law Observance and Enforcement recommended in 1931 that a uniform act be drafted which, when adopted by the states, would provide the basis for good statistics.

The National Conference of Commissioners on Uniform State Laws took heed of the suggestion and promptly appointed, in 1931, a committee to draft such an act. The resulting draft was officially adopted by the conference in 1937. . . .

* * *

BUREAU OF CRIMINAL STATISTICS ESTABLISHED

A Bureau of Criminal Statistics . . . is established. . . . The object of the Bureau of Criminal Statistics is to act as a central agency which collects, analyzes, and publishes statistical information drawn from reports supplied by all local or state officials or agencies concerned in any way with crime and criminals. Most of the states of the union lack such a central service. In a few states the only criminal statistics available are found in the reports of individual institutions or state departments, in which case they refer only to the functions of such institutions or departments. In other states, one or more state departments secure reports from some particular type of county or municipal official or agency. An illustration of this may be found in those states in which the attorney general is required to secure certain statistics from county attorneys and to publish them in his annual report. Or, as sometimes happens, a large number of state departments or boards may be charged with the duty of securing statistics from local sources, each confining itself to one type of source. The result is that a considerable amount of statistical information may be secured for the state as a whole and covering a variety of aspects of the problem, but under such conditions it is inevitable that the published data lack uniformity and comparability. Alabama, for instance, affords a good illustration of such extreme decentralization. In this state the Department of Public Welfare receives annually required reports from public or private state, county, municipal or other agencies or institutions engaged in placing or caring for delinquent minor children. It also receives monthly reports from juvenile court judges on the work of their courts and from probate judges on nonsupport or desertion cases. The Chief Justice of the Supreme Court receives semi-annual reports from clerks of circuit courts or courts of like jurisdiction on the business of the courts and the number of prisoners in jail. The attorney general receives quarterly reports from circuit and county solicitors on the criminal business of the courts. The Department of Correction and institutions receives monthly reports from sheriffs, police chiefs and town marshals on prisoners in county and city jails. Iowa presents another illustration of the same type. In that state the Board of Parole receives reports from clerks of district courts, the Board of Social Welfare, from juvenile courts and institutions receiving delinquent children; the attorney general or the governor from county attorneys, and the Bureau of Investigation from coroners.

CENTRAL BUREAU OF CRIMINAL STATISTICS

A few states have created central bureaus of criminal statistics, empowered to secure information from a wide variety of state and local officials. Such bureaus have been provided for in California, Louisiana, Massachusetts, Michigan, Minnesota, New York, Pennsylvania, Rhode Island, South Dakota, Texas and the Territory of Hawaii. In addition, it may be argued that Illinois, Indiana, Maryland and North Carolina have legislation that might enable the state authorities to set up such bureaus. The various states mentioned exhibit no uniformity in the definition of the duties or powers of these services. Some of these agencies have extremely comprehensive programs, while others are greatly limited by law.

THE ADMINISTRATIVE LOCATION OF THE BUREAU

Strictly speaking, no state of the union possesses, at the present time, an independent Bureau of Criminal Statistics; that is, an agency which is solely devoted to this task and not attached to any specific state department. Most of the present statistical services are administered as divisions of some state department set up to serve some other main function.

* * *

Upon examination, the present situation reveals, then, that two main solutions have been utilized. In most states, either the department in charge of state penal institutions or the state Bureau of Identification has been entrusted with the collection of criminal statistics. In only two states, Louisiana and South Dakota, has the attorney general's office been selected by the legislature as a proper location for a central statistical service, and in one of these, Louisiana, a duplicate service exists in the State Bureau of Identification, while in the other, South Dakota, the choice was adopted in conformity with the recommendations in the Uniform Criminal Statistics Act approved in 1937 by the National Conference of Commissioners on Uniform State Laws.

WHAT SOLUTION SHOULD A MODEL UNIFORM CRIMINAL STATISTICS ACT PROPOSE?

1. Should a Bureau of Criminal Statistics be an independent agency similar to the Minnesota Bureau but devoting its entire effort to criminal statistics? That is, from many points of view, the best solution. Such a bureau receiving an appropriation directly from the legislature would be most unhampered in its work.

2. If this is regarded as undesirable by the legislature, the Bureau should be attached either to the department in charge of the penal correctional institutions of the state or to the Bureau of Identification. This solution has both advantages and disadvantages. The advantages reside in the fact that these agencies already possess a certain quantity of information, or sources of information, which could be explored. In many states today, local police departments are already compelled to

make certain reports to identification bureaus. In others, local jail offi
cials and juvenile court judges are already compelled, by law, to make
reports to state departments of correction. There is one advantage of
having the Bureau in a department of correction. Existing Bureaus of
Criminal Statistics tend to place undue stress upon the administration
of justice and give little attention to offenders and their personal and
social characteristics. While administrative statistics have a certain util
ity, it seems obvious that what must be developed in the future is more
adequate data concerning offenders. Departments in charge of penal and
correctional treatment being, to a considerable extent, concerned with
individual offenders are therefore likely to pay more attention to this
neglected field of criminal statistics. The drawback in attaching a crimi
nal statistical service to these statistical agencies is that the service is
likely to be considered as a sort of stepchild which will suffer from a lack
of funds. This is perhaps the chief reason for advocating an independent
Bureau. If the Bureau is properly organized, however, and has adequate
financial resources, it probably makes little difference in which depart
ment it is located. Obviously, it is desirable to avoid the placing of any
undue stress upon any one aspect of criminal statistics. It is natural to
assume that the Bureau located in the attorney general's department
might be tempted to exploit judicial criminal statistics more than any
other type, or that a Bureau located in the department of correction
might stress penal statistics and pay little attention to police and court
statistics. Similarly, a Bureau identified with a Bureau of Investigation
and Identification might concentrate on police statistics. A completely
independent Bureau would be in a better position to maintain an even
balance. Every effort must be made to keep statistical work from becom
ing a side issue lacking competent supervision.

*   *   *

It is, of course, of paramount importance that the Bureau be given
the authority to collect all pertinent statistics concerning violations of
law, permitting analysis of the condition of criminality and delinquency
in the community. This means that the Bureau should be in a position
also to gather data concerning juvenile delinquency, for instance. If the
Bureau is granted such powers, there is no need to worry about the fact
that the term "criminal" alone is used in the title of the Act and in the
name of the Bureau.

*   *   *

Good criminal statistics result from a carefully selected set of original
data, tabulated in a manner to illustrate or demonstrate significant con-

ditions or trends and interpreted so as to make the importance of the findings clear to the intelligent layman. Every step in this procedure depends on knowledge and skill—knowledge of the crime problem as a whole and of the administrative organization and policies of the agencies which supply the raw data, skill in statistical planning and analysis. Most so-called criminal statistics published today, in various states, possess no conceivable utility, because neither this knowledge nor the skills mentioned entered into their preparation.

It is hardly worth while to establish a central Bureau of Criminal Statistics, unless provisions are made for placing at its head and on its staff persons who have the training and knowledge needed for its proper operation. It may be impossible to write detailed specifications into a statute. California requires the appointment of a "qualified statistician." Louisiana instructs the Attorney General to appoint a criminal Docket Clerk in charge of judicial statistics who shall be "skilled in statistics and a competent administrator." Minnesota has a provision like that of California. The statutes of other states are silent on this point. The illustrations mentioned express the intent of the Legislature, the appointing authority exercising discretionary power which is fairly unlimited.

*   *   *

The movement for the betterment of state criminal statistics will depend for its success ultimately on the efforts made in the various states by individuals and organizations, who recognize the importance of such statistics and can put pressure on legislatures and administrative agencies. If this is not done, the Uniform Criminal Statistics Act will remain buried in the proceedings of the national conference. Unless every effort is made to raise the general level of state statistics and ensure the existence in all states of a competent "bureau" of criminal statistics, there is little—one is tempted to say no—hope for any further major improvement in national criminal statistics, both those which are still hale and hearty and those now moribund or at least in a comatose condition.

Part Two

FACTORS IN CRIMINALITY

CHAPTER SIX

Theories of Some Pioneers
in Criminology

16 · The Positive School of Criminology

by ENRICO FERRI

It was the French philosopher Auguste Comte who used the term "positivism" for the scientific, or inductive method of studying social phenomena. This term was appropriated by the nineteenth-century Italian criminologist Cesare Lombroso for his approach to the study of the criminal. He thus founded what came to be known as the "positive school of criminology." In the following selection Enrico Ferri (1856-1929), a noted Italian jurist and socialist leader and the most distinguished pupil and successor of Lombroso, explains the principles, method, and objectives of this school of thought. [From *The Positive School of Criminology* (translated by Ernest Untermann from *La scuola positiva di diritto criminale*, 1883), Charles H. Kerr and Company, 1913, pp. 14-17, 21-26, 31-32, 34-36, 39-40, 41-42, 44-46. Reprinted by permission.]

THE POSITIVE SCHOOL of criminology was born in our own Italy through the singular attraction of the Italian mind toward the study of criminology; and its birth is also due to the peculiar condition of our country with its great and strange contrast between the theoretical doctrines and the painful fact of an ever increasing criminality.

The positive school of criminology was inaugurated by the work of Cesare Lombroso, in 1872. From 1872 to 1876 he opened a new way for the study of criminality by demonstrating in his own person that we must first understand the criminal who offends, before we can study and understand his crime. Lombroso studied the prisoners in the various penitentiaries of Italy from the point of view of anthropology. And he compiled his studies in the reports of the Lombardian Institute of Science and Literature, and published them later together in his work "Criminal Man." The first edition of this work (1876) remained almost unnoticed, either because its scientific material was meager, or because Cesare Lombroso had not yet drawn any general scientific conclusions, which could have attracted the attention of the world of science and law. But simultaneously with its second edition (1878) there appeared two monographs, which constituted the embryo of the new school, supplementing the anthropological studies of Lombroso with conclusions and systematizations from the point of view of sociology and law. Raffaele Garofalo published in the Neapolitan Journal of Philosophy and Literature an essay on criminality, in which he declared that the dangerousness of the criminal was the criterion by which society should measure the function of its defense against the disease of crime. And in the same year, 1878, I took occasion to publish a monograph on the denial of free will and personal responsibility, in which I declared frankly that from now on the science of crime and punishment must look for the fundamental facts of a science of social defense against crime in the human and social life itself. The simultaneous publication of these three monographs caused a stir. The teachers of classic criminology, who had taken kindly to the recommendations of Pessina and Ellero, urging them to study the natural sources of crime, met the new ideas with contempt, when the new methods made a determined and radical departure, and became not only the critics, but the zealous opponents of the new theories. And this is easy to understand. For the struggle for existence is an irresistible law of nature, as well for the thousands of germs scattered to the winds by the oak, as for the ideas which grow in the brain of man. But persecutions, calumnies, criticisms, and opposition are powerless against an idea, if it carries within itself the germ of truth. Moreover, we should look upon this phenomenon of a repugnance in the average intellect (whether of the ordinary man or the scientist) for all new ideas as a natural function. For when the brain of some man has felt the light of a new idea, a sneering criticism serves as a touchstone for it. If the idea is wrong, it will fall by the wayside; if it is right, then criticisms, opposition and persecution will cull the golden kernel from the unsightly shell, and the idea will march victoriously over everything and everybody. It is so in all walks of life—in art, in politics, in science. Every new idea will rouse against itself naturally and inevitably the opposition of the accustomed thoughts. This is so true, that when Cesare Beccaria opened the great historic cycle of the classic school of criminology, he was assaulted by the critics of his time with the same indictments which were brought against us a century later.

*　　*　　*

The general opinion of classic criminalists and of the people at large is that crime involves a moral guilt, because it is due to the free will of the individual who leaves the path of virtue and chooses the path of crime, and therefore it must be suppressed by meeting it with a proportionate quantity of punishment. This is to this day the current conception of crime. And the illusion of a free human will (the only miraculous factor in the eternal ocean of cause and effect) leads to the assumption that one can choose freely between virtue and vice. How can you still believe in the existence of a free will, when modern psychology armed with all the instruments of positive modern research, denies that there is any free will and demonstrates that every act of a human being is the result of an interaction between the personality and the environment of man?

And how is it possible to cling to that obsolete idea of moral guilt, according to which every individual is supposed to have the free choice to abandon virtue and give himself up to crime? The positive school of criminology maintains, on the contrary, that it is not the criminal who wills; in order to be a criminal it is rather necessary that the individual should find himself permanently or transitorily in such personal, physical and moral conditions, and live in such an environment, which become for him a chain of cause and effect, externally and internally, that disposes him toward crime. This is our conclusion, which I anticipate, and it constitutes the vastly different and opposite method, which the positive school of criminology employs as compared to the leading principle of the classic school of criminal science.

In this method, this essential principle of the positive school of criminology, you will find another reason for the seemingly slow advance of this school. That is very natural. If you consider the great reform carried by the ideas of Cesare Beccaria into the criminal justice of the Middle Age, you will see that the great classic school represents but a small step forward, because it leaves the penal justice on the same theoretical and practical basis which it had in the Middle Age and in classic antiquity, that is to say, based on the idea of a moral responsibility of the individual. For Beccaria, for Carrara, for their predecessors, this idea is no more nor less than that mentioned in books 47 and 48 of the Digest: "The criminal is liable to punishment to the extent that he is morally guilty of the crime he has committed." The entire classic school is, therefore, nothing but a series of reforms. Capital punishment has been abolished in some countries, likewise torture, confiscation, corporal punishment. But nevertheless the immense scientific movement of the classic school has remained a mere reform.

It has continued in the 19th century to look upon crime in the same way that the Middle Age did: "Whoever commits murder or theft, is alone the absolute arbiter to decide whether he wants to commit the crime or not." This remains the foundation of the classic school of criminology. This explains why it could travel on its way more rapidly than the positive school of criminology. And yet, it took half a century from the time of Beccaria, before the penal codes showed signs of the reformatory influence of the classic school of criminology. So that it has also taken quite a long time to establish it so well that it became accepted by general consent, as it is today. The positive school of criminology was born in 1878, and although it does not stand for a mere reform of the methods of criminal justice, but for a complete and fundamental transformation of criminal justice itself, it has already gone quite a distance and made considerable conquests which begin to show in our country. It is a fact that the penal code now in force in this country represents a compromise, so far as the theory of personal responsibility is concerned, between the old theory of free will and the conclusions of the positive school which denies this free will.

*   *   *

In 1832, France introduced a penal innovation, which seemed to represent an advance on the field of justice, but which is in reality a denial of justice: The expedient of extenuating circumstances. The judge does not ask for the advice of the court physician in the case of some forlorn criminal, but condemns him without a word of rebuke to society for its complicity. But in order to assuage his own conscience he grants him extenuating circumstances, which seem a concession of justice, but are, in reality, a denial of justice. For you either believe that a man is responsible for his crime, and in that case the concession of extenuating circumstances is a hypocrisy; or you grant them in good faith, and then you admit that the man was in circumstances which reduced his moral responsibility, and thereby the extenuating circumstances become a denial of justice. For if your conviction concerning such circumstances were sincere, you would go to the bottom of them and examine with the light of your understanding all those innumerable conditions which contribute toward those extenuating circumstances. But what are those extenuating circumstances? Family conditions? Take it that a child is left alone by its parents, who are swallowed up in the whirl of modern industry, which overthrows the laws of nature and forbids the necessary rest, because steam engines do not get tired and day work must be followed by night work, so that the setting of the sun is no longer the signal for the laborer to rest, but to begin a new shift of work. Take it that this applies not alone to adults, but also to human beings in the growing stage, whose muscular power may yield some profit for the capitalists. Take it that even the mother, during the period of sacred maternity, becomes a cog in the machinery of industry. And you will understand that the child must grow up, left to its own resources, in the filth of life, and that its history will be inscribed in criminal statistics, which are the shame of our so-called civilization.

*   *   *

This illusion of a free will has its source in our inner consciousness, and is due solely to the ignorance in which we find ourselves concerning the various motives and different external and internal conditions which press upon our mind at the moment of decision.

If a man knows the principal causes which determine a certain phenomenon, he says that this phenomenon is inevitable. If he does not know them, he considers it as an accident, and this corresponds in the physical field to the arbitrary phenomenon of the human will which does not know whether it shall decide this way or that. For instance, some of us were of the opinion, and many still are, that the coming and going of meteorological phenomena was accidental and could not be foreseen. But in the meantime, science has demonstrated that they are likewise subject to the law of causality, because it discovered the causes which enable us to foresee their course. Thus weather prognosis has made wonderful progress by the help of a network of telegraphically connected meteorological stations, which succeeded in demonstrating the connection between cause and effect in the case of hurricanes, as well as of any other physical phenomenon. It is evident that the idea of accident, applied to physical nature, is unscientific. Every physical phenomenon is the necessary effect of the causes that determined it beforehand. If those causes are known to us, we have the conviction that that phenomenon is necessary, is fate, and, if we do not know them, we think it is accidental. The same is true of human phenomena. But since we do not know the internal and external causes in the majority of cases, we pretend that they are free phenomena, that is to say, that they are not determined necessarily by their causes. Hence the spiritualistic conception of the free will implies that every human being, in spite of the fact that their internal and external conditions are necessarily predetermined, should be able to come to a deliberate decision by the mere fiat of his or her free will, so that, even though the sum of all the causes demands a no, he or she can decide in favor of yes, and vice versa.

* * *

If modern science has discovered the universal link which connects all phenomena through cause and effect, which shows that every phenomenon is the result of causes which have preceded it; if this is the law of causality, which is at the very bottom of modern scientific thought, then it is evident that the admission of free thought is equivalent to an overthrow of this law, according to which every effect is proportionate to its cause. In that case, this law, which reigns supreme in the entire universe, would dissolve itself into naught at the feet of the human being, who would create effects with his free will not corresponding to their causes! It was all right to think so at a time when people had an entirely different idea of human beings. But the work of modern science, and its effect on practical life, has resulted in tracing the relations of each one of us with the world and with our fellow beings. And the influence of science may be seen in the elimination of great illusions which in former centuries swayed this or that part of civilized humanity. The scientific thought of Copernicus and Galileo did away with the illusions which led people to believe that the earth was the center of the universe and of creation. . . .

But men live on illusions and give way but reluctantly to the progress of science, in order to devote themselves arduously to the ideal of the new truths which rise out of the essence of things of which mankind is part. After the geocentric illusion had been destroyed, the anthropocentric illusion still remained. On earth, man was still supposed to be king of creation, the center of terrestrial life. All species of animals, plants and minerals were supposed to be created expressly for him, and to have had from time immemorial the forms which we see now, so that the fauna and flora living on our planet have always been what they are today. And Cicero, for instance, said that the heavens were placed round the earth and man in order that he might admire the beauty of the starry firmament at night, and that animals and plants were created for his use and pleasure. But in 1856 Charles Darwin came and, sum-

marizing the results of studies that had been carried on for a century
destroyed in the name of science the superb illusion that man is the king
and center of creation. He demonstrated, amid the attacks and calumnie
of the lovers of darkness, that man is not the king of creation, bu
merely the last link of the zoological chain, that nature is endowed with
eternal energies by which animal and plant life, the same as mineral life
(for even in crystals the laws of life are at work), are transformed from
the invisible microbe to the highest form, man.

*   *   *

For this reason we believe that the study of the criminal, and the
logical consequences therefrom, will bring about the complete transforma
tion of human justice, not only as a theory laid down in scientific books
but also as a practical function applied every day to that living and suf
fering portion of humanity which has fallen into crime. We have the
undaunted faith that the work of scientific truth will transform pena
justice into a simple function of preserving society from the disease o
crime, divested of all relics of vengeance, hatred and punishment, which
still survive in our day as living reminders of the barbarian stage. We
still hear the "public vengeance" invoked against the criminal today, and
justice has still for its symbol a sword, which it uses more than the scales
But a judge born of a woman cannot weigh the moral responsibility o
one who has committed murder or theft. Not until the experimental and
scientific method shall look for the causes of that dangerous malady
which we call crime, in the physical and psychic organism, and in the
family and the environment, of the criminal, will justice guided b
science discard the sword which now descends bloody upon those poo
fellowbeings who have fallen victims to crime, and become a clinica
function, whose prime object shall be to remove or lessen in society and
individuals the causes which incite to crime. Then alone will justice re
frain from wreaking vengeance, after a crime has been committed, with
the shame of an execution or the absurdity of solitary confinement.

17 · The Criminal—A Born Type

by CESARE LOMBROSO

Cesare Lombroso (1835-1909), an Italian physician and the founder of the positive school of criminology, is considered as the father of modern criminology. Having spent years of research involving anthropological measurements and detailed physical examinations of Italian prisoners (without the use of control groups), Lombroso concluded that the criminal is primarily a born type and is marked by definite physical and mental stigmata. Influenced by the then current anthropological theories, he also maintained that the criminal often represents an atavistic type—*i.e.*, a throwback to the primitive. Lombroso's theories, propounded first in his *Uomo delinquente* (*Criminal Man*), published in 1876, and elaborated upon in many subsequent volumes and articles, made a profound impression on students of crime at the time and, although almost completely discredited at present, they have not ceased to exert an influence on the work of some criminologists (neo-Lombrosians), particularly in Europe. The following excerpts from his work explain the main points of his thesis. [From *Crime; Its Causes and Remedies* (translated by Henry P. Horton from the French edition of *Crime: Causes et remèdes*), Little, Brown, and Company, 1911, pp. 365-370, 373-379, 381. Reprinted by permission. Footnotes omitted.]

ATAVISM

THE BORN criminal shows in a proportion reaching 33% numerous specific characteristics that are almost always atavistic. . . . Many of the characteristics presented by savage races are very often found among born criminals. Such, for example, are: the slight development of the pilar system; low cranial capacity; retreating forehead; highly developed frontal sinuses; great frequency of Wormian bones; early closing of the cranial sutures; the simplicity of the sutures; the thickness of the bones of the skull; enormous development of the maxillaries and the zygomata; prognathism; obliquity of the orbits; greater pigmentation of the skin; tufted and crispy hair; and large ears. To these we may add the lemurine appendix; anomalies of the ear; dental diastemata; great agility; relative insensibility to pain; dullness of the sense of touch; great visual acuteness; ability to recover quickly from wounds; blunted affections; precocity as to sensual pleasures; greater resemblance between the sexes;

greater incorrigibility of the woman (Spencer); laziness; absence of re
morse; impulsiveness; physiopsychic excitability; and especially improvi
dence, which sometimes appears as courage and again as recklessnes
changing to cowardice. Besides these there is great vanity; a passion fo
gambling and alcoholic drinks; violent but fleeting passions; superstition
extraordinary sensitiveness with regard to one's own personality; and a
special conception of God and morality. Unexpected analogies are me
even in small details, as, for example, the improvised rules of crimina
gangs; the entirely personal influence of the chiefs; the custom of tattoo
ing; the not uncommon cruelty of their games; the excessive use of ges
tures; the onomatopoeic language with personification of inanimate
things; and a special literature recalling that of heroic times, when crime
were celebrated and the thought tended to clothe itself in rhythmic
form.

This atavism explains the diffusion of certain crimes, such as the
pederasty and infanticide, whose extension to whole companies we
could not explain if we did not recall the Romans, the Greeks, the Chi
nese, and the Tahitians, who not only did not regard them as crimes
but sometimes even practiced them as a national custom. Garofalo has
admirably summed up the psychical characteristics of the born crimina
as being the absence of the feelings of shame, honor, and pity, which
are those that are lacking in the savage also. We may add to these the
lack of industry and self-control.

To those who, like Reclus and Krapotkin, object that there are savage
peoples who are honorable and chaste, we must reply that a certain degree
of density of population and of association among men is necessary fo
crimes to develop. It is not possible, for example, to steal when property
does not exist, or to swindle when there is no trade. But the proof that
these tendencies exist in germ in the savage, is that when they begin to
pass from their stage of savagery and take on a little civilization they
always develop the characteristics of criminality in an exaggerated form
As Ferrero has pointed out to us, even when honor, chastity, and pity
are found among savages, impulsiveness and laziness are never wanting
Savages have a horror of continuous work, so that for them the passage
to active and methodical labor lies by the road of selection or of slavery
only. Thus, according to the testimony of Tacitus, the impulsiveness of
the ancient Germans frequently resulted in the murder of slaves, com
mitted in a fit of anger, an act which was not regarded as culpable. . . .

*   *   *

We may add that the atavism of the criminal, when he lacks abso lutely every trace of shame and pity, may go back far beyond the savage, even to the brutes themselves. Pathological anatomy helps prove our position by showing in the case of the criminal a greater development of the cerebellum, a rarer union of the calcarine fissure with the parieto-occipital, the absence of folds in the passage of Gratiolet, the gutter-like shape of the nasal incisure, the frequency of the olecranial foramen, extra ribs and vertebræ, and especially the histological anomalies discovered by Roncoroni in the cortex of the cerebrum of criminals, that is to say, the frequent absence of granular layers, and the presence of nerve cells in the white matter, and immense pyramidal cells. In seeking for analogies beyond our own race we come upon the explanation of the union of the atlas with the occipital bone, the prominence of the canine teeth, the flattening of the palate, and the median occipital fossa, occurring among criminals as with the lemurs and rodents; as also the prehensile foot, the simplicity of the lines of the palm, motor and sensory left-handedness. . . .

These facts prove clearly that the most horrible crimes have their origin in those animal instincts of which childhood gives us a pale reflection. Repressed in civilized man by education, environment, and the fear of punishment, they suddenly break out in the born criminal without apparent cause, or under the influence of certain circumstances, such as sickness, atmospheric influences, sexual excitement, or mob influence. We know that certain morbid conditions, such as injuries to the head, meningitis, and chronic intoxication, or certain physiological conditions like pregnancy and senility, produce derangements in the nutrition of the nervous centers, and in consequence atavistic retrogressions. We can see, then, how they may facilitate the tendency to crime, and when we take into account the short distance that separates the criminal from the savage, we come to understand why convicts so easily adopt savage customs, including cannibalism, as was observed in Australia and Guiana. . . .

* * *

EPILEPSY

The same phenomena which we observe in the case of born criminals appear again in the rare cases of moral insanity, but may be studied minutely, and on a large scale, in epileptics, criminal or not. . . . One of the atavistic phenomena shown by criminals is lacking in epilepsy; though epileptics show also certain purely morbid phenomena, such as cephalea, atheroma, delirium, and hallucination. In born criminals also we find, besides the atavistic characteristics, certain others that appear to be entirely pathological, or which at first sight seem more nearly allied to disease than to atavism. Such are, for example, in the anatomical field, excessive asymmetry, cranial capacity and face too large or too small, sclerosis, traces of meningitis, hydrocephalous forehead, oxycephaly, acrocephaly, cranial depressions, numerous osteophytes, early closing of the cranial sutures, thoracic asymmetry, late grayness of hair, late baldness, and abnormal and early wrinkles; in the biological field alterations of the reflexes and pupillary inequalities. To these we may add peripheral scotomata of the visual field, which one never finds in savages, with whom, on the contrary, the field of vision is remarkably wide and regular, as we see in the case of the Dinkas. There is also to be added the alteration of hearing, taste, and smell, the predilection for animals, precocity in sexual pleasures, amnesia, vertigo, and maniac and paranoiac complications. These abnormalities, which are found in greater proportion among idiots, cretins, and degenerates in general, are to be explained by the fact that in these cases alcoholic intoxication is added to the effect of atavism, and still more to that of epilepsy.

However, the participation of epilepsy in producing the effect does not exclude atavism, since they equally involve characteristics at once atavistic and pathological, like macrocephaly, cranial sclerosis, Wormian bones, rarity of beard; and in the biological field, left-handedness, analgesis, obtuseness of all senses except that of sight, impulsiveness, pederasty, obscenity, sluggishness, superstition, frequent cannibalism, choleric and impetuous disposition, tendency to reproduce the cries and actions of animals; and especially the histological anomalies of the cortex, which we have noted among criminals, and which reproduce the conditions of the lower animals; and finally anomalies of the teeth. These latter might appear to have no connection with the brain, but are, on the contrary, intimately connected with it, since the teeth proceed from the same embryonic membrane as the brain does.

*   *   *

COMBINATION OF MORBID ANOMALIES WITH ATAVISM

Very often, moreover, certain common characteristics of criminals and epileptics have been classed as abnormal or morbid and not as atavistic entirely because of the insufficiency of our embryological and phylogenetic knowledge. . . .

Facial asymmetry would also appear to be atavistic when we recall, for example, the flat-fishes (Penta); so likewise the abnormally wrinkled face, taking us back to the Hottentots and the apes. Hernia, also, as Féré

rightly remarks, recalls conditions that are normal in the lower verte-
brates and in the embryo.

* * *

The epileptic background upon which the clinical and anatomical picture of the moral lunatic and the born criminal is drawn (a picture that
would otherwise be lost in vague semi-juridical, semi-psychiatric hypotheses) explains the instantaneousness, periodicity, and paradoxical
character of their symptoms, which are doubtless their most marked
characteristics. Note, for example, in this class, the coexistence and
interchange of kindness and ferocity, of cowardice and the maddest
recklessness, and of genius and complete stupidity.

THE CRIMINALOID

Criminaloids, while quite separable from born criminals, do not lack
some connection with epilepsy and atavism. Thus there are more epileptics among them (10% among pickpockets) than among normal
men, and a greater proportion of criminal types (17%), but there are
also certain specific anomalies, such as left-handedness, common among
swindlers.

In the biology of the criminaloid we observe a smaller number of
anomalies in touch, sensibility to pain, psychometry, and especially less
early baldness and grayness, and less tattooing. But, on the other hand,
we meet with a larger number of strictly morbid anomalies, depending
upon the abuse of alcoholic drinks, such as atheromata, paresis, and
scars. Psychic anomalies are especially less frequent with the criminaloid,
who has not the cynicism of the born criminal nor the passion for doing
evil for its own sake; he confesses his fault more easily and with more
sincerity, and repents more often. But he is more lascivious, and more
often given to alcoholism; and the criminaloid women are more susceptible to suggestion. The criminaloid is more precocious and relapses
oftener—at least this is the case with pickpockets and simple thieves.
They are often drawn into crime by a greater opportunity, although the
lack of self-control which makes the epileptic commit crime without
reason is sometimes found in the criminaloid also. We may recall how
Casanova confessed that when he committed a fraud he never premeditated it, but "seemed to yield to a superior will." A pickpocket said to
me, "When the inspiration comes to us we cannot resist." Dostojevsky
depicts smugglers of the prison as carrying on their occupation almost
without returns, notwithstanding the grave risks they run and in spite of
repeated promises not to relapse. Mendel and Benedict describe the im-

pulsive nature of the vagabond, which keeps him moving without object and without rest.

Criminaloids, then, differ from born criminals in degree, not in kind. This is so true that the greater number of them, having become habitual criminals, thanks to a long sojourn in prison, can no longer be distinguished from born criminals except by the slighter character of their physical marks of criminality.

Still less different from born criminals are those latent criminals, high in power, whom society venerates as its chiefs. They bear the marks of congenital criminality, but their high position generally prevents their criminal character from being recognized. Their families, of which they are the scourges, may discover it; or their depraved nature may be revealed all too late at the expense of the whole country, at the head of which their own shamelessness, seconded by the ignorance and cowardice of the majority, has caused them to be placed. Even this strange species of criminal monomaniac, who seems to differ from the epileptic in the motive of his crime and the manner of carrying it out, shows nevertheless the epileptic and atavistic origin of his criminality by obsessions, interrupted periods of ideation, lack of self-control, exaggerated importance given to certain details, exhaustion after his criminal crises, fondness for symbolism, excessive and intermittent activity, and finally by hereditary stigmata.

CRIMINAL INSANE

Even among the true insane criminals those forms predominate which we may call the hypertrophy of crime, the exaggeration of the born criminal, not only in bodily and functional characteristics but also in the manner of committing the crime and in conduct afterward. These serve to explain to us the extent of the impulsive, obscene, and cruel tendencies of the criminal insane, who are almost always obscure epileptics or born criminals upon whom melancholia and monomania have grafted themselves, according to the natural tendency of different forms of psychic disorders to take root together upon the corrupted soil of degeneracy. . . .

CRIMINALS BY PASSION

Criminals of this class form a species apart, and are in complete contrast with the born criminal, both in the harmonious lines of the body, the beauty of the soul, and great nervous and emotional sensitiveness, as well as in the motives of their crimes, always noble and powerful, such

s love or politics. Nevertheless they show some points of resemblance
vith epileptics, such as their tendency to excesses, impulsiveness, sud-
lenness in their outbreaks, and frequent amnesia.

OCCASIONAL CRIMINALS

Occasional criminals, or better, pseudo-criminals, are those who do
10t seek the occasion for the crime but are almost drawn into it, or fall
nto the meshes of the code for very insignificant reasons. These are the
nly ones who escape all connection with atavism and epilepsy; but, as
Garofalo observes, these ought not, properly speaking, to be called
riminals.

CAUSES

The study of the causes of crime does not lessen the fatal influence to
e assigned to the organic factor, which certainly amounts to 35% and
ossibly even 40%; the so-called causes of crime being often only the last
leterminants and the great strength of congenital impulsiveness the
rincipal cause. This we have proved in some cases by the continual re-
apses occasioned by very small causes, or even without causes, when
ot only the economic environment has been changed, but when all the
ircumstances that might encourage crime have been removed; and we
ave proved it especially by the increasing recidivism in London, not-
vithstanding the great efforts made by Great Britain to suppress the
auses which produce crime. Finally, we have seen that certain circum-
tances have so strong an action upon criminaloids that they are equiva-
ent to organic causes, and we may even say that they become organic.
Among these circumstances should be noted the effect of excessive heat
pon rapes, assaults, assassinations, and revolts, and the effect of alcohol
nd heredity upon the whole gamut of crime; and to these must be
dded the effect of race, which in Italy through the Semitic race, and in
'rance through the Ligurian race, increases the crimes of blood.

A fact of the greatest importance is that the same causes which di-
ninish certain crimes increase others, making it difficult for the states-
nan to devise a remedy. Thus we have seen that education and wealth
ause a decrease in certain brutal crimes, especially homicides and assas-
inations, but at the same time increase others, or even create new
rimes, such as bankruptcy and swindling. And if, for example, too great
density is the cause of many crimes, such as frauds and thefts, a sparse
opulation, in its turn, favors brigandage and crimes of blood. Scarcity
avors thefts from the forests, forgeries, insurrections, and incendiary

fires, while cheapness of grain multiplies the rapes, homicides, and crimes against persons generally.

Alcohol, which next to heat is the most powerful crime-producer, increases, when it is cheap, all the crimes against persons and against the public administration; and if it is dear, all the crimes against property. Yet it presents this strange contradiction, that the more serious crimes are least numerous where alcohol is most abused, doubtless because this abuse takes place in just those localities where there is a higher degree of civilization, and this, by favoring inhibition, decreases the more barbarous crimes.

The school, likewise, is a cause of crime, but where education is most general it diminishes the number and seriousness of the crimes.

NECESSITY OF CRIME

Statistics as well as anthropological investigations show us crime, then, as a natural phenomenon—a phenomenon (some philosophers would say) as necessary as birth, death, or conception.

This idea of the necessity of crime, however bold it may appear, is nevertheless not so new nor so heterodox as one might believe at first sight. Centuries ago Casaubon expressed the same truth when he said "Man does not sin, but he is coerced in various degrees"; and St. Bernard likewise said, "Which one of us, however experienced he may be, can distinguish among his own wishes the influence of the *morsus serpentis* from that of the *morbus mentis?*" And further: "The sin is less in our heart, and we do not know whether we ought to ascribe it to ourselves or to the enemy: it is hard to know what the heart does and what it is obliged to do." St. Augustine is still more explicit when he says: "Not even the angels can make the man who wills evil will the good." The boldest and most ardent defender of this theory is a fervent Catholic and a priest of the Tyrol, Ruf.

*   *   *

THE RIGHT TO PUNISH

Some one replies to us: "But if you deny responsibility, what right have you to punish? You proclaim that a man is not answerable for his conduct, and yet you exact a penalty. How inconsistent, and how harsh!" I shall never forget how a venerable thinker shook his head when he read these pages, and said to me: "Where will you arrive, with such premises? Must we let ourselves be pillaged and murdered by brigands upon the pretext that we cannot decide whether they know they are doing wrong?" I answer: nothing is less logical than to try to be too logical; nothing is more imprudent than to try to maintain theories, even those which are apparently the soundest, if they are going to upset the order of society. If a physician at the bedside of a patient, when there is grave danger, must proceed cautiously even with the best established system of medicine, the sociologist must observe still greater circumspection, for if he puts into operation innovations of an upsetting nature he will simply succeed in demonstrating the uselessness and inefficiency of his science.

Scientific knowledge, however, is happily not at war but in alliance with social order and practice. If crime is a necessary thing, so also is society's resistance to crime, and, consequently, the punishment of crime, which must be measured by the amount of apprehension with which it inspires the individual. Punishment thus becomes less hateful, but also less contradictory and certainly more efficacious.

* * *

One might question whether it is from wickedness or from the effect of their own organism that wild beasts devour man; but notwithstanding this doubt, no one would abstain from killing them than tamely allow himself to be devoured by them. Nor would any one, because of a belief in the right of domestic animals to life and liberty, refrain from harnessing them up for work, or slaughtering them for food. And what right have we to confine the insane, if it is not for self-defense? By what other right do we deprive the conscript soldier of his most holy and noble right of forming his own home and family, and send him, many times in spite of himself, to death?

It is just because the principle of punishment is based upon the necessity of defense that it is really not open to objection.

18 · The Criminal—A Result of Imitation

by GABRIEL DE TARDE

Gabriel de Tarde (1843-1904), a French jurist and social psychologist who is considered the father of social psychology, was a contemporary of Lombroso. Refuting Lombroso's theory of an anthropological criminal type, he postulated that criminal behavior was induced primarily by social rather than biological or physical forces. Of these he singled out imitation as the chief factor. His explanation of crime, being essentially sociological, comes thus much closer than Lombroso's to current views regarding criminal causation. The work expounding his theories about crime and the criminal is *Penal Philosophy*, selected excerpts from which are presented here. [From *Penal Philosophy* (translated by Rapelje Howell from *Philosophie pénale*), Little, Brown, and Company, 1912, pp. 218-222, 251-256, 259-260, 322-323, 331-332, 362-363, 367, 416-418. Reprinted by permission.]

THE CRIMINAL TYPE

WHAT IS a criminal?—At the death of the great Lama, the priests of Thibet agree to seek for the newborn into whom his immortal soul has transmigrated. They recognize him by certain characteristics, by true anthropological description, which they firmly believe never deceives. The Egyptian priests proceeded in exactly the same way, in order to pick out the bull Apis among all the bulls in the Valley of the Nile. Thus, there was for them, as there still is for the clergy and the people of Thibet, a divine type; and it is thus that in the eyes of Lombroso a criminal type exists which will allow of recognizing the malefactor from birth. Such, at least, was his first conception; but we know that in being developed it could not help becoming complicated in order to accommodate itself to the facts that contradicted it. At the present time, what is there left of it? Apparently, there is little, but, at the same time, something essential, as we shall see. If it had only served to give us more precise knowledge as to what the criminal is not, without giving a single indication, moreover, as to what he is, it would not have been in vain. But it has done more. It has accumulated curious observations, which will doubtless be useful later on; it has outlined in characteristics which will not perish the psychology of the delinquent, and has paved the way for a sociological explanation of him.

First of all, owing to the partial failure of its attempt, the school of Lombroso seems to us to have absolutely demonstrated that the criminal is not a product of nature; that is to say, that he does not correspond to any natural idea in the Platonic sense, nor in the scientific sense either. The Chinaman, the Negro, and the Mongol correspond to realistic schemes of this nature. Combine by Galton's processes ten or a dozen photographs of Chinamen, and you will obtain a generic portrait wherein, with their differences blotted out, their similarities alone will appear in a curious relief, a living abstraction and individual incarnation of the ideal rule, of which the individuals are the oscillating deviations. This picture-type has this particular thing about it, that it embellishes that which it combines and it explains that which it sums up. Carry out the same operation with twenty or thirty other Chinamen; the new synthetic picture will resemble the preceding one still more than the photographs which compose it resemble one another.

But now endeavor photographically to integrate in this manner the several hundred photographs of malefactors which fill the album annexed to the French translation of "L'Homme criminel." Assuredly, the thing is possible. Galton's process must always give a result, for the same reason that the repeated looking at external things and the stirring up of recollections in one's memory must always result in the human mind in general ideas. Only, between the violent and artificial fusion of heterogeneous pictures which we can produce in the latter case, and the mutual commingling of congeneric pictures which we have called forth above, there is the same dissimilarity as between a generalization which is purely verbal and a generalization founded upon the nature of things.

One would perceive this by operating separately upon various groups in this album. The number of groups would determine the number of results, which would differ very greatly from one another and would have scarcely any more relation with the elementary portraits which had been violently disintegrated and artificially combined in them. Can one at least hope that in separately photographing groups of malefactors belonging to the same category, — "caroubleurs" (thieves who use false keys), "cambrioleurs" (robbers of apartments), "escarpes" (assassins), swindlers and "stupratori,"—one might be more fortunate? Not at all. Each nation and each race has its swindlers, its thieves, and its assassins, who are bearers of the anthropological characteristics that distinguish it. With any physical type, under certain social conditions, and being given certain cerebral peculiarities that are too profound to reveal themselves in the external anatomy, one can create delinquents of every kind. Thus there are no more *several* criminal types than *one* criminal type in the *Lombrosian* sense of the word; and Marro, when he attempts to substitute the plural here for the singular, is no less conjectural and has no better foundation than his master. One of two things must be so. Either the delinquent is physically, if not physiologically, normal, and in this case he bears the very type of his country, or else he is abnormal, and then he does not belong to any type; and it is his very lack of type that characterizes him. But, to say at the same time that he is an anomaly and that he conforms to a natural model is to contradict oneself. There is another hidden contradiction in looking upon the social life as so essential to man that a human being who is "dishumanized," so to speak, can alone be anti-social, and to assume that nature has taken the pains to make a special creation in order to bring forth this individual who is contrary to nature.

For Topinard, the criminal, when he was not a sick man, would be an individual who was perfectly *normal*, at least as far as he was concerned physically. He finds that the collection of pictures brought together by Lombroso reminds him of the photographic albums of his friends. "With the exception of the filth, the naked breast, and the weariness," he says, "and often the poverty stamped upon his face, the head of a rogue, as a general thing, resembles the head of an honest man." . . .

From the social point of view crime may be a monstrosity, but not from the individual or organic point of view, because it is the absolute triumph of egoism and of the organism over the brakes of society. The man who is a true born criminal could thus be nothing more than a very fine animal, a sample which was a credit to his race. Were the tyrants, were the artists of the Italian Renaissance, who were as lavish with their assassinations as with their achievements and masterpieces, monsters? They were not monstrosities physically, that is certain; and, socially, it is open to discussion. If the social characteristic of this historical phase was, as Burckhardt demonstrates, the fading away of individuality, it was inevitable that it should be fertile in criminal manifestations. The Borgias are not at all an exception in their time. The same lack of scruples and of moral feeling characterizes all the Italian princes of the fourteenth and fifteenth centuries,—born in crime, living in crime, and dying as soon as they cease to be criminals. Crime among them takes on the disguise of punishment. They massacre in order to intimidate, at the same time as they take vengeance. For them crime is a necessary part of government, just as the government is for the people a necessity for order and for existence. Crime has its place, and its place of honor, in this magnificent blooming forth of all the arts in festal array; they are bound up in it "as the pearls are in the dagger."

This is the very thing which was bound to kill this beautiful aesthetic civilization when it was in full bloom. For a civilization which glorifies the criminal is no more capable of living than that which casts the most honest people among the criminals, a spectacle so often met with in times of revolution. The criminal is the man that society, when it is capable of living and is regular, is compelled to eliminate. The criminal is thus, to tell the truth, no more a social product than he is a natural product; he is—forgive me the word—a social excrement. And that is why it is interesting to the very highest degree to examine closely into which are the types of people to be found in the convict prisons and in ordinary prisons, rowing in the galleys or mounting the scaffold, in all times and in all countries. When the nature of these people happens to change it is always a serious symptom. If a society *excretes* excellent elements which it does not know how to utilize,—the Protestants under Louis XIV, the "aristocrats" under the Terror,—it is dangerously ill, rather like a man suffering from diabetes, and for a reason which is at bottom analogous.

*   *   *

THE CRIMINAL TYPE IS A PROFESSIONAL TYPE

If the group of malefactors, which is as variegated as it is numerous, as changing as it is persistent, is not united by a single bond that is truly vital; if there exist between them neither that pathological relationship which a similar form of degeneracy or mental alienation would establish, a same group of maladies with which they would be affected, nor that physiological relationship which their common resemblance to supposed ancestors would bear witness to, of what nature, then, is the bond which brings them together and often gives them a special physiognomy more easily perceived than formulated? In our opinion it is a bond which is entirely social, the intimate relation which is to be observed between people carrying on the same trade or trades of a similar character; and this hypothesis is sufficient to account for even the anatomical peculiarities, especially the physiological and psychological peculiarities by which delinquents are distinguished. Let us first deal with the former.

. . . Every profession, whether it be open to everybody or enclosed in a caste, must in the long run recruit its members from among those individuals best endowed and best fitted to succeed in it, or develop among its members, through heredity, the talents and, consequently, the forms which it prefers. This is so not only with regard to every profession, but with regard to every class and every social category that is more or less clearly defined. For example, a series of the skulls of *distinguished men*—by this is understood the chosen of the liberal professions collectively—is typified, according to Manouvrier, by a face which is relatively small, a fine frontal development, and especially a cubic capacity that is far above the average. When we go into detail in the separate study of artists, learned men, philosophers, or engineers, we shall certainly be led to draw a typical portrait which will have rather strong characteristics drawn from each one of these groups. It is even probable that it might easily be clearer and less doubtful than the famous criminal type.

As a matter of fact, of all careers, the career of a criminal is indeed the one that is least often entered into by a person having freedom to choose, and is the one where, as a consequence of the rapid extinction of vicious families, the hereditary transmission of aptitudes has less time to be carried out. One has been thrust into it from birth; this is the ordinary case. The majority of murderers and notorious thieves began as children who had been abandoned, and the true seminary of crime must be sought for upon each public square or each crossroad of our towns, whether they be small or large, in those flocks of pillaging street urchins who, like bands of sparrows, associate together, at first for marauding, and then for theft, because of a lack of education and food in their homes. Without any natural predisposition on their part, their fate is often decided by the influence of their comrades. However, there are others whom the fatal logic of their vices has driven to the dilemma of crime or death. And, even with regard to the former, one can say, as a general thing, that the preference which they will give to the example set by a small minority of rascals over the example of the immense majority who are laborious denotes in them some anomaly of nature; although one can reply that it is the same thing with imitation as with attraction which is exercised inversely to the square of the distances. Thus it would be permissible for the child who was the most normally constituted to be more influenced by half a score of perverse friends by whom he is surrounded than by millions of unknown fellow-citizens. In spite of everything, there is no doubt that advancement in the trade of murder or theft ordinarily assumes a true vocation, more or less vaguely recognized by an experienced eye. Also, Topinard and Manouvrier are each separately drawn to this conclusion, that criminals form one of those "professional categories" that we have just been discussing.

*   *   *

There is not one of even the most precocious of the young monsters of seventeen or eighteen years whose exploits appall the press who has not behind him years of criminal apprenticeship during his entire vagabond and soiled childhood. For the trade of crime, like every other, has its special schools. Also, like every other trade, it has its special idiom, namely, slang. What old and deep-rooted profession has not its own slang, from sailors, masons, and coppersmiths to painters and lawyers,— to the very police agents themselves, who say that they "camoufler" themselves when they mean to "disguise" themselves, and "coton" for a "resemblance," etc.? We can read Maxime du Camp on this subject. Finally, there are special associations, temporary or permanent, epidemic or endemic. As an example of the former, the rising of the peasants in 1358, and in certain respects Jacobinism, which temporarily ravaged France; as an example of the latter, the Camorra and the Maffia, which are traditionally prevalent in Italy. These are great professional syndicates of crime, which have played a far more important historic part than one might suppose. How many times has a warlike band, organized in the very midst of pastoral tribes, been a society of brigands? How many times has this brigandage been the necessary leaven that has served to raise an empire and establish peace through the triumph of the strong?

*   *   *

PSYCHOLOGY AND THE CRIMINAL

Perhaps one is born vicious, but it is quite certain that one becomes a criminal. The psychology of the murderer is, in the last analysis, the psychology of everybody; and in order to go down into his heart it will be sufficient if we analyze our own. One could without any very great difficulty write a treatise upon the art of becoming an assassin. Keep bad company; allow pride, vanity, envy, and hatred to grow in you out of all proportion; close your heart to tender feelings, and only open it to keen sensations; suffer also,—harden yourself from childhood to blows, to intemperateness, to physical torments; grow hardened to evil, and insensible, and you will not be long in becoming devoid of pity; become irascible and vengeful, and you will be very lucky if you do not kill anybody during the course of your life. And, in fact, the psychological characteristics that I have just enumerated are indeed the most striking ones among the inmates of prisons.

*   *   *

To sum up, the character of the criminal is already very much easier to trace with precision than is his physical type. His type changes according to race; his character scarcely varies. Besides this, we must not exaggerate the psychological differences, especially the intellectual differences, which distinguish the delinquent from ourselves. When we compare the various sorts of books,—fiction, literature, history, science, etc.,—that are read with more or less enjoyment in the Parisian prisons for both sexes with the reading that is more or less preferred in the municipal schools of Paris, we observe that the relative proportion of readers for each kind of writing is about the same in the former as in the latter. More than one-half of the books read by prisoners consist of fiction; the books of Alexandre Dumas chiefly. They also greedily devour the "Magasin pittoresque," the "Tour du Monde," and even the "Musée des familles."

As to the moral characteristics which we have endeavored to point out with some precision, the two most often betrayed, vanity and lack of feeling, are far from belonging exclusively to the criminal and can be the effect of crime as well as its cause. I can say the same thing of laziness and lack of remorse. In the first place, is the criminal as devoid of feeling,—at least, physically,—as Dostoievsky, Lombroso, and the majority of the Italian authors maintain? Their observations seem contradicted by other testimony. "I inquired," says Joly, "at the central infirmary of the Santé, where all the men from the prisons of the Department of the Seine who are seriously ill are taken care of, if they had ever noticed *invulnerability* among them. They replied that, far from it, they always found them very sensitive to pain. They distinctly told me that to one who had worked in this special infirmary and in some of the ordinary hospitals of Paris (as almost all the internes have done) the difference was striking. The brave fellows, the honest workmen, the fathers of families, who go to be cared for at the Charité or the Hôtel-Dieu, undergo operations with very much more courage than the patients at the Santé."

*   *   *

The idea of attributing the lack of pity in the criminal to his relative exemption from pain is thus merely a conjecture without any proof. Another hypothesis seems to me to be more probable. It is, I repeat, that the monstrous egoism, and the prodigious conceit as well, which are noticeable among criminals are perhaps rather the consequence than the source of their crimes. . . .

PREPONDERANCE OF SOCIAL CAUSES

*   *   *

All the important acts of social life are carried out under the domination of example. One procreates or one does not procreate, because of imitation; the statistics of the birth rate have shown us this. One kills or one does not kill, because of imitation; would we today conceive of the idea of fighting a duel or of declaring war, if we did not know that these things had always been done in the country which we inhabit? One kills oneself or one does not kill oneself, because of imitation; it is a recognized fact that suicide is an imitative phenomenon to the very highest degree; at any rate it is impossible to refuse to give this character to those "suicides in large numbers of conquered peoples escaping by means of death the shame of defeat and the yoke of the stranger, like that of the Sidonians who were defeated by Artaxerxes Orchus, of the Tyrians defeated by Alexander, of the Sagontines defeated by Scipio, of the Achaeans defeated by Metellus, etc."

After this how can we doubt but that one steals or does not steal, one assassinates or does not assassinate, because of imitation? But it is especially in the great tumultuous assemblages of our cities that this characteristic force of the social world ought to be studied. The great scenes of our revolutions cause it to break out, just as great storms are a manifestation of the presence of the electricity in the atmosphere, while it remains unperceived though none the less a reality in the intervals between them. A *mob* is a strange phenomenon. It is a gathering of heterogeneous elements, unknown to one another; but as soon as a spark of passion, having flashed out from one of these elements, electrifies this confused mass, there takes place a sort of sudden organization, a spontaneous generation. This incoherence becomes cohesion, this noise becomes a voice, and these thousands of men crowded together soon form but a single animal, a wild beast without a name, which marches to its goal with an irresistible finality. The majority of these men had assembled out of pure curiosity, but the fever of some of them soon reached the minds of all, and in all of them there arose a delirium. The very man who had come running to oppose the murder of an innocent person is one of the first to be seized with the homicidal contagion, and moreover, it does not occur to him to be astonished at this.

*   *   *

. . . Strange as it may seem, there are serious reasons for maintaining that the vices and the crimes of today, which are to be found in the lowest orders of the people, descended to them from above. In every nascent or renascent society when the producing of wine becomes difficult or limited, drunkenness is a royal luxury and a privilege of the aristocracy. It is quite certain that the kings of Homer's time got drunk far more often than did their subjects, the Merovingian chiefs than their vassals, and the lords of the Middle Ages than their serfs. Even as late as the sixteenth century, in Germany "the celebrated autobiography of the knight of Schweinichen furnishes a proof that the coarsest drunkenness did not dishonor a person of rank." He tells us as a matter of course that, the first three nights after his marriage, he went to bed in an absolute state of intoxication, as did all the guests composing the wedding party.

The smoking habit, at present so widespread in every sort of surroundings, perhaps already more widespread among the people than among the socially elect, where they have begun to combat this passion, was propagated in the same manner. James I of England, Roscher tells us, put a very heavy tax upon tobacco in 1604, "because," says the law, "the lower classes, incited by the example of the upper classes, impair their health, taint the air, and corrupt the soil." The irreligiousness of the masses, which today here and there contrasts with the relative religiousness of the last survivors of the old aristocracy, is just as much due to this same cause. Vagabondage, under its thousand and one existing forms, is an essentially plebeian offense; but by going back into the past, it would not be very difficult to connect our vagabonds, our street singers, with the noble pilgrims and the noble minstrels of the Middle Ages.

*   *   *

In our opinion crime is a peculiar social fact, but after all a social fact like any other. It is an off-shoot of the national tree, but a branch nourished by the common sap and subject to the laws which are common to all. We have seen that, taken by itself, it grows in conformity with the rule of imitation from *above* to *below*, just as do all the other fruitful and useful branches of the same trunk. We might have added that, again like them, it becomes changed or develops through the intermittent insertion of new buds or new grafts of *imitation-fashions* which come to replenish and nourish, sometimes to drive back, a stock of *imitation-customs*, but they themselves have a tendency to take root, to swell the legacy of custom and tradition. Every industry feeds itself in this manner by means of an afflux of improvements, innovations today, traditions tomorrow. Every science, every art, every language, every religion, obeys this law of the passing from custom to fashion and the return from fashion to custom, but custom which has expanded. For with each step in advance taken by it the territorial domain of imitation becomes larger, the field of social assimilation and of human fraternity expands, and it is not, as we know, the least salutary effect of imitative cause from the point of view of morality.

*   *   *

It is useless to insist any further. We can draw the conclusion that every social matter, that is to say, all individual initiative, every special method of thought, feeling, or action, put in circulation by a man, has a tendency to be spread through fashion, among primitive peoples as well as among those who are civilized, and after having become widespread, to take root in the form of a custom, among civilized peoples as well as among primitive ones.

The thing which concerns us is to observe that it is not merely language, dogma, industrial and artistic instruments and talents, but moral or immoral feelings, moral or immoral habits as well, which have a tendency to become general and to become fixed in this manner.

*   *   *

Criminality without any doubt, like every other branch of social activity, implies physiological and even physical conditions, but that, like industry especially, it is to be accounted for better than in any other way, by the general laws of imitation, in its local color as in its special force at each period of time, in its geographical distribution as in its historical transformations, in the varying proportion of its various motives or the unstable hierarchy of its varying degrees as in the succession of its changing methods. We have mentioned the importance in our opinion attaching to this demonstration, from the point of view of penal responsibility, from which it results that the offense is an act emanating not merely from the living being, but from the personal individual, such as society alone can make him and cause him to increase in number in its image; from the person more identical with himself, up to a certain point at least, as he is more similar to others; the more willing and conscious as he is more readily impressed by example, just as the better it breathes, the stronger the lung is. It has been said that our body is a small quantity of condensed air, living in the air. Can it not be said that our soul is a small quantity of society incarnate, living in society? Born from society, it lives by means of society; and if the analogies which I have perhaps at some length enumerated are correct, there is no reason why its criminal responsibility should be misunderstood any more than its civil responsibility, which latter is undisputed and assuredly incapable of being disputed.

Moreover, let us clearly understand each other on this important point. I will not deny that, to a greater or lesser extent, the physical or physiological provocations to commit an offense have acted as the determining cause of the will; but their action, being only partial, does not prevent the delinquent from being responsible. On the contrary, they compete with one another, on their part, to demonstrate that he is responsible. No doubt, if they acted by themselves upon the individual, he would not be socially responsible, because this would reveal in him a being absolutely alien to the society of other men; but he might continue to be responsible individually. By this I mean that the condition of social similarity, required by our theory of responsibility, would not really be fulfilled, but that the condition of individual identity, which is above all requisite, might be realized, in spite of the inevitable necessity of external influences.

*   *   *

I would not wish to leave the subject without giving warning that the analogies herein developed as existing between crime and the other social phenomena, especially industry, must not make us forget the differences which exist between them. Crime is a social phenomenon like any other, but a phenomenon which is at the same time anti-social, just as a cancer participates in the life of an organism, but working to bring about its death. And, in fact, if Mitschlerlich was able to say that "life is a corruption," a bitter saying justified to a certain extent by the new school of chemists, according to whom the "chemical diminution of putrefaction and those of the intra-organic combustions offer the greatest analogy," we have a right to say also, as a consequence, that corruption is a part of life, but of the life which kills. Crime is an industry, but a negative one, which accounts for its extreme age; as soon as the first product was manufactured by a laborious tribe, there must have been formed a band of plunderers. A brother and a contemporary of the industry which it fosters, crime does not originally seem to have been any more a disgrace than industry itself. They have developed along the same lines, by both passing from the unilateral form to the bilateral form.

19 · The Criminal—A Product of the Capitalistic System

by WILLIAM ADRIAN BONGER

William Adrian Bonger (1876-1940), a widely known Dutch criminologist, conceived of crime as a social phenomenon caused chiefly by adverse economic conditions. These, in turn, he believed, are the result of the pressures and abuses of the capitalistic system, which frequently lead individuals, particularly those belonging to the poorer classes, to delinquency and crime. The gist of Bonger's theory regarding crime and its causes is contained in the following excerpts from his book. [From *Criminality and Economic Conditions* (translated by Henry P. Horton), Little, Brown, and Company, 1916, pp. 401-404, 407, 420, 424-425, 433-434, 532-533, 669. Footnotes and tabular material omitted. Reprinted by permission.]

EGOISTIC TENDENCIES RESULTING FROM THE PRESENT
ECONOMIC SYSTEM AND FROM ITS CONSEQUENCES

The etiology of crime includes the three following problems:

First. Whence does the criminal thought in man arise?

Second. What forces are there in man which can prevent the execution of this criminal thought, and what is their origin?

Third. What is the occasion for the commission of criminal acts? (As the occasion may be one of the causes of the criminal thought, problems one and three at times form but one.)

For the moment we are still occupied with general considerations with regard to crime; it is clear then that the first and third questions will be examined only when we are treating of crimes according to the groups into which they must be divided because of the great differences which their nature presents.

It is otherwise with the second question. . . . It is certain that man is born with social instincts, which, when influenced by a favorable environment, can exert a force great enough to prevent egoistic thoughts from leading to egoistic acts. And since crime constitutes a part of the egoistic acts, it is of importance, for the etiology of *crime in general,* to inquire whether the present method of production and its social consequences are an obstacle to the development of the social instincts, and in what measure. We shall try in the following pages to show the influence of the economic system and of these consequences upon the social instincts of man.

After what we have just said it is almost superfluous to remark that the egoistic tendency does not *by itself* make a man criminal. For this something else is necessary. It is possible for the environment to create a great egoist, but this does not imply that the egoist will necessarily become criminal. For example, a man who is enriched by the exploitation of children may nevertheless remain all his life an honest man from the legal point of view. He does not think of stealing, because he has a surer and more lucrative means of getting wealth, although he lacks the moral sense which would prevent him from committing a crime if the thought of it occurred to him. We shall show that, as a consequence of the present environment, man has become very egoistic and hence more *capable of crime,* than if the environment had developed the germs of altruism.

a. The present economic system is based upon exchange. . . . Such a mode of production cannot fail to have an egoistic character. A society based upon exchange isolates the individuals by weakening the bond that unites them. When it is a question of exchange the two parties interested think only of their own advantage even to the detriment of the other party. In the second place the possibility of exchange arouses in a man the thought of the possibility of converting the surplus of his labor into things which increase his well-being in place of giving the benefit of it to those who are deprived of the necessaries of life. Hence the possibility of exchange gives birth to cupidity.

The exchange called simple circulation of commodities is practiced by all men as consumers, and by the workers besides as vendors of their labor power. However, the influence of this simple circulation of commodities is weak compared with that exercised by capitalistic exchange. It is only the exchange of the surplus of labor, by the producer, for other commodities, and hence is for him a secondary matter. As a result he does not exchange with a view to profit, (though he tries to make as advantageous a trade as possible) but to get things which he cannot produce himself.

Capitalistic exchange, on the other hand, has another aim—that of making a profit. A merchant, for example, does not buy goods for his own use, but to sell them to advantage. He will, then, always try, on the one hand, to buy the best commodities as cheaply as possible, by depreciating them as much as he can; on the other hand, to make the purchaser pay as high a price as possible, by exaggerating the value of his wares. *By the nature of the mode of production itself* the merchant is therefore forced to make war upon two sides, must maintain his own interests against the interests of those with whom he does business. If he does not injure too greatly the interests of those from whom he buys, and those to whom he sells, it is for the simple reason that these would otherwise do business with those of his competitors who do not find their interest in fleecing their customers. Wherever competition is eliminated for whatever cause the tactics of the merchant are shown in their true light; he thinks only of his own advantage even to the detriment of those with whom he does business. "No commerce without trickery" is a proverbial expression (among consumers), and with the ancients Mercury, the god of commerce, was also the god of thieves. This is true, that the merchant and the thief are alike in taking account *exclusively* of their own interest to the detriment of those with whom they have to do.

The fact that in our present society production does not take place generally to provide for the needs of men, but for many other reasons, has important effects upon the character of those who possess the means of production. Production is carried on for profit exclusively; if greater profits can be made by stopping production it will be stopped—this is the point of view of the capitalists. The consumers, on the other hand, see in production the means of creating what man has need of. The world likes to be deceived, and does not care to recognize the fact that the producer has only his own profit in view. The latter encourages this notion and poses as a disinterested person. If he reduces the prices of his wares, he claims to do it in the interest of the public, and takes care not to admit that it is for the purpose of increasing his own profits. This is the falsity that belongs inevitably to capitalism.

In general this characteristic of capitalism has no importance for the morality of the consumer, who is merely duped, but it is far otherwise with the press, which is almost entirely in the power of the capitalists. The press, which ought to be a guide for the masses, and is so in some few cases, in the main is in the hands of capitalists who use it only as a means of making money. In place of being edited by men who, by their ability and firmness, are capable of enlightening the public, newspapers are carried on by persons who see in their calling only a livelihood, and consider only the proprietor of the sheet. In great part the press is the opposite of what it ought to be; it represents the interests of those who pay for advertisements or for articles; it increases the ignorance and the prejudices of the crowd; in a word, it poisons public opinion.

Besides this general influence upon the public the press has further a special place in the etiology of crime, from the fact that most newspapers, in order to satisfy the morbid curiosity of the public, relate all great crimes in extenso, give portraits of the victims, etc., and are often one of the causes of new crimes, by arousing the imitative instinct to be found in man.

* * *

The proletariat. To be thorough we begin by making mention of one of the consequences of the economic position of the proletariat . . . namely the dependence in which persons of this class find themselves in consequence of their lacking the means of production, a state which has a prejudicial influence upon character. The oppressed resort to means which they would otherwise scorn. As we have seen above, the basis of the social feelings is reciprocity. As soon as this is trodden under foot by the ruling class the social sentiments of the oppressed become weak towards them.

We come now . . . first to the consequences of the labor of the young. The paid labor of the young has a bad influence in several ways. First, it forces them, while they are still very young, to think only of their own interests; then, brought into contact with persons who are rough and indifferent to their well-being, they follow these only too quickly, because of their imitative tendencies, in their bad habits, grossness of speech, etc. Finally, the paid labor of the young makes them more or less independent at an age where they have the greatest need of guidance. Even if the statistical proof of the influence of the labor of children and young people upon criminality were totally wanting, no one could deny that influence. Child labor is entirely a capitalistic phenomenon, being found especially in the great manufacturing countries like England and Germany. And then one of the most salient facts of criminality is the amount of juvenile crime, which is so enormous that England, followed by other countries, has established a special system to combat this form of criminality. Certainly this increase of juvenile crime is chiefly due to the influence of bad domestic conditions (wage-labor of married women, etc.), but the labor of the young people themselves also plays its part.

*   *   *

. . . We come now to the influence of long hours of labor. It has rightly been said that work has a strong moral influence. But it is also true that immoderate labor has the contrary effect. It brutalizes a man, makes him incapable of elevated sentiments, kills as Key says (in "das Jahrhundert des Kindes"), the man in the beast, while moderate labor ennobles the beast in the man.

The housing conditions of the proletariat have also a significance as regards criminality, and for the special group of sexual offenses their importance is very great. We shall speak of this more fully when we treat especially of these offenses, and will, for the moment, note simply their general consequences.

The disorder and squalor of the home communicate themselves to the inmates; the lack of room obliges the children to live, during a great part of the day, on the streets, with the result that they are brought into contact with all sorts of demoralizing companions. Finally, the living together of a great number of uneducated persons in one small dwelling is the cause of constant quarrels and fights. The situation of those who are merely night-lodgers is especially unfortunate, as we have already seen.

*   *   *

From the position in which the proletarians find themselves it follows that, towards each other, it is rather the altruistic than the egoistic feelings that develop; living less isolated than the bourgeois, they see the misfortune that strikes their neighbor, and have felt the same themselves, and above all, their economic interests are not opposed. Forced idleness —at present chronic, and acute in times of panic—modifies these conditions at times; it makes competitors of the workers, who take the bread out of each other's mouths.

The proletarian is never sure of his existence: like the sword of Damocles unemployment is constantly hanging over his head. . . .

*   *   *

Finally we must speak of ignorance and lack of training on the part of the proletariat, as a factor of criminality. As we know, this question of education is one of those which are most debated in criminal sociology. Certain authors have prophesied that each new school would make a prison superfluous, while on the other hand it has been claimed that ignorance and the lack of civilization have nothing to do with the etiology of crime, but that on the contrary knowledge and civilization are even factors of crime. Although these extreme opinions are hardly ever expressed nowadays, the ideas upon the point in question still differ widely.

* * *

I am of the opinion that . . . the illiterates supply, in general, a great proportion of the criminals, a proportion much greater than that of the illiterates in the general population. (In countries with a relatively small number of illiterates, like England, the Netherlands, and Prussia, for example, the difference is naturally much greater than in a country like Italy where the percentage of illiteracy is great. In Prussia for instance, there are thirty-six times as many illiterates among the recidivists as among the recruits.)

However, most of the statistics, aside from the figures for illiteracy, give others which show how many persons really educated are to be found among the criminals. And then we note that a very great majority of criminals are ignorant and untrained. In England, for example, there is among male criminals only 1 to 1,000 who knows more than how to read and write well, and among the women not even 1 to 1,000; in Austria there are a little more than 4 to 1,000; and in France a little more than 20 to 1,000 among the men, and between 4 and 5 among the women. The relation between ignorance and criminality cannot, then, be contradicted. But it is impossible to fix exactly the extent of the influence of the one upon the other, or it is difficult to separate ignorance from other factors with which it is ordinarily found, as poverty, for instance.

The ancient idea that crime is only a consequence of ignorance need not be treated of, for morality and intellect are two distinct parts of the psychic life, even though there exists a certain relation between them.

The first reason why ignorance and the lack of general culture must be ranked among the general factors of crime is this: the person who, in our present society, where the great majority of parents care very little for the education of their children, does not go to school, is deprived of the moral ideas (honesty, etc.) which are taught there, and ordinarily passes his time in idleness and vagabondage.

The second reason which makes ignorance a factor of crime, is tha
generally an ignorant man is, more than others, a man moved by th
impulse of the moment, who allows himself to be governed by his pas
sions, and is induced to commit acts which he would not have committe
if his intellectual equipment had been different.

In the third place, it is for the following reasons that ignorance an
the lack of training fall within the etiology of crime. The mind of th
man whose psychic qualities, whether in the domain of the arts, or o
the sciences, have been developed, has become less susceptible to evi
ideas. His intellectual condition constitutes thus a bridle which ca
restrain evil thoughts from realizing themselves; for real art and tru
science strengthen the social instincts. . . .

*   *   *

Conclusions. In recapitulating now the egoistic tendencies of th
present economic system and of its consequences, we see clearly tha
they are very strong. Because of these tendencies the social instinct o
man is not greatly developed; they have weakened the moral force i
man which combats the inclination towards egoistic acts, and hence to
wards the crimes which are one form of these acts. To mention only th
most important things, in a society in which, as in ours, the economi
interests of all are in eternal conflict among themselves, compassion fo
the misfortunes of others inevitably becomes blunted, and a great par
of morality consequently disappears. The slight value that is attached t
the opinion of others is also a consequence of the strife of economi
interests, for we can be responsive to that opinion only when we do no
see adversaries in our fellows.

The fluctuations of the mind of the person in whom the criminal ide
is born may be compared with the oscillations of a balance; and it i
upon sociology that must devolve the task of examining the forces whic
throw a weight on one side or the other. When the organization o
society influences men in an altruistic way there is then a considerabl
force which can prevent the balance from inclining towards the egoisti
side. In our present society, the organization of which does not exert ar
altruistic influence, this force is very weak, or does not exist at all. Since
however, in every society, man must abstain from a number of egoisti
acts, substitutes have been devised to take the place of the weak or want
ing social sentiments. The hope of reward (whether terrestrial or celes
tial) and the fear of being punished (whether by man or God) ar
charged with the duty of keeping men in order. As believers themselve
know very well, most men are not very responsive to divine rewards an
punishments—heaven and hell are too far off. Is it not believers who ar

the strongest partisans of rewards and punishments here below for human acts? However, this expedient is only a very insufficient one. We know too well that the rewards are very often lacking, and the punishments as well. This is why many persons take the risk of committing the crime they have planned.

* * *

Upon the basis of what has gone before, we have a right to say that the part played by economic conditions in criminality is preponderant, even decisive.

This conclusion is of the highest importance for the prevention of crime. If it were principally the consequence of innate human qualities (atavism, for example), the pessimistic conclusion that crime is a phenomenon inseparably bound up with the social life would be well founded. But the facts show that it is rather the optimistic conclusion that we must draw, that where crime is the consequence of economic and social conditions, we can combat it by changing those conditions.

* * *

CHAPTER SEVEN

Psychological Factors in Crime

20 · The Nature of Psychopathy

by BENJAMIN KARPMAN

Psychopathy is considered by many psychiatrists as the underlying cause of habitual criminality. Some would go as far as to maintain that the fact that one is a habitual criminal proves that one is a psychopath. That psychopathy plays a part in crime causation no criminologist would deny. Yet few matters produce so much disagreement among psychologists and psychiatrists as do the causes and symptoms of psychopathy. Here Dr. Benjamin Karpman, a psychiatrist of note, expounds his views, based on first hand observation and diagnosis, on the nature of psychopathic behavior and how it differs from the psychotic and neurotic. ["The Yardstick for Measuring Psychopathy," *Federal Probation*, Vol. X, Oct.-Dec. 1946, pp. 26-31 Reprinted by permission. Footnotes omitted.]

THE PROBLEM of psychopathy is almost coeval with the problem of crime. Though numerically psychopaths, as a group in the general population, are smaller than the normal, the neurotic, the psychotic, and the mental defective, they contribute more to the criminal group and in general to antisocial behavior than any of the other groups. This explains why the literature continues to have much material written on psychopaths, though unfortunately there is as yet little clarification of the subject.

One of the greatest stumbling blocks in the better understanding of the psychopath as an individual or psychopathy as a disease, is that we group under this heading altogether too many conditions that have little in common with each other except certain outward forms of behavior which we are pleased to call psychopathic. It seems that there is a failure here to appreciate the fact that though some reactions may have a common point of expression, and therefore superficially seem to resemble each other, they may be as different among themselves and divers as conditions could be, the reason being that they have different origins and motivations.

PSYCHOPATHY AND PSYCHOSES

At the present, as concerning psychopathy, psychiatrists are divided mainly into two groups, with diametrically opposed viewpoints. One, and that is the majority, has a most inclusive approach and regards psychopathic behavior as being not only widespread, but nearly universal (Henderson, Kahn, and others). Too, they speak more in terms of psychopathic personality. The other group has a much more limited conception, disregards the term psychopathic personality as having no more justification than schizophrenic, cyclothymic, or psychoneurotic personality; and in contrast, speaks of psychopathy as a disease. The first group emphasizes behavior and symptoms; the other group emphasizes psychogenesis and motivation. The first group speaks of psychopaths as differing from actual psychotics in that they do not exhibit loss of touch with reality, mental conflicts, hallucinations, delusions, impaired memory, disorientation, and the like. This would seem to be a diagnosis by elimination, not by what the subject has, but by what he has not, and yet it is an exceedingly good point to make. All too often, however, we find people who are definitely psychotic, yet exhibit traits of behavior which by common opinion seem so clearly to belong to the psychopath. As for instance, dementia praecox in which such traits as poor judgment, irresponsibility, poor occupational adjustment, criminal involvements are often observed. How then are we to classify such cases? Should we call them schizophrenic psychopaths? That would be silly! It is better to recognize that such psychopathic-like symptoms are not the result or a part of a concomitant psychopathy but rather that such symptoms can equally well flow out of and be an integral part of the dementia praecox disease entity.

Among the symptoms above mentioned, the largest emphasis must be given to the term "mental conflicts," and it is upon these mental conflicts that the other symptoms such as delusions, hallucinations, etc., seem to be predicated. It is wholly unnecessary here to go into the nature and variety of mental conflicts found in schizophrenia, manic-depressive, and other psychoses; the psychiatric literature is full of it. Suffice it to point out that these conflicts being active and dynamic, give rise to and are responsible for all of the behavior and symptoms found in the psychoses. In the case of dementia praecox, for instance, it is out of these conflicts too there often comes the poor judgment, irresponsibility, poor occupational adjustment and criminal involvement. It is unnecessary and illogical as well, to consider these traits as psychopathic or as symptoms of a disease psychopathy. These are psychopathic-like traits (psychopathoid) and may be found in *any* mental disease, and as a part of the disease.

On the other hand, it is characteristic of the psychopath as being the opposite of the psychoneurotic or the psychotic (insane), that he *does not suffer from mental conflicts at all*. When he wants something he goes at it headlong, brooking no opposition, disregarding the difficulties that stand in the way and without concern as to what problems it may create in others; whereas the psychoneurotic or the psychotic individual, even though he indulge in identical behavior, is in constant conflict because his instincts dictate one thing while his conscience is opposed to these aims. While the behavior and symptoms of the psychotic or psychoneurotic, however antisocial, flow out of their conflicts, the behavior of the psychopath seems like a natural development of his original personality. And unlike the psychotic and the psychoneurotic, the psychopath has no symptoms: his behavioral reactions *are* his symptoms.

It is probably not difficult to recognize gross psychopathic behavior, if we ask for no further differentiation; but there are many kinds of subclinical psychopathic conditions which are not easily recognizable as psychopathic. I am sure that in the large group of psychopaths, there are many cases whose behavior is superficially quite psychopathic, yet are basically of psychotic or neurotic make-up.

PSYCHOPATHY AND NEUROSIS

I quite agree with those who believe that psychopaths are not neurotic. Unfortunately in common with many other psychiatric definitions, after such statement is made, the authors persist in including among psychopaths individuals who are definitely neurotic, the reason being that the conception of neuroses differs so among psychiatrists. By far, the greatest number of psychiatrists include under neuroses, the more strictly definable hysterical conditions, more specifically those called conversion hysterias. But they fail to regard as neuroses other conditions which from a more dynamic point of view are definitely neurotic. For instance, nine times out of ten, cases of pyromania which come under the observation of a psychiatric hospital, would be called psychopathic personality; yet more properly they should be called neuroses because the behavior reaction, although definitely in conflict with society, is not willfully enacted by the individual, but is the result of deep-seated conflicts arising from psychogenic difficulties of which pyromania is only one of the more obvious outward expressions. If these authors would enlarge their concept of neuroses to include all cases, however, seemingly psychopathic, that are the result of unsatisfied psychological states and conflicts, I have no doubt that the group of actual psychopaths would become smaller and smaller as indeed it should if we are ever to get the condition clearly delimited.

The reason given for including kleptomania and pyromania in the group of psychopathies is because these people have found an outlet by attacking the environment. I do not believe this is a valid criterion to judge psychopathy by. It is true that psychopaths, as a rule, attack the environment, but I think it is faulty logic to reverse this statement and consider all who attack environment as psychopathic. The paranoid praecox, the excited manic, the hostile neurotic, the disturbed epileptic or the alcoholic who runs berserk, and many like them, attack the environment. One must go beyond and search for the *motivations* back of the reaction. All these individuals attack the environment for widely different reasons. It is about time that we cease making psychopathy, criminal and antisocial behavior, identical and interchangeable.

I do not agree with the statement that the difference between the neurotic and the psychopath is that the psychopath considers himself always right, whereas the neurotic realizes that he—not the world—is wrong. This statement is only partially true and, as presented, is entirely misleading. It is true that many neurotics carry within them a strong sense of guilt, sometimes expressed in confession and atonement but again there are a large number of neurotics in whom the sense of guilt has been absorbed by an unusually large hostility component or by presence of strong inferiority, which obscure or even neutralize all guilt reactions. It is therefore incorrect to say that only a psychopath considers himself right and the world wrong. I have known any number of neurotics who became criminally involved because the hostility component was so strong in them as to obscure the presence of any scruples, and they considered themselves right and the world wrong, yet they were neurotic by all accepted standards. And let us not forget that the delu sional praecox, even though he may be guilty of a serious crime, stil considers himself right and the whole world wrong.

Not unlike the psychotic, the psychoneurotics, too, often give expres sion to mental conflicts and other disturbances and thus often show behavior that looks strikingly like that of the psychopath. The psycho neurotics also may lie, cheat, assault, steal, rob, and even kill. But i would be a great mistake to call them psychopathic. Again, the most im portant difference to remember is the difference in the *motivation* back of it. Whereas all these reactions in the psychoneurotic or psychotic that superficially look so psychopathic, flow out of conflicts, those of the psychopath, though superficially he may actually indulge in like be havior, do not flow out of conflicts but merely out of his desire to contro the environment in his own particular way. This is an important con sideration to bear in mind, for our entire method of dealing with the individual offender should depend upon the causation or motivation back of the reaction. We can do all sorts of psychotherapy with the psy choneurotic and the psychotic, at least there is hope, but in our presen state of knowledge, the one thing to do with a psychopath is not to give him a definite sentence but to confine him, not in a prison, but in a hos pital specially designed to deal with this particular type of personality

TWO TYPES OF PSYCHOPATHY

It is entirely true that psychopaths as a group are superficial. They are so to speak, two-dimensional personalities. Dr. George N. Raines ha correctly observed that what psychopathology you see on the surface o a psychopath is all there is to it. It is just another way of saying that the psychopath has no depth, but this merely comes back to my origina statement that psychopathic behavior is in all probability not the resul of any deep-seated conditionings and conflicts.

On the basis of the presence or absence of psychogenic, often uncon scious, motivations, I would postulate that there are indeed two chie types of psychopaths:

A. Where the presence of psychological motivation is not difficult to elicit, the psychopathy appears then merely as a symptom of some under lying difficulties which can be traced to their basic motivations. When the motivations are uncovered and neutralized, the condition has a good chance of being cured as many have been cured. This is the symptomatic, secondary psychopathy.

B. On the other hand, there is a type of psychopath that no matter how hard and how deep one studies his case, it is quite impossible to find any specific psychogenesis for his behavior. He is what he is and he does what he does by reason of what he always was and always did. The reaction is so deeply ingrained in him that it seems as if it had been with him from birth. This is the primary psychopathy—original, essential idiopathic.

For this reason I should like to use as a yardstick for measuring psychopathy, *behavior* vs. *motivation*. The reason why so much is written on psychopathy without us ever coming to any definite conclusion, is because we have grouped together a large number of people who have only one point in common, this is antisocial behavior, but if we further split this large group on the basis of motivation, we get the two distinct types mentioned above. In further consideration, I personally would call pyromania definitely neurosis, but since many pyromaniacs are socially destructive, they may be called psychopaths but then in an entirely secondary or symptomatic sense. This is nothing new in psychiatry and medicine. We are acquainted with anemia of which there are two types: primary or idiopathic and secondary or symptomatic; we are acquainted with epilepsy which may be essential and secondary, etc., and there is full justification therefore for speaking of psychopathy as primary and secondary. Science moves from the general to the specific, from the diffuse to the concrete.

Once we thus separate psychopathy into two groups, primary and secondary, the whole subject can be handled with greater ease. If, after studying a case, it is revealed as being basically of the symptomatic or secondary type, then that kind of case is obviously hopeful of treatment. All we have to do is find the underlying motivation. In some cases, the cause may not be so deep, though in others it will be so deeply ingrained that it might be very difficult to get at it and require deep psychotherapeutic study. If, on the other hand, after putting forth much effort in that direction, we discover that the individual belongs to the primary type of psychopathy, then obviously we are just wasting time in treatment, for the present at least, and we have to adopt other methods. But in studying all such cases, one must have a great deal of patience.

To repeat, failure to appreciate the difference between the pure or essential psychopathy as compared with and different from the secondary or symptomatic type, has resulted in a clinical therapeutic impasse. For on the basis of studies made, we know that the true, idiopathic type of psychopathy is unable (at the present state of our knowledge), by reason of his particular make-up, to profit in any way by experience. Therefore, giving him a limited sentence of several years can only mean one thing: that on expiration of the sentence, he will be entirely untouched by the experience; and will merrily continue on his own way only to run afoul of the law again. On the other hand, treating the symptomatic type in the same way as the idiopathic type must again result in failure, for punishment only aggravates the situation. If a case study of a criminal reveals that though he has indulged in a great deal of criminal activity, he is basically moved by some emotional drive to commit the crimes in question, then the proper treatment for him is not confinement and punishment, not a limited, specified sentence, but treatment that will attempt to reach the psychological sources of his difficulties. We do not punish a typhoid carrier for infecting others, but we do quarantine him for his own and others' good. Why not treat the mentally ill in the same way as we treat the physically ill!

I have had personal experience in dealing with prisoners who were deeply psychopathic in their behavior, seemingly from any point of view one looked at it, yet a careful study of their life with a therapeutic aim has actually cured these cases. Needless to say, though such procedure is far from being accepted, it is actually by far the most economical we have. For the cost of psychotherapeutic treatment is exceedingly small compared with the cost of maintaining the prisoner in the prison. Limitation of space does not permit the presentation of pertinent clinical material of which there is already a great deal in the literature.

PSYCHOPATHY AND ABNORMAL SEXUALITY

I cannot agree with the view that some psychopaths are homosexual and sex perverts as if the two go together. I think a question is raised here that had better not be raised, for again such opinion speaks in terms of superficial behavior and not motivation. There is absolutely nothing in common between psychopaths on the one hand, and homosexuals and sexual perverts on the other hand. Homosexuals and sexual perverts (paraphilias) are first of all human beings and as such may be variedly organized, which means that they also may be psychopathic but I fail to see any direct connection between psychopathy, and homosexuality and sex perversion. The reason they are often put together is because in common with the rest of descriptive psychiatry, homosexuality here is regarded as an antisocial behavior; hence, by the same token, as psychopathic. I don't think this argument will hold water. It is more than merely a question of a point of view. Antisocial behavior may be due to any number of conditions as already stated. The functionally and dynamically oriented psychiatrists do not regard homosexuality as a form of antisocial behavior, but as a highly specific type of neurosis. I think it is about time that we have grown big enough to realize that people are entitled to their own form of sex life and that we must not brand a psychopathic people different from us merely because they are different. Personal moral judgments should not enter into scientific discussions.

Some time ago I put forth a series of arguments to show that homosexuality and sexual perversions (paraphilias) are basically neuroses and should be treated as such. The social pressure that is being brought upon them often makes it necessary for many such persons to adopt measures which lead them to antisocial difficulties, but that alone is no evidence of psychopathy. Homosexuality and paraphilias (perversions) are neuroses because on analysis they were found to have the psychological structure of neuroses, were treated as neuroses and they have been cured as such. I am sure I am not the only one who has been successful in curing homosexuality and perversions. I think any psychiatrist, working by methods of dynamic psychotherapy, must have to his credit a number of cases of homosexuality and paraphilias which he cured. I have recorded elsewhere the case of an individual who was given to raping little girls. This was a perversion (pedophilia). The case was diagnosed, as one would expect at the hospital conference, as psychopathic personality. The analysis revealed a clear-cut neurosis. This man has been cured and there has been no recurrence for 20 years which again speaks against the condition being psychopathic.

Many psychopaths do not make a normal sex adjustment, but again it seems that we are arguing here *pars pro toto*. While it is true that psychopaths are not normal sexually, I would be the last one to be involved in the faulty logic of reversing it and saying that all those who fail to make a normal sexual adjustment are psychopathic. The woods are full of neurotics with difficult sex life. And is there anyone with a more abnormal sex life than the praecox? Too, the sex life of a psychoneurotic has a different pathology from that of a psychopath. To put it in other words, psychopaths do not make good sex adjustments, but not all who make poor sex adjustments are necessarily psychopathic. Do we have to go back to college logic?

It is often stated that psychopaths are incapable of sincere love. This is true, but again it cannot be said that this by itself is a psychopathic reaction. I have seen paraphiliacs, transvestists, exhibitionists, for instance, who are wholly incapable of meeting the opposite sex on normal terms. They do not know how to kiss, they do not know how to love, or caress; guilt and neurotic inhibitions keep them from it. So we come back to the same statement again that while it is true that psychopaths are not fully capable of normal love life, not all those who are incapable of normal love, are necessarily psychopaths.

One point, however, must be mentioned with reference to the love relations of the psychopaths, or for that matter of any interpersonal relations between them and the opposite sex. They appear to be wholly incapable of developing binding or sympathetic emotions. They do not appreciate what is done for them and they are not likely to return with gratitude what has been done for them. In this respect they are the opposite of neurotics and stand virtually alone among humans.

SOME CARDINAL TRAITS IN PSYCHOPATHY

Occupational maladjustment is charged against the psychopath. It is true that psychopaths do not as a rule hold a job very well. Steadfastness of purpose is not one of their virtues; none the less, it is a great mistake to think of everyone who cannot stick to a job, as psychopathic. Lots of people in this world are occupational misfits for any variety of reasons, psychopathy being only one of these.

It has been submitted that psychopaths are antisocial, that they will lie, cheat, break promises again and again without the slightest compunction. This is entirely true of psychopaths but not of them only. They will sometimes tell the truth, be honest, keep their promises, if they think that by doing so, they may gain a superior advantage; but by and large, it is true. However, I do not believe the psychopath holds a corner on it. Lots of other people will lie, cheat, and break promises, and yet are not psychopaths. Neurotics, for psychic reasons of their own, because of unrequited affection or the presence of a large amount of hostility or strong inferiority-superiority drive, may resort to all these antisocial reactions, but in such a case, their lying and cheating, etc., are only secondary to and an outgrowth of some basic neurotic condition.

The psychopath no doubt is selfish to the extreme, but I have also known a large number of neurotics who driven by psychological motivations were extremely selfish and without the least concern for the welfare of others. In other words, while it is true that psychopaths as a group are selfish, not all people who are selfish are psychopaths.

From all of the above it is evident that there is virtually no single reaction shown by the psychopaths that could not be equally found in other group reactions such as neurotic, psychotic, feeble-minded, and even the normal people. If one wishes to emphasize such traits as extreme irresponsibility, selfishness, dishonesty as being specifically characteristic of the psychopaths, it is obligatory on his part to show in *what specific way* their irresponsibility, selfishness, dishonesty differ from the irresponsibility, selfishness, and dishonesty of neurotics and normal people. Unless one can show that, the statement that psychopaths are possessors of all these traits becomes too diffuse and vague without any significant meaning. But I don't believe they can do that, for they work only on the surface and deal with symptoms and superficialities of behavior. The dynamic psychiatrist possesses finer and more incisive tools to work with, and is able to get at the deeper motivations back of the behavior. And that is why he has a different view and a different approach because by his method he gets different results which in turn influence his point of view.

SUMMARY AND CONCLUSIONS

1. With reference to psychopathic behavior, there exist at present among psychiatrists, two diametrically opposed viewpoints. One may be designated as the behavioral or symptomatic approach and limits itself to the description of conditions as it finds them, but not concerning itself with motivations underlying the behavior and symptoms. For this reason they speak of and include under the term psychopathic, all reactions that appear psychopathic, regardless of their origin. The other approach views psychopathy as a specific mental disease, not to be confused with other reactions superficially resembling it; and in each instance makes a determined effort to search for the underlying motivations.

2. The only way to differentiate these many symptoms and behavioral reactions that superficially resemble each other, is by searching for the underlying motivations back of these symptoms and behavior. It is submitted that these motivations alone can give us a true differential picture of the situation.

a. It can not be claimed as being specific of the psychopath that he always regards himself as right and the world wrong, for the same situation obtains in dementia praecox and other psychoses, and psychoneuroses as well.

b. Such antisocial reactions as lying, cheating, being irresponsible are not limited to psychopathy, but may be found in neuroses and psychoses as well with, however, a different motivation. The same is true of occupational maladjustment.

c. Psychopaths are known to be extremely selfish. However, other cardinal reaction types may show like traits though by reason of different motivation.

d. Psychopaths also are said to be abnormal in their sex life, but that holds equally true of many other conditions as well.

e. Contrary to the opinion generally held that homosexuality, perversions and other sexual reactions of an antisocial character are psychopathic, it is submitted here that they are essentially neuroses, for on psychoanalysis they are revealed as having a neurotic structure, and furthermore can be cured by psychotherapy. They too should also be removed from the group of psychopathic reactions.

3. It is submitted here that making a diagnosis on the basis of superficial behavior and symptoms is fallacious since many divers conditions may express themselves superficially by like behavior and symptoms. Traits, reactions, and symptoms found in psychopathic conditions are with equal frequency found in other psychic conditions as well. Hardly any trait, reaction, and symptom can be said to be entirely and uniquely specific for psychopathy. Therefore, it is not reasonable to put into one group all reactions that look psychopathic.

4. One of the striking characteristics of the psychopath and one that may be said to be uniquely his, is the absence in him of deep mental conflicts and of the ability to develop binding emotions. While in cases of neuroses and psychoses abnormal symptoms and often psychopathic-like behavior frequently results from these conflicts, the psychopathic behavior of the psychopath appears to originate not in conflicts, but, as it were, from the individual's original personality. Pyromania and kleptomania and perhaps other predatory crimes, because of the presence in them of undoubted psychic motivations, should be removed from that group of psychopathies and placed into the group of neuroses. Homosexuality and perversions also should be removed from psychopathies, as they are neuroses.

5. On the basis of motivations observed in various conditions, the following classification is submitted:

a. Symptomatic or secondary psychopathy. These are conditions displaying on the surface psychopathic-like behavior which, however, on study is revealed as being secondary or symptomatic of deeper underlying psychogenic conditions.

b. Primary, essential, or idiopathic psychopathy. In this condition no psychogenetic motivation can be elicited.

6. The differential diagnoses offered above are important for they indicate the attack on the problem and the line of treatment. If the case belongs to symptomatic psychopathy, we have to look for underlying causation and treat the same. The psychiatric literature records cases regarded as being deeply and constitutionally psychopathic, having been cured by psychotherapy. If, on the other hand, a case belongs to primary psychopathy, the treatment, for the present time at least, is indefinite confinement, for it is quite certain that these people cannot profit by any lesson and do not have the judgment necessary for normal social relations.

7. Since many traits presumably characteristic of psychopathy may be found in other reactional types as well, the only way to give those

reactions a specific meaning is by specifically differentiating the reactions from other reactions closely resembling it. Thus it is not sufficient to say that the sex life of the psychopath is abnormal, for this is generally true of other reactions too. There are all sorts of abnormal sex lives. It is obligatory to point out just in what specific way is the sex life of the psychopath abnormal and different from the abnormal sex life of the praecox, the neurotic, etc. This is being done by the dynamic psychiatrists, but not by the behavioral, descriptive psychiatrists.

8. It is submitted further that any psychiatrist who attempts to speak of psychopathy as an abnormal condition, is under obligation to submit such motivational behavior as he has been able to unearth in the study.

21 · The Psychopathic Personality and Crime

by NATHANIEL THORNTON

In criminological literature, as intimated in the preceding introduction, psychopathy is not infrequently considered as one of the chief causes of crime. What, precisely, is a psychopath? Is there only one type or are there several types? Is the psychopath the only defective type capable of committing a major crime? What distinguishes the psychopathic criminal from other types? These are the chief questions that Nathaniel Thornton, a noted psychiatrist, discusses in the selection that follows. ["The Relation Between Crime and Psychopathic Personality," *Journal of Criminal Law and Criminology*, Vol. 42, Aug.-Sept. 1951, pp. 199-204. Reprinted by permission. Footnotes omitted.]

AWARE that much appears to have been made of an alleged affinity between psychopathic personality and the propensity towards crime, I would point out first that the very concept of "psychopathic personality" is itself variously defined, variously interpreted, and variously understood by investigators of behavioral phenomena. Though the affinity just mentioned may well be a perfectly authentic one, it would be insufficient to justify our summarily ruling out the possibility that crimes *are* sporadically committed by human beings other than those who can be strictly referred to the category of "psychopathic personality." Hysteric and paranoid types, for example, are surely capable, under certain precipitating circumstances, of criminal conduct; so, indeed, are epileptic or epileptoid types.

Now precisely what is *psychopathic personality*? How do we recognize and diagnose it? In what essential details does it differ from other defective character-structures?

By the designation *psychopathic personality*, I myself have come, through both observation and experience, to understand a particular kind of characterologic or temperamental make-up characterized by certain diffuse symptoms belonging, strictly, neither to the sphere of neurosis nor to that of psychosis; and—what is perhaps more significant —by an apparent absence of *common moral and ethical sensibility*, or the ability to make a fundamental distinction between what is right and what is wrong according to the generally accepted criteria adopted by society. Among these aforementioned diffuse symptoms, one may enumerate the following: so-called eccentricities of one sort or another; indifference to social demands and unawareness of social responsibilities; flagrant disregard of the needs and rights of other people; excessive selfishness and overweening egocentricity; failures in attempts at adaptation; vagrancy, instability, shiftlessness; etc. I should hardly, of course, care to go so far as to maintain that such characterologic or temperamental traits are invariably found to exist in exactly the same combinations or proportions, or that these same traits inevitably evince precisely the same degree of accentuation, in any given case of psychopathic personality. Furthermore, certain of the symptoms just enumerated might be exhibited no less frequently by persons who could be more accurately classified either as neurotics or as psychotics.

In the ultimate analysis, however, perhaps the chief distinguishing feature in psychopathic personality is nothing but a conspicuously defective or else almost completely undeveloped suger-ego (Freud) which results in the psychopath's being, to all intents and purposes, quite unmoved by any sense of the difference between socially desirable and socially undesirable behavior; or—to couch the matter in different words —by any power to perceive even elementary distinctions between good and evil. In striking contrast, therefore, to the psychopath, the neurotic often suffers, not from an undeveloped super-ego, but rather from repressions (Freud) instituted at the behest of too stern and demanding a super-ego. In cases of paranoia, schizophrenia, manic-depressive reactions, and certain organically determined psychotic disturbances, the conflicts have, on the other hand, been so drastic as virtually to nullify the functions of both ego and super-ego. In my opinion, the absence of super-ego workings in psychopathic personality is to be ascribed rather to constitutional deficiency than to dynamic repression in the sense of

Freud. Psychopathic personalities give us, then, the impression that they are victims of a congenital lack of any foundation on which to construct a super-ego which might serve as a safeguard to preclude acts of a criminal variety.

Should we follow the reasoning of Bromberg, we shall be obliged to recognize no fewer than three separate and relatively independent types of psychopathic personality. To these three types, Bromberg has given the following designations:

1. Psychopathic personality.
2. Schizoid psychopathic personality.
3. Paranoid psychopathic personality.

The three types show symptoms by which they can be differentiated from one another, though at the same time they have in common the same lack of moral and ethical susceptibility, with the result that they prove capable of diverse forms of criminal behavior. Bromberg himself makes the observation that the paranoid psychopathic personality is more especially prone to crimes like that, for instance, of blackmail, since such crimes afford to him an opportunity to bring others under his own control and thus to augment his sense of power. On the other hand, the schizoid psychopathic who has, let us say, committed murder will have a tendency, according to Bromberg's ratiocination, to identify himself with his victim, this having for him the significance of suicide. Bromberg's hypothesis regarding the paranoid type is plausible to the point of being actually logical; the other hypothesis appears, however, to be restricted to the realm of mere theory and speculation. Nevertheless, we must acknowledge the service Bromberg has performed in drawing our attention to the fact that at least three relatively independent types of psychopathic personality can be distinguished.

In our effort to arrive at a few valid conclusions regarding the posited relation existing between psychopathic personality and the proclivity to crime, we may do well enough to recall the words of Goethe, whom Abrahamsen quotes as having once remarked that he never had heard of a crime towards which he could not trace in himself at least some small inclination. Such candor on the part of a gigantic figure like Goethe is delightful and precious for its own sake; and if we ourselves were to think about the matter sufficiently, no doubt we should discover that what Goethe said of himself is no less true of us! The tendency to commit acts of unwarrantable aggression is, therefore, a purely relative matter. In his provocative if sometimes merely speculative *Battle of the Conscience*, Bergler has emphasized that almost anybody is able from time to time to bribe his super-ego by rationalizing his foibles or shortcomings. By this, Bergler means nothing more than that the sense of wrong-doing which ought to be present in *consciousness* has been conveniently *repressed* (again in the sense of Freud) in the interest of sparing the ego a painful realization which might leave a noticeable dent in the ego's idealized concept of itself. In cases of genuine psychopathic personality, on the other hand, we frequently enough are led to assume that feelings associated with guilt do not exist in even a *repressed* form.

We have reached now a consideration which ought to be of some assistance to us in further researches where psychopathic personality is concerned. *So long as we can detect any definite sign of even a latent compunction resulting from criminal behavior, we are justified in believing that the super-ego is by no means really nonexistent, but that the guilt-feelings have been simply relegated to the sphere of the unconscious, where they serve the dynamic and teleologically useful purpose of shielding the ego against the recognition of painful truths.* To repeat a point made earlier in this paper: experience teaches us that such repression is only the rule in neurosis, but that we have little evidence to justify our assuming that genuine psychopaths harbor either a conscious or an unconscious sense of guilt for their misdeeds or their transgressions.

As I have pointed out at the beginning of this paper, we should be grossly mistaken if we allowed ourselves to embrace the notion that psychopathic personalities are the only defective personality-types capable of the commission of major crimes. These other types are, however, differentiated from true psychopathic personalities by the presence of behavior which is indicative of at least some remnants of a super-ego function. When paranoid individuals, for instance, come into conflict with the legal machinery, they are at great pains to rationalize their actions by asserting, sometimes vociferously, but always with strenuous emphasis, that they have done nothing except to take righteous revenge on certain people because of injuries which they have suffered at the hands of those people. They may attempt further to justify their acts by alleging that the Almighty Himself has enjoined them to behave as they have done. Crimes perpetrated by such paranoid individuals appear, then, to have often as their basis a pathologically self-righteous desire for retaliation or revenge, though of course additional factors may be simultaneously operative. (Incidentally, the paranoid types referred to in this paragraph are not necessarily the same as Bromberg's paranoid psychopathic personalities.)

As additional examples showing the variety of deviant types that are driven to crime of one sort or another, victims of sexual anomalies like omosexuality, sadism, fetishism, etc., may be cited here. If, however, ve accept the nearly inescapable view that ethical deficiency is perhaps he prime distinguishing feature of psychopathic personality, then we hall be obliged to exclude from the category of major criminal offenders rather large number of sexual aberrants, because empirical considera- ions teach us that numerous homosexuals, for example, are frequently ubject to deep feelings of guilt, and that they may make a conscious ffort to suppress their sexual drives so far as possible, in the interest f avoiding skirmishes with the law and of not incurring the overt dis- pproval of the community. Even when homosexuals find themselves nvolved in legal proceedings, they generally prove to be mere law- breakers rather than actual criminals—a distinction which Lindner has been the first, so far as I know, to set forth. Indeed, as I myself have pointed out in another paper, genuine homosexuals—or "absolute in- erts" in the sense of Freud—hardly fail to give one the impression that rime, as usually understood, would be beyond them; for they are en- lowed with a soft, feminine, rather artistic temperament which would be almost ludicrously incongruous with acts of undue aggression. More- over, seldom enough do they manifest in conspicuous measure any of he same traits by which psychopathic personality is characterized. This, f course, leaves the objective investigator with some question in his nind as to the justice of indiscriminately equating inverted sexuality vith psychopathic personality. I cautiously suggest, therefore, that it night be more logical to place such human beings in the category of neurotic individuals—a suggestion already made by Karpman—or else to naintain a separate and relatively independent method of classification or those whose sexual instinct diverges from what is accepted as the norm. A homosexual, a masochist, or a fetichist who is conscious of the ocially unacceptable form taken by his erotic impulse, and who is, on his account, a prey to conscious guilt-reactions, is hardly comparable to a real psychopath to whom guilt-feelings are evidently unknown. Of the eal psychopath, the poet Tennyson has intuitively given us a perfect lescription in one of the most beautiful stanzas from his *In Memoriam:*

> "I envy not the beast that takes
> His license in the field of time,
> Unfettered by the sense of crime;
> To whom a conscience never wakes."

For reasons which have been stated quite clearly in this paper, the category now nebulously labelled "psychopathic personality" stands in need of radical re-examination. Some investigators are obviously in the deplorable habit of promiscuously grouping together under the heading of "psychopathic personality" a variety of traits and reactions which indubitably could be more scientifically classified into a number of other categories. On the other hand, an excessively rigid system of classification might do even more harm than the present rather chaotic one. Whenever we are endeavoring to deal scientifically with behavioral variants, we must be prepared to take into account a relativity, an overlapping, or a certain mingling of the individual elements which compose the symptom-structure.

Primarily, the purpose of this paper has been to examine the relationship allegedly existing between psychopathic personality and the tendency towards crime, and to indicate how the concept of psychopathic personality stands sorely in need of clearer, sharper, more rational definition than is currently given to it. This holds true not only with regard to the psychopath but also—as has been likewise suggested—with regard to the classification of personality in general. Though it may well be that mathematical precision is never to be attained in the sphere of personality study, yet surely the loose terminology which so often prevails today in supposedly scientific quarters can on no grounds whatsoever be justified.

22 · Inner Conflicts and Crime

by FRANZ ALEXANDER and WILLIAM HEALY

Although, as we have already pointed out, criminologists tend more and more to regard the criminal as a product of social forces, few of them would deny that certain individuals are led to crime or to pursue a criminal career because they are primarily driven to it by some inner, subconscious motivations and, hence, their behavior can best be understood, and perhaps constructively modified, by psychoanalysis. Two eminent psychiatrists, Franz Alexander and William Healy, discuss here their method of analyzing such cases. [Reprinted from *Roots of Crime*, by Franz Alexander and William Healy, by permission of Alfred A. Knopf, Inc., 1935, pp. 4-12, 14-15. Footnotes omitted.]

Our work represents mainly an etiological study of delinquency and crime. It approached this aim by the method of careful investigations of a limited number of careers. We established step by step how these individuals actually became delinquent and criminal, considering their character-formation in the light of their life-history and particularly as the result of a causally connected chain of psychological processes.

This book will in the first place demonstrate that those factors which, statistically considered, are commonly regarded as major determinants in the causation of crime (such as unfavorable environmental conditions —slum districts, broken homes, alcoholism of the parents, economic uncertainty, etc.) are factors which become effective only in a special setting and in combination with the reactive tendencies of certain personalities. It will also demonstrate that apart from these more tangible factors, other less obvious ones are at least of equal importance. We refer to those ideological trends characteristic of any civilization, trends which determine the individual's attitude to collective life, toward authority, toward law, and which determine his evaluations and ideals. To mention only one example of such ideologies: if in a civilization material success is considered above everything as the highest value, all members of such a society who accept this attitude will be inclined to sacrifice such other values as respect for law if they have to choose between the two. The existence of slum districts alone does not explain the high frequency of criminality; this also requires a certain psychological attitude on the part of the inhabitants. In some other centers of civilization, with a more passive and contemplative attitude toward life, people live under even harder economic conditions than in the poorer parts of American cities and yet criminality may be almost entirely absent. Again, in other civilizations discontent is more likely to lead to collective expressions, such as politically organized revolutionary movements, than to the individualistic form of rebellion which is represented by crime. These psychological group-attitudes which are of such prime importance cannot be studied by methods which consider only surface data, but only by the thorough analysis of individual cases representative of certain groups.

Although this book represents primarily an etiological study of crime, it was possible because of the nature of the psychoanalytic approach to combine the study of causation with some modest attempts at therapy or, more precisely, at readjustment. Since the effect of psychoanalytic treatment is based on a better understanding by the individual of his own motives, the aim of understanding the motives of crime coincides to a high degree with the therapeutic aim.

In projecting our research we agreed for the above reasons to take some apparently exceedingly difficult cases of offenders whom we had long known as being failures under police and court procedure, probation, and the régime of correctional institutions. Only two, one of them a very severe offender, had not received some such forms of treatment at the hands of society. Other kinds of treatment also had been given before and after they were originally seen at the clinic. In most of the cases parents or guardians had stated in the juvenile court or at the clinic that after trying various methods they were at their wits' end to know how to handle the young offender. Indeed, several of the delinquents had been removed from apparently inimical environmental conditions to good foster-homes by child-welfare agencies, a procedure which, as shown elsewhere, has in general seemed relatively to be a most valuable therapeutic measure.

Moreover, most of these offenders at an earlier age had been offered at least some psychiatric help which may untangle, from the standpoint of causation, the interweaving of experience, circumstance, ideas, and emotional attitudes which together form the patterns of delinquent behavior. The social and personal treatment undertaken in a number of the cases, as judged by good standards, was well considered and prolonged, but to very little avail. Evidently the bottom of the difficulty had never been reached.

For psychoanalysis only a few cases could be taken, but even so, it was realized that the body of material that might give insight into deeper motivations of delinquency through this research would be greater than any that heretofore has been presented. Detailed records were made from notes directly after each interview. The publication of these would require several volumes; it has been no small work to epitomize without omitting important issues that appear in the vast amount of ideational and emotional life that was brought to the surface in the analytic sessions.

In order to avoid a mélange of human material, we agreed to exclude mentally defective or mildly psychotic individuals or those classifiable in the ordinary categories of neuroses and psychoses. On the other hand, we selected offenders whose criminal careers apparently were due primarily to internal mental conflicts rather than to external circumstances. These individuals, even if they do not exhibit pronounced neurotic or psychotic symptoms, belong to the larger group of neurotic personalities, since their behavior is to such a high degree determined by their inner conflicts. The unsuccessful effort at previous treatment had seemed to indicate something of the nature of the trouble, and in some instances the story of the individual himself had given intimation that affairs were far from right in his emotional life, even though the difficulty never was verbalized by the delinquent. It would be erroneous to believe that these more or less emotionally unadjusted individuals, whose behavior is largely determined by their inner conflicts, constitute very unusual cases. Though there are no reliable statistical data available, we should be inclined to consider them far more numerous than is ordinarily considered.

The individuals taken for analysis had all been well known earlier, some of them eight or more years previously, to the Judge Baker Guidance Center (formerly the Judge Baker Foundation). The usual careful case studies had been made, including all available social data as well as the family and developmental histories, medical and psychological studies, together with psychiatric interviews—all obtained through the co-operation of members of the family, school authorities, probation officers, and others. In some instances these studies were already voluminous, and in most cases the life of the offender has been fairly well known during the intervening years.

Neither of the analysts at the time of the analysis was acquainted with the full material that had been obtained in the previous case study. For orientation, only a short review of the outstanding data was utilized, with no transcription of the offender's earlier statement of his own problems, attitudes, or conflicts.

An essential part of the research project avowedly was confrontation of material gained through psychoanalysis with the data obtained by the previous more or less thorough study of the individual—and vice versa. This seemed to offer the advantage of comparing the psychoanalytic exploration of the mental processes of the offender with the different type of material contained in the earlier records and obtained through clinical interviews with the delinquent, with parents, agency visitors, and others.

One of the questions we put to ourselves was: could we by delving into genetics learn more about the period or periods of character- and personality-formation as these were related to the development of such unfortunate and costly lives as were exhibited in the cases to be studied? In other words, could we discern what situations and influences and attitudes, if any, might have been altered, and at what age could these alterations have been accomplished, that the development of delinquent trends might have been thwarted? Much of the success of efforts for the prevention of delinquency and crime may depend upon gaining such knowledge.

As far as direct therapeutic aims are concerned, our expectations naturally had to be extremely modest under the time limits and conditions at our disposal: ten months for the whole research project. In only exceptional cases is this length of time considered sufficient to effect satisfactory therapeutic results by the technique of psychoanalysis. To the majority of our cases even considerably less time could be devoted. What has developed during the two years following the analysis is set forth in the epilogues to the individual case records.

Nothing can better illustrate the complexity of the causes leading to criminality than cases where continued criminal behavior appears to be entirely irrational and cannot be explained by the motives which ordinarily induce individuals to violate the law. The following case well illustrates the futility of legal and penal treatment where deep psychological issues are not uncovered—that of an offender whom we particularly had hoped to investigate by the psychoanalytic approach.

More than ten years ago a very mannerly, intelligent boy of sixteen who had been held in jail for three weeks on account of stealing a suitcase which he had pawned was seen for a day at the clinic. In court he first gave the age of nineteen and then acknowledged his true age and that he was on parole from a boys' correctional institution. Physical examination showed a splendid physique; psychological examination gave him full average intelligence. In the juvenile court he told the judge that two correctional institutions had failed to cure him and that he needed more severe punishment and desired to go to the reformatory for adults, whereupon he was committed to that institution.

The history that he gave to us was corroborated later by his father and authorities of the correctional schools. He had begun thieving when he was eight years old, and when he was ten he told his father that there was something, he could not tell what, that drove him to steal. By the time we saw him, there had been an enormous amount of such stealing, with four or five commitments to correctional institutions, where he was always found courteous, well-behaved, and industrious. He readily made friends everywhere by his upstanding qualities. Whenever he was confronted with his delinquencies, he stated that his own behavior was a puzzle to himself.

At the present time his case has become so notorious and has been so much in the newspapers that there is no breach of confidence in giving a very brief sketch of his history with proper disguises. At the reformatory he behaved well and was highly regarded. Paroled from there, he speedily got into more trouble, but then settled down again for a year or so, living at home and being advanced in a certain business concern on account of his good working qualities. This boy came from a fairly well-to-do family where he had all normal advantages. He was an active, outgoing youngster. We learned of no peculiarities in his upbringing. He was the eldest of five children, and no other members of his family had been delinquent. His home and school satisfactions on the surface seem to have been equal to those of any of the others.

After his period of doing well he married and was very proud of his young wife. After his first child was born (by this time he has three), he began again his unreasonable delinquencies while he was doing well in business. He frequently told his wife that he acted under some strange impulse that he could not understand. He stole from his father and from other people and repeatedly took automobiles, travelling long distances in them. He entered the Navy under an alias and soon deserted, was arrested for more stealing and placed in a disciplinary institution, and escaped, getting into more and more trouble. During this time he wrote affectionate letters to his wife begging for forgiveness. It must be emphasized that he might have been living comfortably at home earning a good salary. His father and his wife's parents spent a great deal of money getting him out of various difficulties and tried hard to reform him. He had won the affections of his wife's people by his gentlemanly conduct and ordinarily good attention to business, being a modest fellow and nothing of a high flyer.

Then began more serious affairs. He was arrested in a Western state for burglary because in senseless fashion he stole cheap jewelry from apartments which he entered. He was given a long sentence to the penitentiary, where he was always a hard-working, well-behaved inmate; on the occasion of a catastrophe there he proved himself a hero. A pardon was forthcoming and he was allowed to work on the outside. His wife went to be near him. A few days before the pardon was to become effective and after he had joyously sent word to his parents, he ran away from his wife and pardon. His going away also broke up a new business arrangement which, much to his avowed liking, had been made for him. In another state he soon committed a series of thefts and burglaries which were very easily traced to him and he was given a very long sentence. Once more people became interested in him because of his unusual qualities. A psychiatrist who studied him now felt, as did one who saw him earlier in the other penitentiary, that here was a case out of the ordinary, a man not of a usual criminal type, but rather one who seemed criminal through inner compulsion. Again all attempts to get him placed where he could be studied by psychoanalytic methods were frustrated.

The young man made his escape from a road gang where he was working under atrocious conditions; with aid he then established himself in an Eastern city under an alias. However, he speedily entered into other crimes, taking automobiles and engaging in bizarre stealings and burglaries. With a woman of some standing who was earning well he contracted a bigamous marriage; she knew him only under his alias, and thought him well-to-do. At this time he did such foolish things as having a collar with pendants of gold pieces made for the lady's dog. He adorned their apartment with dozens of clocks which he had stolen, giving much attention to their arrangement and regulation. He remained unknown to the woman as a criminal and undetected by the police for months, but finally was caught in another state where he had also committed several burglaries.

Seen by a well-known psychiatrist, he was once more diagnosed as not having any mental disease. Altogether he has had several most careful examinations at the hands of competent neurologists, who have found no disease of the central nervous system. He has always been abstemious about alcohol and has never had deleterious habits of any kind.

The theory of this young man, here not half told, thus involves ten or twelve incarcerations, numerous arrests, punitive as well as kindly treatment at the hands of many authorities, including, first of all, his own parents. He frankly remains a puzzle to himself as well as to others. He still is a healthy-appearing, generally cheerful individual, strangely optimistic about the possibilities of the future for him, hoping that someone can discover what is the matter with him so that he may alter his conduct tendencies.

This case, however strange it may seem, is only an extreme example of the dynamic power of irrational and unconscious motives which often have a permanent determining influence on behavior, even if this influence does not always appear in such spectacular and dramatic fashion.

*   *   *

These studies represent no attempt to deny or even to discount in the least the important fact that in our day and generation, perhaps more than heretofore, there are many social and other environmental influences which tremendously tend to create delinquency and crime. The many invitations to antisocial conduct which are so plainly offered to children and young people, the many easy avenues open to them for delinquency, the social pressures on them by delinquent companionship, poor parental examples, and the lack of good upbringing make it clear why there is such a defective development of any restraining conscience.

On the other hand, there is no greater mistake than to believe that all human individuals are influenced by the same motives or driven in their conduct tendencies by similar reactions to what would appear to be similar experiences. True, the law, based on its conception of justice, does take this view and judges all men alike—that is wherein the law differs so widely from psychological science. It appears perfectly clear to any careful student of criminology that there are certain offenders not classifiable in the usual psychiatric pigeon-holes, though they may be neurotic personalities, who are most certainly driven to engage in antisocial conduct by the dynamics of their unconscious mental life. . . .

23 · Family Tension and Crime

by DAVID ABRAHAMSEN

Among the various causes of criminal behavior, the disturbed home has been considered by some students of crime and delinquency to be one of the most—if not the most—important. A number of studies—notably those tracing criminal careers—have come to the conclusion that it is a faulty home environment that has led to delinquent or criminal behavior. David Abrahamsen, a noted psychiatrist connected with Columbia University, who specializes in the study of crime and crime prevention, summarizes in the following article the results of a study whose purpose was to determine the extent to which tension in the family is responsible for criminal behavior. Actual cases observed are cited to support the conclusions arrived at, as regards both the causes of antisocial behavior and the preventive and therapeutic measures that should be adopted. ["Family Tension, Basic Cause of Criminal Behavior," *Journal of Criminal Law and Criminology*, Vol. 40, Sept.-Oct. 1949, pp. 330-343. Reprinted by permission.]

IN 1944 Columbia University, supported by funds from the Josiah Macy, Jr. Foundation, sponsored a research project to investigate the psychosomatic factors in antisocial behavior. The project lasted four years and revealed that when criminal tendencies exist, unwholesome conditions within the home and intense physical disturbances among the family members invariably occur also.

PSYCHOSOMATIC FACTORS

Criminal acts, subjectively speaking, indicate an unusual amount of aggressiveness and hostility which is common to warped minds. Because such attitudes usually reflect discord between children and parents, we investigated not only offenders but members of their families as well. Whenever we found psychosomatic disorders, we also encountered distorted emotional patterns in the home, such as over-protection, dominance, rivalry and defense mechanisms. Or if we found the latter, physical symptoms soon showed themselves, if they hadn't already appeared. The one went with the other, inseparably, and often immediately apparent. It was our purpose to find the relation between emotional attitudes and the existence of criminal behavior. As far as we know, this is the first time that this method, with confirmation of Rorschach tests, has been used in such an investigation.

In this undertaking, we worked with 100 offenders and their families and also with 100 non-offenders, or control groups. The latter were abnormal and in need of treatment, but they had committed no crimes.

We used no so-called normal persons in making the comparison, because unfortunately it is not easy to collect such people, inasmuch as no one likes to be examined when it is unnecessary. Beyond this, if we had been able to group together persons usually considered normal, in the final analysis they might turn out to be nothing of the kind.

The offenders we examined were embezzlers, armed robbers, thieves, murderers, exhibitionists, and kleptomaniacs. They were referred to us while they were on probation and on parole from prison. Others were from agencies or direct from private physicians.

It is a common misconception even today that those who commit crimes are arrogantly breaking the law and deriving a fiendish pleasure from getting away with it. Many people in discussing an offender will assume a hostility not too far removed from the original hostility of the person committing the crime. Thus the old idea of revenge is continued and the possibility of understanding the criminal is kept at a minimum.

Perhaps it is even more unfortunate that a vast number of people who deal with criminals believe offenders act out their hostilities and thereby get rid of them entirely.

In fact crime is far from being so simple. Actually, too, those who commit crimes are much to be pitied rather than scorned. Thus the idea of "Pity them, for they know not what they do" can, I think, be applied to the man who commits crime, and to us as well, when we give him more of what may have led him into crime, and then, after a while, turn him loose to commit another, because he is by that time possibly a little sicker than he was before.

My purpose is not to outline remedies for our existing penal system. Such an undertaking would take much more space than I am allowed, and require many people working in many professions with many kinds of experience. It would take the man of scientific theory; that is, the criminologist. It would take the penologist who has actually worked within prison walls; architects, humanitarians and statisticians. And it would take, probably most of all, understanding. It is with the hope of giving a little of this foundation that I am now presenting some of our findings.

In psychiatry we base much of our knowledge upon our discoveries from psychological sessions with patients and the revelations that are made to us within them, together with neurological findings. In research projects of the kind we engaged in, we do the same thing, but we have better opportunity to make comparisons and produce results which are more conclusive insofar as tangible evidence is concerned.

FAMILY TENSION

In this study, for instance, it became clear that there was much more family tension in the 100 offenders we examined, together with their families, than existed in the control group. This was not so easy to detect, for the defenses were heavier and harder to break through. After a while, though, the pieces fell into place in one case after another . . . a mother dominated the family household and/or a father drank, one child was preferred to another, and perhaps the next one wasn't wanted at all.

Oftentimes tension wasn't evident within a household but existed as a strong undercurrent which colored the behavior of the family members. Such was the case with Mr. and Mrs. N. and their little girl, G. This was an exceptionally bright family on a purely intellectual level. The mother and father had no idea that their emotions were infantile and that they were really incapable of loving in an adult fashion; both were fixated, both conflicted. They lived as husband and wife, enjoyed many of the same interests and were looked upon by others as one of the happiest couples in the community. Meanwhile they so successfully buried their inner loathing for each other that they were hardly even aware of it. But their daughter, G., who was only eight years old, sensed it, largely because she was the product of hate, not love. She resented the way both parents gently but firmly ordered her about, and that oftentimes their ideas about G.'s conduct were very contradictory. In such instances, both parents would intellectualize the difference, but nonetheless hold tenaciously on to their point, the ultimate issue being who would win the argument, not what was best for G.

G. began to be a nuisance in school. She wouldn't do her work, and she annoyed the other children when they tried to do theirs. She played truant often and even wrote obscene words in the girls' room. She was able to proceed in her grades only because she had an above average intelligence. Then one day a teacher discovered it was she who had taken several white mice to school and put them in the various teachers' desk drawers. The principal of the school decided to expel her, but her parents asked if she might be sent to a psychiatrist first. This was agreed upon. Psychiatric examination disclosed that G. was reacting severely to an unhappy home situation. She felt rejected, was hostile and depressed, which necessitated psychotherapy. G.'s parents were therefore consulted and soon afterwards put under treatment. G. was sent back to school. Her mother underwent treatment for two years, and the father for some time more than that. In learning about their inner selves, the mother lost her antagonism towards men, who had until then represented her demanding father, and G.'s father discovered it was not necessary for him to outdo everyone simply because he had been made to feel ineffectual as a child.

As a result of this new found self-knowledge, Mr. and Mrs. N. were able to accept themselves and each other, and their daughter in time became one of the leading scholars in the school.

RORSCHACH TESTS

The Rorschachs we took of 31 offenders showed much hostility and aggression and usually sexual or some other kind of conflict as a result of a tense family situation which had not been checked at an early age as in the case of G. Having been permitted to grow, the resentments had become deep and often so devious that the offenders seldom had any idea of the root of their real unhappiness. For it is natural to suppress that which one doesn't like to face, such as contempt for a parent or jealousy of a sister. But emotions such as these, kept in check long enough, can eventually cause illness, and crime as well.

Sigmund Freud developed the concept that the origin of neuroses and psychoses lies within psychosexual conflicts in childhood. Our investigations indicate that criminal behavior, coupled with psychosomatic disturbances, can grow out of early emotional deprivations, not necessarily always connected with the psychosexual type of conflict.

There was one lad of 20 included in our study, who was taken to a psychiatrist because he had stolen a typewriter, sold it, and with the profits had bought many books which he made no attempt to read. As the crime shows, he was not really living in this world. He had, in fact, a very peculiar outlook upon the world as well-adjusted people know it. He thought he should not look for work, but that it should come to him. He wanted to be better and more outstanding than others, and yet he did nothing whatever to bring this situation about. He was ill constantly with infected teeth and still he would not go to the dentist because the dentist might hurt him; but he stayed up night after night administering drugs to his sick mouth because the pain permitted him no sleep. He had the flu on the average of twelve times a year.

Discussion with the boy showed a strong resistance to any reference to his father, except for occasional mention of what an extraordinary person he was. He loved his mother dearly, and as time disclosed, she babied him and pampered him so that it was hardly any wonder he didn't outdo himself to get a job.

The father in this case turned out to be the very real fundamental difficulty in the boy's life. He was a human dynamo, and he enjoyed telling of his accomplishments and then teasing his son for not doing more with the intelligence he must have inherited from his father. All of this made the boy feel so inferior that he felt he could never equal the example set before him, hence he did nothing to escape failure. His mother encouraged his neurotic outlook, and therefore the boy lived in a world of his own making, because there was less pain there.

Both his mother and his father had to learn their mistakes and to change their attitudes. The boy had to be made to understand why he was behaving in such an odd fashion; had to be made to feel he was a person in his own right. The problem rested much more with the mother and father than it did with the boy, for they really created his trouble.

Here, then, was a boy with a schizoid make-up, who was physically ill all the time and who also committed a crime. He was in conflict about sex, as with practically everything else, but his condition was by no means centered around this factor.

PARENTS' ATTITUDES

Another often overlooked feature we found in our study was that a parent's own undeveloped attitude about sex can twist a child's outlook without either parent or child being aware of what is taking place. This would seem not to be a reversal of the Freudian concept, but an addition to it, because, besides or aside from there being a transmission of destructive parental thought and reaction thereto, there would seem to be a kind of contagion of undevelopment that goes beyond identification. In other words, when we found indications of incest or desire for it, invariably it was a reciprocal two-way state of mind, unconscious though it may have been.

In the case of one man who attempted to rape his mother, for example, it was discovered that she was unknowingly being most seductive to him.

Then there was the tragic case of a beautiful young woman who at the time was 22 and looked about 33. At first she seemed very pleasant, charming and eager to please. She was sent to us because she had stolen various articles which added up to quite a few thousands of dollars. It did not seem to worry her. Her father had paid off the amount, and she would in time pay him back. But she was earning only $30.00 a week and could spare him but $5.00 every pay day. She also seemed undisturbed over the fact that she had given birth to an illegitimate mulatto child, who was scorned by her father and the object of great concern to her mother.

After a few sessions with this young woman, it was revealed that C. had a great distaste for all men. She liked to tantalize them, to hurt them and if possible to destroy them. When asked about her father she disclosed an unqualified dislike for him, claiming he always ruled her and, in fact, in saying so, unwittingly said: "he has ruined . . . ruled my life."

After a while C.'s father was consulted. He wanted to do everything in his power to make his daughter happy. So much so that he was sexually interested in her and did not know it. Therefore he dominated the girl, discouraged any interest she showed in the young men who courted her and did all within his power to keep himself near to her. She repaid him by bringing an illegitimate half-breed child into the house, and then by stealing.

Treatment of C.'s father revealed that he was an emotionally immature person who was afraid to go outside of the blood ties in seeking a mate, and that he had in fact also been strongly attached to his mother.

One apparent answer then is that parents cannot expect their children to be like adults and act like them when the parents themselves are still functioning on an immature level, for they are a mirror to the children they bring up, giving them their first ideas, developing in them their first reactions. If the parents' view of the world is distorted, they can hardly expect the children's to be entirely wholesome. Neither can they, if the children become mentally ill or commit a crime, absolve themselves of responsibility and blame it on "the company they keep." For parents, or those who act as such, are a child's first company, that from which his personality is built or destroyed. And if the company he takes up with later on is of the wrong sort, then it can only be because his parents failed him in the beginning.

STATISTICAL PROOF

In our project, of the 29 members of offenders' families who submitted to Rorschach and other psychological tests, all were suffering from mental disturbances of various degrees. Some of these families on the surface were friendly, cooperative, and showed deep concern over the offenders' difficulties. When we went into the situations thoroughly we found hostility and resentment among the family members.

Examination also revealed a high incidence of psychosomatic disorders among offenders and their families as opposed to those found in the control group.

In a cross-section of 60 offenders and 60 non-offenders, just a few of the results were as follows:

Diseases of the gastro-intestinal tract appeared in 55 per cent of the offenders and 45 per cent of the non-offenders. Skin afflictions occurred in 17 per cent of the offenders and five per cent of the non-offenders. And, whereas 20 per cent of the offenders were prone to accidents, this was true of only 10 per cent of those who kept within the bounds of the law.

Psychosomatic disorders are recognized as a turning in of hostility and repressed anger resulting in physical symptoms. It would seem then that in the offender against society you have, in the large majority of cases anyway, the utmost in a basic unhappiness, a basic conflict that more often than not entirely escapes the offender. When he seems to act out his hostilities and thereby rid himself of them, he does so only for the moment, a release the neurotic and psychotic does not have, because they are too inhibited. However, with each new crime the offender commits he builds up a thicker barrier between himself and society, making it the more difficult for him to live in this world. In addition, he also has going on within him those temptations and desires to which he does not and cannot give expression. Therefore he has the fantasies that he acts out, the punishment received therefore and still other fantasies tormenting him.

There is an exception to this, to be found in the genuine psychopath. Having never been able to identify himself with a mother or father, he chose at an early age to live by his own rules, and having never developed any conscience because he had no one to imitate, he always did what he pleased and felt no guilt for it. There are such few people in existence that I mention them only for accuracy's sake, and then go on to maintain that other offenders suffer from acute anxieties arising out of deeply rooted conflicts.

ROOTS OF REBELLION

The first surroundings to which a child is subjected tend to set up reactions within him that will remain throughout life. This is because the child is sensitive and as yet without formed reaction patterns, or pattern of behavior. Hence anything extreme is bound to have a profound effect upon him, just as a dog who was beaten as a puppy will often cringe in the corner in expectation of more of the same. Thus, if a child is subjected to emotional shock such as rejection, he may go on through life looking for shock or for personal rejection. Or, if the situation in which he lives in the beginning starts him off with feelings of insecurity and unrest because of bickerings and quarrels, these may make him tense up, react internally with physical illness, retire partly into a dream world, and in time break out with a crime in pure revolt against the injustice done him.

If a child is overprotected and overindulged in every whim, he will resent it because of the inherent desire within us all to be independent. He may therefore develop such resentment over his dependence that he will commit crime in order to assert himself. Or, he may do so when his means of support and care are taken from him because he considers it an injustice to have to stand on his own. If a child is made to feel unimportant and unwanted, he may in time break the law to call attention to himself, to punish his parents for their neglect and to hurt himself for his own guilt in disliking his parents' behavior.

We all have criminalistic tendencies, and they may be made more acute at certain times. A child, particularly, living in a family where the emotional tension is acute and continuous, will become sensitized to crime. He begins to repress his painful memories about his childhood deprivations with the result that there arises within him a kind of anxiety-tinged, free-floating aggression. When his conscience (or super-ego) has not been sufficiently developed he can commit a crime under the pressure of precipitating factors.

Such sensitization takes place most frequently when emotional tension is present in the family for such an unhappy setting is a breeding ground for crime. We have found that the *emotional relationship* between parents, or between brothers and sisters instigates criminalistic activities more often than the economic or social position of the family. It may then be that the characteristic difference between the criminal and non-criminal has its origin in the degree and type of family tension, as it affects the individual.

Personality make-up is also of importance, not necessarily in terms of heredity, but of constitutional predisposition toward violence instead of, say, to develop a psychosis. That is to say, a person may not inherit the same weakness as a parent, but he may develop a tendency to go in the same direction, all other things being equal.

OUTSIDE FACTORS

Then there is the factor of education. Offenders often come from the lowest strata of society, and there is a curious lack of inhibition in offenders which suggests a lack of education. Yet the offenders in our group were of extremely mixed backgrounds. Some were from very solid and substantial homes and of parents who were teachers, officials and leaders in society. Others were from poor homes and of people who lived in constant fear of complete poverty. Some of the offenders had little actual schooling, and others went through college.

So although formal education seems to answer little, it does seem true that crime may occasionally have its roots in the *home* education. Those cases in which this is most evident have to do with a conflicting form of upbringing in which at least one of the parents is loose and immoral and yet expects the children to be without even normal desires. This is obviously another form of family tension, but it relates to education, too. In such a home a father may live very corruptly and the whole neighborhood may know it, and yet he will tell his son that a boy will go insane if he touches his genitals. The mother may be amoral in her behavior and nonetheless tell her daughter she will become pregnant if a boy kisses her. For a child to have such conflicting outlooks as this may cause him to become so bottled up with anxiety and repressions that a crime will ensue as a result of natural human desires seeking an outlet. This kind of situation—criminality growing out of the asocial home—is possibly one of our greatest battles, and if we do not try to control it when it exists by some sort of enforced segregation of child and parent, it is a problem that is liable to have no end.

There has been much written lately to the effect that children must have more and better recreation if there would be less crime. This is all very well, and I am certainly for healthy activity for youngsters. But the core of crime is within the atmosphere of the home. If we overlook this fact and go on to other things, we are neglecting the real issue and simply missing the fundamental one, for all else is superficial. It is within the home that patterns are formed, and tough gangs notwithstanding, there would be no need of such gangs if relations at home were sufficient and proper guidance were provided.

The insidious factor insofar as tough gangs is concerned is that if there are many homes which provide no emotional security, the boys of the neighborhood will flock together, form a gang and assume a toughness which will act as a shield for them. This then may grow to such an extent that other children who have a half-way decent situation within the home may join up even reluctantly for fear of otherwise being considered a weakling. This, then, is another battle, and a difficult one: the existence of mob reaction to a leader who has developed a false strength through aggression, as for instance the extreme examples of Hitler and Mussolini. Once again, the source, the home, must be reached early before the pattern is so well established that it is difficult if not impossible to break it up. This is not so difficult as it may sound. For just as a man does not become an offender all on his own, so does he not become an offender all at once.

EARLY SIGNS

There are early signs of a budding criminal which should be looked for by parents and in the schools. When a child shows an unusual amount of protest to any kind of authority or suggestion, when he is constantly speeded up whether he works or plays, when he plays truant often, he is indirectly expressing hostility. And it is extreme hostility that we find to such an overwhelming extent in the man who commits crime. Thus if it can be discovered and looked into early enough, the next step, crime, may be brought under our control. If this cannot be done with what general knowledge is before the public, then children must be sent to clinics provided for these things. Parents must also go there, inasmuch as it is adults, who, usually unknowingly and certainly without malicious intent, create the tendency within the children to commit crime.

With those families who refuse to look into their own situation, who refuse to acknowledge their mistakes and thereby continue to make more of the same, there should be provisions within the law that children growing out of these homes should be taken from their parents and placed elsewhere, preferably in a healthy normal atmosphere such as a good foster home. For with help in understanding themselves, children can break up destructive patterns very readily. This understanding together with the emotional security of a home where a child feels wanted, is undoubtedly more distinct assurance of a good solid citizen than that growing out of many another so-called good home.

In illustration of this, there was a man of 50 who started to commit crime when he was forty-five and remained undiscovered for five years. He had been embezzling many thousands of dollars from the company in which he had an excellent and high-paying position. He was taking the money to give to a woman other than his wife. Examination revealed that the woman was older than his wife and not nearly so attractive. But she mothered him within the office, and by an unconscious regression, he did all within his power to have her continue this, inasmuch as his own mother had preferred his little brother to him. This man never had intimate relations with this new-found substitute mother, nor did he understand his feelings about her until he underwent psychiatric treatment.

ECONOMICS

There are a few questions that are frequently asked in regard to our findings that family tension is the basic cause of criminal behavior. The first has to do with economics. It is reasonable to assume, intellectually speaking, that when one is without what is necessary for subsistence and cannot get it, he will simply take it for himself and his loved ones. This is instinctive, and it has to do with self-preservation; therefore there is a measure of truth in it. But it is only a measure, for with a good emotional stability and a proper orientation toward the laws of society and the rights of others, a person will take any kind of job, any kind of relief and any deprivation and humiliation before he will turn to theft. And extremes in this connection are not necessary in this day and age. We make provisions so that they needn't be.

A case in point was one described to us as theft growing out of poverty. Upon investigation, it turned out that the young man in question took things because he had been given to understand at an early age that the world owed him a living. When his father died, his mother sought relief and never made the slightest attempt to work. Therefore the boy became used to the idea that he should receive things without effort. Actually, he probably would have followed his mother's pattern, but there was a complication here. The mother showered her attention upon his sister, so he stole money (an artificial substitute for love) rather than go on relief in order to punish his mother for her neglect of him, and himself too, for resenting her so deeply.

Another somewhat frequent question is, why is it that one boy will be a model son and another will become a hardened criminal? Once more, it is an unbalance within the home. When a child does not receive sufficient attention, he often feigns illness, for which he will have to be well-treated. For the same reason, though usually unconscious, one boy will behave badly to receive the attention his brother receives by being a good boy. Besides this, such a child will often commit crime in a spirit of pure rebellion. With the crime and whatever benefit is gained thereby comes a feeling of power unknown before because the model brother has caused him to feel inferior. With each new crime comes more of a feeling of power, until a false sense of security is built up within the slighted child until, in all his toughness, all his daring and boldness, he is quite a person . . . until, that is, he is caught up with, punished, and again slighted in the eyes of society. These are to him the eyes of his mother all over again, so the hostility grows and so does the spirit of getting even, so that rather than benefiting, he commits crime again because the behavior has not been understood. The pattern has not been broken up.

Still another question that is often asked is—what about intellect? As has already been established, people of good intellect often commit crime, because of twisted emotions and therefore points of view. The outstanding way in which the argument of intellect may make a difference is that a good knowledge of the rules of society, learned often and learned well, is apt to strengthen one's superego, or conscience, so that the primitive instincts which are in all of us are kept in check through fear if nothing else. Thus too the home in which there is no effort made to teach a child what it must or must not do will naturally produce a person to whom the law means little. But this problem is basically one and the same as the one mentioned of criminality growing out of the asocial home. Because it stands to reason that other types of homes at least make an effort, even if the wrong kind, to develop good citizens out of their children.

Over all, especially beneath all, because it is seldom apparent, is the overwhelming importance of the existence of family tension. In the face of this factor, any other cause and any other maladjustment are singularly unimportant. By the same token, any other treatment than that which takes the problem of the entire family in account, is bound to be perfunctory.

RESEARCH RESULTS

Within our project we had absolute proof of this, up to the very end. There were certain obstacles, of course, these being the resistance one always encounters in such matters. All of the 80 offenders were mentally disturbed and all originally said they wanted help, but after a few interviews some of them began to drop out, giving one or another excuse for doing so. Seventy-five had the courage to face their own inadequacies and failures. Of these, some had been completely rejected by their families and therefore had to start over again on their own, which was not easy but not impossible. Those 75 who cooperated were seen one, two or three times a week from one-half year up to two years and some of them are now under private treatment. All of them have received help, some of them more than others. But it is in each case the changing of the *emotional* attitudes within the family group or of the environment itself that has made the difference, together of course with the offender's understanding of himself in relation to the condition under which he grew up.

CRIME PREVENTION

What it means, then, is that we must develop a new general and mandatory treatment for the offender, one which will first of all probe into the emotional difficulties which have caused him to turn to crime as an outlet, and second will discover the cause or causes within the home. This will mean treatment not only for the offender, but for parents, close relatives, foster parents and perhaps wives and husbands.

With such a method of treatment as this as an accepted foundation the next step would be towards the offender's comprehension of his entire situation, and suggestion to replace the original fears and hostili ties with constructive outlooks and forms of behavior, until a kind of character building takes place.

When no treatment of the causative factors is possible—those parents and situations which cannot and will not be changed—then the offender, upon release from treatment, should by law be placed elsewhere.

Then too, there should be classes for parents which will give constructive insight into human behavior, suggestions as to what the needs of children are, and question and answer periods which will deal with special cases.

There should be a family court, possibly outside the jurisdiction of the law, which will put on psychological trial all the members of the family to discover who the offending member or members may be. These persons in turn then should be given no reprimands, but rather insight and understanding of themselves. This, because parents and others who bring up children today cannot be held responsible for what they do. There is not as yet enough knowledge of human behavior. There is not enough comprehension that crime is an expression of individual human emotions, just as is true with the psychotic person, the neurotic one, and the arthritic.

When, perhaps twenty years from today, all this is taught in the schools, as it should be, and the world is as conscious of the evils of family tension as it is of the day's weather, then the responsible parents may themselves be punished for their children's crimes. Until that day comes, it is hoped that we will not go on functioning in an innocent ignorance which first of all creates the sickness known as crime, and then punishes those afflicted with the disease. Measures should therefore be taken to prevent these most dreadful of all crimes: the tension that causes criminal activity and the punishment of the victims of such indignity.

24 · The Schizophrene and Criminal Behavior

by H. WARREN DUNHAM

For a long time it has been assumed by students of crime that criminal behavior is closely connected with various types of psychoses. Numerous efforts have been made by psychologists and psychiatrists, as well as by sociologists, to determine the extent to which this was so. Some studies, particularly the older ones, have concluded that psychoses are the fundamental causes of many types of crime, especially the more serious ones directed against the person, whereas others have found little or no connection. In the article that follows, Professor H. Warren Dunham, of Wayne University, presents the results of a study he made of a sample of criminally insane individuals committed to the Illinois Security Hospital. The purpose of the study was to discover the relationship between schizophrenia and criminality. [From *American Sociological Review*, Vol. IV, No. 3, June 1939, pp. 352-361. Reprinted by permission.]

THIS PAPER proposes to report on one phase of a study which has investigated the schizophrene as a social type. The problems of immediate concern are: Do persons who have a schizophrenic breakdown show delinquent behavior patterns in their adolescent years? (2) Do such persons exhibit criminal behavior in their adult years? (3) Do schizophrenes who grow up in delinquency areas display delinquent or criminal behavior patterns?

These problems concerning the relationship between crime and schizophrenia have not been touched by many investigators. The problem, rather, which has received most attention, is that of the significance of mental disorder as a causative factor in crime. However, the evidence on this point is contradictory in character and consequently has not succeeded in clarifying the relationship of crime and mental disorder. This lack of clarity is partly due to the fact that the inclusive label of mental disorder covers a multitude of clinical symptoms and different forms of behavior. No studies have been confined exclusively to the part which schizophrenia might play as a factor in crime causation.

The most significant studies have been quantitative. Such studies range all the way from reporting fifty-nine percent of a sample of criminals as emotionally and mentally defective, to reporting only five percent so affected. Even when one examines the actual psychoses, the percentages range from 24.0 to 1.5 percent.[1]

[1] J. F. Sutherland, 46-47 *Recidivism*, Edinburgh, 1908. Sutherland's figures on the incidence of mental disorder and types of crime correlate highly with the statistics on this problem reported in the *Illinois Crime Survey*, 757, Chicago, 1928; G. Aschaffenburg, *Crime and Its Repression*, 190-191, Boston, 1913; V. V. Anderson, "The Relation of Mental Defect and Disorder to Delinquency," read at Annual Conference of the Massachusetts Society for Mental Hygiene, January, 1918; B. Glueck, "Concerning Prisoners," *Mental Hygiene*, April 1918, 177-218; A. Bingham, "Determinants of Sex Delinquency in Adolescent Girls," *J. Crim. Law and Criminol.*, Feb. 1923, 494-586; W. C. Sullivan, *Crime and Insanity*, 20-21, London, 1924; W. Healy, *Delinquents and Criminals*, New York, 1926; C. B. Thompson, "Some New Aspects of the Psychiatric Approach to Crime," *Mental Hygiene*, Oct. 1936, 529-545. See also W. Bromberg and C. B. Thompson, "The Relation of Psychoses, Mental Defect and Personality Types to Types of Crime," *J. Crim. Law and Criminol.*, May-June, 1937, 70-89.

In addition to these quantitative studies, this problem has been investigated by others using the case history or clinical method. P. E. Bowers [2] presents the mere outline of a series of cases in which crime and mental disorder were found in the same person. His point of view, following Lombroso, makes the assumption of the existence of a born criminal type. Sullivan,[3] after finding the quantitative relationship between crime and mental disorder of no significance, analyzed the clinical histories of several criminals each having a different psychosis, or perhaps a number of mental patients who have exhibited criminal behavior. Karpman's [4] study of five criminals with mental disorders is significant from the standpoint of detail and case method, but no outstanding results could be reported. None of his cases carried a schizophrenic diagnosis.

The studies which have been cited establish the following points. (1) The quantitative studies show, in general, a decrease in the frequency of mental disorder and emotional defect among criminals. This is similar to the cycle followed in the studies concerning the relationship of mental deficiency to crime.[5] (2) Both quantitative and qualitative studies show that a psychosis is found more often in persons who commit crimes against persons rather than crimes against property. (3) The Bromberg and Thompson study [6] represents the first attempt to investigate quantitatively the different types of mental disorder in relation to types of crime. To date there has been no study of the reverse question, namely, the frequency of criminal behavior among different types of psychotics.

THE CRIMINAL AND THE SCHIZOPHRENE AS SOCIAL TYPES

Unlike mental disorder, the study of crime and the criminal has not been done almost entirely by physicians. As a result, the literature of criminology is filled with the observations and theories of ministers, social workers, lawyers, journalists, political agitators and social scientists, in addition to those of psychiatrists and physicians. On the other hand, the studies and theoretical discussions of mental disorder have come for the most part from medically trained persons because for a long time, mental diseases, like physical diseases, have been regarded as pathological, each form having its own peculiar syndromes and symptoms, which implies an underlying pathology, discovered or to be discovered, and calls for a special type of treatment.

[2] Clinical Studies in the Relationship of Crime to Insanity, Michigan City, Indiana, 1915.   [3] Op. cit.
[4] Psychopathology and Crime, Washington, D. C., 1933 (Private Printing).
[5] E. H. Sutherland, "Mental Deficiency and Crime," in Social Attitudes, 357-375, Kimball Young, Ed., New York, 1931.
[3] Op. cit.

One result of the intellectual laissez-faire in criminology, already referred to, is that a great number of observations and generalizations have been made which aid us in understanding the criminal as a person.[7] The criminal, as a person, in marked contrast to the schizophrene, has a definite feeling of belonging to a certain part of group life. He has developed like other "normal" boys in that he has no feeling of estrangement from the fellows with whom he has contact, but rather, has a strong tie of loyalty to them and to their values. There may be disagreements, antagonisms, or separations, but he feels no uncertainty or anxiety in their company. His personality is likely to be characterized by strong aggressive traits which aid in establishing his status in the group. In competition with his fellows, he makes his adjustments to his victories as well as to his defeats, and, if he cannot assume a position of leadership and responsibility, he sinks back into a secondary position. His hopes, ambitions, ideas and ideals are reflections of the attitudes and values of his social groupings.

The values of his group, of course, run counter to the mores of the larger society and consequently his group tends to develop its own language or argot, and certain ways of thinking and acting, which distinguish it from the larger society. This milieu tends to build into his personality traits which are, in cruder forms, depreciated by the larger society, but which are serviceable to him in competition with members of his own group. Such traits as aggressiveness, vanity, egotism, boisterousness, indifference, and boastfulness, are typical of the criminal as a person. His group opposes itself to that of the larger society and its values with the consequence that the occupation of the criminal consists of an attack upon the most sacred values of this larger society. This attack, which provides the criminal with his livelihood, is, in general, against the sacred value of private property. His attack on property is, for the most part, a social project which he carries on in company with

[7] The literature on the criminal as a social type is voluminous and only some of the most significant contributions are indicated here. Attention should be directed especially to: H. Mayhew and J. Binney, *The Criminal Prisons in London*, 1862; E. W. Burgess, "The Delinquent as a Person," *Amer. J. Sociol.*, May 1928, 657-680; F. M. Thrasher, *The Gang*, Chicago, 1927; C. R. Shaw, *The Jack Roller*, Chicago, 1929; C. R. Shaw, *The Natural History of a Delinquent Career*, Chicago, 1931; Fred Pasley, *Al Capone*, New York, 1930; E. Franklin Frazier, *The Negro Family in Chicago*, 204-219, Chicago, 1932; J. Landesco, "A Member of the '42 Gang," *J. Crim. Law and Criminol.*, March-April 1933, 964-998; H. Asbury, *The Barbary Coast*, New York, 1933; Frank Tannenbaum, *Crime and the Community*, 174-195, New York, 1938; W. F. Nelson, *Prison Days and Nights*, Boston, 1933; E. H. Sutherland, (ed.), *The Professional Thief*, Chicago, 1937. These last two references are especially significant as they were written by criminals and portray the criminal as a professional man.

ther members of his group.[8] He is, in general, loyal and affectionate to he members of his own family, although he is likely to have left home t an early age, for the purpose of being with the members of his own roup. His personality, in terms of his attitudes and values, is organized n such a fashion that his career in crime is a natural result of such organzation and can no more be changed than a "normal" person can change is personality and direct it toward a life of crime. His life is lived much n the surface with no regrets for the past and sometimes an eager, somemes a passive acceptance of the future. His inner and private life is egligible. These, briefly, are the personality traits of the professional riminal.

In marked contrast to the criminal, the schizophrene has practically o feeling of belonging to any phase of group life. He appears definitely s an isolated person who either has been rejected by the group or who as failed to establish the necessary contacts. An intensive study [9] of the ife histories of catatonic and paranoid schizophrenes bears out this oint, and also provides a conceptual scheme of the personality traits of hese two diagnostic types. While the catatonic and paranoid are diferentiated in terms of certain traits, their personalities are in marked ontrast to that of the criminal. The catatonic shows such traits as secluiveness, self-consciousness, anxiety qualities, feeling of difference, seriousess, submissiveness, conformity, and home attachment. In contrast, the aranoid displays the first five traits indicated for the catatonic, but in ddition, shows certain differentiating traits such as aggressiveness, stubornness, quarrelsomeness, suspiciousness, egocentricity and home reellion.

The personality data on both the criminal and the schizophrene indiate that they represent radically different social types. The behavior of ach type, therefore, flows from different motivations regardless of the act that by an abstract, legal consideration, such behavior might be abeled as either criminal or noncriminal.

FREQUENCY OF CRIME AMONG SCHIZOPHRENES

This study is limited to an analysis of criminal behavior among the atatonic and paranoid schizophrenes. As a preliminary step, a statistical

On this point, see especially C. R. Shaw and H. D. McKay, *Report on the Causes f Crime*, 191-199, Washington, D. C., 1931. See also C. R. Shaw, H. D. McKay, nd J. McDonald, *Brothers in Crime*, Chicago, 1938.

This study of the social personality of the schizophrene is contained in a report filed ith the Social Science Research Committee of the University of Chicago. Limitaions of space make it possible to characterize only very briefly here the personality rofiles of the catatonic and paranoid schizophrene.

study was made of the 543 male persons [10] who were committed for th'
first time, 1922 to 1934 inclusive, to the Illinois Security Hospital. Al
were certified as being insane and having committed a major crime. Thi
number is 1.7 percent of the total male insane committed to other Ill;
nois hospitals and 1.3 percent of the male criminals sent to Illinois pena
institutions during this period. These very low percentages, even thougl
inconclusive, indicate the fact, shown by recent studies, that menta
disorder and crime seldom go together.

A comparison of the percentage distribution of the diagnoses of th
543 criminal insane with that of all other male insane persons in Illinoi
state hospitals for 1927, shows that the most important psychoses i;
relation to crime are schizophrenia (all types), (40.3, 23.7); [11] psychos;
with mental deficiency (12.8, 1.8); paranoia (6.4, 0.6); and psychopathi
personality (2.7, 0.4).

These percentages appear to check with the more careful statistica
studies which show that psychopathic personalities and mentally def
cient persons represent a significant proportion of criminals who shov
mental findings even though this percentage is negligible compared t'
the total number of criminals. [12] Schizophrenia appears, then, as the mos
statistically significant psychosis in relation to criminal behavior; murde
appears as the most frequent crime, with larceny and burglary, an'
armed robbery next in order.

These statistical data on the schizophrene and crime are confined ex
clusively to adults. It would be desirable, of course, to know if any o
these male schizophrenics showed any evidence of juvenile delinquenc'
early in their developmental careers. An attempt was made to secur
some data on this point by clearing a sample of 525 catatonics and 34
paranoids, males, 15 to 29 years of age, [13] with the Social Service E>
change, which registers cases of juvenile delinquents appearing in th
Cook County Juvenile Court. Of the catatonics, only nine were regi;

[10] This statistical material is confined exclusively to males. In the complete stud
of this problem, however, the factor of sex takes on considerable significance. I
Illinois, the sex ratio for committed schizophrenes is 100 to 81.7, while for convicte
criminals it is 100 to 6.9. The fact is well established that men are more likely t
engage in crime than women, while men and women are much closer together i
relation to schizophrenic breakdown and subsequent commitment. In schizophreni;
sex is apparently not the differentiating factor that it is for crime.

[11] The first percentage represents the incidence of the psychosis in the criminal insan
group and the second percentage represents its incidence in the state hospital grou
for 1927.

[12] On this point, see R. Gault, Criminology, 155, 175, New York, 1932.

[13] These cases comprise the total number of males from this age group given cat;
tonic and paranoid schizophrenic diagnoses and committed from Chicago to th
Chicago, Elgin, and Kankakee State Hospitals, 1922-1934.

tered at the Juvenile Court. Of these nine, all but one showed that the registration was due to the delinquent activities of the catatonic's siblings.

The one catatonic boy registered at the court was arrested at fourteen in the company of another boy, supposedly the leader, on a charge of burglary. One year from this first registration, he was again arrested for truancy, and nine months later for riding in a stolen car. He was committed to the Parental School in April, 1925, and remained there until June, 1925. The last contact the court had with the boy was in March, 1927. One year later, he was committed to a state hospital and given a diagnosis of catatonic schizophrenia. He remained in the hospital for three and a half years, and was then discharged in July, 1931. Two other brothers and one other sister in this family had delinquent records also.

Five of the eight catatonics who were not delinquents as juveniles had subsequent registrations with the police as adults. This would seem to indicate that the potential catatonic is extremely law abiding in his youth, but as his mental breakdown becomes imminent, he tends to give evidence of criminal behavior.

In the paranoid series of 345 cases, only three were found to have a juvenile court registration. Two of these cases were paranoid schizophrenics. The third case was registered because of the delinquency of a brother. The first boy was brought before the Juvenile Court in March, 1924, charged with stealing a watch. On the same day of this alleged delinquency, he also stole a pay envelope containing $70.00 with which he purchased a railroad ticket to Los Angeles. According to the court record, this boy stated that he did not know why he stole the watch. Five years later, the boy was committed to a state hospital. He was paroled in August, 1929, and later recommitted in February, 1930. He died at the hospital in 1932.

The second boy was arrested on a larceny charge in May, 1927, and on the very next day was apprehended on a burglary charge. He was committed to the Cook County School for Boys, where he ran away a week later and was then committed to St. Charles School for Boys in June, 1927, as an incorrigible. In 1929, he was committed to a state hospital and given a diagnosis of paranoid schizophrenia. He was discharged in July, 1931, and is at present working. He has no further registrations with the police. A court psychiatrist describes him as unreliable, unstable, egocentric, and incoherent in his train of thought.

This same sample of catatonics and paranoids was also cleared for possible criminal charges at the Bureau of Identification.[14] Table I shows

[14] These data were secured through the cooperation of C. R. Shaw, Director of the Department of Sociology, Institute for Juvenile Research.

the percentage distribution of the types of violations, as shown by the police records, for both of these schizophrenic groups.

TABLE I. PERCENTAGE DISTRIBUTION OF TYPES OF OFFENSE
CHARGED IN THE CATATONIC AND PARANOID SERIES

| | Catatonics | | Paranoids | |
Types of Offense Charged	Number	Percent	Number	Percent
No offense charged	446	85.0	227	65.8
Minor violations	53	10.1	90	26.1
Crimes against persons	7	1.3	13	3.8
Crimes against property	19	3.6	15	4.3
Total Cases	525	100.0	345	100.0

These figures show that 34.2 percent of paranoid schizophrenics were charged with some type of criminal activity. This is more than twice the percentage of catatonics (15.0) who showed evidence of criminal activities. In both series, the majority of police charges are of a minor character, and most of the persons were either discharged outright, or subjected to a slight fine. In only three instances were the persons held for the grand jury. All of these persons were paranoids.

It is also significant that approximately 19 percent in each group were sent to the psychopathic hospital immediately following the commission of their criminal acts. In the catatonic group, 44 percent and in the paranoid group, 56 percent, committed their criminal acts at a time before they were sent to the hospital. The remainder in each case committed their acts after they had been returned to the community. It is also to be noted that approximately fifty percent of the persons in each series represented single offenders.

THE CATATONIC AND CRIMINAL BEHAVIOR PATTERNS

Proceeding from the quantitative facts, we now attempt to analyze the relationship between criminal behavior patterns and catatonic schizophrenia. This is of especial significance because the highest rates of catatonic schizophrenia are found in those areas of the city which also have high rates of delinquency and criminality.[15]

The relative freedom from delinquent and criminal behavior of those diagnosed as catatonic schizophrenes has been shown statistically. Part of the problem is to determine how the potential catatonic, growing up in an area of high rate delinquency, regards antisocial or delinquent

[15] See R. E. L. Faris and H. W. Dunham, *Mental Disorders in Urban Areas*, 92-97, Chicago 1939.

behavior. As a corollary, the question can be raised as to whether there is any difference in attitude toward criminal activity among the limited number of catatonics who have been reported for criminal activity.

In the previous study of the catatonic, it was shown that he is a person with an extremely conventional and moral view of the world. The presence of such an ideology might indicate that not only would a marked absence of criminal activity be noted, but also that there would be a definite negative attitude toward such activity. An intensive study of the life career of a number of catatonics reveals both of these points. Of the fifty-six catatonics (mostly from delinquent areas) who were studied intensively, all showed a complete absence of delinquent activity in their early years and only a few showed any such behavior in their adult years. This lack of any delinquent behavior pattern in the catatonic is, no doubt, connected with the traits of inhibition, timidity, and isolation. However, as revealed by his life history, his reasons for not participating in delinquent activities show a high degree of rationalization and indicate an allegiance to the codes of the larger society. In some cases, the catatonic indicates his own timidity and inhibition and a definite nervousness at the idea of engaging in delinquent activity, but without stating that he considers it ethically wrong to steal.

The life story of the catatonic in comparison with that of the delinquent reveals rather clearly that the catatonic lives more in a sphere of fantasy and moody reflection while the delinquent and the normal young man live in a realistic realm of social relationships and do not spend time reflecting on these relationships. The catatonic's behavior is more of the covert type; the delinquent's and normal's behavior, is of the overt type.

Rationalization because of the failure to participate in delinquent activities is often supplemented by a very definite ignorance as to the existence of such behavior in the community. Often the boy knows nothing concerning the delinquent acts of the other young men in his neighborhood and is reluctant to believe such things about the boys he has known.

The interview material with the catatonic and his associates indicates that the catatonic attaches a negative value to delinquency and other activities which run counter to the mores of the larger society; when delinquencies are being planned or discussed by other boys, the catatonic takes no part and is tacitly ignored. Consequently, he feels uncertain as to what he should do or what he should say and this uncertainty of his status in relation to the other young men is brought sharply home to him. This tendency to ignore the catatonic and to exclude him from certain activities tends to increase his isolation and this adds to his increasing mental tension.

While it is noted that the catatonic does not participate in delinquent activities, it nevertheless has been shown that a small percentage of catatonics have police records. These interview data cast some question on the validity of the statistics, and also indicate the necessity of getting beyond the mere figures for any satisfactory interpretation. It is to be remembered that in the catatonic series of 525 cases only twelve percent were found to have records of delinquent behavior after those who went directly to psychopathic hospital were eliminated. Of this remaining twelve percent, certain conclusions will be presented in regard to four cases to show: (1) the manner in which their delinquent behavior figures in their life careers, and (2) a comparison of their personality profiles with those of the non-delinquent catatonics. In three of these cases, the general prepsychotic personality appeared to be of the catatonic variety. In two of the cases, the criminal offense was valid from the standpoint of the legal code, but in the third case the charge was merely incidental to the police system bookkeeping.

Possibly there are several other cases in the statistics where no actual offense was committed or intended, but rather where a charge was entered merely because the police picked the person up on the street or because the family called the police to take the person to the hospital. In the first two cases, the offense was seen to be an aspect of the mental confusion of the young man and was not in any sense a continuation of any previous established pattern of delinquent or criminal behavior. In this connection, the absence of any other offenses should be noted. While it is perhaps impossible definitely to draw this conclusion, it is tempting to assume that all single-offense catatonics were similar to these cases.

The final case deals with a catatonic who had six criminal charges against him. The interview material established the following points: (1) the boy had numerous contacts with other boys in his neighborhood; (2) he was extremely confused as to why he had to go to the hospital; and (3) his delinquent escapades were part of a delinquent pattern of behavior which was also typical of the boys with whom he had contact. In addition, it might be pointed out that his clinical record contained several contradictory psychiatric opinions concerning his diagnosis.

The analysis of this problem would hardly be complete without a consideration of those persons who are incarcerated for a major crime, and also because of symptomatic indication of catatonic schizophrenia. It has already been established that the state hospital schizophrene is not likely to have committed any criminal acts and, of the few committed, the great majority are generally not very serious. However, the fact remains that some catatonics have committed the more serious crimes.

In a thirteen year period, it was found that twenty-four persons had been committed to the Illinois Security Hospital and given a diagnosis of catatonic schizophrenia. At present (1937) residing in this hospital, there were only eleven catatonics who had been convicted of a crime or had been such behavior problems at one of the other state hospitals that they were transferred to the Illinois Security Hospital. In studying these eleven, attention was centered around two factors: (1) the character of the situation in relation to the criminal act; and (2) the presence or absence of a past record of criminal activity.

The data revealed the following facts concerning the criminal records of these men. Four of them appeared to be definitely cases of catatonic schizophrenia with no criminal records. This was ascertained from an examination of both the clinical record and interview with the men themselves. Four other men also appeared to be definite cases of catatonic schizophrenia, but it was impossible to establish from the clinical report as to whether they had a criminal record or not. Two others presented questionable diagnoses. This was shown not only by the clinical report but also by their present condition and personality organization. These two cases had no criminal record. The remaining man also had a doubtful diagnosis, and he had a long history of a petty criminal career.

It is pertinent at this point to mention the subject of terminology. It is apparently more correct to refer to the criminal schizophrene than to the schizophrenic criminal. The schizophrenic person may commit actions of a criminal nature, but the true criminal does not end up as a schizophrene. This latter assertion is made on the basis that the true criminal has social relations of a solidifying character which tend to preserve and protect him from any kind of a schizophrenic breakdown. Just the reverse is true in the case of the potential schizophrene whose social relations are either so weak and casual or so hostile and unacceptable that he eventually has no social contacts whatever and so lacks any social sanctions for his behavior forms.

CONCLUSIONS

From the data presented the following conclusions can be stated tentatively.

1. From a quantitative point of view, schizophrenia appears as a very negligible factor in the causation of crime.

2. In the few cases, however, where crime and mental disorder appear together in the same person, schizophrenia is apparently more significant than all other psychoses as a causative factor in crime.

3. Crimes against the person are the most frequent type when schizophrenia is a causative factor in crime.

4. Both catatonic and paranoid schizophrenes show an almost complete absence of delinquency in their adolescent years.

5. Both the catatonic and paranoid groups, however, show a higher incidence of criminal behavior during the adult years, with the paranoid group showing twice the amount of crime as compared to the catatonic group.

6. The catatonic attaches a negative value to delinquency and all forms of socially disapproved behavior.

7. He is ignored by the other boys when plans for delinquent activity are being discussed.

8. The single-offense catatonics committed their crimes at the point of mental breakdown, which suggests that the crime was merely an aspect of the impulsive behavior which characterizes the breakdown experience.

9. Those catatonics who had numerous charges against them were largely cases in which the diagnosis was doubtful.

10. Among those catatonics who have committed a major crime, there was a noticeable absence of any previous record.

CHAPTER EIGHT

Social and Cultural
Factors in Crime

≡≡≡≡≡≡≡≡≡≡≡≡≡≡≡≡

25 · A Sociological View of Crime Causation

by ALBERT MORRIS

Crime, the violation of the rules of a society, is universal and probably as old as the human group itself. It has always been—to a greater or less degree—a problem which called for a solution. Its dramatic quality, moreover, challenged the members of a society and made them wonder why certain individuals "chose" to disregard the regulations of their group. Throughout the ages, philosophers and scholars as well as laymen have propounded theories explaining the causes of crime. The search to find the causes of criminality is still going on. In this article, Albert Morris, of Boston University, dwells briefly on the nature of crime causation as the sociologist sees it. ["Crime Causation," *Federal Probation*, Vol. VII, July-Sept. 1943, pp.17-20. Reprinted by permission.]

IN HIS *Study of Sociology* Herbert Spencer tells the story of a Frenchman who after spending 3 weeks in England proposed to write a book about it. At the end of 3 months he felt that he was not quite ready and by the end of 3 years he had decided that he knew nothing about it. Anyone who spends 3 years mulling over this question of crime causation may find himself in much the same position. Unlike the Frenchman, unfortunately, some of us are not in a position to avoid writing as though we knew something about it. In order to do this I have drawn freely upon the contributions of others, especially upon the work of Robert MacIver, whose book *Social Causation* is the basic source of the ideas herein expressed on the nature of causation.

NEED TO ANALYZE SPECIFIC CRIMES RATHER THAN CRIME

The first difficulty that confronts anyone attempting to discuss crime causation is that the phrase itself has become so much a part of our technical jargon that we assume that it has a reasonably definite meaning that we have no call to question. *Crime*, whether it be the vague and varied lists of acts which lay persons call to mind when they use the term, or whether it be those acts or failures to act forbidden by the criminal law, includes varieties of behavior which one would not expect, even without study, to find growing out of similar combinations of factors unless they were classified so broadly and included items so fundamental to the understanding of any behavior as to be obvious to everyone and usable in specific instances by none.

If we want precise answers we must expect to obtain them only provided we stop talking about the broad and varied area of crime and, instead, formulate more definite queries about specific types of people and specific types of acts. Why do some people living in isolated mountain areas of the South illicitly distill liquor? Why do some manufacturers, in violation of the law, adulterate the food products they make?

The exploration of such concrete situations is almost bound to raise other queries that may have to be dealt with before the desired answer is found. Are there, perhaps, some southern mountain people who do not make illicit corn liquor? Why not? What are the differences in mentality, or family cohesiveness, or vocational competency, or religion, and so on, between those who violate the law and those who do not? What significant differences are there between the manufacturers of foodstuffs who do not adulterate their product and those who do?

CAUSATION AS A SELECTED COMBINATION OF FACTORS IN ACTION

The nature of *causation* needs also to be examined with care. What is this thing or this process or whatever it may be that we label a "cause"? Is it anything that an ordinary mortal can apprehend by means of his senses? Does the word "cause" mean the same thing when we speak of "the cause of a thunderstorm" as it does when we speak of "the cause of crime"?

In dealing with such questions I am well aware of the danger that we may befuddle ourselves and get lost in an imaginary verbal world that may be mistaken for a real one by those of us whose habit it is to deal in words and who often find it much easier to arrange and manipulate words than the tough conditions which they are merely supposed to call to our minds. Francis Bacon once remarked, "It cannot be that axioms established by argumentation can suffice for the discovery of new work since the subtlety of nature is many times the subtlety of argument." In awareness of this limitation perhaps it would be well to apply to this discussion the suggestion of Oliver Wendell Holmes that words be washed in cynic acid.

The first characteristic of a cause is the element of pressure or compulsion about it. A cause is that which makes something happen. For that reason some philosophers refuse to use the word at all, at least as it applies to the physical world, because it seems to impute to inanimate objects something of human consciousness and volition. Sociologists, though less bold in statement, have been veering in the same direction. They no longer talk about *the* cause of crime but about the interrelations of factors causing crime or they avoid the term causation in favor of factors correlated with it or talk about functional configurations. Must we then discard the term "cause" altogether? The idea does violence to our common experiences. We may not be able to demonstrate just how a combination of such conditions as ignorant quarrelsome parents, a physically deteriorated neighborhood, racial prejudice, a modest intelligence quotient, and an excess of physical energy are bound together so as to produce criminal behavior; but that these items exist as discrete factors we may well doubt. Somehow or other they are organized and interacting. And it is a *combination of factors, tied together,* unified in some way yet undefined, *and in action* that we refer to as "cause."

As MacIver puts it: "In being shot from the bow the arrow is acted upon, motion is imparted to it. But now in motion it is also active, a flying arrow that does things the resting arrow could not do. It is both acted upon and acting at the same time. . . . The two aspects are eternally bound together. Together they constitute the stream of change." [1]

Causation, then, is a continuous and unbroken process in which every cause is also an effect; the effect of its own antecedent causes. When we

[1] MacIver, R. M. *Social Causation*, p. 29. Quoted by permission of Ginn and Company.

search for the causes of crime, therefore, we are seeking to observe the action of that particular combination of factors that happens to have the greatest significance for us.

If sociologists, then, are to lift themselves above the plateau of knowledge about crime causation on which they have been resting now for several years, it will be necessary for them to limit and define more precisely the combinations of factors they are to study. Such terms as poverty, slums, culture conflict, constitutional inferiority, mental deviation, family disorganization, capitalism, hedonistic philosophy, and the like have served a purpose; but now if we are to get on with this business of understanding the sources of certain types of behavior, we must specify the behavior itself more concretely and begin to observe the differences in the conditions under which it occurs in more careful detail. Slums may share gross similarities; so may disorganized families—but one slum also differs from another and one disorganized family differs from another in many ways that probably are vital to any understanding of their influence upon conduct. These are not fixed objects with universally recognized characteristics and boundaries, with a geometry of their own.

THE ROLE OF THE INDIVIDUAL IN CAUSATION

In the sphere of human relations a unique feature of causation is, of course, the so-called "human element" itself. Short of some overwhelming external force such as a moving automobile or an exploding bomb that may knock a man down regardless of his wishes in the matter, a man's behavior is influenced by what MacIver calls his own dynamic assessment of the total situation. For anyone who is interested in the understanding and modification of behavior in particular cases, there is probably nothing that would be more illuminating than an adequate appreciation of what goes on in a client's mind. This has been stressed before by many of us, perhaps first of all by Dr. Healy. It is here, in the mind of a man, that the implications for him of the world about him and of his own glandular and visceral states are developed. It is here, in a man's subjective assessment of the meaning of his experiences, that poverty, and slums, and unemployment, and all of the external factors that get listed as causes of crime begin to influence his behavior. Here, in the mind of a man, all that can have a role in determining his so-called responsible behavior is brought to a focus and translated. Except in the most limited way, it is only through this mental assessment that slums and poverty and acquisitive capitalism can exert their influence as part of an active combination of factors which we label causative.

If a financially successful man returning to his home town after long absence sees an unexpected crowd of people, including the police and the town dignitaries, waiting at the station, he may *believe* either that they have learned somehow of his coming and have gathered to greet him or he may *suppose* that they have unusually long memories about where he got the capital with which to start his career. If he *supposes* that they are a welcoming delegation, he may stand glad and beaming upon the steps of his pullman, or he may retreat in embarrassed modesty; and in doing either of these things he may misinterpret the external situation completely. What the objective facts are may be unimportant. *What he thinks they are and how he evaluates them* is what really determines his behavior.

Moreover, the ends that a criminal seeks may be identical with those sought by the noncriminal: wealth, adventure, sex satisfaction, social prestige. The difference between the criminal and the noncriminal more likely lies in the criminal's disregard of the ways of attaining those ends approved and enforced by whatever majority or minority has legal power. His failure to follow the accepted pathway, his choice of a criminal method, if you like, is influenced remotely by the total universe but more immediately by his capacities and his training or, if you prefer, by his total personality as it exists at the moment. Perhaps he is unaware of the fact that his manner of getting what he wants is socially disapproved; he is ignorant of the value society attaches to its means of maintaining orderly relations among men as they strive to achieve their ends. The cause of the ignorance may be found in his feeble-mindedness which, in turn, grew out of another preceding conjuncture of factors; or it may lie in his lack of exposure to the norms of the larger society in which he is dubbed a criminal because he is a recent arrival from another culture whose norms are different, or because he has been exposed so largely to the special standards of one group (his family or his gang) that he supposes his behavior has more general approval than it in fact has. Or he may be well aware that his methods do not meet with social approval, that they are legally punishable; but his desires may be so overwhelming, the chances of achieving them legitimately appear so remote, and the opportunities for obtaining them illicitly so comparatively easy, and his sense of the need to accept or conform to the methods prescribed by the group in this particular instance so weak that he places a very low value on conformity and a high one on obtaining his ends. Again, both the organically based factors that enter into the making of his total personality, as well as the subjectively assimilated stimuli that originated outside of him, are the elements that are synthesized and assessed as the basis for the course of action that is accepted.

THE SOCIOLOGICAL ELEMENT IN CRIME CAUSATION

Since sociologists have chosen to interest themselves in the nature and interrelations of human groups, that is, of people in association, and of the associated culture pattern which they originate and support and which, in turn, contributes to the stability and regularization of their relations, a sociological view of crime causation must be one that attempts to determine what influence human groups have upon an individual's choice of behavior.

Briefly stated, a view of the sociological element in crime causation might be thus expressed:

Men, by reason of nature and advantage, have come to live in association with one another. Their technical mastery of production has enabled them to increase in numbers and the extension, specialization, and distribution of knowledge and power have produced a well-nigh overwhelming complexity of interdependency among men. In the absence of any organic determination such as might be found among ants or bees, of what their relations with each other are to be, men have had to contrive a system of culturally determined, rather than biologically inherited, ways of providing a working basis for getting on together as a substitute for what might otherwise be a lethal anarchy.

The influence of such codes, of which the United States Criminal Code is a small part, always relative of course to the assimilative capacities of the individual, depends upon *their clarity, their consistency, their ability to satisfy man's needs, and the public acceptance of the authority to which they are ascribed.*

THE NATURE AND CONSEQUENCES OF MORAL CONFUSION AND CONFLICT

As compared with an earlier state of affairs in Puritan Boston, for example, we meet and deal with many more people under more diverse circumstances; we are exposed to a far greater variety of opinions about what behavior is desirable and what is not; the authorities that attempt to guide our conduct are more numerous, and they are often in disagreement as to what behavior is right and what is wrong. Gone is the magnificent authority behind such a phrase as "Thus saith the Lord God Jehovah."

There are many honest citizens who do not know whether they are conducting their businesses in accordance with the law's requirements. There are some among us who see little consistency in the removal of copies of *Life* from Boston's newsstands while *Esquire* goes gaily on.

There are many who accept the Commandment, "Thou shalt not steal," who find it inadequate as a guide to conduct in these days of complicated business arrangements. And there are many who question the authority of the pronouncements of the Unitarian Church or the Roman Catholic Church, as the case may be, with reference, for example, to the practice of birth control.

Where family, church, and State agree upon what conduct is right and when from infancy every child is both instructed and exercised in the simple and uniform applications of the code, within such limits of variation as are set by the differing capacities of the teachers and the taught, it is likely that the individual's acquired sense of values will conform closely to those generally held. If, then, they also serve well the needs of men, their attractive power is great and so also is their power of deterrence upon those whose personalities still move them to make an unapproved choice of behavior, because they find few to support them, their variant behavior is conspicuous, and what they stand to lose is great.

But when, in the course of the intricate interplay of men and their environments, older ways of behavior serve men less well, their values are questioned; alternatives are proposed or tried and accepted by some; new leadership commends itself by its achievements; there is a withdrawal of support from older authorities and a weakening of them, and a conflict between the old and the new that introduces greater possibilities of choice to the individual and gives him the opportunity to find some support for whatever course of conduct may be most congenial to his own biologically and socially conditioned desires of the moment, while at the same time the lack of certainty in the groups to whose pressures he is responsive makes the weight of their disapproval less.

Insofar as the criminal's unawareness of an adequate and compelling sense of social standards is a factor in criminality, the task before us would seem to involve a reintegration of some conflicting parts of our culture and a re-establishment of a strong and generally accepted standard of values as a guide and support to acceptable conduct—a revision and reorganization, perhaps, of our moral codes so as to make them more nearly adequate and serviceable for our daily needs. They may need to have their source and authority more largely in the neighborhood or the community than in the presently unstable family or the church and require a technique for recognizing natural rather than administrative community areas and for developing within them a sense of community pride and loyalty combined with a community code of public conduct.

26 · Social Forces in the Development of Crime

by FRANK TANNENBAUM

The sociological point of view—which is becoming perhaps the predominant one in criminology—regarding crime and the criminal is that they are the products of a society and its culture. In this brief excerpt from his book, Frank Tannenbaum, a professor of criminal law and criminology at Columbia University, shows why crime in this country must be considered as the inevitable result of the American way of life and the philosophy underlying it. [From *Crime and the Community*, Ginn and Company, 1938, pp. 25-28. Reprinted by permission.]

CRIME AND CONFLICT

AMERICAN criminal activity must be related to the total social complex. The United States has as much crime as it generates. The criminals are themselves part of the community in its deeper sense, and are as much its products as are its philosophers, poets, inventors, business men and scientists, reformers and saints. This is a basic fact that we must accept. If we would change the amount of crime in the community, we must change the community. The criminal is not a symptom merely, he is a product, he is of the very bone and fiber of the community itself. The community has given him not merely his ideals and ends, not merely his relationships with the world that make the kind of career he lives a possibility. The community has given him his methods too, whether these be graft, political pull, or the use of a machine gun. The distinction between the criminal and the community drawn in sharp contrast—a distinction between good and evil—is a false distinction and obscures the issue.

The amount of crime in the United States responds to all the factors and forces in American life—it is one way of describing our politics, our police, our civil and judicial administration, our immigration policy, our industrial and social conditions, our education, our morals, our religion, our manners, our culture. It is just as much one aspect of America as is baseball or divorce or anti-union industry or unemployment or Fords or movies. The relationship between the criminal and the community is a total relationship and not a partial one. He is the product of the sum of our institutions and the product of a selective series of influences within them, as are the best and the worst of the non-criminal population. The community does not set out to make a saint, and yet it does occasionally. It does not set out to make a criminal, and yet it does, more than occasionally.

If, therefore, we are to understand what the forces are that make for so much crime in the United States, we must investigate the forces as well as the criminal. It is by manipulating these forces that we may ultimately achieve a control and redirection of the energy that goes into criminal conduct. What, then, are the forces that make the criminal?

The genesis of crime in the United States is to be found in the all-pervasive conflicts that have characterized its history. These conflicts reflect the dynamic quality of American civilization. A glance at the growth of the American community reveals unexampled speed in expansion and growth. Both the settlement of the nation and the increase in numbers were charged with friction. The rapid growth of our industrialism and the congregation of immigrants from widely different parts of the world in close contact produced a species of irritation that embraced all phases of life—religious, political, social, economic, cultural. No appreciation of the growth of American urban life is possible without recognition of the fact that the development of cities (and crime is largely an urban phenomenon) was charged with conflict. The strife was between races, between religions, between political groups, between labor and capital, between new and older immigrants, between the ways of the parents and the ways of the children, between neighborhoods. Manners, customs, language, dress—all of life was thrown into a seething caldron.

The conquest, colonization, and settlement of the continent and the rapid filling of large areas by a heterogeneous population were characterized by a process of disintegration of old mores, by individualization, competition, self-assertion, by a process of carving individual careers against a fluctuating and shifting background where fortune and failure followed swiftly upon each other in the lives of individuals, of communities, of sections of the country. Instability, insecurity, movement, change, flux, have been the rule of American life. This flux has been pervasive. It has included custom, rule, habit, and habituation.

The rapid and large migration to the United States, one of the greatest movements of population in the history of the white race, was a migration of families rather than of organized tribes or races. It was characterized by the immigration of the individual rather than of the family. This fact of personal migration, personal tearing away from a settled and organized world where tradition, law, and custom were age-old, to join restless millions of human beings in a new world where all (including the basic tool of human relationships, language) was different, has had the profound effect of increasing and emphasizing the individualizing process of life in the United States. It has tended to break down ties between families, to make communities temporary habitats for the individual. The settler was a bird of passage.

The breaking down of stability has been and has remained perhaps the most important and the most significant feature of the life of the individual in the United States, and the process has tended to make all law and order a matter of artificial and exterior restraint. Law and order became matters of the outside—foreign, exterior rules. The laws were an attempt to impose a rule upon disorderly movements and processes instead of being an expression of the community's orderly unity of habit. The growth of our large cities has been a process of disintegration of older forms, individualization, and the fusion of temporary culture groups in conflict with each other.

The virtues of the pioneer persisted even in the urban community because life in the urban community, in spite of its physical compactness, lacked the kind of unity, cohesion, common interest, and common culture which pervaded the stable community. The individualism of the American process extended from the conquest of the frontier to the filling of the country and the settling of the large urban communities —except that it was made more pronounced by the lack of personal stability, the rapid change in the character of the communities, and the lack of common mores and unity in the component elements. The personal migration of the individual who came without family increased the shifting and unstable nature of his relationship with the world about him. And where the individual had a family the situation was but slightly improved, because the family itself was in a world of shifting ideals, attitudes, and economic and social relations. The attempts of the multifarious religious, social, fraternal, economic, and professional groups to harness the individual, to root him in some stable form, have mitigated the disintegrating effect of personal and economic instability; but they have not replaced the older pattern. It is in this environment of friction, conflict, and disintegration that our present type of crime and criminal activity has developed, and has set itself in the matrix of American urban politics.

The peculiar quality of American life, therefore, has been individualism, initiative, self-dependence, conflict, and striving. The answer to this phenomenon is success. Success is the alternative to submergence, isolation, deprivation, failure. In the American urban scene success has taken the place which stability held in the older and simpler culture. In the settled community where life is regulated by tradition and law and custom, where the future is known, where rule governs because it is the way of the fathers, the pattern of life is inevitable and makes success an unnecessary virtue; it has no survival value. In the American scene success is the alternative to instability. It is the means of securing those things that come as a matter of course to the individual born into a stable and regulated world: status, a living, possessions, satisfactions.

The pervasive striving for success in the American scene is therefore the counterpart of instability, insecurity. It is upon this food, this spiritual fare, that American individualism has grown strong as a counterpoise to the weakness inherent in the very basis of its existence. The individual had to succeed or be lost, forgotten, thrown upon the scrap heap. The immigrant who could not make a fortune or secure a niche for himself had to face poverty, isolation, neglect, unemployment, and possibly scorn and abuse. Therefore friction was the essence of life. Upon this friction American life has grown strong and powerful. It has sharpened those virtues of ingenuity that make personal achievement conspicuous. Against such a background of experience law is a feeble instrument indeed, and custom has no roots and covers only the most elementary relationships. It is this environment that covers as a surrounding atmosphere the activities which have shaped the growth of all social forms in the United States, including that of the criminal.

27 · Crime and the Frontier Mores

by MABEL A. ELLIOTT

As we have seen in the introduction to the preceding selection, many criminologists hold that it is in the culture of a people that the roots of crime among its members may be found. Culture includes traditions reaching back into the past, and these continue to exert an influence, sometimes to a very considerable degree, on the attitudes and values of a people. In American culture, the frontier, with its peculiar ways of thinking and behaving, is admittedly still influencing present-day life. In the following article, Mabel A. Elliott, a professor of sociology of Pennsylvania College for Women, who specializes in the field of social disorganization and criminology, shows that many of our present criminal behavior patterns had some of their origins in frontier days. [From *American Sociological Review*, Vol. 9, No. 2, April 1944, pp. 185-192. Reprinted by permission. Footnotes omitted.]

ALL SOCIOLOGISTS and criminologists accept the idea that culture in its wider ramifications and that culture conflict in particular provide the matrix out of which much of the modern crime problem emerges. Thus, *e.g.*, we recognize that race, class, national origins and the varying cultural patterns of social behavior provide important sources of cultural conflict and resultant anti-social behavior.

We sometimes forget, however, that the mainsprings of anti-social conduct are as much rooted in the past as they are a function of the present and that in America in particular, crime bears a significant relationship to the folkways and mores of the frontier. As a matter of fact there are numerous evidences that crime itself is written large in these same folkways and mores.

We have all heard the old story of how in Germany all which is allowable is forbidden, whereas in France all that is forbidden is "allowed." In our country we might go even further in asserting that lawlessness has been a part of the devices of social control, and that crimes have been committed which have not only been tacitly allowed, but have had the acceptance and approval of the group. Herein we have an explanation of the confounding confusion presented by the white collar criminal, the corrupt politician, and the ethics of the "robber Barons."

Obviously the American frontier did not develop from any single matrix, nor did they pass on any single matrix to later generations. The frontier folkways and mores of New England contrasted sharply to those of Cavalier Virginia. For Puritan New England paid excessive attention to rigid personal behavior and the penal laws of Colonial New England did not distinguish between vice, sin or crime. With all the intensity with which the Puritans revolted against the laxities and licentiousness of the members of the established Church in England, they set about to exact rigid standards of sex behavior, sobriety and simplicity in dress. Sober zealots that they were, these early dissenters failed to recognize that England was passing through an economic and intellectual revolution occasioned by the tremendous changes of the times. (1) One was transition from the agricultural to an urban economy. (2) Even more important, perhaps, was the development of the mercantile system, the result of the explorations of the new world. (3) But above all was the importance we may attach to the intellectual impact of the extensions in geographical knowledge. Think what it must have meant to the placid clergy and laity alike to have their conception of the nature of the universe completely upset by the discovery of the Americas and the subsequent discovery that the earth was round.

Probably no discovery in history so touched the imagination of the common man or so completely lowered the prestige of the scholar who more often than not was the cleric as well. Today leaders in the church recognize that economic and social upheavals inevitably disrupt the church as a social institution and the church members as individuals in a disorganized society. Our Puritan forebears saw only one explanation, namely the willful sins of the flesh.

While the Cavalier South, generally speaking, was not so rigid in the restraints imposed as was New England, even so, stringent rules soon went into effect in an attempt to curb excesses. The Virginia House of Burgesses organized in 1619 passed many detailed regulations of conduct. One law referred to drunkenness which provided that for the first offense the minister reprove the culprit privately, the second time publicly, the third time the offender was to be put in the irons for twelve hours and fined in addition. For any further offenses more severe punishments were to be inflicted. Here we have a precursor of the habitual offender acts passed in Virginia in 1849 and in Massachusetts even earlier, in 1817 and of course more lately revised in the famous Baumes Laws of New York in 1926.

Despite the differences in religious ideology, the populations of Virginia and New England were both basically British; hence differences were not so deep-seated as the early colonists themselves may have imagined. In Colonial Virginia, criticism of those in political authority was strictly forbidden. Swearing was subject to fine; selling arms to an Indian earned life imprisonment. Any man or woman who played with the affections of another was subject to fine or whipping, while fornication and adultery were severely condemned.

Even so there was a time when the Episcopal Church in Virginia was exceedingly corrupt, when some of the clergy were guilty of the very sins against which they preached. In consequence more than half of the Virginians turned Dissenter by the time of the Revolution. We shall not review the history of Virginia. Suffice it to say here that, even so, the Cavaliers continued to dominate Virginia and after the Restoration of Charles II many Loyalist families came to Virginia to look after their royal land grants. Of course not all of the early Virginians were the landed aristocracy, but nevertheless Virginia society always possessed an aristocratic character, an aristocracy unmatched in the greater austerity and intellectualism that was New England.

Counterpart to the aristocracy of Virginia was the rigid caste system occasioned by the influx of indentured whites and the introduction of Negro slaves. The criminals transported from England and the free but impecunious men who staked themselves to employers for their passage and the Negro slaves all contributed to the development of the caste system in the South. This in turn gave rise to the discriminatory criminal

law of the South. Fears of uprisings and rebellion of the slaves were par
tially responsible for such discrimination. In consequence, statutory
provision was made that a runaway slave might be killed if he resisted
attempts to seize him. He was also liable to emasculation for no white
woman was considered safe. Any master who murdered a slave could
not be punished. Testimony of a slave was not admissible either as
evidence or information save when one of his own race was on trial for
life. Slaves could not be freed except for meritorious service and this or
license of the Governor and Council. By these early provisions the mores
of the Englishman on the Virginia frontier were altered to meet his
rationalizations as to the inferiority of the slave. The laws governing the
colonial slaves set the standard for the treatment of the Negro which
has persisted to the present day. From this cultural heritage present day
discriminations may be traced.

This then was the dual moral code of the Virginia gentleman. And it
is the gentleman, we must remember, that has always been the voice of
the articulate upper and upper middle class which have written the laws
of our nation. On the whole, Virginians were a high type of settler and
generally speaking there was much less lawlessness in Virginia than that
which later characterized North Carolina. Colonial North Carolina was
in a sense Virginia's frontier into which the unsuccessful and shiftless
poor whites from Virginia pushed seeking better times. Here, too, was a
mecca for the escaped outlaws and the runaway indentured servants of
Virginia and South Carolina. Life was simple and rough and in general
lacked much of the polish and refinement so characteristic of life in
Charleston or on the Virginia plantation. It is then in North Carolina
that we have the earliest prototype of what we have come to think of
as the lawless frontier. While crimes ran high on the mainland of North
Carolina, pirates were also ransacking the coast. Threats to life, property
and common decency were so frequent that lynch law became widespread as a popular protest against this flaunting of the rights of free
men.

North Carolina was almost entirely rural, with no urban centers or organized facilities for social control. There was no organized religion; in
fact, Fiske tells us there was not even one clergyman until 1703, while
no schools were opened until shortly before the Revolution. Somewhat
later the Scotch-Irish migrations which began about 1719 altered the
character of social life in the colony by the newcomers' insistence upon
an orderly regime.

Unable to endure the new regulations, the less tractable elements of
the population sought the frontier again. This time the frontier lay to
the west, and the "poor whites" and the more adventurous of the better

stock pushed toward the Alleghenies. Some stayed in the mountains and became the isolated Southern mountaineers. Others pushed beyond the Alleghenies and made their way across Tennessee, others to Missouri and Illinois. In the mythology of American folklore the lineal descendants of the degraded Carolinians are said to have figured in the desperadoes of Memphis and in Quantrill's raid on Lawrence, Kansas, where my own fair university is located.

These stories are undoubtedly gross exaggerations. Certainly no sociologist gives much credence to the biological heritage theory of criminality. Nor can we ascribe the settlement of the West primarily to lawless degeneracy. Out of the West have come some of the finest types of American men and women. But the restive spirit of the pioneer has created much of the pattern of freedom and liberty which has been so characteristic a part of our American way of life. Herein we have the origins of the American rejection of the restraining influences of group life in the cities, a rejection made possible by the existence of the vast open spaces where a man could exist without tribute to tax collectors, or law makers, and if he moved fast enough he did not need to defer even to his neighbor's opinion.

Let us turn for a moment from the escape from law and order which the plains country afforded to the piracy upon the high seas. The freedom of the seas which is one of the freedoms for which men fight today has been the result of the extension of ideas of law and order to the control of ocean traffic-ways. Piracy, or the looting of vessels at sea, ranked high among the economic crimes of the two centuries of our history. The origins of piracy must be traced to the earliest days of seagoing vessels. Piracy was, however, a characteristic type of illegal economic enterprise in our early history. In fact the period from 1632 to 1827 was one marked by excessive plundering of our merchant ships from colonial days until the combined navies of Britain and the United States abolished piracy in the Atlantic.

During the colonial period, piracy developed largely as a result of the attempts of the Mother Country to control American trade through restrictive legislation. In the South such piracy was not only condoned, it was actively supported by at least two governors of Carolina. Political corruption is thus part of our political folkways and mores.

The Navigation Acts of 1661 and 1663, which restricted trade to the Mother Country seemed bad enough, but the subsequent Stamp Act levying a tax on tea, and the Molasses Act which placed such a prohibitive duty on rum, sugar and molasses were virtually non-enforced. Moreover in the development of smuggling and contraband trade there was such popular approval given to illicit trade that it achieved a status very comparable to that of a legitimate trade. To make a long story short, the British attempts to enforce legal restrictions were turned over to American privateers for the simple reason that there was no American navy.

Later, during the Revolutionary War, American privateers played an important part in the capture of British vessels. Following the Revolution these privateers did not long continue to serve the interests of the state, however. After the War of 1812, many actually turned pirates themselves. The spoils of war thus gave a compelling impetus to continue the plundering of merchant vessels in peace time. We cannot digress into any exhaustive analysis of piracy here. As students of crime we recognize the illegal character of piracy, but we may point out that the official support of piracy was also a revolt against the controls and restrictions which the British tried to place on colonial trade. By these same controls the seeds of the American Revolution were sown, hence piracy was in one sense a demand for freedom and liberty. Yet we must also admit that piracy forms an important initial chapter in the trail of the gangster on the American scene. The pirate was in a sense the progenitor of the rum-runner who figured so significantly in the mad lawlessness of the more recent Prohibition era.

It was, as we have stated, the lawless, the reckless and adventurous, who ventured beyond the settled life of the Carolinas to stake out a new existence in the mountain country to the west, and to penetrate into the wilderness beyond. It was restless pioneers such as these who made this venture, who chopped down the trees, plowed the plains, tilled the soil, discovered the mineral wealth and opened up oil fields of the nation. With reckless abandon they and others following in their footsteps exploited the natural resources of our country.

The historical importance of the frontier has found its best expression in the classic work of Frederick J. Turner. None has excelled his description of the Westward course of civilization in our vast commonwealth. For with the ever-receding frontier any man with sufficient energy might clear a spot in the wilderness and secure for himself a goodly competence through the effective assistance of our homestead laws.

In this conquering of the wilderness we may trace the roots of our particular brand of democracy. Here has developed the exaggerated individualism of the plains and mountain country and our much vaunted American standard of living.

Life on the Western frontier presented many variations. Opening up the fertile prairies was a relatively calm and peaceful business. There was, however, sufficient inland banditry and enough piracy in the steamboat trade to lend color and vitality to the tranquillity of the Ohio and Mississippi valleys. The opening up of the great agricultural states of the

North Central area was, in the main, dependent upon orderly men willing to assume the necessary routine tasks. Men engaged in wresting a living from the soil have little occasion for sharp disputes or violent combat. Hence the great agricultural middle west, Ohio, Indiana, Illinois, Iowa, Minnesota and Wisconsin, took on the general orderliness of life characteristic of New England. In these regions the strong motif of Puritanism developed. At the same time the folkways, mores and laws of New England were transplanted to the Western scene. Thus Iowa and Eastern Kansas became more New English than New England.

Those who were seeking a fortune in the Far West and especially those who invaded the mining sections of the Rocky Mountains were pioneers of different character. It is true that many sturdy and courageous men of honor were tempted by considerations of the economic opportunities and advantageous climate to participate in the development of Colorado, Montana, Wyoming, California and the Oregon Country. But here also came the flotsam, outlaws from Eastern states, ex-convicts made bitter by real or fancied injustice, desperadoes. The Western frontier became in fact the haven of refuge for the horse and cattle thief of Nebraska and Kansas, for the escaped burglar from an Eastern penitentiary, for the counterfeiter who might have new opportunity to ply his illicit vocation. Paroled convicts came from Australia, while Mexican outlaws swelled the numbers.

In fact the background of many of our pioneers was so disreputable that a special code of etiquette arose for conversing with strangers. As one Westerner put it:

"Never ask a stranger where he came from or he may draw a trigger. He may very well have come from jail."

Indeed too much inquisitiveness, as Everett Dick expresses it, was "an invitation to gunplay."

In California the signs of the times were well expressed in a song of the day:

> Oh what was your name in the States?
> Was it Thompson or Johnson or Bates?
> Did you murder your wife
> And fly for your life?
> Say, what was your name in the States?

Legal, religious and educational institutions and controls were virtually non-existent in the mining camps and mountain frontiers. Here, too, there were few women. This meant there was little of the conserving influence of good women or the stabilizing values of family life. The distorted sex ratio in the almost exclusively male population was undoubtedly a factor in the frontier crime rates. This distorted sex ratio brought the inevitable influx of scarlet women who became the hostesses of the gambling dens and night clubs and the dancing partners at the "Hurdy-gurdy" houses which offered the combined facilities of a bar, gambling house and dance hall.

Shooting scrapes and jealous quarrels over the attentions of these willing ladies, were a frequent accompaniment of strong liquor, frustrated impulses and the code of the times. According to the latter, no red-blooded man was expected to take silently the curses and insults of his rivals. Personal insults, however much deserved, demanded immediate action. If a mountaineer was denounced as a liar, a thief, or by less mentionable epithets he did not hesitate to annihilate his slanderer. The mountaineer was quick on the trigger, aimed well, and without remorse. Thus we may account for the emotional origins of many a mountaineer murder. Life was cheap, but honor was long on the Western frontier.

Climate, we may say parenthetically, may have added to the murder rate. At least high altitude is said to be irritating, and may have contributed to the resentment occasioning explosive murders.

A large share of frontier crimes were economic in motivation. Vast sums of money were afloat in the West and this, too, stimulated an invasion of outlaws and hoodlums. It was common practice in the cattle country to drive thousands of cattle up the long trail from the Southwest to the markets. First these markets were in Illinois, Missouri and Arkansas, but later as the railroads pushed west, they were in Abilene, Great Bend and Fort Dodge, Kansas, and finally in Utah, Nevada, Colorado and Wyoming. When the cattle were delivered, payment was made in cash and thousands of dollars were turned over to the rangers because of the lack of banking facilities. Often the rangers were forced to protect the gold and silver in their saddle bags with their lives, and many a life was lost. Sometimes the life was that of a cattleman, sometimes it was the quick-shooting outlaw's. Even the United States Marshals appointed to preserve the law and order often had no other recourse than to shoot it out.

Many folktales have grown up in the Western plains country about the quick justice and lynch law of the men who subdued the wilderness quite as often with a six-shooter as with the plow and ax. Old-timers in Kansas can still recount the exciting adventures "West of Salina," at Dodge City and Abilene. In the parlance of the day "there was no law west of Leavenworth," although common law was theoretically enforceable by territorial governments. Boot Hill Cemetery outside of Dodge City is silent testimonial to the days when gambling, hard liquor and hold-ups were outstanding accompaniments of the pay-off at the end of the cattle trail. Men either went about their own business peaceably or met with prompt and decisive lynch law.

In the silver and gold mining camps, riches were more fabulous than in the cattle country. In a Montana mountain valley ten thousand miners extracted more than ten million dollars' worth of gold in a year. Between Virginia City, Montana, and Salt Lake City there lay a wilderness of four hundred and seventy-five miles. Organized crime grew apace. Clever scoundrels posed as honest men. One of the most active outlaws was Henry Plummer who got himself elected sheriff for two communities, Virginia City and Bannock, Montana. As a law enforcement officer he was naturally able to obtain information about shipments of gold by express. He also purported to be an expert mining engineer. In consequence he and his road agents were able to perpetrate some of the most astounding crimes in American history. While pretending to be in the pursuit of robbers fleeing from justice, he and his "road agents" are known to have killed one hundred and two men in their plunderous activities. Finally the outraged citizens organized a Vigilantes Committee for the purpose of eliminating this road agent band. In short order they executed twenty-four of these early racketeers along with other marauders. These two Montana communities are representative of the general lawlessness which flourished all over the West. On the Pacific coast there were mining camps of similar varieties. Here too crimes were settled for the most part by lynch law which afforded the "popular tribunals" of the period.

In Texas a more highly organized group, the Texas Rangers, fulfilled something of the functions of the popular tribunals of Colorado, Wyoming and California. In Texas the frontier problem was both political and geographic. At first the Rangers were a privately financed organization which aimed to overcome the stealing and the interracial conflicts in an area in which Mexicans, Anglo-Americans and Indians were all striving for supremacy. In 1834 Austin called a meeting of American militia-men to put down Indian uprisings and a force of twenty to thirty full time Rangers was created. These men were soldiers in the saddle, but at the same time they were also illegal agents of the United States government, since Texas was at that time under Mexican rule. These Rangers incidentally became known as the "horse marines" because of their capture of some Mexican vessels.

Following Texas' admission to the Union, the Texas Rangers made continuous war on the Indian tribes. Later during the Civil War the Texas Rangers were subordinated to the demands of the Confederacy and virtually passed out of existence. With the carpet-bag government organized in 1870, Governor Davis sponsored their rebirth in the creation of a state police. Murderers and other felons were rounded up with a notorious amount of lawlessness on the part of the police entrusted with the task. Close upon this upheaval the Texas legislature created two military forces for protection of the frontier. One was the Frontier Battalion to control the Indians to the West, the other the Special Force of Rangers charged with suppressing bandits on the Mexican border. As time passed their duties changed. The great cattle country became a mecca for cattle thieves who were dealt with summarily by the pistol. On the Mexican border bandits were continually stealing sheep, cattle, and saddle horses. Mexico was at the same time in the throes of a revolution and this presented other problems.

With our entry into World War I, the menace of German spies crossing the border from Mexico created new problems, and it must be admitted that the Texas Rangers themselves were guilty of many irregular activities. They virtually took the law into their own hands. Following the war a legislative investigation resulted in the Ranger force being drastically reduced. Frontier problems came to be of little importance as friendly relations grew up with our neighbors to the South. In consequence the Rangers were reduced in 1935 to two mounted companies and a headquarters company. Border troubles are now wholly in the hands of the United States Army and a highway patrol is now assigned to take the Rangers' place in regulating public safety.

Thus briefly we may summarize some of the major characteristics of anti-social behavior on the frontier. With the exhaustion of free lands, marked alterations in our social and economic structure appeared and freedom in its more absolute nature was, so to speak, dethroned. So long as there were new wildernesses to conquer any man with sufficient energy and initiative could make a living. No one bothered much about the general laxities in business honesty and financial integrity and in consequence there was little restriction. If a man felt hampered by competitive forces he could always "go West." Social controls were at a minimum and if the sound of the neighbor's ax seemed menacing he could move further West.

Once free lands were exhausted, despite the numerous places which were sparsely settled, the population seemed nevertheless excessive. Immediately demands arose to restrict immigration. Increasingly the defenses of a pioneer democracy shifted from free land to social legislation. Instead of moving when he heard the sound of the neighbor's ax, the sons of the pioneer demanded, as Turner has pointed out, a muffling of the ax!

Our population has settled down and in consequence innumerable measures have been adopted regulating business, health, sanitation, education and, altogether naturally, conduct. Criminal codes have in fact been so expanded as to include many types of behavior previously considered to be within the prerogative of free men. Bankers, once the most respected men of our economic hierarchy, are now languishing in State and Federal prisons for conduct which was once more or less accepted as common banking practice.

The great increase in our urban population and the enormous increase in the nature and variety of our material culture traits have been additional factors which have promoted the need for social legislation in recent years. That the era of social legislation has not ushered in the millennium but has instead created new crimes by redefining old practices is apparent to the least discerning among us. Even so, social legislation is silent witness to an increase in social consciousness. Such legislation does not implement of itself any automatic uprooting of deep seated patterns, however. When the social historian of the future writes the history of the epic period from 1896 to 1950 he will unquestionably find something naively comic in the American belief that "there ought to be a law" and in their attempts to solve their problems by writing laws without reëducation of the populace in the need for reëvaluating basic patterns of human existence.

For out of our lawless heritage from frontier days many of the culture patterns of present day criminal behavior may be traced. Professor Sutherland startled American business men when he delivered his Presidential address to the American Sociological Society on the White Collar Criminal. This White Collar Criminal, whether he be business man or professional politician, is, I believe, a functional product of our frontier mores, the inevitable by-product of the customs and the habits of a people impatient of restraints and controls. The unorganized social processes of pioneer society have left their cultural residue in the opposition to restrictive legislation, and in the amazingly elastic constructions which have been placed upon governmental regulations. This is no place to digress upon the constructions placed upon "constitutional rights," but it should be mentioned in passing that the constitution which was drawn up with the idea of protecting the submerged individual has been so manipulated that it has become the means of protecting the corporation from governmental regulation "without due process of law." This latter term has been so stretched as to subsume practically any unwanted interference in control of industry.

But let us turn to more recent evidences of the persistence of frontier behavior patterns. A few years ago a former Governor of a Western state now serving in the U. S. Senate gave full pardon to a man serving a sentence for embezzlement because of threats made to the Governor by business friends of the embezzler. Unless he did so these friends promised to "tell all they knew about the Governor." The Governor pardoned the man, and kept the matter from the public, although his conduct was strictly illegal and technically made the Governor an accomplice to the crime.

Rationing, which strikes at the heart of the consumer's habits, has been most laxly enforced in the West. Investigate for yourself if you believe that speed rules or gasoline rationing are enforced in the great open spaces of Western Kansas or Colorado. Lynchings of Negroes have been less frequent in recent years, but lynchings still persist in the South and without penalty for the lynchers.

Obviously it is far from this author's belief that the frontier mores explain all or most of our crime rate. Nevertheless, the frontier culture constitutes an important part of our social heritage and explains much of the American's rejection of and disrespect for formal legislative controls. Unlike our European cousins we have had our most serious frontier problems within our own borders. Perhaps, one might add facetiously, herein is one explanation why crime is writ large in the American mores —just as the mores are written in the lack of social consciousness of our forebears. In Europe, on the other hand, there has been much respect for laws within national boundaries, whereas cultural conflicts have led to war. As Turner has pointed out, ours is a democracy born of free land and such a democracy "strong in selfishness and individualism, intolerant of administrative experience and education and pressing individual liberty beyond its proper bounds, has its dangers as well as its benefits."

28 · Crime in a Discordant Culture

by JAMES MELVIN REINHARDT

The factors contributing to crime and delinquency are varied and complex. The home and its immediate environment have been found to be crucial in determining the behavior patterns of the individual, and criminality can frequently be traced back to faulty family relationships and a bad neighborhood. But in the search for a clearer understanding of underlying causes of delinquent and criminal behavior, the total environment—the culture as a whole— must be taken into consideration. In the following selection, James Melvin Reinhardt, a University of Nebraska sociologist whose major interest is in the field of social pathology, presents a brief but graphic description of the

commercialization of our values and the contradictory demands that our society makes on the individual, and notes
the connection between such a state of affairs and criminal
behavior. [From *Journal of Criminal Law and Criminology*, Vol. 41, May-June 1950, pp. 32-35. Reprinted by
permission.]

MUCH HAS BEEN written about poverty, slums, and parental neglect as
contributory to delinquency and crime. These are important, but they
do not operate in isolation. Rangoon has poverty, Bombay has slums,
and some "Appalachians" neglect their children, but the crime rates are
reportedly low. One interested in the environmental genesis of criminality would do well to look to the confusional behavior inherent in the
wider cultural life. The illegal adventures of the "oversanguine temperament," driven by an extravagant optimism and a feeling of feverish
energy may be attributed to "hypomania," but his prototype can be
found among "legitimate" promoters, even candidates for high office
who achieve wealth and influence by making promises they can not keep.

A half orphan "breaks and enters" on the day following the sale of his
mother's household goods to satisfy the "legitimate" demands of a "loan
shark," whose interest charge is 80 percent; and a young man takes to the
road after his father's little business has been squeezed to death by the
"legitimate" operations of a strong armed competitor.

The human nervous system that gives a baby its laugh is also a nursery
house for grudges, anxieties, and fears. There are no ready-made protective devices against destructive forces from the social world. Hence,
a nervous system with the innate capacity for perpetual renewal gets
tangled up in the behavior variants of the cultural life. This fact is clearly
revealed in the scientific literature from juvenile courts, prisons, and
mental hospitals.

The things we do, for instance, frequently have little moral relation
to the things we say about what people ought to do. The juvenile often
is caught in this "interstitial" zone of conflict, and the emotional consequences are sometimes tragic. This theme is too long to develop here.
Its significance, however, may be illustrated.

The radio, for instance, with all its beneficent achievements is a gen-
erator of emotional conflict. As I see it, the telling failures of the radio
are not in the silly little jingles and pietistic evocations jammed between
"Goodbye" and "Dry Those Tears." These are on the order of self-elimi-
nating skin diseases, and if my little polling technique is worth much,
people don't listen to them anyway. Seven out of ten G. H. fans turn
off or engage the censor for sixty seconds of his program.

The real radio pathology lies deeper. It is in the ingenious devices employed to appropriate sacred institutions, noble professions, moral values, respectable titles, high hopes, and the formative dreams of children to "cheap" commercial ends. It is more than that: it is in the "get rich without work" philosophy made to dazzle the imagination of people—some of them young children—who would otherwise be devoting themselves to learning the basic tasks of life.

Take for instance such lavish displays as the radio wedding ceremonies. The "commercials" are woven into the magic spell created by "tender" music, imaginative descriptions, anticipatory moments animated by touching accounts of the first meeting, falling in love, a marriage proposal, and the little "gives" and "takes" of a "timid" boy and a "blushing" girl.

Again, a cigarette is identified with youth's noblest ambitions, and whether one smokes or not, it is a mark of distinction to have the right brand in the house. It protects the household also against the suspicion of being narrow-minded or lacking in altruism. It is all very wonderful, too. There is no "hangover" and the mayor of the town joins in the crusade. Nothing is forgotten. The beautiful "Ave Maria," as well as not, may be wedged in between the "T-Zone" and the "medicine man."

It isn't enough just to entertain the people in the studio audience either. They must be brought into the act. Young and old alike must tell the world, in unison, that a "treat" is not a "treatment." Beyond this, and for "sententious" reasons, endless amounts of time and energy are expended upon efforts to finish extravagant sentences, add last rhymes to silly quatrains, to guess answers to stupid questions, to name that "song," to identify a voice, and on and anon, "world without end." Perhaps never before has so much been given to so few for so little.

This is bad business. It plows deep into the moral fibre of the social life.

Once upon a time honest work done with dignity and self-respect was a "joy forever." It was considered an elemental aspect of the "American Way." The "American Way" can wait while we "give that woman $1,200 cash." And for what? For nothing more than the astounding disclosure that ". . . The world will not long remember what we say here . . ." was said by the immortal Lincoln at Gettysburg.

The radio of itself is not evil. It is an instrument of power insensitive to how it is used. Commercially sponsored radio programs are not necessarily bad. Perhaps, after all, it is the high level performances that sharpen one's sensitivities to the evils.

Less glaringly, but with fearful effect, these "split" moral "in(de)finitives" expropriate the ends of justice and invade the enchanted place of our most cherished institutions. Here is a young man serving a sentence in a state reformatory for putting his name on a worthless check.

At the time the offense was committed he was a homeless, penniless boy wandering the streets of a strange city. Shortly after he entered the reformatory two young college men attempted to blackmail a wealthy philanthropist. The amount demanded ran into the thousands. These young men were sons of prominent, well-fixed families. The blackmailers never entered a penal institution. The matter was "hushed up" and the education of our blackmailers was hardly interrupted.

What has this to do with our young forger? Nothing at all except for the fact that he is human, and being human has a nursery house for grudges: "They're makin' goats out'a us fellas . . . go straight, my eye . . . !"

So the walls of the reformatory crumble before the on-slaughts of "respectability." On some fine day the warden will knit his brow while the judge of an impartial court of justice sentences a second offender. His chance to reform having gone by default, he enters a penitentiary.

I am not suggesting that this sort of moral conflict in childhood and adolescence is the direct or immediate cause of all or even most crimes. I am suggesting that it has a very important causal relation to criminal behavior and that it bears directly upon problems of prevention and reform. This conclusion rests upon case studies of numerous delinquents and criminals in and out of institutions over a period of several years. In many instances these studies involved intimate and confidential personal interviews which led into the secret places of the heart. Not in a "deep therapy" sense was this done, and it was without the exercise of esoteric symbols. This kind of criminological study reveals many warped and twisted personalities, caught early in a cross-fire of values from which there seemed from the individual's point of view, no legitimate escape. Strangely enough, these unhappy experiences are often shown as the products of "rational" judgments of "respectable" men.

The trouble here inheres in the contradictory nature of our standards of "respectability" and the accustomed techniques used in the efforts to conform to these standards. Thus, in many instances original capacity and basic necessity for "one-ness" within the self hasn't a ghost of a show.

The official whose salary was eight thousand a year, and who banked one hundred sixty-eight thousand through business turned to his own firm, while he sent "petty thieves" to the penitentiary, was a divided self; but he was held together by certain "rationalizations" of "value" inherent in our conflicting culture. It may be shown that the very system of rationalizing that preserves the integrity of the official contributes to the formation of the thief. The "rationalizations" are a form of "Hoyle"; and truth, honesty, thieving, and so forth are defined "according to Hoyle."

Perhaps the chief tragedy in the situation arises from the fact that a considerable proportion of the population is never in the position to act "according to Hoyle." They frequently start life as the children of the poor, handicapped by the lack of family prestige and without any naturally protected stairways to the coveted goals of "respectability." These often beat against impenetrable walls; and failing to gain entrance may take flight to the world of pure imagination where events can be juggled at will; or they may—but rarely in modern society—become submissive patrons of privilege; and again they may, as often they do, seek entrance to the "city" by condemned roads.

Not infrequently the failures already characterized come from homes of wealth and social security. The parents of such children are uneasy and constantly fearful of invasion from the cultural "backyards." These are, of all children, perhaps the most unfortunate. The parental attempts to keep them in rigid exclusiveness tends to cut off all avenues to normal childhood enjoyments. In such instances children may seek outlet in the "byways and hedges." But it is done, at first, quietly and on the sly. These children of the "byways" are *real* children to the cramped child of the "reprimand." They may use rough language on occasion. They are not always particularly clean, but they know how to get down to fundamentals. So our sheltered and hedged-in child slips away to play. He slips home again by the back door. Somewhere down under the periphery of consciousness brews a rebellion. The strain of a divided-self becomes too heavy to bear. He finally throws off the yoke of "exclusiveness" and openly flaunts the badge of "irrespectability." Specialists are called in to examine the child—not the parents and not the community. Finally, a perfectly good juvenile court judge sends him back to his "perfectly good" parents, but he doesn't stay. He goes "the way of all flesh" and there is talk about a "black sheep."

29 · Urbanization and Crime

by MARSHALL B. CLINARD

Urban life, with its impersonality of relationships, its anonymity, its rapid change, its cultural heterogeneity, its conflicting moral codes, and other disturbing factors, has been recognized for some time as more conducive to crime than the relatively simple rural mode of life. In the following article, Professor Marshall B. Clinard summarizes the results of a research study he made with the aim of deter-

mining the relationship between urbanization and crime—
particularly crime against property. ["The Process of Urbanization and Criminal Behavior: A Study of Culture Conflicts," *The American Journal of Sociology*, Vol. XLVIII,
No. 2, Sept. 1942, pp. 202-213. Reprinted by permission.
Footnotes omitted.]

SEVERAL WRITERS have recognized that there are quantitative differences
in the incidence of crime in areas of varying degrees of urbanization.
Scientific explanations for this variation, however, have been largely of
an *a priori* nature, since there has been little empiric research on the
factors operating in the violation of legal norms in different types of societies. Durkheim was one of the first writers to state clearly that urbanization inevitably results in a greater amount of crime; and such a position has, in part, been validated by later research which, however, has
usually been restricted to one extreme of the continuum of urbanization, namely, the great metropolitan areas. While these studies shed
much light on the relation of the phenomenon of urbanization and personal disorganization, they have been complicated by the clash of New
and Old World standards of behavior in our great cities. Explanations
for the criminal behavior of persons from rural areas do not necessarily
follow from such findings, even though often tacitly assumed to do so.

This research study sought explanations for the relation of urbanization to property crimes. It suggested, as a general hypothesis, that the
relative incidence of urban features of life accounts for the differential
in crime rates of different areas, and it sought to test various hypotheses
relating to the presence of urban characteristics among offenders from
areas of varying degrees of urbanization. The specific hypotheses tested
involved the incidence of such urban characteristics as mobility, impersonal relations, differential association, nonparticipation in community
organizations, organized criminal culture, and a criminal social type in
the life-experience of offenders from areas of varying degrees of urbanization.

In order to test these various hypotheses, secondary sources were
utilized, and an intensive study was made of a group of offenders resident in the Iowa Men's Reformatory. The interest was not in Iowa as
such, but rather in a selection of offenders who were from a uniform cultural area, which meant that the relationship between urbanization and
crime could be more adequately controlled.

In addition to secondary sources, primary research data were obtained
by means of 200 detailed questionnaires and 116 life-histories. Rapport
was established with each offender during several private interviews.
Because of the care with which relations were established and main-

tained, as well as for various other reasons, it is felt that the data obtained were reliable. In the statistical analyses extensive use was made of chi-square tests, the coefficient of contingency T, and percentage distributions.

The 200 offenders in this study were assumed to be a representative sample of a larger group of 378 men between seventeen and twenty-nine years of age, inclusive, who were white, had been born in Iowa, and had been sentenced to the reformatory between July 1, 1938, and September 1, 1940, for a property offense. In general, the group in this study was found to be of native-born parentage and with some high-school education. These 200 offenders were classified into three categories of urbanization, 60 from areas of slight urbanization (farm), 52 from moderately urbanized areas (village), and 88 from areas of extensive urbanization (city). These categories designated, respectively, open country and places of less than 50 population, places of from 50 to 4,999 population, and, finally, those over 5,000 population. These divisions were assumed to represent ways of life, the most personal intimate relationships being characteristic of the farm. Each offender was classified according to his major type of residence during the period from six until twenty-one years of age instead of by the last residence, as has been frequently done in other studies.

Although the degree of urbanization actually operated as a control factor, an additional control of farm and village non-offenders was added. The control group consisted of 98 University of Iowa undergraduate students from areas of slight and moderate urbanization and 10 farm high-school graduates, all selected as comparable to the offenders in sex, race, age, nativity, and economic status. While no group of persons could ever be perfectly matched, it is felt that this group afforded a fair degree of control in connection with the hypotheses studied.

MOBILITY

The rural offenders were found to have had extensive contacts outside of their home communities, and their mobility, as measured by changes in locality and frequency of outside contacts, was greater than that of the nonoffenders. The farm and village offenders had a significantly larger number of residences, had shorter average residences in one community, and had spent a smaller proportion of their lives in the communities they called their "home towns." The rural offenders seemed to develop a conception of themselves as not attached to a community and a conception of others that was impersonal. The parents of these farm and village offenders, however, exhibited a number of stable characteristics, indicating that their offspring were participating in a different type of social world, a more mobile society, than the one in which the parents interacted.

The offenders from areas of slight and moderate urbanization considered themselves mobile persons. This conception of themselves is of paramount importance in explaining their behavior in a world in which mobility is becoming general. Mobility, facilitated by the auto, gave the rural offenders participation in a larger impersonal world and, in a sense, emancipated them from their home communities and made them dissatisfied with these. The more important contacts of the rural offenders were largely in the area outside their home communities; their attitudes toward other persons tended to be impersonal.

Among the rural offenders the place where the crime occurred was generally not the same as the residence of the offender. The crime frequently was committed in another community in order (1) to avoid detection by those who, because of personal contacts, knew the offender; (2) to secure opportunity for the crime; or (3) in order not to commit an offense against someone whom the offender knew. In the everyday life of those living in the city the opportunity is present for an impersonal relationship in committing a crime, whereas in farm and village communities it must be sought.

COMMUNITY PARTICIPATION

The rural offenders did not participate so frequently in community organizations and groups as did rural nonoffenders. Thus the impersonality in the lives of the farm and village offenders seemed to be not only a reflection of mobility but seemed to be due also to a lack of general participation in community organizations. A large percentage of offenders from areas of both limited and moderate urbanization—36.7 and 21.2 per cent, respectively—were found to have participated in no community organizations. Both farm and village offenders participated in significantly fewer organizations than did nonoffenders; the farm offenders' average number of years' participation was significantly smaller; and there was significantly less group leadership. This seemed to indicate the presence of urban phenomena in the life-careers of the rural offenders.

DIFFERENTIAL ASSOCIATION

Networks of criminal relationships were found to vary directly with the amount of urbanization of the areas from which the offenders came.

In rural areas, as compared with the interstitial areas of a more urban culture, there was a comparative absence of continuity in the criminal culture. The contacts of rural offenders with criminal norms had been either entirely absent or of an occasional or fortuitous nature. The simple techniques of many crimes, such as forgery, committed by rural offenders suggested that prior association with differential criminal norms was not always necessary. Delinquent gangs, where present among farm and village offenders, were of a loosely organized character in comparison with city gangs.

Shaw and Thrasher have emphasized the general importance of the relation of gangs to criminal behavior. In this study, however, delinquent gangs did not appear to be an important factor in the lives of farm offenders, although they were of some importance among village offenders. Among city offenders gangs played a very important role. There appeared to be a definite relationship between the degree of urbanization and the extent of differential association with criminal norms. Moreover, the age at which differential association took place decreased with an increase in the degree of urbanization. This fact is of great importance in explaining the differences in the incidence of crime in rural and urban areas, for the volume and duration of differential association seem closely associated with the development of a criminal social type.

There was a comparative absence of discussions of gangs or of crime in general in the life-histories of the farm offenders—a fact not true of the city offenders. In addition, no significant differences were found in regard to the incidence of boys' gangs in the life-experiences of farm and village offenders and nonoffenders. This seemed to indicate that identification with a group of boys who stole was as important as contact with the differential association.

There was a significant difference between the three groups in the number of partners which the offenders had in their first property arrest. Approximately two-thirds of the farm, one-half of the village, and one-third of the city offenders had no partner. Where the offender had a previous arrest, no significant difference was found between these groups in the number of partners in the last offense. A comparison of the partners' arrest records showed no significant difference either on the first or on the last property arrest. Similarly, there was no significant difference among the offenders with respect to association, prior to the first property offense, with anyone who had been arrested or had served time. As in the case of the other above factors, however, this lack of significance may have been due to the size of the sample. Nevertheless, certain percentage comparisons stood out, for almost half of those from areas of slight urbanization had not had differential contacts of this nature, as compared with slightly over one-third of the village offenders and less than one-third of the city offenders. There was, moreover, a very significant difference in comparing the offenders with the farm and village control groups. Some 85 per cent of the farm and village control groups had never known anyone with a delinquent record, while approximately one-half of the offenders from these same areas had had some contact of this type.

The life-histories indicated that the effects of gossip and other informal controls on the offenders may be a probable explanation for the slight continuity of crime in rural areas. There was a continuous observation of the rural offenders by farmers and villagers, and there were attempts to restrict contacts of others with these deviants. This informal social control tended to destroy the continuity of criminal culture in rural areas. It is difficult for crime to flourish without impersonal disorganized areas such as are found in areas of extensive urbanization.

CRIMINAL SOCIAL TYPE

In the heterogeneity of the urban community the existence of a criminal culture was found to produce a criminal social type, characterized by criminal techniques, criminal argot, and a definite progressive criminal life-history. Offenders from areas of slight or moderate urbanization, in contrast to city offenders, were not definite criminal social types. The rural offenders did not conceive of themselves as criminals; the more urbanized offenders did.

At the time of their first property arrests, offenders from areas of slight and moderate urbanization were considerably older than offenders from areas of extensive urbanization. Over 90 per cent of the farm offenders were first arrested after they were seventeen years of age, while 60 per cent of the city boys were arrested before this age. This late entrance into delinquent behavior appears, in part, to be a product of differential association, which varies with different degrees of urbanization. A similar situation was true for the age at the first property conviction or commitment, although this fact might possibly have been related to differences in the judicial process in less urbanized areas. There was a decided difference in the number of total previous arrests as well as property arrests. In fact, more than twice as many of the farm and village offenders had never been arrested for property offenses prior to their present offenses, as had the city offenders. Data on the number of previous incarcerations revealed a similar conclusion. It is quite likely that the incarcerations of urban offenders, particularly at an early age, had important consequences in the development of criminal attitudes

Crimes having complex techniques were found to be correlated with the incidence of urbanization. The seriousness of the predatory crimes which the offenders committed increased with the extent of urbaniza tion. Such serious predatory crimes as robbery were seldom perpetrated by the rural offenders, indicating a lack of full development in crimina techniques. Thus, the crimes in which those from areas of slight urban ization engaged, in both their first and their last offenses, were of a comparatively simple nature, such as larceny and forgery. Particularly because the latter type of crime is simple in technique, it appears gener ally unnecessary to assume prior differential association with this type of crime. Offenders from areas of moderate and extensive urbanization had a larger percentage of burglary and robbery cases, the figures for robbery increasing among the city boys as they continued to engage in criminal ity. Similarly, more progression in the types of crimes was found with the increasing urbanization of the areas from which the offenders came The use of criminal argot was characteristic of the life-histories of city offenders. As compared with those from areas of slight and moderate urbanization, offenders from the cities had had extensive contacts with other deviant social types, such as prostitutes, "pimps," racketeers, and "fences." This indicated the criminal division of labor, as well as the general social disorganization permeating areas of extensive urbanization

A characteristic of the rural offenders was that they did not regard their actions as crimes or themselves as criminals. It is obvious that thi is very significant in accounting for the differences in crime rates be tween areas of varying degrees of urbanization. The life-histories seemed to substantiate a hypothesis that this noncriminal conception of self i an outgrowth of a limited process of urbanization. To develop a crimina social type there must be in existence some organized criminal culture which is at least tolerated in the area and through which deviant norm are transmitted. Criminal techniques, argot, and progressive association with others having criminal associations are necessary for a crimina career; and without their presence an offender may commit a crime in the legal sense without being a criminal in a sociological sense. The divi sion of labor and heterogeneity of standards of an urban world make possible the existence of a criminal culture independent of the tradi tional culture. Where there exist the opposite characteristics of urbaniza tion, such as general homogeneity of culture and more general persona behavior, it is difficult to identify one's self with a criminal world. Rural offenders are not criminal social types, owing to the fact that in areas of limited urbanization there have been few opportunities to become iden tified with a separate criminal culture.

Among village offenders, in comparison with farm offenders, there was less of the fortuitous element in the criminal act, more extensive criminal differential association, and more of a realization of committing an act against society. In comparison with city boys, however, there was still a marked difference. In fact, the difference was so distinct that one could not call village offenders definite criminal social types. The reason appeared to lie in the differences in the nature of the society from which they came. Although village offenders had become mobile and impersonal, they had continued to maintain a partial feeling of the power of intimate relationships which is the social control of the small town. The fact that they came from traditionally law-abiding families and that they were known in their communities tended to lessen their feelings of being at war with society, as was true in the case of offenders from more heavily urbanized areas. The village offenders did not steal for a living, and the gangs to which they belonged were not so rigidly organized. In brief, they possessed only in an embryonic state the features which criminal social types in areas of extensive urbanization exhibit in their fully developed state.

Definite organized criminal behavior was the outstanding characteristic of offenders from more heavily urbanized areas. They felt that they were playing a criminal role in society and that they were more or less at war with the police. This feeling was not shared by farm and village offenders. Furthermore, large urban communities furnished the city offender with greater mobility and impersonality than was present in the life-experiences of farm and village offenders. Organized criminal gangs appeared to have been instrumental in shaping the city offenders' conceptions of themselves. The stories of the gang, its members, and their activities associated with the gang played a prominent part in their life-histories, indicating that they had come to identify themselves with the gang. Their associations with these gangs usually started at an early age, and there was a developmental process involving progression in criminal techniques and the acquisition of a criminal argot, until crime finally became an occupation—the exclusive method of earning a living. Moreover, the life-histories of the city offenders revealed, in many of their families, a tradition of criminality and general disorganization, which contrasted with the more stable family life of the village and farm offenders.

It is suggested as a hypothesis that the continued existence of an organized criminal culture alongside the traditional culture requires the impersonality of a large population. Otherwise, informal social control would destroy the criminal culture. The life-histories revealed an almost exclusive impersonal control of the city offenders by the use of law rather than by the informal sanctions which still appeared to exert a partial influence on rural offenders. Moreover, the activities of a single city offender are probably more numerous than the combined criminal pursuits of many farm offenders. This probably accounts largely for the quantitative differences in urban and rural crime. If one considers the meaning of the act to the offender, rather than the legal consequences, this quantitative difference would undoubtedly be even more striking.

It may be concluded that, the more individuals in rural areas secure a conception of themselves as partly emancipated from the controls of their home communities, the more opportunities there will be for the development of a behavior situation suitable for delinquent acts. The influence of urban desires will increasingly shift the attention of many rural youths to impersonal relations and also bring about contacts with differential behavior patterns. There will be increasing opportunities for the commission of crimes in an impersonal situation. It appears, however, that, as long as there exists a predominant measure of personal relations and informal social control in the farm and village areas, it will be impossible for a separate criminal culture to exist as is characteristic of large urban areas. For this reason it appears almost impossible to develop criminal social types in rural areas. Without the presence of criminal social types the volume of crime committed by rural residents will continue to be small as compared with that in urban areas. This does not, of course, rule out the possibility that offenders from large cities may increasingly commit criminal acts in rural areas. Cities up to now, however, have offered more fertile fields for crime, and the small town and farm appear unlikely to furnish equal opportunities.

30 · The Rural Criminal

by MARSHALL B. CLINARD

Although almost half of our population resides in rural communities and crime there is by no means negligible, criminological research has been almost entirely limited to the urban areas. Little is known about the rural law breaker. Is he a distinct type? Is he different from his urban counterpart, and, if so, how does he differ? These questions Professor Marshall B. Clinard sought to answer in a study of rural crime. ["Rural Criminal Offenders," *The American Journal of Sociology*, Vol. L, No. 1, July 1944, pp. 38-45. Reprinted by permission. Footnotes and table omitted.]

THE RURAL OFFENDER has been largely neglected in criminological research. While there have been numerous quantitative studies of the incidence of crime in urban and rural areas, very little interest has been displayed in the rural offender, criminal research being largely confined to those from urban areas. Consequently, nearly all generalizations in recent surveys of criminology should be qualified as "urban," even though the 1940 population of the United States was about one-half rural by the Census definition. The assumption appears to be that rural criminal offenders, even though their number is less than in urban areas, should exhibit characteristics similar to city offenders.

Widely recognized differences between the urban and the rural way of life make it questionable that such criminological propositions, derived from purely urban research, are necessarily applicable to rural society. Yet urban ways of life, brought about by an internal and external process of urbanization, are now entering, tending to replace and to coexist with, the general homogeneous features of rural society. Mobility, new means of communication, and an emphasis on a pecuniary nexus are competing with the traditional features of rural life. The rural type of criminal offender reveals, in part, the nature of the processes which are contributing to the breakdown of the rural type of social organization and its social control.

This paper is an analysis of sixty Iowa Reformatory inmates who came from areas of open country and places of less than fifty population. The research sought to determine the role of (1) mobility, (2) differential association with criminal behavior, and (3) criminal social type and conception of self in the lives of rural offenders.

The major type of residence of all the offenders during the period from six until twenty-one years of age was in rural areas rather than simply the place of last residence. The last residence of 73 per cent of farm boys was on farms and, if places up to five-thousand population are included, the percentage would be increased to 90. The research data were gathered over a considerable period of time by personal interviews, questionnaires, and life-histories. Because of the care with which interview relations were established and maintained and in view of the consistency of the reports, it is felt that reliable data were obtained.

At the time of their commitment to the reformatory, seventeen of the offenders were between the ages of seventeen and twenty-one, twenty-two ranged from twenty-one to twenty-five, and twenty-one were from twenty-five to thirty years of age. Thirty-six of the group had completed the eighth grade, eighteen had some high-school education, and six of them had completed high school. Nearly all were of native Iowa parentage: 70 per cent of the mothers and 66.7 per cent of the fathers. Fifteen per cent of the mothers and 5 per cent of the fathers were born in states adjacent to Iowa, while 5 per cent of the mothers and 11.7 per cent of the fathers were born in some other part of the United States. Only 8.3 per cent of their mothers and 10 per cent of the fathers were foreign born. A small percentage—1.7 for the mothers and 6.6 for the fathers— did not report where their parents were born.

THE ROLE OF MOBILITY

In the life-histories of farm offenders there were more references to events and their own activities outside of, than within, their local communities. One of their main preoccupations in the formative years of their lives was to travel, either within a wide zone around their home communities or to more distant places. Twenty-four of the farm boys had visited six or more other states. Almost one-half had spent an average of more than four weeks away from home since fourteen years of age and before their first arrest, while a little over 10 per cent averaged more than sixteen weeks away from home.

Some of the activity associated with their travels was in connection with such occupations as trucking, construction work, migratory farm labor, or work with a circus or carnival. In other instances there had been nomadic drifting through several states to "see the sights," as they put it. Other mobile activity involved going to distant dances, parties, fairs, and similar activities. It is interesting to note that few of their friends, or the girls with whom they associated, lived in the immediate vicinity of their homes.

One of the most striking facts about farm offenders is that they conceive of themselves as mobile persons. A frequent term which they use in referring to their behavior is "fast." This term appears to be a reflection of what other members of the community thought about their behavior. The offenders, moreover, appeared almost boastful of their emancipation from their homes and of the worldly wise attitudes which they had achieved. The emancipation of the rural offender from his home community and an impersonal conception of the world are exemplified in the following life-history excerpts. With the growth of such feelings it can be assumed that the informal controls and restrictions exercised by a farming community over its members had deteriorated. Since several of these comments refer to their "home towns," located near their farm homes, one can assume that the farm offered even less attraction.

I know there's romance in a seed, as the old saying goes, but before I came in here all the farm meant to me was just a place to go back to when I ran out of money. I preferred trucking because I got to see more country and more people. In other words, I wanted to see how other people lived, and I also liked to work in the factories or at trucking because I could make more money than I could on the farm. And I didn't have to get up and milk a bunch of cows, then work ten hours and milk more cows, like you have to do on most farms. I never had to at home because our farm is small and there isn't any need to, but if you hire out to the general run of farmers you're lucky if you only have to work ten hours. Also I liked to run around nights, and I had more leisure when I drove a truck than I did working on the farm. And another thing, how many good looking girls do you pick up while you're working on the farm? I sure picked up plenty of them when I drove a truck. Also I had a lot of good times at different places in different states that I wouldn't have had if I had stayed on the farm. You can see right now that I lived only in the present in those times, and never gave a thought of the future. When I think of some of the things I done back in those days I can see what a damn fool I was, because at that time all I wanted was a little excitement and a good time.

The men that travel with a circus or any other kind of show are just like I am, they like to travel and see the other towns and states and get around through the country and still make a decent living while roaming. . . . I am tired of the hometown and will stay away from there when I get out. I think when people do lots of moving they get so they aren't attached to any one place.

The most important effect of this mobility was that many of the life-histories written by farm offenders made little mention of persons in an intimate sense. References to persons were generally omitted, and frequently people were considered as objects of value only in so far as such association might benefit them personally. This attitude was particularly true of those whom they knew under impersonal relations, such as tradespeople. An impersonal attitude of this type is not only characteristic of most urban life-histories but also generally true of criminal life-histories, as Burgess has pointed out when he terms them frequently "objective" in type. In the following excerpts from life-histories this attitude appears to be almost superimposed upon and in conflict with, the more traditional intimacy of farm living.

I never give people a thought. I never cared what they thought of me just as long as they didn't say anything.

After living in a small town, or rather on a farm near a small town I was amazed at what I saw in sizes of buildings and the differences in people in a large city and a small town. In the large city they seemed very busy and on the go all the time and never would take time to talk, as where in the little town we would stand for hours on the street corner and chat of things that had happened to some particular person or thing.

I thought forgery was better than any other crime, as I used fictitious names on all checks and was hurting no one except the one who cashed them.

In a small community the commission of a crime may present many problems of recognition which are not present in the impersonal life of the city. In this sample the rural offender's residence and the place of his first property crime coincided in only twenty-nine, or about half the cases, while in 37.4 per cent the site of the crime was over fifteen miles away. Eight, or 13 per cent, were up to fifteen miles from home at the time, and about 6 per cent were transient when their first offenses were committed. At the time of their last offenses only 37.1 per cent of the 35 farm offenders who had more than one property offense, committed crimes in their home towns, while over 57.2 per cent committed crimes, more than, and 5.7 per cent up to, fifteen miles from where they were living. Of those boys who committed their last offenses with associates, about one-fourth indicated that their companions had come from some other community. One may venture to suggest, therefore, that, if new means of communication, such as the auto, did not furnish an opportunity for anonymity, there would be even less crime in rural areas.

Why did we always go outside of town to write the checks? Well, for one thing, the people in my town would know us right away and would not cash them, for the guys that run the stores know me too good. They know who I always work for anyway. The people in the other town sometimes they don't even know you, so I think that's the best idea after all.

The towns I went to cash the checks were G——, A——, F——, L——. They were all within twenty-five miles of home. The reason we went to those towns was because it wasn't very far to drive and we were strangers, so more than likely they wouldn't have been able to identify us if they seen us again. But we were both known well in B—— [home town], from our boxing records. We would surely have been recognized right away, so we were afraid to try it.

DIFFERENTIAL ASSOCIATION WITH CRIMINAL BEHAVIOR

Contrary to the contention of Shaw and Thrasher that delinquency is, in general, intimately related to participation in gangs, we found that 39, or almost two-thirds of the farm boys, had not been associated with groups of boys who stole; and, if this role is restricted to serious thefts, 86.7 per cent had never had such previous association. Very little about gang behavior appeared in their life-histories, indicating that such activity is not prominent in the life-experiences of rural offenders. In those few instances where there was such group behavior it was with a group in town which had little cohesion or continuity, existing on a more or less chance basis.

We couldn't thresh for a couple of days, and so I went to town the next day and ran across some boys, and they asked me if I wanted to go to a celebration with them. I said I didn't care, for I couldn't haul bundles because it rained. And that is how it started. They wrote some checks out that day. Then we went to another one the next day, and then I got started to write some. [He continued to write checks until he was caught.] Well, I never did know how to write a check until the gang showed me how to write the checks, for they wrote most of them and cashed them, too, for I was a little bit scared to cash them. Then after a while I thought it was a pretty good idea of getting a little money on the side, so I wrote two or three and tried it out myself and they cashed them every time. So that is how I got all the information about writing checks.

More often, where differential association occurred, it was with one or two companions rather than gangs. At times the companions were chance acquaintances whom they met in town. In fact, in two or three cases one feels that had the farm boy not met up with a certain companion on a certain day he would never have engaged in criminal activity.

I haven't much to say as to what got me into trouble. It was mostly the wrong people, too much liquor, and my troubles at home. I always blamed it onto my married life. If it had been different I think I would have come out better. My first crime was committed in '38. Me and A—— were in a pool hall one night, and we were fairly drunk. A—— and me were playing pool, and A—— saw a large box of cigarettes and he pushed them out the door and had me drive the car around to the back of the building. He put them in my car, and we took them to another town and sold them. We were picked up later and sentenced for it. I guess I learned what I did about this crime mostly from my pal and other persons.

We got the idea of checks because we had heard of two other boys in my hometown who had got off by paying for the checks, I mean by making the checks good.

In several cases the first criminal behavior was not related to any association with others. A set of unusual circumstances, coupled with a general personal irresponsibility, appears to have been involved in the difficulties. Sutherland has alluded to the "adventitious nature" of some criminal behavior, and Ferri has referred to the "occasional" criminal type. The following two cases are good illustrations of such beginnings in "criminal" behavior.

My crime is hard for me to explain. The man I was working for was a good man but I figured he didn't give me quite a fair deal at the time I was laid up with a broken arm. When I went back to work in the fall the job he gave me didn't pay as much as my former job and he didn't let me work as many hours as some of the other men who hadn't been with him as long as I had. I worked three weeks and quit. I forged a check on him.

It was in 1935 that I was arrested for the first time. I found a pocketbook with around $35 in it and instead of giving it back to the owner I kept it even though there was plenty of identification cards and things in it. Some way or another the man found out that I had found it and had me arrested. When I went before the judge and told him all about it he told me that he thought I needed a lesson.

Considering various possible sources, some differential association with criminal norms, however, was observed in 70 per cent of the farm offenders, which means that among one-third of the rural offenders there was no personal differential association with criminal behavior of any kind. The life-histories indicated that it is doubtful that many of these contacts had any bearing on their subsequent criminal behavior. In forty-two of the sixty cases no one in the immediate family of the farm offenders had ever been arrested (excluding traffic offenses), in ten cases one person had been arrested, while in eight cases two or more family members had previously been arrested. Twenty-seven of the offenders had never known anyone with a criminal record prior to their first arrest, four had known someone who had been arrested, while sixteen knew someone who had also been incarcerated. (Thirteen did not mention this.) Of the twenty-five cases who had a partner in their first arrest, eleven of the partners (44 per cent) had been arrested before, while eight had not. In six cases the status was unknown.

CRIMINAL SOCIAL TYPE AND CONCEPTION OF SELF

The farm offenders did not exhibit the characteristics of a definite criminal social type, as defined by (1) an early start in criminal behavior, (2) progressive knowledge of criminal techniques and crime in general, (3) crime as the sole means of livelihood, and (4) a self-conception of being a criminal. In the first place, their criminal activities started late in life, beyond the age at which basic attitudes are laid down. Almost 90 per cent of the offenders were first arrested after seventeen years of age, and a similarly high percentage was also true of convictions and commitments. . . . One-third had never been committed to an institution until they were twenty-three years of age or older. There is only a negligible difference between these figures and the age distribution of first arrests, convictions, and commitments for property offenses.

Moreover, seventeen of the farm offenders had never been arrested before, twenty had been arrested once, and twenty-one had been arrested two or more times. The arrest record of two was unknown. Almost one-half had never been in a correctional institution of any type before, 28.3 had been in one, and 23.4 had been in two or more before. Twenty-five had never been arrested before for a property offense, nineteen had been arrested once, and sixteen had been arrested two or more times.

A second characteristic of a criminal social type is progressive knowledge of criminal techniques and crime in general. Both of these features were found to be lacking in rural offenders. The offenses which they committed were relatively simple. For example, the first property offense was forgery in 26, or 43.3 per cent of the cases; larceny in 16, or 26.7 per cent of the cases; burglary in 8; and auto theft in 5 cases, while 5 committed other property offenses. In only one instance was robbery the first property offense. An indication of slight progression in criminal patterns was the fact that, among the thirty-five who committed more than one property offense, the predominant crime at the time of their last offenses was still forgery (48.3 per cent), while larceny was 20.0, burglary 14.3, auto theft 18.6, and robbery only 2.9. Other property crimes accounted for the remaining 5.7 per cent of the cases. Three of these offenders restricted themselves to larceny, ten to forgery, twenty to various combinations except robbery, and only two combined robbery with other offenses. The opportunities for a serious crime like robbery are by no means lacking in a rural environment with isolated filling stations and other business establishments. In fact, it is interesting to note that the incidence of bank robbery is generally much higher in rural areas than in cities. Rural areas would offer a farm youth the same opportunities for robbery as for any other crime.

Such terms as forgery, larceny, and auto theft, however, do not accurately describe the same behavior when applied to rural offenders, as compared with city offenders, for the stories of their crimes reveal that the techniques were much simpler than one might expect. The type of forgery in which they engaged is not to be confused with the work of professionals who utilize a variety of complex techniques. Forgery among farm boys simply represents, in most cases, the use of a fictitious name or the name, but not an imitation of the signature, of a relative or employer. Checks were not raised, nor were elaborate techniques used in passing them, such as studied attempts to locate and successfully pass a check on a person of means. Forgery is particularly adapted to rural life where farm offenders cash many checks on their trips to town. One might, in fact, contend that, since many of these so-called forgeries were of a most casual nature, almost accidental in some instances, a significant number of the offenders were not by any means criminal types. One might further suggest that if there were not present the mobility required for check writing or an industrial monetary economy that necessitates such transactions, almost half the rural offenders would not have become involved in trouble.

I didn't have any special way in forging checks, but figured it was easy and quick money and could possibly pay the checks off before getting arrested for it.

It was in June, and I had a big debt to pay, and I was sick in bed and could not work. The folks did not know of my debt, so they helped me on my hospital bill and doctor bill, but it was either pay in or lose my car. And it was a new coupe and had a lot of money in it, so you can imagine how one would feel over his car. Dad had a check come in from someone [for a carload of hogs] that owed him $350.00 and they paid him, and he put it in the bank that did business with me. [He wrote his own checks.] So one day I went uptown and wrote one out on him and paid a payment on the car. So they picked me up.

Similarly, auto stealing did not involve knowledge of any of the techniques commonly associated with this type of activity, such as the selection of a special type of car, intimate acquaintance with car locks, "fences," or car-stripping. Cars were not stolen for money but for personal use, since in the country the status afforded by a car is considerable, and the techniques consisted simply of driving away. Even the selection of a particular car was more or less fortuitous, as the following story illustrates.

The crime I done was a few miles from home. Perhaps I would of done it anywhere, as I had to be at a certain place at a certain time. I wanted to go to a dance, and my folks would not give me any money, so I really didn't care what I done. I had a car, but it was getting fixed and I didn't have the money to pay for it, so I stole my neighbor's car, just to show my folks I was not scared. I told them I was going to do it, but they didn't think I would. I have never thought about any crime as far as that goes. Like breaking into a place is way out of my line. I always was honest. My father is one of the best citizens. I consider him one of the best in that county. The boys I went with never stole anything. I never had any experience stealing cars. Guess it don't take any practice. When a boy I would use dad's car without asking him, but he didn't care. Sometimes he didn't like it very well, but he always got over it somehow.

A third reason why farm offenders are not criminal types is that crime was not their means of livelihood. Criminal behavior was often of a fortuitous nature, embarked upon at a particular moment, as, for instance, for a thrill, when intoxicated, or when short of funds for certain immediate monetary desires. The offenses were not persistent but merely supplemented their regular activity. Moreover, it was interesting to note the almost complete absence of criminal argot in their life-histories. One can assume, because of the general pattern revealed in the life-histories, that even in these cases the limited universe of discourse had been largely acquired by prison experience. Reformatory records disclosed that only one farm offender had used an alias. The life-histories showed practically no evidence of association with prostitutes, racketeers, or fences.

Finally, and most important of all, these facts were borne out by the fact that farm offenders, as compared with those from the city, do not regard their actions as real crimes and do not conceive of themselves as criminals. They do not display organized hostility to the police or society, nor do they display any conception that their acts can be formulated into any consistent criminal life-organization. They do not identify themselves with crime; rather they consider themselves as "reckless" and unattached to traditional ways. It is doubtful whether such behavior can actually be referred to sociologically under the general conception of criminality.

I knew nothing about any type of crime until I came in here, that is, I knew nothing about how much time any kind of crime called for. Maybe if I had of known I would of done something that called for less time. I heard the L— police were wanting me. I went to the police station there, walked in, told them who I was. They acted like they were afraid of me the way they got out their handcuffs and locked me up and I was taken to C— that night where I was sentenced.

CONCLUSIONS

The most important conclusion that has resulted from the study of both statistical data and life-histories is that rural offenders do not regard themselves as criminals or their actions as crimes. What we have as a typical process in the lives of farm offenders is, generally, a moral family background and a rather traditional upbringing, with any delinquency largely restricted to pranks. In occasional cases there has been some participation in petty thefts, but, generally, the connection of these actions to later actions does not appear clear. At the age of approximately seventeen to twenty-five, an increased desire to participate in the wider world outside the local community results in local and more distant mobility, which, together with nonparticipation in community organizations, emancipate the individual from many home ties and offer him contacts of an impersonal nature. He considers himself a mobile person. The possession of things becomes more important than the opinion of others. Status becomes measured in terms of urban standards.

At this stage of his life-career he conceives of himself, and is regarded by others, as reckless and irresponsible. He does not typically associate with delinquent gangs or criminals but rather with those who are like himself. Gradually his life becomes more aimless, until finally an occasion or occasions are present wherein an act is committed which is labeled by society as a crime. This act may be committed in the impersonal milieu of a community other than his own. To the rural offender this act does not make him a criminal, for it only fits fortuitously into his life-scheme. He writes a false check, a very simple action, while he is intoxicated or simply because he needs money at a dance. He borrows an auto of a neighbor when deprived of the family car. He happens by chance upon some boys from town who are setting out to pilfer a store and goes along with them. These actions are crimes, not because of the offender's judgment of them, but rather in the light of the legal reaction. The farm offender has developed some of the attitudes of an urban personality, but he is not a criminal social type.

31 · The Negro and Crime

by GUY B. JOHNSON

The crime rate of the American Negro has been, according to official statistics, consistently much higher than that of the white population. To many uncritical people, this has served as proof of the Negro's great propensity to crime, even of his being inherently more criminal than the white man. A distinguished Negro sociologist of the University of North Carolina discusses here the reasons for the greater frequency of crime among Negroes in this country. [From *The Annals*, Vol. 217, Sept. 1941, pp. 93-104. Reprinted by permission. Some footnotes omitted.]

MOST DISCUSSIONS of Negro crime have been concerned with the biases and the inadequacies of criminal statistics as a measure of the actual criminality of the Negro, or with an "explanation" of the Negro's high crime rates. Sellin has aptly said:

It is unfortunate that the belief in the Negro's excessive criminality has made students of Negro crime expend so much energy in attempts to verify the charge. Attention has thus been diverted from much more fundamental matters, such as the causes of crime and the relationship of the Negro to our agencies of justice.[1]

The present discussion proposes to deal with the problem primarily from the standpoint of the causation of Negro criminal behavior and the relation of the Negro to the administration of justice.

SOME ASSUMPTIONS

We shall assume in this discussion that the most fruitful approach to the question of why social groups may differ in the number or distribution of criminal acts which they commit is to inquire into their social interrelations and into the ways in which their social environments differ. We shall assume, further, that the fundamental causes of crime in the Negro are the same as in any other group and that the simple fact of race is not sufficient in itself to explain any important group differences in criminal behavior. We readily grant the possibility that the Negro differs from the white man in temperament or *psyche*, but we assume that by no stretch of the imagination can such a factor be a primary determinant of the amount or nature of crime. Still further, we shall assume that, in view of the advanced stage of the process of acculturation in the United States, culture conflict arising from the clash of the Negro's African heritage with his European heritage is not vital enough to be regarded as an important causative factor in Negro crime.

The most important fact about the relation of the Negro to American society is his subordinate social status. In the South his social position is so rigidly defined as to constitute a caste position, and even in the North and the West, in spite of a certain amount of equality with respect to "civil rights," the Negro is generally subjected to social ostracism and economic discriminations. An analysis of the role of the Negro's social status in the causation of Negro crime will therefore form the burden of our discussion.

CASTE AND HISTORICAL FACTORS

Of all the ethnic groups that have come to this country, the Negro is the only one to experience the degradation of slavery and a persistent status of subordination. Slavery in a sense dehumanized the Negro. It disrupted his native culture and taught him the rudiments of white

[1] Thorsten Sellin, "The Negro and the Problem of Law Observance and Administration in the Light of Social Research," in Charles S. Johnson, *The Negro in American Civilization* (New York, 1939), p. 451.

civilization, but it did not permit him to develop as a whole man. It prevented the development of three things which are generally considered essential for normal group life: stable family relations, stable economic organization, and stable community life. Furthermore, slavery nurtured a set of habits and attitudes which still afflict many thousands of Negroes. Among these are lack of self-respect, lack of self-confidence, a distaste for hard work, a habit of dependence upon white friends, lack of regard for the property of others, a feeling that "the white folks owe us a living," a distrust of the white man's law, and a tendency to "let tomorrow take care of itself."

Emancipation did not mean the end of caste relations, nor did it mean the beginning of an opportunity for the Negro to compete on even terms with other men in the struggle for existence. His cultural retardation, his social and economic disabilities, must be attributed in large measure to historical factors reinforced by the continuing vicious circle of caste barriers. The difference, then, between the experience of the Negro and the experience of other ethnic groups in American society is not merely one of degree but is actually a difference in kind—a fact which certainly has some connection with the incidence of social conditions which are associated with crime.

CASTE AND ECONOMIC FACTORS

The exact relation of economic factors to crime causation is still in dispute, but there is general agreement that they play an important role either as primary or associated factors. Certainly there is a general expectation that the underprivileged economic classes will contribute unduly to the total amount of delinquency.

Economic factors must not be considered merely in the restricted sense of their relation to crimes against property. Their ramifications extend into every sphere of life. There is the whole question of the effect of being born into a barren, dull, underprivileged, lower-class household, of the effect of this upon the choices which a child can make, of the relation of this sort of environment to the personality, attitudes, and philosophy of life which he will develop.

If economic factors have something to do with crime, it is obvious that the force with which they impinge upon the Negro's behavior is much greater than for any other large group in the population. It goes without saying that the Negro is the Nation's Economic Problem Group Number One. The bulk of Negro wage earners scarcely accomplish the satisfaction of the elemental needs for food, shelter, and clothing. In all sections of the country race prejudice or caste attitudes have conditioned the Negro's jobs and wages, his working conditions, his relation to labor unions, his vocational training, his choice of a place to live, and his use of political power as a protection against exploitation. Comfort, home ownership, job security, and the enjoyment of "the finer things of life" are absolutely out of the realm of possibility for the majority of Negro families. On any scale of economic adequacy or inadequacy—measured, e.g., in terms of number unemployed, number on relief, number in unskilled occupations, number in professional work, income levels—the Negro would have to be rated as from two to four times worse off than the white man.

CASTE AND SOCIAL DISORGANIZATION

If it were possible to compute some sort of objective index of social disorder as a basis for predicting probable crime ratios, there can be little doubt that the index for the Negro would be higher than that for any other large group in the Nation. Economic factors and cultural retardation play their part in Negro personal and community disorganization just as they do for other groups, but there are certain ways in which caste status differentially affects the relation of the Negro community to the larger society. For example, there is the well-known fact, almost as true of the North and the West as of the South, that the Negro cannot live where he pleases. Various immigrant groups have come in, lived a "ghetto" existence for a time, and have "graduated" from these areas. Not so with the Negro. Race prejudice tends to make of him a *permanent* "ghetto" dweller. There is the further fact, particularly true in the South, that the Negro community is virtually without political power and thus cannot obtain an equitable share of the benefits and protection of government.

Since the highest Negro crime rates occur in urban areas, the relation of the city to Negro social disorder is a subject which merits much closer study than it has yet had. Ecological studies have demonstrated the relation of "delinquency areas" to the structure and the growth processes of the city.[2] Disorganized areas are selective in that they are populated by people who occupy the lowest social and economic level, and their relation to the larger urban configuration makes it impossible for them to stabilize, to achieve a moral order or a sense of community *esprit de corps*. Vice, crime, and social disorder become traditional. The Negro

[2] See, for example, Clifford R. Shaw, *et al.*, *Delinquency Areas* (Chicago, 1929), pp. 204-6; and Shaw and McKay, "Social Factors in Juvenile Delinquency," *National Commission on Law Observance and Enforcement, Report on the Causes of Crime* (Washington, 1931), Vol. 2.

is our greatest slum dweller, and because of race prejudice his slums have persisted with little change. When one remembers that nearly 90 per cent of all Negroes in the North and the West are urban dwellers and that in all probability about 90 per cent of these live in or adjacent to disorganized areas, the implications for crime causation are rather startling.

CASTE AND THE ADMINISTRATION OF JUSTICE

Let us bear in mind that the process of the administration of justice is not merely a process which by its unevenness may distort the statistics of crime, but is also an aspect of the caste relationship itself and may therefore have a direct bearing on the causes of Negro crime. In this brief article we can do little more than outline the problem and suggest types of relevant data.

Caste definition of crime. There are many acts which are rarely if ever considered crimes when done by white persons but which are frequently defined as crimes when committed by Negroes. In the South the caste definition of crime has the sanction of both law and custom. Numerous laws concerning segregation, vagrancy, labor, etc., create a wide range of possible "crimes" which Negroes can commit. Capital punishment is applied to Negro offenders with relatively greater frequency than to whites, and it is common knowledge that "first degree burglary" is defined as a capital crime in several states as a threat to Negro offenders who enter a white residence after dark.

Quite aside from specific law, every conflict situation between a white person and a Negro has the possibility of being defined arbitrarily as a Negro crime or of leading up step by step to the commission of an actual offense. Forgetting to say "Mister" to a white man, "looking at" a white woman, entering the wrong waiting room, "sassing" the landlord, disputing a white man's word, taking the wrong seat on a bus or street car,[3] riding in a Pullman car—these are some of the things which may define a dangerous situation. If the Negro persists in being "insolent" or ag-

---

[3] Motor buses and street cars are especially productive of unpleasant incidents because the color line is movable. The law usually provides that Negroes shall fill seats from the rear forward, and drivers may take it on themselves to try to see that no Negro moves forward one row until the rear seat or row is filled. For an example of an offense growing out of this kind of situation in North Carolina, see Charles S. Mangum, Jr., *The Legal Status of the Negro* (Chapel Hill, 1940), pp. 212-13. For a detailed account of a Virginia episode leading to the arrest of a young Negro couple, see Harold Garfinkel, "Color Trouble," *Opportunity*, Vol. XVIII (May 1940), pp. 144-52. Incidentally, this "story" was selected for inclusion in O'Brien's *Best Short Stories of 1940*. Perhaps truth is *stronger* than fiction!

gressive, anything from abusive language to homicide may occur, but whatever occurs is likely to be to his own disadvantage. The exact amount of "crime" arising from violations of caste etiquette is a problem which future research will have to determine. Inspection of southern crime statistics shows relatively few offenses booked under "violation of segregation laws," but the writer is convinced, from years of observation and from illustrative cases obtained from Negro acquaintances, that in the South such cases considerably swell the number of Negro offenses booked under "creating a disturbance on a public vehicle," "resisting arrest," "assault," "felonious assault," "manslaughter," and "murder." [4]

Scapegoats and frame-ups. The status of the Negro, particularly in the South, exposes him to the danger of being blamed for crimes committed by whites and of being framed by white criminals. The following types of situations are known to occur: [5] (1) A white person may commit a crime under such circumstances that suspicion will likely fall upon *some* Negro. A special variety of this is the white man's trick of blackening his face before committing his crime. (2) A white person may deliberately arrange a situation so that the guilt of a *particular* Negro will almost inevitably be taken for granted. Sometimes the scheme includes slaying the Negro so as to clinch his guilt and to keep him from talking. (3) A white woman may try to avoid the consequences of sexual delinquency by raising the cry that she has been raped by a Negro.[6] A man-hunt ensues and a Negro is "identified." The Negro may be lynched or legally convicted, while the woman obtains a legal abortion and thus saves her "honor." Sometimes her paramour is a Negro. (4) A neurotic woman may "imagine" that she has been raped by a Negro, or

[4] Such cases do occur in the North, but probably with much less frequency. Last year the writer encountered an instance in an Ohio city. A young Negro woman was standing in line to try to purchase theater tickets to "Gone with the Wind." A young white man approached her, saying, "Why don't you get out? You know you are not wanted here," and gave her a shove. She tried to stand her ground, but in a moment was arrested for "creating a public disturbance." Our investigation convinced us that the theater manager, wishing to impress upon Negroes the fact that they were not welcome, deliberately provoked the affair.

[5] For various examples, see Monroe N. Work (Ed.), *Negro Year Book* (1931-32), pp. 289-92; (1938-39), p. 147; and "Burnt Cork and Crime," a pamphlet issued by the Southern Commission on Interracial Co-operation, Atlanta, n. d. (copyright, 1935).

[6] The notorious Ben Bess case is a good example of the injustice which can be done to Negro men by white women. In 1928 a South Carolina white woman confessed that she had sent an innocent Negro, Ben Bess, to prison on a false charge of rape. Her confession was itself a violation of caste patterns, and pressure was put upon her to get her to repudiate her statement. Finally, in 1929, Bess was pardoned. He had served thirteen years in prison! See *Negro Year Book* (1931-32), p. 292.

she may interpret some innocent action as an insult or "attack" by a Negro.

The exact incidence of these situations will probably never be known because they come to light only when they *fail* to work. It is significant however, that such things do happen, and to the extent that they succeed they are an absolute exaggeration of the Negro's *actual* criminality

The police. The police have an especially strategic position in the administration of justice. Variations in their activities can produce fluctuations in arrest statistics which have no relation to the number of offenses actually committed. By mistreatment or brutality toward any group or class of people they can even provoke or stimulate the commission of crime. The Negro is more exposed to the misuse of police power than any other group.

The police custom of arresting Negroes on slight suspicion or of staging mass "roundups" of Negroes is definitely related to the Negro's lack of security and his inability to exert pressure against such abuses. Police pretty generally feel that in making arrests, handling witnesses, and obtaining confessions they can use brute force against Negroes with impunity. In some places in the South, law officers and magistrates are engaged in a sort of "racket" which involves the rounding up of Negroes on trivial charges for the sake of earning fees. More commonly, however, the police wink at a good deal of petty crime and disorder in Negro communities. Their attitude is: "We can't attempt to control everything that goes on among the Negroes. As long as they keep their hell-raising to themselves and don't let it get too noticeable, we'd rather leave them alone."

In the interplay of behavior between the police and Negro suspects there is a reciprocal expectation of violence.[7] The police too quickly use gun or club, and Negroes—especially those with reputations as "bad niggers"—are keyed to a desperate shoot-first-or-you'll-get-shot psychology. Thus what starts out to be merely a questioning or an arrest for a misdemeanor may suddenly turn into violence and a charge of murder against the Negro.

The experiences of Negroes as victims of police mistreatment or as victims of unpunished depredations within the Negro community must give rise to considerable bitterness and a feeling that the law is unjust These experiences and attitudes deserve careful study, for they are undoubtedly contributory to both the real and the apparent criminality of Negroes.

The courts. The faults and the weaknesses of our courts are well

[7] In this connection, see H. C. Brearley, *Homicide in the United States* (Chapel Hill, 1932), pp. 65-68, 101-2.

known, particularly with respect to the functioning of juries and prose-cutors and the existence of class differentials in the disposition of criminal cases. It is further well known that the Negro's chance of access to bail, to efficient legal counsel, to payment of cash fines instead of jail terms, to appeals, and to all other legal advantages, is on the average very much lower than the chance of the white man. When a Negro goes into court he goes with the consciousness that the whole courtroom process is in the hands of "the opposite race"—white judge, white jurors, white attorneys, white guards, white everything, except perhaps some of the witnesses and spectators. Moreover, in the lower courts, especially in the South and in Negro intraracial cases, Negro defendants and witnesses are frequently subjected to gross insult and are made the butt of various sorts of horseplay and coarse humor. Conditions such as these undoubtedly affect the statistical picture of crime, the efficiency of law enforcement, and the attitudes and motives which enter into the causation of crime.

Discussions of Negro crime almost inevitably get around to the question of whether Negro offenders are more readily convicted and whether they are given longer sentences than whites. It is impossible to obtain a clear-cut answer from judicial statistics at present, for these statistics are especially weak for the southern states and they rarely present us with the necessary data, namely, the details of dispositions by offense, race, and sex. Furthermore, the evidence drawn from such compilations as have been made is sometimes confusing and contradictory. For example, if a national compilation [8] of length of sentences by race for ten important offense categories shows that the average definite sentence for Negroes is actually lower than for whites in six of the ten categories, what is one to think when one feels positively that there *are* racial differentials in the dispositions of cases in the courts? The answer, we believe, is not as difficult as it might seem at first glance, and at this point we wish to present a hypothesis and some supporting data.

Our hypothesis is simply that differentials in the treatment of Negro offenders in southern courts do exist but are obscured by the fact that conventional crime statistics take into account only the race of the *offender*. If caste values and attitudes mean anything at all, they mean that offenses by or against Negroes will be defined not so much in terms of their intrinsic seriousness as in terms of their importance in the eyes of the dominant group. Obviously the murder of a white person by a Negro and the murder of a Negro by a Negro are not at all the same kind of murder from the standpoint of the upper caste's scale of values,

---

[8] See, for example, *Prisoners in State and Federal Prisons and Reformatories, 1931 and 1932*, Bureau of the Census (1934), Table 19, p. 21.

yet in crime statistics they are thrown together. Therefore, instead of
two categories of offenders, Negro and white, we really need four
offender-victim categories, and they would probably rank in seriousness
from high to low as follows: (1) Negro versus white, (2) white versus
white, (3) Negro versus Negro, (4) white versus Negro. It is our contention that, in the South at least, the Negro versus Negro offenses are
treated with undue leniency, while the Negro versus white offenses are
treated with undue severity. There are complicating factors, of course,
such as sex, age, "goodness" or "badness" of the Negro offender, and
the interest of white persons for or against the offender, but on the
whole, if our hypothesis is correct, the differentials which we have suggested should show up in mass statistics based on offender-victim categories.

The probability that Negro intraracial offenses are treated with greater
leniency than Negro interracial offenses has been mentioned by numerous writers, but no one has offered any definitive quantitative data on
the subject. A thorough test of the hypothesis which we have sketched
involves tremendous difficulties, because ordinary judicial statistics are
of no use for this purpose. However, we have been able to secure some
data which serve to check the hypothesis in a preliminary way with respect to one very important offense, namely, homicide. Table 1 presents
data by offender-victim groups on the dispositions of murder indictments [9] in Richmond, Virginia, 1930-39, in five counties in North Carolina, 1930-40, and in Fulton County, Georgia, for the twenty-month
period from February 1938 through September 1939.[10]

One thing which stands out in Table 1 is the preponderance of Negro
in-group murders and the relatively small number of interracial murders. Computing percentages from the first column, one sees that Negro
versus Negro cases account for 88 per cent of the murder indictments in
Richmond, 91 per cent in Fulton County, Georgia, and 75 per cent in
the North Carolina counties. The differences in the per cent convicted
in the N–N and the W–W groups are not consistent, for in the North
Carolina series the per cent convicted in the N–N group is actually
higher than in the W–W group. However, the conviction rates in the
N–N groups are consistently lower than in the N–W groups. Perhaps
the most striking thing as far as sentences are concerned is the tendency
not to apply the death or life sentences to the N–N convictions. Thus

[9] Cases of "manslaughter by automobile" have been excluded.
[10] Detailed analysis of these and other data will be presented in a forthcoming article
on the Negro and homicide, to be published in *Social Forces*. Collecting data of this
sort is an arduous task involving use of trial records, indictments, warrants, and
sometimes newspapers, as well as interviews with court clerks and police. . . .

TABLE 1—DISPOSITIONS OF MURDER INDICTMENTS, BY RACE OF OFFENDER AND VICTIM

(Abbreviations: N = Negro; W = White; N–W = Negro versus White, etc.)

Place and Offender-Victim Category	Total Indictments	Nol Prossed or Acquitted	CONVICTED		SENTENCES					PER CENT OF TOTAL CONVICTED		
			Number	Per Cent	Death	Life	20 Years to Life	10 to 19 Years	Under 10 Years	Life or Death Sentence	Less than 20 Years	Less than 10 Years
Richmond, Va.												
N–N	194	53	141	72.6	0	8	31	43	59	5.6	72.2	41.8
N–W	5	0	5	100.0	0	5	0	0	0	100.0	0	0
W–W	20	5	15	75.0	1	3	3	1	7	26.6	53.3	46.6
W–N	1	0	1	a	0	0	0	0	1	0	a	a
Total	220	58	162	73.6	1	16	34	44	67	10.5	68.5	41.3
Five N. C. Counties												
N–N	247	46	201	81.4	11	1	38	46	105	5.9	75.1	52.2
N–W	19	2	17	89.5	6	2	4	0	5	47.0	29.4	29.4
W–W	61	19	42	68.9	8	2	8	2	22	52.6	57.1	52.4
W–N	3	1	2	a	0	0	0	1	1	0	a	a
Total	330	68	262	79.4	25	5	50	49	133	11.4	69.5	50.7
Fulton County, Ga.												
N–N	87	21	66	75.8								
N–W	1	0	1	a			Details omitted because of small number of cases					
W–W	5	0	5	100.0								
W–N	2	2	0	a								
Total	95	23	72	75.8								

ᵃ Per cent not shown because of small number of cases.

in Richmond, of 141 N–N slayers convicted, not one received the death penalty and only 8 (5.6 per cent) received life sentences. In the North Carolina series, of 201 N–N slayers convicted, 11 received the death penalty and one a life sentence, or a total of 5.9 per cent for these two types of sentences. The contrast between these sentences and the sentences given to the N–W slayers is striking. If the per cent receiving death or life sentences is a good index of severity, the data fit neatly into our ranking of offenses as stated above, with the exception that in North Carolina the proportion of W–W slayers receiving these penalties is a bit higher than the proportion of N–W slayers receiving them. If the per cent receiving sentences of less than 20 years is a fair index of general leniency in sentences for murder, the data again tend to bear out our hypothesis. If the per cent receiving sentences of less than 10 years be used as an index of extreme leniency, the picture is not so clear-cut. The differences between N–N slayers and N–W slayers remain, but the W–W group apparently has as good a chance as the N–N group of drawing these extremely light sentences. However, the fact cannot be disputed that the number of Negro in-group slayers is relatively very large and that the majority of them escape the more severe sentences and thus have a high expectation of regaining their freedom. To a considerable extent they can literally "get away with murder" if they kill other Negroes.

Table 2 pursues the problem a bit further. It deals with death sentences for murder in North Carolina for the period 1933-39 and the extent to which they are actually executed. When the data are tabulated merely by race of offender they show that 71.6 per cent of the Negroes and 69 per cent of the whites get executed. But when they are tabulated by offender-victim groupings the picture is different, for 80.5 per cent of the Negro versus white offenders are executed, as against only 64.4 per cent of the Negro versus Negro offenders.

TABLE 2—DEATH SENTENCES AND EXECUTIONS FOR MURDER
IN NORTH CAROLINA, 1933-39

Offender Group	Sentenced	Commuted	EXECUTED Number	Per Cent
Race of Offender Only:				
Negro	81	23	58	71.6
White	42	13	29	69.0
Race of Offender and Victim:				
N–N	45	16	29	64.4
N–W	36	7	29	80.5
W–W	41	13	28	68.3
W–N	1	0	1 [a]	—

[a] This was a very exceptional execution. It created much comment and was said to be the first such case in the state since Reconstruction days. It involved a particularly brutal murder of a respectable old Negro by a low-class white man, and there was strong public sentiment in favor of the execution.

The data presented here point toward a partial confirmation of our hypothesis, at least in so far as the crime of murder is concerned. Certainly they point toward a fruitful area for further research, and they suggest very strongly that judicial statistics would be far more interesting as well as more useful if a number of courts could be persuaded to experiment with racial offender-victim records.

Studies of less serious offenses than murder would probably show more clear-cut evidence of extremes of leniency in Negro in-group offenses. The implications with regard to the relation of the courts to the causation of Negro crime are clear. The courts, like the police, are dealing out a double standard of justice. Numerous Negro intraracial offenses probably go unpunished or are punished so lightly that offenders feel a real contempt for the law, while the certainty of severe punishment in Negro versus white cases cannot help but make the Negro feel that justice is not entirely color-blind. Undue leniency gives comfort to the disorderly and criminal element, promotes recidivism, and nurtures careers of crime. There is the further implication that if these differentials are very slight in the North, as seems likely, then northern statistics of Negro crime reflect actual Negro criminality in the North better than southern statistics reflect actual Negro criminality in the South, and the statistics are therefore not safe indices of regional differences.

Prison experience. There can be no doubt that jails and prisons are to some extent breeding places for crime. Prison systems in the South are especially backward, and the caste position of the Negro exposes him to the worst which prison experience has to offer. Segregation of prisoners opens the way for all sorts of differentials in accommodations and treatment. The lack of institutions for women and juvenile Negro offenders, the herding together of youthful offenders and hardened criminals, and the turning loose of numerous defective or insane prisoners because of lack of accommodations are all directly related to the crime potential of the Negro group. If there is hard, backbreaking work to be done, it is taken for granted that Negro prisoners will do it. The chain-gang system, which is still used in most of the southern states for highway work, is particularly hard on Negro prisoners. Terrible "accidents," such as the burning of twenty men in a truck cage because they were trying to warm themselves by setting fire to some gasoline, or two convicts' suffering the amputation of their feet after they were frozen during solitary confinement in a cage on a cold night, have a way of happening to Negro convicts almost exclusively. Guards are white, of course, and they share the prejudices of their race. Most of them in their dealings with Negro prisoners are all too quick to use the lash, to use solitary confinement on starvation diet, and to shoot to kill.

There is every reason to believe that the prisons "graduate" an unusually high proportion of Negroes who have been brutalized and have become hopelessly embittered toward society in general and the white man in particular. In this connection it is important to remember that relatively more Negroes than whites get exposed to the "educative" influences of jail, chain gang, and prison for the simple reason that they are unable to escape this experience by paying cash fines.

Release from prison. Aside from execution, death in prison, and escape, prisoners may be released by serving out their time, by being pardoned, and by being paroled. Most Negro prisoners probably serve out their time, with certain allowances for good behavior. But since many Negroes who have committed serious crimes are serving light sentences because their crimes were against other Negroes, there is a quick turnover, so to speak, of prisoners who are potentially dangerous. This would be a factor making for recidivism among Negroes.

As for pardons, Negroes do not share equitably for the simple reason that as a rule they cannot exert the amount of political pressure which all too frequently is needed in obtaining a pardon. There is some evidence that Negroes are discriminated against in the use of parole as a method of release and rehabilitation. This fact, of course, might actually tend to reduce recidivism by reducing the span of freedom of individual offenders. Much more important for our present purposes is the question of the *selection* of such Negro prisoners as *are* given the benefit of parole. Are they selected with a view to the best interests of the parolee and of society? Our general observations point to a decided negative answer. Too many cases fit into the following pattern: The sporty Negro butler for a wealthy white man is circumspect in his work but is considered something of a "menace" by his fellow Negroes. He deliberately murders a Negro girl who has spurned his attentions. Being ably defended by his employer, he receives a light sentence for manslaughter, and he has scarcely begun to serve this when his employer obtains his parole because he is anxious not to lose the Negro's services.

A recent study of parole in Alabama reveals something of the workings of the system in that state. Letters such as the following are "samples of many received by the Parole Bureau":

I can use a Negro full time . . . will see that he has something to eat, and can keep him at work all the time clearing land, cutting wood, and helping cultivate the land. . . .

I am in need of a Negro farm hand and I am depending on one from you. And if you have one for me, you may write what prison I can get him and when. . . .

I understand that the state is letting out prisoners on parole, if so I would like to get a Negro named G—— W——

It seems highly probable that the dominant factor is not the best interest of the individual offender or the welfare of society, but the immediate interest of some white person.

CASTE IN RELATION TO ATTITUDES AND MOTIVES

Criminal conduct, except for accidental or unintentional crimes, is ultimately a matter of personal attitude and motivation. What are the implications of caste status for the motivation of Negro offenses against white people? First, it is well to emphasize the point that many Negro offenses are unintentional in that they get defined as crime only because there is an upper caste to define them as such.

It is scarcely necessary to prove that the frustrations involved in being a Negro in a white-dominated society put the Negro under severe emotional strain and give rise to impulses of hate and revenge. These impulses are undoubtedly related to the causes of crime. Most of the sudden and violent attacks by Negroes on white persons—landlords, bosses, police, prison guards, etc.—are explicable only as the final explosion of emotional tensions which have accumulated over a period of time. But it is not only in violent attacks that hate and revenge play a part. Arson, burglary, injury to livestock, petty thieving, etc., may be direct expressions of revenge; and it is altogether probable that some of the sexual assaults of Negro men on white women have definite overtones of revenge.

No doubt much of the crime of Negroes against whites is merely crime which is motivated in the ordinary way and which happens to involve white persons. However, we would adopt the tentative conclusion that hate and revenge play a dominant role in some of the crimes of Negroes against whites and are contributory motives in many other offenses.

After all, a very large proportion of Negro crime takes place within Negro communities and involves the persons or interests of Negro victims. What role does caste status play in the motivation of such offenses? Let us outline our thesis briefly. First, the frustrations involved in being a Negro bear most heavily upon the members of the Negro lower class. Here one finds people who are utterly hopeless and degraded. They have nothing and know that they will never have anything. Their style of life fits very well into the common white stereotypes of Negroes—shiftless, lazy, impulsive, hypersensual, etc. They contribute the bulk of Negro crime, and their personalities and motives are inseparably tied up with their roles as lower-class members of a subordinate race. They let off most of the "steam" of their frustrated desires among their own group.

Second, social institutions and community controls do not operate with sufficient strength in the Negro lower class to repress the disorganizing influences or to inhibit the rather free letting off of emotional "steam." Violence, for example, becomes almost a positive value and has a high expectancy. The "bad man," the bully, the gambler, the "pistol toter," the pimp, the rowdy woman—all thrive because there are so many of them that they constitute a veritable society of their own. Naturally they thrive best of all in the great Negro "ghettos" of our large cities.

Third, there is lacking, in the South certainly and perhaps to some extent elsewhere, a tradition of strict and impartial justice in Negro versus Negro offenses. The double standard of justice lends positive sanction to violence and other misconduct within the Negro community. The saying that "Negro life is cheap" is tragically real, for even murder is sometimes condoned—one might almost say blessed—by the white man's machinery of justice.

CONCLUSION

The position of the Negro in American society, with all that this means in terms of subordination, frustration, economic insecurity, and incomplete participation, enters significantly into almost every possible aspect of Negro crime causation. Indeed, it is so important as to constitute virtually a special and major set of sociological and psychological factors which can "explain" Negro crime in so far as it needs special explanation.

The administration of justice itself is from beginning to end so much a part of the whole system of Negro-white social relations that it must be viewed not only as a process which discriminates against Negroes and thus biases the statistics of crime, but also as a direct and indirect causative factor in the production of Negro crime.

Our survey of the factors which might be expected to affect Negro criminality lends strength to the presumption that the Negro crime rate is actually considerably higher than the white. We have taken note of several ways in which caste factors bias the statistics to the disadvantage of the Negro, but we have pointed out that compensating factors probably operate, in the South at least, so that it may be that crime statistics, as bad as they are, do not grossly exaggerate the actual criminality of the Negro.

In so far as certain special conditions or characteristics in the usual statistical picture need explanation—for example, that Negroes have higher crime rates than whites, that Negro offenders are younger than white offenders on the average, that Negro women have a relatively high criminality, that Negro crime distributions emphasize petty offenses against property and crimes of personal violence, that Negroes are more likely than whites to be recidivists, etc.—they would all seem to find

sufficient explanation in the implications of the caste factors which have
been discussed here.

32 · Immigration and Crime

by COURTLANDT C. VAN VECHTEN

> There is a widely held and persistent notion that the
> immigrant's share in crime is very high, that the foreign-
> born have a higher rate of crime than the native-born.
> What are the facts? Courtlandt C. Van Vechten, a crim-
> inologist and a statistician for the Navy Department, pre-
> sents here some illuminating data on this subject. ["The
> Criminality of the Foreign Born," *Journal of Criminal Law
> and Criminology*, Vol. 32, July-Aug. 1941, pp. 139-147.
> Reprinted by permission. Footnotes omitted and abridged.]

HISTORICALLY the problem of the criminality of immigrants to this
country is as old as immigration. Certainly the Red Men looked on the
early white settlers as thieves of their land. And from the very first each
group of settlers has looked at the next wave as a rather dangerous and
criminally inclined group. Ninety-five years ago when the great grand-
parents of the Germans and Irish who are now so stable and reputable a
portion of our population were pouring across the Atlantic the Native
American National Convention assembled in Philadelphia and resolved
that the earlier immigrants were superior men and women who had been
"recruited chiefly from the victims of political oppression, or the active
and intelligent mercantile adventurers of other lands"; but they found
the newer immigrants "the worst and most degraded of the European
population . . . victims of social oppression or personal vices, utterly
divested by ignorance or crime of the moral and intellectual requisites
for political self-government."

Most of my readers will recall the things that were said when the
post-war immigration restriction bills were passed. Even though we had
just concluded belligerencies with Germany, we were not unwilling to
accept immigrants from Germany as well as from the rest of Northern
and Western Europe. We based our quotas on national origins as shown
by the census of 1890 so as to exclude the allegedly degraded and criminalistic South and East Europeans. The present situation has tended
to focus attention on immigrants in general and on those from the Axis

powers in particular. For aliens we have gone to the extreme of requiring registration and fingerprinting.

Just what is the basis for our attitudes on the criminality of the foreign born? Before considering statistics let's see what we know. We know that these people were people who had the courage, the ambition, the hope to seek out a new life in a country of opportunity. That should be a credit point. We also know that these were people with different habits, different ideas, different customs. But we must judge them by our laws. We must expect to find some criminality in the areas where legal and moral codes differed. We know also that few immigrants found legitimate success easy. During depressions many of them were unemployed. Even during good times most of them worked at the hardest, most irregular, and poorest paying jobs. That meant that they lived huddled together in the poorest areas. We know enough to know that where we find poverty and slums, there we must expect to find crime.

Turning to statistics we find that we must start by stating assumptions and limitations. The first limitation of our data is that we know only about those criminals who get caught. Detectives have said that they have never seen a perfect crime. This is because the only perfect crimes are those in which no one even suspects that a crime has been committed. There surely are some of these. But far more frequent are the crimes that do not result in arrest. Presumably these are committed by more efficient criminals. What I have figures about, then, is *caught* criminals.

Most police departments record the nativity of the persons they arrest, but the data is hard to make very much of. The difficulty is, of course, that absolute numbers do not tell us very much—we need rates. To know that in a year the city police arrested 100 foreign born persons does not mean anything, unless we know fairly accurately how many foreign born persons there were in the city during that time. This data has not been present in reliable form in most places since the 1930 census. It is not known how many foreign born persons live in the area covered by Uniform Crime Reporting, so national rates have not been possible. There is an additional difficulty with statistics on the criminality of the foreign born based on arrest records—the lack of reliability of the records. The police seldom have any means of verifying the nativity information given by arrested persons and some police officers have peculiarisms—such as recording "Jewish" as a country of birth—which invalidate the record. Back in 1934 Dr. E. H. Sutherland and I published a study on the Reliability of Criminal Statistics. We studied police, court, and institutional records of Illinois inmates and found a little over 10 percent of inconsistencies on place of birth.

Since court data on nativity are scattered and fragmentary, we must turn next to the records of prisoners. This means that we must go to the records of the Criminal Statistics Unit of the Census Bureau, as the one reporting agency with nation-wide scope. There is still the limitation that we are now going to talk not about all foreign-born criminals, but just about those who get to prison.

Since this problem has been attacked before we must consider what conclusions have been reached by those who have seriously studied it in the past. Dr. Sutherland in 1923 considered the question "Is There Undue Crime Among Immigrants"—and concluded that the statistics were so unreliable that no one knew. He found a crude commitment rate considerably higher for immigrants than for the native whites, but for New York City and New York State he found lower rates for immigrants when the rates were based on adult male populations. The National Commission on Law Observance and Enforcement, better known as the Wickersham Committee, conducted an exhaustive survey of the issue and concluded that "In proportion to their respective numbers the foreign-born commit considerably fewer crimes than the native-born; . . . the foreign-born approach the native-born most closely in commission of crimes involving personal violence, . . . in crimes for gain the native-born greatly exceed the foreign-born." This Committee also discovered that the arrest rate, the conviction rate, and the commitment rate for foreign-born constantly bore out their conclusions. The Federal Immigration Commission also stated that, on the basis of all the data it collected "Immigrants are less prone to commit crime than are native Americans." The Attorney General's Study of Release Procedures, Vol. 2, p. 366, notes that "Many studies have concluded that foreign-born whites are less liable to resort to crime than native-born whites." The Gluecks in their study of 500 men paroled from the Massachusetts Reformatory at Concord found that "79 percent of our ex-prisoners were native-born as compared to 54.1 percent native-born in the Massachusetts white population of voting age." Finally Sutherland in his rewritten text says, "The arrest rate per 100,000 adult population in 1937 was 514.2 for native white and 212.1 for foreign white. The native white population had a higher arrest rate in each age group and for all except three types of crime, and in these three types the rates were almost identical."

It would seem then that we have traditional and popular beliefs of the greater criminality of the foreign-born ranged on one side, and the statistically backed assertions of the experts that it is less grouped on the other. In such a situation it is reasonable to mistrust the popular beliefs, but it is imperative to examine very carefully the exact meaning of the assertions of the experts.

At first glance the figures substantiate the contention of the experts that the foreign-born are less criminal than the native-born. In 1938 the Census Bureau received reports of 42,353 native white males 15 years of age and older, and 2,779 foreign-born white males of the same age group who were admitted to prison after being convicted and sentenced for committing various felonies. In order to calculate rates it is necessary to know the total number of men in each of these nativity groups. Since the 1940 Census figures are not yet available in terms of age and race distributions of the population, and since profound changes have occurred in the composition of our national population in the last decade, we are compelled to refer to estimates in order to make rate comparisons. Fortunately, reliable estimates by Thompson and Whelpton, made for the National Resources Committee are available. These varied slightly from earlier estimates prepared by the Census Bureau for the foreign-born and were corrected in terms of the preliminary 1940 total as presented by the Census Bureau. The rates which are given from this point on will be recomputed when final census figures are available, but it is certain that they will not be materially changed. The figures show a commitment rate of 11 per 10,000 for native-born white males over 15 and only 5 per 10,000 for foreign-born white males over 15. The native rate is two and a fifth times as great as the foreign one.

The experts would seem to have demonstrated the greater overall commitment rate of the native-born. But at least one vital factor is hidden in the over-all rates: the critical variable of Age. We all know that prisons receive more men between 20 and 25 than between 40 and 50, even taking into account that there are more 25 year olds than 40 year olds in the general population. Commitment rates drop sharply after 25. So our 11-5 ratio is a good comparison only if the age distributions of the native- and foreign-born are similar. But they are not similar; not by a long, long ways. Depression and restrictions have greatly curtailed immigration in the last two decades; the foreign-born population is an old population. Only when we compare small age groups are we going to get really valid comparisons. The accompanying chart shows comparisons by specific age groups.

COMMITMENT RATES PER 10,000 MALE PERSONS IN THE U. S. BY NATIVITY AND AGE

Nativity	All Ages	15-19	20-24	25-29	30-34	35-39	40-44	45-49	50-59	60-69	70 and Over
Native white	11	11.8	21.5	16.7	13.2	11.7	8.6	6.0	3.9	1.8	0.7
Foreign-born	5	16.7	29.5	22.9	13.2	8.6	6.7	4.3	2.8	1.4	0.4

It indicates that the criminality of the foreign-born is much greater than that of the native-born under age 30, about the same from 30 to 35, and considerably less over 35. But there are few foreign-born men under 30, many in the older age groups. The apparent two to one advantage of the foreign-born is not so much due to their lifelong ability to keep out of trouble, but merely to the fact that most of them are in the upper age groups where, for native and migrant alike, commitment rates are sharply lower than for the younger ages.

* * *

May we say that the argument is a draw? The experts are certainly right when they say that the aggregate criminality of the foreign-born is low; popular opinion seems to be right in the idea that the foreign-born person who arrives here as a child is more likely to commit crime than the native, though here the difference is neither so great nor, such are the difficulties of the data, so certain. And it must be added in justice to the migrants now here that since a large proportion of them arrived here after reaching maturity, namely after the period when the foreign-born crime rate is in excess of the native one, there is no reason to suppose that they, our present foreign-born group, have in fact contributed more to crime in America than our native population of comparable age.

* * *

33 · The Theory of Differential Association

by EDWIN H. SUTHERLAND

Of all the explanations of the causes of criminality given in recent years, the one by the distinguished American criminologist, the late Edwin H. Sutherland, of Indiana University, is considered by many criminologists as perhaps the most plausible. Sutherland's formulation of the reasons why individuals are drawn into a career of crime has become known as "the theory of differential association." In this excerpt from his book, Professor Sutherland describes this theory. [From *Principles of Criminology* (4th ed.), Lippincott, 1947, pp. 3-9. Reprinted by permission.]

THE METHOD OF SCIENTIFIC EXPLANATION

Any scientific explanation consists of a description of the conditions which are always present when a phenomenon occurs and which are never present when the phenomenon does not occur. Although a multitude of conditions may be associated in greater or less degree with the phenomenon in question, this information is relatively useless for understanding or for control if the factors are left as a hodgepodge of unorganized factors. Scientists strive to organize their knowledge in interrelated general propositions, to which no exceptions can be found. The heterogeneous collection of factors associated with a phenomenon may be reduced to a series of interrelated general propositions by two general methods.

First, the multiple factors operating at a particular moment may be reduced to simplicity and generality by abstracting from them the elements which are common to all of them. Negroes, urban-dwellers, and young-adult males all have comparatively high crime rates. What do they have in common that results in these high crime rates? Research studies of criminal behavior have shown that criminal behavior is associated in greater or less degree with the social and personal pathologies, such as poverty, bad housing, slum-residence, lack of recreational facilities, inadequate and demoralized families, feeblemindedness, emotional instability, and other traits and conditions. At the same time, these research studies have demonstrated that many persons with those pathological traits and conditions do not commit crimes. Also, these studies have shown that persons in the upper socio-economic class frequently violate laws, although they are not in poverty, do not lack recreational facilities, are not feebleminded, or emotionally unstable. Such factors are obviously inadequate as an explanation of criminal behavior, and no amount of calculation of the risks of different categories of persons will bring us much closer to an understanding of criminal behavior. An adequate explanation of criminal behavior can be reached only by locating the abstract mechanisms and processes which are common to both the rich and the poor, the emotionally stable and the emotionally unstable who commit crimes. In arriving at these abstract mechanisms and processes, some of the concrete factors can be reinterpreted in general terms. A motion picture several years ago showed two boys engaged in theft; they ran when they were discovered; one boy had longer legs, escaped, and became a priest; the other had shorter legs, was caught, committed to a reformatory, and became a gangster. In this comparison, the boy who became a criminal was differentiated from the one who did not become a criminal by the length of his legs. In general, however, no significant relationship has been found between criminality and length of legs and certainly many persons with short legs are law-abiding and many persons with long legs are criminals. In this particular case, the length of the legs is probably of no significance in itself and is significant only as it determines the subsequent experiences and associations of the two boys.

Second, the causal analysis must be held at a particular level in order to arrive at valid generalizations. Two aspects of this may be mentioned. The first is limiting the problem to a particular part of the whole situation, largely in terms of chronology. In the heterogeneous collection of factors associated with criminal behavior one factor is often the cause of another factor or at least occurs prior to the other. Consideration of the time sequences among the factors often leads to simplicity of statement. When physicists stated the law of falling bodies they were not concerned with the reasons why a body began to fall except as this might affect the initial momentum. It made no difference to the physicist whether a body began to fall because it was dropped from the hand of an experimental physicist or rolled off the edge of a bridge because of vibration caused by a passing automobile. Such facts were on a different level of explanation and were irrelevant to the problem with which they were concerned. Much of the confusion regarding human behavior is due to failure to define and hold constant the level of explanation. A second aspect of this problem is the definition of criminal behavior. The problem in criminology is to explain the criminality of behavior, not the behavior, as such. Criminal behavior is a part of human behavior, has much in common with non-criminal behavior, and must be explained within the same general framework as any other human behavior. However, an explanation of criminal behavior should be a specific part of that general theory of behavior and its task should be to differentiate criminal from non-criminal behavior. Many things which are necessary factors in behavior are not necessary for the criminality of behavior. Respiration, for instance, is necessary for any behavior but it is not a factor in criminal behavior, as defined, since it does not differentiate criminal behavior from non-criminal behavior.

TWO TYPES OF EXPLANATIONS OF CRIMINAL BEHAVIOR

The scientific explanation of a phenomenon may be stated either in terms of the factors which are operating at the moment of the occurrence of a phenomenon or in terms of the processes operating in the earlier history of that phenomenon. In the first case the explanation is mechanistic, in the second historical or genetic; both are desirable. The physical and biological scientists favor the first of these methods and it would probably be superior as an explanation of criminal behavior. Efforts at explanations of the mechanistic type have been notably unsuccessful, perhaps largely because they have been concentrated on the attempt to isolate personal and social pathologies. Work from this point of view has, at least, resulted in the conclusion that the immediate factors in criminal behavior lie in the person-situation complex. Person and situation are not factors exclusive of each other, for the situation which is important is the situation as defined by the person who is involved. The tendencies and inhibitions at the moment of the criminal behavior are, to be sure, largely a product of the earlier history of the person, but the expression of these tendencies and inhibitions is a reaction to the immediate situation as defined by the person. The situation operates in many ways, of which perhaps the least important is the provision of an opportunity for a criminal act. A thief may steal from a fruit stand when the owner is not in sight but refrain when the owner is in sight; a bank burglar may attack a bank which is poorly protected but refrain from attacking a bank protected by watchmen and burglar alarms. A corporation which manufactures automobiles seldom or never violates the Pure Food and Drug Law but a meat-packing corporation violates this law with great frequency.

The second type of explanation of criminal behavior is made in terms of the life experience of a person. This is an historical or genetic explanation of criminal behavior. This, to be sure, assumes a situation to be defined by the person in terms of the inclinations and abilities which the person has acquired up to that date. The following paragraphs state such a genetic theory of criminal behavior on the assumption that a criminal act occurs when a situation appropriate for it, as defined by a person, is present.

Genetic Explanation of Criminal Behavior. The following statement refers to the process by which a particular person comes to engage in criminal behavior.

1. *Criminal behavior is learned.* Negatively, this means that criminal behavior is not inherited, as such; also, the person who is not already trained in crime does not invent criminal behavior, just as a person does not make mechanical inventions unless he has had training in mechanics.

2. *Criminal behavior is learned in interaction with other persons in a process of communication.* This communication is verbal in many respects but includes also "the communication of gestures."

3. *The principal part of the learning of criminal behavior occurs within intimate personal groups.* Negatively, this means that the impersonal agencies of communication, such as picture shows and newspapers, play a relatively unimportant part in the genesis of criminal behavior.

4. *When criminal behavior is learned, the learning includes (a) techniques of committing the crime, which are sometimes very complicated,*

sometimes very simple; (b) the specific direction of motives, drives, rationalizations, and attitudes.

5. *The specific direction of motives and drives is learned from definitions of the legal codes as favorable or unfavorable.* In some societies an individual is surrounded by persons who invariably define the legal codes as rules to be observed, while in others he is surrounded by persons whose definitions are favorable to the violation of the legal codes. In our American society these definitions are almost always mixed and consequently we have culture conflict in relation to the legal codes.

6. *A person becomes delinquent because of an excess of definitions favorable to violation of law over definitions unfavorable to violation of law.* This is the principle of differential association. It refers to both criminal and anti-criminal associations and has to do with counteracting forces. When persons become criminal, they do so because of contacts with criminal patterns and also because of isolation from anti-criminal patterns. Any person inevitably assimilates the surrounding culture unless other patterns are in conflict; a Southerner does not pronounce "r" because other Southerners do not pronounce "r." Negatively, this proposition of differential association means that associations which are neutral so far as crime is concerned have little or no effect on the genesis of criminal behavior. Much of the experience of a person is neutral in this sense, e.g., learning to brush one's teeth. This behavior has no negative or positive effect on criminal behavior except as it may be related to associations which are concerned with the legal codes. This neutral behavior is important especially as an occupier of the time of a child so that he is not in contact with criminal behavior during the time he is so engaged in the neutral behavior.

7. *Differential associations may vary in frequency, duration, priority, and intensity.* This means that associations with criminal behavior and also associations with anti-criminal behavior vary in those respects. "Frequency" and "duration" as modalities of associations are obvious and need no explanation. "Priority" is assumed to be important in the sense that lawful behavior developed in early childhood may persist throughout life, and also that delinquent behavior developed in early childhood may persist throughout life. This tendency, however, has not been adequately demonstrated, and priority seems to be important principally through its selective influence. "Intensity" is not precisely defined but it has to do with such things as the prestige of the source of a criminal or anti-criminal pattern and with emotional reactions related to the associations. In a precise description of the criminal behavior of a person these modalities would be stated in quantitative form and a mathematical

ratio be reached. A formula in this sense has not been developed and the development of such a formula would be extremely difficult.

8. *The process of learning criminal behavior by association with criminal and anti-criminal patterns involves all of the mechanisms that are involved in any other learning.* Negatively, this means that the learning of criminal behavior is not restricted to the process of imitation. A person who is seduced, for instance, learns criminal behavior by association but this process would not ordinarily be described as imitation.

9. *While criminal behavior is an expression of general needs and values, it is not explained by those general needs and values since non-criminal behavior is an expression of the same needs and values.* Thieves generally steal in order to secure money, but likewise honest laborers work in order to secure money. The attempts by many scholars to explain criminal behavior by general drives and values, such as the happiness principle, striving for social status, the money motive, or frustration, have been and must continue to be futile since they explain lawful behavior as completely as they explain criminal behavior. They are similar to respiration, which is necessary for any behavior but which does not differentiate criminal from non-criminal behavior.

It is not necessary, at this level of explanation, to explain why a person has the associations which he has; this certainly involves a complex of many things. In an area where the delinquency rate is high a boy who is sociable, gregarious, active, and athletic is very likely to come in contact with the other boys in the neighborhood, learn delinquent behavior from them, and become a gangster; in the same neighborhood the psychopathic boy who is isolated, introvert, and inert may remain at home, not become acquainted with the other boys in the neighborhood, and not become delinquent. In another situation, the sociable, athletic, aggressive boy may become a member of a scout troop and not become involved in delinquent behavior. The person's associations are determined in a general context of social organization. A child is ordinarily reared in a family; the place of residence of the family is determined largely by family income; and the delinquency rate is in many respects related to the rental value of the houses. Many other factors enter into this social organization, including many of the small personal group relationships.

The preceding explanation of criminal behavior was stated from the point of view of the person who engages in criminal behavior. It is possible, also, to state theories of criminal behavior from the point of view of the community, nation, or other group. The problem, when thus stated, is generally concerned with crime rates and involves a comparison of the crime rates of various groups or the crime rates of a particular group at different times. One of the best explanations of crime rates from this point of view is that a high crime rate is due to social disorganization. The term "social disorganization" is not entirely satisfactory and it seems preferable to substitute for it the term "differential social organization." The postulate on which this theory is based, regardless of the name, is that crime is rooted in the social organization and is an expression of that social organization. A group may be organized for criminal behavior or organized against criminal behavior. Most communities are organized both for criminal and anti-criminal behavior and in that sense the crime rate is an expression of the differential group organization. Differential group organization as an explanation of a crime rate must be consistent with the explanation of the criminal behavior of the person, since the crime rate is a summary statement of the number of persons in the group who commit crimes and the frequency with which they commit crimes.

Part Three

TYPES OF CRIMINALITY

CHAPTER NINE

Sex Delinquency

==

34 · What Makes for Prostitution?

by WALTER C. RECKLESS

Data regarding the prevalence of prostitution and the conditions leading to it are scarce and unreliable because of both the difficulty in obtaining trustworthy information from the girls involved and the poor recording practices of the agencies concerned with the problem. Professor Walter C. Reckless, the author also of a previous selection, has done considerable research on the problem of vice. In this article he presents an account, using a short case history as an illustration, of the reasons prompting girls to enter prostitution, and discusses the effectiveness of certain rehabilitative and treatment measures. ["A Sociologist Looks at Prostitution," *Federal Probation*, Vol. VII, April-June 1943, pp. 12-16. Reprinted by permission.]

IT IS NO exaggeration to say that information on prostitutes usually rates near the bottom for reliability. This is due in large part to the defense reactions of the girls themselves, to the lack of facilities for verification of case information, and to the poor recording practices of persons who deal with prostitutes officially. Consequently, generalizations made from statistical summaries of agency and institutional records of prostitutes must be taken with large grains of salt. There are exceptions, to be sure. But let us, who think our agency or institution keeps good records on prostitutes, not argue over the point that our data is anywhere near as accurately and uniformly reported and recorded as data on births and deaths. The outlook for improving the reporting of data is good only to the extent that more competent agencies and institutions, with careful registrars, deal with prostitutes—whether at the arrest, court, detention, or rehabilitation level.

In the absence of a body of reliable information on prostitutes, it might be pardonable to make some observations. (The writer assumes that an article which "looks at" a problem can dispense with the usual scholarly footnotes.)

PROSTITUTION A TRADE

Although it has been a legal variable throughout the ages, prostitution always has been a trade. In some places and to some prostitutes, it has been a profession. In rare instances, it has been a religious cult.

In years gone by, and still true to some extent, it appears as if the prostitutes formed an occupational caste, frequently set aside as a pariah caste. Special dress, manners, and residence were earmarks of the caste. In some epochs and places, prostitutes had about the same status as university students, mendicants, surgeons, money lenders (usurers), wrestlers, jugglers, and actresses.

Although most of these occupations now have achieved high status, the prostitute has lagged. She may have freed herself to some extent from the indignities of the ancient caste, from association with panders, and from the zoological conditions of the brothel, but she has not advanced her calling in the eyes of organized society. And she has not improved her trade practices and added to its arts, as so many trades have done. Hence, in spite of a long history, the traditions for the practice of prostitution have not perceptibly grown. It could even be argued that prostitutes have lost ground—lost some of the arts which their ancient sisters practiced.

GIRLS INDUCT GIRLS

In various times and places women have been introduced into prostitution by procurers and procuresses. But in the modern American scene I think it best to assume that girls introduce girls into prostitution, although there may be infrequent evidence of procuring. The tradition for procuring has never been as strong in the United States as it has in European, Asiatic, and Latin American countries. Let me cite a recent case which came to my attention, to illustrate the point that girl introduces girl.

A 19-year-old white American-born girl threw herself on the mercy of the juvenile court because she felt the government agents and the police would get her. From the girl's own partially verified story, it seems as if she was released from a children's home and came to the city to find work. She met a very attractive 17-year-old white girl in a movie (complete strangers). They left the movie together and went for a "coke." On the way, the 19-year-old found that the 17-year-old knew her way around the juke-box beer joints and was known by the attendants and clientele. They parted company without further ado. A few weeks later the 19-year-old went to live with a married sister in a nearby city but returned after a week for a Sunday visit to the first city. She did not return that evening; instead she looked up the 17-year-old acquaintance. The 17-year-old was living in an apartment with two experienced prostitutes. These two women formerly had been inmates of a brothel which was closed by law-enforcement action as a result of the Federal policy of suppression near military and naval establishments. They opened a house of their own which was spotted for closing. The girls "beat" the raid. It was to this place that they brought the 17-year-old, whom they in turn accidentally had met at a movie. At this time the 17-year-old had just been in the city a few weeks and already had built up a following among soldiers and other clients at the beer joints. The two older girls invited the 17-year-old to join them at their house. She did. Deserting their own house, the three moved to an apartment. It was here that the 19-year-old called upon the 17-year-old for a place to sleep. And here she stayed for 6 weeks until authorities arrested the 17-year-old and took her to the juvenile court. Then the 19-year-old, fearing further action, gave herself over to the juvenile court. The two older girls skipped the apartment; one leaving town, the other finding new quarters.

During the 6 weeks at the apartment, the 19-year-old hustled; but not very much, as best can be discovered. She already had had some sex experience prior to the experience of prostitution. At the time of appearance in court, she was infected with gonorrhea. The court had no jurisdiction over her because of age and voluntary appearance but the probation worker convinced her to enter the Convent of the Good Shepherd and stay there until treatment was concluded. Later, the court was able to get the Family Bureau to take over the case and make plans for treatment and rehabilitation.

My point is that in America we should expect most of the girls to be introduced into prostitution by their own female acquaintances, casual or intimate.

In recent weeks, I have taken occasion to ask a number of girls detained in the workhouse, "How do girls nowadays get into the racket (their trade name)?" Their answer is that they are "put wise" by other girls already in the racket.

THE SYNDROME FOR PROSTITUTION

The causes of entrance into prostitution are not adequately known. Why some girls enter prostitution and others with practically the same traits and background do not, we do not know. There is no satisfactory answer to this question.

I am going to hazard the tentative statement that previous sex experience together with low resources and differential response to the trade, or to girls practicing the trade, constitutes the syndrome of factors most frequently associated with girls entering prostitution in the United States. In other words, the girl in this country who enters the racket is most likely to be a girl with previous sex experience who lacks resources and responds to prostitution as a vocational opportunity by way of suggestion or help of prostitutes.

I maintain that few virgins in this country enter prostitution. The low resources of girls include items such as lack of education, lack of occupational skills, lack of adequate family backlog, lack of contact with instrumental persons, lack of judgment and sense (including in some cases subnormal mentality), and lack of stability. However, these two items of the syndrome are not enough. The girl still needs a differential response to prostitutes and prostitution—an embrace of the trade and a harkening unto representatives of the trade. This might represent demoralization and a descent from higher status for some girls; however, I am inclined to believe that entrance into prostitution is not a fall for a large portion of the girls. For example, one would not say that the shift from a waitress in a cheap beer hall or restaurant with free or barter sex promiscuity to prostitution is a fall on the social ladder.

Nevertheless, the neophyte must embrace the trade. Just what changes in attitudes toward life take place prior to a girl's entrance into prostitution, making it possible for her to take the step, is not altogether clear. Her value system may not be strong enough to resist the temptation or her value system may actually embrace the opportunity; that is, she may see something in prostitution. Here again, I am inclined to believe that prostitution is not so much of a temptation which ensnares morally collapsed girls as it is a job opportunity and a scheme of life for low resource girls.

TRADE RISKS

Prostitutes ordinarily do not conceive of themselves as criminal, even though they have repeated court, jail, or workhouse appearances. In this respect they are akin to some male criminals (e.g., "bookies") who likewise do not consider themselves criminal although they know their pursuit is a crime. More important than the point that prostitution is not a crime to prostitutes is the point that prostitution, like any other trade, has risks. In this instance, they are social and physical risks. The prostitutes understand most of them in some way or other. The most recent risk to the prostitute in this country is the chance of being reported by the soldier who gets infected, and whose report is routed to the State health department and then to the police who look for Mildred, brunette, 5 feet 2 inches tall, at the Bear Cat Bar; and strangely enough Mildred often is found.

But the girls even know this risk and take it into account. They expect to take a certain amount of beating, bad luck, and infection. The confronting risks and hardships process them and harden them rather than demoralize them.

There are some prostitutes, however, who become hardened but at the same time become demoralized; they become boozers, addicts, and hags. There are others who become hardened but who venture into crime as a supplemental opportunity—pickpockets and shoplifters. Finally, there are those who venture into regular work while in prostitution. The latter avenue is more available now than ever. Reports from observers and the girls themselves indicate that many prostitutes have entered war production factories. Several girls have told me that, in addition to making high wages, defense work has the advantage of giving one an identification badge which is a defense against arrest by police for being a suspicious person or practicing prostitution.

My judgment again is that the typical prostitute is not a demoralized person, not a side-line thief, and not a supplementary worker. She is merely a prostitute.

There is probably much truth in the statement that the unsuccessful operators in prostitution are those most likely to be arrested and that the most unsuccessful of all are those who finally land in the workhouse. The successful practitioners are able to avoid arrest, or if arrested once are able to avoid further arrests. Just how this is accomplished is only partially clear. I suspect that the undetected operators avoid the principal risks of detection such as open and careless solicitation and hustling in the areas of greatest vice raids (i.e. police activity) or of greatest concentration of prostitutes. Some of those who successfully avoid official detection have a special clientele and good operational connections—in rare instances, "pull."

EFFECT OF SUPPRESSION

Suppressive measures which have been applied in the present emergency near military and naval establishments and war industries, confirm the fact that brothel prostitution in American cities yields ground to and can almost be driven out by continuous law enforcement. Soliciting on the streets and in public places likewise subsides in the face of active and continuous suppression. But this form of independent, lone-wolf prostitution is able to survive and persist in spite of the most severe forms of suppression. The call girl type of prostitution probably has not been greatly affected by the law enforcement of the war emergency. This type of operation may be prospering even more than usual.

TREATMENT RESOURCES EVALUATED

A review of the treatment resources available to prostitutes indicates that they have not been particularly rich or effective. Courts have dismissed, fined, sentenced, and, in recent years and in a few places, have placed on probation persons charged with prostitution. While probation work with prostitutes has excellent possibilities, it has not been done adequately. Sentence usually has meant a jail or workhouse sentence and hence mainly a detention program. Within this generation the practice of "holding for clinic" has added to the detention program a required course of treatment for venereal infection. In instances where chronic prostitutes are committed to State-run correctional institutions, a better institutional program is possible than at the usual jail or workhouse level. The free hospitals and dispensaries also have represented an important treatment resource—for the most part voluntarily sought.

REHABILITATION DIFFICULTIES

Rescue workers in the past attempted to rehabilitate prostitutes, but their efforts were largely ineffectual. The fact is that American social work has paid little attention to prostitutes, so great was its concern with family and child welfare. Consequently, very few rehabilitative resources, especially adapted for the handling of prostitutes, are in existence. And clearly very few workers and agencies have ever had a competent rehabilitative experience with girls in prostitution. The exceptions to this might be the few trained workers attached to women's courts, a few competent women's shelters, and, to some extent, Traveler's Aid.

Of course, rehabilitation is now a recognized part of the total social protection program, which is a sort of Magna Charta for prostitutes if they could ever bring themselves to the idea. But to have rehabilitation in the program and to have it in effect are two different things. A special integration of local resources seems to be necessary for effective rehabilitation work with prostitutes (with residence or settlement requirements not interfering). It is my impression that very few specially organized local rehabilitative programs have arisen so far, although there are probably more "rehabilitation referrals" to various social agencies now than in the days before the Federal social protection law (May Act).

AN EXPERIMENT IN REHABILITATION

It is of interest to note the rehabilitation program which is developing in Louisville, Ky. Before a bill of particulars is given, one might describe it as a program which so far combines protective detention with supervision after release in selected cases. The detention center is the workhouse whose program is being improved over and above the usual zoological conditions of most jails and workhouses. The social service department of the workhouse, consisting of one man worker and a recently added woman worker, conducts the post-release supervision of the cases most likely to respond favorably to rehabilitation efforts. The two workers are assigned to the workhouse program from the Muncipal Bureau of Social Service, which is part of the Department of Welfare of the City of Louisville.

With the installation of the Social Service Department a quasi-parole or supervised placement service was put into effect, which service was offered all prisoners. The legal status for this service was derived from a City Ordinance which gives to the Director of Welfare authority to grant special consideration in those cases where such can be proven justifiable and constructive.

In practice, this consideration amounts to trading an unexpired portion of the prescribed term of imprisonment for a much longer period of supervision after release, i.e., if a man or woman is committed for a 30- or 60-day sentence and their petition for release is considered favorably, the subject must agree to, say, six months or more supervision by the Social Service Department at the City Workhouse. Although the social worker has no legal authority after release is effected, the relationship between the Social Service Department and the Police and the Court is sufficient that in cases of violation of agreement, the social worker may appear before the court explaining the parole experience and request its consideration by the Police or Court whether it be favorable or unfavorable.

Obviously, with a limited social service personnel, the standard of selection for parole has been very high. Only those where investigation and observation revealed the better possibilities, were accepted for case work service after release. Average ability, recent development of delinquent behavior, at least a semblance of family interest in the problem, or acceptance by public or private service agencies were the determinants. And as other services, such as transient (when aid was obtained direct from the family), placement in employment after release, referral for hospitalization as psychopathics and medical cases, are also the responsibility of this department, it is apparent that the parole case load has been very small. It is not surprising then, that few of those considered came again into conflict with the law. As a matter of fact, selection was of such character that follow-up was employed as more of a "preventive" than "rehabilitative" in nature.

Our institutional activities program is still in the embryo stage. However, sufficient stimulation has aroused a growing interest in the social work program here . . . and the development has been progressive. Early in 1942, a recreation and handicrafts program was installed under the supervision of this department which has since been accepted as a permanent function. Soon we hope that the University of Louisville will be able to assist us in giving psychometric examinations. One full-time case worker is being added to the staff February first and recently, two religious workers have been assigned to develop a liaison between the institution and the churches of the community.

We know that from among those who received parole service, women of average mental ability, with adequate family resources, with employment opportunities best suited to their aptitudes, where the economic status of the family and their interest in the subject were adequate, and where the delinquent behavior pattern as shown by investigation was a recent development . . . these responded best.[1]

This is a sample of a start. Undoubtedly still wider use and integration of private and public agency resources are indicated in order that the program may expand and ultimately reach its optimum of effectiveness locally.

TREATMENT RESPONSE TYPES

The recognition of treatment response types undoubtedly will play an important role in evolving programs for rehabilitation of prostitutes. That certain types of cases have a better prognosis than other types is now well recognized in the handling of offenders at the institutional,

From a statement communicated to the writer by Mr. James J. Crumley, Social Service Department, City Workhouse, Louisville, Ky., under date of January 17, 1943.

parole, or probation levels. Some are unimprovables; others need close supervision in order to adjust; still others respond well without intensive work. The recognition of treatment types and treatment limits represents half the battle in rehabilitation of human personalities. In her study of prostitutes in New York City,[2] Marguerite Marsh recognizes four treatment types of prostitutes:

The first is composed of those who are "young" in the business, a factor not necessarily related to chronological age, and who have not established habit patterns or personal connections that are hard to break. Rehabilitation may well follow referral to a private social agency *if* it is equipped to ascertain the character of the pressures which resulted in prostitution *and* ready and able to meet the needs both financial and emotional which are revealed.

The second group, usually with a long history of sexual delinquency, is composed of those who are disillusioned as to the satisfactions they once thought were to be found in the business, or who never really wanted to engage in it. Included here are the women who prostitute themselves to obtain money to buy drugs, where prostitution is a secondary effect of the drug habit. This group obviously needs more help of all types—medical and social —and over a longer period than those in the first category. In both, the desire on the part of the individual to change her way of living is the *sine qua non* for effective case work. The complex of emotional problems of most of these women means, however, that the client is not likely to show initiative in the case work relationship, a factor which needs to be faced and dealt with both by the agency and case worker.

A third group is composed of women who engage in prostitution for no other reason than to obtain a none-too-secure livelihood. Provision for comparable financial security with the added satisfaction which comes from living in a socially acceptable fashion, can serve the need of this group. While it cannot be stated with certainty, it is probable that many Negro recidivists, especially those in the early years, are in this class.

The fourth group is composed of those not likely to respond voluntarily to any social plan. It includes the women for whom prostitution has no moral or social significance, but is simply a more successful way of making money by which to obtain luxuries as well as necessities. There are also women whose connections with rackets and racketeers have greater strength and are more satisfying to them than any plan that a social agency can offer. For some the satisfaction may come from the element of danger and excitement that such connections possess. The mentally defective and the psychotic obviously require hospitalization or institutionalization if the community is to be protected, and they, also, fall in this fourth group. In addition certain women, because of psychically traumatic experiences, are suspicious of the good will of others and reject any and all offers of help.

[2] *Prostitutes in New York City: Their Apprehension, Trial, and Treatment*, July 1939 June 1940. Welfare Council of New York City, June 1941.

BREAKING A TRADITION AGAINST REHABILITATION

Attention has been called to the fact that many girls, perhaps most, will not voluntarily initiate rehabilitation themselves and seek the help of social agencies. Some of this is undoubtedly due to the "response type." But a large part of it is due to the fact that the girls in prostitution have no tradition for calling on welfare agencies. In fact, they have a "trade" bias against welfare workers. My impression is that the vast majority of American prostitutes know how to respond to a policeman, a police or workhouse matron, a hospital nurse, a V.D. doctor, but do not know how to "take" the welfare workers of the average social agency. They do not understand the workers or the agency.

If rehabilitation work is once established on a workable and effective basis, the news will travel "down the line." Remember how long it took the public to achieve confidence in our mental institutions, so as to entrust family members thereto. It will take some time for the girls themselves to develop confidence in social protection and rehabilitation programs. Local communities which have advisory committees assisting the rehabilitation program could do well to include a couple of prostitutes in their councils, to give suggestions from the girls' angle and to get 'the word around." Likewise, the fact that male rehabilitation workers in many instances may deal more effectively with prostitutes than the usual woman case worker should not be overlooked.

35 · The Making of a Sex Offender

by RICHARD L. JENKINS, M.D.

What, speaking psychologically rather than legally, is a sex offender? How does he come to be one? Is deviant sexual behavior which is defined by the law as crime due to some inherent propensities of the individual or to external factors? These are some of the questions on which Richard L. Jenkins, an eminent psychiatrist of the Research Section of the Veterans Administration, presents his views in the article that follows. [From *Focus*, Vol. 30, No. 5, Sept. 1951, pp. 129-134. Reprinted by permission.]

IN UNDERTAKING to discuss the making of a sex offender, I shall define a sex offender in terms more limited than those of the law. Our society still shows the marks of its Puritan beginnings in its phenomenal array of blue laws dealing with the subject of sex or with the enjoyment of sex. The sexual preoccupations which so often underlie the Puritan attitude seem revealed in the industry of our lawmakers in listing forms of sexual behavior to be forbidden by law, and penalized with Draconian severity. Such compulsive restrictions, though typically more severe in statute than in practice, serve to confuse an already clouded subject and to make more difficult the problems of protecting the public from what I shall call the real sex offenders.

In the state of Connecticut, for example, anyone using a contraceptive—let me repeat, *anyone using a contraceptive*—is liable to fine and to imprisonment for a year. It is a question as to how far this statute contributes either to popular respect for the law, or to realization of the constructive significance of sex in marriage. However, I shall seek to avoid any controversies in this area and shall not concern myself further with Connecticutians who choose to make themselves sex criminal under the Connecticut law by using contraceptives. I shall restrict my consideration to those sexual offenders who so far invade the rights of others that a majority of us would have no hesitation in agreeing to class them as criminal in their behavior.

There is a story I rather like of a kindly woman whose pastor was so impressed with her good disposition and human appreciation that he exclaimed to her, "Mrs. Jones, I believe you would speak well of the devil himself." Characteristically, her reply was, "Well, I must say I do admire his persistence." While I am not one who likes an identification of sex with the devil, yet sex in human life certainly is characterized by a remarkable persistence, in spite of all legislation.

Modern technology has banished belly hunger as a general source of want in our nation. In relation to sexual hunger, on the other hand, while modern technology has done much to whet the appetite for glamour and romance, it has not made any comparable contribution to the *satisfaction* of the basic hunger. Not that we could ever expect that it would, for sex makes its constructive contribution in life only in a highly personalized relationship, on the basis of love and affection, and not through techniques of mass production. Sexual hunger has probably become a more active force in our well-nourished, healthy population than it has traditionally been over the centuries. By reducing immediate human concern with belly hunger and with imminent danger, technology has increased the relative importance of sexual hunger. This is revealed by the prominence in civilian psychiatric breakdowns of conflicts relating to this instinct of race preservation, compared with the prominence in military psychiatry of conflicts relating to the instinct of self preservation.

It would seem that up and down the scale of life, the male role is the seeking role, while at least in the birds and mammals, the female role tends to be a selective one. This would seem to imply a stronger specifically sexual drive in the male, and a more latent reactivity in the female, which it is the task of the male to arouse by courtship or inducement. It is in keeping with this general principle that the sexual relationship has a typically different significance for men and for women. Men tend to make economic sacrifices to secure sexual satisfaction. Women tend to use a sexual relation rather to attain affectional security and perhaps economic security as well. It is also in keeping with this principle that male sex offenses are typically derivatives of socially unacceptable efforts to obtain sexual satisfaction, while female sex offenses are typically the result of efforts to use sexual attraction as a means toward economic gain. Most so-called sexual offenses in women have either an economic motivation or at most a partially or diffusely sexual motivation; while most sexual offenses in men have a more specifically sexual motivation. And so when we speak of offenses caused by specifically sexual motivations, we are for the most part speaking of offenses committed by men.

Doubtless the simplest and most direct of these is the crime of rape. In a certain sense, a crime is the result of the coexistence of two elements in the offender at the time of the act—the impulse toward the act and a lack of inhibition toward its commission.

Any normal man understands the impulse toward the direct seeking of sexual satisfaction, which may be violently expressed in rape. To lapse into the vernacular, there is nothing queer about rape. The difference between the law-abiding man and the rapist lies typically not in a difference of sex impulse, but in a difference of inhibition and consideration for the personality of others. This makes it worth our while to consider briefly the question of how we get our inhibitions.

No baby is born civilized, socialized, or inhibited. Becoming civilized or socialized—and that means becoming somewhat inhibited—depends upon two elements at least. It depends upon an affectional relation with one or more parent persons through which the capacity to feel for others is developed, and it depends upon social training, social pressure through which certain standards of behavior emerge. The consideration of an older generation stressed the training without adequate popular recognition of the need for affection. Our modern mental hygiene movement is in some danger of stressing the affection to the neglect of training.

The lack of an affectional parent-child relation in early life typically results in a hard, egocentric, bitter personality, lacking consideration and feeling for others and lacking or relatively lacking in conscience. Such an individual is manifestly more likely to offend against the rights of others in any area than is a person with a more adequate development of fellow-feeling.

Crimes of rape are, of course, far from identical. Some occur after strong arousal from sexual play which has been freely permitted or even encouraged by the woman involved. Indeed, with the extent to which the sexual responsiveness of some women is aroused by the play experience—or the suggestion—of being physically overpowered, it may be quite impossible in some cases to determine the exact point at which seduction leaves off and rape begins. At the other end of the scale, we have the unprovoked or planned assault of what I shall call the real rapist. Such unprovoked actions of course bespeak such a gross and conspicuous failure of conscience control as strongly to suggest that we are dealing with a psychopathic personality.

This leads to another problem, rather acute in our attenuating Puritan culture, which tends to associate sex not only with sin, but also with violence. For our Puritan heritage is no longer a substantial obstacle to a considerable sexual freedom in our population, but it does tend to turn the associations of sexual freedom into directions which are far from ideal. It is by no means general practice as yet for parents to give their children information on the subject of sex, and the fragments of information and misinformation gleaned here and there often fit more easily with the associations of the gutter than with the associations of the home. It is not easy for sexual awakening in the young to develop in the healthy surroundings of affection and acceptance in our culture, for since sex is a tabooed subject, it is forced into the company of other things which are tabooed—filth and crime. In fact, since it is often the *most* tabooed subject, filth and crime potentially may become channels more available for the expression of sexual feeling than normal sexual behavior. A matter of great importance in the question of the emotional significance of the sexual act is the further question of what general character of act it is conceived to be.

With a surprising frequency sexual behavior is conceived or fantasied in associations of violence. The Freudians have stressed in this the furtive observation by the child of his parents in coitus and the shocked or excited misinterpretation of the act as one of violence. No doubt this is often a factor, but I believe we must also recognize the association of sexual stimulation with crime and violence in modern cheap literature and particularly in spectacular illustrations. I stepped into a drugstore in close proximity to the White House in the District of Columbia, and looked at the covers on the racks of paper-bound books on sale there

It is a quite respectable drugstore, and despite the iconoclasm of Lee Mortimer and Jack Lait in their recent publication, *Washington Confidential*, not more venal than urban drugstores in this country in general. The books were largely whodunits and I was frankly surprised to find one which portrayed neither a glamorous female corpse nor a partly undressed (or if you prefer, a partly dressed) glamour girl on the cover. Many of them had titles building the same association, *Death and the Naked Lady, Come Murder Me,* and *So Young a Body,* and *What a Body.*

I did not read the volumes, but if I were to characterize what I believe to be our book morality on the subject, it would be that there is no objection to the literary portrayal of a glamour girl gone wrong, providing only that she is foully murdered as a result of her sins. Whatever the justification for this special morality, it seems clear that it tends to build and perpetuate an association of sexual behavior with force, violence, and cruelty, rather than an association with affection, love and marriage.

Such associations may make more difficult the achievement of a sexual adjustment, but by themselves they present little menace. When, however, such associations occur in an embittered, envenomed individual who lacks conscience and has a hatred for mankind in general, and womankind in particular, some women may suffer. Consider, for example, the early atmosphere of the home in which one sex criminal grew up. It is cited in the *Report on the Study of 102 Sex Offenders at Sing Sing Prison* submitted to Governor Dewey in March 1950. When this man was a baby and a social worker visited the home, his mother became angry at the social worker and threatened to slug her with the subject, her small babe in arms. I would raise the question of how much chivalry toward women a son growing up with such a mother might be expected to develop, or how far such chivalry would be likely to curb the impulse toward a sexual crime which might serve the double purpose of relieving sexual tension and furnishing revenge on a representative of the sex which denied him love in his early dependency.

Of course the crime of rape sometimes leads to the crime of murder to silence the potential accuser. It may be associated with murder also in the lust-murder, in which the motivation of the murder itself is sexual. Lust-murder is an expression of the extreme development of sadism. Sadism is the sexual enjoyment of cruelty perpetrated upon another. Here we deal with one of the most disturbed and menacing expressions of the sexual drive. Grotesque as it is, some of its origins are not difficult to recognize.

THE DOMINANT MALE

The masculine role in sex typically involves initiative and the capacity to bring a woman to the acceptance of coitus. Since the male role ordinarily is the more active and dominant, male sexual behavior is usually concerned with an effort to achieve some measure of sexual dominance. The desire to assert such dominance in a direct and even primitive manner is certainly not abnormal in the human male. Nor is the obligation of preserving chastity which society puts upon women always entirely welcome. There is a story of a young woman who dreamed she was lying on her bed in a filmy nightgown, when a powerful man suddenly burst in the door, snatched her off her bed, and carried her into a dark forest. Apprehensively she asked, "Sir, what are you going to do?" The reply was, "That's entirely up to you, miss. This is *your* dream."

Sometimes women fill a gap between desire and morality with a fantasy of being overpowered and violated by a male who cannot effectively be resisted. And probably the fantasy of overpowering women is as common in men as the fantasy of being overpowered by men is in women. This does not mean that such men are likely to try to act out such fantasies seriously, any more than it means that such women would be likely really to find the experience of being raped a pleasant one. It simply means that when we are pressed by others or by ourselves to keep a close control over our behavior, we may not keep as close a control over our thoughts as over our actions. Fantasy is used to circumvent barriers, unwelcome or not entirely welcome, to obtain a shadow of desired experience without the cost and ill effects which would attend the fantasied action if it were carried out in reality.

This does relate to one important point. Sexual passion is, in a way, like the jellied gasoline of napalm bombs. It tends to adhere to whatever comes in contact with it and to set it afire. Many people have erotic reactions aroused or enhanced by particular objects, illusions, or associations. Manufacturers of perfume, cosmetics, and women's clothing base extensive industries on this fact.

It is not therefore difficult to understand that sexual passion may become attached to crude physical domination or to the fantasy of crude physical domination. It may go further and even become attached to cruelty, not as a means to compelling coitus, but as an enhancing factor or even as an end in itself, a substitute for a forbidden sexual act. This is likely to occur when the sexual relation is conceived as one of violence or cruelty, and for some reason, establishing the normal goal of coitus as the culminating realization of sexual desire is impossible. In the warped mind murder may be sexualized, and may be less taboo and less guilt-ridden than what we regard as normal sexual expression.

True rape or its serious attempt is typically a crime of vigorous young men. Men of failing vigor are more likely to be involved in sexual approaches to children. Such individuals in particular deserve careful study, for some are previously upright citizens showing signs of the loosening grip on life and on self which may develop as a symptom of cerebral arteriosclerosis.

NUISANCE, NOT MENACE

Any community is likely to have an occasional Peeping Tom or an occasional sexual exhibitionist. Such individuals are typically nuisances rather than menaces. In most instances they are individuals whose inhibitions to the normal expression of sex are excessive rather than inadequate, and who have through early and repeated experience channeled their sexual impulses through the looking or showing activities which are not uncommon in young children. Of course such individuals frequently cause girls and women to be frightened and may do damage in this way. Many can be treated successfully through psychiatric interviews.

Nuisances are caused by men with the desire to touch, and annoyance by fetishists who collect articles of women's clothing, particularly women's underclothing. Such individuals also can often be benefitted by psychiatric treatment.

There are also those males who, in lay language, are queer, in that their sexual desire is focused primarily or exclusively on their own sex. This is exceedingly common *outside* the State Department. According to Kinsey, a third of males admit at least one homosexual act, and a sixth admit that for at least three years they were more sexually attracted to males than to females. This may be a phase of sexual play with members of the same sex at adolescence, but it persists with remarkable frequency. We should distinguish between that homosexual behavior which is a second choice, a substitute for heterosexual behavior, and that which is primary or preferred. In prison or among rough groups of men there are some individuals, typically vigorous, masculine individuals with strong sexual desires and little inhibition, who, in the absence of women, seek to use softer and younger men to satisfy their sexual desire. Preferential homosexual behavior in men is frequently related to early seduction by an older homosexual man, or to the early development of a feminine identification, or to both. Feminine identification usually begins with an identification of the boy with his mother—not an *attachment for* but an *identification with.* Again psychological taboos to the normal direction of sex desire are at least a common contributing factor.

There remain the large and important group of individuals whose sexual behavior is directed partly or wholly toward their own sex. Probably the problems of homosexual attachments are more common in women than in men. For whatever chivalrous attitudes our culture has, more prestige attaches to the male than to the female sex. The masculine woman enjoys higher respect from both men and women than does the effeminate man. There are as a consequence more inducements toward and fewer social deterrents to a masculine adjustment in women than a feminine adjustment in men. Women are more ready to admit, even more prideful about, close identification with their fathers than men are about close identification with their mothers.

Since homosexual relations are a crime, persons who engage in them are legally sex offenders. Such individuals are extremely numerous, and more often than not, present neither a community menace nor a community problem. There are, of course, instances of homosexual seduction of children and adolescents just as there are instances of heterosexual seduction. Homosexual seduction is perhaps the more difficult to guard against and is likely to be the more damaging, particularly to boys, for homosexual seduction of girls as a rule does not equally throw them out of their normal sexual role. And just as with the heterosexuals, there are those who conceive the sexual relation in violent terms, and who lack inhibition.

The homosexual lives in an intolerant world which places a heavy penalty on his sexual activity. He totally lacks the path commonly available to the heterosexual person of gaining community sanction for a desired relation through marriage. He lives forever in the shadow of exposure and disgrace. However, homosexual tendencies will not be legislated out of existence and the question might be raised whether it might not be well to restrict the penalties of the law to those acts which we recognize as invading the rights of another, and to treat other manifestations on a nuisance basis when they become that.

In summary, the varieties of sex offenders are as numerous as the legal provisions forbidding a wide variety of sex practices. Certainly our knowledge of the making of a sex offender is imperfect. Certainly also, it is fair to stress most strongly early experiences which have resulted in hostility, bitterness, lack of inner restraint and lack of capacity to feel for or to recognize the rights of others. Secondary factors, frequently contributing, include elements, usually overintense parental taboos, which block the normal direction of growth of the sexual drive, and early exposure to unfortunate sexual experiences and sexual stimulation.

36 · The Background of Incestuous Relationship

by SVEND RIEMER

Incestuous relationship is both a religious and a moral taboo as well as a crime throughout the world. The feeling against this kind of relationship is so strong that for a long time it was considered an instinctual aversion. Nevertheless, such a relationship, condemned by both the mores and the law, is encountered in every country and culture, undoubtedly to a much greater extent than is disclosed by court cases. What kinds of person violate this moral and legal prohibition? What are their motivations, their family, social, and economic background? Svend Riemer, professor of sociology at the University of California at Los Angeles, sought to answer these questions by means of an investigation of one hundred cases in Sweden. His findings are presented in the following selection. ["A Research Note on Incest," *The American Journal of Sociology*, Vol. XLV, No. 4, Jan. 1940, pp. 566-575. Reprinted by permission. Footnotes and tables omitted.]

IN SWEDEN every year about thirty cases of incest come to the attention of and are dealt with by the criminal courts. This is a surprisingly low number in proportion to the total population of the country (some six millions). Obviously, however, incest must be assumed to occur much more frequently than the statistics indicate. There is a great likelihood that the crime might be concealed even from the closest relatives. In fact, usually only the persons involved—father and daughter, brother and sister, etc.—would be likely to know anything about the incestuous relationship. The authorities are informed only when childbirth rouses suspicion, in cases of accidental discovery, or when antagonisms within the family go so far as to break down its protective solidarity against interference from outside institutions. There is no doubt that incest, especially father-daughter incest, is very widespread within certain strata of Swedish society, namely, among agricultural laborers of a low cultural standard in districts of large estate farming and within a similarly disorganized group of industrial laborers.

An investigation was carried out in Sweden both from the sociological and from the psychiatric point of view, with an end to discover and analyze the causes for breach of the usually very stringent incest taboo. The social aspects of this research are to be presented here. The basic material was obtained from one hundred intensive case studies. Practically every case of incest in Sweden is, before trial, sent to a psychiatric hospital for a two months' observation and careful investigation. The resulting case studies furnish research material which is particularly useful because the psychiatric interviews reveal significant details about the social environment in which this crime most frequently occurs.

Although the occupational and social backgrounds of incest in Sweden definitely point toward a very limited milieu, it would be misleading to look for a direct connection between agricultural labor and incest. In Denmark incest occurs more frequently among the urban proletariat of Copenhagen, while a German investigation on the same crime contains many records of craftsmen in the small provincial towns of southern Germany.

Dealing primarily with the most frequent type of incest (father-daughter), we have found that the life careers of the fathers involved reveal striking similarities. Moreover the life careers contain peculiar features which definitely exclude the possibility that it might be the "normal" life-career in this environment which leads to incest in some cases and not in others. We are faced with a unique configuration of circumstances, repeated monotonously from case to case and which integrate into every life-history. There can be no doubt as to the influence of this configuration upon the social attitudes of the individuals in question. Hence we may expect to derive an answer from the analysis of the life-career of the individuals involved (58 cases) to the question: What social circumstances allow disregard of the incest taboo?

The typical life-career of fathers who commit incest will be summarily described.

1. *Upbringing and education.*—Patients usually left home at a very early age (generally between ten and fifteen years) in order to make their own living. Parental influences are thus very slight, especially since home conditions are very unfavorable to close contacts with the parents. Some of the patients—illegitimate children—are brought up by the mother's parents until she marries, at which time she takes her offspring to live with her husband. Divorce and separation occur. The home situation is, moreover, influenced by very unstable employment conditions in this environment, which might necessitate rearrangements of the educational background. Thus, very few of the patients are living at their parents' homes all the time before they start out for occupational life.

Primary school, in many cases a country school with children of all ages gathered in a single classroom, is attended by nearly all the patients; they frequently finish their formal schooling after but a few years of not too intensive education. The rigorous winters, the long distances from schools, combined with heavy farm work in the summer, often necessitate absence from school for days or even weeks.

The home atmosphere, moreover, is often characterized by alcoholism of the father and frequent quarreling between both parents.

2. *Occupational life.*—Occupations are almost exclusively restricted to the unskilled, heavy-labor class in agriculture and industry. Characteristic is a very frequent change of jobs and even changes to different kinds of occupations. Many of these people change their jobs almost every year.

In the long run, the occupational career in this environment tends, at the time of best physical development, to lead up to relatively well-paid positions in industries that are widely scattered throughout the rural districts of Sweden. Sooner or later, however, when physical strength wanes, the individual will often return to agricultural pursuits. He has thus reached the stage in life where his career is definitely turning for the worse. Wages decline, and finally he has to sign a "stature" contract, which includes the labor of his wife (milking) and perhaps that of some of his children as well. This action promises wages in kind and thus reduces the free choice of consumption, to say nothing of the extremely low consumption standard, i.e., the actual poverty under which he is forced to live. There are no prospects. Living on the dole or being kept in the community's old people's homes is what he may expect.

The occupational career is, of course, not identical for all men who have forced their daughters into sexual relationship. Even an engineer (of the craftsman type), some industrial laborers, small independent farmers, and others are also included in our data. The frequent change of jobs and occupations, however, and the declining trend of the occupational career at a time when the incestuous relationship begins are in all cases extremely characteristic.

3. *Accidents and troubles disturbing everyday-life routine.*—It is remarkable that, several years before the beginning of the incestuous relationship, in nearly all life-careers the routine of everyday life seems to have been interrupted, although this might have happened in very different ways. If we take into account accidents, diseases, and economic difficulties, there are very few cases which do not reveal one or the other of these interruptions, in most cases some years before the patient begins to make sexual advances toward his daughter. The life-history shows, moreover, that these interruptions have been of considerable importance for the future career. Readjustment to the demands of everyday life seems to be difficult or impossible thereafter.

4. *Sexual experiences.*—Before marriage the young people of the social strata involved in our investigation live almost in a state of general

promiscuity. They have sexual intercourse with one or more of the girls who are staying at the same farm or whom they get to know at dances or other entertainments. Relations of this kind may cease after the immediate desire has been satisfied, or they may continue until the individuals are separated by change of residence or by the choice of another partner. Marriage changes this pattern of sexual behavior radically. Sexual relations with others than husband or wife are very infrequent. The reason seems, however, not to be because of a strong attachment to a certain individual of the opposite sex. There are very few signs indicating experiences of romantic love. Rather, sexual intercourse as such seems to be of overwhelming importance, and the change from promiscuous to monogamous relations is better understood if marriage is looked upon more as a practical arrangement providing—besides other conveniences—the presence of one sexual partner.

With almost no exceptions the patient, shortly before the incestuous relationship begins, finds himself barred from sexual intercourse with his own wife. She may be temporarily absent from home (in hospital) or she may be incapacitated by numerous childbirths and from hard work on the farm and in the household. In connection with this a high-strung psychological tension arises among the members of the family. The man —if he has not been so before—develops into a wife-beater, who holds the terrorized family under the influence of his unbalanced outbursts of temper; the wife nags the husband and thus hinders him from feeling at home with his own family circle. It is impossible to say whether the deterioration of the psychological relationship or that of the sexual relationship should be looked upon as the primary cause.

In this situation of extreme sexual frustration there seems to be no available outlet by choosing another sexual partner outside the family. The country population of Sweden lives a very isolated existence and there is usually very little social activity going on even between members of the same community. The dances function as a meeting place for adolescent boys and girls, and a married man would scarcely dare enter sexual relations through that channel. A long period of monogamous living, moreover, seems to have destroyed the patterns of approaching the opposite sex (shyness).

5. *The final impulse.*—Linked up with the situation immediately leading up to sexual relations with a daughter are circumstances such as alcoholism, overcrowding of rooms, and the sharing of the same bed by persons of the opposite sex, which sometimes have been regarded as the deciding causes of incest. These circumstances certainly give the final impulse which, however, comes into play only given the background of the preceding life-history. In more detail different situations could be

mentioned which have a seducing influence: accidental sight or touch of the naked body, the daughter carrying food to the father who is working alone out in the woods, etc. Obviously it would be wrong to look upon these circumstances as "causes" or "motives" in themselves.

In the individual career, of course, deviations from the foregoing outline appear in one or another respect. As already mentioned, some occupations other than agricultural laborers are represented, but, on the whole, the lower occupational categories predominate.

As to the deviations from the typical life-career it might be noted that the lack of one of the foregoing instances sometimes is compensated for by a particularly extreme situation with respect to one of the other instances. A village shoemaker, crippled from birth, might be obliged to live an absolutely sedentary life, and the frequent exchange of jobs and of places of residence might be missing in his career. But a life-career without any prospects seems to be given here from the very beginning, since the occupation of a village shoemaker scarcely provides a living and it might only be intended to keep the individual busy and make it possible for him to add now and then a small amount to the wages of his wife or to the benefits paid by the community. It might be mentioned also that mental deficiencies can substitute for certain adverse environmental conditions. The son of a city craftsman might be induced to live an unstable life as a consequence of emotional adjustment difficulties, even though the educating forces of his home environment might work for a reverse attitude.

The life-career, of course, is not a social "cause" necessarily leading up to an incestuous relationship between father and daughter. Only the probability may be assumed that, given the foregoing configuration of events in a life-career, incest will be the consequence.

To furnish a full insight into the situation leading up to sexual approaches toward the daughter it is not enough to call attention only to the isolated instances so far considered in the individual life-career as such. They must also be integrated into a comprehensive conception of the social attitudes of the individual concerned.

No attitude has been revealed in any of the case studies which would indicate a special interest on the part of the father to have intercourse specifically with his own daughter. There is no special tension pointing in this direction. The daughter simply replaces the mother, and this becomes possible only under the strain of intense sexual desire combined with a number of environmental circumstances which tend to destroy social responsibility. Thus, the incestuous relationship must be looked upon primarily as a negative phenomenon.

The incest taboo is rooted in a system of complicated social restrictions. It had definite economic implications as far as the patriarchal family and the village organizations were concerned, and in modern society it is supported also by insight into the importance of free and unhampered development of the child's personality. In the disorganized social groups within which incestuous relations arise in Sweden, the values mentioned above are disregarded as a consequence of the life-career. The family relationship does not seem to imply very much more than a relatively convenient arrangement to meet the most elementary demands of everyday life. Children are kept at home only until—at a very early age— they can make their own living. Thereafter the parents may not see them again. At the age of somewhat over forty years, when, on the average, sexual relations with the daughter begin, all social ambitions have been abandoned. The father is psychologically isolated at home. He lacks any privacy that might give him an opportunity to reorganize his life or at least to settle down to the given situation. Although occupational life is quite free from friction, the social contacts established with fellow-laborers are for the most part of a very superficial character and scarcely of constructive influence. As an outcome of these complex experiences the attitude toward social restrictions, especially as far as the family relations are concerned, is one of extreme indifference. The individuals do not care whether they commit a crime; they are even not aware of the fact that they do so when they approach their own daughter. Social obligations seem to be left outside the sphere of intimate family relationship.

The verbal rationalization of their behavior as furnished by the individuals themselves, of course, does not always immediately reflect the foregoing attitude. The subjective experience of "motivation" can be very different, ranging from "protest against society" to "romantic love." Some of them state: "After all I have been through, I just don't give a damn!"

Brought back to some kind of an organized social life, however, by the very imprisonment itself, in many cases it is not too difficult to re-establish the values which have been disturbed. The individual then might have great difficulty in understanding how he could have brought himself to have sexual relations with his own daughter. Where, however, an attempt is made to defend the action, an absurd mixture of surviving values of family solidarity and lack of responsibility is revealed. Sexual intercourse with one's own daughter is justified as being better than "frivolous relations with outsiders." It is mentioned that the daughter in any case would be pregnant very soon at her age; since the father would be the one to take care of her child, it might just as well be his own. There are some attempts to fight the father's "disease" by sexual intercourse with the daughter, and all members of the family agree with this arrangement.

The initiative in this type of incest is nearly always on the side of the father. The daughter is perhaps interested as long as she is not aware of the father's final intentions, but when he attempts to force her, she resists. By and large, however, she is too afraid of the father to scream or to ask her mother for protection. After the first coitus the relationship may develop in different ways. Tendencies on the part of the daughter to free herself and to find a sexual partner of her own age are the normal reactions. For some time, however, she may be prevented from this by all kinds of protective arrangements of the jealous father. There are several cases in which sexual relations between father and daughter developed into a marriage-like state, which lasted for a long time after the daughter's adolescence. She might even take the mother's place with respect to household duties and child care and thus stabilize her position.

The mother does not always fight the father-daughter relationship efficiently. She prefers to be left alone, but she is jealous. Very often, of course, she does not know what is going on. But sometimes she seems even to conceal facts from herself. In other cases it is the mother herself who communicates with the authorities when she finds out about the relationship.

A few words may be added about other types of incestuous relationships. Rather frequent is the incest between brother and sister. This relation, however, is of intermediate character only, arising from sexual experimentation in childhood or adolescence. It does not imply the dominance of one of the partners as in the father-daughter incest, and it is thus very often dissolved without serious damage to either partner. All other possible combinations of incestuous relationship are, however, extremely rare. It is of interest to mention the extremely rare occurrence of sexual relations between mother and son. The mother does not have the same domineering position in the family as the father. He is the one who makes the living and threatens the family by his superior strength. It may be of importance also that the mother even in this disorganized social environment establishes a close relationship with the individual child. This is one of the most important prerequisites for the development of an incest taboo.

CHAPTER TEN

Alcoholism and Drug Addiction

37 · The Alcoholic Personality

by HARRIET R. MOWRER

The alcoholic, one of the major types of disorganized
personalities, has been a challenging social problem in
Western civilization, particularly in this country. He has
therefore been a subject of investigation by medical scientists, psychologists, psychiatrists, and sociologists. Here
Harriet R. Mowrer, a sociologist of wide practical and research experience in the field of personal and social disorganization, summarizes her findings from case studies
seeking to determine the personality traits of alcoholics.
["A Psychocultural Analysis of the Alcoholic," *American
Sociological Review*, Vol. 5, No. 4, Aug. 1940, pp. 546-557.
Reprinted by permission. Footnotes omitted.]

PSYCHOLOGICAL STUDIES of the alcoholic have been primarily from the
psychiatric and psychoanalytic points of view. These studies have been
clinical in nature and, except in a few instances, have not represented
research. They have been instead the reflections of physicians or psychiatrists upon their cases, rather than any systematic analysis of case records.
Among the few exceptions are the studies of Wall of one hundred male
and fifty female alcoholics, Wittman's study of one hundred alcoholics

and Knight's study of thirty cases. This is not to deny, however, the value of other studies characterized more as reflections upon clinical experience than as research, the most recent of which is that of Strecker and Chambers.

As to the etiology of alcoholism there is a wide divergence of opinion among psychiatrists themselves. In fact, theories applied to chronic alcoholism seem to have run the gamut of psychoanalytic theories and most of these have been those worked out clinically in the field of the neurosis and the psychosis. Thus chronic alcoholism, like drug addiction, has long been associated with the neurosis and psychosis and each development or shift in emphasis in analytic theory has been followed by its application to the problem of the alcoholic.

Thus Abraham, in 1908 developed the psychological relations between sexuality and alcoholism and stated that drinking is the alcoholic's sexual activity. He concluded that sexuality, alcoholism, and neuroses are all interrelated. Juliusberger in 1913 stressed unconscious homosexuality as the cause of alcoholism. In 1919, L. Pierce Clark elaborated upon the conclusions of both Abraham and Juliusberger. Alcoholism, he concluded, is a substitute for neurosis and psychosis. In 1925, Sachs characterized drug and alcoholic craving as a compromise between a perversion and a compulsion neurosis. Weiss in 1926 and Kielholz in 1931 showed the relationship between the taking of toxic drugs and paranoid psychoses in which occurred delusions of being poisoned. In 1928, Weijl showed the importance of the Oedipus complex in the analysis of alcoholism and asserted that in drinking there is identification with the father orally (cannibalistic destruction) and attainment of the mother. Chambers in 1937 noted an underlying neurotic condition that makes alcoholism possible in certain individuals—an alcoholic compulsion neurosis.

It was not until recently that there has been any systematic attempt to study the personality characteristics of alcoholics. Since alcoholism was thought to be related to the neuroses and psychoses, then it would logically follow that the alcoholic has some or all of the characteristics of the neurotic and psychotic individual. What these characteristics are, however, is not specifically revealed. In these earlier studies, there are little or no research findings which would give support to the hypothesis that the alcoholic is psychopathic, since no attempt was made to study his personality and background.

Wall's study marks the transition from theorizing about alcoholism as a phase of psychopathic behavior to an attempted analysis of the alcoholic's personality. He found in the family background a doting, oversolicitous mother and a comparatively stern, forbidding father. This produced in the child a feeling of insecurity and helpless dependence, combined with a high percentage of alcoholic excess among the preceding generations. Emotional immaturity or instability, infantilism, passivity and dependence, pathological jealousy, oral eroticism, and latent homosexuality, were characteristic personality traits. Dr. Walter Miles gave greater emphasis to the hypothesis of homosexuality, pointing out that the traits described by Wall resemble in several respects the homosexuals described by L. M. Terman and C. C. Miles.

Generalizations in terms of such extensive traits as have been said to characterize the alcoholic, however, do not seem warranted. In the present writer's research with domestic discord cases, it may be said that many persons with domestic discord display some of these same traits but they cannot be classified either as psychopaths or homosexuals. However, the significance of Wall's study lies not so much in its content as in representing one of the first systematic attempts to study the personality of the alcoholic.

The studies of the alcoholic thus have tended to over-simplify the problem. Causes have been either in the form of data on isolated factors or so general as to apply to other groups of persons including the non-alcoholic. Furthermore, studies have not been comparable. It is impossible to compare analyses of data because of differences in fundamental background and premises, as well as differences in technique and scope. This has been complicated further by the fact that in some instances there have been no specific statements of techniques.

The purposes of this study were: (1) to make an analysis of the personalities of alcoholics in such a way as to reveal the basic reaction patterns which determine their adjustment to the social milieu; (2) to get at the genesis of the attitudes which constitute the personality; (3) to compare the personality patterns of the alcoholic with another group studied and classified as the escape-response type; (4) to compare the alcoholic with a second group studied and classified as showing no personality disorganization.

Case studies of all three groups were made in a comparable way as to frame of reference, interviewing technique, elements of personality genesis and development, social interaction, and later family adjustment. Each group consisted of twenty-five married individuals and their marriage partners; comprising, therefore, seventy-five cases, or one hundred and fifty individuals. None of the marriage partners in either of the three groups showed any personality disorganization. The basis of distinction between the alcoholic and the nonalcoholic was the fact that chronic drinking of the alcoholic constituted a part of his pattern of social maladjustment. Contacts were maintained with each case for an average period of three years, affording ample opportunity for checking upon the reliability of the analysis. Each analysis was made upon the basis of an extensive body of materials obtained through a series of firsthand interviews in response to the desire upon the part of the patient to have the assistance of the writer in the understanding and solution of some problem of personality or of domestic discord.

This analysis has been restricted to twenty-five case studies in each group in order to make it possible to study and compare three groups of cases. The purpose of this comparison is to bring out more sharply the factors in early familial interaction which differentiate the alcoholic personality pattern from other types of personalities. Without such comparisons, as past experience has demonstrated, there is a tendency to look upon common factors as definitive of a particular type. Methodologically, the following procedure is equivalent to the use of a control group in statistical analysis without the attendant loss of the organic unity which characterizes the relationship between etiological factors.

Since this is a case-study analysis, quantitative results wherever utilized have been expressed in qualitative terms and introduced only as they are related to and consistent with the larger organic pattern which can only be portrayed in qualitative language. Quantitative statements, however, may be found in footnotes, but the reader is cautioned against interpreting these data too exactly since the number of cases involved is too small to insure statistical reliability.

In the analysis of the personality pattern, the following factors were assumed to be significant: (1) psychogenetic characteristics, including attachment to parents, rank and role in the family, relationship to siblings, marital adjustment of parents, etc.; (2) the physical pattern; (3) the cultural background, including education and early work history, vocational adjustment, intellectual, and artistic interests, etc.; (4) social and economic adjustments; (5) the sexual and response pattern, including early attitudes toward sex, sex education, sexual experiences prior to marriage, marital adjustments, nature of close attachments carried over from early family group, and the like; (6) cultural setting and circumstances surrounding the first appearance of the behavior which became the basic pattern of response, such as drink, gambling, "illness," attempts at suicide, etc.; (7) later family adjustment, including type of marriage partner, conflict and accord, history of role in the home, attitude of children, and so on; (8) rationalizations.

PSYCHOGENETIC FACTORS

What effect ordinal position has upon familial interaction is not entirely clear. Nevertheless, research has shown that the earliest role of the child in the family has a far-reaching effect upon his life organization and type of adjustment pattern. It is generally accepted that it is usually to a peculiar set of family circumstances that one has to look for an understanding of these reaction patterns.

Several writers have portrayed the alcoholic as more likely to be the only or youngest child. Another has attached no significance to ordinal position. It would seem that ordinal position is of no significance except to the degree to which it may be a factor in determining role. Thus in our culture, the youngest child is more likely to be the favorite and his infantilism is more likely to be prolonged. Witness the number of youngest children still referred to as "Baby," "Junior," "Angel," and so on, by their parents! However, any child in the family, because of various peculiar circumstances, may have the role of the "youngest."

In the cases in this study, the alcoholics in ordinal position clustered around next to the oldest, youngest, and next to youngest. As to role, it is significant that none of the youngest had the role one usually thinks of as typical of this group. The most significant factors in familial interaction, however, were a dislike or hatred for the father, a marked dislike or jealousy toward a brother thought to be favored by the father, a strong attachment for the mother or a sister who in turn favored them. If one can draw any conclusion here, it would seem ambiguity in role is what characterizes the alcoholic—a role in which his status is superior and assured in relation to some members of his family and uncertain and challenged in relation to others.

Comparing the group of alcoholics with those characterized by escape-response through illness, one finds a clearcut distinction. In the latter group, all are either youngest children or have the role of the "youngest." Here the typical family configuration is: favorite of both parents, close attachment of siblings, protection from early responsibility, and no challenge to "favorite" role. Since women constitute the larger number of this group, one may question the validity of comparing all men with a predominantly feminine group. Perhaps the sex of the child is an important factor in the determination of role. With this hypothesis in mind, the escape-response-through-illness group (predominantly women) were compared with the wives of the alcoholics as to ordinal position and role. Here there was a striking difference, the wives of the alcoholics showing a preponderance of oldest and "middle" children. In comparing the alcoholics with the group showing no personal disorganization, this same striking difference was borne out with both the men and the women although the men in this latter group showed a larger proportion of oldest children than did the women.

With the overwhelming preponderance of oldest children in the group showing no personality disorganization and the presence of no "oldest" in the disorganized group under observation, it would seem that one can logically conclude that there must be a definite relationship between adjustment and ordinal position or role in regard to the oldest child. The oldest child usually has the role of one who is taken for granted as conforming to the traditional role of the child, whatever that may be for the particular cultural group. For example, in one cultural group this may mean carrying on the profession or trade of the father even though it may not carry with it a great deal of prestige. Thus in general the American farmer has wanted his oldest son to be a farmer. In another group, it may not mean carrying on the trade of the father, but that glorified by the particular cultural group. The Jewish tailor, for example, does not wish his son to carry on his trade, but dreams of his being a learned man, a lawyer, or a doctor. Many an Italian immigrant laborer, likewise, dreams of producing a Caruso.

The relationship between adjustment and the middle child, while not as striking, is significant. Here he, like the oldest, is more likely to take his position for granted and to demand less recognition for himself than do persons in other ordinal positions.

Of undoubtedly more significance than ordinal position, but closely related to role, is the pattern of family relationships in the so-called organized group, which is characterized by a lesser degree of attachment toward either parent, in some instances, even by extreme detachment, fewer instances of preferential treatment by either parents or siblings, and little or no marked jealousies. In other words, the members of the organized group (predominantly "oldest" and "middle" children) seem on the whole to have accepted the roles assigned to them without conflict and those roles seem not to have conflicted with the rights of others. The result was that theirs were roles which could be maintained without conflict in later interpersonal relationships outside the family.

As to marital adjustment of the parents of the alcoholic group as compared with the group showing no disorganization, there is little significant difference, domestic discord occurring slightly less frequently in the alcoholic group. The parents of the escape-response group, however, show a higher degree of marital adjustment. It is interesting to note that the fathers of the alcoholic group are less often alcoholic than those of the nonalcoholic "organized" group. This would be contrary to the belief that an alcoholic nervous system is transmitted from one generation to the other, about which there is little known. It would more nearly agree with the conclusions of Knight of the Menninger Clinic who did not find alcoholism in the family background as a constant factor and is doubtful that there is an inherited predisposition. The most significant factor suggested, however, by the finding of more alcoholic fathers in the nonalcoholic group is a cultural one. Alcoholism may have a different meaning to the individual reared in a home where a parent is alcoholic. It may be to him a symbol of erratic behavior, shiftlessness, unhappy home life, etc. To the others, the symbol may be the traditional one of masculinity, virility, and strength.

CULTURAL BACKGROUND AND ECONOMIC ADJUSTMENT

The alcoholics show a wide range in cultural background from the clergyman's son to the son of the laborer. In this regard, there is no significant difference as compared with the "organized" group. As to economic status, the "escape-response" group is significantly higher than either of the other groups. Educational background is not essentially different except for a few instances of expulsion from school in the alcoholic group. The alcoholic group is characterized by considerable shifting in occupation, restlessness, dissatisfaction with occupation, and lack of definite drive. The "organized" group shows greater occupational stability and less ambitious aspirations. The alcoholic's background, like that of the "escape-response" type, shows more evidence of reading of an intellectual nature. More of the alcoholic group have artistic interests and when asked what they would most like to have been, the typical reply was, an artist, a musician, or an inventor. This might be said to bear out or throw more light upon Strecker and Chambers' hypothesis that the alcoholic's standards are higher than the average.

THE SEXUAL AND RESPONSE FACTOR

As has already been pointed out, the association of the sexual factor and alcoholism has long been accepted. This has for the most part taken the form of indicating the relationship between homosexuality and alcoholism. Theories have been read into fragmentary factual data on certain behavior reactions of the alcoholic, in an unwarranted fashion. For instance, it has been pointed out that men drink exclusively with men and that this is indicative of a latent homosexual trend. Men, of course, did drink almost exclusively with their own sex during the saloon and prohibition era because of the cultural taboo against women consuming hard liquor. Since repeal this is no longer true. Thus the more plausible explanation of the practice of males drinking with each other is the cultural pattern, rather than organic homosexuality, and this is further borne out by the heterosexual relationships of the alcoholic with the prostitute.

Another evidence of latent homosexuality is said to be that men become affectionate with men friends and swear undying friendship while under the influence of alcohol; but they also become quarrelsome and pugnacious to their best male friends as well as affectionate toward their female drinking companions. There is no behavior reaction here which may be said to be typical. Again it has been observed that most alcoholics have been married and divorced or have had domestic discord which illustrates their characteristic maladjustment with women. That separations and domestic discord are prevalent among the alcoholics there is no doubt, but it is rather ridiculous to contend that this is in itself evidence of homosexuality.

In the writer's study, it was found that an overwhelming proportion of the alcoholics had sexual experience prior to marriage. In the "organized" nonalcoholic group, less than half had such sexual experiences. What can be the meaning of this difference? Since alcohol and brothels have long been associated, and since in several instances the sexual experience had been with prostitutes, one may raise the question as to whether this relationship might not have furnished the social situation for the onset of the drinking. Such a connection was not borne out, however, as none of the subjects either directly or indirectly linked the two together. Furthermore, the age at first sexual experience was invariably given as several years earlier than the onset of the drinking. Both, it is true, are symbols in our culture of masculinity and strength. Perhaps the only conclusion that one is justified in making here is that there is significant evidence that the alcoholic group showed to a much greater degree the urge or necessity for trying to establish through overt expression their strength and masculinity than did the other groups.

The question then may be raised as to how consistent is this behavior with the personality pattern, the genesis of which, as has already been shown, is in familial interaction. Here the alcoholic's status was ambiguous—superior to some, challenged by others. It is only logical to believe that it would be the more favored role the individual would endeavor to maintain and therefore be more demanding than could ever be realized in adult interpersonal relations. Thus his status continues to be threatened, and as the needs for defense expand, he becomes more dependent upon those transitory symbols by which the desired status is achieved.

The transitory character of these symbols of status toward which the alcoholic tends to gravitate is illustrated by the fact that in many instances the individual has made other attempts at maintaining status, and as one has failed he has tried another. Thus one may cite the behavior of Mr. A. who had the typical familial background which has already been presented. He took up boxing, was successful, happy, and adjusted for the period that he was known as "Riley the Fighting Irishman." When he was no longer able to maintain this role, he began drinking and later became a chronic alcoholic. Other cases show a sequence of sexual exploits, gambling, and then alcoholism.

MARITAL ADJUSTMENT

That marital discord is not the result of alcoholism but that both are the result of the same etiological factors, research has demonstrated. This is not to say, however, that the domestic discord does not take on a characteristic pattern which is closely intertwined with the behavior of the alcoholic personality. The alcoholic tends to enter marriage handicapped by some economic insecurity, dissatisfaction with occupational choice, restlessness, and a tendency to resort to substitute adjustment devices. As a husband, his position in the family becomes an inferior one. His feelings of inferiority are reflected in the sexual relationship and his husband role becomes further complicated through chronic alcoholism by actual physical or psychological impotency. Intense jealousy of the husband, excessive sexual demands (which cannot be realized), with frequent sexual practices at variance with the normal, are found to be characteristic of this type of case.

Comparing the groups studied, it is found that the alcoholics seem to have placed more of a premium upon sexual potency than do the men of the other groups and this was borne out by statements of the wives as well. While various types of sexual maladjustments characterized both groups, there were more instances of extremely sexually inhibited wives in the alcoholic group than in the "organized" group. These findings might lead to much speculation as to the use of alcohol as a substitute for sexual relations. However, the women in the escape-response-through-illness group show a characteristic pattern of sexual inhibitions, yet no cases of chronic alcoholism were found among their husbands. This would suggest accordingly, that the factor in itself is not significant but may be of considerable importance when viewed in relationship to the many other factors which go to make up the total pattern. That is to say, the alcoholic husband seems to feel keenly that his difficulty at sexual adjustment with his wife is a challenge to his ego, role in the family, or the like.

DRINKING AND THE CULTURAL MILIEU

In any analysis of the personality of the alcoholic, one must keep in mind the cultural milieu. Accordingly, the reasons men give for drinking and the circumstances surrounding it are in themselves of little scientific value. The alcoholic no more than the person experiencing domestic discord can give unaided the real causes of his difficulty. What he gives is the cultural definition of the situation, that is, those causes approved by the culture of his group. In our culture, such happy occasions as weddings, births, sudden good fortune, etc., call for and furnish excuses for drinking. Likewise, sorrows occasioned by death, financial reverses, disappointments in love and marriage, etc., are crisis situations which can be met and conquered by alcohol, the magic medicine. It keeps those happy who are already happy and makes the sad happy again. Wine is often the symbol of fruitfulness, and drinking to one's health is interpreted as expressing the wish that the life principle in wine may do him good. Alcohol, likewise, is supposed to make the shy become bold and the weak strong. It has long been associated with masculinity and sexual prowess. Quite consistent, then, are the reasons given by the alcoholics: "I drink to make me happy"; "I drink to forget my troubles"; "When I drink I feel like a man"; "Drinking helps me to make a sale"; "Drinking helps me forget that I have no wife"; and so on.

Here, of course, the alcoholic does not distinguish between normal drinking and chronic alcoholism. The average individual probably experiences a satisfying glow and a feeling of contentment and happiness as the result of an occasional drink. But does this average person experience the same reaction in solitude as in the company of friends? This suggests a more general question: How much of the effect attributed to alcohol is due to the physiological response of the organism and how much to the social-psychological setting? This is not to deny that alcohol, particularly the chronic use of it, does not have any effect upon the physiological processes and psychological functions, but this paper is not concerned with this aspect.

It is doubtful, however, whether the chronic alcoholic experiences the oral satisfaction of the occasional drinker because he is inclined to drink hurriedly; in fact, his drinking often takes on the appearance of the performance of a ritual. While it is generally conceded that inhibitions are released through liquor, there is a wide variance as to how people behave under its unfluence. Not all shy persons become bold nor do all persons become happy. Many become sad and despondent; others, taciturn and unsociable; still others remain unchanged while under the influence of liquor. While the chronic alcoholic may say drinking enables him to meet his business associates and put across a deal, the clinical history may show this not to be the case. Alcohol, while it may increase sexual desire, decreases ability at performance, so in reality can hardly be said to increase sexual prowess. Thus it would seem that the chronic alcoholic is in a paradoxical situation. Rather than having been betrayed by his mother through the nursing experience, as some psychoanalysts have contended, he has instead been betrayed by his culture which has held out to him a false panacea for his problems.

THE ALCOHOLIC PERSONALITY PATTERN

It seems apparent that the behavior of the individual under the influence of liquor is not as significant for an understanding of the alcoholic as has been believed in the past. What is more important are the attitudes of the members of his family toward him as a consequence of his alcoholism. The importance of these subsequent attitudes is suggested by the fact that, like the "neurotic" woman, he does not want to be cured of his social handicap.

Instead of slowly ruining his life, as the portrayals of the influence of alcohol would have one believe, the alcoholic, through his drinking, achieves satisfactions which he can realize in no other way. As an aftermath to his drinking, his role becomes equivalent to that played in earlier familial interaction. While some members of his family are disgusted with him, strict in their attitude, consider him an "inferior," a problem, etc., there are others who pamper him all the more, give him unlimited attention, always believe in and fasten hope upon his determination and pledge to "throw away the bottle." Even his wife, vacillating as is her attitude toward him, while inclined to criticize him, yet expresses sympathy and a maternal feeling for him.

How the alcoholic achieves the limelight as a consequence of drinking is illustrated in all the attention which he subsequently receives. Family conferences are held; plans are worked out to help him resist the temptation to drink; new inducements are offered him; and in general he occupies the center of the stage. Thus, for example, a program is worked out by the family requiring him to report each day to a sister, or a wife may meet him at the close of the day's work and thus protect him from the influence of drinking companions. The consequences are that the subsequent exemplary behavior under this regimen convinces those concerned that a cure has been effected. The moment the scheme is abandoned, however, the alcoholic relapses into drinking. Obviously, the cause of the relapse is not that new crises have arisen or that his former drinking companions have reasserted their influence, but that he no longer receives the attention which he got under the regimen of supervision. Observing the collapse of his attention-consuming role, he again reinstates it through another drinking debauch.

How deceptive may be the immediate circumstances surrounding drinking may be illustrated by the following incidents. In one case, the alcoholic became drunk instead of appearing at the funeral of his brother. In another, he failed to go with his children to the hospital to see his wife, becoming drunk instead. At first sight, it would appear that drunkenness in each instance represented an avoidance of the sorrow and pain involved in these circumstances. More thorough analysis, however, revealed that the first person's relationship with his brother had not been such as to call out any deep sorrow and that the second quarreled recurrently with his wife, accusing her of infidelity, as a projection of his own sexual impotency. The more plausible interpretation of both instances is that each was a rebellion against the attention given to another member of the family. The subsequent attention which each received as an aftermath of his drunkenness confirms this interpretation.

Thus it becomes clear that the behavior of the alcoholic cannot be understood except with reference to the basic pattern of personality developed in early familial interaction. Alcoholism provides a way of recapturing at least temporarily the attention-receiving role of the early familial group. This recapturing of the childhood role, however, is much more the aftermath of drinking, than something which is obtained exclusively under the influence of liquor.

The consequence is, that in order to understand the alcoholic, it is necessary to keep in mind this basic pattern of personality. The moment segments of behavior are detached from the total configuration, the picture becomes distorted. In this distortion, single factors are considered causes of alcoholism with little realization upon the part of the researcher that these factors may have a wider application than the alcoholic, or if not, that they are but part of a larger causal complex. Methodologically, therefore, the paramount need in the study of the alcoholic is to see his drinking behavior as a part of the larger pattern of personality disorganization.

Like other forms of personality disorganization, therefore, alcoholism can only be understood as it performs a function in the attempts at social adjustment of the individual. That the consequences of excessive drinking are such as to be only temporarily satisfying, and therefore represent what from an objective viewpoint is inadequate, is of no importance in the understanding of the behavior. What is of importance is the fact that for the moment at least this type of response is within the range of possibilities set by the pattern of personality for the achievement of what to him seem to be essential goals. So long as alcoholism works, he uses it, and when it breaks down, he is likely to abandon it for other devices within this range, or else becomes enmeshed in an ever-increasing drive to make it work until the personality becomes wholly disintegrated.

This does not mean, however, that there are no questions which remain unanswered regarding the character of the alcoholic personality. Of paramount importance in the clearer differentiation and understanding of the alcoholic is the need for comparing more thoroughly this type of personality with other significant types of unadjusted personalities. In any case, the present analysis provides a frame of reference within which comparisons can be made from the psychocultural point of view.

38 · Alcohol and Crime

by ROBERT V. SELIGER

Alcoholism, various studies have demonstrated, is closely related to crime. Both alcoholism and criminal behavior appear to have similar underlying causes, which are to be found primarily in the inner conflicts and urges of a poorly integrated personality. Although in some cases the individual may find release in addiction alone, in others he may resort also to crime, particularly since the locale—*i.e.*, the drinking place—is highly conducive to the scheming of criminal activities. In the following article, Robert V. Seliger, a psychiatrist with experience in prison work and research, discusses the relationship between alcoholism and crime; analyzes the characteristics of the alcoholic and the conditions, both personal and cultural, driving him to excessive drinking; and suggests what must be done to rehabilitate him. [From *Journal of Criminal Law and Criminology*, Vol. 41, May-June 1950, pp. 24-31. Reprinted by permission. Footnotes omitted.]

ALCOHOLISM AND CRIMINALITY are serious national social health problems.

They are also problems in the field of jurisprudence, for the correlation between excessive abnormal drinking and the commission of various aggressive and criminal acts is definitely confirmed by police records and prison statistics which indicate that there is an increase today, of such alcoholic-criminal episodes.

Various measures of a preventive restraint nature, such as fine or punishment for being drunk and disorderly, and for acts of criminal behavior, have not succeeded either in eliminating the source of these problems or in curtailing their extent.

This is not surprising. We would not—in this age—expect "mental illness" to be eliminated or curtailed by threat of fine or punishment.

And, from the viewpoint of medical psychology, alcoholism and criminality are, and should be understood as being, symptomatic of a behavior-illness-deviation, with serious resulting behavior consequences for the individual and for the community.

The premise is that no one in reasonably well balanced emotional and bodily-emotional health will repeatedly drink alcohol to a point beyond control both of his drinking and of his behavior; nor will he commit against society aggressive acts such as burglary, rape, assault, or murder, and so on.

There is agreement among many scientists who have investigated the apparent underlying causations of alcoholism and criminality that the individual dynamics and personality structure are often quite similar. In some instances, these inner conflicts and drives, or primitive inadequately controlled urges of the poorly integrated and unstable personality seem to be released through alcoholism alone; in other instances, through criminal behavior alone; and in still others, through both alcoholism and criminality.

With this latter group, reports have stated that the following factors are found over and over again; and they are, therefore, significant:

1. Crime is often planned in a place where alcohol is sold.

2. The tavern is the place where the criminal seeks his accomplices.

3. The criminal is seldom courageous. He often uses alcohol to depress his inhibitions and allay his fears.

4. The spoils of crime often are divided in the tavern.

5. Alcohol removes the element of self-criticism from the criminal in relation to himself and his acts.

In a recent study of the problem of the criminal sexual psychopath in Michigan, it was found that out of a total group of 237 individuals, 22 percent (nearly one-fourth) were either chronic alcoholics or periodically had become excessively alcoholic. Other studies of other types of a social behavior as well as the practical observations of the policeman on the beat and the night courts unhappily confirm this fact that—although use of alcohol is not involved in all criminal acts—there is a definite and repeatedly found connection between drinking and crime. Further, it is well recognized that juvenile delinquency and drinking are intimately and often associated. The laws are nearly uniform against selling alcoholic beverages to minors or permitting minors to work where alcoholic beverages are sold.

What is needed essentially is more understanding of what constitutes preventive and rehabilitative therapy of these serious and dangerous personality deviations. Inevitably one must advance from the particular to the general—to the community with all its ingredients and change; political, economic, civic, recreational, religious, educational, racial and other corporate tensions and dissensions. And it is, therefore, one feels, the need—as well as the province—of thoughtful justice, embodied in our courts and statutes, to seek a more unified, vital, cooperative understanding of the especial needs of the given community. Existing cleavages, trouble spots, "infected" areas and so on, should not be passively ignored and thus allowed to break down the individual's capacity for self-government; rather, the morale of the community should be such as will increasingly help to reinforce that capacity, upon which all human rights depend.

It is—speaking categorically—impossible to think helpfully in terms of groups if we do not feel in terms of the individual.

And so, in trying to understand the criminal and the alcoholic—in contrast to judging him or to sentimentally "forgiving" and "setting him free" though still unwell—practical experience with many hundreds of alcohol problems, including individuals who have committed criminal acts (whether "caught" or not), leads me to the following thoughts concerning "the causes," prevention and treatment of these problems. I should like to add that these problems are increasing, they are very serious, and they are a very definite, alarming threat to us as a nation and as a people.

These following thoughts apply specifically to the average non-psychotic, non-feebleminded, non-deteriorated alcoholic of today; but they can also be applied to many criminal individuals who present a similar personality structure and who are reacting to outer pressures of our changeful and anxious times.

Medically, there is no one known alcoholic "personality type." Neither is there any one reason or cause for alcoholism. However, in general, one can state that excessive dependent drinking, is symptomatic of an underlying disturbance in personality organization and function and in the interpersonal relationship system.

The alcoholic has not been able to adjust to other people, to past and present troubles, and to daily life with its monotonous requirements. Yet he, himself, usually feels, quite honestly, that it is other people and the troubles of life which are to blame for his disillusionment, unhappiness and drinking. His thinking habits are faulty. Moreover, his emotional reactions dominate him so strongly that his judgment is poor in many spheres and instances. For example, he promises or agrees to do things which are beyond his ability to complete or accomplish. And then, as a result of failure, he renews his quarrels with the environment and blames other people. But he also renews accusations against himself, for the alcoholic usually is prone to marked depressive feelings of inadequacy. He lacks self-assurance except when in a buoyant mood, and he is uncertain in regard to his role in life and in regard to the quality of inner self-reliance and self-government.

As a consequence, he frequently develops protective techniques by which he consciously or unconsciously learns to avoid responsibilities that would require long term perseverance and sacrifice on his part. Often one finds that he appears to pamper himself in many ways, and to behave like a spoiled child when criticized or thwarted or challenged.

These techniques and others tend to increase the difficulties and frictions in his relationships with other people who do not understand why a grown person demands so much from the environment in the way of tolerant understanding. They get "fed up" with him and "tell him off." But, because he usually is completely unaware of these techniques, he fails to understand their attitude, feels hurt with what he considers to be adequate reason, and finds new fuel to feed his inner unhappiness and sense of loneliness.

The resulting combustion frequently ends in another drinking episode. Very often it is felt that these episodes—when the individual has sobered up—add to his sense of inferiority, so that he sinks deeper into his morass. For many indiscreet acts, including psychosexual ones, occur under the influence of alcohol. While sins of omission may plague many of us, the alcoholic individual is often truly tortured by his acts of commission.

The alcoholic also may be one whose drinking is symptomatic of a minor psychoneurotic type reaction or of a major psychiatric reaction, including manic-depressive swings, schizophrenic-like episodes, epileptic equivalents, certain organic states, feebleminded states and conditions of the total or partial psychopath types. Here one might add that many who present varying degrees of this latter classification need not be viewed as hopeless, nor in the light of earlier years when the national and international social structures and populaces were more stable.

Some alcoholics drink because of intolerable physical pain. Others drink for the definite purpose of being free from intolerable psychic pain. And some appear to be at the end-stage of the habit of heavy social drinking, plus temporal, bodily, chemical and metabolic changes, and strains or griefs of life. In nearly all instances, one finds nutritional depletions, as a result of drinking and inadequate diet, along with other faulty hygienic and daily life-habits.

To sum up at this point, the alcoholic of today in many instances may be mildly or seriously psychiatrically ill. His drinking is a symptom

of the difficulties he experiences in his ordinary daily life and life cor
tacts. His thinking, his emotional actions and reactions, and his habi
life in general are faulty. From the physical standpoint he may hav
vitamin and other deficiencies and also conditions of metabolism an
body chemistry which need correction and which affect and are affecte
by his personality make-up and way of life.

The alcoholic of today is a sick person.

WHAT MAKES AN ALCOHOLIC?

An alcoholic is being made when one consciously or unconsciousl
begins to *depend* on alcohol's narcotic effects for a 'pick-up,' to sleep a
night, to feel 'good,' to cope with business or domestic problems, t
enjoy social gatherings, to 'get away' from oneself, to repress inne
urges of rebellion, or resentment, or of a psychosexual nature, to reliev
vague but very disturbing motor restlessness, and so on.

When an individual does depend on alcohol for any of these, or simi
lar reasons, he is substituting fantasy for reality. Because this substitutio
is a subtle one, he usually is *not* aware of it; and his alcohol dependenc
increases at a fairly fast rate. He may not, however, outwardly shov
the signs and harmful effects of this increased dependency for man
years; and because of this, alcoholism can be compared in many in
stances to cancer. Indeed, the average 'alcoholic of today,' can b
described as having 'cancer of the ego.' However, though his is a seriou
problem, it is not hopeless, provided that he can be helped to want hel
and provided that the help can be given by competent workers.

We have now briefly summed up some factors regarding the alcoholic
But, how did the individual become dependent upon alcohol to such ar
extent, in contrast to social drinkers who do not become dependent upo
this easily available narcotic?

From studies of many men and women, representative of nearly al
social, economic, educational, professional, and geographic backgrounds
including racial and religious differences; representatives of the broke
and the unbroken home; and representative also of the better and les
well-known dynamic complexes or motivants, and of the different psy
chiatric reaction types, one reaches the following conclusions:

An alcoholic is developed by many inter-related factors, together witl
his biological make-up and metabolism. We do not yet understand al
the complicated workings of the glands and blood-content but it seem
evident that many individuals must produce more adrenalin, for exam
ple, than do others, and thus are often more than ordinarily irascibl

n their behavior. Sugar metabolic and other disorders, as is well known, often bring about unpleasant mood and other changes and vice versa. The alcoholic individual time after time definitely appears to be 'loaded up' with nervous tension, on the motor side, which is manifested by sweating, stomach sensations and discomfort. All of these are many times considerably relieved by regulated doses of insulin. With the subsidence of the physical or somatic tensions, there is an accompanying calmness in thought and emotion. One feels that this finding, when substantiated by pharmacological research, may provide much help in treatment and also in prevention of alcoholic and other drug addictions which may be, in part produced by faulty body chemistries.

However, the factors of ancestry are equally important, including the geographic, racial, and religious backgrounds, drinking and other life habits. We still do not understand why even third generation Mediterraneans, for example, rarely become alcoholics in spite of the American scene and way of life. This holds true for other groups with a long tradition of wine-using and even of intoxication at festivals and other ceremonies. These groups do, however, produce narcotic addicts.

It is possible that certain highly tensed anxiety types cannot tolerate alcohol because it increases their somatic discomfort in nausea, headaches, etc. whereas other narcotics do not; and hence through trial-and-error they seek out the least disturbing means of acquiring a temporary Nirvana.

Aside from this, the racial background plays an important role, particularly when several racial groups are represented, strains from any one of which may take ascendancy at different times. That this is an actual fact appears to be borne out by the behavior, as, for example, when a descendant of Scotch-Irish ancestry shows alternate thriftiness and expansiveness which his American English wife finds difficult to understand or adjust to. Of course identification and imitation factors are involved here, and the early environmental upbringing of example and family legend. Nevertheless, until we know more about these racial influences, and so are able better to evaluate them, they must be considered in the main as being important factors in the production of different personality types, and different psychiatric problems, including that of alcoholism.

The individual alcoholic's personality make-up also, of course, results partly from his early experiences in life—his hurts and happinesses—and from his later experiences, which may be as profoundly formative.

We must add to all this the present-day stresses of the world we live in. We must also add that it is "normal" today for everyone at times, to

be aware of acute or even panicky feelings of uncertainty, of inner inse
curity, of anxiousness in general and in particular. Many have poo
sleep, and buy packets of sleeping powders at the drug store counters
Many have digestive difficulties. Many have stopped reading the dail
papers because they are too full of sudden political policy change, o
horror, of news of impending or actual disaster affecting large masses o
human beings.

But there is a difference between the majority of people who are re
acting thus to the contemporary pressures of existence in an Atomic Ag
and the millions in early and advanced alcoholism. The latter hav
found that their tensions are relieved by alcohol to a marked degre
and so have developed their addiction with harmful and disruptive con
sequences for themselves, their families, and the community.

Their addiction, and susceptibility to addiction, appear to derive fron
a combination of factors. Outstanding among these are:

1. A hypersensitive nervous system with marked reaction to variou
chemical substances and drugs, including alcohol.

2. A hypersensitive emotional-thinking system which makes the indi
vidual particularly vulnerable to the ordinary and currently extraoi
dinary onslaughts of life and to the inevitable clashes with other people

3. Perhaps as a result of these two factors, histories of patients ofte
reveal a variety of stressful situations which the individual could no
cope with at the time and which he also has not been able to assimilate
that is, their recollection unduly disturbs him and affects his later lif
behavior. Situations like this include family altercations, marital dishar
mony, employer and employee personnel problems, sexual activities an
trauma, unhappy memories of childhood and adolescence, and so on

4. The geographical ancestry already referred to.

5. Unknown physical biological, metabolic, and chemical ingredient
and changes.

6. Frequently, one also finds a lack of consistent active participatioi
in religious and community life which is sometimes due to the indi
vidual's inner personality and attitudes of negativism and sometimes to
definite disjointedness and negativism within the community itself.

In all cases, the so-called dynamics and the problem-clusters whic
the individual seeks to alleviate or escape through drinking are so differ
ent that it is impossible to state scientifically that any one event, or com
bination of events, is responsible for the development of alcoho
addiction.

Nevertheless, there may often be a history of an unstable early emotional life, of shallow and shifting values and goals in life, of inadequate personality disciplining, and, very often, residual effects from some severe illness or operation. One concludes, therefore, that *alcoholism must be understood in every instance as being a special problem relating to a specific individual's psychobiological endowment and functioning, and to his specific life history, his specific life problems, and the specific life setting and relationships with other individuals.*

One feels, at this stage of our factual knowledge, that the average "alcoholic of today" is made by a combination of:

1. His ancestry,

2. Early and later emotional hurts, likes, and experiences, both concious and unconscious,

3. A physical ingredient including his neurological system and the reactions associated with his glandular make-up, blood chemistry content, biological rhythm, and his metabolism,

4. Emotional and personality difficulties in his relationships with other people, and in coping with situations, and,

5. A lack of, or an inadequate, basic philosophy, faith, and conviction in the essential, profound, worthwhileness of life.

The great need, therefore, is first to examine the individual and attempt to understand and treat him as an individual, with attention to his concrete and varied requirements; secondly to be aware of the fact that contemporary history is producing new problems in social adjustment and in psycho-biological adjustment; and thirdly that, socio-psycho-biologically, the values and ideals of mankind cannot be neglected or devaluated without resulting destructive effects upon individual men. The rise in incidence of alcoholism and of crime reflect the current serious disruptions of our social order. We need not be dismayed by this if we remember at all times, and act upon the knowledge, that the social order is created and sustained, or negated and destroyed, deflected or re-invigorated, by its individual members.

Just as any behavior-illness-deviation derives from both physical and psychological components, so does any social behavior-illness-deviation derive from the interaction of individuals and the way of social living that they evolve. "No man is an island unto himself." Neither is any problem wholly insoluble when men of goodwill are determined to work together, using all available means, to work out that problem.

39 · Alcoholics Anonymous

by CHARLES H. UPTON

The rehabilitation of the alcoholic is a problem which the medical, psychological, and social sciences have sought to solve for a long time—without much success. It is interesting to note, therefore, that a movement started by a one time alcoholic and based on the principle of self-help has spread to virtually every state of the Union and even abroad, and claims to have cured thousands of victims. This movement has come to be known as Alcoholics Anonymous. In the following article, Charles H. Upton, the chief probation officer of San Francisco, experienced in dealing with alcoholics, tells the story of how this movement originated and how it works. [From *Federal Probation*, Vol. VIII, July-Sept. 1944, pp. 29-32. Reprinted by permission.]

ONE OF my former "problem children" shook his way into my office and I mean "shook" literally, for he vibrated all over the place and side swiped the door frame leading to my private office. He bore all the outward evidence of a spree.

"Howdy, Jim," I said. "Glad to see you. This is the first time you've been in since you finished your parole."

"I know," he answered, "and I should have been in before, but I was ashamed because I'd slipped on the hootch again."

"Skip it," I went on. "Let's see what we can do for you in the way of a clean shirt."

I dug a shirt that would fit him out of some clean laundry I usually have in the office, and sent him into the lavatory to wash up and put on the shirt.

When he returned, he started to say something, but I shut him off. I gave him two dollars, told him to get two drinks, then a shave, then a shine—by all means a shine. That is one of the greatest lifter-uppers a man's morale can have.

"Be back in an hour," I told him.

Not a word of condemnation; no nagging. This last remark is not intended as a bouquet for myself. I merely was following a precept I had lifted from the Book of Experience as written by Alcoholics Anonymous, that great group of ex-drunkards, of which I have more to say later.

Jim was back in an hour, looking better and undoubtedly feeling better, or at least more at ease. Meanwhile, I had telephoned a businessman friend of mine who is a member of the San Francisco group of Alco nolics Anonymous and who, after hearing my problem, immediately suggested that Jim have dinner at his home that night. Of course, I accepted for Jim.

My former parolee stayed around the office until closing time. Then I gave him another dollar, told him to take one drink—and only one—and go to the home of my friend.

I knew he would arrive there with some control of himself and something bordering on self-determination. I was banking on my own experience with alcohol through the years and with parolees and probationers and hundreds of newspapermen who have passed through my life in the irresponsible manner of the confirmed lush. I knew the clean shirt, the shave, the *shine*, the drink, backed by his own few words of contrition, would perk him up.

The rest of Jim's story came to me second hand. At my friend's home he was met with cordiality, friendship, and a good meal. His host's wife was graciousness personified. She's not an alcoholic herself; but like the wives of many members of Alcoholics Anonymous, she is a staunch ally of her husband in his attitude toward other alcoholics.

Liquor came into their conversation only casually. My friend told the story of Alcoholics Anonymous. It was there for Jim to accept or reject as he desired. No compulsion. No high pressure salesmanship. Just a simple story of men and women who have pulled themselves up by their own bootstraps and then have lent helping hands to others. Jim accepted it. At last reports, he was living an honest, clean life, and devoting his spare time to others who have asked the interest of Alcoholics Anonymous.

THE STORY OF THE FOUNDER OF THE MOVEMENT

How did this movement come about? Here's the story.

Bill, known to thousands of alcoholics as the founder of Alcoholics Anonymous, but who prefers to call himself a co-founder, has just been in San Francisco. I have met him and heard his story. I also have met Mrs. Bill, a nonalcoholic, grayish lady, with young eyes and face and smile. She survived her husband's years of heavy drinking, his on-the-water-wagon and off, his rides on the crest of temporary success, and his plunges into the sink of the outcast, his hospitals in and out, his pledges and broken pledges—until he "recovered" nine years ago.

By word and thought she epitomizes Alcoholics Anonymous, called A. A. by its members. When San Francisco girl reporters asked her how it felt to be the wife of a reformed drunk, she answered:

"I don't know. I've never been married to one. There's nothing worse than a reformed drunk. He's intolerant, crotchety, and altogethe a person to be avoided. I'm married to an alcoholic, a sick man who ha recovered. For alcoholism is a disease of the mind and an allergy of th body. Alcoholics who have recovered—that is, who have arrested th disease, not 'cured' it, for it is ever present—are happy, pleasant, to erant people. They may or may not join the A. A., but they want t help their fellows recover from the ailment they know so well to thei horror."

So Mrs. Bill voiced the thoughts of other A. A. wives I have observed Meanwhile her husband gave his interpretation of alcoholism and ho\ to arrest it before nonmembers and members of groups in the Centra California area.

He is a tall, rangy man with a Down East drawl. Probably no grea shakes as a public speaker before he consecrated his life to aidin fellow alcoholics, he undoubtedly has developed a fluency that, couple with his sincerity, inspires whomever he addresses.

Bill's story runs parallel to that of all alcoholics and because of it similarity to theirs, they recognize in him a fellow creature—one wh speaks the same language—and are willing to listen to him.

After World War I he returned from France to enter Wall Street. H became first a good-fellow drinker, then an habitual one until, as he e> presses it, drinking became an obsession. He was in and out of hospita a dozen times, each time leaving with high resolve to stay dry and eac time falling at the most unexpected time and in the most unexpecte manner. Each time he fell, he rationalized his action with some excus∢ a mental maneuver familiar to all alcoholics. The last time, nine yea> ago, he fell because it was Armistice Day.

Between Bill's next to the last and his last binge, an old-time drinkin companion called on him. The visitor was sober. He said simply he ha been influenced by a group of new friends to get honest with himsel and to square himself with others. No harangue, no shouting religio> Bill thought so well of his friend's program that he tried to think it ou and adopt it. He was doing well—then that fatal Armistice Day.

SOME PRINCIPLES ON WHICH A. A. WAS BASED

During his last visit in the hospital, Bill thought much of his ol friend's new philosophy and pondered the failures of both doctors an clergymen to reach alcoholics effectively. The doctor schooled his patier on the harmful effects of liquor, warned him he was ruining his min and body. The patient granted those things, still could not stop drin` ing. The clergyman opened to him the vistas of a better life, the happ ness to be found in Godliness. The patient granted those things, too, but would not stop drinking.

Then came Bill's thought that grew into a stone in the foundation of Alcoholics Anonymous. Alcoholics would not heed the doctor or clergyman, the mother or father, the wife or best friend. Why? Because the latter were not alcoholics themselves. They could not get a transmission line through to the patient. Perhaps a fellow alcoholic, Bill reasoned, could succeed where the doctor and preacher had failed. Hadn't he listened with awakened interest to his own former drinking companion? Hadn't his friend who spoke the same language aroused something in him that no one else, even faithful Mrs. Bill, had been able to do?

Eureka! He had it. One alcoholic would listen to another. Thus a stone in the foundation of A. A. was laid, and something even greater was to come. As he lay in the hospital that last time he had a sudden spiritual awakening. His friends, he said, call it "Bill's hot flash." Next, Providence placed in his hands a copy of William James' *Varieties of Religious Experience*, and he read of experiences similar to his. Then he realized that a Power greater than himself had come to his aid.

Bill was careful to point out that such sudden inspirations do not come to all, that in most cases the transition is so slow and gradual that it is imperceptible. For this reason A. A. does not overemphasize the spiritual side of its program, preferring to encourage each member to reach his conclusions in his own way.

Bill left the hospital that time inspired with the thought that he was ordained to save all the drunks in the world, but his high hopes were doomed to discouragement. For six months he spoke his piece among scores of alcoholics in New York without recruiting a single one to his banner.

It was not until he was in a mid-western city on business half a year later that he interested a doctor in his ideas—a doctor who himself was suffering the tortures of the damned. The two, gaining strength from each other, went to work on a once prominent attorney who was in a "drying out" hospital for the fourth time in six months. They succeeded in jerking him back from the abyss that yawned before him. Thus A. A. really became an entity, with three inspired members, flanked by Mrs. Bill and Bill's old doctor friend in the New York hospital from which he had last been discharged.

THE GROWTH OF THE ORGANIZATION

As we in San Francisco heard Bill's story and looked back to nine years ago when those "Three Musketeers" embarked on their adventure, we could appreciate only in part those early struggles because we did not take part in them; but on reflection one can see that their self-imposed task was awesome. They were attacking an evil that had afflicted the world for centuries without solution. They were attacking a problem with all the cards stacked against them.

How far they have gone is best shown by the fact that a minimum of 10,000 Americans in most of the States of the union have arrested alcoholism through the A. A. program. The society has more than 200 widely scattered groups. It has come across the Rocky Mountains on its own momentum and has now spread to Canada, Australia, and even India.

"I feel humble," said Bill here, "when I come to California and find 1,500 recoveries in this State alone. That result was reached without a single member of the Eastern groups visiting this coast. It came solely through the printed word—our pamphlets and book and articles published in magazines."

THE PROGRAM AND PHILOSOPHY

What is the A. A. program? The first step is the admission of the prospective member that he is an alcoholic. He must admit to himself first that he cannot control his drinking, that his existence has become unmanageable, that drinking has disrupted his economic, social, and domestic life. He must face the fact that he cannot take a single drink. He cannot take even a beer and then let it alone.

Having made this admission to himself, the alcoholic feels free to discuss his problems with another alcoholic, a fellow sufferer who has laid the transmission line that the doctor or the clergyman could not lay. He learns that A. A. recognizes alcoholism as an obsession of the mind and a disease of the body.

"Alcoholism may result from a number of causes, different and in varying degrees in different people," Bill said. "There may be a maladjustment in youth. A child may be gawky and homely, not one of the crowd. He may obstinately stick at something to prove he can do it. As he grows older, he fortifies himself with alcohol. Or there may be a physical predisposition to alcoholism, as some are physically susceptible to tuberculosis. Years of drinking attack this physical condition until the time comes when a person is thrown out of physical gear by a single drink. Then there is the inferiority complex. A man with such a condition thinks he's quite a fellow after a drink or two; he gets a kick out of the superior sensation and drinks oftener to attain it. As he drinks, his habit becomes an obsession.

"After a drinking man admits his alcoholism and is willing to do anything to overcome it, one of the next steps is for him to get honest with himself, to analyze himself and try to rectify the wrongs he knows exist within him. From time to time," Bill continued, "he should take these personal inventories and continue the self-purging process. One way for him to get right with himself and the world is for him to seek out those he has wronged and try to make amends."

One step in a 12-point program conceived by the early leaders is No. 12 on the list, but it is by no means least. It provides that the A. A. member who has developed his own recovery should try to carry his message to other alcoholics. By this activity he not only helps to keep himself dry, but wins, according to Bill's words, a happiness new to his hitherto drinking world.

The spiritual side of the program is approached without fanfare or evangelism. "We are not crusaders or saints," Bill said. "The point is that we are willing to grow along spiritual lines. The principles we have set down are guides to progress. We claim spiritual progress rather than spiritual perfection."

Bill warned that personality changes or spiritual experiences need not be in the nature of sudden and spectacular upheavals.

"Most of our experiences," he said, "are what William James calls the 'educational variety' because they develop slowly over a period of time. Quite often the friends of the new member are aware of the difference in him long before he is himself. The new man gradually realizes that he has undergone a profound alteration in his reaction to life; that such a change could hardly have been brought about by himself alone. With few exceptions our members find that they have tapped an unsuspected inner resource that they presently identify with their own conception of a Power greater than themselves.

"We believe an alcoholic capable of honestly facing his problems in the light of our experience can recover provided he does not close his mind to all spiritual concepts. He can be defeated only by an attitude of intolerance and belligerent denial."

While the foregoing seems to have referred solely to men, such is not the case. It refers to women as well, for the women alcoholics are as much problems as their male counterparts. In the words of Mrs. Bill: "They are more crafty and more subtle about their drinking, but A. A. does the job for them as well as for the men."

Let us pause to consider how such a movement has grown without formal organization, without money, without taint. Its very simplicity and sincerity, its absence of selfish aim other than recovery from alcoholism, is the answer. It has no officers, no dues, no fees. Its modest expenses are met by contributions in the different groups. Its book and

pamphlets are published by member contributions and a small foundation established by a few nonalcoholics and alcoholics.

CONCLUSION

The A. A. seems to me to be of great significance to the correctional
and penal officer, and to the social worker, because many offenses, probation and parole violations, and social problems may be traced directly
to alcohol. The program may have a far-reaching effect on rehabilitation
throughout the country. It may make progress where medical men, psychiatrists, and penologists have failed. Who knows?

40 · Who Is the Drug Addict?

by ALFRED R. LINDESMITH

As in the case of the alcoholic, so in that of the drug addict
many studies have been made purporting to discover the
causes of an individual's becoming a habitual user of drugs.
The explanation widely accepted is that the drug addict,
who, at least in the United States, is more often than not a
member of the underworld, has become such because of
neurotic traits and other mental abnormalities. In this
article, Alfred R. Lindesmith, an Indiana University professor of sociology whose major field is social psychology
and criminology, subjects various extant theories on drug
addiction to a critical analysis and points out their shortcomings. ["The Drug Addict as a Psychopath," *American
Sociological Review*, Vol. 5, No. 6, Dec. 1940, pp. 914-920.
Reprinted by permission.]

THE PURPOSE of this article is to criticize what is no doubt the most
widely accepted theory of drug addiction today. The significance of this
critique is increased because it deals with topics of general methodological
relevance and because the viewpoint criticized is often assumed with respect to other forms of human behavior than drug addiction.

The "accepted" theory which will be criticized holds that people become addicts because they are inferior or abnormal and because the drug
offers them an artificial support or a means of escape from their problems. A typical expression of this view is found in H. E. Barnes' recent
book:

It is now definitely demonstrated that the most serious cases of drug addiction are the result of neurotic conditions, namely mental and nervous disorders growing out of deep seated mental conflicts in the individual. The narcotic drug produces a sense of euphoria or well being which temporarily removes the sufferer from his mental conflicts and fears.[1]

This statement from Barnes is typical, but the terminology used by various authors is sometimes different. The central idea is that prior to becoming addicts, people are distinguished from the general population by having more than their share of traits which may be taken as evidence of abnormality, weakness, psychopathy, etc. It is frequently assumed tacitly that any trait which distinguishes addicts from nonaddicts must *ipso facto* be an indication of abnormality. In popular opinion, the same view is expressed in the often repeated assertion that addicts have "weak wills" and that this is proved by the fact that the individual uses the drug.

This theory has certain limitations which are at once obvious. It is not specific and is therefore unverifiable. No considerable proportion of abnormal persons (however defined) become addicts, and the fact that in any particular case, abnormality has not led to addiction therefore cannot be taken into account. Moreover, this same explanation has been presented as an explanation of other phenomena, e.g., crime and alcoholism. A theory which purports to explain several different types of phenomena at once with no alteration in form usually explains none of them.

The term "drug addict" will be used in this article to refer exclusively to users of opiate drugs, that is, to users of morphine, opium, and heroin. The use of drugs such as marihuana or cocaine presents an entirely different problem from that of opiate abuse. An indication of the vagueness and all-inclusiveness of the theory being criticized here is the fact that its proponents often have not bothered to exclude any kind of drug in their definitions of drug addiction. Sandor Radó has invented the term "pharmacothymia" for a kind of disease entity which consists of the desire to ingest drugs in any form.[2] Used in this way, the term is an omnibus category referring to many different things rather than to one specific thing. It is necessary to delimit the meaning of this word, for not only is the clinical picture of opiate addiction entirely distinct, but in the social life of the underworld, opiate users constitute a separate class which has little to do socially with other types of drug users. The user of marihuana and the user of opiates ordinarily do not associate with each

1 Harry Elmer Barnes, *Society in Transition*, 806-7, New York, 1939.
2 Sandor Radó, "The Psychoanalysis of Pharmacothymia," *Psychoanal. Quart.*, vol. 2, 1933.

other or feel that they have anything in common, even though according to Radó they are both supposed to be afflicted with the same disease of "pharmacothymia." For the purposes of precise communication, words must refer to one thing at a time. It is a serious error to confound or equate morphine addiction with anything like coffee drinking, tobacco smoking, alcoholism, or the chronic use of aspirin.

The literature on drug addiction contains so many statements like the one quoted from Barnes that one would expect to find a mass of evidence supporting this generally accepted conclusion, but no such mass of evidence exists, and the confidence with which the assertion is made, reflects, not the evidence, but the number of times the assertion has been made. The main factual support of these conclusions is found in the work of two men, Dr. Lawrence Kolb and Dr. C. Schultz.[3] Both conclude that most addicts are abnormal before becoming addicted. Kolb put the percentage at 86 and Schultz put it at about 87 in an independent study.

The first point to be noted about the theories of these two men is that neither of them claims that abnormality is always the cause of addiction, but only that it usually is. Both admit that normal individuals do sometimes become addicts. It may be very useful and important to know that 86 percent of American addicts are abnormal before becoming addicts, assuming that this is true, but from the standpoint of scientific theory such a truth has little significance, for it is precisely the 14 percent of those who are admittedly normal who constitute the most important problem. This is especially true in view of the assumption that the underworld consists mainly of psychopathic persons. Since most addicts belong to the underworld (in the United States), it requires explanation that any considerable percentage of them could be normal at all. Most of the writers who accept the theory under consideration, ignore the problem of accounting for addiction in this group of persons, who, according to the criteria set up, are "normal." Sometimes these cases are dismissed with a sentence or two or are simply called "accidental." A few writers have maintained that those addicts who seemed to be normal before addiction really were not normal at all but had only succeeded in concealing their weaknesses and abnormalities, and so concluded that all addicts were abnormal. By the same logic and method, all human beings can be shown to be abnormal.

[3] "Types and Characteristics of Drug Addicts," *Mental Hygiene*, IX, 1925; "Drug Addiction: A Study of Some Medical Cases," *Arch. of Neurol. and Psychiat.*, X, 1928, 171-83; C. Schultz, "Report of the Mayor's Committee to the Hon. Richard C. Patterson, Jr., Commissioner of Correction, New York City," *Amer. J. Psychiat.*, X, 1930-31.

The studies of Kolb and Schultz represent the best available evidence in support of the theory here being criticized, yet in neither case did these authors use or even mention control groups. If abnormality is assigned as the cause of addiction, it is implied that there is more abnormality among addicts than among those who do not become addicts. It is meaningless to say that 86 percent of a given class of addicts are abnormal before addiction if the same criteria of abnormality are not applied to the nonaddict population to permit comparison. There is no study available to support the theory under consideration which makes adequate use of control groups. On these grounds alone, the conclusions are not supported by the evidence.

It is possible to argue that abnormality in the general population would certainly not run as high as 86 or 87 percent and that these studies therefore do have some significance, even though control groups were not used, if they have actually shown that abnormality is that frequent among drug addicts. It should be noticed, however, that while the authors attempt to draw conclusions about addicts "prior to addiction," they actually studied addicts only after addiction—and in many cases, after many years of addiction. Some of their cases had used the drug for more than thirty years. They do not tell us how those traits which were the result of addiction were separated from those that were causes of addiction. They therefore had no direct information about the "addict prior to addiction" which is what they attempt to generalize about.

When one examines the categories into which addicts were classified in order to establish the conclusions cited, further difficulties make their appearance. Kolb, e.g., in articles cited above, has the following classes:

1. Normals (14 percent) who are accidentally or necessarily addicted in the course of medical practice;
2. Carefree individuals, devoted to pleasure, seeking new sensations (38 percent);
3. Definite neuroses (13.5 percent);
4. Habitual criminals (13 percent) "always psychopathic"; and finally,
5. Inebriates (21.5 per cent).

The largest category, including 38 percent of the cases, is the most poorly defined consisting of "carefree persons devoted to pleasure, seeking new sensations." It is impossible to tell what is meant by such a description. Many persons seek to be carefree; all of us, we suppose, are devoted to pleasure; and W. I. Thomas regarded the wish for new experience as a common human trait. It is to be noted that Kolb assumes that all professional criminals are psychopathic, an assumption which most criminologists would question. In attempts to show that criminality is produced by abnormality or psychopathy, it is assumed that all drug addicts are psychopathic.

Dr. Schultz gives a fuller description of his categories than Kolb does. He classified 318 addicts into the following seven classes.

1. Normal (13.2 percent). In 13.2 percent of the patients treated, little or no evidence could be elicited of psychopathic personality other than the drug addiction *per se*.

2. Inadequate personalities (30 percent). While the majority in this group were probably psychopathic types before using the drug, there were some who appeared to have been fairly normal.

3. Emotional instability (20 percent). Here there is a question as to whether the instability was present before or came as a result of the addiction.

4. Criminalism (13 percent). The dominant feature here is seen to be profound egoism combined with complete indifference to ethical issues.

5. Paranoid personality (9 percent). In this type we find conceit and suspicion and a stubborn adherence to a fixed idea.

6. Nomadism (8 percent). The nomadic or wandering tendency is present in most of us.

7. Homosexuality (6 percent).[4]

In this classification, Schultz like Kolb has the largest percentage of abnormals in the most poorly defined class, "inadequate personality." In the second and third classes, he admits that the trait in question may have followed rather than preceded the addiction. These two classes include 50 percent of the cases. His statement about Class 4 is simply a partial definition of criminality and does not tell why these persons are regarded as abnormal. The last three classes are relatively insignificant in the sense that together they include only 23 percent of the cases. In addition the so-called nomadism and paranoia might very well be consequences rather than causes of addiction. The proportion of homosexuality is close to what one would expect in any class of people. In spite of this author's admission that some of his classes include addicts who were probably normal before addiction, he takes no account of this in stating his final conclusion, that 86.8 percent of the addicts of his sample were abnormal prior to addiction.

It is known that some persons who receive drugs in hospitals become addicts while others under the same conditions do not. This has often been explained by arguing that those who are of psychopathic predisposition become addicts while those who are normal do not. However, when a medical man who accepted this theory gave a patient of his a

[4] The comments on these classes are by Schultz. See article referred to above.

great deal of morphine saying it was not dangerous since the man was not a psychopath, he was solemnly warned by another authority who held the same view that one could not tell whether a person was psychopathic or not and that morphine had, therefore, to be given carefully to everyone.[5] A much simpler explanation of this fact that some individuals in the hospital situation become addicts while others do not, is that those who do not have been successfully kept in ignorance of the nature of the withdrawal distress or of the drug which they were given.[6] This explanation is corroborated by the claims now being made by medical men that it is unnecessary to make addicts in medical practice even though the patient is psychopathic or neurotic and has to be given the drug for a long time. The techniques used to prevent addiction in such cases are directed toward preventing the patient from obtaining knowledge of what is happening to him.[7]

Two mutually contradictory views are often held concerning addicts. One is that the addict becomes what he is because of abnormality, and the other is that anyone can become an addict provided only that he takes or is given the drug. This contradiction is brought out in the remarks made to the author by a narcotic agent. He explained that addicts do not get a "kick" out of the drug, that they are "normal" under its influence. When asked why they used the drug, he was puzzled for a moment and then said, "It's because they are weaklings."

The next question was, "Would you or I become addicts if we took morphine steadily for a couple months?"

"Absolutely," he said.

"Would we be like all the rest of them, or would we quit it?"

"We'd be like any other addict. There's no cure for it. Once they're hooked, they always come back to it."

A basic consideration which only can be mentioned here is the assumption that an explanation of addiction ever can be found by such a procedure as the theory under consideration implies—that is, by comparing the frequency with which a given trait appears in the addict population with its frequency in the nonaddict population. Statisticians usually insist that such a correlation in itself has no causal significance whatever. In the study of crime, positive correlations between poverty and crime and between low I. Q.'s and certain types of crimes have been

[5] E. Meyer, "Ueber Morphinismus, Kokainismus, und den Missbrauch anderer Narkotica," *Medizinische Klinik*, XX, 1924, 403-7.

[6] Cf. A. R. Lindesmith, "A Sociological Theory of Drug Addiction," *Amer. J. Sociol.*, 1938, 48: 593-613.

[7] Cf. *Report of Departmental Committee on Morphine and Heroin Addiction to the Ministry of Health*, London, 1926.

found but no conclusions concerning causal relationships have been established by these facts.

On the basis of the evidence actually presented by Kolb and Schultz and by other scholars, the only conclusion which appears to be warranted is that virtually nothing is known about the addict prior to addiction. Terry and Pellens agree with this after their excellent survey of the evidence.[8]

Finally, a word may be said about viewing the use of morphine as an escape mechanism. It is not entirely clear just what an "escape mechanism" is. The term is one of the popular clichés of psychiatric literature and, like other such terms, is used with more confidence than precision. However, assuming that the meaning is that a drug user forgets his sorrows and his inferiorities by stupefying himself with drugs as an alcoholic does with whiskey, then this conception is entirely wrong. The use of opiates in the beginning, for a month or so, may have escape value in this sense, but after that, such is far from being the case. The person who, let us assume, takes the drug to escape a problem, will find, when he has become addicted, that he still has the original problem plus one even more serious—namely, the opiate habit and all that it involves. His difficulty then would be to find an escape from the habit. During addiction, the user of morphine has insight into the miseries and difficulties which are involved in addiction. He does not spend his time in a dreamy stupor as sensational literature sometimes depicts him. In short, the belief that a man can achieve, by becoming an addict, the same thing that he can achieve by getting drunk is a delusion. For, as a rule, the drug addict does not even maintain the delusion of being carefree and happy. He is, as a plain fact, ordinarily a miserable and harassed person, as all who know addicts are aware.

On the basis of the foregoing discussion, it appears that the theory under consideration is not actually supported by any evidence, and that even if it were, it would still not be a satisfactory theory from the point of view of the etiology of opiate addiction. In view of the weaknesses of the theory and in view of the lack of evidence, how is one to account for the confidence of Barnes and the general acceptance of this viewpoint? The idea of the control group has been well known for many years but was not used in these studies. In spite of this fact, the studies appear to have carried conviction. It seems probable to the writer that the conclusions were not actually based upon the evidence, but were rather independent expressions of attitudes assumed toward addicts. Long before the two studies we have discussed were made, the general public spoke of addicts as weaklings. Addicts, to a greater or lesser ex-

[8] Terry and Pellens, *The Opium Problem*, 513-16, New York, 1938.

tent, always have been a pariah class which has not been in a position to refute any charges levelled against it. Apparently it gives people some kind of secret satisfaction to call names when they cannot understand. We regard the use of such terms as psychopathic, neurotic, weak-willed, degenerate, abnormal, etc., as the representation of an emotional attitude toward the drug user since no research has demonstrated that they are grounded in objective fact. The modern "scientific" theory is, in short, merely a reflection and a rephrasing of old folk attitudes and is, in this sense, moralistic. It did not grow out of any body of tested evidence.

This conclusion is corroborated by other arguments. Drug addiction, it is said, is prevalent in the underworld because there is a large proportion of psychopaths in the underworld. However, Kurt Pohlisch, in a reliable statistical study, found that doctors in Germany were addicts 100 times oftener in proportion to their numbers than the rest of the population.[9] It is well known that the medical profession is relatively often affected by addiction. According to the logic of the position we are discussing, this should lead to the conclusion that abnormality, neuroticism, etc., are much more frequent among medical men than in the general population. However, probably because of the prestige enjoyed by the medical man, this uncomplimentary conclusion has not been drawn. Instead, it is said that the doctor becomes addicted because of the availability of the drug and because of the fatigue connected with irregular hours. But both of these conditions apply equally well to the underworld character who leads an irregular life and has the drug made available to him by the fact that the underworld handles the illicit traffic in drugs. It is much more tempting to call the underworld character a psychopath than to call a reputable physician by that derogatory name.

The same tendency to permit an attitude of disapproval to enter into presumably objective analysis is evident in the unspoken assumption found in studies along these lines, that any trait which distinguishes addicts from nonaddicts is *ipso facto* a criterion of abnormality. Hooton has recently made the same error in his study of the anthropometric characteristics of criminals. Addicts are said to become addicted because they have feelings of frustration, lack self-confidence and need the drug to bolster themselves up. Lack of self-confidence is taken as a criterion of psychopathy or of weakness. But another person becomes addicted, it is said, because of "curiosity" and a "willingness to try anything once" and this too is called abnormal. Thus, self-confidence and the lack of self-confidence are both signs of abnormality. The addict is evidently

[9] Kurt Pohlisch, "Die Verbreitung des Chronischen Opiatmissbrauchs in Deutschland," *Monatschrift für Psychiatrie und Neurologie*, LXXIX, 1931, Pt. I, 1-32.

judged in advance. He is damned if he is self-confident and he is damned if he is not.

It seems more reasonable to suppose that whatever selective influences are at work are much more blind and accidental in character than is usually assumed. The same trait may lead to results that would be called good in one case and bad in another. Thus "curiosity" leads some people to become experimental scientists and leads others to try morphine and become addicts. There is no evidence to indicate that any personality type whatever in any part of the social hierarchy is immune to addiction. In the United States, it is relatively prevalent in the underworld and secondarily in the medical and allied professions. In England and Germany, the great majority of addicts (opiate) comes from the medical class and from the middle classes, not from the underworld. In Formosa, the working classes are mainly affected. The theory under consideration is unable to account for such variations in the incidence of addiction unless one is to assume that abnormality is concentrated in the underworld in one country, in the working classes in another, in the middle classes in another, and so on.

It is the contention of that branch of sociology known as *Wissenssoziologie*, or the sociology of knowledge, that scientific research is often influenced and determined by extratheoretical considerations. This is presumably less true of the physical and biological sciences than it is of the social. This analysis has shown that "scientific" theories of drug addiction may be more adequately understood in terms of the emotional attitudes they express than in terms of the evidence. Theories of drug addiction reflect the unfavorable prestige position of addicts in the class hierarchy. A similar analysis would probably apply to other stigmatized minority groups.

CHAPTER ELEVEN

Gambling

41 · The Forms of Gambling

by OSWALD JACOBY

> Gambling is condemned on moral grounds and, in most
> places, forbidden legally. It is a well-known fact that,
> aside from the demoralizing effect that it may have on the
> individual habitually indulging in it, gambling generally
> involves swindling and corruption on a large scale. It is
> therefore considered by many a social problem of no little
> significance. In the following article, Oswald Jacoby, a well-
> known authority on games, describes the various types of
> gambling in this country. [From *The Annals*, Vol. 269, May
> 1950, pp. 39-45. Reprinted by permission.]

OVER THE SPAN of centuries the definition of gambling has undergone
many changes. For example, what is currently regarded as one of the
world's most prosperous and distinguished industries, namely, insurance,
was once condemned as a forbidden wager on the outcome of an event
—such as the successful completion of a ship's journey and its safe arrival in port, intact, cargo and all. Consequently, insurance was once
conducted clandestinely, among private syndicates, the largest of which
—Lloyds of London—still survives as a venerable institution.

To most people today, gambling means betting on such sport events as horse races, playing card games and the like for money, or taking part in lotteries. This loose definition is open to challenge, but we may consider these activities first, since they represent at least a conception of gambling in America.

BETTING ON HORSE RACES

In many states, legislators have decreed that those who attend horse races may bet on those races. A portion of all the money so wagered is paid over to the state treasury. By contrast, it is illegal to accept away-from-the-track wagers. When such wagers are illegally offered and accepted, no portion of that money is forfeit to the state treasury.

Most people cannot find time to go to the track. They nevertheless insist on betting on the races, laws to the contrary notwithstanding. How many people place bets of this kind? No figures are available. Many men and women who bet regularly take great care to conceal that fact from business associates, spouses, ministers, tax collectors, and other traditional enemies. In these circumstances, any estimate is bound to be a guess.

The technique of placing an off-track bet is quite simple. If one comes well recommended, he may contact a bookmaker and place his bet by telephone. From time to time the bookmaker may find ways to let the bettor know that he has changed his telephone number. From time to time, also, he will send a runner to pay what the bettor has won or collect what he has lost. Such transactions are in cash, and no receipt or written memorandum changes hands. Appointments with a runner are almost invariably private, and sometimes quite secret.

Most bets are not telephoned, but are placed with the bookmaker or his runner. One visits a certain cigar store or barbershop or bar, names his bet, and puts up his money. If he wins, he seeks out the runner and collects his winnings.

How does one locate a bookmaker to begin with? Betting is by no means a completely secret activity. There are always companions with whom one discusses triumphs of the past and plans for the future. The neophyte, fascinated by the dramatic suspense of gambling, its aura of "cloak-and-dagger," or desirous of demonstrating adulthood and oneness with the group, is introduced to a bookmaker. He will presently have his own group of confidants with whom he will exchange comments on bookies as others comment on tailors, hairdressers, and the like.

In a strange town one would ask the hotel bellboy or elevator man. The newsdealer, who sells one a racing chart, would probably know and might tell one. So might the policeman on the beat, although this procedure is not recommended. If the bettor finds a bar or cigar store in which a radio is tuned at track time to racing results, he should have no trouble in establishing contact.

SPORTING EVENTS

A bookmaker is not content with accepting wagers on horse races. He will also quote odds on other sporting and athletic contests, such as football games, basketball games, hockey games, prize fights, and political elections.

Ordinarily this is done by means of handicapping. If Competitor A is thought more likely to win than Competitor B, a suitable handicap is arranged to equalize their chances. The customer may choose either competitor on the basis of the handicap. Thus, a weak football team may be credited with fourteen points against a stronger team. Those betting on the stronger team can collect if it wins by a margin of more than fourteen points. In a one-sided political election, Candidate A may be credited with 15,000 votes to put him on equal terms with Candidate B.

It would be an unusual business office in which one could bet openly on a horse race, but the stigma is not attached to all other contests. For example, football pools are fairly widely tolerated. On a Monday or Tuesday a list of the games scheduled for the following Saturday can be obtained, each game "equalized" with its handicap. The bettor makes a few selections and returns the marked list with his bet toward the end of the week.

Baseball pools are even more widely accepted. Here no outside bookmaker is needed. The names of the major league baseball teams are written on slips of paper, and each entrant draws a folded slip to select a team. Each puts up an equal amount, and the entire amount is turned over to the entrant whose team scores most runs during the week. Some businessmen favor such pools on the theory that they promote office friendship and *esprit de corps*.

Some professional gamblers who concentrate on sporting events—such as football, boxing, baseball, and basketball—follow the traditional habit of trying to assure themselves of a "sure thing." Thus, they have frequently resorted to bribery (or attempted bribery) of one or more of the participants in those events. The most famous such episode was the Chicago "Black Sox" World Series baseball scandal in 1919, as a result of which a number of famous players were banned for life from the game. In more recent years, men have been sentenced to prison in New York for attempts to bribe professional football and college basketball players. These are fairly characteristic of the types of third-party criminality which can, and do, become by-products of certain forms of gambling.

LOTTERIES, PUNCHBOARDS, ETC.

Lotteries based on horse races are slightly more acceptable than ordinary bets on horses, perhaps because such lotteries are often conducted for the benefit of charitable institutions. Even more widely accepted, however, is the raffle for the benefit of a charity. Many of the pious folk who sell raffle tickets to add to church funds would indignantly repudiate the suggestion that they were helping to promote a lottery.

Almost equally common are commercially promoted punchboards. The elevator man or perhaps the switchboard operator asks you to "take a chance on a turkey" at the approach of Thanksgiving or Christmas. You obligingly push out a rolled-up slip of paper from the punchboard and pay the amount indicated thereon. When a winner is declared, one turkey is presented to that person and another to the elevator man (or whoever).

Similar punchboards are made available at other times of the year, but with less success. Storekeepers sometimes use them to raffle off expensive merchandise.

Gambling in stores is made possible also by way of mechanical contrivances of various kinds. In some cases (slot machines) you pull a lever to spin dials. When the dials line up in certain preordained positions you collect from the machine ("hitting the jackpot"). In other devices (pinball machines) you propel a ball onto a surface studded with electrical contacts and springs. You win if you contrive to illuminate certain lights by means of the contacts touched by the ball. Not all pinball games are played for gain, but in many places they are so used.

Slot machines and pinball games have been outlawed in various communities, but often flourish despite such disapproval. Rare is the adult who cannot conveniently play such a machine if he wishes.

A somewhat different type of lottery is known currently as "bingo," although it has been played in many countries under different names. Each contestant is given a card on which numbers are printed, each card having a different selection of numbers. An official draws numbers by lot and announces them as drawn. Each contestant crosses out or covers up any number on his card that is so called out. The winner is the player who first crosses out all the numbers on his card or a particular pattern of numbers (a complete diagonal, horizontal, or vertical row). The winner collects the pool contributed by the other participants, less a percentage for the "bank." Bingo became so popular during the thirties that motion picture theaters organized brief games between showings to attract patronage. Churches and fraternal orders organized bingo nights to supplement their funds.

QUESTION OF PARTICIPATION

The person who bets on the outcome of a race or other athletic event may claim participation to the extent of selecting the most likely winner. The pinball game addict may claim that he can achieve better results, by virtue of his skillful play, than the tyro. For the most part, however, the bettor is a nonparticipant, almost a spectator, in the forms of gambling thus far discussed.

The situation is quite different in such forms of gambling as betting on games of skill, such as chess, checkers, backgammon, billiards, card games, or even dice games. Here the gambler is a true participant, since he is usually in a position to affect the outcome materially by the skill and judgment he exercises.

The case is clearest in gambling on games of chess. There is no large amount of gambling on this game, since skill is so overwhelming a factor that the result of even a single game can usually be predicted accurately. Nevertheless, it is customary in some clubs for amateurs to bet trifling amounts when they play against certain masters. This is more of a subsidy than a gamble. Players of equal ability sometimes bet 10 or 25 cents per game, more to add spice to the game than as a serious wager. Occasionally a strong player will offer a substantial handicap to an opponent, and the outcome may be sufficiently in doubt to make a true wager possible.

The opposite may be observed of dice games, notably the game known as craps. It is very widely played by youths, by adults of little education, and by others who enjoy gambling. When the conditions are fair, the outcome of a single bet cannot be predicted. In casual games, the experienced player may win by superior knowledge of the odds. In gambling houses or in games where all the players are experienced, the skill of the player consists only in knowing when to stop playing.

CARD PLAYING

The popularity of card playing may be judged from the fact that in an average year sixty million decks of playing cards are sold at retail. In a six-month period in 1949 this amount was doubled by the meteoric rise of a new card game (canasta) for which special cards were devised and sold.

Some card games, such as poker, are invariably played for stakes of value. Other games, such as bridge, may be played for no stake at all. It is difficult to estimate how many players should be called gamblers, because many of the same individuals play both types of game. For example, about a million men and women play duplicate bridge with some regularity, no stake being involved; and probably half of the same individuals play rubber bridge for stakes at other times.

Most card playing takes place in the home. Sometimes it is couple against couple, in such games as bridge and canasta. Larger groups of women forgather in the afternoons, taking turns at providing facilities and refreshments. Mah-jongg is another favorite diversion of such groups. It is my informed opinion, based on no careful statistical study, that small stakes are involved in most of these games.

Most country clubs, tennis clubs, and athletic clubs have card rooms, as do also most large social and political clubs in the big cities. It may be that in such a card room a game is sometimes played for no stake, but I am inclined to doubt even the possibility.

Clubs maintained solely for card playing abound in the larger cities. Most bridge clubs, open to the general public, make available the equipment and the space, and serve as a meeting place for players of more than casual skill and interest in the game. The stakes are often quite small in relation to the means of the players, but a stake of some kind is usually involved.

LOCALE OF GAMBLING

The gambling casino plays a very small role in American gambling life. Few but the very affluent, and those in only a few cities, patronize the sort of establishment that provides roulette tables and other mechanical lotteries, such card games as baccarat and *chemin de fer*, and the like.

The poor man's gambling casino is the amusement park, the county fair, or the carnival show. Here he may play any of a multitude of games in which a small investment affords him a chance to win a large doll, a box of candy, or other prize of some value.

The rich man's gambling casino is, in many cases, not a casino at all but a stock exchange. Despite the strictures of legislators and of the Securities and Exchange Commission, a very large number of people still buy and sell stocks regularly for speculative purposes rather than for investment. The practice is not so widespread as it was before 1929, when it appeared that the entire adult population was engaged in it, but it still engages the attention of a large and varied body of customers, customers' men, brokers, and assorted assistants.

It would be possible to demonstrate that little significant distinction can be drawn between investors and speculators; that a stock exchange serves a vital economic function; and that vast upsets would occur if stock exchanges were treated as gambling institutions. But it is difficult to accept the logic or the justice of condemning off-track bets on horse races when track bets are considered legal; of condemning ordinary lotteries when church bingo games are approved; of excoriating the card-player and making a vestryman of the stockbroker. (I have nothing against the stockbroker; but I know some cardplayers who would make excellent church elders.)

THE NUMBERS GAME

The most widely followed lottery in this country is the numbers or policy game. The numbers game is the only form of lottery that has continued on a large scale in the United States. It began as the poor man's lottery—almost, one might say, the pauper's lottery—while the persons at higher income levels bought their tickets in the Irish Sweepstakes and the various Latin American lotteries. In recent years the numbers game has been expanded to reach those who are able and willing to spend a dollar or more for a lottery ticket.

The numbers game is somewhat more than fifty years old. In its earliest form it was called "policy" (and often is still so described), because of the many Italian immigrants who continue to buy tickets (Italian *polizza*) in the monthly Italian lotteries. At first, American "policy" was a true lottery, with drawings of numbers from a bag. Suspicion of chicanery (and well-grounded suspicion, judging by contemporary reports) led to the present system, in which the player can select any three-digit number, from ooo to 999, that strikes his fancy or coincides with a number bearing superstitious significance to him. This he notes on a "slip," which he then gives to a collector (with his wager), who in turn passes it on to the controller, and finally it reaches the "bank." There the collections are tabulated.

If the player wins, he is paid off at some figures from 499 to 534 to 1; that is, for each penny invested he gets back $5.00 to $5.35, depending on the custom in his locality. Thus, a ten-cent ticket would pay fifty dollars if its number showed up for that day.

The pay-off number is determined in a manner that has been shown to be influenced occasionally by the operators of the game. At first, the winning number was taken from the New York Clearinghouse figures published daily in the newspapers. To co-operate with reform groups, the newspapers stopped printing these figures in full, and the operators turned to other sources: the transactions on the New York or another stock exchange; the pay-off figures on pari-mutuel tickets; even the small cards in contract bridge hands reported in the newspapers. (The last-named method is common in the South.) It is essential that the winning number be available somewhere in a daily newspaper. The numbers game is played by so many persons that they cannot assemble in one place to learn the result, and besides, they will not trust operators as they do the newspapers.

As with other forms of American gambling, observers cannot come close to agreement on how much money is bet on the numbers game each year. Few estimates go lower than one billion dollars per year; the highest estimate has been three billion. Most of the estimates appear in public statements and seem to be set unreasonably high. The following analysis may serve to modify them:

The numbers game traditionally thrives in metropolitan centers. The bulk of the slip collections are at 10 to 25 cents. Among those connected with the numbers game, an operator collecting $50,000 worth of slips a week is considered a very big one. There are no doubt a dozen or more such operators in large cities, and numerous smaller ones; but it is improbable that they collect more than a million dollars' worth of slips each week. Assume for New York City a total play of fifty million dollars a year, assume that it represents at least 10 per cent of the national total (since the numbers game is a metropolitan one, and New York's share should be disproportionately high in relation to total population), and one thereby arrives at an annual national volume well under a billion dollars. The foregoing is, of course, based on conjecture (there being no reliable statistics), but because of rough comparisons which we may legitimately make with the known participation in other forms of gambling, it probably comes as close to accuracy as other estimates.

Condemned but tolerated. The numbers game is universally condemned in theory, for four principal reasons: First, its operation is frequently accompanied by political and police corruption; the game entails ticket sales through numerous "runners," or minor agents, and it is difficult to avoid police surveillance. Second, the numbers game preys on the poor. Third, the game is often characterized by swindle. Fourth, it puts large sums of money into the hands of the unscrupulous with which susceptible others may readily be corrupted.

But the numbers game is by some condoned in practice. The small units of betting, the dimes and quarters, do not seem important enough to call for determined public action. Only the aggregate cost to the people is large enough to be impressive, and it is spread so thin that to stanch the total flow is regarded as impossible.

Numerous obstacles exist to rigid enforcement of the law against numbers playing. One is that the organization of a numbers game has been shown to include one or more people highly placed in political circles. Perhaps the most notorious example is that of the James Hines case in New York City. In 1939 Hines, a prominent Tammany Hall figure for many years, was convicted and imprisoned for conspiracy in connection with the operation of a huge numbers syndicate, in which "Dutch" Schultz, a famous gangster, was involved. Governor Thomas E. Dewey, then a special rackets prosecutor, rose to prominence on the basis of his trial of that indictment.

Other obstacles are: many police officers and others who are in position to enforce laws against lotteries; the "bank" which ultimately collects the money received from ticket sales and which pays out the prize money; and an extensive selling organization composed of cigar-store clerks, poolroom employees, newsboys, shoeshine boys, janitors in apartment houses, laborers in large factories, elevator operators in office buildings—almost anyone whose daily work brings him into contact with numerous prospective ticket buyers. There are middlemen who collect from the runners and remit to the bank. Each takes his cut from the gross amount received.

Why they play. During recent years I have asked many numbers players why they participated in the lottery. Few hoped to win substantial sums of money, although several thought that they won more than they lost. A few enjoyed a feeling of contact with a larger world, where the more affluent were able to bet on horse races or buy shares of stock. Some had a feeling of adventure. All enjoyed the suspense.

42 · The Professional Gambler

by ALBERT H. MOREHEAD

Gambling is an activity that is almost as old as mankind and virtually universal. The person who never engaged in any kind of gamble at all is probably quite rare. There is, however, a basic difference between the person who occasionally indulges in a game of chance and one who habitually gambles or makes gambling his profession. In the following article, Albert H. Morehead, the author of many books and articles on games, describes the major types of professional and habitual gamblers and analyzes their motivations. [From *The Annals*, Vol. 269, May 1950, pp. 81-92. Reprinted by permission.]

THE PROFESSIONAL gambling fraternity is a varied one, and the title of professional gambler does not lend itself readily to simple definition. Professional gamblers are not necessarily of the underworld, though they tend to gravitate to underworld society for two reasons: one, because their calling is not conventionally respectable; the other, because their haunts bring them into contact with members of the underworld. Professional gamblers are not necessarily dishonest, but there are few who can long resist the temptation to be so when offered the opportunity. "Professional gambler" seems like a contradiction in terms, because the aim of the true professional is to avoid risk as much as possible, but there are few who can resist an out-and-out gamble, and it is an adage of the fraternity that the gambler wins at the game that is his specialty, only to lose the money at another man's game.

It is most convenient to divide the professional gamblers into several subclassifications: the banker, the percentage gambler, the cheater ("sharper" or "cardsharp"), and the compulsive gambler. Of these, only the last, the compulsive gambler, does not consciously prefer to seek his sole livelihood by gambling.

THE BANKER

The banker is the man who owns or operates a casino—a gambling house. Essential to a proper definition of gambling is the consciousness of risk. One who does not accept risk is not gambling. The proprietor of a gambling house, by this definition, is no more a gambler than is a merchant, and certainly no more than an insurance underwriter; he lets his patrons gamble among themselves, expecting by experience and mathematics that a determinable portion of the money bet will remain with him. But he is or tends to become a "racketeer." He must bribe the law enforcement agencies if he would stay in business; therefore he must condone, protect, harbor, and associate with others who pursue illegal vocations by buying protection.

The American gambling house is most often operated in connection with a cabaret—a restaurant offering some sort of floor show. It is thought that 90 per cent of all American cabarets outside of New York provide gambling in some form. In many of them it is not more than a row of slot machines; in some it is a full-fledged casino. The proprietors usually began as restaurant operators; since the cabaret is one of the most precarious business ventures known, the gambling side line was forced upon them as an alternative to closing their restaurants. The combination of casino and cabaret became the accepted pattern, however, and now anyone who would open a gambling house is more than likely to incorporate a cabaret as an adjunct to it.

The large gambling houses that are not connected with restaurants are, with few exceptions, operated by underworld groups who are implicated in other illicit enterprises. Small gambling houses are often opened by ex-gamblers who acquire the capital necessary to equip an apartment with the facilities for poker games, dice games, or any other form of gambling that does not require expensive paraphernalia. Such gambling rooms pay modest profits to the operators, and are seldom important enough to attract the attention of either the underworld or the police. Operators of gambling concessions in carnivals and at vacation resorts are more of the confidence-man or cardsharper type than of the banker type. In general, there is nothing especially complex or mysterious about the banker; he is no more or less than an unscrupulous businessman.

THE PERCENTAGE GAMBLER

The percentage gambler—the bridge or poker expert, the crapshooter whose brain is unusually agile at probabilities, the skillful player of any game in which skill is the dominant factor and the inferior player must lose in the long run—is a more complex type. The impulse, the psychological necessity, to get something for nothing is one of his characteristics. He feeds on victory, so much that in many cases the money he wins becomes secondary. He may or may not cheat (some percentage gamblers are far more ethical than the average nonprofessional gambler) but he does not gamble in the usual sense. Unless he feels sure that he has an "edge," a better-than-even chance of winning, he does not bet.

The social status of the percentage gambler is even more variable than his psychological make-up. It depends partly on the social status of his game. One of the unusual phenomena of our time is that the expert bridge player not only escapes stigma but is often a social lion, admired and entertained as a celebrated virtuoso in the arts might be. Though it is recognized that he exploits his superior skill to win in games for stakes, he is still welcomed because he is an excellent performer. But the hustler of the crap game would not be so welcomed, because his game is not socially acceptable. The percentage gambler differs from the cardsharper both psychologically and conventionally; for though his chosen profession may be considered unsavory, it is not fraudulent and in most localities it is not contrary to law. With this gentry the cardsharper is akin only in that he does not expect the outcome of his ventures to be controlled by chance.

The percentage gambler has a "feel" for probabilities—the talent that, when applied to cardplaying, is called card sense. It is difficult for an observer to escape the belief that this is an innate aptitude, rather than a result of application and tutelage.

It is almost impossible to trick the percentage gambler into accepting a bad bet (that is, any venture in which the chances are that he will lose, rather than win, in the long run). Skill in most betting and gambling games depends not so much on ability to calculate probabilities as on an almost intuitive facility at translating the probabilities into terms of immediate advantage. The percentage gambler seldom knows anything of permutations and combinations, and he is usually not particularly good at arithmetic. Nevertheless, he could prevail, at most games, over professors of mathematics. These learned gentlemen are, if anything, backward at such games as bridge and poker; the percentage gambler, on the other hand, seems to grasp the niceties of such games with little conscious effort.

The difference between an investment and a gamble is keenly felt by the percentage gambler. A gamble is justifiable when the amount wagered and the possible reward are—by the gambler's scale—heterogeneous quantities. The percentage gambler will not bet two dollars on a horse race to win five or ten; these are homogeneous quantities, and the "percentage" favors the bookmaker, not the bettor. He will not drop a nickel in a slot machine, though he may get five or ten dollars if he hits the jackpot, for five cents and ten dollars are commonplace amounts and measurable in the same terms. But he will risk five cents to win a hundred dollars, just as he may drop a nickel in a blind man's cup "for a break" (this being a superstition of the trade), or take his last two dollars and enter a dice game in which he knows the house figures to win, and he to lose; for if he wins he may win much, and if he loses, he has lost only two dollars. The house advantage (called "vigorish," perhaps from "vicarage") is the percentage gambler's concession to big capital.

Superstition is less characteristic of the percentage gambler than of other gamblers or even of nongamblers. In fact, the percentage gambler tries to take advantage of the superstitions of others. Nevertheless, one does encounter certain tendencies to superstition among this essentially matter-of-fact group. Perhaps it would be super-human never to relate chance occurrences to attendant phenomena. If it rains on three successive Tuesdays and on each occasion the gambler loses, he may involuntarily avoid play on future rainy Tuesdays. A percentage gambler in a losing streak was once offered a "lucky coin." He recoiled from it in horror. "Take it away!" he exclaimed. "If I took it and happened to win tonight, I'd be the slave of that thing for life."

How does one become a percentage gambler? In the case of some games, so profound that their science is capable of challenging any intellect, the ambition to master the game becomes an obsession. Since the study requires all one's time and more, the addict finds it difficult to make a living by conventional pursuits and save as much time as he needs to devote to his study. If his game is such a one as chess, not customarily played for stakes, the obsession may make a ne'er-do-well of him; if it is such as bridge, which offers enough money play to enable a player sufficiently skilled to derive a living income from his winnings, the obsession makes a percentage gambler of him.

Percentage gamblers specializing in less complex games are usually impelled by the same reasoning as the prostitute's: "Why slave away my life like my old woman did? There's no percentage in it; you work hard and you're poor all your life anyway. This way it's an easier life and there's always the chance of a real cleanup."

To this extent the percentage gambler's approach to his profession is the typical underworld one. He has found that he has a measure of skill that he can exploit, just as the thug has found that he has an adequate quantity of recklessness; and each of them has despaired of the future at a respectable occupation. It should be noted here that criminal society in general has that sense of "percentage" characteristic of the percentage gambler; and also a reliance on hope that is characteristic of most gamblers. Professor Edwin H. Sutherland in *The Professional Thief* (Chicago, 1937) remarked that "the patrons of gambling houses are confined almost entirely to the underworld, bootleggers, pimps, whores, and thieves." While this is no longer so, since respectable society furnishes so many gambling patrons that the underworld could hardly outnumber them, it is still true that nearly every member of the underworld gambles.

THE COMPULSIVE GAMBLER

The compulsive gambler, who plays honestly and relies on his luck, also differs both psychologically and conventionally from the cardsharper. Temperamentally this type, and no less the businessman gambler and the percentage gambler, may be more receptive to dishonest schemes than the nongambler, but even this is not necessarily so. When the compulsive gambler does become a cheat, it is usually in the throes of desperation that accompany a long losing streak. In some cases he finds hope in gambling, and is not particularly different in that respect from the housewife who buys a lottery ticket. But more often the compulsive gambler seeks only the risk, without regard to the outcome.

Observation would make one believe that the habitual compulsive gambler is relatively rare, the occasional compulsive gambler quite common. The businessman attends a convention, gambles, loses heavily (as likely as not, to one of our percentage gamblers), is remorseful as if with a hangover, "swears off," and may not fall from grace again until the next convention. Nevertheless, although the turnover is large, the disease afflicts enough of us to assure a supply that is similarly large and quite constant.

THE CHEAT

In the code of the Western world the dishonorable is far more reprehensible than the dishonest, and cheating at cards is the most dishonorable of all offenses. Especially to those subjectively interested, it carries a greater stigma than the seduction of a friend's wife, the misappropriation of property held in trust, or even a show of cowardice when faced with honorable battle. To the exposed cardsharper is meted out a life sentence of ostracism, and seldom is the sentence reprieved.

Among the conventionally respectable classes this might be expected; less easy to explain is almost the identical attitude among classes whose other standards range from unconventional to amoral. No valid conclusions can be drawn from the attitudes of violent criminals, for in their society, as in the most primitive, the penalty for any violation is likely to be death. When Arnold Rothstein was murdered, one theory held that he had been caught cheating in a game, another that he had welshed on a gambling loss, and there were other theories having nothing to do with gambling; we might as readily accept any one of these theories as any other. But in less violent criminal groups, cheating one's fellows at cards is one of the few acts for which self-interest is not adequate justification.

There were, for example, two minor criminals named Maurice and "the Greek" who shared a furnished room. One night Maurice made eighty dollars—untold wealth by their standards—and unwisely boasted about it to the Greek. Whether Maurice was a heavy sleeper or the Greek had the foresight to drug him, the fact remains that when Maurice awoke the next morning the Greek and the eighty dollars were gone. Maurice cursed his bad luck and reproached himself for stupidity, but did not seem to condemn the Greek. This same Maurice displayed righteous indignation when another member of his group was exposed as having cheated Maurice and others in a card game. Though obviously cheating at cards is recognized in Maurice's society as a proper means of livelihood, cheating within the fraternity is barred, perhaps as cannibalism, but more likely as a vestige of conventional ethics.

No less anomalous, perhaps, is a kindred case from more refined circles. Some twenty years ago, a golf club in New Jersey conducted weekly bridge tournaments at which two of the regular players were a real estate man and a college student. The tournaments were played for prizes of no great intrinsic value, and there was little betting on the result, so the reward of victory was no more than transient glory and self-satisfaction. Nevertheless, the college student found this sufficient incentive to falsify some scores. He was caught, and never again was he permitted to play in that or any other tournament or bridge game among players who knew him. The real estate man was tried for falsifying some legal documents to his own financial advantage. He was convicted and served a short term in prison; and upon his release he resumed his place in the regular weekly bridge tournaments.

Despite the severity of the penalty, there are some hundreds of thousands of persons who do, or are willing to, cheat in card games; the extent of their activity depending on the degree of their skill, and their own appraisal of the danger of detection. Furthermore, this estimate of the number who cheat would be many times greater if the word "cheat" were not given a very restrictive definition here.

DEFINITION OF CHEATING

A sharp distinction is drawn, among serious card players, between cheating and unethical conduct. Cheating is manipulation of the cards, marking the cards, or collusion with another player to victimize a third. Unethical conduct is, broadly, intentional breach of the rules or proprieties of play, with a view to giving oneself an advantage over the opponent.

Cheating is universally condemned; unethical conduct is viewed with a range of emotions of which the most harsh is disapprobation, ranging through toleration to outright condonement. Yet the respective offenses have the same motivation, and conscience would call them equivalent. The probable explanation for the difference in attitude is a practical one. Against the usual forms of unethical conduct, one has a defense; he can verify the actual score against an opponent who habitually makes "mistakes" or "oversights" therein, and he can hold his hand up against an opponent who peeks. The offense can be counteracted and the amenities still observed. Against cheating as defined here, the only defense is overt accusation, which is always unpleasant.

The proposed definition of cheating is invariable in the realm of card playing, and applies generally to other games. In dice games a player is cheating if he introduces loaded or improperly marked dice, or if he attempts to slide or otherwise control the dice so that they will fall to his advantage; he is not cheating, but is merely oversharp, if he willfully misreads the faces of the dice or deliberately misconstrues the terms of a bet. A backgammon player is cheating if he palms a stone to remove it prematurely from the board; but he is merely unethical if he attempts an illegal move, one his opponent can see and demand that he retract. A roulette or similar gambling wheel is dishonest if the operator can control its stopping point, and the operator of such a wheel is a cheater; he is merely unduly greedy if he tries to shortchange the winner of a bet.

THE CARDSHARPER

A cardsharper is a person who derives his livelihood, or an essential part of it, by cheating in card games. (The term is not used among the gambling fraternity, to whom a professional player is a "mechanic" if he is skillful at manipulating the cards, and merely a "hustler" if he is not.) The essential ingredients of the cardsharper are that his principal activity is winning money in gambling games and that his method of winning is, by our definition, cheating. Therefore he is by law a criminal, guilty of obtaining money under false pretenses.

All gamblers are predatory, and professional ones are relatively ruthless. The cardsharper, who is more akin to the confidence man than to any form of true gambler, is totally ruthless. His object is to separate victim from money, and he seldom cares how much the victim suffers in the process.

Like any other professional criminal, the cardsharper usually develops by tutelage and example. This requires association with other card sharpers, and leads to some degree of fellowship with them and of group consciousness.

Many cardsharpers, however, begin on their own. They may first be motivated by simple greed. A player in a regular card game sees and covets the money of the others. He finds he cannot win it, or at least cannot win enough of it, by straightforward methods, so he learns to cheat. Having exhausted the possibilities of winning from his original group, or having been detected and banished, he moves out among strangers, seeking games in which to exploit his skill, and eventually he becomes a member of the fraternity.

Then there are those who become addicted to engrossing games of skill. They cannot bear to be doing anything else when they might be playing the game. Sometimes their addiction causes them to lose their jobs. Sometimes they begin so young that they never get around to honest employment. In any case, they have no other means of livelihood and must win to live. The only way to assure winning is to cheat, and they become cheats. Such cases are analogous to that of the drug addict who turns to crime or prostitution to maintain the availability of the drug.

There are the conjurers, who train themselves as performers but as such are not successful—at least not successful enough. The personality that did not quite make a stage presence may be quite adequate in a card game; the dexterity that could not quite deceive a large audience may suffice in a small group who have no particular reason to be suspicious anyway.

Confidence Men. Finally, there are the confidence men who have devised or adopted a scheme involving a card game. To effectuate the scheme they must perfect their cheating technique, at least enough to master the tricks requisite to their plan.

It is the confidence men that are usually thought of when the term "cardsharper" is used. It is to them that the signs in the smoking lounges of transatlantic liners, BEWARE OF CARDSHARPERS, refer. Admittedly they are far more dangerous than the player who merely cheats to give himself a slight but continuing advantage; the confidence man purposes to take hundreds and even thousands from a person who thought he was risking at most a few dollars. But in most cases the card game is only incidental to the routine of the confidence men. They build up to a planned situation in which the victim, in one coup, will lose all his money; after this climax they seek to end the game immediately and to part from the victim as soon as possible. The cardsharper as we define him here has a different object. He wishes to prolong the game and remain in it. The money he wins must seem to come to him from nothing more than good luck in the normal course of play.

There is another notable difference. When confidence men employ a card game to further their ends, their scheme still depends upon the proverbial sine qua non of their profession, "You can't cheat an honest man." Our true cardsharper, on the other hand, wishes to play only with honest men, they being least likely to be suspicious and also least likely to be aware of the several methods of cheating.

Examine typical cardplaying routines employed by confidence men. First there is three-card monte, so simple and so time-honored that it is no less than wonderful that it can still find victims. The dealer pitches his stand like any huckster selling patent medicine or other merchandise, and manipulates three cards until they come to rest face down on his board. One of the three cards is a queen, and the dealer, proclaiming that "the hand is quicker than the eye," offers to bet bystanders that they cannot locate the queen. (Those familiar with the shell game, played with three walnut shells and a pea, will recognize this as the same game.) A good dealer can make money honestly at this game; his hand is indeed quicker than the eye, and the odds are two to one that the onlooker cannot pick the queen at random while the dealer may reasonably offer him only even money. The dealer's object, however, is to make far more money than a stranger would be willing to bet so casually.

To this end, a confederate of the dealer's selects a likely-looking victim and converses with him while both make small bets against the dealer, winning some, losing some. At a propitious moment the confederate "crimps" the queen—gives it a telltale crease in a corner. He and the victim then bet heavily that they can pick the queen. The dealer lays out the cards, the crimped one is turned, and it is not the queen; in the course of his manipulations the dealer has removed the crimp from the queen and put a crimp in one of the other cards.

Here one may see the working of the formula. The victim could not be cheated if he were an honest man; he loses because he is trying to cheat the dealer.

Three-card monte, as aforesaid, is simple, time-honored, and so picayune that it can hardly be associated with the true confidence man, that appellation being somewhat of an honorific in the underworld.

*　　*　　*

PSYCHOLOGY OF THE GAMBLER

It is not within the scope of this article to explore the psychology of the gambler. The broad aspects of the subject are fairly well agreed upon. Generally, the motivation of the compulsive gambler is self-destruction or rebellion; of the criminal gambler, rebellion; of the percentage gambler (the bridge or chess master, for example) the abnormal sublimation of the mock struggle for fear of the real one. The compulsive gambler must be a daredevil, the criminal gambler must get something for nothing, the percentage gambler must have victory regardless of the intrinsic value of the reward.

Some case histories may be of value.

"A" became a contract bridge expert in the usual manner: Vain of his intellectual prowess, he was persuaded to compete in a game with more experienced players; he was inept and suffered; he studied the game until he was far superior to those who had "disgraced" him. He was successful in business, meanwhile, and attained to a high-salaried executive position, a high living standard, and an expensive mistress. The stakes in his accustomed bridge games were 10 to 25 cents a point, and over the course of the year he always won because he was a superior player. Then came the crash of 1929. He lost his job and could not find another. The stakes in the bridge games in which he was accustomed to play dropped to 3 cents a point. At these stakes he could not win enough by mere skill at play to satisfy him. One so long accustomed to handling a pack of cards has considerable facility with it, and he practiced several hours a day on methods that could protect him against ever losing. He put his new-found ability into practice as soon as he felt that he had sufficiently mastered it, and thenceforward cheated in order to win.

"B" was the son of a bookkeeper who made about fifty dollars a week, at a time when that represented a comfortable middle-class income. "B" was a remarkable athlete, and, after two years in a public high school, was offered an athletic scholarship in a famous preparatory school. There he met the sons of the rich and prominent, and, as the school's best athlete, was the subject of their adulation; but he keenly felt the differences of background and his inability to keep up with them in spending money. The only apparent source of extra money was gambling winnings, and he became not only a skillful but also a cheating player of every game at which they gambled. Throughout preparatory school and college he gambled professionally, and with such success that he usually had more money than his schoolmates. After college he remained a professional gambler—a cardsharper by our definition.

"C" was born into an immigrant Italian family: his parents were all but illiterate and could hardly speak English, and their home was in a slum. As a boy of fourteen, "C" hung around a poolroom in whose back room gambling card games were played. He played hooky from school to practice the manipulation of the pack of cards. He watched the games and ran errands for the players. Though he never got through grammar school, he became one of the most proficient of cardsharpers, and has spent the remainder of his life at that profession, though he does not have the surface polish to enter games among those capable of playing for high stakes, and must prey on the lowest classes.

Among the cardsharpers one finds no consciousness of guilt, and often a naïvete that can be amusing. Some years ago Ely Culbertson wrote an article for the *Saturday Evening Post* on the subject of gambling. In the course of the article he attempted to demonstrate, in conventional manner, that gambling (like crime?) does not pay. His fan mail brought him a letter from a man in Brooklyn who took issue with this theme. "I don't see how you can say that," the Brooklynite complained. "My friend and I have been cheating at bridge for years, and it pays very well." There was a P.S.: "We also cheat at poker, and that pays, too."

43 · Gambling: Should It Be Legalized?

by VIRGIL W. PETERSON

Because gambling is widespread and persistent and the gambling laws are difficult to enforce, a question debated for some time is whether it would not be better to legalize it. It would then be possible, it is thought, to eliminate through rigid control, many of the undesirable features now accompanying it and to divert whatever benefits are to be derived from it from the professionals and the criminal gangs to the people. Virgil W. Peterson, director of the Chicago Crime Commission and a former member of the Federal Bureau of Investigation, has studied this question. He explains here the serious effects of gambling and discusses the problems involved in its legalization. [From *Journal of Criminal Law and Criminology*, Vol. 40, Sept.-Oct. 1949, pp. 321-329. Reprinted by permission. Footnote omitted.]

UNDER THE OLD common law gambling was unlawful when the game became an incitement to a breach of the peace constituting a nuisance tended to immorality, affected the interests of others, or were conducted by means of cheating or by fraud. The present status of the gambling laws in the United States is well settled. "Gambling is injurious to the morals and welfare of the people, and it is not only within the scope of the state's police power to suppress gambling in all its forms, but it duty to do so." The laws against gambling which prevail generally in the United States were not based, as frequently stated, on a Puritanical tradition which is now outmoded in the light of present social trends and attitudes. On the contrary, the anti-gambling statutes were based on the well-considered action of citizens in numerous states usually after the professional gamblers who controlled the underworld got completely out of hand. In general, those who were the most ardent advocates of rigid anti-gambling statutes in any locality were the substantial citizens and businessmen of the community. They were not moralists or reformers. They were merely interested in eliminating the widespread criminal activities of the gambling business that threatened their security and future welfare.

Any unbiased study of the history of the gambling business makes it impossible for us to ignore certain salient facts. As a business gambling is entirely parasitic. It is completely non-productive. It creates no new wealth and performs no useful service. One factor common to every legitimate commercial enterprise or profession is that it can exist only because there is an opportunity for a mutual advantage to the operator of the business and the patrons as a class. This is true whether the business is engaged in the manufacture, distribution or sale of a product or a service. Without this element of mutual advantage the business cannot exist. In the business of gambling, even when fraud and manipulation are absent, it still operates on a one-sided percentage basis that makes it impossible for the patrons as a class to derive any benefit. It is self-evident, that if the patrons as a class had an opportunity for any advantage, the gambling business could not survive. But the gambling house patrons are not only confronted with a one-sided house percentage. From time immemorial, the stock-in-trade of gambling houses throughout the country has consisted of fraudulent devices, various cheating schemes and manipulation.

For the most part, criminals, gangsters and swindlers have been the proprietors of gambling establishments. This is inevitable in a business that is tremendously lucrative and which exists only to exploit a human weakness. In addition, habitués of gambling houses are frequently confidence men, sharpers and cheats. This again, naturally results from the nature of the business. The commonplace presence of swindlers in gambling establishments frequently induces proprietors, who would otherwise be content to rely on the inevitable house percentage, to resort to cheating methods as a means of self-protection. Gambling houses have always been rendezvous for criminals. This again is due to the inherent nature of the business. The gambling business has also been recognized as a principal source of crime. In fact, an unusually large number of embezzlements are traceable to gambling activities. Citizens who suddenly become addicted to gambling turn to armed robberies, burglaries or thefts to recoup losses. The conclusion is inescapable that the business of gambling does not properly lend itself to legalization.

The statutes which declare that gambling is illegal are consistent in principle with other laws designed to protect social and economic welfare. Since the enactment of the Blue Sky Laws in Kansas in 1911, many states, including Illinois, have passed similar statutes. On rare occasions, patrons of those operating in violation of the Blue Sky Laws, have reaped huge profits. Likewise on rare occasions, patrons of bucket shops may benefit. But over extended periods of time, the patrons cannot profit and the various Blue Sky Laws and statutes prohibiting the operation of bucket shops are recognized as sound legislation. The identical situation is present with reference to the gambling business.

While it is clear that there is no social or economic justification for the business of gambling, nevertheless, legalization might be worthy of consideration if there was any tangible evidence to indicate this would eliminate existing evils. In an effort to determine whether the legalization of gambling would eliminate the grave abuses that now prevail, an examination was made of the rather extensive experiences in the United States with the licensing of gambling. Legalized lotteries were commonplace in the United States from Colonial times until they were abolished by various states beginning with Massachusetts and Pennsylvania in 1833 and New York in 1834. They were not abolished in Louisiana until 1892. Many of the lotteries authorized by various state legislatures to raise funds for educational institutions, public development companies and for civic improvements, started on a modest scale. Eventually the lottery business reached enormous proportions. It was largely taken over by unscrupulous promoters who were frauds and cheats of the most unsavory character. They made fortunes at the expense of the poor and needy through every type of chicanery that could be concocted in their fertile brains. Bribery of legislatures in various states was frequently resorted to by promoters. Political corruption was commonplace. It was not infrequent that promoters or agents sold the lottery tickets and then vanished with the money. As usual, illegitimate off-springs of the legalized lotteries sprang up. They further bled the poor people for whom they were principally designed. The benefactors of legalized lotteries were largely the racketeers who took over the lottery industry. The political power of the operators frequently became alarming. The frauds and social evils were so enormous that the substantial citizens of the various states determined that action was imperative. They repealed the statutes that authorized lotteries. But they did not stop there. With the evils of legalized lotteries fresh in their minds the people placed provisions in their state constitutions that were designed to make it impossible for legislatures to authorize lotteries in the future. It was this disastrous experience that formed the basis for the provision in most state constitutions forbidding legislatures to authorize lotteries or gift enterprises. An editorial in the *Christian Science Monitor* on June 1, 1945, was on solid historical ground when it said of state lotteries that "No enlightened government resorts to such schemes now. . . . They are a throwback to a type of rule that cared little or nothing for the welfare of the masses. For it is the people that pay. Those who can ill afford it are attracted by such schemes. . . . It is not the rich who suffer, but the poor."

As might be expected legalization of other forms of gambling in the United States has furnished an experience similar to that provided by lotteries. Various experiments with legalization of gambling in New Orleans met with utter failure. For several years prior to 1820, gambling activities were greatly encouraged and spread under legal sanction. The city was without an efficient police force. Adequate control over the municipal regulations enacted was absent. The abuses increased until the legislature found it necessary to enact a statute prohibiting gambling in 1820. The second experiment with legalization of gambling began in 1823. This statute limited the number of licensed gambling houses to six. Each paid an annual license fee of $5,000.00. For a time the six gambling establishments were able to maintain a monopoly. Unlicensed houses were temporarily suppressed. Some of the licensed operators rose to tremendous political power and wealth. The inevitable result followed. The license law was extended and the fee increased to $7,500.00. The number of gambling establishments multiplied with great rapidity and the abuses, together with the rise in crime, increased proportionately. The underworld in all the Mississippi River towns, including New Orleans, was controlled by gamblers. Crime conditions were deplorable. The failure of the licensing law brought about repeal and the enactment of rigid anti-gambling statutes. Subsequent experiments with legalization of gambling in New Orleans brought identical results. The final experiment in New Orleans in 1869 is particularly noteworthy. Upon the legalization of gambling, swindlers from all over the country swarmed to New Orleans. Gambling houses were opened on all principal streets. Most of the gambling establishments even ignored the payment of the stipulated license fee but all of them paid protection money to city officials and the police. The licensing law was a colossal failure and it was repealed at the next session of the Legislature. Similar unsuccessful experiments with legalization of gambling have taken place in California, New Mexico, Arizona and other states. In practically every instance, whenever the population assumed a degree of permanency and the future of the locality appeared secure, the statutes legalizing gambling were repealed.

In Florida slot machines were legalized by the State Legislature in 1935. Two years later the law was repealed. Recent experiments with legalization of slot machines in Idaho and Montana on a limited scale have resulted in numerous abuses. The governor of Montana in 1947 publicly declared that the Montana law permitting slot machines in private clubs and legalized punch boards had created the worst gambling conditions in the state for many years. He urged the repeal of the law. The governor of Idaho asked the 1949 legislature to repeal the statute of that state which permitted local communities to license slot machines on a local option basis. Several Idaho cities canceled all slot machine licenses for 1949 due to grave abuses growing out of the operation of licensed slot machines. Weekly earnings of poor people were being squandered in the slot machines and scandals arose from official corruption. In the past various experiments with legalized gambling have failed.

It is only in the state of Nevada that the general legalization of gambling prevails today. The two principal gambling centers of the state are Reno and Las Vegas. For many years Reno was controlled politically and financially by James McKay and William Graham. They owned the largest gambling establishment in Reno and the biggest one in Lake Tahoe as well. Lester Joseph Gillis, alias Baby Face Nelson, the most dangerous killer of the notorious Dillinger gang which terrorized the nation in 1934, was a close associate of Graham and McKay. After several trials, Graham and McKay were convicted in Federal Court in New York City for mail fraud involving a million dollar horse race swindling scheme. After returning from Federal prison they again became active in the legal gambling business in Reno. Las Vegas is the home of America's most fabulous gambling establishment, the Flamingo Hotel. This elaborate place was built at a cost of several million dollars by Benjamin "Bugsy" Siegel. Prior to the gang killing of Siegel on June 20, 1947, he had been the most powerful gambling boss in Las Vegas. Siegel was one of the most notorious gangsters in the United States. He was closely affiliated with the Frank Costello mob of New York. He was also connected with the Capone gang of Chicago. While in Las Vegas, Benjamin "Bugsy" Siegel was the western representative for the Capone syndicate's wire service, The Trans-American Publishing and News Service, Inc. Siegel and his gangster friends enforced their demands among the Las Vegas gamblers through strong arm and terroristic tactics. Nevada's gambling industry is designed to attract the tourist trade. The same is true of the state's lax divorce laws. Both are revenue measures. A few months ago the legislature enacted a law legalizing prostitution. Sufficient opposition was registered by local residents however to cause the governor to veto the measure. With its small population and large geographical area, the economic, social and crime problems of Nevada are considerably different from those present in states having large metropolitan areas.

On the whole, legalization of gambling in the United States has failed completely. Instead of eliminating abuses it increased them. In many instances the gambling business operating under the sanction of law got completely out of hand. The racketeer element obtained vast political power and wealth. In most instances the abuses under gambling license laws enacted by various states were so great that the people repealed them. Police departments that could not efficiently suppress the business of gambling when it was illegal were, if anything, even more helpless under a licensing setup. On some occasions the legalization of the business of gambling in certain metropolitan areas attracted criminals from all over the United States. Lawlessness generally prevailed on a large scale. The conclusion is inescapable that licensing of gambling has not afforded a solution to the gambling problem.

In fact, attempts to license gambling are wrong in principle. Alexis De Tocqueville in his monumental "Democracy in America" cautioned that governments "must practically teach the community day by day that wealth, fame and power are the rewards of labor, that great success stands at the utmost range of long desires, and that there is nothing lasting but what is obtained by toil." De Tocqueville also referred to fantastic notions of honor during the time of feudalism which "allowed men to enrich themselves by gambling or by war, but not by labor. . . ." The days of feudalism are happily past. Labor in America is honorable. We pride ourselves on an advanced social consciousness that will not permit business practices that are fraudulent or those which exploit the poor and the weak. Why should an exception be made with reference to the most dubious business of all,—gambling? Instead of encouraging gambling through various legalization schemes, efforts should be made through educational programs to discourage that which is the antithesis of thrift and industry. A constructive program would begin with teaching youth in the schools, churches and homes the well established fact that even in gambling houses where fraud is absent, the percentage system makes winning impossible for the habitual gambler and that poverty, hardship and crime are frequently natural products.

Based on past experience and keeping in mind the true nature of the gambling business it is evident that the usual proposals to license gambling would ultimately lead to complete failure. It should be clear that there is absolutely no justification for a license setup that would legally place the control of the gambling business in the joint hands of any local or state political machine and the parasitic professional gambling interests. It has been definitely established that the wide-open illegal gambling business with all its evils can be effectively suppressed whenever those in political authority order it suppressed and mean it, and when the subordinates, including the police, know that they mean it. Only defeatism and a loss of faith in the integrity of local government could make the people resort to further legalization experiments along the lines usually suggested.

Licensing proposals are based primarily on the contention that because of the human desire to gamble it cannot be suppressed and, therefore, it should be licensed and legalized with the people sharing in the profits instead of allowing the hoodlum element to reap all the gains. If these proposals are based on sincerity then it is clear that only one type of proposal is worthy of any consideration at all. *If gambling is to be legalized it should be completely controlled and operated by the state with all the profits accruing to the people.* A state agency should then be set up to operate and control the gambling business. It should be completely removed from politics. A Commissioner of Gambling should be elected directly by the people at a separate election. It is imperative, in view of the inherent nature of the gambling business with its close relationship to lawlessness and crime that only men of the highest possible integrity should be eligible to become candidates for the position. Candidates for office should carry no political party appellation. Rigid restrictions should be placed in the statute to make it impossible for anyone who holds, or has held, any political position, including that of ward committeeman, alderman or precinct captain, from having any connection with the administration of the state agency that is set up to operate the gambling business for the state. It should be illegal for any political party to endorse or actively work for the election of the Gambling Commissioner. The salary of the Commissioner of Gambling should be sufficiently great to attract the most ably qualified men in the state. He should then be empowered to select his own administrative staff. The complete responsibility for the operation and control of the legalized gambling business throughout the state should be fixed with the Commissioner. The law should have sufficient "teeth in it" to assure that there could be no shifting of responsibility. All of the profits would go to the benefit of the people of the state. A scheme of this kind would also fail. In the first place it would be impossible in practice to maintain an honest and efficient administration divorced from politics. Sooner or later political machines would gain control and operate state gambling for the benefit of politicians. This result would be inevitable in this country. In the second place state gambling would encourage mass gambling with its attending social and economic evils in the same manner as other forms of legal gambling. However, there is no justification whatever for the business of gambling to be legalized and permitted to operate for private profit nor is there any justification for the non-productive lucrative business of gambling being operated for the benefit of any political organization.

In many large metropolitan areas wide-spread gambling activities present troublesome problems. But a solution to the problem is not to be found in anything so simple as a correct determination of the licensing question. Licensing does not even touch the real fundamental issues involved. History clearly reflects that whenever widespread gambling activities have been present in any city lawlessness in general, and official corruption, have been commonplace. This has been true whether gambling was operated under licenses sanctioned by law or under the usual illegal system. Extensive gambling has almost always existed contemporaneously with crime, debauchery and lawlessness. Over a period of years Chicago has been the center of extensive gambling activities. But there also prevailed generally a high murder, robbery and burglary rate. Racketeering and lawlessness have frequently been commonplace. This is typical of many other cities. Conversely those cities in which low crime rates have prevailed have also been successful in preventing the business of gambling from flourishing. It is obvious that fundamental issues are much deeper than a determination of whether gambling should be licensed. The welfare and security of the society of any community depends upon the preservation of law and order. Strong, virile, progressive law enforcement agencies that are not subject to the control of the dominant political organization are absolutely essential if any society is to receive adequate protection. Practically all students of the crime problem are agreed on the necessity for a strengthening of the police agencies and removing the interference of politics from their administration. Until we are ready to attack this problem and others of comparable importance which are fundamental, a discussion of legalization of gambling is actually a waste of time. Licensing of gambling is not, has not, and never will be a substitute for the proper performance of duty on the part of responsible officials. It will never take the place of proper respect for law and order on the part of the citizens.

CHAPTER TWELVE

Organized Crime

=====================================

44 · The Nature of Organized Crime

by ALFRED R. LINDESMITH

Much, perhaps most, of the criminal activity in this country is carried on by groups organized for the purpose. The underworld may be said to be organized to exploit the rest of the population. In dealing with the problem of crime, whether from a theoretical or practical standpoint, we must devote most of our attention, therefore, to organized crime. Alfred R. Lindesmith, the author also of a previous selection, describes here the various types of organized criminal gangs and the techniques they employ. ["Organized Crime," *The Annals*, Vol. 217, Sept. 1941, pp. 76-83. Reprinted by permission. Some footnotes omitted.]

THE TERM "organized crime" refers to crime that involves the co-operation of several different persons or groups for its successful execution. Organized crime is usually professional crime. The organization may be loose and general, or informal; or it may be definite and formal, involving a system of specifically defined relationships with mutual obligations and privileges. Crime organizations may involve small or large groups. An organization such as that of Al Capone represents a large-scale formal organization; the profession of picking pockets is an informal organization.

Some types of crimes are relatively rarely committed by organized gangs. Rape, for example, might conceivably be utilized in the white slave traffic by organized mobs, but it is not usually so organized. Murder, also, is usually unorganized, but, of course, a small but significant portion of the total number of murders in the country represents organized crime committed in connection with racketeering and gang activities. Organized crime is devoted almost exclusively to economic ends, to the acquisition of wealth. The criminal is in this respect like most of the rest of us, but in order to obtain his end, he utilizes means which are deemed illegitimate.

STRUCTURE OF UNDERWORLD

In a broad sense, the entire underworld may be said to be organized. It is set apart from the rest of society. It has its own standards, attitudes, and public opinion, and an informal, though effective, means of communication known as the "grapevine." Its members share the common danger of arrest and imprisonment, and when in prison they must perforce live to some extent a common life. The prison experience and evasion of the law bind them together. The "stool pigeon" is everywhere hated. Similar attitudes toward respectable people with "larceny in their hearts" are assumed. Criminals move from one occupation to another within the underworld, according to their opportunities, tastes, and abilities. As stated in the Report of the (Chicago) City Council Committee on Crime:

While this criminal group is not by any means completely organized, it has many of the characteristics of a system. It has its own language; it has its own laws; its own history; its traditions and customs; its own methods and techniques; its highly specialized machinery for attack upon persons and particularly upon property; its own highly specialized modes of defense. These professional criminals have interurban, interstate, and sometimes international connections.[1]

Organized crime as it now exists in the United States requires the active and conscious co-operation of a number of elements of respectable society. It requires the passive co-operation of many other elements. Thus, it is well known that the profits of crime do not as a rule accumulate in the hands of the criminals themselves, but are passed on until they no doubt find their way into the hands of individuals who, unlike

[1] Quoted by E. H. Sutherland in *The Professional Thief* (Chicago: University of Chicago Press, 1937), pp. 209-10.

most thieves, have bank accounts and own securities and property. These persons will be tempted to co-operate with the underworld in one way or another. The legal profession which supplies the prosperous criminal with clever "mouthpieces" is an indispensable instrumentality. Politicians in America have always had connections with the underworld and have derived an important percentage of their revenues from protection money and graft. Many other groups and persons also do their bit. Bondsmen, doctors, businessmen, insurance companies, labor unions, policemen, judges, and even great corporations or financial institutions may sometimes, knowingly or unknowingly, help the work of the underworld.

Arnold Rothstein, who was killed in 1928, was known as a wealthy and powerful gambler and race-track man. He borrowed money from eminently respectable banking institutions, such as the National City Bank of New York, and loaned it to illicit drug dealers and rumrunners. He secured his loans through life insurance policies. Some of the bigger businesses of the underworld require considerable investments of capital. In order to obtain this capital, some sort of intermediary between the underworld and banks is necessary. Arnold Rothstein was such a person. "Dutch" Goldberg of California is supposed to be another.

UNDERWORLD A PART OF OUR CULTURE

The underworld is a big city phenomenon. It is concentrated in certain portions of the city where the defects of our socioeconomic system are most in evidence, and it draws its new recruits mainly from the ranks of the lower economic classes, who also live roughly in the same geographical areas. These classes of legitimate society, which are condemned to life in the slums, naturally often sympathize with the cynicism and disillusionment of the underworld and frequently co-operate with it, join it, or help it in its struggle with the law. An individualistic predatory philosophy of success, indifference to public affairs, general disregard for law, the profit motive, decentralized government, laissez faire economics, and political practice which is often as openly predatory as the rackets, have produced in our great cities a fertile breeding place for organized crime. It is significant that the underworld is not biologically self-sufficient. Many of its members are single and spend much time in prison; children are a liability; family life is casual and without benefit of clergy; and the women of the underworld are often prostitutes. Hence, in order to perpetuate itself, it must draw into itself converts from other classes. It is perpetuated culturally, not biologically. The underworld also serves to meet demands for goods and services which are defined as illegitimate, but for which there is nevertheless a strong demand from respectable people. Prostitution, gambling, and liquor during prohibition are examples. It is, therefore, a mistake to regard the underworld as a separate or detached organization; it is rather an integral part of our total culture. It is implicit in our economic, political, legal, and social organization. It is even biologically dependent. It is in this sense that we have the criminals we deserve.

THE CODE OF THE UNDERWORLD

The following statements by a criminal give a good account of the major underworld code:

In the criminal world every man lives always on the edge of catastrophe. Danger is the norm. Once having put himself into conflict with society, society's rules cease to exist for him. He swiftly recognizes that his life and liberty depend upon the loyalty of his fellows and to get loyalty he must give it. Often it is his only virtue. If he hasn't it he perishes—by one law or another. . . .

The criminal's code is based upon the same fundamentals as the social code; protection of life and property. Though the underworld recognizes no obligation to the upperworld, within the limits of its own world it is absolutely inexorable. It pays its debts and grudges on the minute. The crook, like the businessman, strengthens his position and credit if he meets his bills and discharges his obligations promptly.

A bank burglar assumes an air with a house burglar, a house burglar sneers at a pickpocket, a pickpocket calls the forger "a short story writer," and they all make common cause against the stool pigeon, whatever caste he comes from. He jeopardizes the life and liberty of his own, which is the great unpardonable crime of the underworld code. He is the rattlesnake of the underworld, and they kill him on the "safety-first" principle as swiftly and dispassionately as you would kill a copperhead. Respect for property in the underworld is as deep as it is in the upperworld. The fact that it is upperworld property which is involved makes no difference, for when property is transferred from the upperworld to the underworld it becomes sacred again.

The burglar who shoots his partner for holding out a lady's watch goes up in the social scale of the underworld. . . .

When death comes the underworld turns its face to the wall and dies mute. A criminal punished for an infringement of the code, no matter how treacherously he is dealt with, almost invariably refuses to name his killer. He so hates the law, and the brass buttons and stars which to him are its symbol, that even in death he won't "turn copper." And when the man from the district attorney's office, with pad and paper in hand, prepares to take his dying statement, he most frequently gasps, "Get the hell out of here."[3]

Jack Black, "A Burglar Looks at Laws and Codes," *Harper's Magazine,* February 1930, pp. 306-7, 311.

Another criminal summarized the traits of the successful underworld character as follows:

To get by in the underworld—the world of gamblers, hopheads, burglars, dips, ex-convicts, sluggers, stick-ups, woman beaters, white slavers, snowbirds, crooks of every sort—a man's gotta be tough. He can't have no principles or conscience. He can't have none of them sucker traits that sets the other world apart from the underworld. He's got to be rough and tough, ready to go—and able to go. He's gotta be full of mayhem for any bird who crosses him, whether it's a copper, a squealer, or some dude trying to steal his broad or monkey with his grift. And he must be a winner. He mustn't lose. If a wolf loses, the pack's the first to turn on him and eat him up. It's that way in the underworld.[8]

PREVENTING BETRAYAL BY OWN GROUP

There are two ways in which the criminal attempts to avoid the danger of betrayal by a member of his own group. The most usual way and the traditional way is strictly to limit the size of the actual operating group and carefully to select the members of this small group. The other method is the one used by the modern American racketeer and gangster with such conspicuous success and revolutionary results. It consists in organizing machinery for the forcible enforcement of the code. It involves informal gang trial and ruthless, skillful, impersonal killing, not only of informers, but also of competitors, troublesome characters, gangsters who wish to retire, and sometimes of members of respectable society. Paradoxically, this more efficient organization of force on a wide basis, sometimes nationally, has the effect of reducing the necessity for its application. This organization of underworld police power makes possible a much broader and more formal organization of criminal activity and has sinister implications for the whole social structure, particularly when the underworld power thus organized extends its influence over the traditional agencies of the state and acquires political power. We then have something like a state within a state, an inner enemy, a totalitarian underworld.

The underworld disapproves not only of some informing, but of all informing. There is a significant moral in the story of the gangster who, when asked by a dentist which tooth it was that was bothering him, said, "Find it yourself. I'm no stool pigeon." The convict operates on the principle that someone who "rats" on a "screw" (prison guard) will also "rat" on a convict. Law enforcement agents likewise do not

[8] Quoted by Sidney Sutherland in "Was the Big Fight a Fake?" *Liberty*, December 4, 1926, p. 55.

trust the stool pigeons whom they employ, evidently on the principle that a man who will "rat" on a criminal will "rat" on a policeman. The stool pigeon thus finds himself in the unenviable position of being trusted by no one, not even by other stool pigeons. The effectiveness of gangster strategy is made painfully evident by the difficulty of solving gang murders. No one wants to talk, even though the killer may be known and the motives are self-evident. Witnesses vanish, refuse to appear, or suddenly seem to become deaf, blind, and dumb.

"MURDER, INC."

The confessions of a well-known New York gangster recently shocked the public by revealing the progress which underworld gunmen have made in organizing their business. This gangster, Abe Reles, spoke of the organization which was dramatized by the press as "Murder, Inc.," as "The Combination." It was, he said, "like the Lehman Banks. It is practically one organization and spreads all over the country." Reles himself confessed to something like eighteen murders, although he had some difficulty in remembering them. According to Reles, the whole country was divided into districts and killing in any district, it had been agreed, was to be carried out by the gang rulers of each. The murders were committed in a purely impersonal way for business reasons and for protection by killers who were paid, according to Reles, from $100 to $150 a week, although it was charged by someone else that in hard times it was sometimes possible to have someone bumped off for as little as $5.00. This was denied by Reles. The paid killers, known as "troops" or "torpedoes," were not allowed, under severe penalty, to make any private agreements for killings, on the theory that such practice would ultimately endanger the gang leaders themselves. After a killing, the murderer usually went to Detroit to hide out while the case cooled off, and was there taken care of by a special fund set aside for the purpose. No doubt, to insure quiet, the widows of gang members who were executed for violations of the rules or because they wished to retire were paid the salaries of their deceased husbands—at least during times of prosperity, when the gang could afford it.

In his statements, Reles implicated gangsters in many of the large cities of America, many of whom had acquired their early training in New York in the first decades of the present century and had acquired wealth during the prohibition era. The large-scale organization under these men's direction was no doubt facilitated by the fact that when they moved to other cities, they retained their New York acquaintances. When intergang warfare became too bloody and dangerous, it eventually became clear to these businessmen of the underworld, as other business-men had already learned, that free competition was disastrous and ulti-mately not as profitable as monopoly. Hence, they reconciled their differences and divided up the plunder, first within cities and then on a broader basis. Whether this evolution has reached its limits or whether it still can expand into other and more lucrative and powerful forms remains to be seen. The tie-up with political machines may represent a potent future prospect.

The total number of top-ranking gangsters is not large, although the number of minor thugs is great. They are recruited largely from the ranks of ordinary holdup or "heist" rackets, and come mainly from the slums of large cities. New York's East Side and the Chicago slums have produced many. The enterprising gangster of today finds that monopo-listic control of the rackets, plus the need for capital, inhibits the un-derworld entrepreneur who wants to go into the business independently. The road to success now appears to be to get into an already established mob and work one's way up.

TYPES OF UNDERWORLD CRIME ORGANIZATION

Disregarding certain marginal activities of relatively little significance, such as that engaged in by beggars, tramps, minor clerks and assistants in illicit establishments, and other hangers-on, the main types of under-world activity may be roughly classified as follows:

(1) Thieving, involving either:
    (a) violence or the threat of violence; or
    (b) stealth and dexterity.

(2) Swindling rackets, such as con games, short-con games (some-times called "bunco games"), and blackmail of various types involving the threat of adverse publicity or exposure.

(3) Illicit business and racketeering or gangsterism, involving the organization of legitimate (industrial rackets), quasi-legitimate, or ille-gitimate business, such as those involved in prostitution, bootleg liquor, drugs, gambling, amusements, slot machines, and race-track betting and allied functions.

The degree of organization involved in these three types of enterprise increases from (1) to (3). The number of amateurs diminishes progres-sively from (1) to (3), and the size of the "mob," "troop," or "gang" roughly increases. Racketeers and gangsters are recruited mainly from class one, particularly from (1a). The cheat or swindler cultivates verbal dexterity; he is a salesman, and his specialized abilities as well as his tastes are likely to prevent him from being able or wishing to join the ranks of the gangster.

Theft Involving Violence. Theft by violence (1a) includes such activities as the "heist" (holdup), bank robbery, burglary, kidnaping, "jack-rolling," murder, the looting of stores and warehouses, and other crimes. The size of the "mob" in these activities varies from one to perhaps a dozen or fifteen, although they are sometimes considerably larger. Murder is not usually committed for gain, but now and then instances occur in which it is committed systematically for the sake of profit. Holdups, of which there are very many, are often committed by a single person. The other types of crime listed under this category usually involve groups.

Theft by violence is a traditional form of crime which has been experimented with in many lands for many centuries. In very loosely organized cultures and in frontier days large marauding gangs were sometimes involved. They frequently lived in the woods or villages of their own and used these places as points of departure for their expeditions. Such gangs did not disappear from central Europe until well into the present century, and even later in the case of the United States. The modern counterpart of these old gangs is today represented by such groups as the Dillinger mob, which utilize the anonymity of our culture and particularly the jungles of our large cities as their places of concealment.

Theft Involving Stealth. In the class of thieving without violence, some of the lines of activity are: the "cannon" (picking pockets), the "heel" (sneak thievery), the "jug heel" (sneak thieving from banks), "pennyweighting" (stealing from jewelry stores by substitution), the "boost" (shoplifting), hotel prowling, "moll buzzing" (purse-snatching), counterfeiting, "laying paper" (passing illegal checks, etc.), forgery, and the "hype" (short-changing).

These crimes ordinarily involve groups of about three persons and are often carried out by a single individual. The organization involved concerns such matters as the "fix," professional solidarity and intercommunication, mutual assistance, the passing on of techniques, co-operation in prison, and concerted efforts to foil the law.

Most of these forms of theft are again very old and standardized as to technique, although adjustments are constantly being made to meet new situations and to keep up with the times. A description of the technique of operation of pickpocket mobs in England a hundred or more years ago would be almost identical with a description of present-day technique. German pickpockets use the same methods and have an argot which is much the same as that of English-speaking "guns." It is standard practice for a mob of this kind to use a couple of stalls to distract the attention of the victim and to maneuver him into the proper position to have his pocketbook removed. The man who removes the money is usually a skilled specialist, known as a "wire," "hook," or "tool." One of the stalls may "shade the duke of the wire" (conceal the hand of the thief who picks the pocket). The argot of German thieves designates this man as a *Decker*, or one who covers. Training and skill, as well as practice, are required.

CHEATS

In this category are included those who practice the major con games, such as "the wire" (race-track betting) and the "stock market." The con man is a top-ranking criminal and when successful makes a great deal of money. The major con games are virtually a twentieth-century development and are organized to take advantage of the lust for easy money on the part of those who already have considerable wealth. The victim, or "mark," is contacted by a "roper," or "steerer," who flatters and entertains him and lures him to some city where there is a phony gambling establishment or stock exchange or broker's office. A sure-fire method of making money in a dishonest way is broached, and in the ensuing transactions the victim and his money are parted. The victim may never realize that he has been duped, in which case he can be duped again. If he does catch on and "beefs," there are effective ways of "cooling" him.

The con game requires a rather large personnel: a "fixer," an "inside man," a dozen or so "shills," a "manager," a "big store" (phony gambling establishment), a "roper," and other assistants. Lou Blonger of Denver, who acted as fix for con men in Denver and other parts of the country, notably Florida, operated in the usual way through politicians and policemen to thwart the efforts of Van Cise to break up the con game in Denver, where it was running rampant. Van Cise reports that Lou Blonger annually visited with the chief of a national detective agency at Hot Springs for their mutual enlightenment and benefit—one, in catching criminals; the other, in helping them to avoid getting caught.

One of the incidents which amused the police of Denver was when Blonger complained to them that he had been fleeced by con men.

The lesser forms of swindling are legion. They include the "smack," "the money machine," carnival "gaff joints," crooked dice and card games, the badger games, "dropping the poke," "charity rackets," "slum hustling," "the wipe," "three-card monte," "the strap," "the income tax shake," "the Spanish prisoner bunco," "the muzzle," "fake stocks," "loan sharks," and a great many others too numerous to mention or to explain in detail. In a recent book a police official lists and describes about one hundred such rackets. The principle involved in most of them is the same: an appeal to the desire for a bargain or for easy money, a build-up to inspire confidence, and skillful salesmanship.

RACKETEERING

We have already touched upon this form of crime and indicated that it is the most highly organized of any. The racketeer is primarily concerned with business affairs, legitimate or otherwise, and preferably those which are close to the margin of legitimacy. He gets his best opportunities from business organizations which meet the need of large sections of the public for goods or services which are defined as illegitimate by that same public, such as prostitution, gambling, illicit drugs, or liquor. The prohibition amendment was a great boon to racketeers in that it gave them an enormous market for their goods and gave them enormous opportunities to expand their power and influence and increase their wealth. The peculiar advantage of the racketeer depends upon the fact that most of the business enterprises which he controls are illegal and cannot therefore avail themselves of the usual protection of the law. In contrast to the thief, the racketeer and the establishments he controls deliver goods and services for money received. The racketeer merely exercises control and collects fees. The extension of racketeer control to legitimate industry and to labor unions is one of the most sinister developments in the field of modern crime.

The wide variety of enterprises which may attract the gangster, as well as those in which he specializes, are indicated in the types of rackets ascribed to various gangsters, all of whom were said to have had dealings with a single Tammany Hall politician, James Hines: Owen Madden—beer and rum, race tracks, night clubs, coal and laundry; J. T. Diamond—alcohol, narcotics, night clubs; Louis (Lepke) Buchalter and Jake Shapiro (Gurrah Jake)—garments, furs, movies, flour, poultry, labor unions, and narcotics; Lucky Luciano—narcotics, liquor, Italian lottery, prostitution, and receiver of stolen goods; Philip Kastel—Montreal night club owner, badger game, bucket shop, rum, slot machines; Frank Costello—slot machines; Meyer Lansky and Bugsy Siegel—execution; Larry Fay—milk racket, taxicabs. This is not a complete list of the gangsters who were said to have dealt with Hines, nor does it cover more than a small number of the rackets. It was estimated that at a certain time in Chicago there were as many as 168 industrial rackets in that city.

The assumption of control of ordinary business by racketeers has been facilitated by a number of conditions within the businesses themselves. Employers have sometimes not hesitated to employ thugs to fight labor. Underworld organizations devoted professionally to this cause have been organized. Likewise, labor unions have sometimes employed thugs or gangsters to fight employers. Just as it is said that "If you use a rat, the rat will end up by using you," so it may also be said that if you use a gangster, he may well end up by using you. And that is what happened. Gangsters who were brought in temporarily refused to leave and continued to collect fees. Another circumstance favoring gang control is that competition in some lines has been so fierce that dealers who found themselves unable to do anything about it or make profits called upon the gangster in desperation to "organize" the business. Unhampered by the Sherman Antitrust Law, the gangster ruthlessly eliminates competition and price cutting. The significant point often is, however, that the businessman may make larger profits, in spite of the toll of the gangster, because of the higher prices he can charge. The ones who lose under this system, which is particularly effective when the labor union local in the industry is also in the hands of the gangster, are the consumer and the rank and file of labor. No doubt there is some kind of moral to be drawn from this situation. We shall leave that to the reader.

45 · Organized Crime in America

by U.S. SENATE CRIME INVESTIGATING COMMITTEE

Criminologists and other investigators have been acquainted for some time with the extent to which corruption and crime prevail in this country and the extent to which they reach into high places, involving persons of prestige and leadership. The revelations of the Senate Crime Investigating Committee, known as the Kefauver Committee, came as a shock to the public at large, but they merely confirmed and, at most, added some specific data to what criminologists have known. The hearings of the Committee, held in 1950-1951, dramatized the situation and thus effectively called attention of the public to what was occurring in their midst. The following selection presents excerpts of the findings of the Committee and of the suggestions offered by it for dealing with the problem. [From *The Kefauver Committee Report on Organized Crime*, Didier Publishers, n.d., pp. 125-128, 151-153, 162-164, 167. Reprinted by permission.]

THE SYNDICATION OF CRIME

THE STRUCTURE of organized crime today is far different from what it was many years ago. Its power for evil is infinitely greater. The unit of organized crime used to be an individual gang consisting of a number of hoodlums, whose activities were obviously predatory in character. Individual gangs tended to specialize in specific types of criminal activity such as payroll, or bank robbery, loft or safe burglary, pocket picking, etc. These gangs normally confined their activities to particular areas of the country or particular communities. Occasionally their activities were aided and abetted by law-enforcement officials. The crooked sheriff who aids the outlaws is as much of a stock character as the fearless "law man" who makes justice triumph.

New types of criminal gangs have emerged during prohibition. The huge profits earned in that era together with the development of twentieth century transportation and communication, made possible larger and much more powerful gangs, covering much greater territory. Organized crime in the last 30 years has taken on new characteristics. The most dangerous criminal gangs today are not specialists in one type of predatory crime, but engage in many and varied forms of criminality. Criminal groups today are multipurpose in character engaging in any racket wherever there is money to be made. The modern gang, moreover, does not rely for its primary source of income on frankly predatory forms of crime such as robbery, burglary, or larceny. Instead the more dangerous criminal elements draw most of their revenues from various forms of gambling, the sale and distribution of narcotics, prostitution, various forms of business and labor racketeering, black-market practices, bootlegging into dry areas, etc.

The key to successful gang operation is monopoly of illicit enterprises or illegal operations, for monopoly guarantees huge profits. In cities that gangland has organized very well, the syndicate or the combination in control of the rackets decides which mobsters are to have what rackets. In cities which have not been well organized, the attempt by one mobster to take over the territory or racket from another mobster inevitably breeds trouble, for modern gangs and criminal syndicates rely on "muscle" and murder to a far greater degree than formerly to eliminate competitors, compel cooperation from reluctant victims, silence informers, and to enforce gangland edicts.

Criminal Organization Like Business Organization. Modern crime syndicates and criminal gangs have copied some of the organizational methods found in modern business. They seek to expand their activities in many different fields and in many different geographic areas, wherever profits may be made. We have seen evidence of the operation of the Costello-Adonis-Lansky crime syndicate, whose headquarters is in New York, in such places as Bergen County, N. J., Saratoga, N. Y., Miami, Fla., New Orleans, Nevada, the west coast and Havana, Cuba. We have seen evidences of operations of the other major crime syndicate, that of Accardo-Guzik-Fischetti, whose headquarters is in Chicago, in such places as Kansas City, East St. Louis, Miami, Nevada, and the west coast.

Some indication of how modern crime syndicates operate and how they open new territory is apparent from the facts described under the city story of Chicago elsewhere in this report in relation to the extraordinary testimony of Lt. George Butler of the police department of Dallas, Tex. Lieutenant Butler was approached by a member of the Chicago mob by the name of Paul Jones. According to Butler, Jones stated that he was an advance agent of the Chicago crime syndicate and was prepared to offer the district attorney and the sheriff $1,000 a week each or a 12½-percent cut on the profits if the syndicate were permitted to operate in Dallas under "complete protection." Jones also stated that syndicate operations were conducted by local people who "front" for the Chicago mob. The syndicate, according to Jones, controlled such cities as St. Louis, Kansas City, New Orleans, and Little Rock. In addition the syndicate had connections in every large city, and if Jones ran into trouble anywhere, money and help would be forthcoming.

Lieutenant Butler advised his superiors, and on instructions, played along with Jones and indicated that the Dallas police were interested in his propositions. Jones, therefore, brought Pat Manno, a notorious Chicago syndicate mobster and a partner of Guzik and Accardo, who was labeled as the fifth man in the syndicate, to Dallas to talk matters over with Butler and Sheriff Guthrie, who had been apprised of the situation. Recordings of the conversation between Lieutenant Butler, Sheriff Guthrie, Manno, and Jones were made. Manno stated that he had been in the policy business in Chicago for 17 years and was interested in opening up operations in Dallas. He stated that the Chicago syndicate was definitely interested in coming into Dallas and that he, as representative of the syndicate, was looking the town over to see if they could operate it in collaboration with the police. The work of the Dallas Police in this connection was most commendable.

There are many other criminal gangs and criminal groups throughout the country that have more than a local importance. For instance, the Kleinman-Rothkopf-Polizzi group has operated in many different Ohio counties as well as in the Newport and the Covington area of Kentucky, in Nevada, and in Miami, Fla. Members of the Detroit gang have operated in Miami, Saratoga, and Kentucky. Individual gangsters and gangs in different parts of the country have also frequently worked in close and profitable relationship with each other, particularly in gambling casinos where often members of several gangs participate on a systematic basis. Outside gangs coming into an area will often use local hoodlums and local gangs.

It is apparent, as Narcotics Commissioner Anslinger testified before the committee, that the leading figures in organized crime do business with each other, get together in places like Miami and Hot Springs and on occasion do each other's dirty work, when a competitor must be eliminated and an informer silenced, or a victim persuaded. Commissioner Anslinger did not think that the activities in one part of the country occur as a result of instructions given in other parts of the country as a general rule. In some cases "it is pretty well organized in that particular way but I wouldn't say that one section of the country controls another section." What happens, Mr. Anslinger testified, is that leading mobsters throughout the country "confer together or talk to each other, deal with each other." He agreed with Mr. Halley's characterization that "they confine their dealings pretty well to the family."

As we have seen one of the major areas in which leading gangs cooperate is in enforcing each other's edicts, silencing informers, persuading potential victims through intimidation, violence, and murder. It is obviously far more difficult for local law enforcement officials to detect the work of outside gangsters than the products of their local talent.

Modern gangland operations on any sizable scale cannot be carried on without protection. The gangs have unbelievable cash assets available for this purpose, moreover. Much of the moneys of criminal gangs and syndicates are invested in legitimate enterprises which presents special dangers to our economy and our people.

The Mafia, the committee is convinced, has an important part in binding together into a loose association the two major criminal syndicates as well as many minor gangs and individual hoodlums throughout the country. Wherever the committee has gone it has run into the trail of this elusive, shadowy, and sinister organization. . . .

* * *

INFILTRATION INTO LEGITIMATE BUSINESS

One of the most perplexing problems in the field of organized crime is presented by the fact that criminals and racketeers are using the profits of organized crime to buy up and operate legitimate enterprises.

This committee has no quarrel with the sincere efforts of men with criminal records who have seen the error of their ways and who now wish to earn an honest living by going into some type of legitimate business. The committee realizes that many men sow their "wild oats" in the form of crime, in their younger years, and then settle down to become decent citizens. This process of rehabilitation of offenders should be encouraged in every possible way. What the committee does object to, however, and what the committee finds is fraught with great danger to our country, is the extent to which gangsters and racketeers continue to pursue their vicious careers and invest the spoils of their illegitimate activity in legitimate enterprises.

A gangster or racketeer in a legitimate business does not suddenly become respectable. The methods which he used to achieve success in racketeering and gambling enterprises are not easily sloughed off. Thus, evidence was produced before the committee concerning the use of unscrupulous and discriminatory business practices, extortion, bombing, and other forms of violence to eliminate competitors and to compel customers to take articles sold by the mobsters. Monopoly is the key to big money in criminal activity. It is also sought by mobsters when they enter legitimate business. A racketeer who has contempt for the law and who enters legitimate business has no hesitation in engaging in black-market practices. This gives him a considerable advantage over a more timid competitor and is one of the means whereby the racketeer can push such a competitor to the wall.

There is another aspect of gangster infiltration into legitimate business which troubles the committee. The big-time gamblers and racketeers usually live a life of luxury but they must have some way of explaining their source of income to prying income-tax officials. One of the functions of investment into legitimate business enterprises is to provide a source for income which cannot be impeached by the Internal Revenue authorities. Returns from gambling and other illegitimate enterprises are extremely difficult to check. Some of the winnings may be invested in legitimate business and taxes may be paid on the income from such business. Taxes on the huge returns from gambling and other illegitimate enterprises have not been paid.

Racketeers Prefer Big-Turnover Businesses. It should be noted, however, that gangsters and racketeers have an affinity for enterprises in which there is a large turn-over and in which problems of accounting and control are difficult. Thus, even when the ill-gotten gains of a racketeer or gangster are invested in a legitimate enterprise there is no assurance that the Government will not be defrauded to a considerable degree of its taxes.

There can be little doubt that the public suffers from gangster penetration into legitimate business. It suffers because higher prices must be paid for articles and services which it must buy. This is the result of the monopoly which is often secured and because of unfair trade practices frequently applied. The public suffers because it may have to put up with shoddy and inferior merchandise in fields where gangsters have been able to obtain a monopoly. One such olive-oil dealer, Joseph Profaci, was cited for a series of violations of the pure food and drug laws including one for which he was fined $12,000. The tax load of the general public is increased when gangsters and racketeers fail to pay their lawful return on the enterprises in which they are engaged. Finally, the public suffers because the vast economic resources that gangsters and racketeers control enables them to consolidate their economic and political positions. Money, and particularly ready cash, is power in any community and over and over again this committee has found instances where racketeers' money has been used to exercise influence with Federal, State, and local officials and agencies of government. An official who is beholden to the mob for his election or appointment thinks first of his boss and only secondarily of the people of the community that he must serve. The money used by hoodlums to buy economic and political control is also used to induce public apathy. The committee found that hoodlums, behind the front of their respectable enterprises, contribute enormous sums to hundreds of worthy causes. While the committee in no way wishes to reflect on the worthiness of such causes, it has found that hoodlum contributions do tend to fool uninformed people and thus contribute to the relaxation of public vigilance. The committee has had before it evidence of hoodlum infiltration in approximately 50 areas of business enterprise. These include:

Advertising
Amusement industry
Appliances
Automobile industry
Baking
Ball rooms, bowling alleys, etc.
Banking
Basketball
Boxing
Cigarette distribution
Coal
Communications facilities
Construction
Drug stores and drug companies
Electrical equipment
Florists
Food (meat, sea food, dairy products, groceries, cheese, olive oil, fruit)
Football
Garment industry
Gas stations and garages
Hotels
Import-export business
Insurance
Juke box and coin-machine distribution
Laundry and dry cleaning
Liquor industry
Loan and bonding business
Manufacturing (gambling equipment, broilers, etc.)
Nevada gambling houses

News services	Scrap business
Newspapers	Shipping
Oil industry	Steel
Paper products	Surplus sales
Racing and race tracks	Tailoring (haberdashery)
Radio stations	Television
Ranching	Theaters
Real estate	Transportation
Restaurants (taverns, bars, night clubs)	

While the committee has not been able in the time available to explore fully the situation in these fields, it has developed enough information to clearly indicate the problems and dangers involved in hoodlum penetration of legitimate industry.

One of the most shocking problems in this connection, and one which constitutes a black page in the history of American industry, is the indisputable evidence obtained by the committee of cooperation with major hoodlums on the part of important segments of business enterprise. In Detroit, the committee found leading industrial concerns admittedly cooperating with notorious hoodlums for the purpose of suppressing labor difficulties. In New York, the same situation prevailed in connection with the Phelps-Dodge Co. which invited in hoodlums from the gang of Albert and Anthony Anastasia to help break a strike. Where business uses racketeers, there is a tendency for labor unions to use tactics of violence and vice versa. Finally, the committee found leading hoodlums holding valuable franchises in the liquor and automobile industries.

*   *   *

BREAKDOWN OF ENFORCEMENT MACHINERY

Although the committee has seen and paid tribute to many fine, efficient, honest, and able law-enforcement officers and officials, law enforcement has broken down in many of the communities visited by the committee. Where criminal gangs and syndicates operate openly as they have done in such places as Saratoga; Bergen County, N. J.; the Newport-Covington area of Kentucky; the Miami area of Florida; many of the parishes outside of New Orleans; many of the Illinois and California counties and the area of Jackson County outside of Kansas City, to cite only the most notorious examples, it is apparent that too many local police, sheriffs, prosecutors, and courts are failing to do their sworn duty.

The committee places no stock in the professed inability of many law-enforcement officials to detect violations of the law which are apparent to any informed citizen. The blindness which afflicts many law-enforcement officials in wide-open communities is for the record only.

There can be little question that these officials know perfectly well what is going on. Nor can there be little doubt in the mind of the committee that vigorous, honest law enforcement can put an end to wide-open conditions in a very short time. The fact that Saratoga was run without open gambling in the racing season of 1950; that Sheriff "King" Clancy could give the order to shut down operations in Jefferson Parish; that Pat Perdue, the so-called "one-man vice squad" of Miami Beach, could boast that he could shut down operations in Miami Beach in 24 hours if he were given the order to do so, is an indication of what can be accomplished where law-enforcement officials really wish to act.

It can be assumed that this failure of law-enforcement officials to suppress gambling and vice conditions in their community affects their law-enforcement responsibilities in other fields. By refusing to act against the racketeers who run bookmaking operations, slot machines, gambling casinos, and houses of prostitution, law-enforcement officials give aid and encouragement to some of the worst hoodlums and criminal gangs in this country. These hoodlums and criminal gangs do not restrict their operations to exploiting the human desire to gamble.

They also engage in activities which are even more devastating to the community and to the welfare of the people; the sale and distribution of narcotics, various forms of extortion and shake-downs, various types of business and labor-union racketeering, as well as outright robbery, burglary, and larceny. Inevitably, their operations in gambling and other fields bring in their train aggravated forms of violence against persons and property. The ultimate weapon that these mobsters have is murder and they have not hesitated to use it in communities all over the country.

Nor should it be assumed that law-enforcement agencies, which are ineffective in suppressing gambling operations, suddenly become efficient instruments of justice when confronted with other crimes. The record is clearly the other way. Police officials, sheriffs, and district attorneys who refuse to do their duty in enforcing the gambling laws because of corruption or the use of political influence do not prosecute vigorously when the racketeers and gangsters operating gambling enterprises become involved in other crimes.

If money or political influence will fix a gambling case, it will also fix a case involving a more heinous offense. The creeping paralysis of law enforcement which results from a failure to enforce the gambling laws, therefore, contributes to a breakdown in connection with other fields of crime.

It is axiomatic in the underworld that once a public official allows a case to be fixed, thereafter the underworld owns him.

One other aspect of this breakdown must be noted. Wherever organized criminal gangs are entrenched in a particular community and have been given the green light to operate, it is not unusual to see the forces of law enforcement being used against their competitors, while protected operations are left severely alone. This fact helps to explain the growth of such vast bookmaking conspiracies as the S and G Syndicate in Miami, the Guarantee Finance Co. in Los Angeles, and the Gross bookmaking empire in New York. Only too frequently, bookmakers, slot-machine operators, policy bankers and punchboard sellers have been given to understand that they must come to terms with the "syndicate" or the "combination" that has the "in" with law enforcement. The penalty for failing to come to terms is continual harassment by the police and other agencies of law enforcement. . . .

The breakdown in law enforcement is not entirely due to corruption of law-enforcement officials or to the use of political influence to paralyze law-enforcement processes. Much of the responsibility must be placed upon the present organization of law-enforcement agencies. In metropolitan communities like Cook County, Ill., Los Angeles County, Calif., or Bergen County, N. J., there is a congeries of independent local police forces covering the county. In addition, a sheriff's office with wide law-enforcement responsibilities and the State police with a wide jurisdiction to enforce State laws, may also operate within the county.

There is no centralized direction or control and no centralized responsibility for seeing that a single uniform law-enforcement policy is applied over the entire geographic area of a county. The situation lends itself to buck-passing and evasion of responsibility which can only inure to the benefit of gangsters and racketeers. It makes it possible for hoodlums to find those cities and towns where law enforcement is lax and to concentrate their operations there.

It is obvious that many factors contribute to the breakdown of law-enforcement agencies. No single panacea can make law-enforcement agencies more efficient and effective in dealing with organized crime. It is suggested, therefore, that each State make an over-all survey of its law-enforcement agencies to see whether or not they are adequately organized and equipped to cope with modern racketeering and gangsterism. It is obvious that a survey of this character must not only inquire into the organization and operations of law-enforcement agencies, it must also determine whether they are so beset by corruption and political influence that no matter how they were organized, they would continue to be ineffective.

Surveys in each State are necessary because of the difficulty of making suggestions which are applicable to the entire country.

The peculiar problems of each State vary and there are significant differences in the organization of their law-enforcement agencies. However, there is sufficient administrative know-how in the various States to make it possible to lay out a plan and a method for dealing with organized crime which will considerably curtail this threat to our institutions.

*   *   *

The committee has been most gratified by the tremendous interest which the general public has demonstrated in the hearings conducted by the committee over the past 11 months. That interest has confirmed anew the committee's fundamental faith that the heart of America is basically sound.

The active participation of an informed public is essential to the correction of the conditions which the committee's investigation has shown to exist throughout the country. The committee has emphasized time and again that organized crime cannot exist without political protection. It is the responsibility of the voting public to insure that their representative governments at all levels are made up of men who are not open to corruption or persuasion by criminals and racketeers.

46 · The Menace of Organized Crime

by ADLAI E. STEVENSON

In the selection that follows, Adlai E. Stevenson, former governor of Illinois and Democratic presidential candidate in 1952, depicts and thoughtfully analyzes organized crime in Illinois. After pointing out that commercialized gambling and other forms of vice are rampant, he dwells upon the factors responsible for the situation and offers specific suggestions for alleviating it. These involve far-reaching reforms in the law-enforcement agencies and, above all, a change in the attitude of the public. ["Crime and Politics," *Journal of Criminal Law and Criminology*, Vol. 41, Nov.-Dec. 1950, pp. 397-405. Reprinted by permission.]

COMMERCIALIZED GAMBLING IN ILLINOIS

A FEW MONTHS ago the Illinois State Police, acting upon my orders, launched a program of raiding notorious gambling establishments throughout the state. This action was widely heralded as a "crackdown" against commercialized gambling in Illinois. It was not only a crackdown; it was a breakdown as well—the breakdown of local law enforcement, the breakdown of decency in government in many parts of the state, the triumph of greed, corruption and, perhaps worst of all, cynicism.

In ordering these raids, I did not feel the joyful exhilaration of a knight in shining armor tilting with the forces of darkness. I felt more like a mourner at a wake. For something had died in Illinois—at least temporarily. And what has happened in Illinois is by no means unique. The formation of the Senate Crime Investigating Committee, under Senator Kefauver's able and effective leadership, as well as the fact that you have chosen this subject for your annual meeting, indicates that organized commercialized crime is in reality a menace throughout the country.

In Illinois, as in most states, the enforcement of the general criminal laws traditionally has been a local matter, with responsibility resting squarely upon local officials—the county sheriff and state's attorney, and the mayors and city police. That is as it should be. Government should be as small in scope and as local in character as possible. And, if all local officials in Illinois had done their sworn duty, as many of them have, there would have been no occasion to use the State Police. But almost from the moment I took office I was besieged by urgent requests from outraged citizens who complained that open gambling and other forms of vice were rampant in their communities, and that they could secure no action from local officials. I was reluctant to use the State Police, despite insistent demands. For over a year prior to the first raids, Attorney General Elliott and I attempted to stop commercialized gambling by several methods. We found direct talks with local officials of offending counties and personal persuasion the most effective method. The local authorities cooperated with us in many cases. In others we were successful only temporarily, or in part, or not at all, although on the whole, the results were reassuring, and commercialized gambling dried up in many counties. Some local officers, however, failed to act. Hence the raids by the State Police.

The evidence obtained by the State Police is turned over to local prosecuting authorities. They can no longer claim to be ignorant of the existence of organized gambling in their counties or that they have been unable to obtain evidence upon which to base a prosecution. The evidence is there. If these officers fail to do their duty now, they must answer to the people, and, if nothing happens, it is the people's own fault, because the people are stronger than the gamblers or any other criminal element.

IMPROVEMENT OF LAW ENFORCEMENT

Our campaign against commercialized gambling has resulted in what the *St. Louis Post Dispatch* referred to recently as a "new kind of pay-off"—the pay-off of success, of new and increased respect for law enforcement, the pay-off of the satisfaction which every decent citizen can take in the fact that commercialized gambling, with all of its poisonous effects upon the quality of local government, is at its lowest ebb in Illinois. As evidence of this change, the Collector of Internal Revenue for the central and southern Illinois counties reports that federal tax stamps for gambling devices have declined forty percent in one year.

Some people have urged that the state take over the enforcement of the criminal laws, and that the State Police should make wholesale raids and arrests. Apart from any constitutional and legal considerations involved, I have three objections to this, at least so far as our situation in Illinois is concerned. First, the state does not now have the resources to assume this responsibility. Our State Police force has its hands full patrolling the highways, enforcing traffic laws, and cracking down on overweight trucks—in other words, in performing the functions for which it was primarily intended. Second, the use of state officers to enforce the general criminal law when local officers are already charged with that responsibility would mean that the public would be paying for law enforcement twice—and this at a time when both state and local governments need more revenue, and the public is demanding economy in government. The third and most fundamental objection is that such a move would be one more step in the abdication of local governmental responsibility, one more example of the growing and dangerous tendency to look to higher levels of government for the solution of problems that could and should be solved closer to home.

For the state to take over local police powers seems to me a dangerous acknowledgment of the failure of local government. However, organized crime with its attendant corruption and corroding disrespect for law enforcement is even more dangerous, and, if local government cannot or will not meet the challenge, the people will demand and receive help from other levels of government, just as they have demanded and received other services which were not provided on the local level. But whatever our views as to who should enforce the laws, we are, I take it, all agreed that law enforcement can and must be improved.

What are some of the obstacles to better law enforcement, and what are some of the things that can be done to improve it? Securing better personnel is part of the answer, but only part.

Crime and politics must be divorced! Police forces, on whatever level of government, must be severed from partisan political control. In Illinois one of the first things I asked from the Legislature was the removal of the State Police from politics—and we now have a force which functions under a merit system. The old system was intolerably expensive and inefficient. Every time the Governor's office changed political complexion, virtually the whole police force of five hundred was discharged and a new one of the proper political faith recruited and trained, only to go out when the state changed its politics again. It is obvious that a man cannot be a good police officer and owe a greater measure of loyalty to his political sponsor than to his superior officer.

Safeguarding against political interference does not in itself guarantee a competent police force; the fact that a man is honest does not necessarily make him a good policeman. Amateur crime detectors cannot cope with the professional criminals of today. We need more police forces that are truly professional in the best sense of that term. Recruiting and training practices must be improved. We have made progress along these lines under our new merit system in Illinois, too, and hope to make more.

Our police must be paid adequate salaries—salaries that are not an invitation to graft and corruption. In many of our larger Illinois cities, policemen have not had a salary raise for several years, despite skyrocketing living costs. Here again, this salary problem is tied up with the pressing need of local governments for more revenue, thus emphasizing the interdependence of so many of our governmental problems.

Another thing we can do to improve the quality of law enforcement is to re-examine our entire law enforcement structure. Obsolescence and duplication present formidable obstacles to efficient law enforcement, and diffusion of authority makes it difficult to fix responsibility. Where responsibility cannot be fixed, public opinion has no chance to operate effectively, and the democratic process is weakened.

The basic pattern of our law enforcement structure is an inheritance from a bygone day. To this, some latter day accretions have been added more or less haphazardly. In some instances, state, county and municipal officers have overlapping or conflicting authority. The duties of the office of sheriff and constable, for example,—to say nothing of the coroner—have been largely inherited from medieval England. Some law enforcement officers are so burdened with other unrelated duties that they can give only a fraction of their time to the apprehension or prosecution of criminals. They are, at best, only part-time law enforcement officers. Some elective offices have constitutional or statutory restrictions as to succession, making it impossible for them to be manned by professional career men. I do not say that all of these things are necessarily bad, but I do say that they need to be constantly re-examined in the light of present day conditions.

This problem of obsolescence and duplication is not peculiar to our law enforcement machinery. It is a problem of government generally, and the Hoover Commission report, followed by the formation of "little Hoover commissions" in approximately one-half of our states, shows that the public is acutely aware of the general problem. There should be similar studies with a view to improving our law enforcement machinery. Of course, there have been studies like that in the past, and I am not unmindful of the invaluable work that the organized bar is constantly doing to improve the administration of criminal justice. But there is need for a larger, more comprehensive study, and the problem must somehow or other be dramatized for the public.

Among the questions to which answers should be sought are these: What should be the respective roles of state and local governments in law enforcement? What controls, if any, should the state have over local law enforcement officers? Should these controls be direct or indirect? In Illinois, for example, the state's attorney is a county officer, but he is charged with prosecuting violators of state laws, and he receives part of his salary from the state treasury. Yet no state officer exercises any control over him. In some states, although not in my own, the Governor may remove any local law enforcement officer who fails to do his duty; and this has proved to be a most potent instrument for improving local law enforcement. Given some such power, I have little doubt that commercial gambling could be quickly and inexpensively ended in Illinois for keeps.

There is another means for securing good law enforcement which appears to me to have been too little used—and that is the weapon of disbarment. In Illinois, for example, I should say that it represents as effective an instrument as we have for disciplining attorneys who hold law enforcement positions. This is, of course, an area where the organized bar can be of the greatest help, and I was greatly interested in the action of the Illinois State Bar Association a few months ago in filing disbarment proceedings against the state's attorney of a county where organized gambling had been permitted to flourish under a cynical system of periodic fines. I know of no duty more clearly comprehended

within our obligations as members of this profession than to live up to
our oaths of office when we occupy public posts with law enforcement
responsibilities.

What federal laws should be enacted in aid of state laws? Parenthetically, I am gratified that Congress seems disposed to close the channels of interstate commerce to slot machines and racing information.

To what extent should the functions of investigating and prosecuting
be separated? In some states, the prosecuting attorney prosecutes only
upon complaint. In other states, he is expected to take the initiative in
discovering violations of the law. And in many localities the public insists that he conduct investigations but refuses to allow his office to
have any investigators. The result is that the average prosecuting attorney must rely for his evidence upon a police force over whose activities
he has little, if any, direction.

Combining the functions of investigation and prosecution in one officer may possibly lead to abuses, but this division of authority makes it
easy to escape responsibility and encourages "buck passing." We have
some counties in Illinois, for example, where the bi-partisan approach
has been used with singularly devastating effect. The managers of the
two parties, in collaboration with the gamblers, see to it that there is
always a Republican sheriff and a Democratic state's attorney, or vice
versa, with the result that the citizen who wants action is told by the
one that it is the responsibility of the other, and is shunted back and
forth between them to no purpose whatsoever.

THE PLAGUE OF CYNICISM

These are only a few of the questions which are worth considering. In
a sense, however, they are secondary and superficial, for the greatest obstacles to effective law enforcement are public indifference and cynicism.
The greatest menace of organized crime is not the crime itself nor the
criminal. The greatest menace is that the public will come to accept organized crime as something inevitable, as a necessary part of our social system.

Cynicism toward law enforcement is as old as government itself.
When Solon was writing the laws of Athens, he was told that laws were
like spiders' webs and would only entangle the poor and the weak, while
the rich and powerful would easily break through them. This attitude
toward law enforcement has persisted throughout the ages and, unfortunately, has not always been without some justification. In a democracy, however, there is no justification for such helpless cynicism. Nor is
there any use to place the entire blame for crime and lax law enforcement upon a real or supposed alliance between criminals and politicians.

and to assume that the members of the public are helpless bystanders. Organized crime cannot thrive without the active support of many elements of the community, nor without the passive support of many more elements. The respectable businessman who falls for the myth that a wide-open town is good for business is just as effective an accomplice of the criminal as is the politician who seeks to win friends by influencing people. The solid citizen who thinks that illegal slot machines are just fine for his country club but bad for the corner saloon does not realize what difficulties he is making for the persons he has elected to enforce the laws.

Of the 2,700 gambling machines presently registered for federal tax purposes in 76 Illinois counties, only 800—less than one-third—are in taverns and other public places. The other 1,900 are in the country clubs, the fraternal organizations, the veterans' clubs, the Army posts and other places with which we do not customarily associate law violation, organized or unorganized. Consider the effect on the public mind, and the vexatious problem of law enforcement, through this wholesale violation of the law by the most responsible elements of our communities.

While we are on the subject of "organized crime," let me say that one of the most disheartening things that I have encountered is what might be termed "unorganized crime." One example of this which we have had to battle incessantly and expensively in Illinois is the persistent and flagrant violation of our very liberal laws regulating maximum truck weights on our highways. It appears, I can only conclude, that at least some otherwise reputable businessmen prefer to overload their trucks and pay the occasional and meager fines when they are caught because it pays.

To what point, I inquire, does violation of the laws have to go, or what character does it have to take, before it achieves the status of "organized crime"? I have a feeling that this category has been a little too exclusive.

The phrase "organized crime" has, in the ears of the average citizen, a horrendous ring and conjures up visions of masked men with tommy guns, bank robberies, murders and similar high and unspeakable crimes. Our average citizen also feels, probably as a result of this lurid conception, that organized crime does not touch him very closely and is something that can safely be left to the F.B.I. Senator Kefauver would, I am sure, be very quick to join me in my assurance to you that this is a highly mistaken concept. The most powerful and affluent in the world of organized crime operate in much more prosaic fields and in much less dramatic ways. They move where the money is, and this too often seems to be in such twilight zones as that of gambling where there are prohibitory laws on the books but no unanimity of moral conviction. The happy hunting ground of organized crime is in the area where too many people are disposed to participate in the breaking of a law. What these people seem not to realize is that the law cannot be broken without the connivance of elected officials, and that open and long-continued viola tion inevitably means that there is corruption—a pay-off in some form or another. And corruption is a cancer which cannot be confined—a public official who has gotten in on the take for one purpose has become a captive and his usefulness as a public servant is largely at an end.

I am new in politics, but I happen to believe in the value and impor tance of partisan political organization. I think that strong and healthy political parties are essential to our democracy, and I think also that a broader and more active participation in them by all good citizens is one of our greatest needs. But I can understand the discouragement and despair which assails those who find their own party machinery domi nated by those who can fight with the aid of money supplied by the gamblers—who can, if you please, buy up all the billboards, bribe or bid highest for the services of election workers, and do all the other seem ingly trivial but highly practical things which can snuff out the hopes of decent people in politics.

These are some of the facts of life about the menace of organized crime in a democracy. These are the reasons why the dropping of a fifty-cent piece in a slot machine is too often not merely a matter be tween you and your own conscience or budget. This is why a double standard of law observance is no more feasible in the gambling field than it is in that of burglary.

Law enforcement doesn't exist in a vacuum, and it can't be considered in isolation. The crisis in law enforcement is but one aspect of the crisis of representative government. Good government is indivisible. You can't expect good government in other departments along with dishonest or ineffective law enforcement, and you can't have effective law enforcement without honest, efficient, responsible government all down the line. And I suspect the major problem of our age is whether or not we have enough citizens who are willing to labor unceasingly to achieve good govern ment. Wherever law enforcement continues lax over an extended period of time, it is so only because a large segment of the population does not want effective law enforcement, at least not badly enough to labor for good government as diligently as those who want bad government labor for it.

We speak glibly of the necessity for ending the alliance between crime and politics. But so long as the support of the lawless element of the community is reckoned a more potent political asset than the suppor of the people who are willing to labor for effective law enforcement, this alliance will be a constant threat.

One of the most disheartening things that any conscientious official has to face is the lethargy and apathy on the part of most of the public. The malicious criticism that is leveled against us does not hurt so much. We have come to expect that. Every man in public life knows that his words and deeds will be twisted by knaves to make a snare for fools. The truly disheartening thing is that so many people—people who are neither knaves nor fools—just do not have enough interest, enough sense of civic responsibility, to take the trouble to make their government work better.

The ultimate answer to the menace of organized crime and to the problem of lax law enforcement is public opinion. And, above all, it must be continuously active. Too often public opinion is a sleeping giant. We have already had too many cycles of reform and relapse, too many moral crusades followed by business as usual. Just as our nation can no longer withdraw into an isolationist shell until some Pearl Harbor stirs us to vigorous action, so we can no longer afford to postpone effective law enforcement until lawlessness becomes a national scandal.

Today there are signs that the public is awakening to the twin menaces of organized crime and corrupt law enforcement. Let us hope this time that it will not be another ephemeral crusade but a true rebirth of citizen responsibility.

17 · The Inside Story of a Crime Trust

by JOSEPH FREEMAN

One of the most relentless as well as most efficiently organized crime rings on record is what came to be known as Murder Inc., with headquarters in Brooklyn. This organization was tracked down by the then Brooklyn district attorney William O'Dwyer in 1940. Although "busted up" some years ago and presumably out of existence, it was probably typical of criminal networks operating at present. This graphic account of the operations of the ring is based on the testimony of one of the members of the gang who turned state's witness. It offers a glimpse into the ways in which large crime syndicates conduct their "business." ["Murder Monopoly: The Inside Story of a Crime Trust," *The Nation*, Vol. 150, No. 21, May 25, 1940, pp. 645ff. Reprinted by permission.]

AGAINST A BACKGROUND of violence, sensation, and sadism—all tending to obscure its real import—Brooklyn's District Attorney, William O'Dwyer, has run to earth a criminal network which puts in the shade the great racketeering organizations of a generation ago. "Murder, Inc.," is journalese for the ring, and the name is an inspiration; it shows that to some extent at least the press has caught the meaning of Mr. O'Dwyer's discovery: that crime, like business, has outgrown the forms of rugged individualism and moved on to the greater glories of monopoly. Confessions by leaders of Murder, Inc.—its own name for itself is "the Combination" —show that it is a nation-wide, highly organized business which operates major rackets from coast to coast, trains its personnel, has its own code of conduct, and kills on contract. It is a grotesque caricature of American big business, and its ramifications are almost as manifold: labor unions, politics, and industry all covertly recognize the racketeer as a functionary of American society—though they may not be aware of the extent to which his activities center in Murder, Inc.

Today it is almost impossible for a gangster, big or small, to conduct an independent racket. Whether he runs a policy game which nets him millions or a peanut machine which brings him in $30 a week, he can work his racket only with the permission of the Combination. The leaders grant each racketeer his territory, just as an automobile manufacturer grants a dealer his territory. If a racketeer leaves New York for Chicago, he can set up in business only with the consent of the Chicago leader of Murder, Inc. Similarly, no murder can be committed without the okay of the boss of the zone. The boss even reserves the right to choose the killers.

The killings—and they are numbered by the score—are by-products of widespread business operations involving millions of dollars. The Combination exercises control over gambling, prostitution, the illicit traffic in narcotics, the policy game, bootlegging, and the loan-shark racket, to cite its outstanding spheres of influence. By sheer force it also dominates certain trade-union locals, and has a financial stake in various night clubs and cabarets. It operates certain legitimate enterprises and muscles in on others, where it exacts tribute from business men by threats or use of violence. Through its control of slot machines it collects pennies and nickels even from the school children of the nation. And not least, through its connection with corrupt political machines, it plays an important and sinister role in urban politics.

The Combination even has its own banking and credit system designed to lend racketeers money—at an exorbitant rate—with which to start in business. It protects the member racketeer against unauthorized rivals and punishes him when he violates the laws of Murder, Inc. The punishment is usually a violent and horrible death.

At the moment public attention is centered on the first trial which has come out of O'Dwyer's investigations. The defendants, Harry (Happy) Maione and Frank (the Dasher) Abbandando, are charged with killing a fellow-gangster named George Rudnick in 1937. The victim was wiped out because he had turned police informer. According to the prosecution, the defendants strangled Rudnick with a rope, perforated his head and other parts of his body with sixty-three jabs of an icepick, and, to make sure, bashed in his skull with a meat-chopper. Technically the trial is concerned with only one killing, but it is merely the opening gun against Murder, Inc. So far the prosecutor's investigations have shed light on fifty-six hitherto unsolved murders in New York, and he has leads, he told me, which will uncover the bodies of scores of men whose murders were not even recorded on the police blotters. He believes Murder, Inc., can explain the mysterious disappearance of Peter Panto, progressive waterfront union organizer, and of many other members of the waterfront union.

Although his work has just got under way, O'Dwyer has already forged links between various branches of Murder, Inc., in New York. He has related the Combination to Lepke and Gurrah's racketeering in the garment and fur industries, flour trucking, the bakery trade, and narcotics; to the gambling, bootlegging, extortion, and trucking rackets headed by Charles (Bug) Siegel and Meyer Lansky; to the prostitution, policy, loan-shark, and narcotic rackets of the Bronx heirs of Dutch Schultz, whose mob continues to do business as part of Murder, Inc.; and to the various criminal and political activities of the Brooklyn underworld headed by Albert Anastasia and Joe Adonis. From New York the lines lead to other cities and other big shots: to the Purple Gang of Detroit; to Frank Nitti, former aide of Al Capone, who now runs the rackets in Chicago and Miami; to Frank Costello, boss of the New Orleans underworld; and finally to Dutch Goldberg of California, who is believed to be the biggest shot of them all.

Much of the information which enabled O'Dwyer to piece together the pattern of social decay that is Murder, Inc., has come from Abe (Kid Twist) Reles, now state's witness in the case against Maione and Abbandando. This slight, kinky-haired, brown-eyed gangster, with the flat nose, low wrinkled forehead, and heavy lips, began his criminal career in 1920, at the age of thirteen, as a professional racketeer of the prohibition era. He has been arrested forty-three times on every charge ranging from juvenile delinquency and disorderly conduct to murder (no less than five times), and in the course of the present trial has confessed to eighteen murders, six of which he calmly described on the witness stand. In all but five arrests Reles went scot free.

He is known in Brownsville as a cruel, sadistic slugger. His voice is harsh; the words come rapidly; the language is clipped, full of that underworld argot in which money is "sugar," confessing is "singing," and lending at high rates of interest is "shylocking." Behind this lingo are a shrewd, predatory mind and a strange rationale. Reles considers himself and his associates cool, calculating business men operating a vast enterprise.

"The Combination," he boasted to O'Dwyer, "is operated like the Lehman banks. It is practically one organization and spreads all over the country." Reles compares Murder, Inc., to a "tree with all its branches branched out," and in a less idyllic mood to the "airplane trust." He emphasizes that it extends from coast to coast, with headquarters in cities like New York, Chicago, New Orleans, Detroit, and Los Angeles. In the entire United States there are hundreds of thousands of people in the Combination, and in the five boroughs of New York alone there are several thousands. According to Reles, the nation-wide crime syndicate is an outgrowth of the fierce competition in the alcohol racket during the era of needled beer and bathtub gin. "There was no price regulation," Reles told O'Dwyer. "The rule was, I'll do you and you'll do me." Profits ran into the millions, and that was bound to create war. Prohibition gang shootings are now part of American legend, like the predatory excursions and killings of the frontier cattle rustlers. Reles looks back on that era with horror, but for other reasons than the public. He feels that machine-gun competition was in the long run unprofitable for the racketeer.

"Nobody cared how he moved around," he said. "I looked to kill you and you looked to kill me. Somebody did something out of the way and got shot, and then his friends went gunning for the man who did the killing and *he* got shot. There was no sense in that. So the leaders of the mob said, 'Why not stop this crazy competition and go out and make money instead?' So six or seven of the leaders got together and said, 'Boys, what's the use of fighting each other? Let's put our heads together, all of us, so that there can't be a meeting without one another.' That's how they all got together, to make no fighting."

Reles claims that the crime trust was from the beginning organized on a nation-wide basis. Modern means of communication and transportation made this logical. The syndicate developed its own hierarchy. Gradations in income, power, and authority were based on original accumulations of capital. When prohibition went out, the gangs had to seek other sources of income—race tracks, cabarets, gambling joints, bordels, policy games, the corrupt sections of the labor movement, the fur and poultry industries, the trucking business. Everywhere the mobs "muscled in" and chiseled off "a piece."

The ordinary small-time mobster was in no position to muscle in. In crime, as in other modern enterprises, the day of the small entrepreneur was over. He might have "brains" as Reles put it, but "he didn't have a chance because he didn't have a dime." He needed capital or credit to start a racket. Failing that, he was forced to become a "worker" for wages, employed by the bigger racketeers. That is how the hierarchy started. In the prohibition era Tim Murphy, a witty Chicago labor racketeer, used to say that Smith and Wesson made all men equal. Now the racketeer with the money had the last word.

A gangster who wanted to run his own racket had to borrow money. He would go, let us say, to Henry (Dutch) Goldberg. During prohibition, Dutch had done quite well running beer; he had wiped out rivals and piled up millions. After the great show was over, he invested some of his money in legitimate distilleries. He also became, according to Reles, head of the Broadway syndicate known as the Big Six. Dutch Goldberg has a police record in New York of four convictions for grand larceny and manslaughter and has served time in Elmira and Sing Sing.

Secure in his millions, Dutch acted as banker for other racketeers; he financed gangsters who started various legitimate and illegitimate enterprises, and received in return a big slice of the racket. In the credit system of the crime trust Reles sees the operation of a natural law. "If you haven't got any money," he remarked philosophically to District Attorney O'Dwyer, "you can't go any place. So the main thing is, you must have money." It was this credit system which first gave wealthy racketeers like Dutch Goldberg, Frank Nitti, and Joe Adonis their leadership in the crime trust. After that, rule was maintained by rigid organization and discipline, with murder the ultimate instrument of control.

As Reles describes it, the racketeers in each zone are governed by an "inner circle" of overlords whose decisions are law. These are the big shots who direct the various "business" enterprises, arrange murders, and acquire heavy bank accounts. Below them are "vice presidents," like Happy Maione, Pittsburgh Phil Strauss, who is to be tried separately for the Rudnick murder, and Abe Reles. The word "mob" is no longer used to designate the rank and file. They are now "troops" or, less glamorously, "punks," in the employ of the top men. Big shots operate in terms of profits—all the traffic will bear. Secondary leaders and punks work for wages. Reles emphatically denies that Murder, Inc., triggermen have committed murder for as little as $5. "That's just newspaper stuff," he says indignantly. "You don't get paid for that kind of work. When you kill, it's duty. When you work in a shop, and the boss wants you to do something, he doesn't say, 'I'll give you five or ten dollars.' He is paying you a salary, and you've got to do what he tells you." Similarly, the trig-german is on the pay roll of the Combination; any work he does is "part of the routine."

The salaries of Murder, Inc., employees vary from $100 to $250 a week. In addition, some of them are given small rackets of their own: running slot machines or collecting tribute from storekeepers and pool par-lors. If the income from these is small, the "trooper" may keep it all: if it runs into real money, he has to kick back part of the take to gangsters higher up. Salaries are paid regularly all the year round, according to Reles, and all the boys make a "good living."

That is the optimistic view natural to a foreman; he resents any im-plication that his men are underpaid. "Punks" like Pretty Levine and Duke Maffetore, now caught in the O'Dwyer net, tell another story. They say that "troopers" make little money. They are often broke; they are compelled to borrow at fantastic interest rates from the syndicate; and they commit murders for as little as $5, or even for coffee and cake. They have no choice, because once they are in the gang they can't quit. And Reles admits that nine times out of ten when a mobster wants to quit he is killed. The widow is not told what happened to her husband, though she may learn about it from the newspapers. However, she re-ceives his salary as long as his gang is making money. This is Murder, Inc.'s own form of life insurance.

In his confession Reles has insisted that the Combination is a "busi-ness" outfit, an economic syndicate whose main object is not murder but money. The murder is incidental to the struggle for money, just as in the moral world wars may be incidental to the struggle for markets. Since Murder, Inc., obtains its money by illegal means, it must purge rivals, code violators, and renegades by illegal means. Under the laws of the community this is murder; from the viewpoint of the crime trust it is just execution.

The economic setup of Murder, Inc., apes big business; its "troops" ape the military machine; its internal justice fantastically mimics our official courts. Charged with violating mob law, a gangster may under certain circumstances demand and obtain a trial by his peers. Here the leaders are judges, and various gangsters appear as prosecutors, wit-nesses, and "lawyers" for the defense. On several occasions, Reles will tell you proudly, he appeared as counsel for fellow-gangsters on trial before a Murder, Inc., court. He has a flair for legal jargon; he has had plenty of opportunity to hear it in the forty-three times that he has been brought into the official courts. He has defended fellow-gangsters by arguing, "This ain't admissible evidence," or "There ain't no corroboration for this."

Verdicts of Murder, Inc., courts and executions ordered by its leaders are accepted without question by the membership. Loyalty to the group transcends all friendships, all blood ties. The big shots may inform a gangster: "Your brother was a rat; we had to shoot him." The gangster, knowing what is best for him, accepts his brother's execution in silence. Fifteen years ago Louis Capone's own gang killed his brother. Louis, no relation to Al Capone but a powerful figure in the Brooklyn underworld, has known this all along and has done nothing about it. It all happened within accepted mob regulations.

The crime trust, Reles insists, never commits murders out of passion, excitement, jealousy, personal revenge, or any of the usual motives which prompt private, unorganized murder. It kills impersonally, and solely for business considerations. Even business rivalry, he adds, is not the usual motive, unless "somebody gets too balky or somebody steps right on top of you." No gangster may kill on his initiative; every murder must be ordered by the leaders at the top, and it must serve the welfare of the organization.

A murder by the crime trust can be arranged only by one of the big shots. An ordinary citizen cannot hire Murder, Inc., to do away with someone he does not like. You may, of course, approach a minor triggerman with a proposition to bump off someone for $5,000. But if he did that, Murder, Inc., would kill him. Such a triggerman, Reles says, is not safe to have around. Any member of the mob who would dare to kill on his own initiative or for his own profit would be executed. "Suppose," Reles says, "I come to a triggerman on my own hook and give him $5,000 to rub out someone I don't like. What's to stop him from taking $10,000 from someone else to rub me out?" The crime trust insists that murder must be a business matter, organized by the chiefs in conference and carried out in a disciplined way. "It's real business all the way through," Reles explains. "It just happens to be that kind of business, but nobody is allowed to kill from personal grievance. There's got to be a good business reason, and the top men of the Combination must give their okay."

In support of this contention, Reles gives examples of "good business reasons." George Rudnick, whom Happy Maione and Frank Abbandando are accused of having removed from this earth, had turned police informer—a simple instance of cause and effect. Willie Weber, the policy racketeer, rated death because he bucked the Combination's attempt to organize the policy racket along trust lines. All other policy men entered the Combination. They had one boss, Lucky Luciano; they all turned in their profits to him, and he paid them a salary. Weber held out for the old laissez faire system; he kept his own policy bank and insisted on continuing in business for himself. The Combination decided to execute him. Weber turned out to be tough; he escaped death, though they managed to blow his shoulder off with shotguns. Pittsburgh Phil Strauss was bitter about the failure to rub out Weber. It was a great financial loss to the Brooklyn mob. Under the verbal contract with Luciano the killing of Weber would have given them 50 per cent of his policy racket—perhaps a million dollars clear.

Another clear case cited by Reles was that of Walter Sage. The boys liked Sage. "He was like one of us," Reles explained, "hanging around the corners of East New York making a living this way and that." Pittsburgh Phil staked him to the peanut-machine racket on a percentage basis. But Sage disappointed everybody. He double-crossed his patron and ran away with Strauss's share of the profits. Accordingly his friend Big Gangi was detailed to visit him in Sullivan County. Later handsome green-eyed Pretty Levine, an unfeeling triggerman, was sent up to meet the boys. They took the unsuspecting Sage for a pleasure trip through the wood in a 1937 Oldsmobile sedan. Without warning Big Gangi and Pretty Levine stabbed Sage with an icepick fifty-four times, tied a slot machine around the corpse, and threw it into Swan Lake. "There's the motive," Reles added, "when you have no respect."

Under syndicate rules it is "illegal" to kill a man outside your own territory. If New York wants a man rubbed out and he escapes to St Louis, the job must be done through the St. Louis branch. The St. Louis leaders must give their okay and choose the killers. For strategic reasons they may call in triggermen from out of town, "so the man who will be killed won't know them," Reles explains, "and they can put him on the spot. You go to St. Louis and you don't know a thing about the man you are going to kill or why he is being killed. When you get there you are told what to do."

Often the killer has to read the newspaper to find out whom he has executed. Then he goes into hiding, usually in Detroit. There is a special fund to take care of him, to cover his living expenses in hiding, to defend him if he is caught. Every branch of Murder, Inc., contributes to it.

Reles insists that any murder committed in the United States which has not been solved within a reasonable length of time is a murder committed by the Combination. It has got to be, he says; a private killing is broken sooner or later by the police, usually within six months or a year. If a killing remains unsolved for five or ten years, you may be sure it was the work of Murder, Inc.

CHAPTER THIRTEEN

White-Collar Crime

48 · White-Collar Criminality

by EDWIN H. SUTHERLAND

In studying crime and the criminal, criminologists have
traditionally concentrated on the convicted law-breaker or
the inmate of jails or prisons. These, they have found, were
drawn mostly from the lower socioeconomic classes, and
they therefore concluded that crime is mostly associated
with the poorer classes. They have known, to be sure, that
an upper-class person may become a criminal, but they
have thought such a case to be rather rare. In recent years,
however, they have become increasingly aware of the widespread criminal practices of upper-class persons in business
and the professions, and doubts have arisen as to whether
the lower-class individuals on whom they have concentrated their attention are really typical criminals and, hence,
whether their generalizations were valid. It was primarily
Professor Edwin H. Sutherland, in a presidential address in
1939 before the American Sociological Society on "White-
Collar Criminality," who called for a reconsideration of
the problem. His paper and subsequent book on the white-
collar criminal had a far-reaching effect on the study of
crime. The selection that follows presents Sutherland's
original statement on white-collar criminality. [From *American Sociological Review*, Vol. 5, No. 1, Feb. 1940, pp. 1-12.
Reprinted by permission.]

THIS PAPER is concerned with crime in relation to business. The economists are well acquainted with business methods but not accustomed to consider them from the point of view of crime; many sociologists are well acquainted with crime but not accustomed to consider it as expressed in business. This paper is an attempt to integrate these two bodies of knowledge. More accurately stated, it is a comparison of crime in the upper or white-collar class, composed of respectable or at least respected business and professional men, and crime in the lower class, composed of persons of low socioeconomic status. This comparison is made for the purpose of developing the theories of criminal behavior, not for the purpose of muckraking or of reforming anything except criminology.

The criminal statistics show unequivocally that crime, *as popularly conceived and officially measured*, has a high incidence in the lower class and a low incidence in the upper class; less than two percent of the persons committed to prisons in a year belong to the upper class. These statistics refer to criminals handled by the police, the criminal and juvenile courts, and the prisons, and to such crimes as murder, assault, burglary, robbery, larceny, sex offenses, and drunkenness, but exclude traffic violations.

The criminologists have used the case histories and criminal statistics derived from these agencies of criminal justice as their principal data. From them, they have derived general theories of criminal behavior. These theories are that, since crime is concentrated in the lower class, it is caused by poverty or by personal and social characteristics believed to be associated statistically with poverty, including feeblemindedness, psychopathic deviations, slum neighborhoods, and "deteriorated" families. This statement, of course, does not do justice to the qualifications and variations in the conventional theories of criminal behavior, but it presents correctly their central tendency.

The thesis of this paper is that the conception and explanations of crime which have just been described are misleading and incorrect, that crime is in fact not closely correlated with poverty or with the psychopathic and sociopathic conditions associated with poverty, and that an adequate explanation of criminal behavior must proceed along quite different lines. The conventional explanations are invalid principally because they are derived from biased samples. The samples are biased in that they have not included vast areas of criminal behavior of persons not in the lower class. One of these neglected areas is the criminal behavior of business and professional men, which will be analyzed in this paper.

The "robber barons" of the last half of the nineteenth century were white-collar criminals, as practically everyone now agrees. Their attitudes are illustrated by these statements: Colonel Vanderbilt asked, "You don't suppose you can run a railroad in accordance with the statutes, do you?" A. B. Stickney, a railroad president, said to sixteen other railroad presidents in the home of J. P. Morgan in 1890, "I have the utmost respect for you gentlemen, individually, but as railroad presidents I wouldn't trust you with my watch out of my sight." Charles Francis Adams said, "The difficulty in railroad management . . . lies in the covetousness, want of good faith, and low moral tone of railway managers, in the complete absence of any high standard of commercial honesty."

The present-day white-collar criminals, who are more suave and deceptive than the "robber barons," are represented by Krueger, Stavisky, Whitney, Mitchell, Foshay, Insull, the Van Sweringens, Musica-Coster, Fall, Sinclair, and many other merchant princes and captains of finance and industry, and by a host of lesser followers. Their criminality has been demonstrated again and again in the investigations of land offices, railways, insurance, munitions, banking, public utilities, stock exchanges, the oil industry, real estate, reorganization committees, receiverships, bankruptcies, and politics. Individual cases of such criminality are reported frequently, and in many periods more important crime news may be found on the financial pages of newspapers than on the front pages. White-collar criminality is found in every occupation, as can be discovered readily in casual conversation with a representative of an occupation by asking him, "What crooked practices are found in your occupation?"

White-collar criminality in business is expressed most frequently in the form of misrepresentation in financial statements of corporations, manipulation in the stock exchange, commercial bribery, bribery of public officials directly or indirectly in order to secure favorable contracts and legislation, misrepresentation in advertising and salesmanship, embezzlement and misapplication of funds, short weights and measures and misgrading of commodities, tax frauds, misapplication of funds in receiverships and bankruptcies. These are what Al Capone called "the legitimate rackets." These and many others are found in abundance in the business world.

In the medical profession, which is here used as an example because it is probably less criminalistic than some other professions, are found illegal sale of alcohol and narcotics, abortion, illegal services to underworld criminals, fraudulent reports and testimony in accident cases, extreme cases of unnecessary treatment, fake specialists, restriction of competition, and fee-splitting. Fee-splitting is a violation of a specific law in many states and a violation of the conditions of admission to the practice of medicine in all. The physician who participates in fee-splitting tends to send his patients to the surgeon who will give him the largest fee rather than to the surgeon who will do the best work. It has been reported that two thirds of the surgeons in New York City split fees, and that more than one half of the physicians in a central western city who answered a questionnaire on this point favored fee-splitting.

These varied types of white-collar crimes in business and the professions consist principally of violation of delegated or implied trust, and many of them can be reduced to two categories: misrepresentation of asset values and duplicity in the manipulation of power. The first is approximately the same as fraud or swindling; the second is similar to the double-cross. The latter is illustrated by the corporation director who, acting on inside information, purchases land which the corporation will need and sells it at a fantastic profit to his corporation. The principle of this duplicity is that the offender holds two antagonistic positions, one of which is a position of trust, which is violated, generally by misapplication of funds, in the interest of the other position. A football coach, permitted to referee a game in which his own team was playing, would illustrate this antagonism of positions. Such situations cannot be completely avoided in a complicated business structure, but many concerns make a practice of assuming such antagonistic functions and regularly violating the trust thus delegated to them. When compelled by law to make a separation of their functions, they make a nominal separation and continue by subterfuge to maintain the two positions.

An accurate statistical comparison of the crimes of the two classes is not available. The most extensive evidence regarding the nature and prevalence of white-collar criminality is found in the reports of the larger investigations to which reference was made. Because of its scattered character, that evidence is assumed rather than summarized here. A few statements will be presented, as illustrations rather than as proof of the prevalence of this criminality.

The Federal Trade Commission in 1920 reported that commercial bribery was a prevalent and common practice in many industries. In certain chain stores, the net shortage in weights was sufficient to pay 3.4 percent on the investment in those commodities. Of the cans of ether sold to the Army in 1923-1925, 70 percent were rejected because of impurities. In Indiana, during the summer of 1934, 40 percent of the ice cream samples tested in a routine manner by the Division of Public Health were in violation of law. The Comptroller of the Currency in 1908 reported that violations of law were found in 75 percent of the banks examined in a three months' period. Lie detector tests of all employees in several Chicago banks, supported in almost all cases by confessions, showed that 20 percent of them had stolen bank property. A public accountant estimated, in the period prior to the Securities and Exchange Commission, that 80 percent of the financial statements of corporations were misleading. James M. Beck said, "Diogenes would have been hard put to it to find an honest man in the Wall Street which I knew as a corporation lawyer" (in 1916).

White-collar criminality in politics, which is generally recognized as fairly prevalent, has been used by some as a rough gauge by which to measure white-collar criminality in business. James A. Farley said, "The standards of conduct are as high among officeholders and politicians as they are in commercial life," and Cermak, while mayor of Chicago, said, "There is less graft in politics than in business." John Flynn wrote, "The average politician is the merest amateur in the gentle art of graft, compared with his brother in the field of business." And Walter Lippmann wrote, "Poor as they are, the standards of public life are so much more social than those of business that financiers who enter politics regard themselves as philanthropists."

These statements obviously do not give a precise measurement of the relative criminality of the white-collar class, but they are adequate evidence that crime is not so highly concentrated in the lower class as the usual statistics indicate. Also, these statements obviously do not mean that every business and professional man is a criminal, just as the usual theories do not mean that every man in the lower class is a criminal. On the other hand, the preceding statements refer in many cases to the leading corporations in America and are not restricted to the disreputable business and professional men who are called quacks, ambulance chasers, bucket-shop operators, dead-beats, and fly-by-night swindlers.[1]

The financial cost of white-collar crime is probably several times as great as the financial cost of all the crimes which are customarily regarded as the "crime problem." An officer of a chain grocery store in one year embezzled $600,000, which was six times as much as the annual losses from five hundred burglaries and robberies of the stores in that chain. Public enemies numbered one to six secured $130,000 by burglary and robbery in 1938, while the sum stolen by Krueger is estimated at

[1] Perhaps it should be repeated that "white-collar" (upper) and "lower" classes merely designate persons of high and low socioeconomic status. Income and amount of money involved in the crime are not the sole criteria. Many persons of "low" socioeconomic status are "white-collar" criminals in the sense that they are well-dressed, well-educated, and have high incomes, but "white-collar" as used in this paper means "respected," "socially accepted and approved," "looked up to." Some people in this class may not be well-dressed or well-educated, nor have high incomes, although the "upper" usually exceed the "lower" classes in these respects as well as in social status.

$250,000,000, or nearly two thousand times as much. *The New York Times* in 1931 reported four cases of embezzlement in the United States with a loss of more than a million dollars each and a combined loss of nine million dollars. Although a million-dollar burglar or robber is practically unheard of, these million-dollar embezzlers are small-fry among white-collar criminals. The estimated loss to investors in one investment trust from 1929 to 1935 was $580,000,000, due primarily to the fact that 75 percent of the values in the portfolio were in securities of affiliated companies, although it advertised the importance of diversification in investments and its expert services in selecting safe securities. In Chicago, the claim was made six years ago that householders had lost $54,000,000 in two years during the administration of a city sealer who granted immunity from inspection to stores which provided Christmas baskets for his constituents.

The financial loss from white-collar crime, great as it is, is less important than the damage to social relations. White-collar crimes violate trust and therefore create distrust, which lowers social morale and produces social disorganization on a large scale. Other crimes produce relatively little effect on social institutions or social organization.

White-collar crime is real crime. It is not ordinarily called crime, and calling it by this name does not make it worse, just as refraining from calling it crime does not make it better than it otherwise would be. It is called crime here in order to bring it within the scope of criminology, which is justified because it is in violation of the criminal law. The crucial question in this analysis is the criterion of violation of the criminal law. Conviction in the criminal court, which is sometimes suggested as the criterion, is not adequate because a large proportion of those who commit crimes are not convicted in criminal courts. This criterion, therefore, needs to be supplemented. When it is supplemented, the criterion of the crimes of one class must be kept consistent in general terms with the criterion of the crimes of the other class. The definition should not be the spirit of the law for white-collar crimes and the letter of the law for other crimes, or in other respects be more liberal for one class than for the other. Since this discussion is concerned with the conventional theories of the criminologists, the criterion of white-collar crime must be justified in terms of the procedures of those criminologists in dealing with other crimes. The criterion of white-collar crimes, as here proposed, supplements convictions in the criminal courts in four respects, in each of which the extension is justified because the criminologists who present the conventional theories of criminal behavior make the same extension in principle.

First, other agencies than the criminal court must be included, for the criminal court is not the only agency which makes official decisions regarding violations of the criminal law. The juvenile court, dealing largely with offenses of the children of the poor, in many states is not under the criminal jurisdiction. The criminologists have made much use of case histories and statistics of juvenile delinquents in constructing their theories of criminal behavior. This justifies the inclusion of agencies other than the criminal court which deal with white-collar offenses. The most important of these agencies are the administrative boards, bureaus, or commissions, and much of their work, although certainly not all, consists of cases which are in violation of the criminal law. The Federal Trade Commission recently ordered several automobile companies to stop advertising their interest rate on installment purchases as 6 percent, since it was actually 11½ percent. Also it filed complaint against *Good Housekeeping*, one of the Hearst publications, charging that its seals led the public to believe that all products bearing those seals had been tested in their laboratories, which was contrary to fact. Each of these involves a charge of dishonesty, which might have been tried in a criminal court as fraud. A large proportion of the cases before these boards should be included in the data of the criminologists. Failure to do so is a principal reason for the bias in their samples and the errors in their generalizations.

Second, for both classes, behavior which would have a reasonable expectancy of conviction if tried in a criminal court or substitute agency should be defined as criminal. In this respect, convictability rather than actual conviction should be the criterion of criminality. The criminologists would not hesitate to accept as data a verified case history of a person who was a criminal but had never been convicted. Similarly, it is justifiable to include white-collar criminals who have not been convicted, provided reliable evidence is available. Evidence regarding such cases appears in many civil suits, such as stockholders' suits and patent-infringement suits. These cases might have been referred to the criminal court but they were referred to the civil court because the injured party was more interested in securing damages than in seeing punishment inflicted. This also happens in embezzlement cases, regarding which surety companies have much evidence. In a short consecutive series of embezzlements known to a surety company, 90 percent were not prosecuted because prosecution would interfere with restitution or salvage. The evidence in cases of embezzlement is generally conclusive, and would probably have been sufficient to justify conviction in all of the cases in this series.

Third, behavior should be defined as criminal if conviction is avoided merely because of pressure which is brought to bear on the court or substitute agency. Gangsters and racketeers have been relatively immune in many cities because of their pressure on prospective witnesses and public officials, and professional thieves, such as pickpockets and confidence men who do not use strong-arm methods, are even more frequently immune. The conventional criminologists do not hesitate to include the life histories of such criminals as data, because they understand the generic relation of the pressures to the failure to convict. Similarly, white-collar criminals are relatively immune because of the class bias of the courts and the power of their class to influence the implementation and administration of the law. This class bias affects not merely present-day courts but to a much greater degree affected the earlier courts which established the precedents and rules of procedure of the present-day courts. Consequently, it is justifiable to interpret the actual or potential failures of conviction in the light of known facts regarding the pressures brought to bear on the agencies which deal with offenders.

Fourth, persons who are accessory to a crime should be included among white-collar criminals as they are among other criminals. When the Federal Bureau of Investigation deals with a case of kidnapping, it is not content with catching the offenders who carried away the victim; they may catch and the court may convict twenty-five other persons who assisted by secreting the victim, negotiating the ransom, or putting the ransom money into circulation. On the other hand, the prosecution of white-collar criminals frequently stops with one offender. Political graft almost always involves collusion between politicians and business men but prosecutions are generally limited to the politicians. Judge Manton was found guilty of accepting $664,000 in bribes, but the six or eight important commercial concerns that paid the bribes have not been prosecuted. Pendergast, the late boss of Kansas City, was convicted for failure to report as a part of his income $315,000 received in bribes from insurance companies but the insurance companies which paid the bribes have not been prosecuted. In an investigation of an embezzlement by the president of a bank, at least a dozen other violations of law which were related to this embezzlement and involved most of the other officers of the bank and the officers of the clearing house, were discovered but none of the others was prosecuted.

This analysis of the criterion of white-collar criminality results in the conclusion that a description of white-collar criminality in general terms will be also a description of the criminality of the lower class. The respects in which the crimes of the two classes differ are the incidentals rather than the essentials of criminality. They differ principally in the implementation of the criminal laws which apply to them. The crimes of the lower class are handled by policemen, prosecutors, and judges, with penal sanctions in the form of fines, imprisonment, and death. The crimes of the upper class either result in no official action at all, or result in suits for damages in civil courts, or are handled by inspectors, and by administrative boards or commissions, with penal sanctions in the form of warnings, orders to cease and desist, occasionally the loss of a license, and only in extreme cases by fines or prison sentences. Thus, the white-collar criminals are segregated administratively from other criminals, and largely as a consequence of this are not regarded as real criminals by themselves, the general public, or the criminologists.

This difference in the implementation of the criminal law is due principally to the difference in the social position of the two types of offenders. Judge Woodward, when imposing sentence upon the officials of the H. O. Stone and Company, bankrupt real estate firm in Chicago, who had been convicted in 1933 of the use of the mails to defraud, said to them, "You are men of affairs, of experience, of refinement and culture, of excellent reputation and standing in the business and social world." That statement might be used as a general characterization of white-collar criminals for they are oriented basically to legitimate and respectable careers. Because of their social status they have a loud voice in determining what goes into the statutes and how the criminal law as it affects themselves is implemented and administered. This may be illustrated from the Pure Food and Drug Law. Between 1879 and 1906, 140 pure food and drug bills were presented in Congress and all failed because of the importance of the persons who would be affected. It took a highly dramatic performance by Dr. Wiley in 1906 to induce Congress to enact the law. That law, however, did not create a new crime, just as the federal Lindbergh kidnapping law did not create a new crime; it merely provided a more efficient implementation of a principle which had been formulated previously in state laws. When an amendment to this law, which would bring within the scope of its agents fraudulent statements made over the radio or in the press, was presented to Congress, the publishers and advertisers organized support and sent a lobby to Washington which successfully fought the amendment principally under the slogans of "freedom of the press" and "dangers of bureaucracy." This proposed amendment, also, would not have created a new crime, for the state laws already prohibited fraudulent statements over the radio or in the press; it would have implemented the law so it could have been enforced. Finally, the Administration has not been able to enforce the law as it has desired because of the pressures by the offenders against the law, sometimes brought to bear through the head of the Department of Agriculture, sometimes through congressmen who threaten cuts in the appropriation, and sometimes by others. The statement of Daniel Drew, a pious old fraud, describes the criminal law with some accuracy, "Law is like a cobweb; it's made for flies and the smaller kinds of insects, so to speak, but lets the big bumblebees break through. When technicalities of the law stood in my way, I have always been able to brush them aside easy as anything."

The preceding analysis should be regarded neither as an assertion that all efforts to influence legislation and its administration are reprehensible nor as a particularistic interpretation of the criminal law. It means only that the upper class has greater influence in molding the criminal law and its administration to its own interests than does the lower class. The privileged position of white-collar criminals before the law results to a slight extent from bribery and political pressures, principally from the respect in which they are held and without special effort on their part. The most powerful group in medieval society secured relative immunity by "benefit of clergy," and now our most powerful groups secure relative immunity by "benefit of business or profession."

In contrast with the power of the white-collar criminals is the weakness of their victims. Consumers, investors, and stockholders are unorganized, lack technical knowledge, and cannot protect themselves. Daniel Drew, after taking a large sum of money by sharp practice from Vanderbilt in the Erie deal, concluded that it was a mistake to take money from a powerful man on the same level as himself and declared that in the future he would confine his efforts to outsiders, scattered all over the country, who wouldn't be able to organize and fight back. White-collar criminality flourishes at points where powerful business and professional men come in contact with persons who are weak. In this respect, it is similar to stealing candy from a baby. Many of the crimes of the lower class, on the other hand, are committed against persons of wealth and power in the form of burglary and robbery. Because of this difference in the comparative power of the victims, the white-collar criminals enjoy relative immunity.

Embezzlement is an interesting exception to white-collar criminality in this respect. Embezzlement is usually theft from an employer by an employee, and the employee is less capable of manipulating social and legal forces in his own interest than is the employer. As might have been expected, the laws regarding embezzlement were formulated long before laws for the protection of investors and consumers.

The theory that criminal behavior in general is due either to poverty or to the psychopathic and sociopathic conditions associated with poverty can now be shown to be invalid for three reasons. First, the generalization is based on a biased sample which omits almost entirely the behavior of white-collar criminals. The criminologists have restricted their data, for reasons of convenience and ignorance rather than of principle, largely to cases dealt with in criminal courts and juvenile courts, and these agencies are used principally for criminals from the lower economic strata. Consequently, their data are grossly biased from the point of view of the economic status of criminals and their generalization that criminality is closely associated with poverty is not justified.

Second, the generalization that criminality is closely associated with poverty obviously does not apply to white-collar criminals. With a small number of exceptions, they are not in poverty, were not reared in slums or badly deteriorated families, and are not feebleminded or psychopathic. They were seldom problem children in their earlier years and did not appear in juvenile courts or child guidance clinics. The proposition, derived from the data used by the conventional criminologists, that "the criminal of today was the problem child of yesterday" is seldom true of white-collar criminals. The idea that the causes of criminality are to be found almost exclusively in childhood similarly is fallacious. Even if poverty is extended to include the economic stresses which afflict business in a period of depression, it is not closely correlated with white-collar criminality. Probably at no time within fifty years have white-collar crimes in the field of investments and of corporate management been so extensive as during the boom period of the twenties.

Third, the conventional theories do not even explain lower class criminality. The sociopathic and psychopathic factors which have been emphasized doubtless have something to do with crime causation, but these factors have not been related to a general process which is found both in white-collar criminality and lower class criminality and therefore they do not explain the criminality of either class. They may explain the manner or method of crime—why lower class criminals commit burglary or robbery rather than false pretenses.

In view of these defects in the conventional theories, an hypothesis that will explain both white-collar criminality and lower class criminality is needed. For reasons of economy, simplicity, and logic, the hypothesis should apply to both classes, for this will make possible the analysis of causal factors freed from the encumbrances of the administrative devices which have led criminologists astray. Shaw and McKay and others, working exclusively in the field of lower class crime, have found the conventional theories inadequate to account for variations within the data of lower class crime and from that point of view have been working toward an explanation of crime in terms of a more general social process. Such efforts will be greatly aided by the procedure which has been described.

The hypothesis which is here suggested as a substitute for the conventional theories is that white-collar criminality, just as other systematic criminality, is learned; that it is learned in direct or indirect association with those who already practice the behavior; and that those who learn this criminal behavior are segregated from frequent and intimate contacts with law-abiding behavior. Whether a person becomes a criminal or not is determined largely by the comparative frequency and intimacy of his contacts with the two types of behavior. This may be called the process of differential association. It is a genetic explanation both of white-collar criminality and lower class criminality. Those who become white-collar criminals generally start their careers in good neighborhoods and good homes, graduate from colleges with some idealism, and with little selection on their part, get into particular business situations in which criminality is practically a folkway and are inducted into that system of behavior just as into any other folkway. The lower class criminals generally start their careers in deteriorated neighborhoods and families, find delinquents at hand from whom they acquire the attitudes toward, and techniques of, crime through association with delinquents and in partial segregation from law-abiding people. The essentials of the process are the same for the two classes of criminals. This is not entirely a process of assimilation, for inventions are frequently made, perhaps more frequently in white-collar crime than in lower class crime. The inventive geniuses for the lower class criminals are generally professional criminals, while the inventive geniuses for many kinds of white-collar crime are generally lawyers.

A second general process is social disorganization in the community. Differential association culminates in crime because the community is not organized solidly against that behavior. The law is pressing in one direction, and other forces are pressing in the opposite direction. In business, the "rules of the game" conflict with the legal rules. A business man who wants to obey the law is driven by his competitors to adopt their methods. This is well illustrated by the persistence of commercial bribery in spite of the strenuous efforts of business organizations to eliminate it. Groups and individuals are individuated; they are more concerned with their specialized group or individual interests than with the larger welfare. Consequently, it is not possible for the community to present a solid front in opposition to crime. The Better Business Bureaus and Crime Commissions, composed of business and professional men, attack burglary, robbery, and cheap swindles, but overlook the crimes of their own members. The forces which impinge on the lower class are similarly in conflict. Social disorganization affects the two classes in similar ways.

I have presented a brief and general description of white-collar criminality on a framework of argument regarding theories of criminal behavior. That argument, stripped of the description, may be stated in the following propositions:

1. White-collar criminality is real criminality, being in all cases in violation of the criminal law.

2. White-collar criminality differs from lower class criminality principally in an implementation of the criminal law which segregates white-collar criminals administratively from other criminals.

3. The theories of the criminologists that crime is due to poverty or to psychopathic and sociopathic conditions statistically associated with poverty are invalid because, first, they are derived from samples which are grossly biased with respect to socioeconomic status; second, they do not apply to the white-collar criminals; and third, they do not even explain the criminality of the lower class, since the factors are not related to a general process characteristic of all criminality.

4. A theory of criminal behavior which will explain both white-collar criminality and lower class criminality is needed.

5. An hypothesis of this nature is suggested in terms of differential association and social disorganization.

49 · Our Law-abiding Law-breakers

by JAMES S. WALLERSTEIN and CLEMENT J. WYLE

As we have pointed out in a preceding selection, crime statistics indicate only a fraction of the crimes committed. There are a number of reasons why many crimes are not reported and do not even become known to the police. Lawbreaking, much of which is technically serious crime, is so common that perhaps the majority of our "law-abiding" citizens, young and old, would at one time or another be in jail were it not for the fact that their breaking of the law remained unknown or, for one reason or another, was overlooked. In the article that follows, a glimpse into this situation is offered by two students of crime, James S. Wallerstein and Clement J. Wyle. [From *National Probation*, March-April 1947, pp. 107-112. Reprinted by permission.]

WE HAVE no accurate gauge of the extent of delinquency and crime in the United States. What we know comes to our attention through admittedly inadequate statistical data gathered by some police departments, juvenile and adult courts, and correctional institutions. There are no comprehensive figures which cover the entire country even for this imperfect measure.

We can only hazard guesses at the incidence of hidden delinquency and crime. Most law violations are probably unknown to juvenile and adult courts, and hundreds of thousands of offenses never are reported to the police. In a paper given at the annual conference of the National Probation Association in June of 1946, Fred J. Murphy, speaking of "delinquency off the record" on the basis of findings of the Cambridge-Somerville Youth Study, reported that of a total of some 6000 offenses admitted by youths who were subjects in the study, a scant 1.5 per cent were actually brought to public attention by arrest or juvenile court hearing.

Another slant on this subject appears in the report of a study made in Fort Worth, Texas by Austin L. Porterfield of Texas Christian University. Mr. Porterfield's interest was in the social factors which may be back of this hidden delinquency. He compared a group of college students with a group of delinquents who came to the attention of the local juvenile court for commission of one or more of 55 specific offenses ranging in seriousness all the way from making a disturbance in church to homicide. The 237 students (both men and women) received little or no attention from the public authorities. (One ministerial student got by with 27 and one with 28 of the listed offenses.) The delinquent acts of these students were apparently as serious though not as frequent as those which brought other young people into court. Why did they enjoy relative impunity? Mr. Porterfield states that their behavior is an expression of the same fundamental wishes—for new experiences, adventure, recognition, for instance—which motivated the court group. The varying socioeconomic status of the family is undoubtedly important, as is family disorganization which was notably higher in the court cases.

CONCEALED CRIME

What similar ratios might be revealed among adults? The authors, interested in Mr. Porterfield's study, set out to get some descriptive data by distributing questionnaires listing 49 offenses under the penal law of the state of New York. All of these offenses were sufficiently serious to draw a maximum sentence of not less than one year; fourteen were felonies, seven might be felonies under certain conditions, the rest were misdemeanors. Replies were returned anonymously to insure frankness. The study was not a rigidly scientific one, but was carefully and critically prepared and tabulated. Some effort was made in distributing the questionnaires to secure a balanced racial and religious community cross-section, although this could not be done with precision. Economically the group was probably weighted on the upper income side.

SELECTION OF SUBJECTS

The subjects were requested to check each offense and to circle their "yes" answers if the offense was committed before they reached the age of sixteen, the upper limit for juvenile court jurisdiction in New York.

This sample of citizen opinion was drawn from men and women in the following occupational groups deliberately picked for diversity:

VOCATIONS OF THE SAMPLE OF 1698 INDIVIDUALS

Occupations	Men	Women
Business and law	13	12
Teachers and social workers	80	117
Scientists and doctors	63	15
Writers and artists	80	55
Ministers	17	—
Sales clerks and office workers	59	71
Military and government employees	53	11
Mechanics and technicians	239	32
Farmers	44	—
Laborers	100	10
Housewives	—	276
Students	148	79
	1020	678

RANGE OF OFFENSES

The offenses covered in the questionnaire were in the following general groups:

Malicious mischief
Disorderly conduct
Assault
Auto misdemeanors
Health law violations
Indecency
Gambling

Larceny
Burglary and possession
of burglar's tools
Robbery and illegal possession
of firearms
Bribery
Perjury

Falsification and fraud   Conspiracy and compounding
Election frauds   a crime
Tax evasion   Criminal libel
Coercion and extortion

MEANING OF CATEGORIES

Malicious mischief included such offenses as removing ferns, flowers, vegetables, fruits from other people's property, intentional injury to property, opening mail without permission; the auto misdemeanors listed were reckless driving, driving without a license and driving while intoxicated; by indecency was meant showing or giving an obscene, lustful or passion-provoking picture, object or writing; by gambling was meant, not the Saturday night gin-rummy session, but operating gambling devices or selling lottery tickets; larceny covered taking property under or over $100 in value from the person of another, auto theft (including unauthorized borrowing of a car), issuing checks without sufficient funds, spending entrusted money in an unauthorized manner; burglary denoted unauthorized entry by violence or guile into a room or building with intent to steal; robbery meant taking property under threat of force; bribery included bribing a public officer or a witness; perjury was in two categories, making a false statement in a legal document (a felony under New York law) and making a false statement under oath.

Questions under the heading of "falsification and fraud" covered obtaining employment, credit or other advantage by false written statement, using falsehood to induce another to sign a document benefiting you, making a false statement to affect the price of stock or merchandise; conspiracy and compounding of crime was covered in two questions, conspiring to injure person or property, and agreeing to conceal a crime; criminal libel, as used meant maliciously printing or writing anything derogatory about another person.

WHAT CRIMES WERE COMMITTED

Replies were received from 1698 individuals, 1020 men and 678 women. Geographically most of the responses came from the metropolitan area of New York, Westchester and Long Island, but there was a scattering from upstate New York, Pennsylvania, Ohio and California. Ninety-nine per cent of those questioned answered affirmatively to one or more of the offenses. The percentage of individuals admitting to these offenses, excluding those committed as juvenile delinquencies, is shown in the following partial list:

Offense	Per cent Men	Per cent Women
Malicious mischief	84	81
Disorderly conduct	85	76
Assault	49	5
Auto misdemeanors	61	39
Indecency	77	74
Gambling	74	54
Larceny	89	83
Grand larceny (except auto)	13	11
Auto theft	26	8
Burglary	17	4
Robbery	11	1
Concealed weapons	35	3
Perjury	23	17
Falsification and fraud	46	34
Election frauds	7	4
Tax evasion	57	40
Coercion	16	6
Conspiracy	23	7
Criminal libel	36	29

The high rate for assault may be explained by the inclusion of such episodes as fist fights and the more violent shoving in the subway. Probably most males don't mind admitting this type of offense. The low rate on election frauds suggests that New Yorkers may be more conscientious citizens in exercising the ballot than one would expect. However, interpretation of these figures is necessarily speculative.

Businessmen and lawyers were highest in perjury, falsification, fraud and tax evasion; teachers and social workers in malicious mischief; writers and artists in indecency, criminal libel and gambling; military and government employees in simple larceny; mechanics and technicians in disorderly conduct; farmers in illegal possession of weapons; laborers in grand larceny, burglary and robbery; students in auto misdemeanors.

The number of offenses per person ran high. The mean number of offenses committed in adult life (over sixteen) for men, classified according to occupation, ranged from 8.2 for ministers to 20.2 for laborers, with a mean of 18 for all men. For the women, excluding again acts committed under the age of sixteen, the range was from a low of 9.8 for those classed as laborers to a high of 14.4 for those in military and government work, with a mean of 11 for all women. In addition, the men reported a mean of 3.2, the women 1.6 of juvenile offenses.

Returns from the questionnaire were classified according to the age of the subjects in six groups: under 21, 21-30, 31-40, 41-50, 51-60, and over

60. For both men and women the rate of crimes admitted increased progressively in the first three groups and then progressively diminished. Perhaps age has a short memory.

AS THEY SAW IT

Personal comments appearing on some of the questionnaires reflected the ethical viewpoint of the individual and sometimes the human situations which may have been duplicated innumerable times in the lives of those who are convicted daily in our courts. A housewife over sixty, admitting to false testimony, added this statement: "It made no difference in the outcome, and I did it to spare someone pain." An artist made this comment on the same question: "It was a divorce action and I'm a gentleman." A doctor, admitting to taking a car without permission, pencilled in the word "emergency." A businessman who opened someone else's mail appended this explanation: "Tried to keep my son from making a fool of himself, but he did it anyway." A girl student justified illegal opening of somebody else's mail with the explanation, "She (room-mate) opened my mail first." A minister who confessed to making false statements about a commodity that he sold, betrayed traces of his moral struggle in the comment, "I tried truth first but it's not always successful." Annoying letters were sent by a social worker to her husband, by a student to his teacher and by a salesclerk to his boss. A laborer who had broken in and taken property took pains to note that he "put it back later."

Several persons stated that they had had to falsify their religion to get a certain job, others reporting violation of birth control or gambling laws regarded the laws themselves as stupid and therefore they saw nothing wrong in violating them. Larceny of objects under $100 in value covered such items as towels, a bathmat, a spoon and stamps. One man asserted that his high bill gave him at least a moral right to steal from the hotel where he was staying. Another excused himself for stealing from his employer by observing, "My boss is a jerk." A mechanic who falsified to get someone to sign a document explained that the paper in question was his marriage license. Another man learned that crime did not pay when he used a falsehood in the matter of signing a document. He added to his admission, "My uncle's will, but got nothing, anyway." A farmer faced with the issue of whether or not he had been guilty of assault without provocation wrote "no" in the designated space, but added the comment, "Thrashed a lot of men in my time but they all jolly well deserved it." A woman artist decided to call herself guilty of assault but with the qualifying phrase, "Threw ash tray at an unbearable cad." A self-styled criminologist over sixty gave up after reading the questionnaire and returned it with the sweeping comment, "Too much trouble, I've done them all."

WHAT MIGHT HAVE HAPPENED

Under New York law conviction of a felony is ground for deprivation of citizenship rights. Analysis of the replies on the fourteen felony offenses brought out the fact that the felony rate for the group as a whole was 64 per cent for men and 29 per cent for women, that is, considerably more than half of the men and nearly one-third of the women admitted to committing at least one felony. If we can envisage law enforcement machinery which could detect all law violations, the ultimate result would be loss of franchise for a substantial proportion of our citizens, and deprivation of other civil rights such as special licenses for business operations. While this carries us somewhat into the realm of fantasy, the solid truth remains that there is a large chance element in our administration of justice and it's the unlucky ones who are caught.

INTERPRETATION

We cannot, of course, accept without reservations the percentage results of an inquiry like this. Many of the offenses were no doubt committed against friends and relatives and thus were not likely to result in apprehension and prosecution, unless as happens to some unlucky mortals, friends and family in a vindictive moment report the incident to the police. What is technically an offense and therefore within the scope of this study may actually be a relatively harmless act. Thus the threat of an irate householder to smash his neighbor's radio if the volume was not lowered, was technically coercion, though hardly likely to result in prosecution. Borrowing without authorization, though it may rise to the seriousness of a felony as in the case of a car, in practice is often a minor matter. The very broad wording of much of our penal law seems designed less to insure rigid and uniform enforcement than to make it easier for law enforcement authorities to obtain convictions when desired.

With all due allowance, the figures in this study indicate, however, that the number of acts legally constituting crimes are far in excess of those officially reported. Unlawful behavior, far from being an abnormal social or psychological manifestation, is in truth a very common phenomenon. Environmental factors important in the commission of a crime may be even more so in determining whether a particular act will be overlooked or reported to the police. The social stratum of the individual may determine how much criminal behavior he can get away with.

SOCIETY'S ATTITUDE

Whether a man becomes a confirmed criminal may well depend less on what he does to society than on what society does to him. Pranks that cause a college student some uncomfortable moments in the Dean's office may send an East Side youth to the reformatory. Unlawful possession of a revolver may result in a warning to a suburban home owner, a prison sentence to a tenement dweller. Taking a sum of money as "honest graft" in business or public life is vastly different from taking the same amount from a cash register.

THE POINT OF VIEW

Perhaps the principal conclusion to be drawn from this study is the revelation of the prevalence of lawlessness among respectable people. It is perhaps less important to show that good citizens are not always good than that these same citizens can commit crimes and still become eminent scientists, intelligent parents, leading teachers, artists and social workers, or prominent business executives. The absence of a police record for many citizens arises not from their individual virtue but from sheer accident and from less than one hundred per cent law enforcement. From this angle the punitive attitude of society toward the convicted offender becomes not only hypocritical but pointless. In time to come men may be rated not by their past mistakes but by their assets and potentialities.

50 · What Is Behind Embezzlement?

by VIRGIL W. PETERSON

Embezzlement figures high among the lone-wolf white collar crimes. Huge sums of money are misappropriated annually. Virgil W. Peterson, author also of a previous article analyzes here the reasons why people who are generally considered honest "suddenly" become embezzlers. Although the factors responsible for one's becoming an embezzler are personal, laxity and lack of proper precaution on the part of the concern or institution involved play a not unimportant part. In other words, the victim bears to some extent responsibility for the crime. ["Why Honest People Steal," *Journal of Criminal Law and Criminology* Vol. 38, July-Aug. 1947, 94-103. Reprinted by permission.]

IT HAS BEEN estimated that annual losses resulting from the offense of embezzlement will approximate the astronomical sum of $400,000,000. A large share of this amount is taken by trusted employees who have previously enjoyed excellent reputations.

The embezzler is an anomaly in the field of crime. Previous arrest or prison records are frequently wanting to act as warnings of possible dishonest conduct. Steady work records many times conceal the instability that may be present in the person's make-up. Yet, there is usually an explanation for the embezzler's conduct. And through an understanding by employers of some of the factors that frequently contribute to embezzlement, it is believed that business losses as well as the crime of embezzlement can be materially reduced.

In view of the frequency of embezzlement cases involving losses of large sums of money, an attempt has been made to determine some of the factors that contribute directly or indirectly to the offense of embezzlement. In this connection it was felt that surety companies are the best source of accurate information in view of their long and intimate experience with this problem. Surety companies in every part of the United States were requested to rank in order of their importance those factors that appear to cause employees to embezzle or steal from their employers. Replies were received from over twenty approved surety companies and fidelity bond departments of insurance companies located in various parts of the United States. These companies engage in business in every state of the Union, Canada and foreign nations. An analysis of these replies would indicate that the factors most frequently present in embezzlement cases are: (1) Gambling; (2) Extravagant living standards; (3) Unusual family expense; (4) Undesirable associates; (5) Inadequate income. The need, and thus the motive to commit embezzlement, is created by one or more of these factors as well as others, and the embezzlement is made possible through lax accounting methods and improper or inadequate supervision over employees having custody of funds. A summary of the information obtained from the various surety companies follows:

GAMBLING

Based on the experience of over twenty of the largest surety companies, it would appear that the two principal factors contributing to employee dishonesty are gambling and extravagant living standards. Some companies estimated that gambling on the part of employees has been responsible for 30% of the losses of those companies. Other companies blamed gambling for as high as 75% of their total losses. The manager of the bonding department of one company wrote, "Gamblin; is one of the greatest evils sureties must contend with under their fidelit bonds." Another manager stated that "Gambling appears in more em bezzlements than any of the other causes." The secretary of one larg; company, based on the experience of 100,000 case histories, placed gam bling next to extravagant living standards as the most important facto in causing embezzlement of funds by employees in connection wit] losses of $5,000 or over. The same company expressed the opinion tha with reference to the smaller losses, i.e., under $5,000, gambling ranke third as the cause of employee dishonesty. Gambling was said to be re sponsible for about 15% of the smaller losses while it caused approx mately 25% of the larger losses. Several other companies likewise diffe entiated between embezzlements in small amounts and large losses. On surety manager wrote, "Gambling is probably the greatest single cor tributing factor that we know of and this is particularly true with claim of large size."

Several years ago the United States Fidelity and Guaranty Compan; Baltimore, Maryland, published an excellent booklet entitled "1,00 Embezzlers—A Study of Defalcations in Business." In a statistical anal; sis of mercantile embezzlements committed by 963 men involving losse totaling $6,127,588.48, "gambling and/or drink" was listed as the mos frequent cause of defalcation. Ranking next in importance was "livin above their means," followed by "accumulation of debts," "bad busines managers," "women," and "speculation." "Gambling and/or drink" an "speculation" were responsible for 26.3% of the embezzlement offense under study.

One surety company stated that "Gambling losses in large amount are more frequent now than ten years ago." This is the natural conse quence of the growth of gambling in America during the last decad; The upward surge of gambling since World War II ended undoubtedl; adds to the hazard of embezzlement in business today.

Almost every type of gambling has been responsible for employe dishonesty including horse race betting at the tracks and at handbook dice, roulette, slot machine, black jack and many other forms of gamin; as well as stock market speculation. In recent years, however, wagerin on race horses has been the most prevalent type of gambling that ha been involved in embezzlements attributed to gambling. One large ban embezzler was referred to as a "super sucker" in connection with gam bling on race horses at various handbooks. On some days when as man; as 16 race tracks were operating, he would place bets on horses runnin at each of the 16 tracks and frequently on more than one horse in a rac; This case received nationwide publicity.

Some surety companies expressed the opinion that while a large portion of stolen funds involved in their losses is used in gambling, that gambling itself is not the primary cause of the embezzlement. On the other hand it was suggested that many times the employee may feel the impact of a sudden financial strain such as illness in the family and embezzlement may follow. The employee may then resort to gambling to recoup his losses. He inevitably loses. Additional money is stolen in the hope that luck may enable the embezzler to make one big "killing" on the horses or at the roulette wheel which will enable him to pay back all the money he has surreptitiously "borrowed." As his losses mount, the need to win becomes more and more acute. He becomes reckless to a greater degree than ever and his chances of winning accordingly decrease. His situation eventually becomes hopeless. Disgrace and prison or suicide almost inevitably result.

Regardless of whether gambling is the direct or indirect cause of employee dishonesty, it is one of the most important factors contributing to embezzlement. It is commonly agreed among surety company officials that a person who is addicted to the gambling habit is a poor risk for any position which places in his care the funds of his employer. So well recognized is this risk that no fidelity bond underwriter would knowingly approve a bond for a gambler.

EXTRAVAGANT LIVING STANDARDS

Some surety companies attribute more of their losses to extravagant living standards than to any other single cause. Inquiry into the causes for defalcation on the part of many employees has determined that the embezzler was living beyond his financial means. He stole to supply the necessary income to maintain his mode of living.

The necessity for maintaining living standards that he cannot afford does not always originate with the embezzler himself. His wife may make extravagant demands. Attempting to "keep up with the Joneses" has frequently caused trusted employees to borrow funds entrusted in their care. They may fully intend to pay back the money taken but are never able to do so. Instead, further peculations frequently become necessary until the embezzler is hopelessly involved. Likewise, doting fathers may be subjected to demands from children that are beyond their financial means. The employer himself is sometimes responsible for the extravagant living standards maintained by the defaulter. Occasionally the employer may require some of his employees to associate with a wealthy class of people for the purpose of increasing business and to enhance the reputation of the company. The income of the employee may not be sufficient to enable him to meet the demands of his association with people in the higher income bracket. Yet he must do so if he expects to maintain the approval of his employer. The employee may steal from his employer to furnish him with the necessary funds to meet the social requirements of his job. The employee who lives beyond his means usually incurs obligations he is unable to meet. He may become heavily indebted to finance companies for the purchase of furniture, automobiles, radios or jewelry. When the obligations become due he feels the necessity for "borrowing" from his employer. He intends to return the money he has taken when he receives his next paycheck but he is too heavily indebted to make this possible. Having stolen once it becomes easier to do so again and in time he is unable to extricate himself from the vicious cycle that he has set in motion.

Careless spending habits are very similar to extravagant living standards as a cause of embezzlement. Such habits may result from poor management or through exercising bad judgment in personal or family affairs rather than from attempting to live extravagantly. The results are often the same. Many embezzlements have their origin in careless spending habits of employees.

UNUSUAL FAMILY EXPENSE

Perhaps the most pathetic cases are those of employees who steal to meet some unusual family expense that may have suddenly arisen. One surety company reported the case of an employee who had a very sick wife. All of his savings had been exhausted to pay for medical services. She required further medical care. So great was the desire of the employee for his wife to regain her health that he insisted on providing her with the best available medical aid. He could not afford this unusual expense. The strain upset him emotionally and he stole from his employer. Such cases are not unusual. Several companies listed illness of a member of the family as one of the important causes of employee dishonesty.

UNDESIRABLE ASSOCIATES

Frequently the cause of embezzlement may be traced to undesirable associates. It was stated by some surety companies that the two most frequent causes of embezzlement are (1) slow horses, and (2) fast women. Not infrequently the "other woman" figures in embezzlement cases.

Employee dishonesty is also many times attributed to association with companions who drink heavily and who run with a fast crowd. The expenditures necessary to maintain himself in this company may be considerably beyond the income of the employee. The bad influence of his association and the development of habits of carousing may result in a general breakdown of moral standards. Stealing from his employer may follow.

A number of embezzlement offenses involving large sums of money are the result of collusion between employees holding positions of trust and persons with criminal backgrounds. In some instances employees who frequent gambling establishments have become quite friendly with the proprietor. Realizing that the employee has access to sizeable funds of his employer, the gambling house proprietor may influence the employee to steal from his employer and to gamble on some "sure thing." The employee may be permitted to win temporarily until the time is ripe for the "kill." He is then so hopelessly involved that it is only a matter of time until he must choose prison, suicide or flight.

INADEQUATE INCOME

In many criminal court cases the defense is presented on behalf of the embezzler that his income was inadequate to support his family and consequently he was driven to stealing. It is undoubtedly true that inadequate salaries have frequently contributed to employee dishonesty. The employee, to his partial satisfaction, is able to justify in his own mind his peculation on the ground that his employer actually owes him the money he is stealing. Once he has started to take the money of his employer it becomes increasingly easy to steal again and to enlarge the individual amounts embezzled. This may account for some of the cases in which the embezzler advances the defense of inadequate income and yet the amount stolen may greatly exceed any salary that he could have reasonably expected.

The official of one surety company advised, "It has been our experience that whenever economic conditions are bad, fidelity losses increase in number and size. This is particularly true among the so-called 'white collar classes' whose income is not normally increased to meet an increase in the cost of living. This does not necessarily mean that embezzlements by this class are attributed to increased living expenses. On the contrary, most of the money embezzled is spent for other purposes, the outstanding one being gambling." Several surety companies listed inadequate income as a major cause of defalcation.

OTHER MOTIVES

In many instances the employee may have become an embezzler as a result of a combination of several of the factors previously mentioned. Many other factors also contribute to embezzlement. Surety companies have attributed employee thefts to such factors as financial pressure due to losses in other business activities, a past criminal history, mental irresponsibility, low morals, improvident investments and revenge. An official of one surety company stated, "We have seen several cases where resentment was the cause of a dishonest act. A young messenger who had been severely reprimanded, and, as he thought, unjustly so, tore up a large certified check that had been given to him for delivery. Another employee asked for a raise in pay. He was refused and thereafter he stole $10 each week from the cash drawer."

In attempting to determine the causes of embezzlement or any other type of crime, it should be borne in mind that human behavior is extremely complex. Some criminologists would vigorously protest that the actual causes of embezzlement lie much deeper than such factors as gambling, extravagant living standards, unusual family expense and undesirable associates. They would assert that these factors merely precipitate the criminal offense while the true cause of the embezzler's activities is to be found in the personality make-up of the offender which is besieged with internal conflicts and maladjustments. It is undoubtedly true that the employee would not become addicted to the gambling habit nor would he try to live beyond his means or associate with undesirable companies if he did not have a basic weakness in his personality make-up. But it makes little difference whether we refer to such factors as "causes" or "precipitants." They are extremely important in any consideration of embezzlement and methods designed to reduce it.

LAX ACCOUNTING METHODS AND SUPERVISION

Frequently the employee who embezzles funds has advanced himself to a position of trust by faithful application to duty throughout a long period of employment. Over a period of years he has earned a reputation for honesty and trustworthiness. Due to his extravagant mode of living, illness or gambling, he may find himself desperately in need of money. Because of the position he holds he may be in custody of funds of considerable size. But the motive or desire to steal will consciously or unconsciously be weighed against the risk of prompt detection. Proper accounting systems with checks and balances and efficient personnel supervision will serve as a deterrent against employee dishonesty. A manager of the fidelity and surety department of one company stated,

"Just as industrial accidents can be reduced through the installation of proper safety appliances, so can fidelity losses be reduced in number and severity by installing internal systems and rules designed to reduce temptation and make embezzlements more difficult." The importance of efficient accounting and supervision methods was further stressed by the experience of another company which reported that "During the war years we have attributed some . . . losses to rapid turnover in help, the replacement of experienced workers with inefficient substitutes and the shortage of auditors which together with the increased volume of business compelled many employers to cut down either on the frequency or extent of audits. This was in effect a deficiency in supervision which increased the chances for stealing and a number of our fidelity losses were attributed to this cause." Incidentally, it is expected that many employee thefts that occurred during the war years will continue to be discovered for some time.

The problem of reducing employee dishonesty to a minimum is an important one. Many employers who have never suffered losses through embezzlement may be inclined to minimize the threat that is always present. They may point to the fact that burglaries and robberies are reported daily in the press whereas newspaper accounts of embezzlements are relatively few. It should be borne in mind, however, that perhaps most of the embezzlement cases are disposed of through the discharge of the employee without the initiation of prosecutive action. Some companies have a definite policy against prosecuting dishonest employees. In addition, the losses in the exceptional cases that are publicized are frequently minimized in newspaper accounts. The employer may withhold many facts in order to avoid unfavorable publicity. The total amount of money lost annually through embezzlement, if the truth were known, would reach astronomical sums. Available statistics of surety companies reflect annual losses which run into millions of dollars. But such figures do not show the complete picture since many employers do not carry fidelity bond insurance. And the total losses of those employers who do bond their employees are far in excess of the amount of the obligation of surety companies.

The true losses, however, cannot be computed in terms of dollars. Most embezzlers were respected and valuable employees prior to their defalcations. They were without criminal propensities and in many instances they would never have turned dishonest had reasonable precautionary methods been exercised. To take steps that will successfully prevent embezzlement is to save many human lives from ruin. The employee, as well as the members of his family, is saved from the stigmatizing effect of a criminal record.

CHAPTER FOURTEEN

Juvenile Delinquency

51 · Psychological Factors in Juvenile Delinquency

by WILLIAM HEALY and AUGUSTA F. BRONNER

Juvenile delinquency, which, legally considered, is a violation of the law by children between the ages of seven and sixteen, is frequently the precursor of adult crime. Juvenile delinquency may, therefore, be considered as crime in its incubatory state. As in the case of crime, the causative factors underlying juvenile delinquency are varied, complex and not readily diagnosed. Internal as well as external—*i.e.*, psychological as well as environmental—forces seem to be involved and intertwined in the process leading to delinquency. In the following selection, the eminent American psychiatrist William Healy and his collaborator, who have made extensive studies in this field, analyze factors entering into the making of a delinquent. [*New Light on Delinquency and Its Treatment*, Yale University Press, 1936, pp 1-13. Reprinted by permission.]

FOR BETTER attacks upon the problem of juvenile delinquency, that forerunner of adult crime, new points of view are obviously needed. Since the results of dealing with the offender are so frequently disappointing, it must be that the basic forces producing delinquency and the obstacles to treatment have not been sufficiently considered and made clear. And most solutions proposed, embodying, as they usually do, some one idea about cause or cure, are easily seen to be not based on established fact, often unconsciously biased, and mainly futile. When scientific methods of investigation seek to connect cause and effect, the complexities of causation and the common weakness of treatment methods in vogue are unavoidably brought to light.

It has gradually been borne in upon us that a better conception of the significance of delinquency as one form of human behavior is an essential offering vastly better vantage points for its control. This appears in great contradistinction to the attitudes of those who dwell only upon the negative or destructive aspects of delinquency, who see delinquency merely as wrong-doing, as behavior which injures society—and consequently are concerned with nothing more than utilizing some means to put a stop to this social injury.

Our present research, with its long continued treatment program for serious offenders, has centered on the family life of delinquents and a comparison of the delinquent with a non-delinquent child in the same family. Our collected material reflects the growing emphasis, largely taken over from psychiatry, which all workers in the social sciences have found themselves forced to place upon human relationships and upon the emotional issues involved therein. The findings have much interest in and of themselves, but their chief value lies in their contribution to practical formulations. It is in the spirit of our inquiry to regard it as highly fortunate that through it some new and valuable outlooks on delinquency have been derived. Indeed the culmination of our study is represented by these new orientations.

The first of these is a new orientation concerning the general significance of delinquency as a phenomenon. As a mode of behavior which is one part of the stream of life's activities, it must have as much meaning in the total order of happenings as socially acceptable forms of conduct. It must in some fashion be equally as purposive from the standpoint of the individual's needs and urges. Stated in terms of a general principle, the origins of delinquency in every case unquestionably represent the expression of desires and urges which are otherwise unsatisfied. For the onlooker, delinquency merely signifies misconduct; for the offender it is just as much a response to inner drives and outer stimuli as any other kind of conduct. The sequence of causes leading up to delinquency we deal with later in this chapter.

Second, from this understanding of the general background of causation we may best discover the nature of the special personal experiences and the reactions thereto which have activated the delinquency of the given delinquent. Realizing that delinquency has purposiveness the question arises: for the individual what is the specific meaningfulness of his delinquency? Analysis of our research material . . . demonstrates the possibility and practical value of a new orientation relating to such meaningfulness.

Third, from our experimental studies of treatment we undertake a reorientation with regard to treatment possibilities.

Upon the personality of the delinquent much attention has been centered in the last few decades. Delinquents have been studied in order to determine their deviations, if any; their constitutional, physical, mental, and emotional peculiarities have been scrutinized. And it still remains, as will be seen in the present material, that the importance of these factors is not to be gainsaid. The serious consideration of the case begins with all available data about constitutional and acquired characteristics. By constitution we mean the equipment with which the individual is born; acquired peculiarities are the result of what has happened to the individual, notably the diseases, injuries, endocrine imbalance, or nutritional privations that may have affected the individual in any way, particularly the functioning of the central nervous system.

Then we also have to reckon with the phenomena of early established reactive tendencies. These are established as the result of response to stimuli in early life situations, particularly within the family circle. These stimuli originate almost entirely through human relationships, and how powerful they may be in creating behavior trends is demonstrated very clearly in our comparative studies of delinquents and nondelinquents.

*   *   *

Delinquency is one small part of the total stream of the individual's life activities and in its significance represents, equally with other behavior, a response to inner or outer pressures. In common with all voluntary activities, it is one variety of self-expression.

The terms by which delinquency is designated—larceny, truancy, breaking and entering, and so on—are descriptions of behavior which do not in the least indicate what is expressed by the offender in the delinquent act. While it seems necessary to have labels for such types of conduct, yet it must be recognized in all common sense that naming the offense reveals nothing of the determinants of the behavior. It would seem equally obvious that it is just these determinants which must be known and coped with if effective treatment is to be undertaken.

Nor does it serve a better purpose to speak of delinquent, criminal, asocial, dissocial, or antisocial individuals. The prime matter for consideration is the fact that in only part of their activities are they delinquent or antisocial and that these particular behavior trends need explanation in terms of causation.

Contrast cases of the simple offense, truancy. One boy may be avoiding a situation in which he feels inadequate and discouraged; another has developed out of family life antagonism to all forms of authority—school representing one form; another has such need of recognition that, even though he does not dislike school, he truants in order to be "a regular fellow" with his companions; still another is the victim of peculiar anxieties which make the classroom hateful to him. However, in spite of the diversity of determinants, the authoritarian attitude toward all truancy and all truants is very likely to be the same, whether on the part of the school principal, the attendance officer, or the juvenile court.

This general principle applies to practically all offenses; the label of the offense gives little or no clue to its meaning as an activity which though swerved from the stream of socially acceptable behavior must originate in the desires, wishes, or urges that are fundamental in human nature.

The great driving forces which have strong emotional concomitants are the general fundamental desires for ego and affectional satisfactions. Specifically we must consider the desire for feeling secure in family and other social relationships, for feeling accepted by some person or group, for recognition as having some standing as a personality, for feeling adequate somehow or somewhere. The wish for various sorts of affectional response is allied to, though distinct from, desires for recognition, security, and adequacy. And there are other urges, such as those for accomplishment satisfying to oneself, for new experiences and adventures, for outlets for physical and mental energies, for ownership of possessions, for having, seeing, and doing. Normally with increasing age there is also the urge of self-assertion showing itself, for example, in desire for emancipation from childhood and family restrictions—the desire for independence and self-direction.

Interferences with these fundamental wishes are felt by the young person as thwartings and deprivations causing keen dissatisfactions. And since fundamental wishes as driving forces are integrated with the stream of active life, thwartings and deprivations tend to draw a part of the stream strongly into currents of activity which for the individual constitute substitutive satisfactions. Some activity must offset dissatisfactions, and delinquency offers one of the possibilities. Indeed a striking finding of our present study has been the immense amount of discoverable emotional discomfort that clearly has been part of the story of the origins of delinquency. On the other hand an acute contrast was brought out by the disclosure that very few indeed of the non-delinquents in the same families had in their emotional lives any such frustrations—and those few had found in channels other than delinquency some modes of compensatory satisfactions.

Now what form substitutive activities will take, whether or not they will be antisocial, depends partly on external circumstances, but mainly upon the acceptance of certain ideas. So far as ideas of delinquency are concerned, it is perfectly evident that in our stage of civilization these are derivable from many sources and that the potentiality of their virulent growth upon the fertile soil of youthful dissatisfactions is not to be denied. Of course it is the individual who has not primary or substitute satisfactions of other sorts who is prone to succumb to an impulse toward delinquency as the result of a combination of dissatisfactions and ideas about delinquency. The combination is found to show many varying aspects as either of the components differ. A boy, for example, feeling himself inadequate in other relationships finds himself accepted and gains recognition with a gang if he takes up with the suggestions they give him of stealing with or for them. Another may seize upon notions that he has gained from his reading and by entering into some hazardous solitary form of delinquency set out to prove merely to himself that he is not white-livered. An idea much dwelt on by many youngsters centers about the possible pleasures of independently making one's own way in the world—then, given a situation in which family discords make home life irksome, running away is the understandable result. The special temptations that the environment offers—the display of goods that can easily be stolen, the unlocked automobiles that are readily driven away, the observation of money that can be pilfered—make their impress upon the ideational life sometimes long before delinquency is entered upon.

But how does it happen that some young people living in the same family environment as the delinquent, with the desires common to youth, with the same social pressures, and always with ideas of delinquency easily obtainable, are able to refrain from antisocial conduct? We have often turned to consideration of the non-delinquent with the thought that it is more astonishing to discover that they have refrained from delinquency than that a brother or sister has developed antisocial behavior. It has been part of our task to study the personalities and lives of these non-delinquents for comparative purposes. In endeavoring to answer the question why ideas of delinquency have never been considered, or if considered why they have been rejected, we have had to take account of various differences in personality characteristics but in the main we have found the behavior derivatives of emotional satisfactions to be the answer. When there have been no intense feelings of deprivations, inadequacies, or thwartings as related to either ego-impulses or desires for affection, the individual has been able readily to find sufficient satisfactions in socially acceptable behavior. Our comparative studies of two children in the same family bring this out clearly and especially our studies of twins, one of whom was delinquent and one not delinquent.

As cause and effect most closely linked to the deeper satisfactions and dissatisfactions of children are the behavior attitudes of those in contact with the children. This stands out very plainly as we have compared the emotional lives of the delinquents with a brother or sister who has avoided delinquency. Many of the families from which the delinquents came lived in situations that could be considered thoroughly inimical for the upbringing of a child, yet even under these conditions it was clear that the non-delinquents had distinctly more satisfactory human relationships than had the delinquents.

It would be easy to generalize that parents through their own dissatisfactions arising from discrepancies between cultural or economic desires and the realities of their life situations could reasonably be expected to display asocial attitudes, even as exhibited in their behavior toward their children. But for our research it was most enlightening to uncover the additional fact that there had been great differences in their feelings and behavior toward their different children—more sympathetic understanding, more fulfillment of fundamental needs, less inconsistent treatment very frequently indeed having been exhibited from early years toward one child as compared to another.

As investigators of the stream of life's activities we are led to wonder why at various points there have not been dams or barriers which might have prevented the current from flowing in the direction of delinquency. We can readily understand that when a channel has been formed by habits of thought or by established social contacts the difficulties of checking the flow of activities are great. How often we have heard, "I got in the habit of stealing," or "I couldn't stop going with those fellows!" Some more introspective youngsters have related to us their story of how thoughts, once started in this direction, returned again and again in idle or half-waking moments to ideas of delinquency—they had nothing else to absorb their interest, nothing else that gave them commanding satisfactions.

But aside from this matter of the strength of habit formation there remains the question why the delinquent early or later did not find in himself inhibiting forces strong enough to check delinquent impulses. As we looked into the lives of these young people, it was clear, for one thing, that social restraints and inhibitions were in many instances absent because of poor formation of what is so aptly termed an ego-ideal. There had been no strong emotional tie-up to anyone who presented a pattern of satisfactory social behavior. To put it in another way, the child had never had an affectional identification with one who seemed to him a good parent. The father or mother either had not played a rôle that was admired by the child or else on account of the lack of a deep love relationship was not accepted as an ideal.

. . . If from nowhere else, it would have been made clear to us from our present comparative studies that the effectiveness of moral teaching and of good example is dependent on emotional values attached to them by the child. The feeling tone about right conduct derives most powerfully from the emotional side of human relationships. Ethical concepts that have no personification have little force in the lives of young people.

But in contrast, when studying the non-delinquents we came across many striking evidences of influential ties to some person, nearly always a parent—sometimes an unworthy parent though not felt as such by the child—whose esteem was desired and was obtained and retained if the child remained non-delinquent. The importance of building up standards through such personal relationships can hardly be overstated.

We might go a step further in inquiring why the young individual finds in himself no barriers preventing his ideas and activities from flowing in channels of delinquent conduct. In particular we may ask, why has the delinquent in and of himself, arising from his own sense of what is right and wrong, no strong feeling about the wrongfulness of delinquency? Now it is very true that we constantly find the delinquent fully able to express his conscious belief that delinquency represents wrong conduct, but evidently his *feeling* about its wrongfulness has not been sufficiently strong to function as a preventive. How then does it happen that the delinquent's personality is possessed of such an impotent categorical imperative, conscience, or superego? Why, for example, has "Thou shalt not steal" no strong sanctions for him?

To be sure, we have partly covered this point in the preceding discussion. We know that the introjection, as the analysts phrase it, of parental prohibitions, the absorption of parental ideas of right and wrong, is the anchorage of conscience long before the principles of good conduct are taught by church or school. Through the earliest prohibitions, even with regard to bodily functions, family possessions, or behavior in the family circle, the child develops a conscience or superego long before it comes to any question of social behavior outside the family. This is obvious, but it leaves the whole matter of the growth of the sense of right and wrong an extremely complicated problem.

The fact seems to be clear that the barrier which we call conscience or the superego is universally found, but in different individuals plays various and partial rôles in determining or motivating behavior. Hence conscience may cover only certain areas in the field of conduct. In one case of our series a young boy evidently had a strong conscience about being mannerly and doing his school work well, while stealing seemed really to mean nothing to him except as he might be caught for it. And we have noted in some instances that lying was quite condoned by conscience while stealing was a sin, and that in other cases this was exactly reversed.

A final consideration in this discussion of the development of delinquency as one special manifestation of behavior is the origins of the attitudes and beliefs of parents—just because these have so much to do with the development of conduct trends in their children. Quite apart from the knowledge we gained of the parents' scale of values resulting, more or less unconsciously, from the influences of their own early lives, there is another matter of vast import to general social welfare. Though we made no special study of this, it often cropped out that certain undesirable attitudes and behavior tendencies exhibited by parents were related, sometimes vaguely and sometimes explicitly, to prevalent asocial ideologies. Our population in general is well acquainted with the exploitations, unfairnesses, and dishonesties which are current in many spheres of activity. From this it follows that parents who feel deprivations and discomforts and who have not ideals that prevent can readily rationalize the situation. They may easily persuade themselves that, such being the state of things, the sensible behavior is to get what one can by whatever means are available, to consider one's own personal advantage at the expense of anything else, to enjoy oneself as best one can. It goes without saying that these sentiments based on current ideologies of self-considering individualism militate against the proper upbringing of children and specifically tend to pervade the household, spreading—though, for various reasons, differentially—from parents to members of the younger generation.

52 · Sociological Factors in Juvenile Delinquency

by MARSHALL B. CLINARD

In the following selection, Professor Marshall B. Clinard shows how juvenile delinquency may be traced back to the corrupting influences of the broad social environment—*i.e.*, the adult world in which the child moves and to which he is relentlessly exposed. Clinard singles out a number of institutions and agencies, which, because of their serious shortcomings and malfunctioning, may be considered as "moral hazards." Among these, he points out, are the police and courts; the school; the mass communication media, such as the newspaper, movies, radio, and comic books. He also calls attention to the inconsistent value system in our society and the wholesale flouting of our laws on the part of the public as factors in juvenile delinquency. ["Secondary Community Influences and Juvenile Delinquency," *The Annals*, Vol. 261, Jan. 1949, pp. 42-54. Reprinted by permission. Footnotes omitted.]

DESPITE the fact that there is increasing evidence to link the problem of the juvenile with the adult world through the larger community in which both juveniles and adults participate in the standards of the culture as a whole, many writers in this field persist in regarding the delinquent as a product almost exclusively of personal maladjustment. The delinquency of the juvenile is explained with little reference to the social and cultural realities or to the fact that there are indications of widespread social disorganization in the general adult society.

Most of those with this belief write of maladjusted personality traits, and a few who are Freudian psychoanalysts invent a mystical world of innate animal drives, Oedipus and various other guilt complexes to explain the delinquent. Others tend to look chiefly at the family as though it were the sole source of value judgments. Still additional writers seem to concentrate their analyses, with much more validity, on the boys' associates to the exclusion of the larger outside world, either in the form of the neighborhood in which the gang functions or, in turn, the over-all society and culture whose standards are reflected and found in the behavior of the family, the gang, and the neighborhood.

THE POINT OF ATTACK

The results of such one-sided emphases are seen in the panaceas that are recommended. Those who look at the individual personality believe that testing and clinical guidance programs in our schools should be stressed. Many stress more and better psychiatrists, psychoanalysts, and psychologists who, by diagnosing and treating the deviations and stresses and strains of youth, will put them soundly on the road to social health. Some who regard the family as the basic cause stress family training and counseling, while the more radical believe that the parents should be punished. Those who see the nexus of the problem in the boys' gang believe that organized recreation and the diverting of the delinquent group into more acceptable social patterns will offer a complete solution. Co-ordinating councils and neighborhood councils have been offered in turn as the most adequate means of dealing with problems of delinquency at the neighborhood level.

While the evidence seems to indicate that the neighborhood, particularly in more socially deteriorated areas, is a more logical basis for an attack on delinquency, it is well for us not to confine our efforts solely in this direction. The larger society, as it impinges on the community and also upon the adult and the juvenile alike, must be dealt with in any realistic analysis of juvenile delinquency. Moreover, the attempt to draw a line between the world of juveniles and young adults (as seen in the current enthusiasm for Youth Correction Authorities) and the larger adult world is theoretically indefensible, for both secure their values within the social framework of our culture. In fact, such a position of separating the behavior of certain age groups from that of others resembles the attempt of persons formerly to see only problems of the individual rather than of society.

In general, secondary influences such as the police, judges and penal institutions, the schools, the newspapers, the movies, radio programs, and comic books are largely administered or controlled by forces outside the immediate local community or neighborhood. To evaluate and deal effectively with these secondary influences requires a much broader perspective than the family, the gang, or the immediate neighborhood. In fact, the behavior of almost the entire adult world, whether in the neighborhood or not, constitutes a moral hazard to the juvenile.

POLICE, COURTS, AND PENAL INSTITUTIONS

Numerous studies have indicated that the police and other agencies of law enforcement constitute, in many communities, one of the chief moral hazards to both juveniles and adults. It is doubtful, however, that in terms of typical adult standards, such agencies are any different from what the public deserves. The employment of police personnel and the election of judges who in no way exemplify the type of conduct required of juveniles add both directly and indirectly to the production of delinquency. A great many police officers, both urban and rural, are still political appointees, intellectually unfit, inefficient, frequently willing to accept bribes even from juveniles, and brutal in making arrests and securing evidence, whether of juveniles or adults. Their attitude is not one to encourage respect for law or to aid in the rehabilitation of the juvenile.

Similarly, many judges do not deserve the respect of juveniles, for both their attitude on the bench and the general demeanor of the courtroom seem to indicate a lack of understanding. This is understandable when we realize that neither law schools nor the legal system itself provides adequate, if any, training for juvenile rehabilitation work by jurists. The fact that a middle-class jurist has children of his own does not necessarily provide him with an adequate comprehension of juvenile delinquency problems. Experience achieved by mistakes made in dealing with innumerable delinquents is a process costly to society.

Recently a police judge in Newark, for example, pleaded guilty to stealing over $630,000 through a rigged-up series of fictitious mortgages. The money was used to cover his losses in horse-race bets. The really serious injury to society in this case, as in the many others like it, was the effect such disobedience of law must have had on the majority of potential delinquents or those already delinquent residing not only in Newark but perhaps elsewhere.

The failure in most communities to provide separate juvenile detention facilities of an acceptable type and the tendency to incarcerate juveniles with adults in our local jails represent a serious hazard to any juvenile placed in them. Our jails are one of the most disgraceful aspects of our society, most of them being unable to receive a satisfactory evaluation in terms of minimum human welfare standards from state or Federal inspectors. It is fortunate that our Nation is not judged by its jails and by its treatment of the tens of thousands of juveniles incarcerated in them. Although not affecting as large a number, the so-called boys and girls schools for delinquents are, for the most part, little more than junior prisons, and the boys who enter leave marked as much by its education in crime and by the stigma of society as any criminal released from a penal institution.

All these agencies, police courts and penal institutions, are still largely staffed with untrained persons, filled with prejudice and folk knowledge.

The evidence is so overwhelming on all these scores that social scientists are frequently faced with the dilemma of either delinquency unapprehended and untreated or delinquency apprehended but made worse by the social situation of arrest and incarceration. The public must sometime come to the conclusion that all persons dealing with human beings in a preventive or corrective capacity must be trained in the social sciences, whether they be police, judges, or correctional officers, as otherwise they frequently constitute a menace to juveniles. Such training is now chiefly in techniques of criminal identification and apprehension, in the technicalities of the law, or in custodial care which too often emphasizes confinement, at the same time sacrificing rehabilitative treatment.

THE SCHOOL AND TRUANCY

It is a curious commentary on our modern world, which emphasizes education, that the school is a large contributing factor in delinquency. Truancy, for example, constitutes a considerable proportion of delinquency in itself, and if we recognize that it in turn is related to stealing and sex delinquency, it becomes even more important. By definition, truancy implies that school is an unsatisfactory experience.

Schools are generally not operated with the purpose of developing interested, creative minds with some degree of individuality. Most professional educators would agree that in reality schools are places where juveniles, during a process of several hours a day, are routinized, bored, crushed in their individuality, and thrown into needless competition with others rather than aided in the development of co-operation. The preoccupation with competitive grades, beginning at the first grade, is illustrative of this.

Many schools are staffed by persons who inspire neither creative intelligence nor respect for the values of our society. The influences of the school and the teacher may sometimes be personal, but in general, at least in many urban areas, they are secondary, nonintimate, and categoric.

The school situation is a social situation; and the learning process takes place in a situation of personal interaction. Not a few of those selected to educate the young are themselves maladjusted, teaching being, if anything, a neurotic adjustment to life. Wickman demonstrated that those behavior elements which the majority of our teachers feared most were precisely those regarded by mental hygiene experts as least likely to result in behavior disorders. But our teachers act as if their fears were well founded; and the inquisitive, creative student is silenced by the demands for obedience. It is no wonder that part of the function of juvenile gangs engaging in delinquency is to furnish new experience, the thrill of the cleverly executed act of vandalism or auto theft.

THE NEWSPAPER

The style and contents of many newspaper stories represent a continual glorification of and preoccupation with crime, the delinquent, and the criminal. By continually playing up crime it is likely that newspapers are important in making us a crime-centered culture. They make crime seem probably more frequent than it is. The treatment is such as to imply adventure and excitement, and in many cases indirectly the glorification of the criminal participant is achieved. Pictures and stories of juveniles and criminals apprehended in crime give publicity and status; perhaps to some juveniles these resemble the folk tales of frontier bad men. They provide vicariously emotional thrills not provided by home or school. In some the vicarious becomes the real. The newspapers also furnish knowledge of techniques of committing crime, although this is probably not too important.

Unusual events are newsworthy and gain ready access to the printed page, for the urban American reader is little concerned with the ordinary happenings in everyday life. Only the unusual, the different, the new, can attract his attention. He dotes on war, rape, murder, crime. The breaking of the law is an event that can capture reader interest. The amount and prominence of space devoted to crime in the newspapers, and the amount of conversation based on these stories, must present a bewildering picture of immorality even to a delinquent child.

Though the line is difficult to draw, there is a difference between reporting verifiable facts about an event, such as crime, and loading the story with emotionally charged words that convey to the reader but one impression. Crime is given a specific prominence in our newspapers through the amount of space given its reporting, as well as through the position of the news stories on the front page. The total percentage of crime stories is not an adequate basis for comparison, for the front page sells the paper. Even a juvenile on his way to the comic section in the paper cannot help noticing front-page crime stories and pictures. If he misses them there, he is sure to hear them included in the dinner-table conversation.

Under the guise of supplying what the reader demands, crime is not merely made prominent, but is supplied to the reader in colorful exposition and frequently with on-the-scene lurid photographs. A person is not merely murdered or slain, he is brutally slain with a blunt instrument. The suspect does not merely attempt to escape capture; the desperate killer, his cunning increased by his emotional stimulation, gives the inept police a terrific run for their money.

There is general indifference in newspapers to the serious moral implication of the offense or to the necessity for bulwarking society against such behavior. Admittedly, this statement raises the problem of the function of the newspapers. On the one hand, the conception of "free enterprise" condones the collection of sordid tales as a valuable vehicle for selling advertisements; on the other, the conception of social responsibility suggests that these newspapers should be re-evaluated in terms of the role they play in determining human behavior.

Unfortunately, the actual effect of the newspaper on delinquency, while giving an impression of a crime-centered society, has not been accurately ascertained. Probably the crime emphasis has only a minor direct influence, for considerable delinquency starts before the reading of newspapers, other than comics, becomes frequent. . . .

Like the motion picture and the radio, the important influence of newspapers is that they furnish rationalizations for deviant conduct learned in the gang or by other personal associations. This is not to underestimate the importance of the newspaper in making some positive contributions to crime control. The point to be made here is that crime stories both reflect and further influence the general culture. It is hoped that the newspaper may be able to develop sufficient professional ethics to compromise the desire to sell more papers for profit by playing up crime stories, and recognize the interests of the general public welfare which is now of secondary importance in this connection.

MOTION PICTURES, RADIO, AND COMIC BOOKS

The great interest of juveniles in motion pictures, the radio, and comic books has caused some persons to overestimate their importance, while others in their explanations of delinquency tend to discount them. It is conceivable that were all three media to disappear from our culture, we would still probably have almost as much delinquency. Certainly we had delinquency and crime before any of the three were considered of consequence. Yet today there is a great wave of public indignation against so-called and misnamed "comic" books for their emphasis on the morbid aspects of life and particularly on their vicious crime content. It is reported that nearly fifty cities have taken steps to ban objectionable comic books. The same acute public interest was and still is to a less degree centered on the crime stories on the radio and before that on the motion picture, and if we go still further back, on dime novels.

All these entertainment forms probably have some effect, with the motion picture, due to its visual imagery, probably having the most. There is no question that the motion picture often presents a version of our culture emphasizing wealth, materialism, and immoral conduct, both crime and sex, which, as far as juveniles are considered, furnishes to them approved models conducive to delinquency. Research indicates that while both delinquents and nondelinquents attend the movies, the delinquents attend more often and exhibit greater interest in them. In some recent studies marked differences were noted between delinquents and their control groups in this regard. While this may have significant implications, yet careful additional study would be required to ascertain them. The radio, the motion picture, and comic books tend, on the whole, to glorify the criminal or immoral girl. All three offer knowledge of techniques of how to execute crime or delinquency.

It has long been noted by both lay and professional publics that the growing child needs an outlet for imaginative thinking. In answer to accusations of the harmful effects of the radio thrill drama and the sordid comic books, some people are prone to point out that a generation ago the children acted out much the same roles in a play world, and the radio and the comic book, it is alleged, give a vicarious experience in these comparable situations. One need, however, only observe children listening to or reading such stories to note a significant difference. The child listening to the exploits of his favorite hero can only sit and squirm as his emotional tensions are aroused, for in guiding his imaginative process along perilous routes and all sorts of dangers the radio program leaves the juvenile's tensions unsolved. It is conceivable that overt physical activity of a delinquent type may result in some cases, provided there is a prior pattern of deviant behavior.

Limited Influence. A realistic appraisal of these forms of entertainment indicates that while there are cases in which they may be important, on the whole their direct influence on the juvenile is either almost nil or serves only to aggravate already existent attitudes and personality traits. Blumer and Hauser found in their study of some fifteen years ago, which is still our chief source of information, that motion pictures were one of the factors that was important in only about one out of ten of the delinquent males and one out of four girls.

Present evidence seems to indicate that the process of acquiring conduct norms, both deviant and conventional, is primarily through intimate association with others and personal experiences of a face-to-face nature. Delinquents who have already had differential association through companions with deviant norms may be further stimulated by bad motion pictures, by certain radio programs, or by comic books. In his study of 1,313 gangs in Chicago, Thrasher found that comic strips influenced these groups and their activities. Not only did many of the gangs obtain their names from the comic strip, but suggestions for vandalism and other destructive activities were directly traceable to this source. In fact, such sources may even furnish rationalizations for deviant behavior. Similarly, persons with abnormal psychogenic traits may be morbidly influenced by such media.

It is doubtful that many cases can be found where, even though there was no evidence of prior deviant behavior, it occurred as a result of such contacts of a secondary nature. Much of this material represents a world of impersonal fantasy rather than having personal reality. Nondelinquents are not likely to succumb to such influences, any more than the average adult readers' attitudes are too greatly changed by editorials in newspapers as compared with the opinions of their friends. The problem is chiefly one of differential response.

*　　*　　*

OTHER AGENCIES OF MORAL RISK

There is much public discussion but little research on taverns and roadhouses and their relation to delinquency. Reckless has termed places of this type "agencies of moral risk" and has included also poolrooms, pawnshops, junk yards, criminal fences, dens of vice, gambling parlors, and cheap dance halls. While some of them may be located in the immediate neighborhood, some are at considerable distance from it and beyond its immediate control. It is doubtful whether taverns and roadhouses constitute a very serious problem as far as alcoholic beverages are concerned, since these may be secured by other means; but rather they may serve as centers for the dissemination of deviant value systems because of their anonymity and, in the case of roadhouses, freedom from the social control of the family and the neighborhood. This may be the result of the attraction to them of juveniles and adults who previously possess these attitudes, or it may be that the owners of these concerns are themselves persons of ill repute and with an unsavory past. Certainly, while the chief influence of these places is probably impersonal, in the hands of deviant persons their influence may be that of a personal relationship.

Such establishments do perform a function for the juvenile as social gathering places, and by providing recreation varying from pinball machines to dancing. Realistic thinking must recognize this fact, and society should closely supervise them and their management or else it must provide alternative social situations. In rural areas as well as many urban areas, it is likely that taverns and roadhouses exert far more influence on the lives of many juveniles and young adults than traditional organizations, including the church.

In a nation-wide rural opinion survey, the question was asked: "Which of the following are doing the greatest harm to young farm people: liquor, tavern dances, gambling, petting?" Some six million farm neighbors were of the opinion that liquor was the most important, and a strong second was tavern dances. Interestingly enough, the opinion of farm youth itself was more lenient toward tavern dances, yet still ranked them second to liquor. Curiously, rural sociology works contain virtually no mention of such agencies. Rather the discussion centers around Four-H clubs and church groups. The author is now engaged in a study of taverns and roadhouses as factors in social disorganization but with potentialities for social reorganization.

THE ADULT WORLD

Studies of peoples living in folk or provincial types of society have so far brought in limited but rather consistent evidence that juvenile delinquency, crime, suicide, chronic alcoholism, and many other forms of disorganization among us, while not nonexistent, are relatively rare. This furnishes considerable but not conclusive evidence that juvenile delinquency is not a product of personal inadequacy. Further evidence has been furnished by studies of disorganization among some people living under varying types of society, such as the Negro or the Polish people. Thomas and Znaniecki conducted a monumental study of the Polish people which had, in addition to a theoretical interest, a practical purpose in examining the validity of discriminatory immigration laws. The authors showed clearly that juvenile delinquency, for example, was rare in peasant villages, moderate in Polish cities, and high in Chicago.

Inconsistent Value Patterns. There are several factors in the patterns of these societies of different types to account for this, including a minimum amount of individualism and impersonality in social relations, which our society stresses, emphasis on kinship, other status values than materialism, and less mobility both spatial and mental. One of the most important factors, however, is the general consistency in their value structure, a relative absence of differential attitudes on basic social relationships among most members of the society. This is not to say that there are no differences, but that these differences are neither numerous nor as pronounced on important questions of conduct.

But what is most important is that either there are not pronounced differences in acceptable conduct between the different age groups in the society, or the society carefully prescribes the behavior and takes it for granted that everyone will eventually assume certain rights and obligations with increasing maturity. In our society, on the other hand, there is great inconsistency between the behavior of a child and of an adult, these differences not being clearly defined as a correlate of age. In fact, as will be indicated shortly, an adult is permitted increasing transgressions of the conduct norms, while juveniles are expected to obey even the ideals.

In many simpler societies the situation is reversed, for it is the juveniles that have considerable freedom, whereas the behavior of adults is one of rigid conformity. The inconsistent value patterns of the adult world constitute one of the chief moral hazards to the juvenile in the modern world.

The term "delinquency," in fact, refers to prohibited forms of conduct ranging from behavior ordinarily designated as crime, including theft, to such as truancy, being ungovernable or beyond parental control, late hours, malicious mischief and destruction of property, intoxication, gambling, sexual misconduct, and violations of the traffic laws. The relation between the differing degrees of latitude allowed in the behavior norms of the adult world and the juvenile can best be illustrated by the fact that if we were to insist on the same or comparable behavior standards among our adults, neither the police, the jails, nor the courts could possibly deal with the consequent avalanche of cases that would ensue. There are few adults, certainly very few in large urbanized areas, who in their conduct approach the standards set by that ideal for juveniles, the Boy Scout code.

Flagrant Law Violation. The wholesale flouting of many of these taboos by the general adult population, including labor, farmers, and business and professional men, is self-evident. The Kinsey report, for example, even if the sample were only partially representative, shows that sexual misconduct is both extensive and flagrant among all sections of the adult population. There is considerable indication both from government reports and from a limited number of research studies that there are extensive violations of law not only by adults of the lower socioeconomic groups but among business and professional men and politicians as well.

Crimes committed by the latter groups include the sale of fraudulent securities, black market activities, sale of adulterated and misbranded foods and drugs, violations of the antitrust, Federal trade and labor relations laws, fraudulent income tax returns, fee-splitting in medicine, illegal abortions, and bribery. The crimes committed by these groups are both flagrant and willful, and the social and monetary damage to society far exceeds that of ordinary crime. Most important is the damage to general law obedience through violations of laws by white collar criminals, since they occupy positions of trust and public importance.

An illustration of adult noncompliance with law was the flagrant disregard for law by businessmen exhibited in the black market during World War II, in which over half chose to violate the law and in which the government found over 1,000,000 violations and imposed serious penalties upon more than 200,000 businessmen. Although many have failed to see the connection, black market activities for individual material gain, as well as other white collar crimes, are intimately tied up with the problem of juvenile delinquency in our society.

The typical apprehended criminal is usually between 14 and 20 years of age, and over one million juveniles and youths come annually to the attention of the police. The tendency at present is to approach the problem by asking what is wrong with youth and trying to study them without reference to the behavior of the larger social world.

Following the Adult Model. Conversations with many young offenders readily reveal the fact that they do not regard their actions as different from the behavior displayed by many ordinary citizens, politicians, businessmen, and other professional groups. A large number can recite cases they know or have read of in the newspapers. Some perhaps were learned around the dinner table where a father may have bragged about how he defrauded the government either on the black market, his income tax, or some other regulation, Federal or otherwise. It is obviously impossible to rear law-abiding children in a world where their adult models disobey the law.

One may suggest that there is a difference between political and business crimes and the more overt acts that are commonly committed by juveniles. It appears, however, from social-psychological experimentation that children and young adults frequently do not distinguish between similar situations which may appear to an adult as different or as actually representing a distinction in kind.

*   *   *

One might question whether juveniles are familiar with the delinquent or criminal activity of adults. It is true that juveniles may not be actually as aware as an observer might think, but we would still be reasonably safe in assuming that the effect of adult criminality, at least in the form of rationalizations, is considerable. Certainly there was extensive knowledge among all age groups of the existence of a black market. The arrest of police, judges, or prominent politicians for corruption soon reaches the attention of most people, young or old. Criminal behavior in the sports world, especially among leading contenders, becomes common knowledge. And in the case of a juvenile play model, such as the Air Forces, the arrest and conviction of a high-ranking officer such as General Meyers may create a serious moral hazard in the community.

In stating this there is no intention to deny that delinquency, like crime, is primarily the outgrowth of personal association with those having deviant standards, but rather to point out that such delinquency among adults furnishes rationalizations both for the delinquent group and for the individual delinquent, to support, probably unconsciously, their deviant behavior. The conclusion is obvious that no successful program for dealing with delinquency can leave out the larger adult world.

Public Attitudes. In addition to the example of law violation, the adult world furnishes juveniles with patterns in the general public attitude toward law obedience and toward the agents of the law, the police. This attitude is either that all laws except those dealing with very serious offenses should be violated if one can get away with it, or that laws should be selectively obeyed according to one's interests. The first can be seen in the public attitude toward intoxication, taxes, gambling, traffic law, and general disorderly conduct. The second can be seen in the selective obedience to laws by labor, business, and the farmer. Laws governing labor, such as injunctions against strikes or the prohibition of violence in picketing, can be violated by labor; laws governing the conduct of commerce, ranging from the securities laws to prices and rationing in wartime, can be violated by business; and farmers may use violence to dump milk trucks to keep up prices. In each instance the group requires obedience to the laws by all other groups. The juvenile likewise is expected by all groups to obey the regulations of society even though some of these rules may furnish controls over peculiarly juvenile aspects, such as school attendance and recreation in the form of malicious mischief.

Linked with this differential morality of adults which at the same time requires almost ideal behavior by the juvenile, is the lack of extensive generation interaction which we term the adolescent conflict. The person from age 12 to 18 has a vague role of duties and obligations in our society. The result is a separate culture of adolescents. This failure of the adult to encourage the participation of adolescents in the larger world, keeping them half adult and half child, results frequently in the diversion of their activities into unconventional patterns. To this extent the social controls of the adult world are weakened and the violations of conduct norms are frequently seen out of context by the adolescent, who witnesses the adult world deprived of intimate knowledge and adult responsibilities.

Adult attitudes of the larger community toward minority groups, particularly racial groups, add to the difficulties in dealing with juveniles from these groups, particularly where the boys' delinquent gang, consisting of members of a minority group, secures for its members status and material gain. The segregation of minority groups in areas fostering delinquency is a problem of the larger adult world, and must be dealt with as much on this level as in the immediate neighborhood where the group resides. Certainly the individual delinquent or family is not the proper unit.

CONCLUSIONS

There is no question that those who in studying delinquency concentrate almost exclusively on the personality characteristics of the juvenile or on the influence of the family are in an extremely vulnerable position theoretically. Although not nearly to as great an extent, the same error of limited perspective is made by those who see the exclusive cause of delinquency in the companions and gang associates of the juvenile. Even those approaching the problem of delinquency entirely through the local neighborhood are faced by social forces emanating from beyond this small world.

While agreeing that delinquency is chiefly a product of personal contacts, the world of secondary relationships can by no means be completely eliminated from an investigation of delinquency. Such secondary contacts may furnish models and rationalizations which become part of the set of beliefs of the juvenile delinquent as he sees the world. Among those contacts having a possible influence, there is no question about the police, courts, penal institutions, and the school. While the relationship seems obvious, there is only limited evidence to indicate that the newspaper, magazines, movies, the radio, comic books, and various agencies of moral risk produce delinquency. Similarly, the immorality of the general adult population, its extensive violation of law while at the same time it requires model behavior of juveniles, must not only be bewildering but must have a relation to delinquent behavior.

Most of the very few studies which have been made of secondary influences either represent findings which have not been substantiated by other studies or are more than fifteen years old and do not necessarily embody improved research techniques. Considering the seriousness of the problem of delinquency, the amount of largely scientifically unsupported public discussion of the relation of secondary contacts and the large financial investment in such media as the movies and the radio, it is surprising that there is not more valid evidence of relationship today. One reason for this is that research problems have been set up to look only for certain factors, with the obvious result that if secondary contacts are not included in the research, no evidence of their relationship is found.

Perhaps if more research were done, this important problem would be taken out of the realm of speculation into the scientific world of fact, process, understanding, and control. Of primary concern to such research is the question of the extent of contact of nondelinquents with each of these influences. Certainly no definite conclusion can be reached as to causation by confining ourselves to delinquents and not including as well the frequency of the same experience among those who have not engaged in delinquency.

53 · The Family and Juvenile Delinquency

by HARRY MANUEL SHULMAN

In the following article, Professor Harry Manuel Shulman, of the City College of New York, who has done extensive research as well as practical work in the field of juvenile delinquency and crime, discusses the disorganized family as a factor in juvenile delinquency. After pointing out the major functions that the family fulfills, he shows how the presence of unfavorable conditions, physical, economic, and psychological, prevents their fulfillment and thus creates a situation conducive to delinquent behavior. [From *The Annals*, Vol. 261, Jan. 1949, pp. 21-31. Reprinted by permission. Abridged, and footnotes omitted.]

JUVENILE delinquency is more than a formal breach of the conventions; it is indicative of an acute breakdown in the normal functions of family life. The loss of parental control represented in the formal breach of the law is usually the culmination of a period of heightened tensions arising from severe conflict over patterns of rearing—disagreement over duties, restrictions and limitations, standards of education and training, selection of associations and places of association, and so forth—culminating in a breakdown of emotional attachment between parent and delinquent child, and leading often to a break in essential communication of attitudes between the generations.

Juvenile delinquency is thus a circumstance of acute emotional disturbance both to parent and to problem child, involving usually several aspects; among them, the parent's sense of helplessness in the situation, his ambivalent desires to protect the errant child and at the same time to injure it physically for rejecting the parental protection, and the shame and sense of social degradation that accompany the exposure of family incompetence. The shock is often productive of complete emotional rupture and of rejection of the wayward child, although unconscious emotional rejection of the child may have long preceded the outward break in relationship.

FACTORS IN FAMILY INFLUENCE

The family fulfills at least three major functions: it provides organic sustenance and habit-training in survival patterns; it affords primary group association for the experiencing of socializing interpersonal relationships; and it is a major source for the transmission of the values and knowledge of the culture. We shall therefore have to consider the influence of aspects of each of these upon juvenile delinquency.

Among the conditions which we shall consider are physical factors such as family size and crowding; economic and social factors such as the economic status of the house and the structure of the family; sociopsychological factors such as transmission of delinquent attitudes and the role of discipline; and cultural factors such as the role of social class in patterns of rearing, and the influence of ethnic group upon the solidarity of family structure. The importance of any single one of these as an agency in juvenile delinquency may be minimal; it is the cumulative impact of a large number of these factors that constitutes the multiple causation pattern and, at the same time, the complex treatment problem of the delinquent situation.

*   *   *

PHYSICAL FACTORS

In the earlier history of juvenile delinquency research there was preoccupation with the physical and economic concomitants of delinquency. Several studies of family size indicated that a disproportionate number of delinquents spring from large families. Merrill, in a very recent matched control study, verified this point for her sampling. But it has been pointed out that family size is related directly to socioeconomic status in terms of per capita income, and that the child from a large, poverty-stricken family may become delinquent not necessarily because of size, per se, but because of the crowding, poor housing conditions, bad neighborhood, and early cessation of education and early beginning of employment that accompany the living conditions of such families.

Adverse economic conditions in the home appear to have, in combination with other influences, some relationship to delinquency. The majority of studies of court samples of arraigned delinquents bring out the low socioeconomic status of the families and the fact that a large proportion of them have been recipients of aid from public and private social welfare agencies. Burt, in his London study, discovered more poverty in the homes of his delinquents than in those of his control group of nondelinquents from the same neighborhoods and schools. Merrill also found sharp differences in economic status among a sample of delinquents carefully matched against a control group of nondelinquents. There is the possibility that family economic status is entirely an outcome of skewness of court intake; as against this interpretation is the finding of Glueck and Glueck, that among their "juvenile delinquents grown up" there were marked differences in the economic status of the parents of the delinquents who succeeded compared to those who failed following treatment.

The occupation of the parents is important in relation to economic status. Studies of the occupational backgrounds of fathers of court-arraigned delinquents indicate an excess number with slight skills or unskilled, and relatively fewer in semiskilled and skilled occupations. This is indicative of the greater occupational precariousness, the less secure income, and the lower social status of many of the parents of delinquents. Similarly, most studies of delinquents bring out the greater extent of total unemployment among parents and the greater number of families in which the mother is the sole support or where both parents are employed. In the latter case, there is a marked effect upon the capacity of the parents for supervision of the children.

Crowding, as determined by the number of persons per room, has been shown in several studies to be greater in families of delinquents than of nondelinquents in congested areas. Shulman, in his New York State Crime Commission study on truants, discovered that the median number of persons per room was 1.7 as against an estimated housing congestion of approximately one-half of that amount in congested areas generally. Crowding, while an effect of large family size and economic marginality, has its own significant social and psychological effects in contributing to a lack of privacy, to breakdown of barriers to sex experience within the family, and to limitations of activity, leading to quarreling and to the flight of children and adolescents from the home to the

street or to public and commercial centers for recreation and companion
ship.

* * *

BROKEN HOMES OF DELINQUENTS

Breckinridge and Abbott, reporting on 13,000 cases studied between
1899 and 1909, found 34 per cent from broken homes. The United
States Children's Bureau, in successive reports, has indicated high per
centages of broken homes among court cases. In 1939 it reported broken
homes in 36 per cent of boys' cases and 50 per cent of girls' cases disposed
of in sixty-four courts in 1936.

Among children committed to institutions there has been an even
higher proportion from broken homes. In 1923 the United States Bu
reau of the Census reported that 56 per cent were from broken homes.
In Wisconsin 63.5 per cent of girls committed to correctional school
were from broken homes. The factor of the family break may have in
fluenced judges in the direction of institutional commitment; but this
must be taken together with the fact that institutional commitments
usually represent either severer offenses or more persistent offenders
especially in urban jurisdictions, from which the bulk of systematic
court reports originate.

Thus, the increase in the frequency of the broken home as we progress
from court arraignment to commitment may be taken as one evidence
of a relationship between family disorganization and delinquency. In
general, percentages of broken families among children arraigned in
juvenile courts appear to be higher than for known samples of the gen
eral population.

Collateral evidence on this point is available from private researche
based on individual case study. In a study of 966 cases presenting specia
problems of diagnosis, referred by the Boston Juvenile Court to Dr
William Healy and his associates at the Judge Baker Foundation, Shel
don and Eleanor Glueck found that 48 per cent came from broken
homes. The same authors, in their earlier study of the family back
grounds of 500 youths committed to the Massachusetts Reformatory for
serious offenses, reported 60 per cent from broken families.

* * *

LIMITED SIGNIFICANCE OF BROKEN HOMES

. . . The majority of research studies are in agreement with official
court reports, that the incidence of broken homes is higher for delin

quents than for nondelinquents, even when such factors as age and ethnic background are taken into account. This does not necessarily prove a causal relation, but strongly suggests one.

Significant as the hypothesis of the broken home may be for the objectives of a broad social welfare program of delinquency prevention, its framework is too broadly conceived to be useful as a guide in the study of the dynamics of individual delinquency in the family setting.

*   *   *

DELINQUENCY AND FAMILY DISCORD

The interpersonal conditions of family relationship leading to delinquent behavior stand out as more important than general background factors. Numerous studies have shown that uncongenialities, tensions, marital triangles and sexual breaches, frictions over income and expenditure, projections of frustrated ambitions, losses of authority and standing, and many other broken threads in the tangled skein of family relationships are as important as, if not more important than, physical breaks in family structure, are usually antecedent to physical breaks, and contribute largely to delinquency. Clinical experience has demonstrated that rarely does a child become delinquent where the members of a family have successfully maintained love and affection for one another. The treatment of delinquency involves the treatment not of the individual but of the whole family constellation.

Carl Rogers, in a discussion of the Smith College studies based on 697 case records from the Institute of Child Guidance in New York City, has pointed out that Miss Witmer and her associates, in studying the factors associated with success and failure in treatment, both at the time of disposition and several years later, reported negative findings for such items as the child's age at time of clinic study, sex, school placement, ordinal position in family, even the child's symptomatic behavior, and but slight significance for such factors as intelligence, economic status of home, and family size. What did have a striking relation to the clinic's success in dealing with children were the marital adjustments of parents, the emotional tone of the home, and the behavior and attitudes of parents toward the child.

The adjustment of parents to each other was alone significantly related to successful treatment, distinctly better results having been achieved where parents were living together in a satisfactory relation than where they were definitely dissatisfied with their marital life. Intermediate results were obtained in homes where the parents were divorced or separated or where they had a resigned or neutral attitude toward the frictions of their married life. From these results Rogers concludes that so far as children's behavior is concerned, a broken home is probably less injurious than the tensions of a home in which the parents are deeply dissatisfied with each other.

*   *   *

SOCIAL DIFFERENCES

Findings which place emotional frustration at the root of juvenile delinquency have for the most part been based on studies of clinic and court samples drawn from lower socioeconomic levels. New light recently shed on different patterns of child training in different social classes in American society suggests that these differences may have their effects on patterns of social behavior, including delinquency. They suggest that a stricter regimen with more frustration of direct pleasure impulses is distinctly a middle-class characteristic, and that in contradistinction, lower-class rearing is distinctly permissive in its practices. Thus middle-class parents tend to initiate tensions in child-rearing patterns earlier and sustain them longer than poor parents. Habits of sphincter control and weaning are established earlier and more rigidly among the middle class, and later and more permissively among the poor. Middle-class children are more closely supervised than children of the poor. They are expected to participate in home duties more frequently. These facts raise a question.

If frustration is closely allied to delinquent behavior, and if middle-class rearing involves sustaining of many tensions, why do these tensions not result in frustrations leading to officially recorded delinquency? The answers may lie along at least three lines of reasoning:

1. The frustration patterns in middle and lower classes appear to be differently organized. The middle-class child is forced to maintain tensions leading to discipline, learning and utilization of skills, and is concomitantly guarded against early pleasure behavior of unapproved type. The lower-class child is less restricted in his range and choice of activities, being permitted greater freedom with regard to distance allowed from home, choice of companionships and recreation, and time of entering upon both part-time after-school and full-time posteducational employment. The child of lower socioeconomic background more frequently has earlier heterosexual experience.

Thus, the frustrations of the lower-class child are not in relation to severe checks upon his freedom. He achieves the partial independence of a wage-earning status earlier, whereas middle-class children remain in school and economically dependent on their parents longer. Middle-class rearing delays social maturation longer, while establishing parental authority earlier. The middle-class child appears to accept his frustrations more philosophically as part of his life pattern. The pattern differences, one may suggest, lie in the earlier onset and greater consistency in establishment and maintenance of tensions in middle-class rearing. The middle-class child accepts his harness of tension patterns on a habitual basis because he has been less indulged and less subjected to ambiguous and inconsistent rearing practices.

To the middle-class child, frustration involves obedience which gives him a status, as inheritor of the parental status, to which he may aspire. The child of the poor, if obedient, has a status as inheritor of his parental status, to which, in our culture, he usually does not aspire. Thus tensions are endured by the middle-class child more consistently because they lead to a goal acceptable in our culture, but are less consistently endured by children of the poor as leading to an unacceptable goal.

2. The delinquencies of the lower-class child arise from the conditions of his rearing—greater deprivation of material means to pleasure, and greater clash of temperaments in family life owing to the inconsistencies and lack of discipline in rearing. His offenses (among boys) consist largely of various types of stealing, and (in girls) of waywardness and ungovernability—behavior for which the penal code and its counterpart in children's court acts have well-defined statutes and rulings. In contrast, and in the absence of scientific data, we may speculate from scanty evidence that the characteristic offenses of middle-class children consist of malicious mischief occurring under group stimulus, and sex offenses that are privately dealt with.

3. The characteristic offenses of the middle class do not show up in criminal statistics until adult life, and are then occupationally differentiated from the offenses of the poor, tending toward fraud, in contrast to assault and theft among the poor. Aside from occupational opportunities, it may be pointed out that the personality structure involved in successful fraud is wholly consistent with middle-class education and training, depending not on a single successful attack or raid, as in the case of assault or theft, but on a more carefully controlled aggression involving knowledge and application of a wide range of technical skills and patience and fortitude in planning and carrying out extensive frauds as nearly within the letter of the law as technical skill will permit. This suggests that the middle-class child who in later life resorts to crime does so in the light of earlier experience which has taught him that the social

order has few loopholes and many restrictions; whereas the poor child
resorts to types of crime which suggest that earlier experience has taught
him that the social order has many loopholes and few restrictions.

54 · The Juvenile Court as an Institution

by FREDERICK W. KILLIAN

The juvenile court was established only a little more than
a half century ago, in response to a more enlightened view
of the nature of the child. During this relatively short
period it not only has been instrumental in bringing about
a more humane treatment of the child gone wrong but has
served to call to the attention of the adult world the special needs of the child and the responsibilities of parents
and of the community toward him. In the following article
Professor Frederick W. Killian, of Clark University, a sociologist and lawyer of wide experience in the field, describes the character, procedure, and function of the juvenile
courts. [From *The Annals*, Vol. 261, Jan. 1949, pp. 89-100.
Reprinted by permission. Footnotes omitted.]

WITH THE establishment of the juvenile court, approximately fifty years
ago, a policy design was put into operation in which the idea of public
security with reference to the offenses, neglect, and dependency of children was to be implemented through a separate, special, and sometimes
exclusive jurisdiction. This was the first recognition by the law of a separate area of legal control for a distinct field of behavior. Implicit in this
policy design, unlike the criminal court emphasis, *treatment consequence* was to predominate rather than *behavior circumstance*, and the
norms and standards of common law and equity, as well as of social and
administrative necessity, were to find an operating relation in a new
synthesis of experience. The laws establishing these courts have, as policy
designs, been hypotheses for action and experimentation.

THE CONFLICT OF NORMS

During fifty years of experience, these factors have led to a sharper
delineation between behavior circumstance and treatment consequence
than perhaps was first contemplated, certainly more than in any other

court, and have even effected a change in the predominance of behavior circumstance in the criminal courts. From the juvenile court come also theories for the newly established youth authorities or commissions.

The conflict of norms and standards is the court's bane today; it has been apparent both within the court itself and between the court and other community agencies. The policy design of the court has necessarily brought it nearer to other agencies, correlating its work with theirs in implementing the public security with reference to children. This sharpens conflict, as the norms and standards of courts and of agencies are still in the stage of formulation.

The court, established in 1899, graced by charity, reform, and progress, each too vague and speculative to provide more than an atmosphere of good will and good intentions, each increasingly to be rejected, therefore fell somewhat short of expectations, and too often worked, and still does, behind a façade of hope, looking for new ideological supports in a fuller development of the social disciplines and of social work.

The limitations as well as the advantages of each normative system embodied in its structure have come to be more apparent in the struggle for equilibration. Case work functions and judicial functions vie with each other. Active, or potentially active, in the court's ideology are doctrines and hypotheses concerning the nature of law or of some control area, as well as their specialized terminologies, and confusion results. New logical applications are being sought for the analysis, formulation, and reformulation of norms and doctrines of substance, procedure, court structure, and operation. The emphasis on treatment demands clarification between judicial function and case work function as old legalities and new inductive concepts pervade the court's operation on all levels.

For the purpose of analysis, it seems advisable to classify the norms as structural norms, substantive norms, and procedural norms. The first includes form, arrangement of components, and the court's connection with the judicial system; the second, the norms of behavior or conduct which may be applied to particular situations; and the last, the procedures for making the applications of substantive norms. The purpose behind the adoption and use of a norm of conduct and of the procedure for its application will ultimately determine the norms of structure; all normative levels are interrelated in operation.

What, then, has been the experience of this court, and what does it offer as experience? The selection of norms and standards as the unit of attention reduces the analysis to an operational level which will therefore proceed from intake to disposition, after certain preliminary considerations have been examined.

STRUCTURE AND WORK OF THE COURT

Students of the court will find considerable differences from place to place in the organization of the courts, in the emphasis on various stages of procedure, in the competence of staff, judge, and officials, and also in tone and atmosphere.

The Court's Structure. For purposes of discussion and to give a general picture of this special jurisdiction, its organization may be classified under four general heads:

1. Independent courts with jurisdiction over children: with city, county, or state-wide jurisdiction and with probation services supplied by the court or by city, county, or state agencies; mostly in large urban centers (or state-wide courts, as in Connecticut and Rhode Island).

2. Family courts with jurisdiction over specified offenses and relations and over specified types of family conflict, including jurisdiction over children; services attached or separate; urban centers largely. (Of 33 family and domestic relations courts listed in *The Book of the States* only 19 possess divorce jurisdiction.)

3. Juvenile and domestic relations courts: independent or parts of courts with more general jurisdiction; rarely having jurisdiction over divorce and separation; services attached or independent; in urban centers largely.

4. Juvenile courts as sections or parts of courts with more general jurisdiction: judges of the court holding juvenile parts or divisions by designation sometimes in rotation (usually probate, county, circuit, or common pleas courts); services attached or separate; more common in nonurban centers.

Operation for all these courts could easily be uniform from a normative point of view; indeed, they largely resemble one another as to the jurisdiction conferred over children, the differences being largely due to community needs, understanding, and resources, which determine good or poor operations, functionaries, and facilities.

Sources of Intake. To all of these courts, children come on petitions alleging delinquency, dependency, or neglect. Generally, parents or any interested person, including the police, school officials, or social agencies may make a petition informally alleging the offense or difficulty. Children may be brought directly to the court by the police; if arrested after court hours, they are taken first to a detention home (where such exist).

Very many delinquency cases come to the court through the police. Police departments, including juvenile aid bureaus, where properly organized, furnish indispensable aids to the court in sifting out those cases that need court action; many complaints—particularly of neighbors watchmen, janitors, foremen, railroad guards, and others to whom other people's children are a nuisance, often whether good or bad—indicate little if any need for special treatment, but rather for recreation and play facilities or for a warning. This service, as the New York City and Detroit experiences show, save the court many valuable intake interviews in disposing of such cases. Most of these cases come from low income families and areas of the city—the juvenile court being primarily an urban institution with a population heavy in this category.

Indispensable to the court, its functions centered around the intake process, is the detention home. Sometimes an independent service and sometimes under probation direction (as in the Toledo juvenile court), it serves the court in and out of hours as a protection for neglected and dependent children as well as for serious or questionable cases of delinquency where the child cannot be released to a parent's or relative's custody. It furnishes a first view of the child, his needs and temperament, and the conditions of his difficulty. This home is by no means a jail substitute, but a treatment-initiating and study center, and relations between it and the court must be highly integrated through proper procedures.

The schools rely on the courts for truancy control, for cases of unmanageable children, and sometimes in cases where further schooling seems inadvisable. The authoritarian setting of the court and the quasi-authoritarian setting of the school tend toward a common emphasis (often that of functional autonomy) on discipline and responsibility, but may conflict because attention is to different values. The schools referring children to a court too often expect it to achieve in a week, by some mysterious operation, what it, with more extensive facilities, could not do in years. Good schools and good courts alone, through the conference method, can define a proper relation.

Procedures. All of what has been said suggests the importance of formulating procedures to define the methods of work between the court and other agencies and between divisions of the court itself. These should be made, co-operatively, in a conference of qualified agency representatives. This is a procedural norm perfected in social work, through which referrals based on co-operative and overlapping functions are defined. The trained social worker assumes the necessity; the judge tends to regard it as a matter for authoritarian attention—is he not superordinate? The answer is, No. This function is nonjudicial; it relates to treatment consequence, to intake, to agency relations, and not to jurisdiction. However, the judge should participate in such conferences. In this process the judge waives no prerogative, as here he performs an administrative function. Too frequently court procedures are established (and procedures are very few) by judicial directives, either as parts of rules of the court or as temporary instructions.

The Judge—Focal Norm of the Court. All lines of operation in the court either lead to or emanate from the judge. No court can rise above its judge—particularly a separate and independent court. He is chief administrator, adjudicator, policy maker; also the public relations man for the court, and the reconcilor of disputes. It cannot be too plainly asserted that no condition—of selection, of preparation for office, of tenure, of salary—is favorably defined for the judge of this court.

His education, legal, and general, has probably been of little use. Criminal law, a short one-year course, is usually a formalistic study of remedial categories, not of normative development. Juvenile court judges more than others must learn on the job and acquire judgment with respect to the exacting application of legal and social norms, and experience in a dawning sense of the law in relation to the social disciplines.

Judges are generally selected by election or by appointment. Both are hazardous, and separate effort is always essential to obtain a qualified judge. By either method, demands of politics enter into the selection and later into the judge's work. Nor is performance of work for one or more terms necessarily a guarantee of re-election or re-appointment.

Relegated to the lowest level of the judicial hierarchy in an inferior court, the office does not, as a rule, attract men of maturity or ability. Pressure is insistent at the lower levels, and selection for quality is more difficult because public sensitivity tends to be directed to higher offices. Nor is this work regarded as adequate preparation for the coveted status of a judgeship on the superior or appellate benches, but rather as specialized and not demanding extensive legal experience.

In courts of mixed jurisdiction, judges frequently avoid assignment to the juvenile division as unprofitable, particularly in terms of promotion and legal achievement; only a few prefer it. Rotation of work is therefore often resorted to in order that no judge shall be deprived of common law or equity experience. Several such judges may have to learn the trade, so to speak. Generally they will not regard it worth while to make this effort, and, in any event, such experience will be spotty and discontinuous.

The fact that this judge may practice law in many jurisdictions, mostly outside the large urban centers, indicates a lack of community resources or of awareness of job demands, or both. This is closely correlated with salaries, which range from under $1,000 in rural areas to generally fair competences of $10,000 and over in large cities, as in New York.

Short tenures do not encourage men of ability to seek this inferior position. Five-year terms (in New Jersey, for instance) have demonstrated that no sooner is a judge in command of the situation than his office may be filled by a novice. In short, the judge of this court is now faced with an impossible definition of the situation.

Intake, Jurisdiction, and Power. The sources of intake and referral above described are preludes to entry into the court. But before the court can begin to function, two norms of procedure must be given weight—intake and jurisdiction—each fixing its own standards for admission to the court. Unity between them is found in the concept "public security," a concept of social control. The two definitions were formulated in different areas of control at different times—jurisdiction out of the King's peace, intake as a limit of services in a social-agency policy-design; both out of experience. Each is organized around its own principle of authority, with jurisdiction superordinate; a norm carried over from criminal law emphasizing behavior circumstance.

The social worker sees ordering and commanding as attendant upon the requirements of treatment consequence, a norm of case work, based on service, which in the court, therefore, tends to function to the limits of this definition, which is its own. Judges may tend to refrain from power exercise as a concession, in lieu of punishment—"giving another chance," an expression which is anathema to the trained social worker.

Thus intake and jurisdiction are too often irreconcilable, each operating as a unit of taught and of operational experience and conditioning. Each exercises a sifting function designed to protect its respective area of operation—intake, the social; jurisdiction, the legal. Jurisdiction, in certain respects a substitute for self-help, defines the exercise and limits of power applied from ideas of behavior circumstance and is concerned with rights and duties, largely with a mechanical application thereof, while intake defines the client need in relation to agency resources. These norms operate simultaneously and tend to be mechanically related, and in most courts the judicial process dominates, as none is present to dissent.

In the better courts having trained staff, it is unlikely that judge and case worker can, in the foreseeable future, possess an identity of taught and of operating experience; and here responsibility falls heavy on the judge, while the case worker often overemphasizes professionalization.

From Intake to Disposition. From whatever source, the child entering the court is handled by a staff which in good courts consists of skilled professional workers, chiefly trained in social work techniques and supported by medical, psychological, and psychiatric services. The interjection into the case of any such service, including the judicial process, should be made only at stated intervals and through channels estab-

lished by carefully prepared procedures. When treatment is being emphasized, the case work process must be the predominant norm, subject only
to considerations of public security. Unusual circumstances may demand
a departure from a defined process sequence.

Sometimes the procedures themselves call for revision; and in good
courts, procedures will be continually evaluated in terms of experience,
and all unnecessary interference with the case work process eliminated.
Staff conferences in better courts help to interpret these definitions. In a
properly organized juvenile court, probation workers and staff can clear
most matters of interpretation, legalities, jurisdiction, and so forth informally, as parties to the proceedings rarely insist on the observance of
strictly technical forms.

Social agencies insist upon skilled and tested workers for intake; in
the court, the intake worker should have all the skills of the case worker
in addition to a comprehensive knowledge of the court's jurisdiction.
This requires continual training, and is only one reason why training-on-
the-job conferences—another case work norm—are imperative and are
held in good courts at least monthly.

However, in the great majority of courts throughout the United States,
intake, in any technical sense, is almost completely neglected; even clerks
of the court, frequently miserable hacks, are sometimes allowed to hold
first interviews. Clerks, bailiffs, and uniformed attendants have no place
in a juvenile court. Even in many common law and equity courts, certain clerks have for some time had legal training and are in a sense judicial administrators and professional employees. In this sense, a clerk is
a useful official.

Treatment consequence, if stressed, must begin at intake and continue
as defined, with the few exceptions made necessary by serious offenses,
for instance, homicides and adult-linked larcenies. In these cases it may
be essential, and actually advisable and appropriate, initially to emphasize the public security by bringing the child directly before the judge.
He may then make a referral to intake, as is frequently done in good
courts, if behavior circumstance, in his estimation, need not be emphasized at that stage of the proceedings to meet the needs of public
security.

Actually, this method, thoughtfully used, may strengthen a later case
work process, and it interrupts no process begun. For many judges, the
hardest lesson to learn is that an undefined interjection into the case
disrupts treatment; for many social workers, that their norms of process
must be flexible in an authoritarian agency.

At intake the case begins to fall into one of two categories—official
cases and unofficial cases (used by almost all courts). No uniform defini-

tion of these terms can be stated, as a considerable difference of opinion prevails from person to person and from place to place as to whether an offense belongs in the area dominated by behavior circumstance or by treatment consequence. The definition of delinquency, rarely specific, influences all that happens to a child from intake, through hearing, to disposition, and later in treatment. Someone, either the judge himself or a staff member, must determine whether an adjudication shall be made with treatment to follow (official) or whether adjudication is unnecessary, the child to be carried for treatment (unofficial) or the case dismissed. This reflects a conflict of norms which will be discussed shortly, but a view of the hearing and disposition stages is essential for the analysis.

If a case is not designated as unofficial, and if behavior circumstance marks it for the judge's attention at some stage, it is docketed for the court. In good courts the judge hears the case on a staff report with the worker present together with parents, very occasionally legal counsel, and interested parties. Medical, psychological, and psychiatric reports may be included, or, if needed, may be required by the judge and the case may be continued. School and recreational experiences are included. But hearings in these courts vary from strictly legal exhibitions to careful studies—sometimes sixty or seventy children or more herded through the court in a single day.

Referees. In about one-third of the courts, referees are provided for by statute. In other courts they are designated, in lieu of such provision, under the judge's power (as chancellor) to designate masters in chancery; but a wide variety of referee use, mostly poor, is found to exist. A well-developed use of the referee system is found in the Toledo court, where the judge, also possessing divorce and domestic relations jurisdiction, sits in juvenile cases on rehearings from a referee's decision; in that court, the staff is of the highest quality in training and education. In the vast majority of cases in that court such rehearings are not demanded. The Standard Juvenile Court Act (Sec. 10) provides a definition for the use of referees correlating judicial with case work functions, allowing flexibility and inventiveness.

It is not too much to say that the referee system, contemplating highly trained and carefully selected functionaries, will in the final analysis prove to be the most promising device for resolving the conflict of norms in this court and for overcoming the difficulties facing juvenile court judges. This device has the advantages of reducing political pressures, providing for career service, retaining the essential legal safeguard of judicial review, and ultimately allowing an appeal on questions of law.

Seen as part of Dean Pound's proposal for a unified court system (now in effect in New Jersey under the new constitution), the referee system holds a place for juvenile, domestic relations, and family jurisdictions within a unified court structure but with a separately defined area for the indispensable administrative and case work functions. In this way a member of the bench of a unified court could be assigned to a part of that court dealing with family matters, with reasonable assurance that the difficulties now impeding juvenile court judges, as above described, would be eliminated in great measure.

A judge cannot perform all functions. If he hears all or nearly all cases in courts where the referee system is not developed, he is actually involved in administrative work. Since present-day legal education does not measurably deal with behavior problems, and since a new type of legal-social mind and approach is needed, it would seem that the referee function, institutionalized, might more easily provide it than a re-education of judges.

Trials, in a more formal sense, are sometimes necessary in juvenile courts for older children involved in serious offenses in terms of behavior circumstance or (and this seldom occurs) where a child denies having committed the offense alleged. Some laws provide for such trials, and some for transfer of such cases to adult courts.

Disposition. Because a child is not charged with crime in this court, disposition of the case is not necessarily a terminal stage, and of course does not impose on the child any civil disabilities, nor does it, legally speaking, work against his interests, the theory being treatment in which discipline, where needed, is related to estimated needs. The disposition favored is to keep children in their own homes, if possible, under probation supervision if necessary. It is also generally possible for the courts to commit to designated guardians (foster home placement) or to public or private institutions, which are rarely satisfactory, or to order treatment which is deemed to be to the best interests of the child.

But it is obvious that the decision, whatever it be, cannot be mechanical or, as is more general in the criminal law, move directly from behavior circumstance to a particular penalty. The laws neither define a penalty nor a necessary, specific consequence following a stated and determined offense. Disposition is a function of clinical judgment, of which treatment is the consequence. Notwithstanding, in many courts (how many, it would be difficult to document), probation and institutionalization are mechanically and impatiently applied with little or no thought, induced through careful study, given to human needs. Moreover, institutional and foster home resources are often meager, and where the child's own home is not to be considered but action must be taken, a devil's advocate argument often determines the decision.

FUTURE DIRECTION

Four urgencies now press for attention and for solution, and may be thus stated:

1. Should the juvenile court continue to provide complete services for dependent and neglected children (including placement)?

2. Should it continue to provide treatment for delinquent children after (and before) adjudication?

3. Should the definition of delinquency be made more specific?

4. What form of organization should the juvenile court seek to follow in the future?

It should now be apparent that each of these questions is related to the other; that each is dependent on the factors stated in the suggestive analysis above. Because space is limited and because the present interest is to suggest possible solutions, these questions will be considered within certain established trends bearing on the juvenile court and, for convenience, will be handled in reverse.

Three developments, all bearing upon the juvenile court and affecting its work, are materializing: (1) the youth correction system, (2) a growing demand and trend toward a new separate and special jurisdiction over divorce, separation, and family matters, and (3) the gradual acceptance of unified state-wide court systems.

It is not difficult to see that family matters as heretofore handled, children's cases, divorce and separation (as suggested that they be handled), and youth matters, all lend themselves to the referee device. As now operating or as proposed, much of this work will be administrative, most of it an incident of equity jurisdiction, and all of it needs protection by judicial review and by appeal on matters of law.

Three separate areas of behavior stand out here: youth, child, and adult family. However, in a real sense, all are family subdivisions. Maybe the proper line of thought for organization utilizing the best that experience has to offer, as well as contemporary needs, will lead to a plan for allocating all these jurisdictions within the framework of a court of general jurisdiction with administrative and service areas fixed in referee divisions of the court, these divisions responsible to a judge presiding over a division of such court. The advantages seem to be many as Dean Pound has observed.

Services of the Court. Concerning the other questions raised: in the early days of the juvenile court, it was necessary for the court to develop services for children.

Social services have now expanded outside the courts, and where such agencies serving dependent and neglected children are now well developed and adequate (including foster home placement) and where proper definitions can be worked out between courts and agencies, it appears the better practice to divorce any extensive work in this field from the court. There should be reserved to it, of course, the hearing of petitions for changing guardians (natural or otherwise), for removing children from homes, for institutionalization, and for incidental relief.

Social services should be rendered by private or public agencies, the private agencies being frequently better equipped than the court for this purpose. In this respect the court would retain its strictly judicial function on an informed social basis, with the agency protected by proper procedures of operation.

Study Needed. The second and third problems are actually difficult and will need detailed and careful consideration before any action is taken. This much is certain—they will not be satisfactorily settled without better documentation than now exists. The fact is that since Lou's book no general study of the juvenile court has been made bringing together the chief types of experience. Most of the critical and pressing questions arising since his study (1927) are reviewed in materials cited herein.

Many particular practices, devices, and forms need summarizing. Moreover, no recent, fully scientific, objective study of particular courts and court types has been made. We badly need such detailed studies (not made by special arrangement for the purpose of immediate improvement of some one court) as Professor Tappan's work on an adolescent court for girls—the only thoroughly competent, scientific, and wholly objective treatise concerning a special jurisdiction based on a separate control area. How a reformulation of normative factors can be made without such studies is difficult to see.

Definition of Delinquency. Inadequacies are apparent in the definition of delinquency. Professor Tappan points out that, with a vague definition of delinquency, judges and probation officers are allowed scope (harmful in proportion to their lack of skill, training, and knowledge) for moralizing. Thus, what offense will, as an offense, require treatment (perhaps actually lead to an unreasoning and even diabolic reaction) may vary from judge to judge, from officer to officer, from court to court.

Tappan's point is well taken and carefully documented for the court he studied; empirical observations of juvenile courts in operation tend to confirm it. It is certain at least that behavior circumstance has been neglected. It is not suggested that a predetermined result should follow a particular offense, but rather that the offenses which symbolize the conduct desired to be prevented or modified be carefully defined, weighed, and seen as part of what Dr. Jenkins, for instance, calls behavior syndromes.

Children, and often adults, do not comprehend the meaning of metaphysical designations such as felony, even of terms like larceny, or the various degrees of crime. The present classification of crimes is totally inapplicable to this court's task; in fact, is outworn in criminal courts.

The juvenile court has been thinking in terms of the child's interest and welfare. This is a fine purpose, but does not offer much for adjudication. Determinations of welfare may vary considerably. More intelligent is the concept "course of conduct," which Tappan expounds. It has the advantage of representing concrete behavior as an identifiable area of psychological experience related to the public security, and thus ties in the Jenkins' behavior syndromes as relatively predictable patterns implicit in which is *the* treatment reflecting *the* disorder.

Bringing the petition for entering this court to the level of behavior-circumstance language and, with it, using a common name to designate the offense or conduct, a specific, meaningful statement of the reasons for court attention could be made. Course of conduct also should be retained as a reason for exerting jurisdiction, and can be illuminated by the syndrome descriptions. In passing, the terms "wayward child" and "minor" are vague and, for that reason, useless.

As Tappan shows from the adolescent court experience, vagueness in jurisdictional terms leads to vagueness in the exercise and the results of jurisdiction, and thus, for reasons stated above, affects intake policy adversely; but intake and jurisdiction must center on the same norms for initiating court activity. The full extent of moralizing to a disposition-conclusion in juvenile courts is perhaps little understood. A wealth of experience from the criminal law bears on this subject, and, aside from that, it is common experience to one familiar with juvenile court proceedings. New formulations of policy design cannot escape this problem; its partial solution is implicit in a referee system, which itself depends on high quality of staff.

Psychiatric, most often psychological and medical, services are furnished the court on a part-time basis; in some places, by city or county units. Urban centers have largely established child guidance clinics, and many hospital facilities and special services are at the court's disposal. It is generally convenient to utilize such services by referral, conference, and definition. This would certainly be so if the court included no treatment staff consequent upon adjudication.

Social agencies—family societies, public welfare units, boys' and girls' clubs—work closely with the court, particularly in urban centers. The growth of the council of social agencies, or community council, has stimulated a definition and practice of total community need expressed as community organization.

Continuation Services. The question is now asked whether the court should continue to service children on probation, and the answer has been in part suggested through the analysis in terms of the conflict of norms. Ideally, probably it should not; but, retaining a diagnostic staff, presently handled unofficial cases could be referred to other agencies (many could be handled in juvenile aid bureaus), and later, upon adjudication when course of conduct or public security violation was determined, cases could be referred to separate, specialized treatment agencies or to institutions. But this is an ideal projection, as much still remains to be accomplished in securing proper institutions as well as new service areas.

What may be regarded as semantic confusion—the question whether adjudication should follow or precede investigation—is referred to by Professor Tappan. In the New York Children's Court (New York City) and the Boston Juvenile Court it is insisted that an adjudication be first made. In most courts this is not the theory of operation; and in terms of a balance between treatment consequence and behavior circumstance as applied to the offenses of children, investigation first would seem to be the sound procedure, depriving no child of any right but rather illuminating obligations of society to children. This confusion of procedure has not been adequately discussed.

It would seem, too, that probation departments find a more acceptable definition of operations apart from the court, and, continuing to supply intake personnel or working close to intake (which must remain at the court), could expand into adequate treatment services. This seems to be agreeable to certain structural arrangements now present in the courts, and certainly to the idea of the juvenile court as part of a uniform jurisdiction including the referee system.

The conflict of norms is now in process of accommodation, with the separate jurisdiction over children certain to remain, however, related or reorganized.

Part Four

TREATMENT OF THE CRIMINAL

CHAPTER FIFTEEN

The Police

55 · What's Wrong with the Police?

by FRED J. COGSHALL

> At various times during the past few years, the police have been under severe criticism on numerous grounds. Although some of their shortcomings may be blamed on outside factors—notably the attitude of the public toward law enforcement—others are due to internal weaknesses in the system. Writing from firsthand experience, Fred J. Cogshall, of the Institute of Criminal Law Administration at Indiana University, discusses here the peculiar problems faced at the present time by the police and suggests ways of overcoming them. ["Are We Buying the Trojan Horse?" *Journal of Criminal Law and Criminology*, Vol. 42, July-Aug. 1951, pp. 155-162. Reprinted by permission.]

THE POLICE PROFESSION as a whole is being assailed by forces such as it has not encountered actively within its history. The invention of the Trojan Horse was mere child's play compared to modern techniques of deception and subterfuge—but it set a classic pattern. These forces are known by many names, but they all tend to the same end: Control of persons and government by one person or by a small clique that is responsible to no one. Call the technique by whatever ideological name which may come to mind, the form proposed is not the way of living as set up by the forefathers of our nation.

Never before in history has this country been so big, so wealthy, so powerful, and so thoroughly disliked by others. Never before has it been so necessary that all police departments protect the rights and privileges of the citizen regardless of race, creed, or political faith against intrusions from without. It is necessary that these rights be protected, for they are the entire basis of our government, and the loss of these rights would constitute an entirely new type of governmental control. The American Constitution has remained relatively unchanged, especially in its Bill of Rights since its adoption. Through court decisions and police practices we have set a pattern of criminal law administration. These decisions and practices are not the foundation of our living, rather they are the structure above the foundation within which we must live and work.

To effect a breakdown of this structure and an uprooting of the foundations of American society, it will be necessary to destroy it a piece at a time. The strategists and tacticians call this principle, "divide and conquer." Examination of the pattern of "divide and conquer" shows that in the recent world war in Europe in every instance the control of police and police functions was of paramount importance to the attacking force. This police control covers not only the daily activities of the citizens but goes on into their rights; rights of which, in many instances, the citizens possess only meager knowledge.

Further examination shows the pre-attack pattern in somewhat this fashion. Police are encouraged to operate without legal restrictions particularly in cases that arouse public indignation such as arson, murder, and rape. This non-legal type of operation, backed by public sentiment to a degree, tends only to retract further the knowledge of rights within the minds of the public. The public loses an awareness of its liberties while the hue and cry is in full sway. These operations set a precedent that will be enlarged at a later date by those assuming despotic control. Police are further urged to violate civil liberties of the citizen particularly in the field of search and seizure, some of the citizens even being willing victims, in order that dissatisfaction with the manner of performance of duty may be created in the public mind. The police are beset constantly by pseudo friends who spread this propaganda and encourage the use of illegal tactics only for ulterior motives.

Another method of creating internal friction should not be overlooked. Police officers as a professional group are prone to gossip—not only of cases but of administrative matters as well. This practice perfectly fits the pattern that is desired by the forces without the law. Gossip is the fertile field for the growth of the budding half truth into the ripened falsehood. Such falsifications are most difficult to combat as they are generally accusatory in nature, and the truth of the situation is not sufficient to counteract the element of doubt created in the minds of the police officers. Some departments have been successful in combating this habit of the policeman, and all departments should make greater attempts to eradicate this evil. The motives of the above two courses of action are basically the same; a desire to create unrest and dissension within the department itself.

Such dissension and violations of civil and criminal rights creates a low morale factor within a police organization, and the organization becomes easy prey to the more overt changes of administration. Thus, in a relatively short period of time, a police organization is ready for a change of administration and welcomes any change with the feeling that "anything would be better" than the preceding regime.

What allows this state of mind to occur? It is simply a lack of knowledge of basic constitutional law and a strong tendency to do the job the easy way or just "be lazy." It is the product of ignorance and lack of self discipline. It is much easier to third degree a confession from a suspect than to spend the time and energy gathering evidence that will convict him without his confession. It is more satisfying momentarily to inflict punishment on a prisoner than to stand by quietly and wait for due process of law. These are only two of the more common police techniques that aid directly in creating the moral dissolution so dear to the hearts of those who would set up a police controlled and fear dominated form of government. These techniques are the mark of the lazy and ignorant as well as the despotic minded.

In order to counteract these factors the police administrator must set up a system of education within his department that will indoctrinate thoroughly the individual police officer in the civil and criminal rights of suspects and accused. The acknowledgment and enforcement of these rights should be a matter of paramount importance to all supervising officers as well as to the titular head.

Many will say that this close adherence to the rules will hamper seriously the work of the police organizations. The obvious answer to this complaint is that such close adherence has never been tried by all police departments. It has been given lip service only; never has it been truly practiced.

Our Federal agencies are more prone to adhere to the rules of proper procedure and constitutional law than are the state and local establishments, and the respect that is accorded to these Federal agencies as well as their court records are sufficient proof that close adherence to the rules will work. Though the occasional lapses in protecting the rights of the people often have been corrected by court action, too often the correction has been detrimental not only to the morale of the police agency involved but has created a greatly lessened respect on the part of the public whom they serve.

It has long been known that persecution of a cause will increase its growth while laughter has killed many worthy ideas. The expansion of Christianity is an outstanding example of an idea whose growth was vigorously cultivated by the persecution of the Roman emperors. All police organizations should be extremely careful that they are not lured into a trap where the charge of persecution can be leveled at them by groups whose only idea is to obtain persecutory publicity. These groups flourish on a diet of persecution and because of persecution draw to their banners many who otherwise would look only with disdain upon their cause. Again this is only one phase of the Trojan Horse method of obtaining control of the police establishment.

Charges of persecution can be avoided by impartial dealing with all persons and groups. Impartial attitudes may be obtained only by knowing the rights of all parties involved. A few of the many situations in which charges of persecution frequently are made are: Labor difficulties, racial troubles, political parties, and religious groups. These are the most common and fertile fields of endeavor for those who seek to control police systems and, as a natural consequence, the form of government and way of living.

In addition to this study of civil and criminal rights of the citizen, a thorough study of the article "Ethics in Police Service" [1] is strongly recommended. This code is outstanding in its simplicity. Yet it will apply many years in the future even as it might have been applied for many years past. The knowledge of the citizen's fundamental rights, administered in the light of this code should go far in preventing the police establishment of our country becoming a victim of those who seek control of our government by violent strategy.

Certainly this is a danger that is to be faced. The American police systems can become a victim of the Trojan Horse just as did the European systems in the recent war unless the twin steps of self preservation are taken: Education and self-discipline.

[1] Don L. Kooken, *Jr. of Crim. Law and Criminol.*, 38(1):61-74, and (2):172-186 (1947).

56 · Progress in Police Administration

by O. W. WILSON

Formerly a chief of police of Wichita, Kans., and now professor of police administration of the School of Criminology in the University of California at Los Angeles, O. W. Wilson surveys in this article the changes that have occurred in the American police system during the past hundred years as a result of the appearance of new needs. He then assesses the progress made to date and predicts the modifications that are likely to occur in the future. [From *Journal of Criminal Law and Criminology*, Vol. 42, July-Aug. 1951, pp. 141-154. Reprinted by permission.]

A COMPLETELY OBJECTIVE appraisal of progress in police administration in the U.S. during the past 100 years is not possible. Changes in police administration do not represent progress except as they have increased police effectiveness in the accomplishment of their purpose. Since this country is a democracy, "effectiveness in the accomplishment of the police purpose" means more than the repression of criminal activity and the apprehension and conviction of criminals. The American police purpose may be defined as the protection of life, liberty, and property, and the assurance of a peaceful, convenient and pleasant life for all persons in accordance with law by preventive means.

Failures in the accomplishment of the police purpose invariably make some law-abiding person's life less satisfactory. Progress, therefore, may be measured in part by public satisfaction with police service. But public opinion is fickle; it is sometimes quickly changed by relatively unimportant incidents. A more objective and constant measure of the value of changes in police administration is needed. Crime and accident rates and the proportion of crimes cleared by arrest and of stolen property recovered give some evidence of accomplishment by individual police forces, but incomplete statistics and lack of uniformity in their compilation make impossible an accurate appraisal of police progress during the past hundred years. Analysis of the most reliable police records seems to indicate an increase in the crime rate in the last 50 years, a conclusion that appears to be substantiated by penal statistics.

Even though crime and accident statistics had been uniformly and accurately compiled, the apparent police success or failure reflected in them would not be an accurate measure of police progress. This is so because the inventions and social changes of the past decades have imposed many new tasks on the police, have added to the complexity of their old problems, and appear in some instances to have promoted criminal behavior. Police administration today is one of the most difficult tasks confronting government at all levels. The accomplishment of the police purpose 100 years ago was simple as compared to the task now confronting the police.

THE MODERN POLICE TASK

Police progress must be appraised in the setting of modern police problems. A brief review of the changes that have complicated the police task will make this apparent.

During the past hundred years, the population of this country has grown rapidly and has become more and more concentrated in urban areas. Population density apparently promotes criminal behavior. This, together with the rapid growth and urbanization of the population, has made more difficult the assurance of a peaceful, convenient, and pleasant life. In consequence the police have had forced upon them many new tasks designed to accomplish their purpose.

Improvements in transportation (especially the automobile and a nation-wide network of good roads) have provided the population with a mobility that has complicated the repression and successful investigation of crime. These improvements have also fostered a migrant class which lacks the community roots that provide a desirable control for those who lead more settled lives. Automobiles have otherwise added to the police burdens: they have stimulated and facilitated the commission of certain types of crime, and the regulation of their movement and parking is a task, unknown 100 years ago, that today occupies as much as 25 percent of police effort in some communities.

Improvements in communications are also leaving their mark on modern society; whether for good or bad is not agreed by all. The radio, television, and a glut of comic books, all devoting a disproportionate share of their attention to crime, must affect their audience; perhaps only future events will prove whether their influence promotes or retards the accomplishment of the police purpose. Modern communications are used in both organized and unorganized crimes; police efforts towards their repression are made correspondingly difficult.

Improvements in transportation and communication facilities have likewise affected the rural police problem. These devices have, in a sense, moved some of the crime-inducing influences of the city to the farm. In consequence, the lag of rural crime behind urban crime has been shortened; just as urban crime has increased, so has rural crime, but at a faster rate.

The improved lot of those in the lower income brackets has enabled the purchase of automobiles, radios, television sets, comic books, and liquor, and has provided an increased leisure time in which to enjoy these commodities. The social-welfare concept and the application of early delinquency-prevention theories have provided compulsory education beyond the mental capacity of some as well as group recreation activities and other government-provided facilities not in existence 100 years ago. It is not intended to imply that these conditions and services result in more harm than good. It is clearly apparent, however, that many of them have increased the burdens of the police.

Modern concepts of police responsibility have also imposed some new tasks on the police and have increased the proportion of police effort directed at others. Police administrators are devoting increasing attention to the problem of the juvenile delinquent; special divisions charged with the control of juvenile crime and some form of treatment of the problem child, while unknown fifty years ago, are commonplace in police departments today. A recognition by both the police and the public of the relationship between vice and organized crime with its concomitant corruption and acts of terrorism has resulted in an increasing proportion of police effort directed at their repression. A recognition of the need for public support has also resulted in the direction of police effort into new channels: informing the public, organizing the community, and improving their public relations are tasks that are recognized today by progressive police administrators as essential to the effective accomplishment of their purpose.

In the setting of their modern tasks, are the police today accomplishing their purpose of protecting life, liberty, and property and assuring a peaceful, convenient, and pleasant life to all law-abiding persons as effectively as they did 100 years ago? In other words, are the police holding their own? An affirmative answer would be proof of police progress. A negative answer, however, does not prove lack of progress; the police may have progressed in effectiveness but not at the rate of their added burdens.

The changed conditions mentioned above, and some others, have resulted in changes in police organization, procedure, and philosophy of service. These changes, in most instances, represent progress in the sense that had they not been made the quality of police service would be greatly inferior today. In some instances, however, an "improved" technique designed to facilitate the accomplishment of a specific purpose has retarded the achievement of other objectives made possible by the "old" technique. "Progress," therefore, has not invariably been an unmixed blessing.

THE POLICE SYSTEM

The police system in this country 100 years ago was not simple; nor was it completely adequate to meet the needs of the time. The multiplicity of local police agencies with overlapping jurisdictions and duplications of responsibility was a system poorly adapted to deal with local crime. It was even more ineffective in coping with crime whose ramifications extended beyond the local jurisdiction. Its ineffectiveness was aggravated by the wide expanse of territory and the independence of the several states.

As police problems increased in number and complexity with changing social conditions and as the nature, volume, and severity of crimes fluctuated from time to time, efforts to increase the effectiveness of the police in dealing with them included attempts to improve the police system. These efforts were principally directed at providing new police agencies to meet specific needs. Little attention was given to the elimination of a system that had proved unsatisfactory, to removing from an agency a law enforcement responsibility that it was discharging indifferently well or not at all, or to consolidating any of the existing agencies among themselves or into a newly created agency. The system has consequently grown more complex; overlapping jurisdictions and duplication of responsibilities have been increased instead of diminished. These results are apparent at all levels of government: national, state, and local.

National.   Five of the nine Federal police agencies were born during the past 100 years. Although of the nine, five are in one department (Treasury), they remain unconsolidated, and their efforts are poorly coordinated.

The increase in the number of Federal police agencies is only one manifestation of the increased activity in law enforcement at the national level. Federal laws have been enacted that have substantially increased the scope of Federal law enforcement. These laws of necessity have been restricted to matters over which the Federal government was granted authority by the Constitution: the power to impose taxes; to regulate interstate and foreign commerce; to make laws on naturalization and bankruptcy; to coin money; to establish a postal system; to exercise exclusive jurisdiction over areas and places owned by the U. S. government; and to suppress counterfeiting, piracies, maritime offenses, and treason.

Many of the Federal laws, and especially those enacted during the past two decades, have been directed at offenses that have interstate ramifications. In this way the Federal police agencies (notably the FBI) have been able to assist local authorities in dealing with their crime problems. The Federal agencies have also provided law enforcement assistance to local police in crimes not having interstate ramifications but involving violations of other Federal laws. This is especially true of the Narcotics Bureau, Alcohol Tax Unit, U. S. S. S., Immigration Service, and Postal Inspectors. Federal police agencies (notably the FBI) have provided a variety of other services to state and local enforcement agencies: crime statistics, identification and crime laboratory services, and assistance in training.

No serious effort has been made to nationalize U. S. police service or to extend the authority of Federal law or its enforcement agencies beyond the restrictions imposed by the U. S. Constitution. Neither does it seem likely that such effort will be made in the future. The existence of highly centralized police systems in the principal enemy totalitarian countries in the past decade serves as a warning to those who would exchange American freedom for increased police effectiveness.

State. The states have attempted to patch up weaknesses in their system of local police by creating new agencies to meet special needs. The needs have evolved from changed social conditions, from failure in law enforcement on the part of existing agencies, and from the desire to provide certain central services to assist local agencies with police problems. All of the state agencies concerned with crime and safety have developed in the past 100 years, except the Texas Rangers which was created in 1835.

The need for an enforcement arm of the state first became apparent when some local police agencies demonstrated indifference in the enforcement of vice laws. Labor disturbances created a similar need. Without some form of police under their control, governors charged with the enforcement of the laws of their states had no instrument of enforcement except the state militia. For example, the Governor of Indiana found it necessary to call out the militia to enforce a statute prohibiting race track gambling. The use of the militia in dealing with labor disturbances was at one time quite common in many states.

The failure of the county sheriff to provide an effective patrol in rural areas added to the need for a state police. The advent of the automobile and the phenomenal growth of the highway system created a need for a police agency to enforce regulations governing their use, principally in the interest of safety. There is no state today that does not have a uniformed police engaged in some form of patrol. Approximately a quarter of them, however, restrict the authority of their police to the enforcement of laws regulating the operation of motor vehicles and the use of highways. The state police agencies generally restrict their operations to unincorporated areas as a matter of policy although some such restrictions are imposed on them by statute in some states.

The provision of central services to local police has developed principally during the past 50 years. A system of criminal identification by fingerprints, adopted by the American police shortly after the turn of the century, made apparent the need for a central clearing house; many states created identification bureaus to meet this need. Some bureaus also served as clearing houses of information regarding crime as well as criminals and had the responsibility of compiling state-wide crime statistics. In more recent years an increasing number of states are providing crime laboratory services to local police. Many states that have not given general law-enforcement authority to their state police have investigators to assist local police in the investigation of more serious crimes (usually only on request). The investigators are assigned to bureaus created for this special purpose in some states; in others they have been assigned to existing identification or other bureaus. Many states today also provide some form of training for the local police.

The states have been reluctant to deprive existing agencies of their law-enforcement duties even when new agencies are created to perform them. They have also failed to provide effective machinery to discover and deal with law enforcement agencies that are derelict in their duty. A system has not yet been developed to assure suitable standards of local police performance by means of a reward for acceptable accomplishment or penalty for failure, implemented by periodic inspections. The system of grants to local police authorities conditioned on the maintenance of acceptable standards that has apparently worked effectively in Great Britain for nearly 100 years has not been tried in this country.

A noteworthy but futile effort was made by many states to control local police forces through state appointed administrators. During the last half of the last century most large cities were thus placed under state control. Inevitably conflict between the state and local authorities led to the virtual abandonment of the plan. Today such control is exercised in only four cities of more than 250,000 population and less than a dozen smaller sized cities; six of these have populations of less than 25,000; only one has a population of more than 100,000.

Many states have strengthened their offensive against criminals who take advantage of the poor interstate coordination of law enforcement efforts by legislation and inter-state compacts enabling reciprocal action. Noteworthy advantages thus gained include fresh pursuit across state lines, simplification of extradition of criminals and rendition of witnesses, and the supervision of out-of-state parolees and probationers.

Local. Urban law enforcement has been recognized in this country as a responsibility of local communities. More than 90 percent of them have populations under 50,000. Although some state police forces are authorized to serve incorporated areas on a contract basis, few towns have availed themselves of this opportunity. Practically all incorporated communities, and some unincorporated areas as well, have their own police forces. Park police and special district police that operate independently of the regular force have been created in some cities.

Although there have been isolated instances of groups of communities banding together informally to provide some central services to all, this has consisted principally of a large city making its identification, records, laboratory, communications, training, and some other facilities available to its satellites. Consolidation of police forces in metropolitan areas and in other adjoining communities has not been undertaken. In consequence, the principal responsibility for urban law enforcement rests on completely independent forces, all but a few hundred of which are of such small size as to make efficient operation impossible.

The characteristics of the small police forces charged with this responsibility account for much of the inefficiency of the American police. Their small size makes it impractical to provide suitable training, equipment, and technical services for their members. Police salaries are nearly always lower than those in the larger forces. In consequence, the small town police officer is usually not well qualified for police service in spite of the fact that the performance of police tasks in a small community is more difficult than in a large city where the individual officer enjoys the counsel of ever-present supervisors and the ever-ready assistance of specialists and a large and well equipped force.

Rural law enforcement presents an equally disturbing picture. State police forces are inadequate in strength to provide the desired level of service; with some notable exceptions the sheriff has failed to provide satisfactory police service for rural areas. Some few exceptional counties have created county police forces, usually but not always under the direction of the sheriff. To further complicate the situation, county prosecutors frequently have a staff of investigators to participate with other police agencies in the investigation of serious crimes.

TECHNIQUES

The American police have been quick to adapt to their needs many of the inventions and developments in other fields. They have developed techniques for detecting deception through the use of drugs and mechanical devices that record physiological reactions to questions. They adopted the motor vehicle, radio, telegraph, telephone, teletype, sound and visual recording devices, mechanical tabulating and other modern office equipment, and an almost unlimited array of laboratory instruments. The American police have the well-earned reputation of being "gadget minded."

The mechanization of patrol during the past three decades has perhaps been the most revolutionary change in police operations. The relatively low cost of radio-equipped automobiles as compared to rising police salaries, and the greatly increased effectiveness of the officer when motorized, have made this method of patrol economically sound. A failure to recognize that the motorized officer is fundamentally a foot patrolman who has been supplied with an automobile to enable him to move speedily and without fatigue from the location of one task to another, and that he must spend a substantial part of his time on foot if he is to perform a satisfactory patrol service, has impaired the quality of motor patrol in some communities and created a demand for the return of the foot patrolman. In recent years an increasing number of police administrators have recognized the true character of motorized patrol and its important economy. Present trends are toward more complete mechanization.

During the past two decades the American police have become increasingly conscious of the value of scientific aids in crime investigation. Crime laboratories, many of them well equipped and staffed, have been created in police agencies at Federal, state, and local levels. While some crime laboratory staffs are not granted the powers of peace officers, no serious objection has been raised to the testimony of police laboratory experts on their examination of physical evidence. Police laboratory operations have been improved in some communities by procedures that assure the prompt search for physical evidence by well trained officers who are on duty on each shift in suitably equipped automobiles. The trend in all but the small departments is toward the provision of laboratory equipment and staff adequate to assure an effective search for physical evidence and to enable screening from it, for reference to a better equipped laboratory, evidence whose examination involves techniques beyond the local facilities.

In the late 1920's, the International Association of Chiefs of Police developed a system of uniform crime reporting on which is based a national system of crime statistics maintained by the Federal Bureau of Investigation. The absence of suitable crime statistics before this time had made analysis of the crime situation and the discovery of crime trends practically impossible. The situation was aggravated by the lack of uniformity of laws in the several states, the classification and compilation of crimes in a variety of ways by thousands of independent police forces, and the absence of a central clearing house for the assembly and analysis of such statistics. The present system of national crime statistics is based on voluntary monthly reports submitted by local police agencies to the FBI. The compilations are no more accurate than the submitted reports, and there is evidence that some police departments fail to submit complete reports. There is no law requiring the submission of the crime data, no administrative machinery with the power to audit police records to assure accuracy of reporting, and no penalty that may be assessed for failure.

Records in individual police forces have been expanded and improved; their completeness has substantially increased both the operational and administrative use that is now made of them. Indexes maintained in progressive departments facilitate maximum use in operations; the follow-up made possible through records has improved administrative control over police operations; and the analysis of the data compiled has improved the quality of police planning.

The advent of the automobile imposed tremendous traffic-control tasks on the police that have been substantially lessened in recent years by mechanical control devices and by the elimination of points of traffic friction by improved highway design. With continuing success the police are increasing the use of schoolboy patrols to assist in traffic control in the vicinity of schools. In spite of the continued high accident rate, the police are probably applying as progressive principles in traffic control as in any other field of police responsibility.

Police departments have accepted some responsibility in assuring suitable treatment for problem children, and some actively participate in the treatment with the voluntary consent of the child and its parents. Many departments provide recreational and character building activities for children under the guise of preventing delinquency; the activity is frequently not directed at the most delinquent segments of the youth population and consequently it usually has a greater public relations than crime prevention value.

ORGANIZATION

The control of police forces by boards, popular during the last century, has been discontinued in favor of a single head in all but a few forces. The appointment of a layman as the head of the force, tried in many departments, has given way almost completely to the appointment of professional policemen to this post. The rapid extension of the city manager form of government has simplified police control in most instances and has consequently improved the quality of police service in most cities where it has been adopted.

The organization of individual police forces has been subjected to marked changes in the past 100 years. The modern police organization structure, when compared to its predecessor, reflects somewhat the complexity of the police task today compared to the simplicity of police work in the past. The many mechanical and electrical devices used by the police and the varied tasks imposed on them by their modern problems have created the need for specialists in police service. Modern forces must have criminalists for their laboratories; communications and traffic engineers; mechanics, statisticians, and persons trained in social and psychiatric work.

In addition to the staff specialists, the line officer has also specialized; some are engaged exclusively in traffic or vice control, others in crime investigation or juvenile crime control. The specialists are inclined to be empire builders; they demand (and usually receive) specialized organization units whose members devote their attention exclusively to the specialized tasks. In consequence, the simple police organization, in which nearly all members were assigned to patrol a beat with only a few assigned to crime investigations and headquarters duties, has developed into a complex structure composed of many specialized units at both operating and service levels. The complex modern police organization structure is marked by organic units dependent from the chief in a number far beyond his span of control.

Recent years have brought organization reforms strongly influenced in many departments by the experience of their members in military service. The wide span of control has been diminished by grouping related tasks in a smaller number of organic units. The concept of line and staff has been adopted in many departments and increasing attention is being given to staff planning and control by inspection.

While specialization, especially at the staff level, is undoubtedly needed to deal successfully with the complex modern police problems, the extent of specialization at the level of execution raises serious question as to whether it has not been carried to the point where the effective accomplishment of the primary police purpose has been jeopardized. The proportion of police force devoted to preventive patrol has sunk to a low ebb, and in many departments overlapping specialized patrols are provided by traffic officers, detectives, and juvenile division members. According to some specialists, the incompetence of beat patrolmen in the field of special interest makes specialization essential. As the competence of beat officers is improved by superior methods of selection and training, the need for specialization is likely to diminish.

PERSONNEL

Modern techniques of personnel administration have been adopted by many progressive police administrators while others have had these procedures imposed upon them through independent civil service boards. Improved recruitment and selection methods and standards have raised the quality of police personnel during the past two decades. Noteworthy are the higher intelligence and educational requirements, the more thorough character investigations, and the appraisal of the personality of candidates by psychologists and psychiatrists to eliminate those not emotionally qualified for service. Pre-employment residence requirements for police candidates have been substantially relaxed in recent years. The practice of nation-wide competitive examinations to fill the position of police chief has become commonplace. In contrast, the other supervisory and command positions in police departments are invariably filled by promotion from within the force. Determined efforts to base promotions on merit have resulted in over-emphasis of readily scored objective information tests with diminished attention to the less easily measured qualities of leadership.

All departments large enough to support such a program provide recruit training and some a continuation training also. Many take advantage of training facilities provided by state police and boards of education, the FBI, and such University-sponsored programs as the Northwestern University Traffic Institute, the Delinquency Control Institute of the University of Southern California, and the Louisville University Southern Police Institute. Pre-employment training is provided in a score of universities and colleges. American police service seems to be on the threshold of professionalization.

The welfare of the police has improved beyond the average. While there is lack of uniformity of salaries among the independent forces, pay has increased on the average more rapidly than for workers in private enterprises. The work week has been shortened; the present trend is toward forty hours of work each week. During the past decade many departments have adopted the practice of paying overtime in cash or by granting time off to compensate. Most departments now have generous pensions, some supported by the state in such a manner that service on more than one department may be accumulated to fulfill pension service requirements. Agreements between states to enable police service in one state to be counted toward a police pension in another have not been made.

Dissatisfaction of the police with pay made inadequate by post-war inflation caused the American Federation of Labor in 1919 to lift a 20-year ban on the admission of police unions into the Federation. Police strikes occurred in Cincinnati (1918) and Boston (1919). The right of the police to affiliate with labor unions was challenged and nearly all departments now have regulations that forbid this practice. Police professional organizations exist at national, state, and regional levels. Local forces frequently maintain social and benefit organizations. In some communities these associations have organized public opinion in support of legal enactments designed to raise salaries, shorten the work week, improve pension provisions, assure promotion on the basis of merit and service, and protect the police from unmerited disciplinary action. Grievance committees created in many police departments have demonstrated their value to the administrator in discovering and correcting morale-destroying influences.

The desire to protect the police from pernicious influences has resulted in the sharp curtailment of the power of the American police chief to manage his personnel. Such formidable legal safeguards have been thrown around the rights of the policeman, and even of the police candidate, that the chief of police in many communities has little voice in the selection of men for appointment and promotion, and in their discipline. The protection thus afforded has not invariably improved personnel administration. Depriving the responsible head of a force of essential authority over its members and vesting this power in independent agencies that lack both the responsibility for police operations and an appreciation of the unique police personnel requirements has resulted, in some communities, in the appointment and retention of persons unqualified for police service.

During the past 50 years the use of policewomen and of both male and female civilian employees has substantially increased. Policewomen have demonstrated their value in the service. The need for technical and clerical skills not likely to be found in policemen, police salaries increasing beyond the level of pay for office workers in private enterprise, and the simplification of some personnel management problems have stimulated the employment of civilians.

The increased cost of police manpower has stimulated attention to economies made possible by its wise direction. Efforts have been made to measure the need for police service as a guide in its deployment. The distribution of the force equally among three platoons, in order to simplify a periodic rotation of the men among these shifts, is gradually being eliminated in favor of a distribution of the force in proportion to the need for service.

THE FUTURE

Weaknesses in police administration, aggravated by the increased complexity of police tasks, have become more readily discernible in recent years, and some trends toward their correction are evident. On these may be based some conjectural future developments.

The future will probably bring substantial consolidation of Federal law enforcement agencies. Present agencies, deprived of general law enforcement responsibilities, will then be restricted to policing Federal employees and property. Federal law enforcement may become more intensive but it is not likely to expand. Control of local enforcement agencies by the Federal government does not seem likely.

Crime control will continue to be considered a responsibility of local government, but it is possible that the need for increased effectiveness and economy will force the consolidation of small local forces on a regional basis. The county may undertake a more active role, especially those under county-manager control; county forces, comparable to the English county constabulary, may be expected to emerge to police rural areas and some urban areas on a contract basis as well.

The states, too, are likely to participate more actively and effectively in local crime control than they have in the past; it is not inconceivable that some may provide incentive to local law enforcement in the form of grants to jurisdictions that maintain acceptable standards of police performance. While the states may provide administrative machinery to assure suitable performance standards, it seems unlikely that they will undertake an operational or even an administrative control over local forces.

The future will probably restore to the police chief some measure of his lost control over police personnel. Greater attention will be given to the provision of staff services in police departments, but the present trend toward extreme specialization at the level of execution will probably be reversed. Police activity in the prevention of delinquency and the assurance of suitable treatment for problem children will undoubtedly increase.

In conclusion, a fair appraisal of the American police must recognize that none of their major problems has yet been solved. The police, with the other agencies concerned with the administration of criminal justice, continue to muddle along repeating the mistakes of the past with little consideration to the fundamentals of their task. The need for research to discover the underlying factors in crime and other police problems is becoming increasingly apparent. Real progress cannot be expected until professional training becomes a prerequisite for service in police departments throughout the country. The next 50 years may see the American police emerge as a true profession.

CHAPTER SIXTEEN

Legal Procedure and the Courts

---

57 · Errors of Justice

by OTTO POLLAK

Error in the administration of justice, particularly in a case involving a capital offense, is obviously a most serious matter. Cognizant of this, many objective students of crime and law have been arguing against the death penalty. On the other hand, there are scholars in jurisprudence and the social sciences who believe that the existing safeguards are sufficient to prevent errors of justice in serious cases of crime. Otto Pollak, formerly a practicing lawyer and now a professor of sociology at the University of Pennsylvania, has done research in the field of criminology and other social problems. He shows that errors do occur at not infrequent intervals and suggests that this fact be given recognition by our legal system and that the proper conclusions be drawn—that is, that capital punishment should be abolished. [From *The Annals*, Vol. 289, Nov. 1952, pp. 115-123. Reprinted by permission. Abridged. Some footnotes omitted.]

To RECOGNIZE the fallibility of human judgment and still to act, but act wisely in the light of such fallibility, is one of the great challenges of mankind. For this reason the fact of irrevocability has always been among the arguments for the abolition of the death penalty. It was brought up in the French National Assembly of 1791. In 1948 it was brought up in the debate on the Criminal Justice Bill in the British House of Commons. It was brought up on all conceivable occasions in the time span between these two cornerstones of legislative consideration of the abolition of capital punishment. In all probability it will continue to be brought up until capital punishment has disappeared from the practice of civilized society.

The strength of this argument is revealed by the counterarguments which it has evoked. Apparently very few opponents of the abolition of capital punishment have had the courage to say: Yes, errors of judgment have led to the execution of innocent persons and may do so in the future, but this is a necessary item of social cost. Significantly enough, many efforts to meet the argument have followed other lines. They have resorted to avoidance or to the denial of the obvious. Thus they have shown reactions typically associated with fear, and it is this fear which suggests that the argument is considered as serious even by those who try to deny its validity.

RISK OF ERRONEOUS EXECUTION MINIMIZED

The records show that French, English, Belgian, German, and American lawyers have repeatedly made statements to the effect that because of the safeguards of the jury system, because of the protection furnished by the pardoning power, or because of the possibility to resort to the alternative punishment of lifetime imprisonment, the risk of executing an innocent person did not exist or almost did not exist. A district attorney in Worcester County, Massachusetts is reported to have said in the 1920's: "Innocent men are never convicted. Don't worry about it, it never happens in the world. It is a physical impossibility." Sir John Anderson, for ten years permanent Head of the Home Office, said in the British House of Commons on April 14, 1948:

It is fair to say, and there was a wealth of testimony to that effect in the evidence before the Select Committee, that the risk, under the conditions as they exist in this country, of the capital penalty being executed on any one who was not in fact guilty of the crime of which he had been convicted is so small, indeed so infinitesimal, that that consideration can be dismissed.

Statements of similar nature have been made not only by practicing lawyers in the heat of public pronouncement, but also by professors of criminal law. Even a man of the international reputation of Wilhelm Kahl asked, on the occasion of a lawyers' convention, where those cases of executing innocent persons had occurred which justified stressing the argument of human fallibility in discussing the pros and cons of capital punishment. Interestingly enough, in 1910 the *American Journal of Sociology* contained an article in which the following statement can be found:

It is said that the death penalty is irrevocable and thus an innocent man might suffer it. It is well known to prison officials and the police that such instances are mostly mythical and seldom, if at all, can be proved beyond a doubt.[1]

If such denials can be made by practitioners and scholars alike, the argument apparently cannot be countered with Bentham's question: "Is there, or could there be devised, any system of penal procedure which could insure the judge from being misled by false evidence or the fallibility of his own judgment?" The obvious must be corroborated by facts, and such attempts have been undertaken repeatedly and in various countries.

REPORTS OF MISCARRIAGES OF JUSTICE

Actually, by the time Kahl and McDonald made the statements quoted above, they could have found books devoted to reports of miscarriages of justice. The number of these books is large enough to make their disregard or lack of knowledge by these scholars an interesting psychological phenomenon. Certainly McDonald might have been expected to be acquainted with the writings of Charles Phillips and Alfred H. Dymond. Equally, Kahl might have been expected to be acquainted with the works of Mühlfeld, Katscher, Lailler and Vonoven, and Péan.

Since McDonald's and Kahl's statements were made, there have appeared Sello's careful analysis of 153 cases, and Borchard's classic *Convicting the Innocent* which carries the identification of erroneous verdicts in the United States into the first three decades of the twentieth century. To be sure, these works show some overlapping in their reports and show various degrees of reliability. However, they contain a sufficient number of solidly documented reports on actual executions of innocent persons to make the questioning of the real risk in this respect a hardly tenable position. They contain, further, a large number of cases which show to what degree life imprisonment, because of the time element involved and because of the continued interest in the victim

[1] Arthur McDonald, "Death Penalty and Homicide," *American Journal of Sociology*, Vol. 16, pp. 91-92.

which such life terms safeguard, permits the discovery of errors in convicting a person of a capital crime. They show, finally, that the sources of errors in judgment are frequently the same whether the error has led to an actual execution or to a life sentence. Thus they dispel the notion that errors may have occurred in the past but do not occur in the present, and also the notion that errors might occur in the cases of sentencing a person to a life term but do not occur in the cases of actual execution.

Meaningful examples which might illustrate all this can, of course, be taken only from a time span in which the principles of procedure and the rules of evidence were sufficiently close to the present to make the risk which these cases demonstrate a still plausible one. Because of this consideration, the illustrations given below do not go beyond the period of the French Revolution. In order to show the persistence of the same sources of error over the time span, the procedure followed in this paper will be to give for each source of major error an example from the late eighteenth or early nineteenth century on the one hand, and one from or close to the twentieth century on the other.

CIRCUMSTANTIAL EVIDENCE

As might be expected, circumstantial evidence is a frequent source of error in judgment. This category might be illustrated by the two following cases.

Case 1

On January 31, 1811, the barns of the mayor of a French village, Noyelles, were destroyed by a fire which had all the appearances of arson. Public opinion directed suspicion immediately at Maximilien Flament, who was a relative of the mayor. He was known to have lived in enmity with the latter, and some witnesses reported that three days before the fire Flament had voiced threats against him. Others reported that at the time of the fire the wind had blown in a direction such as to drive away the flames from Flament's house, which was situated close to the barns which were consumed. Flament increased suspicion against himself by repeatedly declaring himself innocent before a direct accusation had been made. Finally, the detectives discovered in the hedge which separated Flament's property from that of the mayor's a hole big enough to permit the arsonist to get through; and close by were footprints which fitted Flament.

On the basis of this circumstantial evidence Flament was arrested. He attempted to establish an alibi by only one witness, who first supported him but later showed uncertainty in his depositions. During the trial thirty-one witnesses testified against Flament; only the one produced by him in his defense supported him, and that one only weakly. On that basis he was found guilty and sentenced to die. Clemency was denied to him by the

Emperor, and he was executed. Six years later his innocence became manifest in the following manner.

On October 20, 1817, a certain Felix Moreau was executed for murder in the same place. Immediately before the dropping of the knife Moreau, who was attended by the same priest who had stood by Flament at his last hour, confessed having committed the arson for which Flament had been executed, and asked for forgiveness. In recognition of the error in judgment which had sent his father to the guillotine, the National Assembly of 1850 granted Flament's son a pension.[2]

Case 2

On the morning of October 17, 1901, a railroad engineer, H. E. Wesson, was found dead in the shop yard of the Florida Southern Railway at Tilgham's Mill in Palatka, Florida. He had been shot at close range in the back of his head and his pockets had been turned inside out. Close by a .38 caliber pistol was found from which one shell had been fired. Under the pressure of public indignation the authorities right away rounded up a number of suspects and put them into jail. Among them was a yard night watchman, Lucius Crawford. Apparently on the afternoon after the arrest, the jailer observed a colored man approach a crack in the fence of the jail yard and call for Lucius Crawford who happened to be in the yard at that time. The jailer reported that the colored man was J. B. Brown and that he had heard him say to Crawford, "Keep your mouth shut and say nothing."

Brown was arrested and a chain of circumstantial evidence began to form against him. First of all it was reported that two months earlier Brown had had a fight with the murdered man and had threatened to kill him. On October 16, the day before the murder, Brown was reported by one witness as having been without money and having tried to borrow a quarter from him. In answer to the witness's refusal of his request, Brown was reported to have said "Never mind, I'll catch 209 away from here tonight, that is the train going south to meet 208." Two hundred and eight was the train on which the murdered man had worked as an engineer. On the morning after the murder, Brown had been observed to have money when he joined in a card game with a number of men, among whom there was one by the name of Johnson. Brown was reported to have been excited when he arrived for the game and to have taken Johnson aside for a whispered conversation.

After these items of apparent evidence had been collected against Brown, the other suspects were released. The clouds over Brown thickened further when two cell mates of his reported to the authorities that Brown had confessed to them that he had, together with Johnson, committed the murder for purposes of robbing Wesson of his money.[3]

[2] Condensed from Erich Sello, *Die Irrtümer der Strafjustiz und Ihre Ursachen*, Berlin, 1911, pp. 6–7.
[3] Condensed from Edwin M. Borchard, *Convicting the Innocent*, New Haven, 1932, pp. 33–39.

On the basis of all that, Brown and Johnson were indicted for murder in the first degree and Brown was brought up for a separate trial in which he was convicted and sentenced to be hanged. His appeal for clemency having been denied, he was finally led to the gallows. However, at the last minute, the rope having been put around his neck, the executioner was interrupted because of an almost unbelievable event. When the death warrant was read in the course of the execution procedure it was found that by mistake it ordered the execution, not of Brown, but of—the foreman of the jury which had found Brown guilty. Brown was returned to jail, and under the impact of this occurrence his capital sentence was commuted to life imprisonment. The prosecution seemed to have lost the taste for continuing against Johnson, for the case against the latter was nol-prossed.

More than ten years later, Johnson confessed on his deathbed that he alone had committed the murder and that Brown had not been connected with the crime at all. On October 1, 1913, Brown, on the basis of Johnson's confession, was granted a full pardon, and in 1929 the Florida legislature granted him "For faithful service . . . during the period of his wrongful imprisonment the sum of $2,492 to be paid in monthly installments of $25."

FALSE IDENTIFICATION

Another possible source of errors in judgment of criminal cases is false identification of the accused by witnesses. This phenomenon of faulty perception is well known to lawyers, and on occasional instances also reaches the awareness of the public because of the weight of tragedy with which its consequences may strike an innocent person. . . .

* * *

FALSE CONFESSION

It is probably true that nothing alleviates doubt in jurors and judges as much as a confession on the part of the defendant. It is probably even more true that nothing is harder to believe than the possibility that a person accused of a capital crime would wrongly confess to having committed it. Yet this seems to have happened a number of times. . . .

* * *

EXTENT OF RISK OF ERROR

* * *

For an evaluation of the quantity of risk of executing an innocent person, we must turn to the following considerations. As far as the nineteenth century is concerned, a survey of the literature shows that the col lections which have been made of such instances fill books. This, of course, was a period of time in which the number of capital crimes and the number of executions were greater than they are today.

For the twentieth century, no such collection has come to the atten tion of this writer except Borchard's book, which has for its emphasis the problem of indemnification of persons who have been erroneously convicted. This work, therefore, is concerned also with offenses other than capital crime. As the examples presented above show, even this work, with its different focus, contains material showing that the danger of executing innocent persons has not yet completely passed from the American scene. On the other hand, if reports published in the literature are taken as an index of the extent of this problem, executions of inno cent persons for capital crimes in this country must have become very rare indeed during the last few decades.

It is the opinion of this writer, however, that no collection of cases known to have been miscarriages of justice can reveal the true extent of such occurrences.

FACTORS IN CONCEALMENT

The effort of the truly guilty person to escape punishment is in itself a force which may lead to error in judgment by keeping correct informa- tion away from the courts. Furthermore, if crime goes together with strenuous efforts at concealment, so does erroneous judgment in a capital case. If it has led to the execution of an innocent person, the feelings of guilt and regret on the part of those involved in such a judgment cannot but work against the acceptance of the fact of error. Borchard reports that pardons are granted on occasion "without indication or admission of an erroneous conviction probably in order to save the prestige of the prosecuting officials." If such face-saving comes into play where a meas- ure of reparation to the innocent person is still possible, how much stronger must the same factor be in cases when reparation can no longer be made! We are justified, therefore, in assuming that the efforts of the police and of a district attorney's office cannot be relied upon to reveal executions of innocent persons to any extent which might approximate reality.

Even in cases where innocent persons have been sentenced to a life term, it is usually the deathbed confession of the murderer or some effort of an outside person which brings about the elucidation of the facts. However, if an innocent person has been executed, the interest of out- siders will probably be much less active than it will be in cases where

here is still the motivation of saving a person from the continuation of his wrongful punishment.

CRITERIA OF RELIABLE REPORTING

It is now accepted theory in criminal statistics that a crime in order to be reliably reported must have three characteristics: (1) it must be considered serious enough to ensure intensive effort on the part of law enforcement officers to elucidate it; (2) it must ensure the co-operation of the victim, or those interested in the victim, with the police; and (3) it must leave public traces.

If one were to apply these criteria to the question whether executions based on errors in judgment are likely to be reliably reported, it is clear that the answer would be negative on all three counts. Such cases will not arouse law enforcement officers to great effort, because that would mean enthusiasm for professional self-indictment. Obviously, they cannot ensure the co-operation of the victim. Furthermore, the impossibility of reparation to the victim of the error will probably weaken the effort also of those who were interested in him as long as there was hope. Finally, the efforts of the actual killer to remain undetected, together with the fact that the case has been decided and led to the punishment demanded by the law, tends to conceal a miscarriage of justice rather than leave public traces of its occurrence.

Thus it is highly probable that erroneous convictions for capital crimes are greatly underreported. This does not mean, however, that we have to assume any considerable number of occurrences every year. The actual figures, absolutely taken, are probably very small—as are the figures of actual executions at present.

THE ETHICAL ASPECT

However, this does not meet the core of the problem, which is ethical and not utilitarian. Ethics cannot be argued in figures. It shows the strange humor of history that the essence of the ethical position involved has never been better expressed than by Robespierre in the National Assembly of 1791. Participating in the debate on the abolition of capital punishment, he said:

Listen to the voice of justice and of reason! It tells us and tells us that human judgments are never so certain as to permit society to kill a human being judged by other human beings. . . . Why deprive yourselves of any chance to redeem such errors? Why condemn yourselves to helplessness when faced with persecuted innocence?

58 · Society Is Wonderful People

The article below records an actual case of miscarriage of justice in Illinois. Although the reader will derive from it an insight into the tragedy of a person accused of a crime he did not commit, he should bear in mind that this article and the one that follows it are written on a popular rather than a scientific level. [Courtesy of *Time* (Aug. 22, 1949, pp. 14-15). Copyright Time, Inc., 1949.]

JIM MONTGOMERY remembers Nov. 15, 1923 very clearly. He had just quit his steel-hustling job at a Waukegan machine plant and was having a game of 10¢ black ball at the Aggressor Pool Hall with his friend, Finis Moore. But Jim and Finis got to arguing and suddenly they were heaving pool balls at each other.

Jim's wife, Sentoria, heard about it and came rushing down to take him home. But she couldn't keep him there—Jim strolled back to the poolroom for a while, then sauntered over to the Busy Bee for a cup of coffee. That was when the cops came. They hauled Jim to Waukegan jail and started talking. "All right, you black sonofabitch, tell the truth," demanded one. "We know you done it."

"Done what?" asked Jim. "Raped that white woman," the cop replied. That, swears Jim Montgomery, was the first he knew that he was in real trouble. Mamie Snow, a 62-year-old white woman who peddled doughnuts in Waukegan's squalid Negro district, had been found, beaten and moaning, near the Oakwood cemetery. Mamie vowed that she had been raped and the police told Jim that she had named him as her attacker.

One Day True. At first, Mamie was a little confused about identifying Jim. (It was "forgetfulness," explained relatives, a trait which made it necessary several years later to send Mamie to the Elgin State Hospital for the insane, where she died in 1947.) But later she got quite positive about it. At the police station, Montgomery recalls, he was beaten up by the cops and the prosecutor told him, "if you were down in Georgia or Mississippi . . . we would turn you over to the K.K.K. and we are liable to do it up here." The Ku Klux Klan was strong in the Midwest in those days. Jim Montgomery's trial, on a capital charge, lasted only one day. The prosecution offered no convincing medical proof of rape, but the jury convicted him anyway. He was sent to Joliet for life.

In prison, Montgomery tried to make the most of his ride on the slow train to nowhere. He struck up a friendship with a more famous prisoner,

Nathan ("Bebe") Leopold of Chicago's sensational Leopold & Loeb slaying, and from him learned how to read and write. After that he kept pretty much to himself, read a lot and spent his leftover time hoping for justice.

Back home in Waukegan, Sentoria Montgomery did more than hope. She worked part-time as a cook, spent about $7,000 of her own and her brother's money trying to get her husband out of prison. For 24 years she found only frustration; but two years ago she found Luis Kutner, a flashy, wealthy Chicago lawyer.

After Kutner took the case (he likes to take on "charity cases" which intrigue him), he discovered that all important court records were destroyed or missing. But Lawyer Kutner's investigators did obtain a medical report submitted by a Dr. John E. Walter of Waukegan the day after the crime. It showed that Mamie Snow had not been raped. The prosecution, ruthlessly bent on convicting him, had suppressed the report.

The Doctor Explains. Called into federal court last June during a hard-won review of Jim Montgomery's trial, old Dr. Walter testified that he had indeed examined Mamie Snow; he could testify positively that she had not been raped. Why had he kept quiet about this vital fact while Jim Montgomery wasted in prison? ". . . You don't know our prosecutor at that time," testified the doctor lamely. "He wanted his way and if he did not get it, there was trouble . . . and I'm not a fellow who looks for trouble." The state called no witnesses, refuted none of Kutner's evidence.

Last week, Jim Montgomery sat uneasily in federal court while Judge Michael Igoe read his ruling. "James Montgomery," said the judge, "has gone the merry-go-round of Illinois justice . . . His conviction was secured by the use of false testimony, fraud and suppression . . . The court finds that the trial was a sham . . . The issue was not the guilt or innocence of rape—but that of racial subjugation."

A messenger from Joliet handed Jim a $10 bill—the usual parting gift from the prison—and he walked from the courtroom a free man.

Steady Praying. No one could give back the lost years, but Kutner thought the State of Illinois should have the decency to award Jim Montgomery some money for his trouble ("My talking figure is $100,000," said the lawyer).

But big Jim, gulping at freedom, was too happy to worry about that for the moment. "I ain't holding no grudge," he smiled. "I still think society is wonderful people. Man, I'm living for the first time. I prayed steady, seems like, for 26 years. Took the good Lord a long time to get around to me."

59 · It Could Happen to You

by PEGGY KRIEG

This is another popularly written story which brings out perhaps better than a formal account what it means for a person to be wrongfully convicted and imprisoned for a lengthy period. In addition to the obvious carelessness on the part of the law, the story also offers an illustration of how disgraceful the behavior of the police may be at times. [From *U.S. Crime*, Feb. 27, 1952, pp. 66-74. Reprinted by permission.]

NANCY LOUISE BOTTS, of Brazil, Indiana, had been married five months to the day on October 12, 1934. As she bustled around in her kitchenette getting supper for her young husband, she planned the way she'd break the wonderful news the doctor had just given her. First, there'd be the extra special meal, everything William liked. Then very casually—just as if it weren't the one thing they'd both hoped for—she'd make her announcement.

After William arrived, and as she was putting the last dish on the table, she remarked: "By the time our first anniversary rolls around I'll be too busy getting ready for the baby to cook like this— Oh!—"

They both had a good laugh over her "slip of the tongue." And, since they were really too excited to eat, they soon left the table to talk about possible names for the child, deciding where the bassinet should go, and so on.

Around 9 o'clock they were startled by a terrific pounding on the door. When William opened it, the sheriff of Clay county and a deputy from nearby Howard county brushed past him and seized Nancy. Before they knew what was happening, she was charged with issuing forged checks at the Montgomery Ward store in Kokomo.

"But I've never even been there!" she protested. "I've never been in Kokomo and I can prove it—"

The arresting officers didn't give her a chance. They seemed interested only in getting a confession: she was taken to local private detective Guy Bolin's house and questioned for several hours. Then she was turned over to the state police in Indianapolis. When they finished with her, the police matron started in all over again . . . trying to make her admit her guilt.

It wouldn't have been quite so terrifying if William had been allowed to come along. But when she heard that her bail had been set at the impossible sum of $2500, she knew that she'd have to wait out the long weeks before trial in the dirty county jail cell, alone.

On November 23, 1934, a jury of local citizens found Nancy guilty and Judge Joseph Gripe sentenced her to the Indiana Woman's Prison for not less than two years nor more than fourteen years . . . in spite of her protestations of innocence and in the face of evidence that she had been in Brazil, Indiana, at the time the checks were alleged to have been passed in Kokomo.

Two years later the woman who actually passed the forged checks in the Ward store confessed and Nancy Botts was given a full pardon by the governor. She had her freedom but she'd lost her most precious privilege—the chance to be a mother. The records show that she suffered a miscarriage while in prison and, because she was denied proper medical care, she became permanently invalided. In 1939 the State of Indiana took unprecedented action in awarding her $4,000, to be paid in $60 monthly installments, as compensation for injuries to the mind, body, and reputation of this unfortunate young woman.

This is the *only case* in the history of Indiana in which indemnity has been paid to a wrongfully convicted person. Even so, Indiana is doing better than three-fourths of our states which have never made *any* move to reimburse victims of unjust imprisonment.

A search through the records of the Secretaries of State turned up many cases like Nancy Botts'. Some of them were even more appalling—Vance Hardy spent 26 years in a Michigan prison, 10 *of them in solitary*, before his recent pardon—but only a handful of indemnity bills had ever been enacted. Less than a dozen in all the United States, in fact. California, Wisconsin, and North Dakota provide for such relief by general statutes, but these laws are so narrowly interpreted that little has been accomplished by having them. For instance, one California man was turned down (although proved innocent of any crime) because the examining board didn't think his "character" was good enough. Any prisoner who makes a confession is automatically disqualified from receiving compensation even though the confession may have been the result of third-degree methods. (One New York psychiatrist says that the new psychological treatment, in which the mind is gradually broken down, should be called "menticide." In his opinion, anyone can be made to confess to anything if the pressure is great enough.) As early as 1913 legal reformers presented bills to Congress calling for "State Indemnity for Errors of Criminal Justice" and spasmodic attempts have been made since then to secure some sort of uniform legislation. It seems strange that nothing has resulted—*social* justice has made such marked advances during this period. Why, then, has this most flagrant of all publicly-imposed wrongs been by-passed?

There are a number of reasons ranging from highly involved legal polemics about "the accountability of a sovereign state" to the very simple fact that most of the victims are poor people, members of a weak social group whose voice is almost unheard. Up to the present time, our feelings of law and equity have been directed more toward property than toward liberty . . . because the owners of property are powerful and are accorded legislative recognition.

One of the most important reasons why there has been little action on this problem is the commonly held belief that the victims are few in number. While it *is* impossible to state the exact number of innocent men and women in our prisons, we do have estimates (from responsible individuals who have made a study of the situation) to guide us in our thinking:

Attorney Luis Kutner of Chicago, a practicing corporation and criminal lawyer and Yale visiting professor, has personally freed 1,011 *wrongfully convicted men.* He told me that he believes approximately 30 per cent of the men in prison today did not commit the crimes for which they were convicted.

Robert Daru, the New York district attorney whose special investigation freed Bertram Campbell in 1945, says: "Every prison in the country contains some innocent men. Persons who believe that innocent men are never convicted are the cause of such injustice." He charges that jurors who hold such views are easily swayed in their verdicts by judges and lawyers. "Lip-service alone is given to the fine American principle of the presumption of innocence in many of our courtrooms," Mr. Daru, himself a prosecutor, asserts.

The leading authority is undoubtedly Professor Edwin M. Borchard of the Yale Law School. His book, "Convicting the Innocent," based upon his life-long study of this problem, contains a collection of 65 incredible miscarriages of justice selected from hundreds of cases on record. There is the story of Stephen and Jesse Boorn of Manchester, Vermont. They were about to be hanged when the "corpse" turned up to watch! (Compensation for this harrowing experience was denied by the legislature.) J. B. Brown of Palatka, Florida, was sentenced to hang and the rope was placed around his neck, but a technical error on the death warrant resulted in commutation of his sentence to life imprisonment. Twelve years later another man confessed and Brown was released. Because he was by then, "aged, infirm, and destitute," the State of Florida appropriated $2,492, to be paid him in $25 monthly installments.

John A. Johnson of Madison, Wisconsin, was lucky to get off with life after he was convicted of murdering a little girl; the citizens of that good city wanted to lynch him. Eleven years later a neighbor finally got up enough courage to report that the father of the little victim was the real murderer. Investigation proved this to be true but the father was not sentenced because second-degree murder is not punishable after ten years due to the statute of limitations. After Johnson was pardoned, bills to compensate him under the existing Wisconsin Indemnity Law were introduced but failed of enactment because he had contributed to his conviction by confessing! This was another case of a rather weak individual, terrified by the howls of the mob outside the jail and the threats of the police inside, breaking down. When last heard from, Johnson was in ill health and aging rapidly.

One of the most amazing cases is that of Will Purvis. He was indicted for murder and sentenced to be hanged on February 7, 1893. When the trap was sprung, the knot around Purvis' neck slipped and he dropped unharmed. Later, friends rescued him from jail. He voluntarily surrendered to the next governor who promised to commute his sentence to life imprisonment. Two years later the State's star witness said he might have been mistaken about Purvis and he was pardoned. About 20 years later, another man confessed and Purvis was completely vindicated, but the fact remained that he had forfeited four valuable years of his life in hard manual labor and had lived for a quarter of a century in the shadow of guilt. In 1920 Mississippi gave him $5000 for "services rendered."

These are some of the more widely-publicized cases, of course, and one might say . . . "It can't happen to me . . ." But it does happen to ordinary people all the time; and, while the majority of them are poor and uneducated, there are still many who come from the ranks of the business and professional classes. Take Edward A. Kimball of Maryland, for instance. He was a deeply religious man, a student of philosophy, law and medicine, an ardent supporter of the Salvation Army, and he had an annual income from an estate which supported him and his wife handsomely and enabled them to send their son to Bowdoin College. One Michael Funicielo of New York City picked Kimball out of the crowd at Pennsylvania Station one day and he found himself charged with grand larceny: the theft of $15,000. He was convicted and served time and it was only through a considerable expenditure of his fortune that he was finally proved innocent. The judge said upon releasing him: "This case illustrates how possible it is for any man to be picked up on the street and placed in jail to suffer the tribulations of the damned. I regret that the State of Maryland does not provide for restitution."

Some things can never be compensated for: the loss of loved ones who have died or deserted (this happens in almost every case) or the ruination of a career. Consider the case of Madge Meredith, the young actress. She was recently freed in California *after almost five years* in Tehachapi Prison on a frame-up!

Many doctors have been mistakenly convicted on narcotic charges. Others, like Robert MacGregor of Huron County, Michigan, are the victims of gossip and circumstantial evidence. Just because several members of one family he was treating died within a few years of each other, MacGregor was charged with murdering them for the insurance money. As a matter of fact, he collected only a modest fee for his professional services; yet he served five years in the penitentiary before he was pardoned by the governor. No effort appears to have been made to compensate him.

The most generous compensation payment ever made—$113,142—did little for Bertram Campbell of New York. Before his conviction as a forger he had been a customer's man and salesman of stocks and bonds. He and his wife and three children lived in middle-class respectability on Long Island. Five witnesses, men and women trained to identify the human face in their work as bank tellers, identified him as the man who had given them bad checks, and he served four years in the penitentiary before Alexander Thiel signed a confession to the crimes. After his release, Campbell, a sick and broken man, eked out a miserable existence as a bookkeeper.

When the state awarded him compensation he didn't live long enough to enjoy it; he died 82 days later.

FREEING THE INNOCENT

The fight to free a wrongfully convicted person has long been a popular subject for writers and movie-makers. The movie, "Call Northside 777," was based on the Joe Majczek case and depicted the sacrifices his loyal mother made in his behalf; she scrubbed floors to raise money during the 12 years he served at Joliet. Finally she had enough to advertise a reward for information leading to the real killer of policeman William Lundy. This tale, unlike so many others, had a happy ending: Joe was freed and paid $24,000 indemnity by the State of Illinois.

Innocence, however, by no means provides even reasonable assurance for a man that he will some day be vindicated and released from jail. Many serve their full sentences before fresh evidence is uncovered to prove their innocence. Others are only slightly more fortunate. Rudolph Sheeler was freed in 1951 after serving 12 years for a murder he never committed. He says: "That old maxim about everyone in prison saying he's innocent doesn't stand up. For one thing, it wouldn't do them any good. The guards pay no attention to such claims and if they did believe you they couldn't do anything about it. *A man in prison is like a man on an island—everything you want is on the mainland, but you can't reach it.* And every day you are in, means one more door locked behind you."

Sheeler, now that he is free, plans to devote his life to helping others wrongfully convicted. This has been a popular hobby with wealthy lawyers and professors down through the years but they have to spend so much time and money investigating claims, collecting evidence and cutting red tape, that the total number of people pardoned is pitifully small. Probably the best organized effort along these lines today is Erle Stanley Gardner's Court of Last Resort. The famous lawyer-mystery writer is assisted by a staff of skilled detectives, medico-legal experts, and crime lab technicians. Even so, only half a dozen men have been freed in the three years of the Court's existence.

CAUSES OF INJUSTICE

Because gaining one's freedom is next to impossible, the causes of errors of criminal justice merit close study so that methods of preventing them might be used more widely. The "causes" can be divided into three main classes: *faulty judgment* which leads to mistaken identification and erroneous inference from circumstantial evidence; *evil intent* which motivates malicious prosecution, perjury, and the "frame-up"; and just plain *carelessness* which causes records to be lost and scientific tests to be inaccurate. Included under this last category is public indifference to the slipshod justice meted out in all too many of our courts.

Mistaken identification was found to be a common factor in most of the cases studied. In one instance, involving Herbert Andrews of Boston, 17 non-conspiring shopkeepers were positive that he was the man who had given them bad checks. Yet when the real culprit was found, he bore not the slightest resemblance to Andrews; in fact, the two men were almost as dissimilar in appearance as possible. The old German saying— "As unreliable as an eye-witness"—is well-founded. As the elementary psychology professors have pointed out for years—seeing is *believing* but it is not *perceiving*.

If police officers kept this in mind, they would never do some of the things they do: drag suspects before complainants handcuffed—this naturally implies guilt; dress suspects up and change hair styles to conform with descriptions offered by witnesses; show pictures of suspects to victims before presenting them in person—of course, they then look familiar. Most of these practices result from thoughtlessness rather than a desire to make an arrest at any cost, although pressure from "higher up" to get-the-culprit-or-turn-in-your-badge has been a factor in a number of cases of wrongful arrests. The over-zealous prosecutor, eager to point to a spectacular record of convictions, also contributes to this condition.

Authorities agree that we probably will continue to suffer tragic errors in criminal justice as long as we have people. The number of such occurrences can be reduced by utilizing scientific methods in crime detection, for example, and substituting the medical examiner for the coroner, but such advances are a long time in coming.

In the meantime, innocent men go to prison.

The least we can do in such circumstances is pass the indemnity bills presented in their behalf when they are pardoned . . . so very, very few of them ever get that far. Perhaps some day public interest and support will result in a uniform Federal indemnity law. Most European countries had passed such laws by the end of the nineteenth century!

60 · Limitations of the Lie Detector

by MAURICE FLOCH

In recent years the lie detector has been used, always with consent of the person involved, in a variety of criminal cases as a means of getting at the truth. The lie detector, a mechanical device attached to the arm and chest of the suspect, records his emotional reactions to questions put to him, and thus presumably proves his guilt or innocence. How reliable is the lie detector as a device for extracting the truth from an alleged criminal? Maurice Floch, clinical psychologist attached to the Detroit House of Correction, presents his views in the following article. [From *Journal of Criminal Law and Criminology*, Vol. 40, Jan.-Feb. 1950, pp. 651-653. Reprinted by permission.]

THERE WAS a time when there was considerable enthusiasm about the possibilities of the lie detector. It was believed that it would furnish considerable scientific help in determining innocence or guilt in criminal cases. It was to mark a new era, free from the crude third degree methods, when the mere threat of being placed under the lie detector test would bring about confessions more certainly and quickly than any amount of violence inflicted by burly police detectives. Since then the clamor died down somewhat, and the lie detector was relegated to the role of one among many other useful instruments for the detection of crime.

The Lie Detector, as is well known, is based on the principle that an emotional disturbance will register in the physiological reactions. It is assumed that, if an individual should lie about some matter, he will develop a certain amount of anxiety due to pangs of conscience, and this anxiety in turn will cause his blood pressure to rise, his respiratory and pulse rates to increase.

It would seem, however, that theoretically there are some significant deviations in reactions to the test which should make the findings of the lie detector somewhat dubious. For example, there is the asocial, childish personality type, the individual who has no appreciation of the significance of falsification. He has either not learned the commandment, "Do not bear false witness," or else has failed to develop an understanding of the important difference between falsehood, based on his own desires, and reality. This individual can very well utter any number of lies without pangs of conscience or anxieties.

The second exception would seem to be presented by the antisocial characters who consciously embark on a criminal career and believe that the main purpose of their lives is to please themselves. On this account, a lie to them is a perfectly acceptable instrument preferable to any silly concept of truth. Thus, the antisocial types, because of their philosophical orientation—if one can call it that—have absolutely no anxieties when uttering falsehoods.

Finally, we come to the pathological liar type which, owing to a serious emotional derangement, lost the ability to differentiate between reality and fiction. The pathological liar certainly will not show any significant reaction to the lie detector test.

Prof. Fred E. Inbau in his *Lie Detection and Criminal Interrogation* makes adequate mention of these exceptions. However, he maintains that it is chiefly the fear of detection, rather than any other factor, which produces the measurable physiological reactions. The present writer would put conscience in the same class. After all, psychologically conscience is also fear of detection. Only the fear is of the superego or moral principles which, in the final analysis, represent the father or authority in general. In brief, conscience is fear of detection and retribution and not an abstract concept.

Much depends, therefore, on the sophistication of subjects. The asocial, childish individual is certainly unsophisticated. At the same time, he also finds it difficult to envision future consequences. Every experienced examiner is acquainted with the simple subject who will lie with the greatest unconcern even in the face of the weightiest evidence. The fact is that, not desiring to see the truth, he cannot comprehend why others would see it.

Apropos the antisocial character's fear of detection, he is not infrequently quite sophisticated and is contemptuous of the abilities and methods of legal authorities. Often, he knows that the apparatus is not acceptable to the courts. Hence, if he had not much conscience to begin with or had rationalized it away, he is not apt to show any significant lie reactions because of any fear of detection.

Considering then these possible deficiencies, it is surprising to note that, of late, at least one state parole board is making use of it as an aid in the determination of innocence or guilt for commutation recommendations. In referring to two lifers, a man and a woman, the following statement was made in the Detroit News of June 22, 1949:

. . . "Mrs. Storick has maintained through her long years of imprisonment that she was innocent of poisoning her first husband in 1923.

A recent lie detector test indicated she was telling the truth.

The board also announced that it will interview William H. Padgett, who was convicted of first degree murder in Ann Arbor but successfully passed recent lie detector and truth serum tests. Padgett was sentenced for shooting Clifford Stang, Ann Arbor policeman, during a store robbery in 1935. He maintains he was in York, Pa., at the time . . ."

Such employment of the lie detector test is even more objectionable than its utilization for trial evidence because, outside of the already mentioned defects, it has an additional and still more important weakness. Specifically, the lie detector test does not make allowance for the condition called "circumscribed amnesia" so well described by a physician of the Ionia State Hospital for the Criminally Insane of Michigan. This doctor noted from his many years of experience that there were individuals to whose conscience or superego the crime they committed was so thoroughly unacceptable and reprehensible that they go through an immediate, unconscious process of repression which leaves them with a complete forgetfulness or amnesia of the events of the crime. These individuals, then, could calmly sit through a lie detector test and deny the crime without showing any physiological changes inasmuch as the instrument does not tap the unconscious itself.

There is still another type occurring in parole work which the lie detector cannot successfully reach. Here the present author draws upon his many years of experience in institutional work. He refers to lifers who, shortly after the crime for which they were imprisoned, emotionally rejected the act itself and succeeded in hypnotizing themselves, during the many years of their imprisonment, by sheer wishful thinking into a denial of their crime. These cases are similar to the so-called "circumscribed amnesia" cases except that the amnesia of the crime does not come about with the dramatic abruptness of the former but rather through a gradual process of self suggestion. Members of this last group when facing the lie detector test, having as was said before hypnotized themselves into a denial of the act, will naturally behave as if they had been altogether innocent. Significantly, this exception is also recognized by Prof. Inbau.

Should the lie detector test be widely utilized in parole work, it would assist in the liberation of many guilty but pathologically inclined individuals in preference to those who admitted the commission of an act and have since then gone through a process of emotional re-education and re-evaluation. This latter group should make far better prospects for community adjustment than the pathologically inclined, unrehabilitated individuals who continue to deny their offenses. These, having rejected the reality of the crime itself, will obviously never make an attempt to obtain understanding of their personalities through psychotherapy.

61 · Psychiatry in Criminal Trials

by JOHN ERIC NORDSKOG

Testimony by a psychiatrist in a case involving alleged insanity is now accepted practice in our courts of law. The psychiatrist has unquestionably a great deal to offer toward the just disposition of such a case—and, for that matter, in many other types of cases. But, under the present system of court procedure, are the services of the psychiatrists and other scientifically trained experts utilized properly? This is the question which John Eric Nordskog, a professor of sociology at the University of Southern California, attempts to answer in the following article. [From *Southern California Law Review*, Vol. 17, June 1944, pp. 371-380. Reprinted by permission. Footnotes omitted.]

THE EVILS growing out of the so-called insanity defense have too long constituted a problem for both the legal profession and the public, and, noting modern developments in criminology and penology, sociologists have become increasingly concerned. The attitudes toward factors in criminality have been greatly revised in recent years, and sociologists have contributed not a little to reveal the true status of the criminal in society. Legal traditions and trial procedure have, however, been modified so slowly—and in some particulars to such a minor degree—that the findings of the social sciences have largely been disregarded. Psychiatry, of course, is essentially medical, although psychology has contributed to that profession, but, as it has thus far functioned in criminal trials in this country, it appears often to serve as a tool or weapon by means of which opposing attorneys may wage a battle, the judge or jury being the umpire to declare the winner. Meanwhile, justice hangs in a delicate balance.

It would not be the purpose of a sociologist to disparage the achievements of psychiatry, and he would gladly give due credit to psychiatry for its emphasis upon the role of human relationships and upon the emotional issues involved therein. It is the view of the writer, however, that psychiatry merely stands on the threshold of its usefulness to society, especially as its functions are limited in the courts of today. Psychiatry would have no quarrel with a rational and modernized brand of criminal law, but it certainly does have a quarrel with conventional criminal law, which is based upon the theory that the criminal is a free moral agent, punishment being measured quite specifically for definite crimes. So far apart are the legal and medical concepts involved that there is little possibility that psychiatry can be adapted to the conventional jury trial, or even to a trial before a judge.

It should be admitted, at the outset, that our national and state constitutions stand as obstacles to a fuller use of psychiatry in criminal trials, owing to the emphasis on jury trial and "due process of law" along with other features in the Bill of Rights. Changes in jurisprudence which require amendment of constitutions, let alone ordinary legislation, are not easily accomplished at any time. Society tends to resist change and is slow to accept new ideas; and in the realm of jurisprudence we find one of the best examples of cultural lag. Lawyers and public alike hesitate to "break the cake of custom," as Bagehot expressed it; hence trial procedure observes "due process of law" in ways that are centuries old. Old laws and traditions stand as barriers to a more enlightened and socialized jurisprudence. Society continues to fear and hate the criminal, and the negative attitudes which prevail have grown up as defense mechanisms. Many views are mere rationalizations founded on ignorance. Nevertheless, the advancement in humanitarian treatment of the criminal, influenced by the leadership of Beccaria, Voltaire, John Howard, Jeremy Bentham, and others who have pioneered reforms in penology, is one of our best criteria of social progress. It is necessary for our jurisprudence also to be accommodated in this direction, so that the social worker, the sociologist and the psychiatrist may contribute more largely and concertedly to the trial and disposition of criminals.

We have come a long way since primitive and early historic times, when criminals were regarded as persons whose acts were instigated by evil spirits, and yet the many theories of criminality have been inconsistent and refute each other at many points. Therefore, the influence of heredity, rationalization of biological inferiority, compensation for physical defects and abnormalities, the influence of alcoholism and drugs, psychopathy, and other factors, have been grossly overrated and misrepresented as causes of criminality. As an example, Lombroso's theory that criminals are born and are a distinct type has been refuted by Goring and others who have shown that there is no such thing as a physical criminal type. Generalizations regarding mental types of criminals are also subject to criticism. Feeblemindedness is no longer regarded as inheritable in Mendelian fashion, and there are serious fallacies with reference to the inheritance of insanity.

The above remarks do not imply that there are no mental pathologies or psychopathic personalities. There is quite a respectable literature dealing with mental pathologies, such as feeblemindedness, psychosis or insanity, and neuropathic conditions, which include epilepsy, post-encephalitic personality, psychopathic personality and the psychoneuroses. And psychopathic personality may be of many kinds: the egocentric, the inadequate, the vagabond; also, schizoid, paranoid, cyclothymic, sexual, drug addict, constitutionally inferior, epileptoid, and others. Psychoses may be represented by dementia praecox, paresis, melancholia, senile dementia, paranoia, mental conflict, blocking of wishes, et cetera. The above enumeration indicates how complex and intangible are the mental data of psychiatry, and how vastly different from legal terminology. Under existing limitations, whatever the findings of the psychiatrists as submitted in reports to the court, they resolve themselves into answering the question of whether the defendant was sane or insane before the criminal act, or during the criminal act, or what his mental condition is after the act. The insanity of the defendant, insofar as it is a matter of law, concerns his knowledge of right and wrong, the existence of delusion, or the presence of an irresistible impulse, or, briefly, whether the defendant is responsible for his action; so that the very word "insanity" has become pernicious and confusing in legal and medical usage.

Studies loaded with statistics regarding the many pathological conditions which exist, whether for the general population or for criminals, have not been very dependable, but, allowances having been made, they are somewhat indicative. It may be safely remarked that none of these factors in criminality has been as important as earlier studies led us to believe. Sutherland, a leading criminologist, shows that psychiatric examinations of criminals on admission to state prisons generally show not more than five per cent. to be psychotic, and in many institutions less than one per cent. would be so classified. Barnes and Teeters, whose comprehensive survey is the most recent, say that it appears "rather well established today that not more than a quarter of our convicts go into crime because of mental and nervous diseases, and such disorders may be rendered acute or aggravated by adverse living conditions." Conclusions of this kind are reached after careful perusal of many studies which are sadly lacking in common denominators for comparison; but, whatever the figures cited, it is the consensus among criminologists and sociologists that causal relationships in criminality have been much exaggerated in the past. It should also be noted that psychopathies are often the results rather than causes of criminal behavior, and that social processes and relations generally underlie the psychopathies. Criminals are not born, but are now regarded as the product of their social environment, although the physical and mental endowment of the individual must be taken into account along with the environmental influences. Individuals vary in their suggestibility and response, yet what they become depends on the culture area and social influence.

It has therefore become increasingly evident that the criminal should be studied completely as an individual, so that justice may more surely be rendered him in the courts or in some penal or corrective institution. This would require the services of the social worker, the sociologist and the psychiatrist, the last mentioned being medical and psychological in nature. Psychiatry and psychology, of course, are closely related and complement each other at the treatment level as well as at the diagnostic level, and their respective services are known to overlap at many points. It is sometimes difficult to distinguish between what is termed abnormal psychology and psychiatry, and it is likely that the distinction is largely academic. The psychiatrist, as his profession has developed, must be also a pathologist, neurologist and serologist; he must have at his command the main data of medicine.

Now, psychiatry, as launched by Charcot, Bernheim, Janet, Kraepelin, Freud, and their successors, was designed to heal mental disorders. But it is further acknowledged that psychiatry may give us insight into the mental causes of crime when these actually exist; and in court trials, the psychiatrist is the only one who may *offer as evidence his opinion* as to the sanity or insanity of the defendant, such an exception being significant because it opens the door to the evils growing out of the insanity defense.

No one today would eliminate the factor of responsibility for a criminal act. Even in our most ancient codes such recognition was emerging. The Code of Hammurabi (*ca.* 2100 B.C.) reveals little of this nature and is, furthermore, characterized by class partiality, whereas the Assyrian Code, which overlaps it in time but tends to be later, not only provides for equality before the law regardless of class, but definitely recognizes intention and responsibility for criminal acts and qualifies punishment accordingly. Contemporary views concerning insanity have an interesting history which may be traced back through early English law, Justinian's *Institutes*, Bracton, the Twelve Tables of early Rome, ancient Greek, Hebraic and Egyptian law; and the philosophers and medical scientists have influenced each stage of legal development. We thus have had about four thousand years of legal background, along with its social philosophy, from which to evolve a more enlightened and practical solution of the problem of responsibility for crime, and yet the psychiatric process in contemporary courts is decidedly elementary. Incidentally, Russia, under the U.S.S.R., appears to be ahead of this country in the use of psychiatry in criminal proceedings.

Only a small minority of the courts in the United States are served regularly by psychiatrists or psychologists employed by the court on a full-time or part-time basis or furnished by some other public agency, and a minority of the courts call upon expert service for assistance in the sentencing process. Certain States are particularly well equipped along psychiatric lines, insofar as we may compare California, Illinois, Massachusetts, Michigan, New York, Ohio and Pennsylvania, with other States of the Union. Psychiatry is employed least in the States to the South, West and Southwest. The trend of comment, however, is favorable for the use of medical and psychiatric reports as an aid in the disposition of criminal cases. In this connection, it may be pointed out that the use of psychiatry in penal institutions is also on a minority basis, the institutions in the South and Far West lagging in this particular; but there is growing a favorable opinion for such service as an aid to the classification and disposition of prisoners. Since old-style prison systems are slowly yielding to the classification clinic with its trained personnel, it may be hoped that conservative members of the judiciary may turn to the pre-sentence clinic for assistance in sentencing.

It is clear, then, that, with such limited acceptance of its role in the courts, and the quality of its participation in presenting evidence, the position of the psychiatric profession in criminal trials is quite elementary and introductory. Even so, the medical aspects of jurisprudence, particularly the insanity pleas, have grown to be a regular defense technique, and the alienists sometimes are merely the pawns by means of which the attorneys play a legal game of chess. The judge or jury may find the defendant legally guilty of a heinous crime, but the fate of the defendant depends upon the success of his insanity plea. It is not facetious to remark that it is a matter of luck whether the alienists agree as to the defendant's state of mind—who the alienists are on the one side or the other is important, owing to the methods they use, their technique of investigation, their selection of persons for interview, and so on—and yet the "opinions" of the psychiatrists have more weight than, under the circumstances, they should have. Their findings are sometimes so incompatible with the other evidence submitted during the trial that the psychiatric reports are frankly ridiculous, yet the judge or jury may give them full credence. If the judge were to take the legal point of view, he might have to set aside the findings of the psychiatrists; if he takes the medical point of view and accepts the reports, it may appear to him and to the public as contrary to common sense. Thus it happens that cases are often won not in terms of law so much as through the manipulation of psychiatric reports. There may be technicalities far beyond the grasp of either judge or jury, but in that case the ultimate decision should not be made by the judge or the jury. Should the decision, then, fall upon the shoulders of the psychiatrists? Not, in the opinion of the writer, in the present state of development of psychiatry. The entire routine would more properly belong to a scientifically trained Board of Criminologists, including also social workers, sociologists and psychiatrists, for only thus can a composite knowledge of the social, physical and mental factors of the defendant and his crime be attained, and justice meted out accordingly.

The Briggs Law of Massachusetts passed in 1921, marked a step in the right direction when it took the psychiatrist out of the courtroom and ordered him to make an examination of the defendant and submit his report in a complete form prior to the trial. Some of the States have followed this pattern. California and Indiana, for instance, make it mandatory for the court to appoint experts in all cases where the issue of insanity is pleaded. Similar laws in Michigan and Illinois were found unconstitutional. The Briggs Law was an effort to meet the deficiencies of judge and jury in handling insanity pleas; but in a sense it opened the door to the clever attorney to manipulate the psychiatric report which is drawn up altogether outside the courtroom. The attorney can, by suggestion, influence it to show amnesia or some disorder suitable for his use as counsellor.

The suggestion would not be novel, and yet it would be shocking to many, to recommend that the jury be eliminated from criminal trials when there is an insanity plea; such a step would, of course, be unconstitutional except insofar as already made optional, and further change would require amendments. It may be further suggested that not even the judge should have jurisdiction in trials depending on psychiatry, and certainly there should not be a battle between attorneys as is now so characteristic. Psychiatry belongs more properly with a Board of Criminologists having jurisdiction throughout the criminal proceedings. Then the findings of the psychiatrists would form a part of the information collected by the highly-trained members of the Board, and the "opinions" of the psychiatrists would be seen in their full perspective, free from the influence of battling attorneys, although attorneys, as criminologists, may participate on the Board.

This would require taking the question of insanity away from the jury, which, as has been indicated, could not be done without amendment to constitutions of the several States. It would require basic changes in criminal law and procedure; but the system now in effect is so archaic that even the legal profession should welcome changes. There would remain a wide range for legal practice anyhow; what is before us for consideration is the criminal trial involving an insanity plea, which, it appears, could be handled better by a Board of Criminologists. Since the criminal attorney is often subject to criticism for his methods, and since, all too often, he is not regarded as a defender of the public welfare, perhaps, through a Board of Criminologists, free from politics and the drama of the courtroom, we may come closer to rendering justice to the defendant and also protect society.

In order to give credit where due, it should be mentioned that the American Bar Association, in 1929, passed a resolution calling for psychiatric service in all juvenile courts, criminal courts, and every penal and correctional institution. This resolution, which was approved by the American Medical Association and the American Psychiatric Association, appears to fall short of the real problem of psychiatry in criminal trials. In Pennsylvania, a Joint Medico-Legal Committee of the Philadelphia Medical Association and the Bar Association launched a program of intramural training in psychiatry, under which service began in 1939, but this instance also fails to meet our problem. California's new legislation as of 1944 is an outstanding example of penal reform, and in Section 5079 of the Penal Code it is provided that the Director of Correction shall establish a psychiatric and diagnostic clinic at one of the state prisons. The work of the clinic shall include a scientific study of each prisoner, his career and life history, the cause of his criminal acts and recommendations for his care, training and employment with a view to his reformation and to the protection of society—all of which is good as far as it goes, but it does not deal with the function of the psychiatrist in the trial which may decide whether the defendant is to become a prisoner in an institution or be set free.

That which is necessary to correct the evils of the insanity defense, therefore, remains practically untouched. There should be as complete a study of every defendant as possible, before he is brought to trial. If the defendant pleads insanity, he should be tried not in the traditional manner through which so many evils arise, but before some more modern medium, such as a Board of Criminologists; and if he is to undergo a program of rehabilitation, a clinic like the one provided in the new California law may supervise the classification and rehabilitation of the defendant. The entire process of the Board would use the lawyer, the social worker, the sociologist, the psychologist and psychiatrist, but there would be no battle of lawyers to confound the issue.

An extensive and continuous educational program would be required to work out such far-reaching changes, for, with all due respect, resolutions by any number of associations may point in the right direction and yet achieve little. The writer does not say that it is the lawyer's ignorance of psychiatry which permits wrongdoers to escape both penitentiary and asylum; more significant is the failure of the medical and legal professions to work out something that is compatible and clearly defined. It is, nevertheless, doubtful how far the members of the legal profession itself would support such an educational program asking for amendments to the several constitutions and a new definition of the function of our courts in criminal trials involving the insanity defense. Anything gained in this direction would modernize the legal profession in social values that are commonly recognized as desirable. It would identify the legal profession with humanitarian methods in trials as well as in the rehabilitation of criminals, and render the profession more definitely a servant to society. It would help rid us of the criminal lawyer who ruthlessly exploits society by having countless criminals turned loose by using, among other things, the insanity defense.

CHAPTER SEVENTEEN

Punishment

═══

62 · The Concept of Responsibility

by ARNOLD W. GREEN

Is the criminal responsible for his behavior in the sense
that he could, if he chose, have avoided acting as he did?
Present-day criminologists, and some of the earlier ones,
deny this. What are the implications of such a denial?
These are pointed out in the following article by Arnold
W. Green, a professor of sociology at Pennsylvania State
College. [From *Journal of Criminal Law and Criminology*,
Vol. 33, Jan.-Feb. 1943, pp. 392-394. Reprinted by per-
mission. Footnotes omitted.]

I

It is the thesis of this paper that many modern criminologists have
injected more than semantic confusion into their body of theory by
simultaneously using the concept "responsibility" on two different levels
of meaning. This practice has no logical consistency or scientific validity,
is consistent and valid only in terms of humanitarian value-judgments, as
will be demonstrated.

With the effective refutation of all "free will" theories of personality,
and the wide-spread acceptance among social scientists of deterministic

theories of conduct in terms of heredity and life-experience, the realization has dawned that from a strictly scientific point of view it is absolutely impossible to attach praise or blame to any individual act. Probably more than any other group of social scientists, students of criminality are acutely aware of this.

But demonstrating the invalidity of "free will" has a limited applicability. Life, in all societies of which we are cognizant, is made up of a system of rights and duties, differentiated according to class, sex, age, etc., for the various segments of a given population. These rights and duties are arbitrarily prescribed to individuals and groups. Some philosophy, or, if you will, series of rationalizations, always buttresses the system.

The system of rights and duties could not function if the individual were not held responsible for his actions. But the meaning of the term has been shifted: as used above, "responsibility" explicitly refers to some mysterious "inner power" over "individual destiny," which most criminologists justifiably deny; here, reference is made to man's being held accountable for his personal behavior. The first is a fiction, the second a fact necessary to society's functioning. The first is a rationalization, used to buttress the system of rights and duties, the second is the very cornerstone of the system's structure.

Although *some* fiction, some non-logical explanation, is necessary to inculcate a given society's system of rights and duties, it need not necessarily be the idea of "responsibility" (free will) current in our society. If displaced, a new fiction would supplant it. "Responsibility" as personal accountability is, however, a different matter. Only on the basis of personal accountability can prediction of behavior take place, without which all social relations would be impossible.

We know, for example, that A will act thus and so in a given situation because his deviation from expected behavior would redound to his discredit or disadvantage, in a word, punishment, in the form of loss of reputation, ridicule, or in extreme cases, expulsion from the group in which he is currently interacting. Only by accepting responsibility (accountability) for his actions can the individual invoke upon his fellows their common system of rights and duties, offer them the assurance of being able to predict his future behavior on the basis of his past and present actions, and thus preserve the relationship.

But when the humanitarian criminologist refutes the concept of responsibility (free will), he is attempting to relieve the criminal of responsibility (accountability). It is difficult to see how the humanitarian criminologist is to achieve this goal when non-criminals are, and must be, held accountable for their behavior in the home, at school, on the job. The humanitarian criminologist is making the fundamental error of positing a specialized treatment for those who have violated society's norms most flagrantly, a specialized treatment it would be impossible to accord the general population.

II

The difficulty in attacking the humanitarian value-judgments and pseudo-logic of social reformers is that one runs the danger of being labeled a reactionary, and in this instance, of "advocating punishment." But this is not so. While the author agrees with Emile Durkheim and George H. Mead that the *function* of punishment is far more subtle and deep-rooted in social organization than the humanitarian criminologist is aware of when he blandly proposes banishing it as archaic and irrational, no one knows what the "most effective" forms of punishment are as apart from specific situations and specific goals.

Certainly, without punishment, organized society is inconceivable. Accountability for personal action ceases to exist when sanctions are not applied. But the realization of this is not necessarily followed by advocating cruel and unusual punishments. Those criminologists who have pointed out that extremely harsh punishment has historically been associated with periods of excessive criminality cannot be refuted. And yet, on the other hand, that some forms of punishment are necessary to a functioning social order cannot be gainsaid.

Finally, the humanitarian criminologist's lack of certitude about justice, even the justification of punishment, is in and of itself symptomatic of a social order that is lacking certitude, lacking vigorous beliefs in its own tenets, faiths, its own entire way of life. The anguished fulminations of the humanitarian criminologist are part and parcel of that uncertainty, indeed, of the very complex of causes in which much of modern criminality is rooted.

63 · Mental Disorder and Criminal Responsibility

by SIDNEY J. TILLIM

The inability of a person to distinguish right from wrong with respect to a specific criminal act he has committed is, legally, considered as proof of his not being responsible for his crime. Is the concept of insanity as currently defined

and applied in the courts consistent with psychiatric knowledge? Is it just, from the point of view of the individual
involved, and effective as far as society is concerned? A psychiatrist of wide experience with the mentally ill, Sidney
J. Tillim, critically analyzes this problem in the article that
follows. [From *Journal of Criminal Law and Criminology*,
Vol. 41, Jan.-Feb. 1951, pp. 600-608. Reprinted by permission. Footnotes omitted.]

THE MOST WIDELY accepted test of irresponsibility for a crime, on a plea
of insanity, is whether the accused had "capacity and reason sufficient to
enable him to distinguish right from wrong as to the particular act in
question . . ." Conviction on the charge results in a verdict of either
"guilty," or "not guilty, by reason of insanity." The acceptance of this
test makes the formula the measure of justice rather than an independent consideration of the accused's capacities for responsibility,
which is the basis of selection for responsible tasks in our society. Capacity for responsibility is a qualitative faculty not equally bestowed by
the Creator, and can be materially altered by life experiences. It is proposed to show that the present method of fixing criminal responsibility
is not just, is not especially protective of society, and is not in con-
sonance with present knowledge of human behavior.

The aim of law is protection of society and justice for the person convicted of crime against the particular society or one of its members. A
society which cannot afford justice for individuals is either so insecure or
so depraved as to null the very purpose of its organization. A formula
defining responsibility or irresponsibility in human behavior cannot do
justice to individuals of unequal endowment in intellect, emotional
stability, or probably intervention of various mental illnesses. These differences are often expressed in substantial disabilities which are not exposed by mere knowing right from wrong, and disregard of these must
lead to legal perpetration of injustices.

The present yardstick of criminal irresponsibility discloses nothing
affirmative about possible mental handicaps at the time of the criminal
act, unless it shows that the accused possessed the consciousness and
physical force to wield the lethal weapon. Paradoxically, the required
knowledge of right from wrong is generally held to be of a moral rather
than of a legal nature; goodness from badness or evil in a social sense in
interhuman relationships. The legal presumption that everyone has the
requisite knowledge of criminal law precludes tests for determination of
such knowledge.

Moral concepts are largely formed in infancy and early childhood.
The wrong in doing injury to others, even killing of some domestic ani-

mals, and the Ten Commandments are indoctrinated by home, school, and the churches. When mind is perverted by injury, disease, or failure of function, the earliest instructions are the last to fail. Senile dementia is peculiarly marked by failure of memory for recent events with fair retention and recall of very remote memories. Amnesia victims who may not recall their own identity generally answer correctly questions about moral right from wrong. Mentally dilapidated patients (chronic psychotics, functional type), after years of confinement in mental hospitals, have astounded lay persons with their retention of skills and learning acquired prior to the mental breakdown. Thus, the musician can recall much of his musical repertoire; a minister can deliver some of his tried sermons; the artisan some of his special skills, and so on. These findings are the rule rather than the exception. Moral concepts and trained behavior are generally demonstrated as automatic responses; only on special occasions does the individual require deliberative mentation to express them. Persons in ambulatory delirium, from whatever cause, may condemn themselves by the prevailing test; drug and alcohol delirium are well known to have been associated with grave crimes. Although wilfully induced intoxication is generally held as no excuse for crime, it seems certain that the condition of delirium or pathologic effect is neither intentional nor anticipated. Besides, there are many other causes for ambulant, delirious states which are completely of an involuntary nature. The important point is that such obviously sick people can answer correctly to the right from wrong test, but will show gross defect in reasoning "as not to know the nature and quality of the act" charged against them which relates to intent, premeditation, and deliberation requisite to a first degree murder conviction.

The magic power of precedent, the lack of agreement on more flexible principles, and the morbid social hostility towards criminals are the probable causes for continuing the M'Naghten rules as the yardstick of criminal irresponsibility. These rules were formulated by 14 of the 15 highest Judges of England in 1843 as answers to five hypothetical questions posed by the House of Lords. Of immediate interest is the answer to questions II & III, to wit: "to establish a defense on the ground of insanity, it must be clearly proven that, at the time of committing the act, the party accused was labouring under such a defect of reason, from disease of the mind, as not to know the nature and quality of the act he was doing, or if he did know it that he did not know he was doing what was wrong." Mr. Justice Maule wrote a separate opinion. He first protested the burden of answering to hypothetical questions without arguments on the subject, and that the answers may embarrass the future administration of justice. (His foresight was prophetic.) He nevertheless gave as his opinion "To render a person irresponsible for a crime on account of unsoundness of mind . . . it has long been understood and held, (the unsoundness of mind) be such as rendered him incapable of knowing right from wrong."

The M'Naghten rules intended a firmer footing for the legal thinking of the period. Law is interested primarily in the collective security and an orderly functioning of a particular society. Application of law should take cognizance of changes in public policy and keep abreast of scientific progress relating to human behavior. The law concerned with criminal liability is behind the times many years, perhaps, because the public would rather despise than understand a known criminal. A formula based upon "what has long been understood and held" over one hundred years ago determines today whether a person accused of murder shall live or die.

Crime often results from perversion or aberration of a sane mind. It may follow sanctioned social activity, like the pathological reactions from alcoholism, or the "oiled" tempers of inebriate celebrants. Neurotic and psychopathic persons clash with the law largely as a result of prevailing social pressures. Psychopaths are adversely influenced by the inconsistencies in our moral, religious, and social practices. Among the youth of Central Europe must be thousands of malignant psychopaths, products of a hateful ideology and a protracted merciless war. They understand the accepted right from wrong, but respond with perverted attitudes towards social values; the preciousness of life is greatly discounted, and the sacredness of private property even more discounted. Combat trained soldiers returned to civilian pursuits may harbor hatreds and a taste for blood. Press reports indicate a post-war rise in criminal activity, most marked among those of military age of World War II, in this country and abroad. Increased criminal activity and psychopathologic behavior are well known aftermaths of wars.

Social resentment of crime is justified, but the criminals are entitled to be understood. Society should recognize its share in the precipitation of criminal behavior, although not entirely to blame. Fuller understanding of the criminal would lead to a higher level of justice while still providing the desired protection for society. When crime is due to a mental illness which is amenable to treatment, the criminal should be placed under treatment; those handicapped by mental deficiency or organic brain damage beyond remedy should be segregated under effective control; whether in a hospital or an institution with maximum security facilities is a matter of secondary consideration.

These views have been widely accepted in dealing with juvenile delinquency and non-capital crimes. It is shown by the increasing number of institutions to deal with such offenders, and the growing popularity with courts of mental hygiene clinics and psychiatric consultation services. There is no factual support for the legal presumption of uniform capacity for responsible conduct in a conglomerate population, nor for the myth that individuals are possessed with a "free will." The fallacy of the first is within common knowledge. Every population has persons of exceptional intellects, from the idiot to the superiorly endowed. It has been reliably determined that about 10% of the general population is of moronic or lower intelligence. During the last war it was evident in dealing with millions of troops that intellect alone is not a sufficient criterion for attaching responsibility; even those with superior intellects may lack capacity for discharging responsibility. Knowledge about human behavior has progressed far since "the wild beast test" and "the child of fourteen years test" were the measuring rods for legal responsibility.

The assumption that man functions by a "free will" is a myth thoroughly exploded. Psychoanalytic studies of human behavior have revealed beyond question the dynamic influence of the subconscious. It is within common experience that daily behavior is largely performed thoughtlessly, that behavior patterns are often directed by undisclosed motivations. The subconscious of the normal individual is finely regulated to a working balance between primitive or infantile goals (the *id*), the aspirations or desired esteem (*super-ego*), and the mediator (*ego*) between the two relatively conflicting drives. Social behavior expresses the effectiveness of ego control. This effectiveness may be readily disturbed by disease, intoxication, and sudden change in emotional tension. Predominance of the *id* suppresses inhibitory controls, permitting primitive or socially unaccepted behavior. Under such behavior the elements of premeditation and intention may be reduced to the type and quality found in beasts. This is already recognized in jurisdictions which permit a plea of "heat of passion" as a defense.

The inhibitive mechanism in human behavior is protective against self-debasement. Failure of function may indicate a powerful *id* or an inflated super-ego; the former generally results in an amoral or lawless character, the latter, in behavior of opposite extreme such as exaggerated piety and honesty. Chronic alcoholics, drug addicts, and persons with other pronounced behavior disorder often evidence powerful demands from the *id*, as well as from the super-ego. Thus alcoholics and psychopathic personalities may voluntarily reduce themselves to the lowest dregs of society and yet be ready to fight over the slightest aspersions upon their persons or characters. This sensitiveness, of course, may also be due to inadequacy of the super-ego. Murder is one of the most debasing crimes against society. Yet, there are more would-be murderers than the records can show; the wish is not unknown even to completely normal persons. The threshold for criminality varies with individuals and in the same person at different times. Through factors beyond control of the individual the "free will" may become "the will of the wisp."

Clearly, the test of insanity based upon knowing right from wrong can do grave injustice to many accused. Most psychotics (insane, in legal language) retain indefinitely approved ethical concepts in relation to specific deeds, and to the wrongness of murder in particular. This presents an incongruous and an untenable legal situation which should be resolved. An accused person may die if he knew right from wrong at the time he committed the act, even though he may have been at the time mentally disordered, as judged medically; he may yet escape punishment, if he is found insane (committable to a mental institution) before, during or after trial. A man might be found guilty because he knew right from wrong but may not be executed because of being medically insane. This generally requires that the insanity shall be manifest, which must be taken to mean obvious, at some time after the crime, and, of course, before execution. A patient on temporary leave from a mental institution who commits murder or rape, knowing such acts are wrong and punishable, will be punished in those jurisdictions which hold the "right from wrong" test as the only criterion for responsibility. Practically all jurisdictions hold that an insane person is not to be executed, yet the concept of responsibility which may lead to capital punishment bears no determining relation to the concept of mental illness warranting civil commitment to a mental institution. Why should there be different standards of irresponsibility for the same person at different times? The present formula for irresponsibility, indeed, gives a tenuous support to the justice in our laws; a human life is balanced against it, suspended by a hair.

The special defence of "partial delusion" is no improvement. It is inconceivable in the present state of our knowledge to speak of anybody as partially insane and otherwise normal. Only relatives of insane persons may be heard to speak of mental patients as being, say 85 percent normal, to feel encouraged about the outlook. Such partially insane persons, presumably delusional, must meet the standards of judgment in relation to criminal acts as is expected from normal persons, according to the M'Naghten rules. If the accused does not meet this protective standard, "and is not in other respects insane," he is punishable as a normal person. If relief is sought from "in other respects insane," the probable outcome has already been considered.

The present application of the law does not provide maximum protection for society. Criminal law is punitive and also exemplary, primarily to safeguard individuals in a society, and the orderly functioning of the society itself. Capital punishment has not served well to materially reduce the incidence of murder. Religion with its promise of reward in the hereafter for good deeds and, most unattractive, everlasting punishment for grave sins has not effectively discouraged criminal activity even in religious persons. The annual rate of legal executions and the increasing population in our penal institutions is evidence that the present system is not successful despite its long history of operation, that it is a system created out of fear rather than as an intelligent approach to a problem. It cannot be said that it is the best system or that it has not yet received sufficient trial. In other social endeavors experience and newer knowledge have caused social, political and legal changes.

The answer to the present dilemma is not for more indiscriminate executions. The desired security and greater justice in our penal system would be as well, if not better, served by a fairer and fuller consideration of the criminal's mind at the time of the crime, and not alone by whether he knew "right from wrong." Society has known a long time about institutions of maximum security; many men have died in such institutions as proof of their effectiveness. A verdict and judgment based upon capacity for responsibility at the time of the crime would avoid absolvence for some doubtful cases, while allowing a greater measure of justice for mentally ill persons accused of crime but who cannot be squeezed under the line of the protective formula.

The degree of guilt which attaches to a deed cannot be separated from the state of mind of the accused at the time of the crime. Under the established tests persons with severe forms of mental disorder may be held responsible. Such practice ignores realities concerning human behavior, and cannot be justified by the mere lack of more adequate tests or any difficulties in applying more just principles. This point of view has been variously recognized for a long time, in instances too numerous to recite. . . . Legal minds are frequently slaves to time-honored rules, and quite indifferent to a reasonable evaluation of the life under consideration. It is not unusual for the prosecution to pass over or ask exclusion of collateral information and demand that the verdict be based entirely on the established test. Members of appellate bodies have been known to summarize expert testimony on the probable state of mind of the accused by asking "Well, did he know right from wrong at the time?" Answers have had to be given in the affirmative, even though the degree of mental disorder at the time precluded an appreciation of the nature and quality of the act. A moment of reflection will convince that the two conditions are not synonymous and may co-exist.

*   *   *

SUMMARY AND CONCLUSIONS

A concept of mental disorder in relation to criminal activity is presented. Medical appreciation of the problem supported by statute and judicial opinion warrants considerable broadening of the present tests of criminal irresponsibility. The principle of guilt for a criminal act according to mental capacity for responsibility, is supported. The whole issue so important to the basic tenets of the Federal constitution, as the question of life or death for inhabitants of this country, should not be left to state jurisdictions but controlled by Uniform Criminal Liability Law. It should be abhorrent to judicial minds that any human being might suffer legal death by the sheer accident of residence in a particular jurisdiction. One of the prime purposes of law is justice. No just law can be ageless; it should bear relationship to a specific time and society. It cannot have literal application for a changing and unpredictable civilization. Law in essence is a book of rules by which a society seeks security and order. The judiciary *interprets* the rules, passes judgment, and imposes penalties for violations. This power vested in the judiciary should not be exercised without regard for the human beings affected, without awareness of change in the social and economic pressures upon the persons involved, or without notice of newer knowledge about human behavior. A just application of law would seem possible only through the instrumentality of thinking, living and feeling minds, in relation to persons rather than acts or things. It is suggested that the punishment be set to fit the accused or criminal, not the man of one hundred years ago but the man of today, under modern conditions of social responsibility. Society could be more adequately protected under such a rule; there would be less likelihood of abuses than is possible under the present system which often permits premature freedom for murderers. Any difficulties in the application of the enunciated principles can be resolved once recognized as a sound and just approach; mere difficulty in application is not a warranted basis for rejection.

64 · The Deterrent Influence of Corporal Punishment

by ROBERT G. CALDWELL

Throughout the ages, the assumption has been that punishment is an effective way of deterring criminals from further breaking the laws and potential offenders from committing crimes. In this article, Professor Robert G. Caldwell, a sociologist at the State University of Iowa who specializes in criminology, presents the results he obtained from a study of the effectiveness of corporal punishment on prisoners in the State of Delaware, the only state in the union retaining corporal punishment in its prisons. ["The Deterrent Influence of Corporal Punishment upon Prisoners Who Have Been Whipped," *American Sociological Review*, Vol. 9, No. 2, April 1944, pp. 171-177. Reprinted by permission. Footnotes omitted.]

DELAWARE, ALONE among the forty-eight states, has continued to prescribe corporal punishment, in the form of public whippings, as a penalty for a large number of crimes and today in each of her three counties there stands a whipping post as a warning to those who are tempted to violate the law. At the present time, Delaware's laws provide that public whippings may be inflicted as a part of the punishment for male prisoners for the following twenty-four crimes, here listed with their prescribed lashes:

1. Poisoning with intent to murder, 60 lashes;
2. Maiming by lying in wait, 30 lashes;
3. Assault with intent to ravish, 30 lashes;
4. Wife-beating, not less than 5 nor more than 30 lashes;
5. Robbery, first offense, not more than 40 lashes, subsequent offense, 40 lashes;
6. Assault with intent to rob, not more than 20 lashes;
7. Burning a court house or office where public records are kept, 60 lashes;
8. Burning a vessel, mill, granary, church or school, not more than 20 lashes;
9. Burglary with explosives at night, person in building, not less than 20 nor more than 40 lashes;
10. Burglary with explosives at night, no person in building, not less than 15 nor more than 25 lashes;
11. Breaking and entering a dwelling at night with intent to commit a crime other than murder, rape, or arson of the first degree, not less than 20 nor more than 40 lashes;

12. Other forms of breaking and entering with intent to commit a crime, 20 lashes;
13. Larceny of horse, ass or mule, or larceny by breaking a lock, 20 lashes;
14. Bringing a stolen horse, ass or mule into the State, and selling or attempting to sell it, 20 lashes;
15. Knowingly buying, receiving, or concealing a stolen horse, ass or mule, 20 lashes;
16. Grand larceny, not more than 20 lashes;
17. Embezzlement by carrier or porter, not more than 20 lashes;
18. Embezzlement by a cashier, servant or clerk, not more than 20 lashes;
19. Fraudulent misapplication or conversion of funds, not more than 10 lashes;
20. Counterfeiting, 39 lashes;
21. Wilfully and feloniously showing false lights to cause a vessel to be wrecked, 39 lashes;
22. Unlawfully obstructing railway tracks so as to make them unsafe, 20 lashes;
23. Perjury or subornation of perjury, 40 lashes;
24. Tampering, altering or destroying legislative bills or acts, not less than 10 nor more than 30 lashes.

The criminal code of Delaware requires that the punishment of whipping shall be inflicted publicly by strokes well laid on the bare back. In New Castle County it is administered by the warden of the New Castle County Workhouse, or by one of his subordinates; in Kent County, by the sheriff or his deputy, or by a constable; in Sussex County, by the warden of the county jail. The court in every case must so graduate the sentences imposed upon a prisoner that the total lashes to be inflicted will not exceed sixty.

Although during recent years some important moves have been made toward curbing the use of the post in Delaware, there certainly has been no definite tendency to reduce the number of different kinds of crimes for which lashes may be inflicted. In fact, since 1900, seven offenses have been added to those for which the state's laws prescribe the possible penalty of whipping.

During the period 1900 to 1942 inclusive, over 7300 prisoners were convicted of crimes in Delaware for which they might have been whipped in accordance with the provisions of the state's criminal laws. However, only 1604, or about 22%, of this total were whipped. Of those who received lashes, 79% had been convicted in New Castle County, 86% had been found guilty of either breaking and entering, with intent, or larceny, 68% were negroes, 66% belonged to the age group 17 to 35 inclusive, 89% were American, and 68% were either unskilled laborers or farm hands. Since the beginning of the century there has been a considerable decline in the use of the whipping post in Delaware, so that although in 1900, approximately 70% of the prisoners who had been convicted of crimes for which they might have been whipped were actually whipped, in 1942, only about 7% of such prisoners received lashes.

When the study of the whipping post in Delaware was undertaken, it was hoped that the criminal careers of all whipped prisoners could be analyzed in order to determine the extent to which the infliction of lashes acted as a deterrent influence in each case. However, an examination of the condition of the existing records made it quite clear that this aspect of the study would have to be restricted to the criminal records of those who had been sentenced to be whipped by the courts of New Castle County between 1920 and 1939 inclusive. The criminal careers of prisoners whipped for the first time after 1939 were not included in this part of the study so that in each case in the analysis, which was extended down to the end of 1942, there would be a minimum of three years between the first whipping and the conclusion of the study, during which time the effects of the lashes could be observed. Of course, for each prisoner involved all available information regarding his criminal record from the time of his first contact with the court to the end of 1942 was secured. This meant that whippings given to these prisoners before as well as after 1920 were taken into consideration.

In this study of criminal careers, the records of 320 different prisoners, all of whom had been whipped at least once and 74% of whom were negroes, were examined. As a result, it was found that 62% of them (52% of the whites and 65% of the negroes) were again convicted of some crime after their first whipping. It was further revealed that after the first whipping 52% of the men (37% of the whites and 57% of the negroes) were convicted of crimes committed in Delaware, and 49% (45% of the whites and 50% of the negroes) were convicted of major crimes. In addition, it was ascertained that after the first whipping 42% of the total 320 (32% of the whites and 45% of the negroes) were found guilty of crimes for which whipping was prescribed by the laws of Delaware (some of these did receive lashes), and 31% (15% of the whites and 36% of the negroes) were convicted of crimes that not only were punishable with whipping according to Delaware's laws, but also had been committed in that state. Of the 320 prisoners included in the analysis of criminal records, 20% (5% of the whites and 25% of the negroes) were whipped at least twice, and 65% of these (50% of the whites and 66% of the negroes) were again convicted of some crime after their second whipping. Furthermore, of the ones who were whipped at least twice, 57% (50% of the whites and 58% of the negroes) were convicted of major crimes after their second whipping.

Anyone who has given much thought to the subject of corporal punishment will undoubtedly raise a question regarding the analysis that has thus far been presented. It may well be asked at this point whether the amount of recidivism among those who have been whipped should not be compared with that of some other group, that is, with a group of prisoners who have not been whipped but who have been punished in some other way. For example, it may be contended that even though a large percentage of prisoners are again convicted of some crime after they receive lashes, nevertheless, whipping exerts a greater deterrent influence than imprisonment. Obviously, therefore, this comparison must be made if the study of the subject is to be complete.

An examination of Delaware's criminal records for those who were not whipped revealed that any analysis of such records could not be a very satisfactory one if it were used for any county except New Castle County, or if it were extended back beyond 1928. Therefore, it was decided that the criminal careers of those who were convicted in 1928 in New Castle County of crimes for which they might have been whipped but were not, would be used since that would give the maximum number of years during which the effects of such punishment could be accurately observed.

During 1928, there were 93 persons convicted in New Castle County of crimes for which they might have been whipped but who were not. Of these, 98% had been found guilty of either breaking and entering, with intent, or larceny, 57% were white, 71% belonged to the age group 17 to 35 inclusive, 87% were American, and 58% were either unskilled laborers or farm hands. If a comparison is made between the foregoing characteristics and the same characteristics of the 1,259 prisoners who were whipped during the period 1900 to 1942 inclusive, after having been convicted in the courts of New Castle County, it will be seen that a higher percentage of the former (unwhipped) had been convicted of offenses of breaking and entering, with intent, or larceny (98% to 85%); that more of the unwhipped were whites (57% to 31%); that more of the unwhipped were in the age group 17 to 35 inclusive (71% to 66%); that more of the whipped were Americans (93% to 87%); and that more of the whipped were either unskilled laborers or farm hands (72% to 58%).

A further examination of the criminal records of the 93 unwhipped prisoners convicted in 1928 showed that 34% (32% of the whites and 38% of the negroes) had been convicted of some crime before 1928, and that 27% (26% of the whites and 28% of the negroes) had been convicted of a major crime before 1928. A similar examination of the records of the 349 different New Castle County prisoners who were whipped during the period 1920 to 1942 inclusive revealed that 69% (73% of the whites and 68% of the negroes) had been convicted of some crime before their first whipping, and that 62% (71% of the whites and 59% of the negroes) had been convicted of some major crime before their first whipping. Thus, a much higher percentage of the whipped had previous criminal records.

Of the 93 prisoners who were convicted of crimes for which they might have been whipped but were not, 26 (only 1 of whom was a negro) were placed on probation and the remaining 67 were imprisoned in the New Castle County Workhouse for definite terms varying from less than one month to five years. A study of the subsequent criminal careers of these unwhipped prisoners showed that 51% (53% of the whites and 49% of the negroes) were convicted of some crime after 1928, and that 40% (42% of the whites and 38% of the negroes) were found guilty of a major crime after 1928. The subsequent records of those who were placed on probation in 1928 were better than those who were imprisoned in that year, 42% of the former and 54% of the latter being again convicted of some crime after 1928, and 31% of the former and 43% of the latter being found guilty of a major crime after 1928. It will be seen from this analysis, therefore, that *the percentage of prisoners that were again convicted of some crime was greater for those who were whipped than it was for those who were not* (62% as compared with 51%).

However, there remained the possibility that 1928 was not a representative year and that a study of the criminal careers of persons punished but not whipped in that year would not show what usually happens in subsequent years to those who do not receive lashes. Hence, it seemed advisable to select another year which would not only allow enough time between it and the end of 1942 to make possible the observation of the behavior of released prisoners, but also reflect more recent conditions. For this purpose, the year 1940 was chosen, although rather arbitrarily it is true.

During this year, 120 prisoners were convicted in the courts of New Castle County of crimes for which they might have been whipped but were not. Of these, 58 (12 of whom were negroes) were placed on probation and 62 (33 of whom were negroes) were sentenced to imprisonment. An examination of the criminal records of these men indicated that 34% (45% of those imprisoned and 22% of those placed on probation) already had been again convicted of some crime before the end of 1942. The passage of a few additional years will undoubtedly raise these percentages. Apparently, then, although the amount of recidivism for this type of prisoner who was placed on probation in New Castle

County dropped between 1928 and 1942, there was no material alteration in the criminal tendencies of those who might have been lashed but who were imprisoned without having to undergo this punishment.

It now seems possible to summarize, in the following manner, some of the conclusions that may be drawn from the preceding discussion:

1. Criminals who were convicted of crimes for which they might have been whipped but were not, tended to be better educated, younger, less hardened in criminal habits, more often white, and more often found guilty of crimes against property (rather than crimes against the person) than those who were whipped.

2. The whipping of criminals did not effectively deter them, after their release from prison, from again committing a crime. Not only were many such persons (62%), after their first whipping, convicted of crimes, but a large number of them (49%) were found guilty of major offenses. Moreover, a high percentage (42%), after their first whipping, were convicted of crimes for which the laws of Delaware prescribed the penalty of whipping, and many (31%), after their first whipping, were found guilty of having committed such crimes in Delaware.

It is interesting to observe here that although many Delawareans are convinced that whipping is an efficacious punishment, the laws of Delaware, wherever they prescribe the possible penalty of whipping, also in every such case, except that of wife-beating, require the court to sentence the convicted person to imprisonment. In the sentencing of wife-beaters, a fine may be imposed instead of a term of imprisonment. Apparently, then, the legislators believe that some penalty in addition to that of whipping is needed to curb criminal tendencies.

3. The subjection of criminals to more than one whipping was not effective in changing their criminal habits. After having received at least two whippings, many (65%) were again convicted of some crime, and a large percentage (57%) were found guilty of major crimes.

4. Negroes who had been whipped showed a greater tendency to continue their criminal careers than did whites who had been similarly punished. After their first whipping, 65% of the negroes, as compared with 52% of the whites, were again convicted of some crime. Thus, the belief held by many in Delaware that the punishment of whipping is especially effective in dealing with negro criminals is not supported by the facts.

5. The use of imprisonment as a punishment for those who might have been whipped but were not, proved ineffective in deterring them, after their release from prison, from again committing a crime. Of such persons who were imprisoned during 1928 and 1940, 54% and 45% respectively were again convicted of some crime.

6. Probation was used with apparently mixed results in the handling of some of those who might have been whipped but were not. Of such persons who were placed on probation during 1928 and 1940, 42% and 22% respectively were again convicted of some crime.

7. The amount of recidivism was greater among those who had been whipped (62%) than it was among those who might have been whipped but were not (51% and 34% of those convicted in 1928 and 1940 respectively), and those who might have been whipped but instead were only imprisoned (54% and 45% of those convicted in 1928 and 1940 respectively); and there was the least amount of recidivism among those who might have been whipped but instead were placed on probation (42% and 22% of those convicted in 1928 and 1940 respectively).

It must be recognized, however, that this comparison is somewhat obscured by the combination of a number of factors. There was, in the first place, the element of selection in the processes of apprehension, prosecution, and punishment. Not all persons who committed crimes for which they might have been whipped were apprehended and prosecuted. It may be that the most skilful and hardened in crime eluded the law enforcement agencies and so their activities were not reflected in the police, court, and prison statistics. Furthermore, there was the tendency, as revealed by the examination of the prisoners' criminal records, of not whipping the better trained, the younger and the less hardened in crime. This tendency possibly accounts to some extent for the lower rate of recidivism among those who were not whipped.

In addition, it should be remembered that those who were whipped also received terms of imprisonment as part of their sentences so that there is the possibility that both these methods of punishment affected the subsequent behavior of the prisoners. The problem is further complicated by the fact that some of those who were whipped were not only imprisoned but also fined.

Finally, there were other more subtle factors, many of which were not involved in the processes of law enforcement, that greatly affected, in varying degrees, both those who were whipped and those who might have been whipped but were not. The love of dear ones, the hatred of enemies, the encouragement of friends and relatives, the security or insecurity of economic and social position, the attitudes of guards and wardens—these and many other influences played in an unending stream upon the lives of those whose criminal careers were statistically analyzed in this study.

All this, of course, is just another way of saying that human beings do not live in a statistical vacuum and that each of us is a product of a multiplicity of environmental and hereditary influences. Even a slight insight into these congeries of human relationships could have been achieved only by an intensive case study of each prisoner. Nevertheless, despite the complexity of the problem, the available statistics do seem to indicate that neither whipping nor imprisonment effectively deterred those who had been so punished from again committing crimes. Perhaps it is significant that those who received the greatest amount of personal attention; i.e., those who were placed on probation, subsequently had the lowest rate of recidivism.

Delaware does not stand alone in her inability to cope with the problem of recidivism. All other states have been similarly unsuccessful, and, in fact, some have higher rates of recidivism than Delaware. This nation-wide record of failure is not surprising since the United States continues to handle her prisoners in accordance with the outmoded principles of the philosophy of punishment. Despite the modifications that have been made in this philosophy during the past few decades, its chief aim is still the infliction of suffering upon the convicted criminal. The application of its principles has failed in Delaware just as it has failed in the other states, but Delaware's failure has been rendered conspicuous by her persistence in the use of the whipping post, a spectacular method of punishment. To attack the lash and to say nothing in condemnation of the philosophy of punishment, of which the "post" is but an expression, is, therefore, futile and misleading. There is needed, not some change in the methods of punishment, but the elimination of the entire program of punishment itself, and the establishment, in its place, of a system of scientific treatment, with its emphasis upon the understanding of the causes of crime, the rehabilitation of the individual in terms of such causes, and the modification of the conditions which produce criminality. Until this can be accomplished, no real progress will be made in society's efforts to deal with criminal behavior.

65 · A Prisoner's View of Punishment

by "FRISCO"

In the article that follows, a seventy-year-old convict who has spent approximately a quarter of a century inside the walls of a prison expresses, in an interview with a penologist, his ideas regarding the "New Penology" and its implications for the prisoner—ideas which are strikingly penetrating and realistic. ["Old Mike States the Case," *Raiford Record*, Vol. 12, Aug. 1950, pp. 10-13. Reprinted by permission.]

OLD MIKE took his time and read it carefully, stopping once to wipe his glasses and once to light his pipe. He's over seventy—been here since '24. Never hurries for anything, not even chow line—even the guards know that. His conversation is slow and deliberate and he won't talk at all unless he has something to say, but he's read everything in the prison library—two or three prison libraries, and he got around in his younger days. I waited quietly while he read.

We were in the print shop office behind the school where I help get out this rag, and he had come in on the off chance that we might have some coffee going. We didn't, but it was hot outside and he sat down.

That's how I happened to show him the circular. It had been lying on my desk in a pile of other stuff ever since the warden gave it to me. I'd made myself a half promise to knock out something and send it in —knowing perfectly well, of course, that I would never get around to it.

Mike said: "American Prison Association, eh? That's *scientific* penology—I remember when they started, back in the '30s, I guess it was— they've been going good. Lasted longer than most."

By the way he had accented that "*scientific*" penology, I knew he wanted me to react to it. Old Mike uses subtle gambits in his conversational excursions—so I did the straight for him. "Scientific penology? How do you mean, Mike; I thought *all* penology was based on scientific approaches. Is there any other kind?"

That's what I was supposed to ask. He kept a dead pan, but his eyes showed that he appreciated my picking up the cue.

"Scientific penology comes out of libraries, universities, laboratories, and clinics," he explained. "It reduces crime and the consequences of crime to charts and graphs and statistics—great stuff for the pamphlet publishing industry, and it's the number one hobby for people like statisticians and psychiatrists and dieticians and vocational guidance experts."

He lighted his pipe again, carefully and at length, then he sat back with his legs outstretched and closed his eyes meditatively. That was to see if the mood was right. If I had spoken it would have broken the spell. Mike had set forth a premise, now he chose to sound his audience before expounding. There may be a little touch of the ham in Mike, but the years have made him extremely wary of blunt-wits who know nothing of listening.

Satisfied that my attention was both valid and sincere, he resumed: "Scientific penology is the most harmless. They have a good time with it, and once in a while one of its followers gets into a spot where he can do a little good."

I asked him what kind of a spot.

"Some part of actual penology," he explained, "—in the big league. Probation officer or parole supervisor or prison psychiatrist. Even captain or warden. Scientific penologists go for schools and planned recreation and prisoner-classification, and they oppose strong-arm discipline and rank food."

He paused, leaning his head back and closing his eyes.

I remained silent, and presently he resumed, right on the beat, as though there had been no stop: "They make good conditions—especially when they're new and not discouraged yet."

"Discouraged?"

"You know—busted illusions. They get their heads and their hearts full of theory and ideals, then they get on the scene in one of these joints and gradually begin to learn what the score really is—the futility, the hypocrisy, all the rest of it; then they either turn bitter or quit, or they harden up and go along with Big Penology."

He paused expectantly, but he had confidence in me and I didn't disappoint him. I came in on cue: "Big Penology? what's that?" It wasn't altogether an act, either—I didn't know exactly what he meant. "Big Penology," said Mike patiently, "is the gag—the big-industry, heavy-money aspect of crime and imprisonment. It starts with the hustling bail bond broker who's shilling for a shyster lawyer on the side; it covers legions of bovine fat men with cigars, frustrated and threadbare lawyers, thin-lipped, untrained and fanatical Emissaries of Right—all of whom have in common a connection in the upper levels of a city or state administration."

"You mean special investigators, public defenders, and all them?"

"Those, and assistant D.A.'s and probation officers and county jail doctors and social and welfare workers—all the way up to the Boards and Committees and Commissions," he added. "It's the most powerful thing in the world, a foolproof gimmick for employment and production and political power. It's even better than a war, because there is practically no bloodshed and no danger of an armistice or surrender to interrupt or stop the action. The public is nuts about it."

It sounded pretty radical, but I'd seen a lot of it myself and knew that it was also pretty true. He leaned forward and pointed his pipe stem at me.

"Best of all," he went on, "there's no limit to it and no end to it. All they have to do is keep grabbing ignorant young punks who steal cars for joy rides and scared working stiffs who get out of work and broke and hungry and grab a spare tire or something in desperation. There are hundreds of them in every town everywhere. They run them through the mill and dress them into these joints by the dozen, then they scream to the public 'Crime increase . . . desperate criminals in overcrowded prisons . . . danger . . . more money . . . more prisons!' "

"What about the scientific penology you mentioned? Where do they fit in?" I asked.

"They throw it wide open—that's why I say they do good. They make better conditions for guys like us and they fatten up Big Penology. They have shown the big-business boys about classification . . . segregation . . . analysis . . . custody . . . treatment . . . training . . . parole preparation . . . surgery . . . therapy . . . school . . . recreation . . . time and motion study—the works. All that takes wardens, associate wardens, doctors, psychiatrists, sociologists, instructors, engineers, sanitarians, dieticians, instructors, athletic directors—and college-trained guards who understand practical psychology and judo."

I started to answer, thought better of it, and let him go. He did. "It calls for more and bigger jails and penitentiaries, more prison farms, road camps, reformatories, industrial schools—more and more—because when one state sets up a machine like that and opens all those plum jobs to be tossed around for votes, other states catch on and start their own penal reform programs with multi-million dollar building schedules and the jobs and all the rest of it."

This time when he stopped he looked at me and I knew it was time for me to say something again. I asked, "What about the prisoners for all these joints? If Big Penology keeps setting up factories for reform and rehabilitation, and scientific penology keeps running down the causes of crime and correcting them, eventually there won't be enough convictions to populate the institutions they have now, let alone building more. Do you think crime is on the increase?"

Mike said gently, "The crime industry is on the increase. People, and the things they do, don't change much. In any given segment of population—a regiment of soldiers, a chapter of a fraternal organization, the congregation of a church, there will be a certain percentage of intellectuals and dullards and neurotics; some who are emotionally stable and some who are not. Those percentages will hold true in any region and they will change only as humanity changes through progressive generations."

". . . and," I interposed, "there is always a certain percentage who are potentially criminal?"

"If by 'criminal' you mean potentially capable of breaking a statutory rule of conduct," he replied, "I'll have to ask you to remember that everybody who took a drink during prohibition was criminal, as is everybody who has ever driven an automobile faster than prescribed regulations."

Mike paused, it seemed to me that he sensed he was in danger of belaboring a trite point, then he switched his tack. ". . . but you mean felonious crime—murder, rape, assault, robbery, embezzlement. Every human being has within him or her certain basic instincts, dormant and suppressed, which, if heeded, would result in felonious crime. The influence that holds them in check is our civilization and culture. The more civilized and cultured the individual, the deeper are these atavistic instincts suppressed—but they are always subject to breaking through to the surface under the pressure of emotion, opportunity or circumstance. That is the reason it's considered shrewd business to paint up a worn out and broken down jalopy and palm it off on some sucker as an excellently-cared-for car formerly owned by an old maid school teacher. That's larceny by opportunity."

. . . .

I saw what he was leading up to. "A fraud, you mean, that isn't a fraud because there is no law describing it as such?"

He ignored me, continuing: ". . . likewise with circumstance and emotion—that's the reason respectable people of refinement get grabbed every so often for betting a chunk of their boss' dough on a cinch horse —or they throw a jealous wing-ding and murder their rivals. That's why nice clean-cut American college boys still get a kick out of telling how they shot Japs on Okinawa who had their hands up in surrender. Circumstances . . . Opportunity . . . Emotion—they can awaken instincts in anybody, anytime, that are usually good for headlines."

It was getting close to time for the bell, so I nudged him toward a conclusion. "So what's the answer, Mike? You've seen it all, in here and outside as well as in other joints—aside from the politicians with their Big Penology, what about the scientific penologists—the sincere ones, who are looking for the answer? What is their answer . . . ?"

He was ready. First he prodded his pipe with a match stick, then he sat back and studied for a moment. Old Mike's innate sense of theater would never permit him to go into a second-act finale without first tensing up the scene with a brief stage-wait. "It would be easy," he said, "if the Big Penology boys would let it be done. First, they would have to cut down the field—eliminate that big seventy or eighty percent of harmless unfortunates who hate crime and are afraid of it, but yield to it in weakness because they have to live even if they are incapable mentally or emotionally of getting a job and holding it. Their only crime is that of being unable to manage their lives and themselves. Every joint like this is full of them."

"But how?" I couldn't tell whether he already had a solution in his mind or whether he was ad libbing as he went along.

"About half of them are mental defectives—psychopaths, mostly borderline paranoia. That's one of the first things the Scientific Penology boys discovered years ago. Big Penology could divert some of the budget that keeps these characters stumbling around prison yards and set up treatment clinics. Some could be cured, and others could be given gainful employment under normal conditions but with supervision—huge co-operative farms, canneries, various types of light industry. They could even coin a new name for it: Penological Socialism."

"How about competing with private industry?"

"State and federal agencies could use most of the output, saving the necessity of purchasing it with tax money. Private industry would lose some fat state and government contracts, but it would save correspondingly on the tax bill for supporting scores of over-crowded and unproductive prisons."

"How about your social misfits who aren't necessarily nuts, but resort to theft because they can't get into gainful employment and stay on the job?"

"Big Penology again. An expanded probation and parole system, but with the emphasis on guidance and job placement. It's easy—during the war the Army grabbed up thousands of just such people, limited education, no special skills, unimaginative, drifters—and in swift months they were dynamited through training that taught them how to handle and service weapons and machinery, operate technical equipment, follow instructions and carry out orders. Similar methods in peacetime could qualify them in trades and crafts, special aptitudes could be discovered and developed."

. . . .

I thought I saw a flaw and tried to nail it: "Where are all the jobs for these salvaged miscreants coming from?" I slipped in. "You know and I know that people in business want no part of ex-cons."

Mike brushed it off in stride. "They'll hire them if there is something to be gained by it. During the war when business was yelling for help ex-cons were doing everything from baby sitting to cashiering in banks. Give the average business man a tax discount for every state-sponsored man or woman he employs and he'll start putting on extra shifts."

"Swell," I said. "Now what are you going to do about the rest—the ones that insist on stealing—heavy guys who want the big dough and don't want any part of square shooting?"

"There are a few dozen or possibly a few hundred in each state," Mike answered. "One large institution—say as big as San Quentin—could accommodate all the professional thieves who are doing time right now. How many guys do you know in here—or in any other joint—who are actually able or inclined to support themselves exclusively from the proceeds of any sort of crime?"

I had to admit there were few, if any. Everybody I've ever talked to in prison has always been a working man of one kind or another whose experience with crime was incidental to his job.

"You see," Mike pressed on, "when you are in here on the scene you find there really isn't any crime problem at all—it's a social problem, the problem of what to do with uneducated, unskilled unfortunates who get hungry and steal a bag of groceries, and assorted neurotics who crack up under emotional stress, and perfectly normal people who get a bad break, like believing a girl is twenty when she is only a mature seventeen. Of course, if you blanket them all in under the label 'criminal' it looks pretty sordid and awesome—but actually it's just a matter of dealing with people . . . smart people and dumb people . . . psychopathic people and normal people—the same kind of people you find everywhere."

The bell rang then and Mike got up. "Nobody will change things much in our time," he said, "so don't worry too much about it. They'll keep bringing them in and they'll keep turning them out. Some will come back and some will not. Meanwhile, Scientific Penology will break it all down on charts and graphs, and Big Penology will use the charts and graphs to prove that more and bigger joints are needed, with more and bigger payrolls for people to handle classification . . . segregation . . . analysis . . . treatment. . . ."

"See you later, Mike. . . ."

"Yeh, so long."

66 · Why Is the Death Penalty Retained?

by ROBERT G. CALDWELL

The grounds on which capital punishment is advocated have been challenged for a long time. Despite the admittedly plausible arguments advanced against the practice, however, many jurists and scholars claim that there are good reasons for retaining it. In the following article, Professor Robert G. Caldwell, author also of a preceding selection, evaluates the arguments in favor of capital punishment in the light of our present knowledge and attitudes. [From *The Annals*, Vol. 284, Nov. 1952, pp. 45-53. Reprinted by permission. Footnotes omitted.]

THE ARGUMENTS for and against the death penalty have been analyzed, dissected, lacerated, mangled, and pulverized, in legislative halls, forums, churches, classrooms, newspapers, journals, and pamphlets, by law-makers, orators, clergymen, lecturers, journalists, pamphleteers, and schoolboy debaters. It seems that everything that can be done to these arguments by all kinds of people in all kinds of places has already been done; and yet the controversy goes on, now and then bursting into flames as prison riots and heinous crimes deeply shock public opinion and pro-voke indignant protests and clamorous demands for action. In the face of this, we must conclude that the controversy has many more sides than it appears to have at first glance, and that many who have engaged in it have tended to give simple answers to problems that are very complex.

In our discussion of the death penalty it will be helpful to remember that both crime and punishment are functionally related to the culture in which they occur. That crime is so related and that it varies in kind and incidence from society to society is usually recognized; but that punishment likewise has such a relationship and that the efficacy of its methods is affected by what the people in a particular society feel, want, and believe is sometimes overlooked. We shall therefore seek to conduct this analysis with reference to the following important tendencies that exist in various degrees in many countries of Europe and the Western Hemisphere: (1) the spread of humanitarianism with its emphasis on the value of the individual, the protection of human life, and the reduc-tion of human pain and suffering; (2) the increase of the impersonality of social relationships; and (3) the growth of the belief in the powers of science.

Capital punishment is a subject on which many people are likely to have very decided opinions, and both opponents and advocates are in-clined to express their views in vigorous and emotional language. How-ever, despite this, some arguments susceptible of analysis are used to de-fend capital punishment, and to these we shall now turn our attention.

THE ARGUMENT OF RETRIBUTION

An argument which is persistently advanced in support of the death penalty is that the criminal ought to die because he has committed a terrible crime and perhaps killed or seriously injured someone else. If this is not done, say those who employ this argument, friends and rela-tives of the victim, as well as the general public, who demand and expect satisfaction, may take the law into their own hands and try to lynch the criminal.

It is recognized that the desire to "get even" is a natural human tendency and that it exists in almost everyone, but we must inquire about the extent to which this feeling should influence our actions against the criminal. Should we be satisfied with a mere execution? Why not torture the criminal first—put out his eyes, cut out his tongue, beat him into insensibility and then revive him so that at last he will know the agony of being flayed alive and boiled in oil? If it is pain that is wanted, why should we not make sure that we get as much as possible?

Now as a matter of fact, in harmony with the humanitarian movement, the tendency has been to make the method of execution as swift and painless as possible. Thus, in the United States by the beginning of 1951, the District of Columbia and twenty-four of the forty-two states which used the death penalty had adopted electrocution. Eight other states had provided for execution by lethal gas, and in one of the ten states where hanging was still used, the convicted person was permitted to choose shooting instead of hanging. The trend away from hanging, which we see here, is due largely to evidence that it may cause a slow and painful death.

But, an advocate of the death penalty may insist, the punishment must be made to fit the crime. Well, if this be true, which crimes should be punishable with death? Should an offender who is convicted of armed robbery be so punished? Apparently only a few of the states in the United States believe so. Indeed, in 1950 only eighteen states prescribed the death penalty for so revolting a crime as rape, and only in the case of first degree murder do we find the death penalty prescribed by all states that have capital punishment. Furthermore, of the 42 states whose laws provide for the execution of criminals, 20 prescribe it for only one or two crimes, 29 for only one, two, or three crimes, and only 1 for as many as seven crimes.

Thus, it can be seen that the argument for retribution in defense of the death penalty is not strongly supported in practice in the United States. In fact, it seems to be of declining influence not only in the United States but throughout western civilization. However, this does not necessarily mean that public opinion no longer wants to keep the death penalty in the criminal code. On the contrary, the public strongly supports its retention in some countries. For example, this is apparently true in both Great Britain and the United States, where all but six states still use it.

Lynching and Other Considerations. But do the facts support the contention that if certain types of offenders are not executed, people will take the law into their own hands and lynchings will result? Although the experience of Colorado, where lynchings increased after the abolition of the death penalty and then decreased after it was restored, has been cited to substantiate this view, it is probable that the increase of lynchings there was a mere coincidence, and that the presence or absence of capital punishment had nothing to do with it. Certainly, none of the other states had a reign of lynch law after the death penalty was abolished, and the number of lynchings actually decreased in Washington, Oregon, North Dakota, and Arizona after the death penalty was removed from their codes. Besides, in general, lynchings have been most frequent in the states which have continued to execute criminals. It appears, therefore, that lynchings are correlated with factors other than the death penalty, and that, furthermore, since they now occur so seldom, they no longer constitute a serious problem. Thus, the possibility of lynchings need not be considered as an obstacle to the abolition of capital punishment.

Finally, it should be obvious that the demand for retribution cannot be permitted to control the policy of the state in its treatment of criminals, for this would tend to encourage and strengthen the very motives that might destroy all collective action. Of course, the injury to the victim of the crime and the interests and desires of the public must be considered, but so must the causes of criminality and the rehabilitation of prisoners; and since the abolition of the death penalty does not mean that the offender escapes all pain, any desire that the victim, or his friends and relatives, and the general public have for the suffering of the offender can be taken into consideration even if the criminal is not executed.

THE ARGUMENT OF SOCIAL SOLIDARITY

Another argument in favor of the death penalty is that an execution constitutes a spectacular exhibition of law and order which helps to unify society against crime and criminals. By providing a symbol around which law-abiding citizens can rally, the infliction of the death penalty, it is claimed, gives them renewed strength and courage to carry on the fight against crime and to furnish greater support to law enforcement officials.

Even if we grant, for the moment, that an execution does accomplish this, we may inquire whether there are not better methods of increasing social solidarity. War also helps to unify a people, but there are few who will advocate plunging a nation into war to achieve this purpose. Opponents of the death penalty may well ask, Wouldn't it be better to increase social and economic opportunities for all persons so that greater loyalty and respect might be fostered for the established standards? Furthermore, it can be seriously questioned whether executions unify society against crime and criminals. Executions are closed to the public, and no special effort is made to give them publicity. Then, too, since there is an increasing impersonality in western civilization, particularly in the United States, even serious crimes often attract little attention, and directly affect or injure only a few people. Under such circumstances, an execution can hardly be expected to exert a major influence in modern society.

And here another point may be raised. The humanitarian movement has made many conscious of the suffering of their fellow human beings and filled some with an earnest desire to reduce pain and suffering everywhere. Is it not possible, therefore, that among those who are aware that a criminal has been sentenced to death, there will be a tendency to reduce rather than solidify opinion against the condemned prisoner? May this not cause many, who would otherwise be strongly in favor of the criminal's punishment, to rush to his defense? Does an execution thus actually divide rather than unify the law-abiding members of society?

THE ARGUMENT OF ECONOMY

Some who favor the death penalty claim that it is cheaper than the cost of maintaining a prisoner for life, or for a long period of time, at the taxpayers' expense. Even though this can be shown to be true in some cases, the argument should be carefully examined. One may ask, for example, whether it is not more of an argument against the poor management of our correctional institutions than against the abolition of the death penalty. Might it not be possible, at least in many cases, to modify our correctional policies in such a way that if a person were imprisoned instead of being executed, he could not only pay for his maintenance, but actually contribute to the support of his dependents and, if necessary, make payments to the victim of his crime or to the relatives of the victim?

Furthermore, how far should this argument be pressed? If it is valid in the case of those who now may be condemned to die, may it not also be applied to all prisoners—yes, even to all types of persons who are being maintained at public expense in our federal and state institutions? At the close of 1950 there were 167,173 in state and federal prisons and reformatories for adult offenders. Thousands of these prisoners undoubtedly were not self-supporting, and therefore, on the basis of the economy argument, might have been selected for execution. Obviously, the possibility of such executions cannot be seriously considered. The humanitarian feelings of our country would be outraged, and public opinion would shrink in revulsion from the procedure.

Then, too, there is still another side of this argument that should be scrutinized. Is it really cheaper in most cases to execute the prisoner than to imprison him? In the first place, it must be recognized that although a prisoner may not be self-supporting, he can usually contribute something to his upkeep. And in the second place, it should not be assumed that the process in sending a man to his death is inexpensive. When the penalty may be death, the legal battle is often fierce and prolonged as each side struggles for an advantage. Much time and money may be spent in the selection of jurors acceptable to both sides, in the employment of experts and witnesses, and in the successive new trials and appeals that may ensue. Add to this the cost of constructing, maintaining, and staffing a suitable place of detention for those awaiting execution, and it can be seen that the cost of inflicting capital punishment may be very great—greater, in fact, than it may be to keep a person in prison "for the remainder of his natural life."

Thus, an examination of the argument of economy causes much of its effectiveness to vanish, and one is left with the conviction that it cannot be given a great deal of weight in the controversy over the death penalty.

THE ARGUMENT OF PROTECTION

A fourth argument for the death penalty is that it protects society from dangerous criminals. This it accomplishes, according to those who reason in this way, by ensuring that they will never return to society to commit other crimes and to spread their undesirable hereditary traits. This is a complex argument and requires careful analysis. However, at the very beginning, we must admit that a state has the right to take the life of a criminal who threatens its security from within, just as it has the right to send its soldiers to their death in battle in order to defeat those who threaten its security from without. But we must also point to various reasons which compel us to ask whether the state should exercise this right to execute prisoners.

For example, it is clear that the possibility of releasing dangerous prisoners into the community could be reduced by improving the rehabilitative facilities of our correctional institutions and by strengthening our pardon and parole procedures. An execution, it is true, absolutely eliminates this possibility; but since it is to be prescribed as punishment for a crime, one can hardly maintain that in a given case it should be used not so much because a certain offense has been committed but because we are too lenient and inefficient in the operation of our correctional systems. To do so would appear to place one in the position of arguing that all persons who have recidivistic tendencies, regardless of the crimes that they have committed, should be executed. Such drastic action, of course, would not be tolerated by public opinion. Moreover, on the basis of our present knowledge, we cannot be sure that a person is incorrigible. Many persons who might have been executed for their crimes, but instead have been imprisoned, not only have caused little trouble while incarcerated, but have become law-abiding citizens after their release.

*   *   *

The Eugenic Aspect. Now let us look at the part of this argument which claims that capital punishment exerts a eugenic influence. Unquestionably, many of the criminals who commit capital crimes have mental or physical defects; but, it should be added, so have many prisoners who have been convicted of crimes that are not capital. Besides, it is one thing to say this, but quite another to say that such defects are the cause of criminal activities. Sometimes physical and mental defects do contribute to crime, but on the other hand, many persons who have them never come into conflict with the law at all. The fact is that crime is a very complex phenomenon, and is produced in the individual by the interaction of many factors as he seeks adjustment with his environment. Further complicating this situation is the fact that although heredity may cause a certain type of defect in one individual, environment may cause the same type of defect in another; and at the present time, science in many cases cannot determine which caused the defect.

Moreover, since many persons who are apparently normal may carry recessive defective genes, and consequently may have defective children, it is clear that even if all persons who have hereditary physical and mental defects could be identified and were killed, the next generation would produce a whole new group of defective individuals. And here we are assuming that public opinion would sanction the killing of all such defective persons, regardless of whether they have been convicted of capital crimes or not—indeed, regardless of whether they have been convicted of any crime or not. This, it is clear, public opinion is not prepared to do.

However, if a program of eugenic executions were instituted, the overwhelming complexity of the problem would provoke a public demand for nothing less than a very carefully planned and administered series of examinations based on the best knowledge that science can provide. And here one should not overlook the possibility of using sterilization as a substitute for execution in many cases, since sterilization would be just as effective as death in preventing procreation.

Our System Does Not Protect. But it is obvious that we are not condemning prisoners to death on the basis of their hereditary traits. Our courts, of course, are neither designed nor equipped to do this. In fact, they are not condemning many prisoners of any kind to death. The available records indicate that in the United States we are executing only a small percentage of the persons who have committed capital crimes. For example, although it is estimated that in 1949 there were 6,990 cases of murder and non-negligent manslaughter and 16,380 cases of rape in the United States, in that year we executed a total of only 119, of which 107 were for murder and 10 for rape, and in the following year a total of only 82, of which 68 were for murder and 13 for rape. In view of this, we can hardly say that our system of criminal law is contributing in a significant way to the elimination of the "undesirable" or the "dangerous" from our society.

Furthermore, the death penalty may not be imposed equitably upon all offenders. The man of wealth, education, and position can secure able attorneys and use every legal device and technicality for delays and mitigation of penalties, while the poor, the illiterate, and the friendless can avail themselves of no such resources, and so suffer from greater exposure to the death penalty. Thus, factors other than those which make prisoners a threat to society may determine whether or not they are executed.

There is always present, also, the possibility that an innocent man may be sent to his death. Mistaken identification, perjured testimony, fallibility of the senses, lapses of memory, errors in judgment, undiscovered evidence, public clamor for a conviction, inordinate zeal on the part of investigators and prosecutors—all these and many other factors contribute to the miscarriage of justice. And yet the death penalty is irrevocable. How can a life once taken be returned? How can the relatives of an innocent man be recompensed? How can the public's faith in justice be restored? Even though it can be shown that the execution of an innocent man rarely occurs, the very possibility, when measured by the humanitarian standards of western civilization, compels us to consider it in an evaluation of our use of the death penalty.

THE ARGUMENT OF DETERRENCE

The most frequently advanced and widely accepted argument in favor of the death penalty is that the threat of its infliction deters people from committing capital offenses. In analyzing this argument, we must admit at the outset that human behavior can be influenced through fear, and that since man tends to fear death, it is possible to use capital punishment as a deterrent. We must admit, also, that many who have had contact with convicted criminals have testified that almost all of them fear the death penalty. Virtually every trial involving a capital offense becomes a desperate struggle to avoid this punishment, and petitioners continually urge governors to reprieve condemned prisoners.

But the real question is whether individuals think of the death penalty *before* they act, and whether they are thereby deterred from committing crimes. If for the moment we assume that the death penalty does this to some extent, we must also grant that certain human traits limit its effectiveness as a deterrent. Man tends to be a creature of habit and emotion, and when he is handicapped by poverty, ignorance, and malnutrition, as criminals often are, he becomes notoriously shortsighted. Many violators of the law give little thought to the possibility of detection and apprehension, and often they do not even consider the penalty. As a matter of fact, it appears that most people do not regulate their lives in terms of the pleasure and pain that may result from their acts, and obviously, the mentally deranged, the mentally deficient, and those who commit crimes in the heat of passion are not in any significant way influenced by thoughts of the future.

Human nature, moreover, is very complex. A criminal may fear punishment, but he may fear the anger and contempt of his companions or his family even more, and the fear of economic insecurity or exclusion from the group whose respect he cherishes may drive him to commit the most daring crimes. Besides, fear is not the only emotion that motivates man. Love, loyalty, ambition, greed, lust, anger, and resentment may steel him to face even death in the perpetration of crime, and impel him to devise the most ingenious methods to get what he wants and to avoid detection.

However, if the death penalty were surely, quickly, uniformly, publicly, and painfully inflicted, it undoubtedly would prevent many capital offenses that are being committed by those who do consider the punishment that they may receive for their crimes. But this is precisely the point. Certainly, the way in which the death penalty is being administered in the United States is not fitted to produce this result.

Factors Hindering Deterrence. In the first place, in addition to the uncertainty of detection and apprehension, long delays often occur in court procedures as each side, spurred on by the fact that a human life is at stake, furiously fights for victory. It is also true that when the penalty may be death, some juries are not inclined to convict, and some witnesses are not willing to testify. Furthermore, there has been a tendency to give the jury or the court, or both, the power to decide whether the prisoner should receive the death punishment or a lesser penalty. In fact, at present only one state—Vermont—makes the death penalty mandatory by law, and then only in the case of first degree murder. Moreover, comparatively few criminals are executed each year in the United States. The greatest number of executions for any one year in the United States during the period 1930 to 1950 inclusive was 199, in 1935, and the smallest number was only 82, in 1950.

Thus, it can be seen that today the infliction of the death penalty is not an important method of punishing criminals in our country. Besides, as we have already pointed out, the executions that do take place are closed to the public, and the tendency has been to make them as swift and painless as possible.

And yet, if we know how to make the death penalty more effective as a deterrent, why do we not take the necessary steps to do this? Indeed, if this is all that is needed, why do we not increase the number of capital offenses? The reasons are to be found in the complexity of our society, which makes quick action in the detection, apprehension, and conviction of criminals impossible, and in the fact that our society is less inclined than ever before to support a program of severe punishment. Our impersonal social relationships do not demand such a program. Our scientific attitude cannot sanction it. Our humanitarianism will not tolerate it. In other words, as Professor Sellin has concluded: *"The death penalty probably can never be made a deterrent. Its very life seems to depend on its rarity and, therefore, on its ineffectiveness as a deterrent."*

But do the facts substantiate the line of reasoning that has led us to the conclusion that the death penalty as it is administered in the United States is not an effective deterrent? Although the results of the best statistical studies are not entirely conclusive, they do indicate that capital punishment in our country does not have any significant effect on the frequency of crimes punishable with death. Similar studies conducted throughout western civilization point to the same conclusion regarding other countries.

* * *

CONCLUSION

Punishment is an art which involves a balancing of reformation, deterrence, and retribution in terms of not only the court and the offender, but also the values of the society in which it takes place; and in the balancing of reformation, deterrence, and retribution, first one and then another of these receives emphasis as the accompanying conditions change. It is clear, therefore, that a form of punishment which is suitable today may have been unsuitable in the past and may become unsuitable in the future. In the United States, with its humanitarianism, increasing impersonality in social relationships, and growing belief in the powers of science, the death penalty has become an unacceptable and ineffective method of punishment and has been largely replaced with imprisonment, in which the emphasis is being put more and more upon a scientific program of rehabilitation.

But more important than this, there is a growing recognition that it is the desire to find love, respect, and security among relatives, friends, and business associates, rather than the fear of legal penalties, that keeps the majority of persons from violating the law. This is the principal form of social control, and it will always exist, regardless of what methods are used in dealing with criminals.

67 · Punishment of War Criminals

by DONALD R. TAFT

Are war criminals in the category of ordinary criminals? Are they products of forces and circumstances similar to those creating the ordinary offenders? Should they be punished, and in what manner? What results may be expected from punishing them? May we expect positive results from punishing them—*i.e.*, the determent of similar aggressors in the future? These are the main questions which Professor Donald R. Taft, a criminologist of the University of Illinois, attempts to answer in the following article. [From *American Sociological Review*, Vol. II, No. 4, Aug. 1946, pp. 439-444. Reprinted by permission. Bibliographic footnotes omitted.]

THERE APPEAR to be both similarities and differences between the conditions surrounding the punishment of war criminals and those surrounding the punishment of domestic criminals. Most criminologists agree that punishment has a limited place in any program of crime prevention, but that its use has been generally ineffective. It must be admitted, however, that the effects of punishment on the apprehended criminal are better known than its effects upon the potential criminal. We are also agreed that the sole purpose of punishment is the prevention of crime, delinquency and exploitative behavior generally. It will be the thesis of this brief and all-too-dogmatic paper (1) that the principles of domestic criminology apply generally to the field of international behavior. (2) That where they do not apply, because of differences in the surrounding conditions, those differences argue for even less effectiveness of punishment in the international than in the domestic field.

There are two major general types of war crimes: aggressive attacks and atrocities. The test of the effectiveness of the punishment of war criminals is seen, then, in its effect upon the prevention of World War III, IV, or V, or possibly upon the degree to which men fight cleanly or atrociously in those wars. There is a good reason, however, for confining attention to the prevention of the crime aggression rather than the crime of atrocity. The next world war will be fought either with atomic bombs or some other weapons of terrific destructive power—whether legal or illegal at that time. The explosion of an atomic bomb, even of the early vintage of 1945, kills its tens of thousands so indiscriminately that in terms of its lethal effects, at least, it makes the ghastly atrocities even of Dachau appear, by comparison, as rather petty misdemeanors.[1] The latter war crimes were different indeed in being more futile and less directly connected with the need to put the enemy out of action. But the point is that warfare of the future will be a matter of competitive atrocity. The hope to make war nice—always rather unreal to the realistic military man—vanished forever in those few diabolical seconds at Hiroshima and Nagasaki. May we not, then, test the social value of punishment of war criminals solely in terms of its effect upon the aggressive act of initiating World War III?

In passing we may suggest that in a sense there is no such thing as a single isolated aggressive act. Aggression is always *re*action to a pre-existing condition. No social scientist need be reminded that the war did not begin at Pearl Harbor nor at any single moment in the accumulation of tension between the nations of Europe. War is rather a process of slow development. It is not wholly illogical that men hardly bother to declare war any more. Our friends the political scientists are never quite so ludicrously unrealistic as when they fix upon a single act—such as refusal to arbitrate an issue—as determining responsibility for modern war. Hence we must test the value of punishing war criminals in terms of its effects upon those international tensions which lie *behind* any decision to initiate a war of aggression.

There are two contrasts between war crimes and domestic crimes which call for brief comment. Many war crimes are said to be either

[1] It is not intended to imply that total casualties from the Nazi policy of extermination were less than those resulting from the use of the atomic bomb. The former seem to have been measured in millions, the latter only in tens of thousands. The comparison intended is rather between the relative destructiveness of the two methods in a given period of time.

more terrible or more deliberate than individual domestic crimes. Hence, some would argue, they are outside the stream of cause and effect, are not amenable to constructive treatment, and call rather for deterrent or even vengeful punishment in accordance with the emotions they arouse among their victims or friends and fellow-countrymen of victims. Sheldon Glueck appears to approximate this position. The argument is, we believe, unsound. No scientific criminologist holds acts to be uncaused either by reason of their extreme viciousness or their callous deliberateness. Felonious behavior is a product as truly as is the petty misdemeanor. The neo-classicist—not traditionally seeking causes—is more likely to investigate the sanity of a brutal rapist or of a Rudolf Hess than that of a drunk or petty thief. The positivist, of course, sees both types of behavior equally as products, and the sanity or insanity of the actor, to him, does not determine the criminal's responsibility, though it may help define his future dangerousness. Nor does the true positivist accept the distinction between the impulsive and the deliberate act as basically significant. Deliberately planned crimes may indeed be found to result from more complex causes than do acts growing out of ignorance, impulse, or immediate group patterning; but their causes are as impelling and may be discovered. John Landesco has shown how the professional gangster chooses his vocation, compelled by the same type of cultural conditioning as others who enter a more legitimate profession. By the same token the deliberate extermination of thousands of Jews or Poles, the attack on Pearl Harbor and the development of the atomic bomb, were as much by-products of the world social process as are so-called "acts of the moment." If so, the fact that some war crimes were ghastly indeed, or that some were deliberately planned as part of a long-time conscious policy—such facts do not remove these crimes from their setting as part of a world process. They do not, therefore, in themselves make punishment either appropriate or effective.

We may note a further difference between the crime of aggressive war and domestic crimes. Aggressive war, even more than some individual crime, is a group phenomenon. When a juvenile delinquent steals it is indeed often possible to show that he merely expressed a gang pattern or behaved as most any boy in his neighborhood would behave in the search for social status. Nevertheless there is not a little crime which is in a way individual. It is individual not in the sense that it is uninfluenced by group relations, but in that the choice of crime must at times be explained in terms of some detailed aspect of an individual's life experience which differentiates it from that of some non-criminal or from a particular group pattern. Not every slum-dweller becomes a criminal. To that extent the particular individual crime may not be explained merely as part of a general social norm. Aggressive war, however, grows out of the norms of the national culture and of international relations, rather than out of particular details in the lives of individuals. It is true that in the explanation of a Hitler, as in the explanation of Shaw's Jack Roller, the influence of experiences more or less peculiar to the individual enters in. But the explanation of why Hitler was accepted as leader, and of his influence as a leader, is evident from an analysis of group relations involving not only the German people as a whole, but their relations with the peoples of the world. The point is, of course, that international crimes are even more evidently products of a social process than are individual acts. A Hitler may indeed in some degree manufacture his following through propaganda, but that propaganda must be couched in terms of group experience or group attitudes. It must appeal to the resentments of a defeated people or to a people of frustrated ambitions—the "have-nots desiring to be haves." Hence the positive approach is more and not less easily justified in the analysis of international aggression. Aggressive war is more obviously a product of conditions precedent than is much domestic crime because its origin in group relations common to many, is more evident.

It should be unnecessary to call the attention of sociologists to one fallacious conclusion sometimes drawn when one suggests that domestic or war criminals are products. It is a popular view that, if so, they may not justly be punished. But if punishment is a preventive act and not an act of retribution or abstract justice, this conclusion is, of course, a *non-sequitur*. The positivist will urge punishment of war criminals when, but only when, it seems probable that it will reduce the likelihood of aggressive war.

It remains to examine the probable effects of the punishment of war criminals on World War III. Since history never exactly repeats itself, and since the principles of penology may not be quite the same in the international as in the domestic field, we cannot know with full certainty what the actual effect of this punishment will be. Yet just as a parole board must try to predict whether parolees will or will not go straight; so United Nations leadership has had to try to predict the effects of punishment or other treatment of war criminals. The decisions have already been made. War criminals are being punished. Nevertheless some consideration of probable effects is significant for future policies. It is also significant because any adverse effect of the punishment of war criminals should be offset by constructive aspects of our program to prevent future war.

It is the writer's contention that punishment of war criminals will increase the probability of World War III. It is his contention that (1) what we know about the effects of punishment in other settings; (2) what we know about the particular conditions surrounding the punishment of war criminals; (3) what we know about previous experience with the punishment of war criminals; and (4) what we know about the nature of the causation of aggressive war—that all these things argue for the failure of punishment in this area. We can only list our arguments dogmatically. We deal chiefly with the first two of the above-mentioned arguments.

1. Punishment fails when the potential criminal feels that the punishers are themselves also criminals. If some among the United Nations feel that some United Nation acts were war crimes or causes of war, then, of course, many of the defeated and some neutrals will also feel this to be true. There seem to be five kinds of evidence to support this feeling: (a) Individual United Nations soldiers violated the laws of war without sanction from their superior officers. (b) In such situations as the Battle of the Bulge and in the war on the Japanese it has been said that violations of the laws of war were at times commanded. Enemy soldiers who might have been taken prisoner were, it is said, not infrequently shot. The writer speaks here, however, of individual testimony —not of fully documented evidence. (c) The use of the atomic bomb can hardly be called a legal act, however justified on other grounds. (d) There is evidence of "aggression" or plans for "aggression" on both sides before Pearl Harbor. Finally (5) United Nations citizens were "accomplices" in the causation of war in the broader social sense of the word. American racial doctrines, discrimination against Japanese immigrants in public policies and primary relations, the failure to achieve the Wilson program in 1918—these are but three examples of the two-sidedness of international relations. All this does not imply anything concerning the relative frequency, severity or military necessity of these acts on either side. Nevertheless these facts create a condition unfavorable to successful deterrent or reformative effect of the punishment of war criminals.

2. Punishment is apt to be ineffective when inflicted by those who are not the "peers" of the punished. Apparently great effort has been made to make the war criminal trials fair in terms of accepted criminal procedures; but trials imposed by victors upon the vanquished can hardly be accepted by the latter as just. They will thus arouse bitterness, rather than approval. Recommendations that war criminals be tried by truly international courts might well have been heeded.

3. Punishment is ineffective when the pain inflicted is less impelling than the social approval created by the criminal act. Goering, facing probable execution, is said to have declared that if again given the oppor-

tunity he would again follow Hitler. His attitude presumably had considerable support among other Germans.

4. Punishment is ineffective if many committing similar acts escape punishment. Quite apart from United Nations soldiers, the vast majority of Nazi war criminals will escape punishment. Moreover the potential criminal is notoriously a gambler. This extremely important and well-known characteristic of criminal and indeed human motivation seems to have escaped the attention of many who confidently expect the trials to succeed. The international criminal gambles for the world's hugest stakes. The recent war teaches the lesson that with a bit more luck Hitler would have won, more effectively than it teaches the lesson that aggression does not pay. What a gambling chance of diabolical success the potentialities of the atomic bomb have introduced! Moreover war which of necessity uses the power of might, cannot teach the desired lesson that might does not make right.

5. Punishment is ineffective when acts similar to the crimes punished, or acts which cause crime, go unpunished. To propound a dangerous racial doctrine; to discriminate against an alien; to spit upon a Jew; to accept a subsidy or other unfair advantage in foreign trade; to organize a monopolistic cartel; to deny citizenship or an immigration visa because of color of skin—such dangerous criminalistic acts are not and cannot be punished as crimes. Ultimately they are among the world's most dangerous acts, but many of them occur with impunity both in former enemy lands and in our own. Such acts are a part of the war process. It is arguable that the majority of the people of the United States accept the essentials of Hitler's fallacious race doctrine, and that in that doctrine every war crime of aggression and atrocity is implicit.

6. To be effective punishment should be accepted by former enemies and by potential supporters of the punished as just. The ineffective trials of war criminals after World War I nevertheless took place under conditions which in this respect were favorable. German courts tried Germans. Few were punished, but at the time many Allied students felt some good had been accomplished. Punishment by victors has, of course, a contrary effect.

7. Closely related to this last fact is the evidence that punishment is ineffective when the punished are supported by a gang. The nation is the gang in modern wartime. Just how far the criminals under trial have support from fellow nationals seems not yet wholly clear. Much indifference is reported, Germans—not so surprisingly—being more interested in whether they and their children will starve than in the outcome of the trials. Apparently, however, this indifference does not indicate any anti-Nazi attitude. If the report that we have been unable to find even one

percent of true anti-Nazis in Germany is anywhere near true, it appears that the lesson of the trials will be largely lost on the Germans. Perhaps the situation is not the same in Japan, where greater docility is reported. Anyway, it is not the immediate but the later reaction of enemy peoples and their potential imitators which is important. If the new world order is truly accepted and nationalism is truly dead, this ill effect will not be significant. But if any nationalism survives, it appears that German and Japanese nationalism will surely survive, and tend to make punishment of war criminals ineffective.

8. Perhaps as important as any consideration is the knowledge that punishment by itself never changes attitudes from antisocial to social. It is not punishment itself but the total situation—the gestalt—that determines future behavior. In a home with friendly inter-personal relations punishment may work, because the child feels that an essentially constructive home experience has been interrupted by his delinquent act. In a home characterized by conflict and bitterness, punishment merely increases family tensions. The same is true of the world scene. In other words the meaning of the punishment of war criminals will depend far more upon the general peace and world settlements, than upon the punishments themselves. Punishment is effective when a solution of problems which is more acceptable than crime, is offered along with it. It is ineffective when the punished feel life to be hopeless and have no confidence in the new order. To put this point slightly differently, it will be the punishment of defeat, rather than the punishment of war criminals which will chiefly determine the future behavior of potential aggressors. Essentially similar principles apply to this punishment of defeat, however. Not defeat in itself—though defeat was absolutely essential—but the settlement which follows defeat is all important.

9. Punishment is ineffective when it expresses the hatred of the punisher. At the close of a horrible war such hatred is in some degree inevitable.

10. Finally punishment of war criminals is ineffective because it is in practice moralistic rather than scientific. A moralistic policy is one which is satisfied with determining guilty parties without going behind them to ask why they were guilty. The defense of "superior orders," so much discussed in legalistic articles on war criminal trials, may or may not be legally sound. The sociologist as such does not know which and does not much care. That defense does, however, suggest a far more important consideration. Back of the war criminal there may or may not have been a superior order. But back of his act there was always a series of causes. Back of aggressive war there is a similar series. This series of causes constitutes the war-peace process. To center attention on the punishment

of war criminals as individuals, detracts attention from the basically important need. That need is to understand and attack the war system —the social process by which aggressive war is produced. The more eagerly we seek to hang a Goering or a Yamashita, the less eagerly we seek to prevent the recrudescence of Nazism or racism. The less likely, too, are we to realize that the roots of these and other causes of war are in our own lands as well as among the enemy.

Our discussion has been mostly in the area of the application of penological principles to the punishment of war criminals. Space does not permit us to refer adequately to the evidence from history. Nor can we refer to evidence as to the nature of war's causation.

We close with one final point. When we thoroughly individualize the treatment of domestic criminals we always make a discovery. It is that however unique a particular case may prove to be, its explanation has been found not only in the unusual social experience of that individual but also in the nature of the general culture of which you and I are a part. The same is even more true of war criminals. When we really discover why a particular soldier committed an atrocity, or why Hitler initiated World War II, we find that the explanation transcends the life history of an individual. We find the roots of aggressive war and atrocity in the nature of the world system. It is that system which needs change. It is too late to stop the punishment of war criminals, if we wished to do so. It is not too late to see and teach the need for a change in conditions making for international tension. If we can make the needed changes before the atomic bomb destroys us all, the evil effects of the war criminal trials will be unimportant. If we cannot effect these needed changes the trial of war criminals will not prevent and may help cause World War III. The subject of punishing war criminals thus leads quite logically to the subject of the type of world order we need to prevent world aggression. If we can think less of punishing war criminals and more of reducing international tensions, there is possibly a chance for avoiding war.

CHAPTER EIGHTEEN

The Prison and Its Inmates

68 · The Sociological Study of the Prison Community

by F. E. HAYNES

In the following article F. E. Haynes, a criminologist and penologist of the State University of Iowa, presents an account of the new methods and techniques employed by the sociologist in studying the prison community and of the effects that the findings of sociological studies are having on the penal policies of our prison systems. The results of studies of this kind, he believes, are bound to influence the attitudes of the prison authorities and personnel toward the prisoner and to bring about a more scientific view of the objectives of penal institutions. [From *Journal of Criminal Law and Criminology*, Vol. 39, Nov.-Dec. 1948, pp. 432-440. Reprinted by permission.]

A NEW FORM of prison study has developed in the United States during the last quarter of a century. It is the outgrowth of an effort to make sociology more exact or scientific and less abstract or theoretical. Social organizations and institutions are studied by sociologists for the purpose of analysis and the making of generalizations that may be used in the interpretations of social situations. Social problems are investigated and the reasons for their existence are examined. The sociologist in contrast to the social worker is interested primarily as to *why* social problems exist and not merely in the *fact* of their existence. Instead of armchair study, the modern sociologist goes into institutions to find out what are the actual individual and social factors that cause the failure of our penal institutions to reform a larger proportion of their inmates. This phase of sociology is responsible for a new approach to penal problems and treatment. It has given rise to what is in reality a new form of prison study—resident study by criminologists of conditions in prisons and the analysis of the prison as a community. This new approach has been described as *the technique of the participant observer,* because it has been found by experience that the only way to determine what causes bad conditions in social relations is to put oneself in a place of observation where social processes are in operation. To understand the prison community one must be in a position to observe from the inside, and still not be involved in responsibility for what goes on in the institution.

Three other developments have contributed to the establishment of this new method of approach: (1) the work of Thomas Mott Osborne from 1913 to 1926; (2) the reforms in penal administration in New Jersey from 1918 to 1925 under the leadership of Dr. W. J. Ellis, and in the Federal Prison System from 1930 under the leadership of Sanford Bates and James V. Bennett; and (3) the influence of psychology and psychiatry upon the use of classification in our more progressive correctional institutions. The result has been the introduction of trained personnel with a more objective attitude to the administration of these institutions than can be expected from purely custodial officials.

THOMAS MOTT OSBORNE

A pioneer in the development of this new form of social study of prison conditions—prison visiting for the purpose of scientific study rather than for purely humanitarian results—was Thomas Mott Osborne, who in 1913 attracted wide attention by spending a week in Auburn Prison. Osborne lived all his life in Auburn and as a public-spirited citizen had been familiar with the famous institution. As early as 1905 Osborne began his criticism of the prison system. In 1912 he was made chairman of a state commission on prison reform. As a result of his experience and study he conceived the idea of spending a week in Auburn as a prisoner. Originally he had planned to conduct his experiment anonymously, but was persuaded to let it be known to the inmates, whom he addressed upon the Sunday preceding his incarceration. He served under the name of Tom Brown and was treated like any other inmate. His action was severely criticized because a voluntary prisoner could not be expected to see things from the point of view of a sentenced prisoner. He recognized the truth of the criticism, but he believed that he could learn how to improve the situation by such an experience. He brought the prison problem to the attention of the country. He emphasized the fact that prisoners are human beings, and that if reforms were to be accomplished the attitudes of inmates must be considered. Osborne had an unusual ability to form friendly relations with all sorts of people. He established personal relations with prisoners and introduced a new relationship between prison officials and prisoners by the development of Mutual Welfare Leagues in three prisons. These leagues were organizations of inmates, sanctioned by the prison authorities, to facilitate inmate participation in prison administration.

Osborne's association with prisoners was not based upon any abstract scientific principles. He liked people and he had an unusual ability for forming social relations. He believed that by forming friendly relations with prisoners reforms could be accomplished better than in any other way. More or less unconsciously he set the pattern that has resulted in the technique of the participant observer. The most permanent result of his own work has been the establishment of an organization, first known as the National Penal Information Society, and later as the Osborne Association whose objective was to prepare handbooks of American prisons, containing accurate information as to penal conditions as a basis for intelligent reform measures. This objective was identical with that of the participant observer. Osborne as a penal reformer prepared the way for the sociological study of the prison community. He was not a trained student of sociology, but instinctively he pioneered the way for the prison interne of today.

Much of the penal reform in recent years was inspired by Osborne and some of it has been carried out by persons associated with him during his lifetime. His genius for personal relations was not confined to prison inmates. The work of the Osborne Association has been carried on by persons associated with him.

Recent reforms also owe much to the work of psychologists, psychiatrists, and social workers. The development of a great variety of tests for individuals and groups during and since World War I has made possible more exact studies of personalities and their social relations. These tests have formed the basis for the wider use of classification in many correctional institutions. Individualization of treatment of prisoners has become a reality in place of a goal to be hoped for but rarely attained. To administer classification a new type of personnel has become essential in our prisons. This personnel is not primarily concerned with discipline and administration. The Federal Prison System has recognized this fact by the appointment of associate wardens who head up classification and allied activities as distinguished from deputy wardens who are traditionally responsible for discipline.

The introduction of a trained personnel into our penal institutions has facilitated the entrance of scientific observers. These observers are men trained in our colleges and universities and often of the same generation as the psychologists, psychiatrists, and social workers. Regular visitors to the congresses of the American Prison Association in recent years have noticed the presence of many young university men. These are representative of the new type of prison workers. Recruits to their ranks come from our higher institutions of learning. From the same sources come the participant observers. They are the end results of all the factors just enumerated and described.

SOME ILLUSTRATIONS OF THE TECHNIQUE OF THE PARTICIPANT OBSERVER

The work of the participant observer was carried on under various conditions. Sometimes graduate students acting as internes or student assistants used their opportunities to study and record various aspects of prison life. One graduate student became a voluntary prisoner and served a "term" in a state prison. Illinois has so-called "sociologists" who study individual prisoners and make recommendations to the parole board to aid in determining the time of release. In Michigan a sociologist is a member of the classification committee of the state prison. Students in training from the University spend periods of ninety days as assistants in classification. In Indiana graduate students from the State University and Notre Dame also have assisted in classification work. In Iowa from 1937-1942 four graduate students from the State University of Iowa served as voluntary workers at the State Penitentiary in return for the opportunity to interview inmates and collect materials to be used in theses presented for Ph.D. degrees.

Professor Norman S. Hayner and his assistant, Ellis Ash, of the University of Washington have published studies of the prison community as a social group based upon the technique of the participant observer. The junior author spent four months at the State Reformatory and in addition short visits were made for over a year to supplement the period of residence. Mr. Ash was accepted by inmates and officers. Leaders among the prisoners were discovered and their acquaintances cultivated.

The confidence of the officers was won. Aid was given in the organization of a classification clinic.

It was some months before the pattern of the prison community began to appear as something distinct from the official organization of the institution. Work was divided on the basis of crews. Place of residence in cell houses was determined by crews. Men were under rigid supervision. The population was made up of incorrigibles, trusties, and the "fish" (newcomers). The organization of the inmates was a sub-rosa one aimed at the obtaining of goods and services denied by the administration. "Conniving" constituted a basic process in the interaction of the inmates. It provided daily training in a code of deception. Gambling was facilitated by the inmates who made the rounds of the cells to deliver study papers or aid in school work. "Politicians" are the key men in the conniving process. They may or may not include "the right guys," the small, select group of natural "con-wise" leaders.

The prison community with its conniving, its perversions, and exchange of crime techniques re-enforces the behavior tendencies which society wishes to prevent. We cannot expect to break down anti-social habits in an atmosphere that is distinctly anti-social. If the function of a prison is to protect society, the prisoner must learn during his incarceration how to live in society. Individual treatment is not the solution of a situational problem. The punitive attitude has been tried and found wanting. Constant hostility between guards and inmates—"cons" vs. "screws"—results only in what sociologists define as accommodation, not in assimilation. Symbiosis, that is, living together, may be satisfactory for plants and animals, but it is not the solution for human relations. Prison stupor or "stir simple" and "con-wise" represent the results of the "machine-gun school of criminology." A sociological study of the prison community emphasizes the need for a more socialized approach to these problems.[1] Why not try the ideas of inmate participation and less expensive minimum security institutions? Analysis and study of the prison community seem to point in that direction.

Hans Riemer, a graduate of the University of Chicago, served three months in 1936 as a voluntary prisoner in the Kansas State Penitentiary. The legal and formal commission of an offense, conviction and commitment by a criminal court, and admission to the State Penitentiary were the steps involved. Neither officials of the court and of the institution nor the inmates of the prison were aware of the nature or purpose of the commitment. The study was conducted under the direction of O. W. Wilson, chief of police of Wichita, Kansas. Arrangements were

[1] Hayner and Ash: *The Prisoner Community as a Social Group, American Sociological Review*, June 1939, pp. 362-369.

made, and advice and sponsorship were secured from Professor E. H. Sutherland of Indiana University.

Three months were spent in the prison and two weeks in a county jail. In both institutions Riemer lived according to the ordinary routine and was treated as an ordinary inmate. The objective was a study of the social life of the inmates. The study was undertaken because of an interest in the plans and theories of inmate participation in the administration of penal institutions.

The basic theory of the study is that the behavior of convicts is determined by the convicts themselves. The reaction of convicts to the prison situation is outlined by "traditions, a social hierarchy, mores, attitudes, and a mythology."

The existence of a social hierarchy becomes apparent early in the period of commitment. The prison population is broken up into cliques and groups. Each man is classified and acquires status in terms of his reaction to the prison situation. Association with a "rat" or a "punk" results in a suspicion of like tendencies by other inmates.

The prison population is largely controlled by two groups of leaders. The "politicians," who hold key positions in the administrative offices, who can distribute special privileges and make possible the circulation of special foods and other supplies. The other group is made up of the "right guys," who can always be trusted, do not abuse or take advantage of other inmates, and are always loyal to the interests of the convicts.

The mythology of a prison community is a strong educative force in determining the behavior of new inmates. Stories of remarkable escapes and accounts of riots are passed on from one generation to another. The characters become legendary heroes and their exploits are described in exaggerated terms. "Big shots" who have committed spectacular crimes are admired by other prisoners. The myths and legends are built on opposition to the law and its enforcement and the administration of the prison.

Traditions, attitudes, and mores of the prison community are directed against the prevailing order of society, personified by the institutional administration. The conflict situation influences all members of the prison community. Punishments and withdrawals of privileges are the instruments for enforcing regulations. Organization of work and production are governed by officials. Hence there is a constant conflict between the officials and the inmates.

The convict functions under two general influences. If he desires a favorable status in the opinions of his fellows, he must adopt patterns of behavior in line with their culture. And since there is a very keen awareness of all his acts, he must be very careful unless he does not care for the ill will or ostracism of his fellow inmates. If he accepts a specific group, he tends to adopt their behavior. "Daily incidents and daily conversations mold reactions that fit into the mold of the conflict situation which is the life of convicts." [2]

Another study made by a graduate student in the State University of Iowa based upon some months of experience as a psychologist at the Fort Madison Penitentiary points out that the prison is interesting as an example of an autocratic group, where policy is, for the most part, determined by the top members of a hierarchy. It is clear that no program aiming at anything more than segregation and punishment can be effective without taking into consideration the reactions of its subjects.

The prison group run according to authoritarian lines has neither "the desire nor the opportunity for the development of those self-imposed responsibilities which make possible the smooth conduct of a free society." Prisons, consequently, have "an almost infinite capacity for the anti-socialization of their inmates. And the more onerous one makes prisons, the more will he facilitate the process of atomization and social disruption." [3]

The most comprehensive study of the prison as a community has been made by Donald Clemmer and published in 1940 under the title *The Prison Community*. One reviewer described it as "the first life-size portrait of the prison community processually analyzed."

The author worked in a large prison system (Illinois) for nine years. He was a professionally trained sociologist and enjoyed relative academic freedom and political immunity. In addition to his routine duties as a member of the classification board, he coached prison football teams, acted as a father confessor, assisted inmate journalists, and participated in many other activities. He functioned as a member of a group of psychiatrists, psychologists, physicians and sociologists in the service of the state. His assignments have taken him into every branch of the penal system. The book covers a period of three years and is a by-product of his routine duties.

The purpose of the book is to present an accurate picture of an American prison. The institution studied (Menard, Illinois) has many features common to all American prisons. It is typical in size varying only 200 in population from the average of fifty-one major correctional institutions. The study covers the period 1931-1934. There were at that time

[2] Riemer: "Socialization in the Prison Community," in the *Proceedings of the American Prison Association*, pp. 151-155.
[3] Polansky: "The Prison as an Autocracy," in the *Journal of Criminal Law and Criminology*, May-June, 1942, pp. 16-22.

about 2,300 inmates and 230 employees, including 160 guards, eight or nine captains, and a warden and two assistant wardens.

The book aimed at a description of the culture of the prison. It is more concerned with social processes than with incidents or events. Attention is focused on such phenomena as class stratification, informal group life, leadership, folkways and other social controls. The author hoped "to make clear the pattern of prison life woven of those salient social forces which influence and prescribe the attitudes and behavior of prisoners," and "the extent and degree to which the culture of the institution determines the philosophy of the inmates."

After three preliminary chapters on the culture antecedents of the prisoners, the composition of the penal population, and the organization of the penitentiary, Clemmer describes the social relations in the prison community, social groups, leadership phenomena, social controls, the social implications of leisure time, sexual patterns, and the social significance of labor.

A final chapter on culture and the determination of attitudes summarizes the manner in which attitudes of prisoners are modified as the men spend month after month in the prison. Structural aspects of the prison community are important in the determination of attitudes. The greatest cleavage is between officials and inmates. Next in importance is the existence of spontaneously formed primary and semi-primary groups. These cleavages are by no means absolute. The relations are symbiotic rather than social. The prisoner's world is an atomized world. Social controls are only partially effective. Daily relationships are impersonal. It is a world of "I," "me," and "mine," rather than "ours," "theirs," and "his."

Assimilation into the prison world may be described as *prisonization.* "Every man who enters undergoes prisonization to some extent. He becomes at once an anonymous figure in a subordinate group. A number replaces a name. He wears the clothes of the other members of the subordinate group. He is questioned and admonished. He soon learns that the warden is all-powerful. He soon learns the ranks, titles, and authority of various officials. And whether he uses the prison slang and argot or not, he comes to know its meaning.

"Acceptance of an inferior role, accumulation of facts concerning the organization of the prison, the development of somewhat new habits of eating, dressing, working, sleeping, and the adoption of local language, the recognition that nothing is owed the environment for the supplying of needs, and the eventual desire for a good job are aspects of prisonization which are operative for all inmates."

These aspects of prison life are important because of their universality, especially among men who have served many years. Their influence is "sufficient to make a man characteristic of the penal community and probably so disrupt his personality that a happy adjustment in any community becomes next to impossible."

These aspects, however, are less important than the phases of prisonization "which breed or deepen criminality and antisociality and make the inmate characteristic of the criminalistic ideology in the prison community." Every man feels the influence of the universal factors, but not every man becomes prisonized by the other phases of prison culture. Whether or not complete prisonization occurs depends upon a number of determining factors. It depends: (1) on the man himself, his personality; (2) the kind and extent of relationships which he had outside; (3) his affiliations with prison groups; (4) chance placement in work gang, cellhouse, and with cellmate; (5) acceptance of the dogmas or codes of the prison culture. Other determinants are age, criminality, nationality, race, and regional conditioning. All determinants are more or less interrelated.

Most men in prisons have no chance of being salvaged if they become prisonized to any appreciable extent. Clemmer concludes from a wide acquaintance with hundreds of inmates that those who were improved or rehabilitated were men who should never have been committed to prison, and who were prisonized in only the slightest degree. The rehabilitation of habitual criminals is more likely to be the result of treatment which keeps them in prison until they reach such an age that they no longer have sufficient physical or mental vigor to commit crime. A few men are "scared out of" further adventures in crime, and consequently become prisonized to a lesser degree. A few seem to develop a new sense of loyalty and responsibility toward their home folks. Their prisonization has not progressed very far. Many concrete examples are known where subsequent behavior proved the genuineness of the change.

"The adoption of religion usually occurs among a few men who are relatively unprisonized. They take up religious teachings because they are prisonized only to a mild degree and the adoption of religion, in turn, prevents further prisonization. We have no information to offer as to the permanence after release of the religious influence, although it is important in the penal community because it reflects the attitudes and adjustment of men in reference to prisonization." [4]

[4] Clemmer: *The Prison Community*, preface and Chapter XII, The Christopher Publishing House, Boston, 1940.

69 · Aspects of the Prison's Social Structure

by S. KIRSON WEINBERG

To what extent do human relationships in a prison community reproduce those prevalent in society at large? On what basis are they carried on? How do prisoners react to the subordinate position imposed upon them by the officials, and how do the officials react to their position of superiority and power? What conceptions do the prisoners and officials have of each other? S. Kirson Weinberg, a professor of social psychology at Roosevelt College, sought answers to these questions in his study of a penitentiary, the results of which are presented in the following article. [From *American Journal of Sociology*, Vol. XLVII, No. 5, March 1942, pp. 717-726. Reprinted by permission. Footnotes omitted.]

THE PRISON is often regarded as an institution with a punitive, segregative, deterrent, or rehabilitative function. It can also be considered a closed milieu with many primary features of community life. The attitudes which emerge from inmate-official and interinmate relationships are continuations of cultural conflicts antecedent to incarceration and permeate the formal discipline in the penitentiary. While many studies have concentrated upon these formal phases of prison life, some recent inquiries have veered to its dynamic social aspects. This investigation, following this latter trend, considers the results of the conflict process upon (1) the prison's informal social structure and (2) upon the opposing ideologies of the inmate and official groups.

I

The inmates and officials are two segregated strata whose relations and attitudes, like those of other castes, result from previously unresolved conflicts. Their relations are impersonal, and the individual members of the respective groups are considered as stereotypes. Modes of deference and obedience are expected by the officials, and expressions of authority are anticipated and tolerated by the inmates. Castes which are long subservient acquire inferiority feelings from traditional displays of deference, but groups in a less-resolved conflict situation, such as the prisoners, also consider the upper groups as out-groups; consequently, their respect remains superficial and external.

Before imprisonment, the criminals and law-enforcing personnel are mutually unrestrained in their hostility. When incarcerated, the criminals are placed in an obviously defensive and helpless position. They are compelled to restrain direct conflict expressions and to divert these into more subtle, less discernible channels. The prisoners' submerged hostility finds outlet in criticism and condemnation of the administration and in intensified intrigue against it.

But the administration, through repressing and countering the inmates' inimical attitudes, makes for the continuation and intensification of this conflict. For conflict met on its own level does not abate but seems to revolve in a vicious cycle. The antagonistic relationships extend the social distance between the two strata and relatively isolate them. Through isolation the members of each group assume logically extreme positions. Each selects and exaggerates the defects and weaknesses of the opponent and overlooks or minimizes his merits. Each abstracts certain traits and imposes them as a group stereotype upon the opposing individual members. This impedes a sympathetic understanding of the individual qua individual. In reacting to the others in terms of the stereotype, the respective members of each stratum reinforce and sustain the conflict process.

But, in condemning the other, each group seeks to sustain morale by a collective self-elevation. While this type of self-praise would be apparent among the officials who are in a dominant position, it also obtains among the inmates. The added defensiveness of the latter places more vigorous demands upon the individual members and compels them to conform to the group norms. While Hargan has shown that the inmate argot "softens an otherwise too unpleasant reality into something bearable," their vernacular also is anti-administration and through idiomatic meanings changes words to add rather than to detract from their prestige.

Vogelin and Copeland in previous studies of conflict groups have shown that, when an upper stratum wishes to reinforce its social position and to justify its behavior with reference to the subordinate group, the "contrast-conception" arises and is diffused among the members. This "contrast-conception," as the authors point out, defines the lower group in "negative polarity" to itself. The whites of the South, as Copeland shows, regard the Negroes in direct contrast to the "character and properties of the white man." Negroes are considered "subhuman in temperament, lacking in emotional control and restraint . . . incapable of continuous affection and mental concentration," and "beyond the pale of human sympathy." This negative depiction makes the white group all the more impressive to itself.

Both writers, however, neglect to describe the conceptions which the lower group has of the superordinate one. In the prison situation the inmates as a subordinate group oppose, negate, and even nullify the ideology and symbols used by the officials. They tend further, as has been indicated, to denounce and to deride the officials as they converse among themselves. This opposition is verbalized in their "conflict-conceptions." These "conflict-conceptions" are one of their media of contradicting the notions of the dominant officials and of justifying their behavior with reference to these persons. Also, the conceptions channelize the perspectives of the individual inmates and control their conduct and relations to the official group. Both countering ideologies— the "contrast-conception" and the "conflict-conception"—emerge in a situation of group hostility and define and articulate the positions and attitudes of the opposing collectivities.

II

Within the scope of these ideologies, the inmates are labeled "cons," but the guards are contemptuously referred to as "screws" or "hacks." The custodians believe and claim that they are "always right" and that the prisoners are "always wrong." The prisoners, however, state among themselves and at times to the officials that the administration is "never right" and, as Nelson has also shown, "make carping criticism" of the administration "the order of the day." Prevention of escapes and the imposition of discipline are the objects of admiration among the officials and form the nucleus of many anecdotes. "Breaks," strikes, and riots are the pervasive and admired myths among the inmates. As guards might delight in detecting and in relating the inmates' frustrated attempts at illicit activity, the inmates, conversely, exult when they tell how they "put one over" on the custodians.

The officials, especially the guards, regard the convicts as "criminals after all," as "people who can't and shouldn't be trusted," and as "degenerates who must be put in their place at all times." "You can't be too easy with them," states one custodian. "You can't be too soft with them. They're on the go to put one over on you. They don't think of us when they try to get over the wall." "There must be something wrong with every man here," states another, "else he wouldn't be here. They're scheming all the time, soon as you give them an inch. That's because there's something wrong with every one of 'em." Convicts are considered "born bad," as mentally, emotionally, or morally deficient. Their only language, "the language they understand, is punishment." Attempts at rehabilitation usually are considered as futile. In exceptional cases, only in cases where the inmates are "not really convicts," reform does occur. Prisoners are "unfit, failures," and hard men without human feelings.

They are considered calloused because they were unable "to make their way in life like honest folk." Hence when they become recalcitrant, they must "be softened and broken" to get them "back in line." They are thought of as unintelligent and lazy, and, consequently, they stall in their work at every opportunity. Further, those with abilities usually have other undesirable qualities to offset their merits.

Because they are unable to care for themselves, they must be held under leash. Because they are "wild" and uncontrollable, they require the sternest measures of discipline. Homosexuality is almost considered "natural" among inmates. As one custodian claimed, "It's in them. I couldn't believe it could happen till I saw it, and I had to give them both the hole." The "punk" and sex pervert are thus natural products of a degraded group and "prove" that the convicts are depraved and animalistic, for they resort to practices abhorred by conventional persons. Hence "to act like an inmate" denotes derogatory behavior. "To look like an inmate" indicates disagreeable appearance. Convicts in their dress, speech, and walk are "different." They are enemies of and outcasts from society. Resultantly, they diverge from noncriminal persons in all the above-mentioned characteristics.

The officials, on the other hand, consider themselves honest, law-abiding men. They are the servants and the protectors of society. As home-loving individuals who are devoted to their families, they can assume responsibilities without breaking laws or getting into trouble like the inmates.

The inmates have a definitely reverse conception of this order of things. As one typically writes: "Convicts still think pretty well of themselves in spite of their present social status. And this is as it should be, for they are in the main no different from the man on the street." From their vantage point almost all people are potentially or actually crooked. Convicts are distinguished from others because they have been detected. As Tannenbaum puts it: "If a man is not a thief, he is a fool, or a poor 'simp' like the keeper who cannot make a living at anything except torturing better people and smarter men than himself . . . the poor, ignorant, simple-minded 'screw' knows nothing but brutality, is simply a person beneath his own class worthy of nothing but contempt." They consider officials as "economic failures" "who couldn't get a job on the outside." Consequently, they are compelled to work in the prison. The wardens and deputies are mere political appointees, "ignorant sheriffs." The doctor is a "quack," a "croaker," or from a "B school at the most." The chaplain is insincere and "full of witchcraft." Further, the custodians have either committed crimes on the outside or have resorted to sadistic practices which they regard as more cowardly and detestable than property offenses. These guards, according to the inmates, derive their greatest pleasure "from telling you what to do or turning you in." An inmate upon being reminded that his name was similar to a high official indicated that the similarity was a misfortune. Another reluctantly granted that one particular custodian might be all right, but the "only thing wrong with him was being a screw." One tersely summarized his attitude toward the situation as follows: "Where would they be without politics? All they're interested in are elections and cuts. How about us? How about rehabilitation? It's all a phony."

Criticism and condemnation of the administration thus range from prison personnel to penal policy, from a contemptuous portrait of the guard to an indictment of the social order. Some more intelligent inmates may become radical, indict the whole order, and almost welcome an upheaval. Society, according to their version, is responsible for crime. Men are not born criminals but often become so through adverse circumstances. Society is blamed for the present penal system, and they are "victims of society." Society, "the true criminal," if differently arranged, would reduce crime and revise its penal practices. Further, some leaders of conventional society, the financiers, the "real crooks," are almost never arrested.

III

The truth of these mutual claims and tirades is significant in so far as it reveals and reflects the conflicting perspectives of the two groups and governs the behavior of one in respect to the other. The intense emotion with which the "negative aspects of the administration" are expressed by the inmates are, if anything, only mildly presented; for the coercive character of the group representations are so intense that at times they tend to become diluted when an inmate is released or converses with an objective outsider. No longer subject to the collective pressure of the other inmates, he may become more objective and detached from the situation.

The nature of these group representations allows some individuals to have neutral or, in some circumstances, friendly attitudes toward some officials. Similarly, officials pick favorites from among the inmates. This inevitable variation comes with individual differences. But the fact emphasized is that these representations, inherent in the prison situation, are larger than individuals, antecede them, and continue to persist despite the attitudes of certain few individuals. These representations are beyond individual power to control or modify. Rather, persons must adjust and conform to them.

The idealistic or timid guard, for example, acquires these attitudes in more or less degree or becomes a variant. He cannot be too friendly with the inmates because he may be suspected of being "queer," soft, or susceptible to collusion. Even the custodians of the newcomers ("the fish"), while somewhat exceptional, in this respect are also on the alert. This situation is more adequately understood in the light of the contriving tactics of the prisoners. Their mischief occurs in a setting where their subservience is a customary and expected social fact. Indeed, their apparent subordination and deference are so expected that some guards derive a haughty feeling of power, of dogmatism, and of intolerance. These men hate the outwardly troublesome prisoner who resists them, discuss him among themselves, and "get it in for him." Though annoyance of the guards may be a mark of prestige among the inmates, the adjusted inmate aims to achieve his purposes without being detected; he resorts to mischief in, as it were, an underground fashion. Some inmates may become aware that the custodians, who are accustomed to simple situations, become confused in complex or quickly maneuvered situations. They thus plan resourceful media for outwitting the guards during critical situations. By a timely question or by having another inmate distract his attention, they have the "damage done" before the guard discovers the trouble. Some inmates also would have no scruples in betraying an official to a higher authority. Some play one official against another by telling each mutually unfavorable stories about the other. Others plan illicit activity of varied degrees of gravity. The potentiality of an escape or a betrayal by the inmates reflects in some measure the ingenious resourcefulness of the inmates and the needs of the guard to remain wary of these plots so as to be able to cope with them.

In general, the inmates acquire attitudes of condemnation and implement their contriving tactics against the administration in the process of institutionalization. This implies a dual attitude. Through an external deference, the inmates accommodate themselves to the officials, but the former group continue to harbor inner grievances as they assimilate into the inmate society. These views operate as reciprocal checks and determine the likely path of adjustment for the incoming prisoner. They also mean that conformity to prison rules is no criterion of rehabilitation but is rather an index of prison adjustment. As a result, the more experienced and sophisticated criminals tend to violate the prison rules less frequently than the unknowing first offenders.

Just as the custodian cannot be too friendly to the prisoners, the convicts cannot always become too friendly with the guards. For the friendly inmate may be suspected of informing and be considered untrustworthy by the other convicts. In fact, through defection, the informer releases the fierce pressure of the group representations. The informer, however, is a necessary expedient by the administrators to assure order by anticipating plots and conspiracies. He becomes a burden and worse than useless to them, however, when his identity becomes known. He then may create certain disturbances which he is used to avoid. The inmates may plan retaliation; they may blame him for previous penalties imposed upon other inmates; they tend to distrust him in the future. Consequently, he is made miserable in many ways. He may be shunned or denounced, ostracized or framed, when feasible, beaten, and, in some serious situations, killed. Suspect for a long time, he may also become so beset with anxieties and fears in regard to reprisals from the offended inmates or their friends that mental breakdown is not improbable.

IV

This description, in general, has aimed to show that the conflict between the criminals and law-enforcing groups, although modified, persists in the prison despite the formal administrative setup. This conflict is expressed not only through their relationships but also through their reciprocal conceptions. The officials negate and derogate the inmates, while the inmates deride and condemn both the officials and the whole penal policy. These respective ideologies verbalize the opposing perspectives and attitudes of the two groups. Because these attitudes are inherent in the prison situation, they can neither be controlled nor modified by any single individual of either group. In fact, the individuals who do not conform to these group representations are considered variants and subject to the controls and pressures of their respective stratum.

Methodologically, the intent of this inquiry was to indicate that this institution, like other institutions, is, in its inner dynamic sense, a configuration of social relationships and can be regarded as a dynamic social process.

70 · Prison Practices and Policies

by NEGLEY K. TEETERS

Below is a summary of the results of a survey covering fifty-eight state and federal penitentiaries, conducted under the supervision of Professor Negley K. Teeters, of Temple University, with the objective of discovering penitentiary practices and policies regarding prisoners. The survey, which consisted of a questionnaire submitted to the wardens, dealt with a variety of practices—from shaving to solitary confinement—and the replies received reflect, to a considerable extent, the present trend in the treatment of prisoners. ["A Limited Survey of Some Prison Practices and Policies," *Prison World*, May-June 1952, pp. 5-8, 29. Reprinted by permission. Footnotes omitted.]

AT THE 81st Annual Congress of Correction held in Biloxi, Miss., a group of delegates held a bull session one night and the conversation gravitated to the dearth of material on prison practices and policies. Not since the publication of the *Survey of Release Procedures* has source material been available dealing with overall prison practices. The group felt that it would be valuable if some effort was made to gather, from time to time, information dealing with penal practices although it was agreed that such data could, at best, be limited in scope.

Through the efforts of Edmond G. Burbank and Albert G. Frazer of the Pennsylvania Prison Society, the various questions compiled by the Biloxi group were formulated into a questionnaire. It was decided that this should be sent to the wardens of the state and federal penitentiaries only. Sixty-eight institutions were included. The response was most gratifying; 58 responded from 38 states and the Federal Bureau of Prisons. Another gratifying feature was that many wardens wrote that they were interested in the project and wished to receive the tabulated results. In the questionnaire, it was stated that no institution would be singled out in the results for any specific policy or practice followed. The information gathered from these schedules follows:

The questionnaires were sent out in March. The total population of the prisons submitting replies was 96,837. In attempting to compute the number of first offenders, we could take only those institutions that ventured a guess or which had a compilation. These represented a total population of 85,350. Of this number, 36,880—or 42%—were labeled "first offenders." Of course this is not an accurate figure, since many informants stated that many of these inmates had served time in reform schools or reformatories. The question as stated was, *"How many inmates—according to your own or F.B.I. records, are serving their first sentence in a penitentiary?"* We are in no position even to venture a guess as to whether 42% is a high figure for first offenders or not.

In these 58 institutions, we find 7,535 lifers. The question was phrased, *"How many inmates are now serving a definite term or minimum sentence of life?"* Four institutions failed to answer this question and two prisons stated that they held no lifers. During the past five years, it was

croaches on their own specialty or because of fear that it undermines their own effectiveness with inmates. This is certainly an area that needs careful study.

GRATUITIES AND CLOTHING FOR RELEASED PRISONERS

In the matter of gratuities, the prisons vary widely:

$5—eight institutions.
$10—seven institutions.
$20—six institutions.
$25—four institutions.
$50—three institutions.
No money at all—two institutions.
$2—one institution.

In two states, the released inmate who has served his entire sentence receives $50, whereas if he is paroled, he receives only $25. Following are some variations noted:

$10 plus transportation and $2 extra per year over a five year term; up to $40 plus transportation; up to $50 depending on need; minimum $25, maximum, $50; less than two years, $10, more than two years, $20; (one peculiar variation was $10.95); railroad fare plus $15 in clothing; $5 to $10 according to distance from prison to home; one state, $50 to $100; in one state, $1 per month of sentence; one state, no definite amount, depending on decision of board of correction. Several, but by no means all of the prisons, add carfare to the amount of the discharge money.

Transportation money is presumably meant to mean from the prison to home or city where sentence was imposed.

In practically all states, this discharge money is allocated from public funds. There are a few states in which the discharged inmates may borrow from welfare funds upon discharge.

In the great majority of the states, the discharged inmate is given a complete outfit of clothes. In winter he is also given an overcoat, or topcoat. In a few states, he is given only his own clothing in which he appeared at the prison. One informant stated that the prison cleans the inmate's clothes before he leaves the prison. A few states give the men, in addition to a complete outfit, a bundle of work clothes. One state indicated the inmate was given what clothing "is necessary." In one state he may "buy his own clothes" if his own are not suitable. One state gives a khaki outfit of clothes, plus work clothing.

POLICIES REGARDING CORRESPONDENCE

The number of letters a prisoner may write varies widely throughou the country. In quarantine we find the following:

8 institutions—no limits placed on correspondence
12 institutions—one letter per week
7 institutions—two letters per week
10 institutions—three letters per week
2 institutions—one letter per day
1 institution—a "reasonable" number
1 institution—two letters per month
2 institutions—six letters per month
1 institution—a total of one letter during quarantine period.

Six institutions did not answer this question and four prisons stated they had no quarantine period.

Correspondence privileges after quarantine period:

5 institutions—no limit
11 institutions—two letters per week
10 institutions—two letters per week
11 institutions—three letters per week
1 institution—varies "with grade"
5 institutions—no limit
1 institution—"reasonable" number
3 institutions—one per day
1 institution—one per month
1 institution—two per month
1 institution—six per month
1 institution—eight per week
1 institution—six per week
1 institution—ten per week
1 institution—"depends on conduct"
1 institution—no answer

Several institutions make special allowances for special circumstances A few states place "no limit on business letters." Many prisons naturally pointed out that lists of correspondents must be approved.

POLICIES REGARDING MONEY AND COMMISSARY

To the question, "What restrictions are there on how much an inmate may spend in the commissary per month?" we find the following:

Only two prisons stated they had no commissary.

13—no limits placed on amount spent
12—$5 per week
5—$10 per week
2—$6 per week
5—$4 per week
1—$3.50 per week
3—$2 per week
7—$15 per month
1—$7.50 per month
3—$12 per month
1—$4.50 per month
1—"half their earnings"
2—"depends on conduct"
1—"depends on grade"

To the question, *"If inmates may earn money are they required to save toward date of release?"* we find the following: In 21 institutions, they are required to save something; in 21 they are not. In five establishments, the inmate cannot earn money. Two prisons did not answer this question. In one institution, the inmate need not save until he has been designated for parole and then only one dollar per month.

As to the percentage of earnings that must be set aside, 9 prisons expect fifty per cent; 4 institutions expect 20%; one prison each for 10%, 33%, 70%, and 75%. One prison stated "depends on inmate's needs."

To the question, *"Are inmates permitted to have cash in their possession?"* 45 prisons stated "no" and 3 prisons answered "yes." A few institutions did not answer.

To the question, *"Do you permit transfer of funds between prisoners?"* the results showed: "No"—33 prisons; "yes"—4 prisons. Two prisons permit transfer of funds between brothers or blood relatives. Four prisons permit transfer "on rare or limited occasions."

EXTENT OF CARD PLAYING

Twenty-seven institutions permit card playing and 26 do not. A few noted: "under special conditions" or "farm group only."

CLASSIFICATION CLINICS AND PERSONNEL

Of the 57 institutions answering the question, *"Do you have a Classification Committee?"* eleven answered "no."

To the question, *"Who sits on the committee?"* there was so much variation that it is difficult to make much tabulation. In only four of the institutions having a classification committee do we find only the warden and deputy sitting. In all others, there are one or more treatment officers included, although in some cases these are designated as superintendent of industries, road camp supervisor, or warden's secretary. A few states have as many as 10 or more officers on this important committee. Only three institutions specifically mentioned a psychiatrist, although several put down "chief medical officer" or physician. Those services appearing most frequently were: classification officer, superintendent of education, psychologist, chaplain, guidance director. In only one state do we find sociologists mentioned.

SERVICES TO PRISONERS

The question dealing with services to prisoners was stated, "*What provision do you make for providing the following—artificial limbs; dentures; glasses; hearing aids?*"

About two-thirds of the prisons indicated that their states, through the prison administration, supplied dental work and glasses; at least to any prisoner who needed such services. In almost the same proportion the prisons supply artificial limbs and hearing aids.

Several institutions give free dental service or eye glasses but stated that artificial limbs or hearing aids could be supplied only through some special fund or through recommendation of a physician. In a few institutions, artificial limbs could be furnished only if the amputation occurred while in the prison.

Eight of the total number of prisons responding stated that no provision is made for the above needs. At least, answer to the question was "No." Several added that any of the services indicated could be supplied at the prisoner's expense. In some cases, the services were paid for out of special funds such as "commissary funds," "state rehabilitation funds" or "educational and recreational funds."

Special remarks included—the services could be furnished: "on loan"; "up to a certain cost"; "inmate pays for material"; "necessity only"; "dentures only for long termers"; "hearing aids only in excessive cases"; "on physician's recommendation"; "no appropriations for hearing aids or artificial limbs"; and "for indigents only."

It may be assumed from the above that hearing aids are not furnished in too many prisons; that artificial limbs are none too frequently supplied; and that eye trouble and dental work are, in the tradition, widely accepted as a state responsibility.

It may be further suspected that not too many institutions may draw from appropriations for hearing aids or artificial limbs but do have fund for routine optometry and dental work. But there are still several institutions that make no provision whatsoever for any of these services, although there are several that may meet prisoners' needs if such inmates pay for them out of their own money.

DETAINERS

One of the questions dealt with detainers: also the policy of paroling inmates who had detainers. It was found that of the 44 institutions answering this question (representing a population of 67,218), 5430 or 8 per cent had one detainer and 918 or 1.36 per cent had two or more. One institution stated it held 20 per cent of its population under detainers. This seems an unusually high number if it is compared with the overall figure of only 8 per cent.

Out of the total number of institutions answering (58), four stated that parole is not granted to those having detainers. In the vast majority of the institutions, parole is possible—subject, of course, to the detainer. Answers from other prisons not covered above were: "Very rarely"; "except for deportation"; "commutation possible"; and "only with permission of detaining jurisdiction."

EMPLOYMENT OF INMATES IN VARIOUS CAPACITIES

It has long been a question whether inmates should function as clerks, typists, or mail censors, or in any capacity where they have access to confidential or personal information. The questions asked were: "Do you employ inmates as: mail censors; turnkeys; guards; instructors?" and "Does inmate clerical help handle confidential material from: (a) district attorney's office; (b) probation office; (c) psychiatrist's office; (d) welfare reports?" Tabulation follows:

As mail censors: none in any of the 57 institutions
As turnkeys: in only five prisons
As guards: in only one prison
As instructors: in 28 prisons (in many, limited to some degree)
District Attorney's office: five answered in the affirmative
From probation office: three answered "yes" (some have no probation officer)
Psychiatrists: seven answered in the affirmative
Welfare reports; nine answered "yes."

There were some qualifying statements regarding these questions. A few stated "no confidential information"; "under limited conditions"; "under supervision"; "only as clerical help."

The next question dealt with designation of some person on the staff to whom the inmate could come with confidential information. To this question, all prisons stated there was some person designated. In the vast majority of the prisons it was the chaplain. In a few it was the classification officer. In several instances it was the warden or the "warden or his deputy" or the "warden's secretary." Some specific remarks were: "warden, deputy and chaplain will hear and keep in complete confidence any matter not pertaining to the security of the prison"; "the psychologist, as long as information does not concern life of another individual or physical destruction of the prison." This informant added: "Has happened only once in past ten years. No secrets between staff members; ordinary things kept secret but none where life is at stake."

NEGROES AND SEGREGATION PRACTICES

Most of the prisons have a fairly large percentage of negroes and segregation is the rule in eating and housing, but seldom at work except in some southern prisons. However, there are several large prisons in the North having a good proportion of negroes that have no segregation whatsoever. In at least two northern states where the negro population runs almost half, there is no segregation. It is of some interest to note that, in a few prisons where the population is small and the negro population extremely small, segregation obtains—and in the North.

A few institutions stated that segregation at meals was "voluntary." Some, which scrupulously maintain individual housing, state there is no segregation on cellblocks. A few prisons stated also that segregation is maintained in cellblocks but not in dormitories.

Cases of prisons with large proportion of negroes in which no segregation occurs: case A, 33 per cent; case B, 54 per cent; case C, 43 per cent.

It is interesting to note that in a few southern prisons there is no segregation while inmates are at work.

POLICIES ON SHAVING

The purpose of this question was primarily to ascertain just how men shave. In by far the majority of prisons, inmates may have their own safety razors. In almost all of them, however, men may be shaved by inmate barbers. In many institutions, barbering is one of the trades maintained. Several questionnaires stated that single edge safety razors were not permitted—only double edged razors. In two institutions, inmates may use electric razors if they furnish their own. Only one prison stated specifically that blades are furnished only for the time of shaving and then must be returned. In one prison, men in segregation may not have razor blades although there are doubtless many institutions where men under discipline may not shave themselves. In one prison, it is stated that those considered "psychopathic" are denied blades; in still another, those having "suicidal mania" many not shave themselves.

In some prisons, inmates must shave themselves at least once a week, but in most cases they are required to shave daily or "keep shaven" or "look neat." In a few prisons it was specifically stated that no mustaches are permitted, but in a few others they may. A few prisons stated "no goatees," and one prison specifically stated "no sideburns." Some prisons merely answered the shaving question with "no rules" or "no restrictions."

CONCLUSION

Those who conceived the idea of this questionnaire feel there is a need for gathering penal information. It is almost impossible to know what policies are followed in prison practice, except in isolated institutions. There is a crying need for a central collecting agency that can collect data on many of the areas so often overlooked. . . .

71 · So You Know About Prisons?

by JOHN C. BURKE

Most visitors to a prison see the institution as outsiders, and few have even the slightest conception of its meaning to the prisoner. What does life in prison feel like to the insider, the inmate? From this thought-provoking article by the warden of Wisconsin's penitentiary, the reader may perceive what an individual confined within the four walls of a prison and completely cut off from the free world for years must think and feel. [American Prison Association Pamphlet, Fall 1949. Reprinted by permission.]

So YOU KNOW about prisons, John, you and your good wife, Mary? You have read about them in the papers, in magazines and books, and have heard about them over the radio. . . . Then too, John, I believe you and Mary saw the "lugs" in the "big house" when you went through the prison the time your club held its annual meeting at Fond du Lac and you all went over to the prison to see the "animals." Yes, I knew you had!

You saw the ball diamond, the busy shops, the men talking in th dining room, everything just as you knew it was going to be.

But there is another prison, John, that I would like you to see an know. No, not an imaginary prison, nor a prison in another state. Thi is the same prison you went through, seen from a slightly differen angle than when you went through before.

No, Mary, you can't come along. But don't worry, you will have chance to learn a lot more about prisons than you now know.

Let us, you and I, John, take a walk down into one of the cell halls Here we are, John. See how nicely the cells are arranged, twenty-five o them in a row and four rows stacked one on the other.

Notice how the fronts of the cells are barred. One half of the cel front is covered by a sliding, barred door. Take a good look at that door John, because doors like that play a big part in the prison I am going t show you. Just step inside. That's it. Now I will pull the door shut an lock it, and then lock another lock, and then another. Yes sir, John, yo are securely locked up! Just sit down and look around.

Notice your cell, John. Take a good look at it, because it is going to b your home for the next ten years. Sure! You have just gotten a ten-yea "jolt," John; so settle down and be a good prisoner.

Mary?

Oh, now don't you worry about her. She will be all right, and she wil be waiting for you when you get out . . . I hope. And she will come u to see you once every month . . . if she can come up.

Notice, John, that your cell isn't a bit like it seemed that day you vis ited the prison. It's somewhat smaller than you thought. Yes, they d seem smaller from the inside, don't they? Probably an optical illusion Notice, when you lie on your bed you can touch both of the side wall without any stretching. That makes it handy when you want to swat flie and mosquitoes. Yes, that cell is 60 inches wide and 90 inches long. Bu you will get used to it in time . . . maybe. One thing is sure, the cell' narrowness will not bother you much . . . or it will crush you.

Notice that you can see out through the cell hall windows. True, yo can't see much; just the front of the dining room and a patch of sky— tiny triangular patch of sky. But don't scorn that little patch of sky John. Before you finish up your ten years in here, that little bit of sk will mean a lot to you.

But let us get started on your ten-year journey, John. It isn't so bad You may get a parole in two or three years, if you keep your record clear Sure, the Judge said so, didn't he? In any event, with good time grante you will get out on a discharge in about six years and three months. That's not long . . . or is it? See that man out there on the cot in front of your cell? He's been here seventeen years and society says that the pound of weary flesh it has taken from him is not big enough. No, he is a trusty now, has been for six years or so. He works outside a great deal of the time and is one of the best carpenters in the prison.

You ask what are your chances of getting a parole after two years. Frankly, they are rather slim. About half of the men never get a parole at all. Those who do, often serve at least half of their time and many all but a few months, before they are granted parole. Who can tell; you might be lucky, though. Better figure on doing five years, John, and you won't be disappointed.

Now it is time for you to go to bed; ten o'clock and the lights are being turned off. You're not sleepy you say? Well, that is all right, because you don't have to go to sleep, you merely have to go to bed. You can lie awake all night if you wish, only stay in bed and keep quiet. No, you can't have a light to read by; but you can lie flat on your back and wonder what Mary is doing and so on—and so on. That may be a comforting thing to think about . . . *and it may not.* However, just to cheer you up, the odds are at least fifty-fifty that you will not have your Mary at the end of your "jolt." *Sure, I know Mary is different.* Every Mary is different; but six years and three months is a whale of a long time for a woman to wait alone. Isn't it, Mary? Yes, it is at that.

No, John, don't jump out of your skin. That is just the morning gong and that means it is time for you to get up. Sure you slept. You feel like you'd been up all night? Yes, you will feel that way lots of nights. But come on, get up. It's ten minutes to six and in just forty-five minutes you have to have your bed made, get washed, have your cell swept out, and be ready to leave when the gong rings for breakfast line. Why do we get up so early? Why not; you can't sleep anyway. And then, one must get up early to harvest the crop of wild oats one planted. Yes, that's an old stir joke.

There goes the gong; and now follow and you will learn something. You will learn one of the first lessons about doing time. You will learn about the endless marching to nowhere; the ceaseless marching to the dining room, to work, to the cell hall—always over the same route. You will march many a weary mile, John, before you march out the front gate.

We won't worry about what you work at; we will be glad if there is work for you to do. Industry and labor take a rather dim view on work for prisoners.

But here you are, John, back in your cell. You have served your first day at work.

Stand up to the door until you are counted. Yes, it does make you feel sort of funny, the way you are counted and recounted. That is doing time, John.

And now, John, you get a break. Mary is coming up to see you! You will have the pleasure of seeing her across a wide table, that is at least four feet wide; then there is a nice, heavy, half-inch screen for you and her to peer through. No, John, you can't kiss nor touch her. You *might* tell her all that is in your heart . . . but you *won't*. You won't because there are other men having visits and they are sitting right alongside you, and you wouldn't want them to hear all the things you would like to say. But you *do* get to see her.

You get to see her brave little smile and you get to hear all the brave pitiful little things she has saved up to tell you . . . and they will cheer you no end . . . or will they? Anyway, you got to see her; and that will give you something to think about tonight. Yes, indeed, John; her visit will give you something to think about tonight.

But this is a modern prison, John. You know you have read how the prisoners are being pampered these days. Sure! In your cell there is a toilet just back of the head of your bed, your bed which hangs from the wall. No old-fashioned cell bucket here. And there is the wash bowl with two kinds of water—running and cold. That's another of the old stir jokes.

And then there is the radio, John. That is fine. Might as well put the earphones on and get a load of what is coming in. A little bit early yet. There is a kid program just signing off. Funny how that kid's voice brings a lump to your throat, isn't it? Sounds just like your little Johnny's voice. Well, lumps in your throat . . . that's all part of the game.

Yes, it is kind of tough, but you'll get hardened up as time goes on. If you don't get so that the sound of children's voices leaves you sort of cold; if you don't get so that Mary's visits don't upset you (if she is still visiting you); you're going to have a tough time of it. In fact, if you don't raise a good, tough callus over your finer feelings, you might wind up hanging onto the bars and screaming at the wall.

It isn't so bad now that you have been here two years, is it? The world you used to know is beginning to fade, and the world of prison is beginning to seem sort of natural.

Sure, you get used to anything. Notice how easy it is to lie on your bunk and dream the hours away. Sure, a regular country club, John.

Well, John, six years and three months have rolled around and you take the last march in prison . . . the march out the front gate.

Remember, John, that time you went through here as a visitor. It took only an hour to march in and then march out again. But it took you six years and three months this time, didn't it? Funny how different the prison you saw on the second march looked from the one you saw as a citizen touring through the place.

As a visitor you saw the ball diamond, the busy shops, the men talking in the dining room, just as you knew it was going to be.

But when you started to live here it was so different. You saw heartbreak . . . your heartbreak. You saw a man working away at meaningless labor for six years and three months . . . you. You saw a man talking in the visiting room, saying empty nothings for fear his voice would make a monkey of him . . . your voice. You heard a lovely voice over the radio, a voice on the "Hour of Charm," singing, "Sweet Hour of Prayer" . . . and you didn't feel so good because that was your mother's favorite song before she died last year. *Your* mother . . . and *you were here.*

It is nice to think, John, that you have paid your debt to society.

Of course, you haven't seen much of prisons in your short stay. You really must look at prison through a lifetime glass before you can really see it. You don't get the really exquisite flavor, John, in a small dose. At any rate, you've seen enough to know that prisons are *not* "country clubs."

72 · County Jails

by JAMES A. TRACY

The primary function of the jail is supposed to be the detention of suspected or arrested offenders awaiting trial. In many instances, however, it serves also as a place where misdemeanants of all kinds—alcoholics, drug addicts, prostitutes, and derelicts in general—are kept for periods of varying duration. Because of this, and because of its usual lack of proper facilities, the jail has been subjected to severe criticism for some time. In the following article, James A. Tracy, a student of the penal system, offers an analysis of the country jail, pointing out its serious defects and making suggestions for its improvement. [From *The Atlantian*, Fall 1947, p. 6ff. Abridged. Reprinted by permission.]

THE DEFENDANT is committed to the County Jail in lieu of bond! Thus with these words many an American citizen is summarily sent to jail. And the particular type of citizen we have in mind at the moment has not been found guilty of any breach of his country's laws. Yet he is sent to jail. Why? Because his only "crime" in this instance is an inability to provide bond in the amount levied by the court to assure his appearance in court at a later date when the worth of the charge against him— whether or not he is guilty—is determined.

"Of course," many will quickly point out, "if he is innocent he will be released when the case is tried." And certainly this is so. But in the meantime, assuming for the sake of argument that the hapless citizen *is* innocent, he is placed in jail. And while technically he is a free citizen entitled to the protection of *all* of the provisions of the Constitution of the United States, he actually is deprived of most of them. He is not free to come and go as he pleases. He has no say in what and where and when he will eat. He cannot choose his place of abode. And on and on ad infinitum.

Most uninformed Americans are certain, if they have ever given the matter any thought at all, that no one is ever placed in such a position unless he has, almost without doubt, violated the law. They are badly mistaken. Any citizen can, merely by visiting the proper authorities, accuse any other citizen of violating the law and bring about the arrest of the so accused. And when the victim appears before a court for hearing any indication that the charge against him might be authentic results in his being held for trial at some later date, and, with the possible exception of a murder charge, he must furnish bond in order to retain his freedom until that time. If he is not financially able to provide the required bond he often is remanded to jail for "safekeeping" until his trial.

Theoretically, of course, the authorities are supposed to be disinterested personally—duty bound to examine the evidence presented by the person bringing the charges and, unless that evidence presents proof of wrongdoing beyond a reasonable doubt, refuse to act. However laudatory this premise appears not always does the accused receive such consideration. The only pressing concern, from the standpoint of the average prosecutory authority, is that it not be liable for any subsequent suit for illegal arrest, defamation of character, etc. A safeguard against this is established when a private citizen makes the complaint, swears out the warrant and signs it, and thereby demands the arrest and trial of the accused. Thus this process relieves the arresting authority from any liability in the event the accused is later found to be the victim of unfounded charges. Unfortunately, in too many jurisdictions such avoidance of liability is the only measuring rod that determines many arrests.

Many variations of the above occur throughout the country, too, and in far greater numbers than the average citizen realizes. The police in most communities are able, in a case in point, to arrest and jail a citizen for no other reason than that of "investigation." The person so arrested may or may not have committed any overt act for which he can be legally charged, but that determination never enters into the picture until hours, days, or often weeks later. And the maltreated citizen has almost no hope or opportunity for recourse from such an action due to the fact that he is not formally charged with a violation of the law.

The most outrageous of all circumstances wherein a citizen may be jailed we have purposely saved until last. This occurs when a citizen is put in jail although he is not even *suspected* of violating the law! Believe it or not, an American citizen can be put in jail for nothing more than being in the wrong place at the right time, or is it the right place at the wrong time—for merely being the luckless *witness* to the commission of a crime on the part of someone else. To insure the witness' testimony when the perpetrator of the crime is to be tried the court may rule, and often does, that the said witness must provide bond to that end. If the witness happens to be unable to provide the bond required by the court he may be, and often is, remanded to the county jail until the trial. That the actual culprit is often able to furnish the required bond in his case and win his freedom pending trial seems to mean nothing to the court that so blandly sends the innocent and helpless witness to jail.

Of course social position in the community determines, to a great degree, one's susceptibility to such outrageous treatment. But *no* man is entirely free from the threat of such imprisonment.

Thus, briefly, we have tried to convey the fact to you that a sojourn in jail is ever present on the horizon of your daily life regardless of how blameless an existence you may lead. And no American, irrespective of the charge against him, or his guilt or innocence, should be subject to incarceration in some, or rather most, of the archaic jails that are to be found in the United States today. Geographical position has no bearing on this national disgrace for some of the vilest jails in the United States are found in some of the richest sections of the country, and some of the finest in the poorest.

Democratically—to coin a pun—regardless of race, color, creed, sex, age or social position these jails offer the same foul environment to all. Paradoxically, these filthy jails—lacking proper sanitation, serving poor food, vermin ridden, rat infested and ill smelling—are found to be in the majority rather than in the minority. This statement is based on authentic reports made by trained and qualified jail inspectors who *know* what to look for even in those jails that offer a surface appearance of adequacy, but reveal the shallowness of their screening veneer when intelligently examined. Of course, hundreds of America's jails will so reveal themselves to even the most cursory and uninformed of examinations. . . . For every jail in the United States that even comes close to adequacy there are at least 6 jails that are rated as unsuitable for federal prisoners. Significantly, approximately 80 percent of America's jails inspected by the U.S. Bureau of Prisons' Jail Inspection Service were disapproved for use by federal prisoners.

An explanation of the why of this circumstance often boils down to indifferent, ineffectual jail administration by untrained, inefficient personnel. Of course, in the final analysis, it is the community itself that is really to blame. By not taking an active interest in the administration of the jail, by not allocating adequate funds to maintain the institution properly, or by allowing a dishonest sheriff or jailer to pocket a substantial portion of the funds that are furnished, the community actually furthers this infamy. . . . We'd like to think that were responsible citizens in the community aroused to a point where they would examine the running of their institutions something would be done to right these situations. Of course, as long as America's 3,500 jails are individually administered just so long will these deplorable conditions tend to prevail.

*   *   *

In reading over what we have written we notice that we haven't mentioned those citizens who are committed to jail by the courts after being tried and found guilty. We mention them now because many of them should not be jailed. For instance, did you know that, roughly, one-third of the inmates in America's jails are there because they are "debtors"? These citizens are committed to jail because they are unable to pay fines levied against them by the courts. The alternative is working the fines out at a predetermined rate per day—some jurisdictions credit the debtor-inmate with as little as 50 cents a day, some as much as 2 dollars. Also among jail inmates may be found those convicted of various misdemeanors; for intoxication; for disturbing the peace; for traffic and motor vehicle violations; for contempt of court; etc. These misdemeanants constitute approximately 75 percent of America's jail population. Thus we find there are three broad categories into which jail inmates fall: 1) Witnesses whose testimony is needed and who are unable to furnish bond to guarantee their availability; 2) Inmates convicted of minor violations and held for non-payment of fines or to serve short sentences; 3) Citizens charged with law violations and awaiting trial who are unable to furnish bond.

However, all of these citizens, regardless of which category they fall into, are Americans, and as Americans they surely deserve decent treatment. Criminologists and penologists have recommended for years that sorely needed intelligent jail administration be established. But their voices seem to have fallen upon deaf ears. Their recommendations cannot accomplish anything worthwhile unless communities shed their hands-off attitudes.

In many sections of the country a spoils system has given unscrupulous officials the means whereby they can reap a golden harvest at the expense of the helpless citizens in their charge and the taxpayer. Exploitation of inmates committed to the mercies of these men, together with misappropriation of funds allocated for their upkeep, offer a virtual bonanza for some officials. But, whenever and wherever the citizenry of the community takes a hand, these situations clear. Intelligent and periodic check-ups are vital, however, if this desirable circumstance is to maintain once it is accomplished. What needs there are indicate themselves to the intelligent reader who will carefully study the jail rating chart compiled by the Bureau's inspection service. This service of the U. S. Bureau of Prisons has been instrumental in bettering conditions in many jails throughout the country. Most of the notorious "Kangaroo Courts" have been abolished, but only after a thorough airing of the evils perpetrated by them brought community action. For years inmates were beaten, robbed, and terrorized by inmate bullies who operated without interference from jail officials who, in some cases, were actually working with them. Scores of jails were cleaned up, began to provide better food, sanitation and administration in order to comply with federal requirements. A few sheriffs and jailers have been altruistic in their advance toward better jail standards but many of them were spurred to action only when they saw the monies ordinarily received for the care of federal prisoners disappearing when their jails were disapproved due to bad conditions reported by the jail inspectors.

But federal prisoners only constitute a small proportion of the total jail population found in the United States. The government looks out for her charges but has no jurisdiction over others. No violations of standards for the treatment of federal offenders are allowed to continue. The jail that fails to provide decent treatment is quickly dropped from the approved list. But many thousands of Americans are at the mercy of local authorities. They need help. The well formulated, tried and proved jail program devised by the U. S. Bureau of Prisons is available to any community for the asking, and experienced personnel to set the program up will be furnished if requested. But, unfortunately, in many communities (and especially is this so in those offering the most infamous circumstances) the people are generally apathetic to jail conditions, and certainly those in charge of these jails don't desire any change that would curtail or end their pattern of administration. So it is up to the responsibile citizens in each community to determine whether their jail is up to par and finding it wanting demand a change.

73 · Imprisonment as a Source of Criminality

by DONALD CLEMMER

Criminologists have for some time expressed grave doubts regarding imprisonment as means of rehabilitating criminals or of deterring potential law-breakers. Some have maintained that, far from helping the offender in getting back to a law-abiding existence, the prison is frequently responsible for perpetuating criminal behavior in the individual confined. Donald Clemmer, a penologist and criminologist and at present Director of the Department of Correction of the District of Columbia, expresses his thoughts on this subject in the following article. ["Observations on Imprisonment as a Source of Criminality," *Journal of Criminal Law and Criminology*, Vol. 41, Sept.-Oct. 1950, pp. 311-319. Reprinted by permission. Footnotes omitted.]

THE RISE of humanitarianism during the last two centuries has had its influence on penal practices in noticeable ways. Earlier societies employed corporal punishment strictly as personal retribution and with deterrence as only a vague and secondary purpose. The development of imprisonment as a form of penalty for violation of laws is, in the historical sense, rather new. As humanitarianism has in minute and almost indescribable ways edged slowly into all human relations, so also has it influenced penal programs. The doctrine of humanitarianism has, for example, added a new concept to penal practice within fairly recent times—the concept of rehabilitation. This doctrine or trend has also recognized the youthful offender as a "juvenile," and it has been instrumental through modification of criminal codes, in reducing the single and absolute responsibility towards the offender. There have been many exceptions according to locality, and the humanitarian influence has been jagged in its slow, upward climb.

It is important to recall the historical newness of imprisonment as a penal method, and it is especially important to recognize that rehabilitation as a serious purpose has only a few decades of experience behind it. These views are needed for perspective as we lay bare in a descriptive way the manner in which American prisons contribute in some degree to the criminality of those they hold.

No scientific evidence exists to show in what precise manner or to what degree the influences of the prison culture mould the lives of those subjected to its culture. There can only be observations and rather crude deductions from those observations. Reference is indicated here, of course, to the well-understood condition that the tools of research for understanding in a scientific way how a human being comes to be exactly what he is, are limited. Human nature is too complicated a phenomenon to dissect and analyze, and locate with certainty the precise set of causes of any particular human reaction. There are too many and too complicated individual differences among people. Neither the psychiatrist nor the sociologist, in contrast to the chemist or mathematician, can claim full, logical understanding of casual factors. While it is a common-place to stress this view, it is pertinent as we attempt to survey in what manner imprisonment affects the personalities it holds.

WHAT HAPPENS AFTER RELEASE?

We do have certain fundamental information as to what happens to men after they are released from prison. We know, for example, that in the United States varying numbers, between 40 and 80 percent, are returned to prisons for additional offenses. We know precisely that 83 percent of the inmates admitted to the jail in Washington, D. C. in the fiscal year 1949 had some type of prior criminal record. Of the 19,980 admitted in the year mentioned, 46 percent had a prior felony record, and the balance a misdemeanor record only. In one of the revealing studies having reference to imprisonment it was found that four-fifths of the inmates of a reformatory in Massachusetts turned out to be failures so far as post-parole criminality was concerned, when the cases were followed up for a period of five to fifteen years following their release from the institution. This study by the Gluecks though now quite common knowledge created, when it was published, great concern because it revealed that annual reports of penal administrators dealing with imprisonment had not distinctly showed what happened to ex-inmates after release from institutions.

Statistics currently being cited in America by parole authorities indicate the country over that between 10 and 20 percent of inmates placed on parole, violate it. These figures are accurate so far as they go, in that the calculations are made according to the length of time an individual is on parole. Thus, if a man is released from prison and has nine months to serve on parole, he is tallied as making a successful parole if he completes the nine months, even though the next month he commits a new crime. It requires studies such as those made by the Gluecks to reveal the real facts. Such facts are also known to observant penal officials through their experience.

In the Federal parole system covering some 25 penal and correctional institutions, warrants for arrest have been issued for violations of regular parole, as follows, over the last several years, by percentage of all those placed on regular parole: 1941, 7.7 percent; 1942, 9.8 percent; 1943, 6.7 percent; 1944, 10.8 percent; 1945, 13.6 percent; 1946, 10.0 percent; 1947, 13.1 percent; 1948, 19.2 percent. These figures are cited to indicate that even in what is probably the most progressive prison system the world has ever known, almost one-fifth of men paroled in a recent year—men who are ordinarily considered the "good risks"—violated their parole.

PRISON CULTURE MAY PLAY A PART IN THESE RESULTS

It is unnecessary to belabor the point further, that the inmates flocking out from American penal and correctional institutions, go forth in tragic numbers to engage in crime again. Though no tangible facts are now presented, the later crimes of those who have been in prison are frequently more sophisticated or heinous than the offenses for which they were first committed. Just what part the prison itself plays in what appears to be this advance in criminality is not known. Certain basic conditions of the prison culture are understood, however, and it is reasonable to presume that the culture of a prison influences the people participating in it, in the same way as culture anywhere plays a part in shaping the lives of men.

It is not possible to characterize the culture of a prison community in specific detail here. Some of its characteristics are easily discernible, such as the recognition that it is a community of persons of one sex, that those held in it have been stigmatized by the broad society because of law violation, and that the persons who make it up hold, or have held, attitudes which are predatory or sexually unconventional or assaultive in nature. We know further that the prison usually concentrates these people in a restricted area, without privacy of any real kind, and that they mingle and interact in personal ways. This writer, after struggling through 300 tedious pages attempting to depict the prison culture, attempted even more futilely, to summarize it in a few brief paragraphs.

The social world of an average prison was characterized thus. The prisoners' world is a confused world, he said. It is dominated and it submits. Its own community is without a well-established social structure. Recognized values produce a myriad of conflicting attitudes. There are no definite communal objectives. There is no consensus for a common goal. The inmates' conflict with officialdom and opposition toward society is only slightly greater in degree than conflict and opposition among themselves. Trickery and dishonesty overshadow sympathy and cooperation. Such cooperation as exists is largely symbiotic in nature. Social controls are only partially effective. It is a world of individuals whose daily relationships are impersonalized. It is a world of "I," "me," and "mine," rather than "ours," "theirs," and "his." Its people are thwarted, unhappy, yearning, resigned, bitter, hating, revengeful. Its people are improvident, inefficient, and socially illiterate. The prison world is a graceless world. There is filth, stink and drabness; there is monotony and stupor. There is disinterest in work. There is desire for love and hunger for sex. There is pain in punishment. Except for the few, there is bewilderment. No one knows the dogmas and codes notwithstanding, exactly what is important.

It is not surprising, if the foregoing evaluation is even reasonably accurate, that men or women in durance vile are influenced by the culture in which they find themselves and which, by their basic personality traits, they help to make. Prisons and prisoners are what they are because of what they have been in the past, and because of the mood and temper of society concerning them. Institutions could be so organized as to be less deleterious, it is believed, but society is not ready for this step. Modern and progressive penological methods have done much in recent years to alter and counteract the harmful influences which are inherent in them. Certain paradoxes, society-wise, are apparent, however.

. . . Even our modern prison system is proceeding on a rather uncertain course because its administration is necessarily a series of compromises. On the one hand, prisons are expected to punish; on the other, they are supposed to reform. They are expected to discipline rigorously at the same time that they teach self-reliance. They are built to be operated like vast impersonal machines, yet they are expected to fit men to live normal community lives. They operate in accordance with a fixed autocratic routine, yet they are expected to develop individual initiative. All too frequently restrictive laws force prisoners into idleness despite the fact that one of their primary objectives is to teach men how to earn an honest living. They refuse the prisoner a voice in self-government, but they expect him to become a thinking citizen in a democratic society. To some, prisons are nothing but "country clubs" catering to the whims and fancies of the inmates. To others the prison atmosphere seems charged only with bitterness, rancor and an all-pervading sense of defeat. And so the whole paradoxical scheme continues, because our ideas and views regarding the function of correctional institutions in our society are confused, fuzzy, and nebulous.*

Director James V. Bennett in this statement has put the problem well. The confusion of the free community ramifies to the prison or correctional institutions. None-the-less, important progressive measures have been taken. Yet in the prisons of America, in spite of classification, vocational and social education, psychiatric service and all the other efforts to treat inmates, prisons continue to "breed crime," to use a moralistic phrase.

The manner and way in which the prison culture is absorbed by some of its people can be thought of as a process of "prisonization." Prisonization is here regarded as similar to the sociological concept of assimilation. When a person or group of ingress penetrates and fuses with another group, assimilation may be said to have taken place. Assimilation implies that a process of acculturation occurs in one group whose members were originally quite different from those of the group with whom they mix. It implies that the assimilated come to share the sentiments, memories and traditions of the static group. It is evident, of course, that men who come to prison are not greatly different from the ones already there, so far as broad cultural influences are concerned. There are, however, differences in mores, custom folkways and group behavior patterns. As these are encountered, and when absorbed, some aspects of acculturation or prisonization are occurring.

Every man who enters the penitentiary undergoes prisonization to some extent. The first and most obvious integrative step concerns his status. He becomes at once an anonymous figure in a subordinate group. A number replaces his name. He wears the clothes of the other members of the subordinate group. He is questioned and admonished. He soon learns that the warden is all-powerful. He soon learns the ranks, titles and authority of various officials. Even though a new man may hold himself aloof from other inmates and remain a solitary figure, he finds himself within a few months referring to or thinking of keepers as "screws," the physician as the "croaker" and using the local nicknames to designate persons. He follows the examples already set in wearing his

* Federal Bureau of Prisons, *Annual Report*, 1948, p. 5.

cap. He learns to eat in haste and in obtaining food he imitates the tricks of those near him.

After the new arrival recovers from the effects of the swallowing-up process, he assigns a new meaning to conditions he had previously taken for granted. The fact that food, shelter, clothing, and a work activity had been given him originally made no especial impression. It is only after some weeks or months that there comes to him a new interpretation of these necessities of life. This new conception results from mingling with other men and it places emphasis on the fact that the environment *should* administer to him. Supplemental to it is the almost universal desire on the part of the man, after a period of some months, to get a good job so, as he says, "I can do my time without any trouble and get out of here." A good job usually means a comfortable job of a more or less isolated kind in which conflicts with other men are not likely to develop. The desire for a comfortable job is not peculiar to the prison community, to be sure, but it seems to be a phase of prisonization.

In various other ways men new to prison slip into the existing patterns. They learn to gamble or learn new ways to gamble. Some, for the first time in their lives, take to abnormal sex behavior. Many of them learn to distrust and hate the officers, the parole board, and sometimes each other, and they become acquainted with the dogmas and mores existing in the community. But these changes do not occur in every man. However, every man is subject to certain influences which we may call the *universal factors of prisonization.*

Acceptance of an inferior role, accumulation of facts concerning the organization of the prison, the development of somewhat new habits of eating, dressing, working, sleeping, the adoption of local language, the recognition that nothing is owed to the environment for the supplying of needs, and the eventual desire for a good job are aspects of prisonization which are operative for all inmates. It is not these aspects, however, which concern us most but they are important because of their universality, especially among men who have served many years. That is, even if no other factor of the prison culture touches the personality of an inmate of many years' residence, the influence of these universal factors are sufficient to make a man characteristic of the penal community and probably so disrupt his personality that a happy adjustment in any community becomes next to impossible. On the other hand, if inmates who are incarcerated for only short periods, such as a year or so, do not become integrated into the culture except in so far as these universal factors of prisonization are concerned, they do not seem to be so characteristic of the penal community and are able when released to take up a new mode of life without much difficulty.

The phases of prisonization which concern us most are the influences which breed or deepen criminality and anti-sociality and make the inmate characteristic of the criminalistic ideology in the prison community. As has been said, every man feels the influences of what we have called the universal factors, but not every man becomes prisonized in and by other phases of the culture. Whether or not complete prisonization takes place depends first on the man himself, that is, his susceptibility to a culture which depends, we think, primarily on the type of relationships he had before imprisonment, i.e., his personality. A second determinant effecting complete prisonization refers to the kind and extent of relationships which an inmate has with persons outside the walls. A third determinant refers to whether or not a man becomes affiliated in prison primary or semi-primary groups and this is related to the two points already mentioned. Yet a fourth determinant depends simply on chance, a chance placement in work gang, cellhouse, and with cellmate. A fifth determinant pertains to whether or not a man accepts the dogmas or codes of the prison culture. Other determinants depend on age, criminality, nationality, race, regional conditioning, and every determinant is more or less interrelated with every other one.

INFLUENCING FACTORS IN PRISONIZATION

With knowledge of these determinants we can hypothetically construct schemata of prisonization which may serve to illustrate its extremes. In the least or lowest degree of prisonization the following factors may be enumerated:

1. A short sentence, thus a brief subjection to the universal factors of prisonization.
2. A fairly stable personality made stable by an adequacy of positive and "socialized" relationships during pre-penal life.
3. The continuance of positive relationships with persons outside the walls.
4. Refusal or inability to integrate into a prison primary group or semiprimary group, while yet maintaining a symbiotic balance in relations with other men.
5. Refusal to accept blindly the dogmas and codes of the population, and a willingness, under certain situations, to aid officials, thus making for identification with the free community.
6. A chance placement with a cellmate and workmates who do not possess leadership qualities and who are also not completely integrated into the prison culture.
7. Refraining from abnormal sex behavior, and excessive gambling, and a ready willingness to engage seriously in work and recreative activities.

Other factors no doubt have an influencing force in obstructing the process of prisonization, but the seven points mentioned seem outstanding.

In the highest or greatest degree of prisonization the following factors may be enumerated:

1. A sentence of many years, thus a long subjection to the universal factors of prisonization.
2. A somewhat unstable personality made unstable by an inadequacy of "socialized" relations before commitment, but possessing, none-the-less, a capacity for strong convictions and a particular kind of loyalty.
3. A dearth of positive relations with persons outside the walls.
4. A readiness and a capacity for integration into a prison-primary group.
5. A blind, or almost blind, acceptance of the dogmas and mores of the primary group and the general penal population.
6. A chance placement with other persons of a similar orientation.
7. A readiness to participate in gambling and abnormal sex behavior.

We can see in these two extremes the degrees with which the prisonization process operates. No suggestion is intended that a high correlation exists between either extreme or prisonization and criminality. It is quite possible that the inmate who fails to integrate in the prison culture may be and may continue to be much more criminalistic than the inmate who becomes completely prisonized. The trends are probably otherwise, however, as our study of group life suggests. To determine prisonization, every case must be appraised for itself.

Among inmates who are prisonized to the least degree, the agencies of reform existing in many American correctional institutions take hold, and it is these individuals who do not recidivate. That is, among the individuals who do not return again and again to prison, it is reasonable to presume that some force during their incarceration has acted as cause or partial cause to prevent recidivism. By case study methods it can be demonstrated that a trade learned in prison, or re-directed attitudes, or by surgical or psychiatric treatment, many inmates have been "cured," as it were, of their criminality. Others who do not recidivate, refrain from further crime simply because the one experience in prison has been so painful and unpleasant, that further desire or impetus towards crime is blocked.

Prisons do affect the people who live in them. They "breed crime," it appears, but they also retrain some few people and scare others. The culture of the prison with its unseen environment does these things through many of the same processes that operate in any social group. It is fundamentally a learning process.

In a scientific sense, the exact and precise role of the prison as cause of criminality can not be determined. Most persons admitted to prison already possess "criminality" in various degrees. After they leave, and if they engage again in crime the "location" of criminality for such subsequent crime is difficult to determine. Presumably, the criminality which the individual brought to prison was intensified as a result of prisonization, and remained as a potential in the personality upon release. Also, when released, no forces of sufficient strength in the free community existed to thwart or divert the potential,—and thus it may be said that the post-release community was conducive of crime. By observation and presumption, however, it can be stated that imprisonment, even in progressive institutions with their carefully developed training programs, frequently increases the criminality of the individuals it holds.

As humanitarianism increases and as the sciences which deal with human nature improve their techniques of treating the maladjusted, and as other better methods than prison are found to deal with violators of the law—the criminality of the offender, which is currently increased by the methods used, may well be decreased in that brave, new world somewhere ahead.

CHAPTER NINETEEN

Probation

74 · Principles and Practices of Probation

by JOHN OTTO REINEMANN

In the selection that follows, John Otto Reinemann, Director of Probation of the Municipal Court of Philadelphia,
explains the meaning of probation and its implications for
the individual and society, touching upon such problems
as selection for probation, probation as a treatment process,
the administration of probation, and what needs to be done
to improve the system. [From *Federal Probation*, Vol. XIV,
Oct.-Dec. 1950, pp. 26-31. Reprinted by permission.]

PROBATION is a method of treating offenders by releasing them on good
behavior upon conditions prescribed by the court and under the guidance
of a probation officer. Probation is being used in cases of juvenile as
well as adult offenders.

Probation in Adult Cases. In criminal proceedings against *adult*
persons the courts, when placing the defendant on probation, may either
suspend the imposition of the sentence or impose a sentence and suspend its execution.

Probation in Juvenile Court Cases. In *juvenile* courts, probation is
one of the various forms of case dispositions which are available to the
judge. Juvenile courts have jurisdiction over children (in most instances

under the age of 18 years) who have violated a law or otherwise have manifested delinquent behavior. Juvenile courts are further concerned with neglected, dependent and physically or mentally handicapped children and with cases of contributing to the delinquency and dependency of children, and in some jurisdictions also with cases of adoption and illegitimacy. Probation may be used in all these instances. There is also an extensive field for probation in the domestic relations or family courts, or in other courts dealing with marital problems, such as desertion, separation, divorce, and neglect to support.

Probation should not be confused with "parole." Both include supervision and guidance of the offender in the community but parole is a conditional release of an offender from a penal or correctional institution, while *probation* is used *instead of commitment* to an institution.

Advantages of Probation. What are the advantages of probation compared with institutional commitment? The following are some of the advantages in the case of *adult* offenders: the probationer remains in a free society; his social status is not impaired; he can continue to support the members of his family who often become public charges when the breadwinner is in prison; he can pay restitution to the victim of his unlawful act; he can be rehabilitated through the efforts of the probation officer; in order to achieve such rehabilitation, the resources of the community can be utilized; and the community saves money due to the fact that it costs at least 10 times more to keep an offender in prison than to supervise him on probation.

Regarding *children*, the advantages of probation compared with commitment to an institution are the following: it is an individualized form of treatment; it applies the methods of social casework; it leaves the child in its normal home surroundings; it enlists the help of community resources; and it is not considered punitive and therefore is free of social stigma; as in the case of probation for adults, it is much less expensive.

Probation in recent years has developed in an atmosphere of changing ideas and attitudes concerning crime and punishment. Its growth has been promoted by (1) a weakening of our belief in the deterrent effect of punishment upon convicted offenders and upon other potential law violators; (2) a growing realization of the deteriorative effects of imprisonment upon many prisoners, making them more dangerous when they are released; (3) the belief that each offender should be studied individually and given treatment adapted to the circumstances of his case, instead of punishment predetermined by a code of prescribed penalties for each offense; (4) a growing awareness of community responsibility for crime and its causation; (5) an ever-increasing appreciation of the worth and dignity of the individual.

SELECTION FOR PROBATION

Probation treatment is not a legal right but is determined by judicial discretion. It should not be thought of as an act of leniency or clemency. It is governed by a regard for justice for the individual and for society.

The Need for Social Investigation. In order to enable the judge to apply probation in the proper cases, it is necessary to supply him with all the necessary information regarding the personality and the social background of the offender. Such an investigation should be made in all cases coming before the court, whenever it can be of assistance to the judge in determining treatment. It should be understood that this investigation does not concern itself with the question of guilt or innocence of a defendant regarding the specific offense for which he is brought before the court. In cases of adult offenders, therefore, the investigation usually follows conviction or plea of guilty. In juvenile cases, it customarily is made prior to the hearing. To make social investigations is the task of the probation officer. These investigations should cover the following items:

1. Vital statistics as to date and place of birth, etc.

2. Family history, including a description of the members of the immediate family household (father, mother, brothers, sisters, etc.) and all the positive and negative factors apparent in the family situation

3. Physical history, including such information on physical factors that may have contributed to the present problems and, if possible, report of any physical examination

4. Mental status, including information on the emotional stability and the mental capacities of the person, and preferably a psychological and a psychiatric report

5. Education, including a résumé of reports of educational background, indicating factors of retardation or exceptional merits

6. Work record, including the history of employment, reliability and earning capacity

7. Religion, including an indication of the degree of church participation

8. Leisure time activities, if any

9. Personality traits and habits, providing as detailed a picture as possible of the person's make-up, his weaknesses and strength

10. A report from other social service, health, educational and related agencies regarding the individual and the family

11. A summary, pointing up the assets as well as the liabilities in the personal make-up of the individual and in the total situation

12. A recommendation regarding the most promising disposition of the case

Criteria for Selection of Probation as Court Disposition. Who shall be placed on probation? In adult cases, the law may limit the use of probation by excluding individuals convicted of serious offenses or repeaters. (This often proves to be an unfortunate restriction and will be discussed later in connection with desirable probation legislation.) In juvenile cases, there usually are no legal limitations.

Within the framework of the law, therefore, the selection of a probationer depends upon that individual's potentiality to adjust. Probation should be granted to all those who, upon investigation and analysis of the total situation, seem likely to be good subjects for rehabilitation and re-education under supervision. Selection should not be indiscriminately based upon haphazard choosing, or as a reward for an informer or as a substitute for a more suitable disposition of the case, only because other community facilities are not available. The protection of society, dignity of the individual, available resources and adequacy of supervision are factors to be considered. Distinction should be made between the incidental delinquent and the professional criminal or habitual offender. Psychopaths, alcoholics, drug addicts, and offenders with long criminal records are among those who may be poor risks. There is no precise formula for selecting probationers that can guarantee success with mathematical accuracy. Every case must be determined on the basis of its own merit.

The most desirable practice is to have the court place the individual on probation for an indeterminate period and to have it clearly understood that the probationer must earn his release through definite and acceptable improvement in his attitude and his conduct.

PROBATION AS A TREATMENT PROCESS

Since probation is a treatment process, it is important that the probation officer at the beginning formulate as soon as possible some kind of treatment plan. In many instances, he already knows the individual and his family from the previous investigation.

Conditions of Probation. There are certain conditions attached to probation. In view of previous faulty social attitudes and antisocial acts, it is usually necessary to impose various restrictions upon the behavior and activities of the probationer for his own good and that of society. When wisely applied, this use of authority has real therapeutic value. In order to bring about a real change in the individual's attitudes and character, the conditions should be reasonably flexible and adjusted to each case. It is also necessary to inform the probationer about the conditions of probation and to let him know that the probation officer, as an officer of the court, is required to see to it that the rules are lived up to by the offender and that a serious violation of any of them may require that he be returned to court for further disposition by the judge who had placed him on probation.

The conditions, in cases of juveniles on probation, include obedience to the parents, regular school attendance, keeping of early hours, staying away from undesirable companions and from disreputable places, notification to the court of any change of address, and compliance with all the instructions given by the probation officer. In addition to these general requirements other special conditions may be imposed, as, for instance, payment or restitution for damages, living with a relative due to the inadequacy of the parental home, attendance at a special school, affiliation with an approved recreational agency and carrying out medical recommendations.

In adult cases these conditions may consist of payment of a fine or restitution, regular support of his family, steady work at suitable employment, staying away from persons of disreputable character and from disreputable places, refraining from the excessive use of intoxicants or the use of drugs, living within a specified area, the requirement of asking permission from the probation officer regarding change of address, application for marriage license, automobile driver's license, etc., and regular reporting to the probation officer as directed.

Contacts With the Probationer. Contacts with the probationer can be established either through home visits or through the reporting of the probationer at the office of the probation officer. The home visit enables the probation officer to see the individual on probation as a part of the family. In the case of a child on probation, the probation officer wins an insight into the attitude of the parents toward the child and the child's role within the whole family set-up. In the case of an adult offender, too, his status within the family can be more easily perceived by contacts in the home.

The physical and moral environment of the home and neighborhood thus becomes known to the probation officer supervising a child or an adult. The probation officer often finds himself in the position of undertaking reconstructive work with the whole family. The picture of the family unit seriously damaged by the death or desertion of one or both parents or by divorce, poverty, ill health, alcoholism, etc., is familiar to most probation officers. Finally, there is another reason which speaks for the necessity of home visitation. It is the most readily available means of affording the family a sense of participation in the treatment process and responsibility for carrying it forward.

Reporting to the office by the probationer has several values. Contact with the probationer in the office provides the probation officer with an opportunity of getting better acquainted with the person on probation; it particularly affords privacy, not always attainable in the home of the probationer. Finally, it has a disciplinary value in that it gives the probationer training in responsibility and regularity and that it creates in him a feeling of participation in the treatment process. But office contacts never should be considered a substitute for home visitation, particularly in cases of children on probation.

The Wide Scope of Probation Service.   Probation service should also include attention to health needs, to the development of sound recreational activities, to the development of moral concepts and practices, and to attendance at school or adult education courses to prepare for economic advancement and cultural pursuits. Encouragement must be given to the development of economic responsibility and stability, and the acceptance of personal responsibility as a member of society, not only to be a good citizen but to contribute to the welfare of the local community and the Nation.

In this, probation officers constantly co-operate with a great variety of community agencies and resources, such as school authorities, health centers, hospitals, mental hygiene clinics, family welfare agencies, public relief agencies, recreational and character building organizations, and churches.

The Treatment Process.   The success of supervision of a probationer depends largely upon the establishment of real rapport between the probation officer and the juvenile or adult on probation. The methods of modern social casework have been helpful in probation treatment. The functions of social casework are to relieve tensions within the individual, to help him find acceptable outlets for his drives, and to guide him in overcoming his frustrations. Fundamentally, casework is founded upon respect for the individual as a unique personality and recognition of his worth; equally, probation is based upon the idea of the dignity of every human being.

The relationship between probation officer and probationer should be one of mutual respect, understanding, sincerity, and confidence. This is not in conflict with the use of authority, since all treatment in correctional work must be carried on in an authoritarian setting, just as all activity in any properly organized and disciplined society must be carried on within the framework of government. The psychology behind the authoritarian approach in probation is not different from the generally accepted principle which recognizes that in every group setting, such as family, school and club, office and factory, any behavior of an individual which is harmful to the group calls for discipline of the individual. In a democratic society authority and freedom are complementary to each other. To teach respect for the rights of every person, for his well being and for his property, has been one of the essential concepts of probation treatment. The misuse of authority in the form of threats, carping imperatives, bullying, shouting, and condemnation on the part of the probation officer will not achieve the desired results. It is necessary to interpret to the probationer in a way that he understands and accepts, the meaning of authority, the need for discipline, and the consequences of nonconforming behavior.

Termination of Probation. Probation may be terminated in various ways. In those cases in which a definite time limit is set, it expires automatically; however, as we pointed out before, it is desirable that probation should not be limited as to time in advance. If the length of probation is indeterminate, particularly in juvenile cases, it is left to the probation officer to determine when the objectives of probation are met and consequently to petition the court for discharge from probation.

Violations of probation also may lead to its termination. Upon a finding that a probationer has violated the conditions of his probation, the statute should provide that the court may impose any penalty or sentence that it had the authority to impose at the time that the individual was originally placed on probation. In juvenile cases, when the probationer has seriously failed to live up to the conditions of his probation, he is returned to the court for further planning or treatment. The probation officer in these situations should acquaint the child and his family with this decision and prepare both for their impending appearance before the judge. This may lead to temporary detention, foster home placement, or commitment to a training school.

The commitment of a new offense is considered a violation of probation per se.

ADMINISTRATION OF THE PROBATION SYSTEM

Probation facilities should be available to every court dealing with offenders. Probation in the United States is administered under varying state laws and systems; and for offenders against federal laws under a national system. Two major administrative systems are in effect. The system which developed first and still is the prevailing one in the larger states, is based on the establishment of county or local court units of administration, with appointment of probation officers by judges or local authorities—the local units being co-ordinated and supervised by state agencies. The second plan, more recently developed in many states of the United States, consists of a central state department which provides probation services for all courts throughout the state. This has the advantage of making a uniform and centrally directed probation service available to all parts of the state, urban and rural alike.

Staff. The main requisite of a well functioning probation program is an adequate staff. In the juvenile court, more than in any other judicial branch, the judge must rely on the work of court aides. But in cases of adult criminals, too, an increasing number of judges request presentence investigations and use probation as a promising form of case disposition. The men and women who function as aides to the court are called "probation officers" or sometimes "probation counselors." In the majority of instances they are appointed by the judges except where other provisions are made, as for instance, for appointment by central state agencies.

The Job and the Qualifications of the Probation Officer. The probation officer has, as a rule, two main assignments: (a) investigation of social facts and pertinent data concerning the personality of the adult or juvenile offender prior to the court disposition and (b) supervision on probation.

Because probation involves the study and diagnosis of human behavior, the guidance of young impressionable individuals, and the counseling of adults in need of help and rehabilitation, knowledge and skill are required to render such service effectively.

The personal qualifications of a probation officer, therefore, should include good health, physical endurance, intellectual maturity, emotional stability, integrity, tact, dependability, adaptability, resourcefulness and sincerity, humor, ability to work with others, tolerance, patience, objectivity, capacity to win confidence, respect for human personality, and genuine affection for people.

As to the probation officer's educational qualifications, it has been held that the best training for probation work is graduation from a school of social work or (where such an institution is not available) equivalent training in a department of sociology of a college or university offering courses in criminology, penology, social economy, applied psychology, and related subjects. It is also desirable that before being appointed to the position of a probation officer, the candidate should have a certain period of experience in social work or related fields, such as teaching, public health, law-enforcement, child welfare, correctional institutions, vocational guidance, legal work concerned with social welfare, group work, or work with rehabilitative agencies.

The selection of a man or woman for the position of probation officer should be exclusively based upon his or her qualifications regarding personality, education, and experience. His or her religion, race, nationality origin, social status, and political affiliation should not be considered as determining the appointment.

Training is necessary not only in order to qualify for entrance into the probation service (pre-service training), but also in order to keep the job performance on a high level (in-service training).

Volunteer workers in probation work can be valuable, especially in smaller towns and sparsely populated areas, but they should serve under a well-equipped probation supervisor. Volunteers should not be used to avoid the appointment of needed salaried and qualified probation personnel, or for reasons of false economy.

Case Load, Case Recording, and Case Evaluation. It has been considered desirable that the maximum number of persons to be supervised by one probation officer at one time should not exceed 50. There should be objective and factual case recording of the contacts with the probationer. The probationer's attitudes and problems, his family and neighborhood relationships, and his interests, inclinations and activities should be analyzed. Every probation department ought to have devices for measuring the effectiveness of its work. The progress of treatment should be measured periodically, preferably by someone other than the person or persons who directly administer it.

Behavior Clinic. Wherever possible a behavior clinic should be established to serve each probation organization. Where no such court clinic is possible, other clinic facilities in the community should be made accessible for use by the probation organization.

PROMOTING THE IDEA OF PROBATION

Legislation. Successful administration of the probation system, like other governmental services, requires basic legislative authority and efficient organization. Probation should be administered under laws providing the basic and broad power needed by judges and probation officers to discharge their responsibility. Probation laws should be enacted to authorize the judges of all courts dealing with adult offenders and juvenile delinquents to utilize probation. Specifically there should be no provision in the law confining the application of probation to cases in which specific offenses were committed or in which the individual is for the first time accused of any crime or delinquency. Rather the judge should be entrusted with broad discretionary power with respect to using probation. This should include the power to prescribe indeterminate periods of probation or at least periods sufficiently long to make possible a well planned program of rehabilitation. In the field of juvenile court legislation the widest possible discretion regarding the use of probation should be given to the judge as well as the power to impose specific conditions and to alter at any time previous decisions whenever changes in the personality development or the home situation of the juvenile warrant.

It is necessary to convince the legislative bodies of the value of probation as a modern, scientific, and humanitarian approach to the problem of the offender as well as a procedure that is saving public expenditures. It always should be pointed out that probation is not a device of mollycoddling the offender—juvenile and adult—but that it combines the best features of rehabilitation of the offender and the fullest consideration for the protection of society.

Public Opinion. Naturally, in order to promote such legislation, public opinion must be molded into the acceptance of the ideas underlying the use of probation. The history of social legislation in many countries has shown that in various fields of public policy the concern for children and their welfare has preceded—sometimes by long periods—interest in adults. Curtailment of working hours and protection against hazards to health and morals in certain occupations, are examples in the field of labor legislation. In the field of penology, it is a truism to say that what seems good and sound for children in one generation is likely to be adopted for adults in the next. The public usually is emotionally more inclined and prepared to approve of progressive legislation affecting children and youth. But in recent years modern ideas on the cause and treatment of juvenile delinquency have increasingly entered the orbit of handling the adult offender. It is, therefore, reasonable to assume that probation, if thoughtfully applied and efficiently administered, will be accepted by the public-at-large as an equally valuable and promising instrument of treatment of both juvenile delinquents and adult offenders.

75 · Social Dynamics in Probation and Parole

by G. I. GIARDINI

The following article, by G. I. Giardini, Superintendent of Parole Supervision, Pennsylvania Board of Parole, analyzes the factors involved in crime and delinquency. He discusses matters which must be taken into consideration by those dealing with probation and parole—from the administrative to the workers' level as well as by the public at large—if methods of treatment are to be just and effective from the point of view of the individual involved and of the community. [From *Federal Probation*, Vol. XII, March-April 1948, pp. 41-45. Reprinted by permission.]

BEHAVIOR is the product of heredity and environment. Neither can have meaning without consideration of the other. No matter how good the environment, if the individual does not have the capacity to make use of the opportunities it offers, he will not achieve what might be expected of him. Contrariwise, despite mental or other potentialities with which the individual may be endowed, he is not likely to develop those potentialities to the utmost unless the environment provides the opportunity. It is true that the very able person, by his very abilities, manages frequently to make his own opportunities for development. We say that genius will out. But we all know of capable persons who lead relatively useless or definitely antisocial lives largely because the right kind of opportunities or the right kind of influences were not present at critical points in their development.

THE ROLE OF ENDOWMENT AND ENVIRONMENT

Opportunity serves for something more than just to bring out the talents or lack of talents of the individual. The kind of opportunities which present themselves to him determine the kind of development he will follow. To put it differently, the kind of environment or situation will determine the direction of the individual's behavior, while the distance he will travel in that direction, how much he will achieve, will be determined to a large extent by the intellectual and emotional equipment which he inherited. This applies whether we are concerned with criminal or law-abiding behavior.

Men like Al Capone, Sitamore, Kruger, Insull, and others, were men of talent—some of them had great intellectual endowment and certainly all were as sane as many honest citizens. But the environmental circumstances under which they were reared, the peculiar nature of their life experiences, largely determined their behavior. Under a different set of circumstances, they might have turned out to be honest business men, professional men, or remained honest administrators.

Frequently what appear to be insignificant episodes in the life history of an individual are actually important turning points. One glass of beer more, at a given moment in his life, may turn a law-abiding individual into a murderer.

The social environment is equally significant for those of limited abilities. The moron is not likely to be the successful leader of a criminal gang, nor will he be an embezzler or a high-grade robber any more than he is likely to be a bank president, a lawyer, or a physician. But if he is exposed to a favorable environment and is trained properly and protected through childhood and youth, it is not likely he will be delinquent. Many morons walk the streets as law-abiding citizens.

In other words, the native endowment of the individual is primarily responsible for the proficiency attained in any activity, occupation, or form of conduct. But the environment is the primary determinant of the kind of activity, occupation, or form of conduct which an individual follows. Whether you can do only second grade arithmetic or are an Einstein will depend largely on your native endowment, provided, of course, that you are given the opportunity to learn numbers at all; but whether you are an honest bookkeeper or a clever embezzler will depend greatly on the circumstances of your bringing up—that is, your social environment. Whether you are an honest store clerk or an Einstein, a petty thief or an Insull, will depend largely on your native equipment, but whether you are an honest store clerk or a petty thief, an Insull or an Einstein, will depend to a great extent on the sort of experiences that you will have gone through during the period of your life.

DYNAMICS OF THE SOCIAL ENVIRONMENT

Both for the poorly endowed and for the richly endowed, by necessity, the dynamics of the social environment are extremely important. In the final analysis, the environment determines in a very definite way the patterns of behavior that an individual acquires and defines his character and conduct.

What constitutes the environment? The physical aspects of the environment, such as air, water, sunshine, food are, of course, necessary to health and survival. Everyone knows that good conduct is contingent upon good health. The ancients recognized this fact many centuries ago when they said *mens sana in corpore sano*—a sound mind in a sound body. But even these physical aspects of the environment are not exempt from sociological influences. Water becomes polluted as a by-product of social organization in certain localities, or because of defective sanitation laws or inadequate enforcement of these laws. Increased social contacts in urban centres increase contagion. The processing of such basic needs as food becomes a major social problem requiring the promulgation of many laws for the protection of the health and the pocketbook of the individual.

In the formation of character and personality, these physical aspects of environment are perhaps the least important. What we are, within the limits of our native capacities, depends a great deal more upon the way different social institutions influence us. To enumerate only the more common ones of these, we have the family, the neighborhood, the school, the church, marriage, the press, the employer, the movies, the club, the baseball team, the gang, the police, the courts, the prisons, the automobile, the library, the museum, the tavern, the beauty parlor, the brothel, the number writer, the liquor store, the service club, the doctor, the clinic, the hospital, etc. In addition to these tangible forms of institutions, we have a host of customs, mores, beliefs, and superstitions which influence our behavior in very definite ways.

If we would understand why an individual is a delinquent or a criminal, we must study his life history in great detail and must determine the kind of institutions, customs, beliefs, and superstitions to which he has been exposed and his reactions to them. Many go to church, but not all are affected in their behavior by the teachings of religion. The individual's interest may not be deeply engaged by religious rituals. On the other hand, his interest as well as talent may be keenly aroused by the activities in a poolroom. To the extent that attention and interest are aroused and activities are engaged in, the development and fixation of habits along certain lines take place. Whether these habits are good or bad, social or antisocial, will depend upon the nature of the activities around which they are built, and the associations and attitudes prevailing during the process. Established community customs and beliefs have even more direct bearing on conduct. Depending on the content of customs and beliefs, the effects can be very devastating.

THE SOCIAL SITUATION AS A FACTOR IN CRIME

Obviously the individual is exposed to various institutions throughout his life. Some of these are more influential at certain periods of the individual's life than at others. But the important thing is that the person is under pressure at all times. At any given moment his conduct will depend on all of the habit patterns and attitudes he has acquired up to that time, plus the way he is affected by the present situation. The particular situation, in fact, can be of such paramount importance that it may cause the individual to cast aside all of his previous habits and beliefs and may cause him to commit an act which is entirely "out of character."

Modern criminologists tend to agree that in classifying criminals we must recognize three groups of factors, namely, heredity, the social environment and the situation. But no act is exclusively the result of heredity or environment or of the situation. The feeble-minded suffer from definite biological limitations, but whether they become delinquent or not will depend on social factors and situations. The normal criminal is as much the result of heredity, as far as his native equipment is concerned, as the feeble-minded. The individual who remains law-abiding in every respect until he is 40, then commits a murder, is likewise biologically and sociologically determined, although the uniqueness of the situation is the factor that precipitated the criminal act.

One implication of all of this is that in rearing children we must be always on the alert to see that only desirable social institutions, customs, and beliefs exert their influences upon them, at least until we are sure that desirable habits are sufficiently well established and character sufficiently well knitted to enable the child to reject harmful and undesirable influences of his own accord.

If this principle is valid in the rearing of children, it should be valid also in the guidance of probationers and parolees after due allowance is made for the social requirement that adults must be held responsible for their acts to a degree not expected of children. The immediate concern of the probation or parole officer, as well as every agency concerned with the improvement of human conduct, is to focus upon the individual all of those influences in the community that can be counted upon to reshape the habits of the subject and rebuild his character. The agencies that will be chosen to exert such influences will vary with the individual.

UTILIZATION OF COMMUNITY RESOURCES

It follows that the parole or probation officer must be thoroughly familiar with the resources of his community. He must be familiar not only with the agencies that can help him to rehabilitate the subject, but also with those agencies that can harm the probationer or parolee and from which the subject must be frequently weaned, and which he must avoid in the future.

In obtaining the co-operation of institutions and agencies that can be of assistance in the rehabilitation of parolees and probationers, it frequently is necessary to do missionary work in an attempt to convince them of their share of responsibility in the rehabilitation of the delinquent. For example, it sometimes is necessary to work at length even with the home that has rejected the parolee or probationer, and attempt to bring about a reconciliation along with a necessary change in attitude, so that in the future that home may be restored to its expected usefulness in the readjustment of the subject. Schools have been notoriously guilty of failure to accept responsibility in the prevention of delinquency as well as in assisting juvenile court wards, probationers, and parolees in their readjustment. An instance actually has been reported where a high school principal placed a boy who had just been returned from a juvenile institution before the assembly of high school children as the boy

vho had just come back from the reform school, implying that he was
o be watched, if not avoided by the rest of the student body. While it
s admitted that a maladjusted child can disrupt the program of any
choolroom, it is nevertheless the responsibility of the school, as it is
hat of any other public agency dealing with children, to do something
or that child other than throw him out on the street.

All men have problems. Parolees and probationers have daily problems
hey must face. The way they face these problems and the way they
esolve them frequently will determine whether they revert to crime or
ıot. The parole or probation officer must be ready to assist with informa-
ion and guidance, sometimes with coercion. If the problem is one of
ıealth, the officer must be ready to give information as to where and
ıow medical assistance may be obtained. If it is a question of unemployment the officer should be ready to inform where and how a job can be
ɔbtained. In some instances he must practically take the probationer or
ɔarolee by the hand to the job. If work is not available, guidance is given
ɔn how to obtain relief. If there are domestic problems, it may be neces-
;ary to seek the aid of family agencies. If there is suspicion of mental
listurbance in a probationer or parolee or a member of his family, the
ɔrobation and parole officer must know where and how psychological
ınd psychiatric services can be obtained.

It has been established by actual experience that the greatest success
n the control of crime has been achieved in those communities where
here has been co-operation not only between agencies interested in the
ɔroblem but also organization and co-ordination of all of the community
esources under a central authority so as to present a solid unbroken
ront against vice and crime at the prevention as well as the remedial
evel. In such an organization and co-ordination of effort, the parole or
ɔrobation officer should assume a dominant role.

FACTORS WHICH SHOULD GOVERN THE EXTENT OF SUPERVISION

The question often is raised as to how far a probation and parole
ɔfficer should go in aiding a probationer or parolee. This can be determined only after knowing the abilities and resources of the subject him-
elf. A good principle to follow is that of letting the subject take the
nitiative as much as he is capable.

Some workers in this field have the view that probationers and parolees
;hould be left entirely to their own devices as long as they do not com-
nit any crimes. Supervision consists merely of having the probationer or
ɔarolee report every so often. There is no authentic information as to

the actual adjustment of the subject. Under such a system, it is remark able that more subjects do not go astray in any serious manner. It ma be that no supervision is better than the bad supervision which migh result if such probation and parole officers would attempt a more positiv approach.

Another view is that everything should be done for the parolee an probationer. We should find him a job; fight for him to get relief whe he needs it; we should protect him from prejudice and embarrassmen by hiding the fact that he is on parole or probation; we should even fin friends for him. This view, of course, does nothing to develop initiativ and responsibility in the individual and, as soon as supervision is ended the subject is likely to relapse into his old habits and weaknesses.

A third school of thought advocates the use of the club—"You do a I say or else." This view relies entirely upon the authority of the parol or probation officer to keep the probationer and parolee on "the straigh and narrow." Many subjects respond to coercion and maintain a recor which complies with the letter of the rules, but which can in no way b taken as indicative of a changed and improved character. Like the on just described, this system of supervision fails to bring about any desir able change in the attitude of the individual towards his responsibilitie and place in society with the result that when coercion is removed, i not before, the subject reverts to crime.

Although none of the three views described is desirable as an exclu sive system of supervision, each has its place in the supervision of individ uals. On which one the emphasis is placed will depend upon the re sources of the particular subject we are supervising; assuming, of course that the parole or probation officer is skilled in the use of all three methods. Many probationers and parolees need little supervision an little direction. They are largely self-reliant and require only a hint now and then to keep them "on the beam." Others must be helped consider ably because of their limitations. Still others must be pushed, threatened and even punished merely to keep them from kicking over the lega traces, let alone developing self-reliant social adjustment.

CASEWORK IN AN AUTHORITARIAN SETTING

There are certain professional people, social workers, and some psy chologists who believe that no subject can grow into a self-reliant socially adjusted individual, in an authoritative setting. Some go so fa as to say that the probation and parole officer is hopelessly handicapped in his attempt to bring about genuine readjustment in probationers and parolees because of the police power bestowed upon him by law. They say that we cannot wield the club and do casework at the same time.

It seems to us that this is a very unrealistic view. It not only fails to face facts but, if carried to its logical conclusion, it would foster license rather than law-abiding conduct. The activities of every one of us are circumscribed by laws, customs, and consideration for the rights of others. Authority in one form or another is all about us. We are forbidden to spit on the sidewalk. We cannot park our cars where we like or as long as we wish. Speed limits are set by laws. We cannot own a dog, a car, or even a bicycle without a license. We cannot hunt or get married without a license. We cannot sell without a license. We cannot build or repair our homes without a permit. We must send our child to school. If we are law-abiding, we will not play the numbers, gamble, attempt to buy liquor on Sunday. In many places we cannot go to the movies or play baseball on Sunday. When we look at the situation closely, we find that the ordinary citizen is surrounded by all the restrictions that surround the parolee or probationer with one fundamental difference, and that is that in the case of the parolee or probationer the restrictions are more likely to be enforced.

So the social worker who believes that he or she is doing casework with his clients in a nonauthoritative setting is working under a delusion. Only Robinson Crusoe might feel that he could do as he pleased on his Island, and even he had to give his dog some consideration. As long as one lives in society one cannot escape restrictions and curtailment of his activities. We can live in society only if we are willing to forego the indulgence of many of our impulses to the extent that we expect others in the group to do likewise.

After all, is this not what we as parole and probation officers are trying to get our parolees and probationers to do? The individual who can refrain from committing acts which would infringe upon the rights of others is by and large the socially adjusted individual. If we should succeed in inducing the parolee and probationer to accept this principle and to behave in accordance with it, we would not need to fear for his reverting to delinquency.

Contrary to the view of the nonauthoritarian caseworkers, the view we have just expressed does not limit freedom of choice or growth on the part of the individual. We all live and move within a framework of restrictions, but within this framework there is ample room for freedom. In fact freedom, in the best sense of the word, means the acceptance of the restrictions that the social order imposes upon us all for the good of the whole group. The individual will grow and become adjusted to the extent that he will accept these restrictions and impose them upon himself by his own choice. Although parole and probation officers occasionally must resort to force, we know that reactions brought about by force do not result in any permanent change. On the other hand, they are not entirely without value. Sometimes acts induced by force form an opening wedge into the consciousness of the subject and cause him to awaken to his responsibilities. This form of treatment partakes of the nature of shock therapy and may result in what is sometimes called traumatic learning.

MUST CHANGE NECESSARILY COME FROM WITHIN?

We do not share the view that rehabilitation and change in the individual must come from within himself, if by this is meant that habit patterns, beliefs, and ideas are initiated from within. A naïve interpretation of this view is probably responsible for the "do nothing" philosophy encountered in some penologists and correctional workers. It scarcely needs to be stated that such structural elements of the personality as habit patterns, beliefs, and ideas are never determined by the genes of the individual. They are acquired. While we no longer believe in the Lockian view that the child's mind at birth is a *tabula rasa*, it is axiomatic that the child is trained from without, that this training is done by the imposing of all sorts of restrictions from without, and that the goal of the training is to help the child accept these restrictions as though they were self-imposed. As habits, beliefs, and ideas accumulate and become systematized, the person is in increasingly better position to cope with the environment and with his own impulses. In other words, the process is one of slowly transmuting external prohibitions into internal inhibitions. It is in this sense that we may say that changes in conduct must come from within. The process is not unlike the process of osmosis. It is relatively slow and imperceptible, but inexorable. It will go on as long as the individual remains immersed in the solution of social pressures which will impinge upon him on all sides. Once these pressures have been absorbed and assimilated, they make for growth in some direction. Our task is to see that the solution—the social milieu—contains the proper ingredients which, after absorption and assimilation, will lead to the kind of growth that will meet the standards which have been set up by the group as a whole.

The essential task of the probation and parole officer, therefore, is that of helping the probationer and parolee to face the restrictions which are placed about him, just as the parole and probation officer himself and all the rest of us must face them. The officer must constantly point out to the parolee the limits within which he may move, not as something arbitrarily imposed from without, but as something already ac-

:epted by the community of which the officer is a representative, both
by official designation and as one who has already accepted the standards of the community. If the probationer or parolee really desires to
become a member of that community, he will see the need of accepting
the limits within which he can move and be happy.

76 · Probation Work Requires Special Training

by CLARENCE M. LEEDS

As in a number of other fields of social work, so in probation work, having a "nice personality" and experience in
dealing with people was at one time deemed sufficient as a
qualification for anyone seeking a job in it. This no longer
holds true. Much more than that is thought to be necessary
now. An assistant chief probation officer of a domestic-rela-
tions court in New York, Clarence M. Leeds discusses in
the following article the training and the personal qualities
necessary for effective probation work, which increasingly
is coming to be considered as a career requiring special
preparation and skills. [From *Federal Probation*, Vol. XV,
April-June 1951, pp. 25-28. Reprinted by permission.]

THE EDUCATION and training necessary to make a good probation officer
has been broadening as our knowledge of the field has grown. Not too
many years ago the general impression was that all one needed was a
"good personality" and some experience with life. Retired police officers
seemed, too frequently, to fit these qualifications with questionable results for probationers and probation generally. Consequently, interested
people both in and out of the field demanded standards for probation
staffs that would meet the specific requirements of the tasks performed.
Today, there is growing agreement that one must be not only a college
graduate but also must have completed a full graduate program in this
field in a graduate school of social work.

CASEWORK SKILLS REQUIRED

Increasingly, it has become evident that sound practice in this field
requires that the probation staff have education and training in the

basic skills of casework and that their general orientation be toward the social work field. Correctional work, like family casework or medical social work, has aspects which differentiate it in detail from the other specific fields of casework, but in approach and skills required it has a common base with all of the others—family, medical, psychiatric child guidance, and the rest.

Professor Gordon Hamilton, in 1940, clearly saw the casework nature of the service required of those who come to the attention of probation departments and indicated the relationship of the function of such probation work to other social work services being rendered in the Community. She wrote,[1]

If one considers the concern of social casework with standards of living and constructive social relationships, one can see certain broad groupings of agencies around objectives which, in turn, suggest functions. One might express these objectives as maintenance, guidance and therapy, protection and supervision, and correctional education. . . . Protection and supervision are common aspects of child caring work, of case work attached to State Hospitals, of probation and parole. There is usually a strong component of authority and much of it is public. . . . There is, of course, considerable overlapping as among maintenance, guidance, therapy, protection, and correction. Nevertheless, it is possible to think of these objectives as furnishing one clue to function.

VARIETY OF APPROACHES IN PROBATION WORK

When we look at probation work, which is only one segment of the field of correction, we find that while there is a common setting—the court—there is some variety in the approaches, in the people and problems they meet, in legal requirements with respect to the handling of these probationers, and in community attitudes with respect to that handling.

First, there are the children's courts. Here has developed a minimum of legal practice and procedure, an attitude that the function of the court is the protection of the child, as well as of society, a departure from the merely punitive to that of understanding the child and his family and through psychiatric treatment and casework service bringing about an adjustment of the child and his situation. A worker in this setting should be a psychiatric caseworker, skilled in the problems of children and family relationships.

[1] Gordon Hamilton, *Theory and Practice of Social Case Work.* New York: Columbia University Press, 1940. Pp. 261-2.

Next, there are the family courts which vary in their jurisdictions but which primarily focus on the problems of adults, particularly husbands and wives. Whether it is a question of support or, in some jurisdictions, an issue of divorce, the service must be directed at understanding the motivations of the adults if real help is to be given. Here, again, is a need for studying the emotional make-up and behavior of people and a psychiatric base is required of the probation counselor. In addition, there are problems of budgeting, medical care, home management, child care and training. One gets the feel of the need for a family caseworker with psychiatric orientation.

The courts to which adolescents go are expanding and developing their probation services. The individual problems of these young people are, truly, emotional ones combined with a number of situational problems which require help by a caseworker. This group presents in more intense form, perhaps, the usual variety of emotional problems characteristic of all adolescents. These relate to problems of sex, breaking away from parental control and establishing their independence, employment and vocational guidance, and education and training in relation to their future employment and progress. Too, there are also matters such as the management of money, wholesome spare-time activities, and housing, all of which may be quite difficult to handle when one considers that many of these youngsters are living away from home on their own with no help in solving them.

The older probationers present some of these same problems and others of their own. Many of the difficulties of this group have their basis in the emotional maladjustment of these individuals. The growing interest and concern of the community and the courts with this behavior is demonstrated by the increasing developments of psychiatric services in courts for adult offenders. These clinics, in order to be of maximum value, require the services of caseworkers who have been trained and who are experienced in psychiatric treatment. Providing this service should, and probably will, fall upon the probation staffs. Therefore, requirements for such staffs are clearly established.

We can conclude, then, that fundamental in the education and training of a probation counselor is casework with a psychiatric focus. There has been occasional criticism that training of this sort, which requires a minimum of 2 years in a graduate school of social work, imposes a hardship upon many who might be qualified in other respects to enter this field of work. That is true. However, the training is essential to sound practice and those who do not have it or cannot acquire it will not be suitable. That is a fact in all professions. Undoubtedly many more than do would become physicians if the standards for entering that profession were reduced. Few, if any, would consider that a satisfactory solution of the problem.

Another factor also is involved. It is that of the age of the probation counselor. It has been my experience that a staff member under 25 years of age is handicapped in establishing relationships so necessary in treatment. Those who are just out of college, having completed only their undergraduate work, are too young to carry out the responsibilities of probation work. An additional period of graduate work not only gives them needed technical knowledge and skill but also adds to their age and makes them better qualified in that respect, too. It is not uncommon, when very young staff members are employed, to have mothers of children or wives who are in court ask for an older worker. I am sure all of us have heard them say, "I feel like I'm talking about my most intimate personal affairs with my young daughter."

TRAINING FOR PROBATION

In the training of personnel for probation there also should be introduced in the classroom work, a course which will cover an introduction to our judicial system and our laws. Students need to be made familiar with the philosophy of our system of justice and the framework of our laws, as well as the mechanics by which the system works. They should be sufficiently acquainted with these to be comfortable when working with them. The uncomfortable feeling which some social workers have concerning the law and legal process must be overcome particularly when training for work in probation. Along with this might go a historical review of the development of probation, and the accommodation of the law and legal procedure to the treatment approach to the offender as contrasted with earlier methods of extreme punishment as a deterrent to delinquent behavior. The gradual evolution of the offender from an outcast to a human being before the law and the community is important and illustrative of real progress being made by courts and society in dealing with offenders.

In general, otherwise, the classroom work in the training of probation counselors should not vary a great deal from that planned for other caseworkers in a graduate school of social work. The very important part of the training of probation counselors, like that of other caseworkers, is the supervised field work. For probation counselors, a part of this total field work experience should be in a probation setting; the remainder, I think, should be in a freer setting and, too, should be in a program where there is emphasis on the treatment of behavior.

The requirement that part of this field work training be carried on in probation setting creates a difficulty for graduate schools of social work to meet inasmuch as there are few probation services organized to meet the high standards required of such a program. Undoubtedly, there will need to be special arrangements worked out between schools and probation departments to meet this situation. As standards rise in existing probation services and more qualified supervisory personnel become available to them, the conditions with respect to training will be relieved.

Part of this responsibility for training probation personnel is that of the courts and existing probation agencies. They have an obligation to develop along with this program and should begin now, if they have not already done so, to move toward meeting it. What are a few of the problems that courts and probation services must meet and overcome in this respect?

A probation counselor must be looked upon as a specially trained staff member, equipped to do a particular kind of job in dealing with the personal and social adjustment of offenders. Just "anyone" cannot do that. It takes years of preparation and training in order to learn to do it even reasonably well. The process is costly and time consuming but it produces benefits in the long run. Courts and probation services must come to recognize the need for professionally trained staff, be ready to pay them a salary sufficient to attract and hold the best of those entering the casework field and afford them working conditions and tenure that will enable them to function in a manner that accords with sound professional practice.

CONDITIONS OF WORK

Low entrance salaries paid for probation counselors make it virtually impossible to recruit qualified personnel. Trained, competent probation staff cannot be attracted at salaries prevailing in many communities today. Probation services have not been given sufficient money to enable them to compete for staff with other casework agencies and, as a result, have been forced into taking personnel who are not fully qualified by experience and training. This situation must be corrected if there is to be improvement. Salaries high enough to attract and hold trained and experienced staff are basic to the building of a sound, professional probation service.

It must be recognized, too, that the qualified staff member must be provided with conditions which will permit him to perform in accordance with good practice. Excessively high case loads militate against this. Case loads of 100 to 150 cases per worker are found today in too many places. No staff member can do anything worthwhile with such fantastic loads. A trained probation counselor would be wasted on such a load. Individualization of cases, and a personal approach on a basis of human understanding cannot be undertaken with these loads and they must be reduced or the probation service saddled with them will be merely probation in name only. With the introduction of trained staff, there should be a readiness to meet this problem of high case loads and to deal with it effectively and constructively.

The probation counselor should be recognized for what he is—a trained specialist—and should have some tenure on his job and reasonable opportunity for advancement. He should not be expected to participate in the campaigns of judges or parties in order to secure or retain his position as a probation counselor. I think it should be stated that this practice is no longer as common as it was in this field at one time, but so long as it remains in even a single jurisdiction it should be deplored.

Probation counselors should have protection against removal resulting from political changes in administration. They should have full opportunity to pursue their work without unwarranted interference. Continuity of service in staff is desirable and there should be reasonable rights of tenure which will provide added incentive to trained people to make probation work their career.

PROBATION IS A CAREER SERVICE

A few words are necessary, I think, on career service. Frequently, in Civil Service, this is interpreted to mean promotions exclusively from among those in the service, years of service being the only or major qualification. A career probation service cannot, I believe, justify itself if it places the vested interests of its own group above the sound requirements of its department and the needs of its clients. Promotions on a career basis can be justified where the department has a staff which is fully trained and qualified for the higher positions to be filled. Only on such a basis can a good probation service be maintained and clients' needs be met adequately. Opportunities in probation must be made available to qualified supervisors outside of this field when a probation service cannot supply them itself. Only in this way can a trained staff of probation counselors be spared the frustrating and stultifying experience which inevitably will develop when an unqualified supervisor is given responsibility for their direction.

It is evident, I think, that as our knowledge and skills for treating behavior deviations have grown, higher standards of training and experience are required for those entering and qualifying as probation coun-

selors, supervisors, and executives. Graduate schools of social work are
showing an increasing amount of interest in the preparation of personnel for this field. Communities, courts, and probation departments have
the obligation and responsibility to create conditions within their own
probation services which will enable them to make effective use of the
growing number of trained people who will be entering this field.

77 · The Shortcomings and Needs of the Probation System

by ERIC KENT CLARKE, M.D.

Probation as a treatment measure for the offender has been
practiced in this country for a considerable length of time,
and its importance in our legal system is universally recognized. Although it has proven its value, however, much
remains to be done to achieve greater effectiveness. A director of the Minnesota Psychiatric Institute, Eric Kent
Clarke, a psychiatrist who has had considerable experience
in dealing with probation problems, presents here his views
on the probation system as it is now administered and
carried out, pointing out its chief defects and offering suggestions for its improvement. ["Observations of a Psychiatrist on the Probation Program," *Federal Probation*, Vol.
XI, Oct.-Dec. 1947, pp. 25-28. Reprinted by permission.]

IN THIS postwar period of rehabilitation, all of our community services
are under review with the aim that programs may be strengthened. In
all fields there are weak spots that are accepted as being inevitable. The
war created personnel shortages that stopped new developments. Now
that we are in the period when new workers are becoming incorporated
into the various areas of social work, it is timely that the different programs be studied carefully and evaluated so that traditional weakness
will not be perpetuated. Probation services have been in operation for
a sufficiently long period to have demonstrated their value. However,
as in all programs of this size, and because of its gradual growth to meet
a specific need, weak spots exist which reduce the potential value and
often nullify the results that might be obtained.

The comments offered in this paper are based on many years of experience in working closely with probation departments in several cities

and coming to accept the limitations of a system as unchangeable. For a considerable period during the war I had the privilege of being one of the large team who co-operated in building and making community life bearable in the development of the totally new city at Oak Ridge, Tennessee. The sociological importance of the evolution of this remarkable community has been largely overlooked. It was a city without tradition forced into rapid expansion to meet a specific need. . . . My concepts of the changes that might evolve in the present transitional stage of probation programs grew out of my observations of what was accomplished under forced draft at Oak Ridge, where none of the traditional handicaps of the average community existed. My views are presented with the desire that they be received as constructive criticisms.

ISOLATION FROM COMMUNITY RESOURCES

Probably the greatest single handicap of most probation programs is isolation from other community resources. In this the probation department is not the sole offender. The criticism applies equally to most of the social agency groups, the private and public family and welfare agencies, the health services, the medical and psychiatric services, and the school system. Each group has evolved its own delineated field of responsibility, and as a result has jealously guarded its prerogatives. The result has been that the individual is frequently lost in "the system," for there is little consideration given to a total integration of the various segments that go to make up the individual's daily life. This strict delineation of agency function leads to duplication of effort, contradictory advice, and confusion. Such isolation of a program is unnecessary, cumbersome, and ineffectual, and at Oak Ridge it was reduced to a minimum, because of the necessity of spreading a small, well-trained professional staff as effectively as possible to keep pace with the innumerable and inevitable problems that arose. A small but effective coordinating group with responsibility to give practical guidance to the individual in distress and his family was the solution—whether the problem was one of delinquency, marital discord, psychiatric disorder, or any other of the conflicts that create social maladjustment. It was the general policy in any problem that involved more than a single sphere of an individual's life to orient other community workers who should have an interest in the situation, to avoid later confusion and duplication of effort.

SUPERFICIAL NATURE OF MUCH OF PROBATION WORK

While the majority of the results obtained by the present probation systems are commendable, the criticism that much of the work is superficial cannot be denied. Inordinately large case loads preclude anything beyond superficiality. Unless the seemingly satisfactory results obtained by perfunctory methods are analyzed critically, unjustified complacency is frequently the result. Possibly the undifferentiated intake policy would indicate that many "successes" would have been so without a probationary period. An appraisal of the failures of the probation program is a more valuable indicator of efficiency and effectiveness. The cause of failure will probably be found to be a combination of insufficient time, inadequate diagnosis of the problem, rigidity of the system that prevents sound individual casework procedures, and isolation of effort from other available community resources.

LACK OF DIAGNOSTIC FACILITIES

Lack of facilities for accurate diagnosis of the individual problem is a tremendous handicap in many probation programs. Investigations by the majority of probation officers are usually excellent in gathering data about the individual. However, the collection of data in itself is not sufficient unless it is carefully correlated into a useful working plan which will alleviate the pressures operating to induce nonconformance. Usually the individual probation officer has the full responsibility of collecting the data, trying to compile and analyze them, and evolve a working plan in a brief period and without assistance. Frequently he lacks the professional training and experience in diagnostic methods to do this adequately; yet he must assume the responsibility of developing a plan that will have tremendous influence on the future life of the individual under investigation and probation. The data are frequently incomplete and inadequate because of a deadline that does not permit full evaluation. The present system can be compared with an attempt to run a hospital with only a staff of nurses without any medical staff. The nurses might be quite efficient in passing out aspirin tablets and sedative capsules to keep the patients comfortable, quiet, and from causing a disturbance; but unless there was some diagnostic service that would establish whether the patient was suffering from a cancer or pneumonia or some other obscure and malignant disease, such a hospital would not remain long in existence. Why should we be content to do likewise in the field of human behavior?

INELASTICITY OF PROGRAM AND PUNITIVE NATURE OF GOAL

Other handicaps of the present program are the lack of elasticity and the fact that its goal is largely punitive. This is a relic of the traditional legalistic domination. Most probation officers speak in terms of helping the probationer find himself, but really mean helping him as long as he stays within very rigidly defined limits. The arguments used to support such rigidity are that the probation office has to deal with large groups and that policies must be uniform to prevent chaos, and that after all the probationer is on probation instead of being incarcerated through the generosity of the community. Therefore it is the duty of the probationer to conform to whatever restrictions are placed upon him. He is in no position to protest. However justified this theory may be, it must be admitted that in practice rigid uniformity often is the factor that leads to failure.

RIGIDITY AND INFLEXIBILITY OF PROBATION CONDITIONS

Frequently the inelasticity of probation rules prohibits activities that would be of reconstructive value. In this category is a man of 33, accused of an indecent assault based largely on an insinuation of homosexual activity that was never established. Because of the excessively violent reaction toward all sexual offenses, the worst possible interpretation was placed on his questionable behavior and he was given a long prison sentence which was suspended with 5 years' probation in its stead. At the request of his family he was referred for psychiatric supervision. It was extremely doubtful if this man could have been considered an active homosexual, although he was a potential homosexual. He was an illegitimate child, who had always lived with his mother and stepfather, and was the ill-favored oldest child in a family of four half siblings. The circumstances of his birth were common knowledge in the small community in which he grew up. Later the family moved to a large city. This man had a good work record, as he was a conscientious, hard worker, whose main motivation was an attempt to justify his existence. He had many schizoid characteristics in that he was solitary, had few social contacts, and led a lonely, empty life. There was little in the home that was constructive or stimulating. His arrest alienated him further from the family, so that he then lived alone in a housekeeping room in a boarding house. Psychiatric effort was directed toward helping him eliminate his many emotional conflicts and effect better socialization. The usual terms of probation forbade him to go to dance halls and places serving liquor; he had to be home at ten-thirty in the evening, and had to avoid the company of minors. These regulations completely eliminated all the things he might have done to assist himself to develop a more healthy outlook on life. He worked until eight in the evening so that it was impossible for him even to go to a movie and be home before ten-thirty. It would have been desirable for him to find some companionship in women, yet he could not invite any of the young women he had met through the church to go out because they liked to dance. Even the large restaurants were ruled out because most of them served liquor. This man's rigidities made him strongly opposed to drinking or smoking, so that the risk of his indulging in alcohol actually was remote. On one occasion, when he invited a young lady to dinner at an expensive restaurant with the probation officer's permission, he saw the judge who had sentenced him seated at an adjoining table. Although he had permission to be there, he expected to be re-arrested and sent off to prison, as he was sure the judge had recognized him and would revoke his probation.

On another occasion when he was to meet a young lady for dinner at another acceptable restaurant, but one where liquor was served, he saw the detective who had arrested him standing on the corner in front of the restaurant. He did not dare go into the restaurant as his old suspicions were aroused. The detective had been very rough on him at the time of his arrest and the probationer was convinced that the detective would welcome the opportunity to crack down on him. He left the young lady standing inside the restaurant until he could call her from a nearby drugstore to meet him elsewhere. There have been repeated episodes of a similar nature. The man's conscientiousness made it imperative to him that he live up to the letter of probation. The probation officer had been most co-operative but was bound down by the rules and regulations of his department. The probationer was discouraged and was giving up his efforts to live a normal life because at every turn he encountered restrictive measures that prevented him from doing the things that would have helped. He was developing more clear cut ideas of persecution and many of the schizoid traits were being reinforced rather than modified by the probation program. Rigidity and inflexibility of the rules here seemed to defeat the very purpose of probation.

ARBITRARY TERMS OF PROBATION

The terms of probation are often so arbitrary as to lose sight of the individual, the length of the duration of probation being based on the seriousness of the delinquent act rather than on the individual's response to probation. Thus a disturbed youngster from a chaotic home, who needs every bit of understanding and assistance our community resources can give him, comes before the court for a trivial offense and is placed on probation for a minimum period. Because the offense is trivial and the probation officer is overworked, the youngster gets scant attention. This youngster, in spite of the trivial offense, may offer the greatest opportunity to do good reconstructive work, but the opportunity is missed because the offense itself is trivial, and is no indicator of the human volcano that exists close under the surface. Such a youngster could benefit by probation supervision over a long period.

On the other hand, a youngster from a stable, well-integrated family, who impulsively becomes involved in some serious act, may draw an unduly long period of probation supervision that is both unnecessary and harmful. One such lad from a very stable home, but who was maturing more rapidly than his family recognized, was involved in borrowing a neighbor's car, as a means of asserting his desire for freedom. The car was reported missing by its owner and the youngster was picked up as he was leaving a fashionable and respectable night spot with a young girl of fine background. Although the charge of driving a stolen car was serious, a period of 4 years' probation with a suspended sentence to a correctional school seemed out of all proportion to the actual needs of the situation. Sufficient punishment occurred in the arrest and embarrassment his impulsiveness occasioned in his home community, and the long period of reporting weekly to the probation office seemed more harmful than constructive.

LACK OF INDIVIDUALIZED PROGRAM

The delinquent is usually an individualist, whose pattern of nonconformance is the result of his resistance to pressures in the home, the school, and the community, which leads to rebellion. To him the rebellion is justified, for it is an expression of his inner dissatisfactions. Arbitrary regimentation of his freedom and actions may serve to curb his activity with superficial acceptance but make no fundamental change in his personality. It does not make him a better citizen at heart, beyond learning to conform because he must. The same burning resentments that motivated his original nonconformance continue without abatement. This is a lesson we never seem to learn. It is the weakest spot in the entire system of management of nonconformists and proves to be one of the most expensive luxuries of modern community life. A century ago many commentators on the system of jails and penitentiaries wrote extensively on the shortcomings of the correctional institutions as they then existed, and yet today the same shortcomings are still in existence. Some latitude in evolving a probation program that would fit the individual would help a great deal. Yet in most cities the same set of probation regulations must apply to all under probation supervision. Often the supervision could be much better carried out by other agencies than one affiliated with the court and without the unfortunate stigma that court affiliation so generally connotes.

There is great need for diagnostic service composed of specially-trained staff who are experienced in diagnostic work and who have time and resources to do a complete study of the individual, his home, his school or work experience and relationships, his recreational and other interests. This complete study is a necessary starting point of reconstruction of behavior patterns. Diagnostic services have been slow to develop, chiefly because they are expensive; trained personnel have been scarce and often the senior probation staff, who have held office for many years, are vigorously opposed to innovation. In advocating the establishment of diagnostic service, I am not attempting to impose psychiatric service specifically upon the probation field. There are too few trained psychiatrists, and will be for years to come, to begin to fill the need. The appointment of well-qualified and mature psychiatric social workers, social caseworkers trained in family casework, and experienced clinical psychologists to serve as a nucleus of the organization is essential.

Present probation practices evolved too rapidly to meet an urgent need; and because the results have seemed satisfactory, the stimulus to progress has been lacking. There is too often contentment with palliative measures that do not go below the surface. There is need for a more intensive program which will offer real treatment to the individual whose personality difficulties find expression in antisocial behavior. This change in program calls for an additional well-trained staff and an acceptance of the newer philosophies that have emerged during the war period in sociology, psychology, and psychiatry. The opportunity to move ahead and improve probation techniques may be postponed indefinitely, if complacency continues. Probation service can be strengthened only by a program based on treatment of the individual and the administration of such a program by a staff well-trained in the understanding of human behavior.

CHAPTER TWENTY

Parole

━━━━━━━━━━━━━━━━━━━━━━━━━━━━━━━━━━━━━━━

78 · Group Therapy for Parolees

by JUSTIN K. FULLER, M.D.

Group psychotherapy is becoming increasingly accepted as one of the most effective ways of rehabilitating incarcerated offenders. Little, if any, use, however, has been made of this method with paroled prisoners, even though it is agreed that this method could be utilized on them to great advantage. Justin K. Fuller, a former medical director of the U.S. Bureau of Prisons and now a consultant to the California Department of Correction, discusses the methods and techniques employed in group psychotherapy in prisons, the need to extend this kind of service to the parolees, and the means to be taken to accomplish this. ["Extension of Group Therapy to Parolees," *Prison World*, July-Aug. 1952, pp. 9-11. Reprinted by permission.]

FOR MANY YEARS, medical service [1] in federal and in some state correctional systems has diligently sought for ways to assist in retraining

[1] "Medical service" is an inclusive term covering the general practice of "medicine," surgery, dentistry, psychiatry, and all allied specialties and skills. A "medical" examination implies both a physical examination and a mental examination—a *complete* examination, in other words.

offenders, to the end that an increasing percentage of them will be enabled to follow acceptable methods of living after release from incarceration. At first, the effort followed the easiest and most obvious channel, which was correction of remediable physical disabilities. The philosophy governing this effort was largely concerned with the supposition that physical deformity or disease begets warped and unhealthy trends of thought and reaction, whereas a healthy body is likely to encourage a healthy way of living and thinking. The one is more likely to result in conduct disorder, delinquency, and crime, than the other, and anything that can be done to improve physical health will also improve reactions to the problems of life and thus directly or indirectly reduce the tendency to offend.

Another factor of equal significance is that physical disability often serves as a handicap to obtaining work and holding a job, and that anything that can be done to reduce this handicap will increase the individual's ability to earn an honest and law-abiding livelihood.

This part of the program is unquestionably significant to penology. It is also satisfying to the conscientious worker because it is *obvious* and *physical* in nature—something that can be seen, and grasped, and understood, and appreciated; one *knows* what is being done and the results that are being obtained. In this sense, it is tangible and can be recorded statistically as an indication of honest effort and an evidence of how appropriated funds are being expended.

On the other hand, its ultimate reflection on conduct disorder is both indirect and intangible and must, to a certain degree, be taken for granted. Therefore, it usually happens that no sooner has an institution developed this part of a medical program to the stage where it is working satisfactorily, than the thoughtful medical officer begins to look for ways in which his science may have a more direct bearing on conduct disorder, delinquency, and crime. He usually concludes that the most obvious channel is psychiatry and allied disciplines.[2] A few years ago, this channel seemed so hopeful, and penologists were so anxious to take advantage of anything that promised help in the solution of its problems, that psychiatry came to be rather badly oversold. Promises were made and hopes were entertained that could not be fulfilled. Many psychiatrists attempted to approach the problem on the basis of individual psychotherapy rather than group psychotherapy, because, in the early heyday of psychoanalysis, group methods of therapy were frowned upon. It soon became evident, of course, that there were not enough

2 "Discipline" in the sense of "teaching; instruction; that which is taught to pupils; training which corrects, molds, strengthens, or perfects," not in the sense of "punishment or chastisement."

psychiatrists to treat even a small fraction of those offenders who needed psychotherapy, and, gradually, group methods of treatment have come into their own.

Realizing that the typical incarcerated offender is in one way or another mentally abnormal and therefore in need of help, the psychiatric staff, assisted and supported by all the rest of a modern prison's staff, have bent every effort to give psychiatric treatment to as many as possible during incarceration. Group counseling, group psychotherapy, pertinent psychological education, are nowadays commonly applied in combination to both the free staff and the inmate population of a progressive prison setup. The employe thus comes to have a better understanding of the inmate and to be a better employe. The inmate learns to depend upon the help offered by an intelligent staff. He has been taught the value of it and has come to place reliance upon it. It is an understandable and promising discipline in his simplified intramural environment.

This has been demonstrated at the California Department of Corrections Medical Facility, temporarily located at Terminal Island while the permanent Medical Facility at Vacaville is being constructed. The Medical Facility is one of the seven major institutions of the California Department of Corrections: it is a specialized hospital prison, devoted in its entirety to examination, study, care, and treatment of prisoners afflicted with chronic mental or physical diseases or disabilities.

The superintendent of the Medical Facility, Dr. Marion R. King; the clinical director, Dr. Nathaniel Showstack; and all the rest of the staff, with the interest, approval, and encouragement of Richard A. McGee, director of the State Department of Corrections, Walter Gordon, chairman of the Adult Authority, and his colleagues, and Walter Stone, chief state parole officer, and his staff, and others, have developed a program of group psychotherapy that is in many respects unique. Dr. Showstack describes it in part as follows:

"At an actual meeting of group psychotherapy, the therapist, after greeting the patients, invites one of them to come to the front of the room and tell his story to his fellow men. One of the first things the therapist tells the group is that whoever decides to go into his case in detail can feel thoroughly protected because he does not have to say anything he does not want to say, and he does not have to answer any question from the group he does not want to answer. At no time is a patient forced to present his case. Intimate details he does not want to discuss before the group may be taken up later with the therapist in a private, individual session of psychotherapy. Rarely does a patient fail to come before the group. He is given about half an hour to present his life history, and then the meeting is opened to general questions and discussion. The therapist, for the most part, sits in the rear of the room observing what is going on.

"The method used is an analytical one, based on the existence of unconscious emotional circuits present in the patient's mind of which he is totally unaware, which lead to abnormal behavior. By raising these circuits to the surface of consciousness so that they are observed by the individuals in whom they occur, and by members of the group, the patient gradually becomes aware of the immature, even infantile emotional circuits in his unconscious mind. . . .

"This is a long process and does not take place in one or ten sessions. It might take several years, depending upon the amount of emotional trauma that the patient has been exposed to in his past life . . ."

The first groups of 40 to 50 inmates organized by Dr. Showstack and his associates, with the approval of Dr. King, have gradually been reduced to numerous smaller groups of 10 to 15 patients. Attendance is, of course, voluntary. Severe psychotic cases, the senile, aged and tuberculars do not participate.

As of this writing, there are 39 psychotherapy groups, each meeting at least once a week with Dr. Showstack or one of his colleagues. At certain of these sessions, tape recordings have been made at the request of the patients themselves so that later they could listen to what they had said in a more objective fashion. Many of the 500 individual inmates who regularly participate in this program would attend more sessions at their own request than are now available.

Of added special interest is the fact that the psychiatric council, of which Dr. Showstack is chairman, sits monthly to talk with and examine all patients who are to appear before the Adult Authority for parole consideration. The council then discusses the case, reaches a psychiatric diagnosis and submits a written report to the Adult Authority on each patient.

The regular program summarized above is supplemented by joint, weekly round-table discussions with the educational staff on Mondays and with other employes on Thursdays, to the end that the entire staff will be made conversant with its nature, purpose, and progress.

Dr. Showstack states that ". . . the ultimate objective of psychotherapy is to bring the patient back to living in accordance with the laws of God and nature and the laws of the land. The speed with which this can be attained and good results obtained in this program obviously depend upon the amount of treatment each patient can receive. . . ."

While the Medical Facility program of group psychotherapy is remarkably effective within the limitations imposed by the numerical strength of the psychiatric staff, it has become evident to the staff that the therapeutic gains achieved by the intramural program are frequently entirely lost when the patient is released and steps into a much more complicated environment in which he has nowhere to turn for psychiatric counseling, advice, and support to help him over the rough spots and out of his emotional and other difficulties and frustrations.

Existing public and private outpatient psychiatric clinics are not sufficient to provide anything like adequate service to the parolees and probationers that need this kind of help. No public funds are available to increase these facilities. All such clinics were organized to meet certain problems (e.g., child guidance clinics), none of which were concerned with the peculiar problems that characterize the parolee group.

GROUP THERAPY CLINIC

Therefore, an effort is being made to obtain private endowment funds for establishing a group therapy clinic essentially for parolees in the Los Angeles area. A draft of the plan which has been formulated by Medical Facility staff members for operation and staffing of the first such clinic, together with an approximate budget for funds and other supporting details, is being assembled for this purpose. Preliminary investigation has indicated that of the 1,300 parolees in the Los Angeles area, at least 200 would benefit from additional consultation and therapeutic service and that a majority of this group are not only willing but anxious to have these services extended from the Medical Facility to the outside for those who are released on parole.

This preliminary sampling was so suggestive that a much more intensive survey of the group is now being made which will (1) identify by name and number how many parolees are in need of and would profit by such service, (2) find out how many of them will cooperate in the program (3) and where those who need it and are willing to co-operate live in order that a spot map may be developed, (4) determine the time of day they work and when they would be available to attend the clinic, and (5) find the best place in which to locate the clinic.

It is assumed that much of the clinic's work will be in the evenings and on Saturdays and Sundays, and that the budget should include an item to cover travel expenses of a certain few patients from outlying sections who find transportation expenses burdensome.

Therefore, the clinic should be located in relation to the following factors:

(1) Near the numerical center of the parolee population of the area served.

(2) In pertinent relationship to the geographic center of the population served.

(3) Most convenient to the common methods of transportation used by the population served—private car, bus, street car, train—and with due consideration given to the schedules of the common carriers.

It would appear at the moment that the most appropriate location for the first office of the clinic would be in metropolitan Los Angeles or nearby in Los Angeles County, because at present this is the area of greatest need and, too, because of its geographical propinquity to the Medical Facility. This is important, since the chief psychiatrist of the clinic would administer the immediate details of the clinic but would be responsible to the superintendent of the Medical Facility. The clinic, therefore, would be an extension of the Medical Facility even when the permanent Medical Facility is moved to Vacaville.

It is anticipated that minimum space required would consist of:

1. One administrative office, approximately 12 x 15 feet.
2. One reception office, approximately 14 x 14 feet.
3. Six soundproof treatment rooms, approximately 12 x 15 feet each.

It is anticipated that minimum staff required would consist of:

One chief psychiatrist (administrative director of the clinic)
Two consulting psychiatrists (second consulting psychiatrist to start second year)
One clinical psychologist
Two psychiatric social workers (second psychiatric social worker to start second year)
Two stenographers

It is also assumed that, no matter how carefully the location of the first clinic is planned, there will be a sizable number of potential patients unable to attend because of time consumed, travel expense, general inconvenience, and so on. It is hoped that, through including a staff automobile, with no addition to the professional staff until the second year, it would be possible, beginning with the second year, to extend the services of the clinic to Medical Facility parolees residing in Orange, Riverside, San Bernardino, Ventura and Santa Barbara counties.

The larger communities in each county named would be the gathering point for group psychotherapy sessions of one to two hours, the staff persons concerned making the arrangement for the time, place and attendance at the meetings with the staff of the Bureau of Paroles.

If the clinic contemplated for the Los Angeles area is successful, a similar clinic may be established in the San Francisco area. It is hoped that private support of the project may be assured for a period of *not less than five years*. If at the end of such a reasonable demonstration period, the accomplishments of the clinics are sufficiently gratifying, a request will be made to provide for their continuation with the utilization of publicly appropriated funds.

COST

Authoritative hope can be entertained that operating the clinics as they are proposed will result in a substantial saving to the taxpayer. It is estimated that the cost for treating a parolee outside the prison in the group therapy clinic would be a little less than $67 per year. This, when added to $138, the present approximate cost of maintaining one man on parole for one year, would make the cost total $205, or just over 21 per cent of the average cost of $956 per year for maintaining an inmate at one of the California state prisons.

Group psychotherapy has the potential promise of achieving parole readiness much earlier than other methods of intramural treatment, *provided* continuation of adequate psychotherapy and other supervision can be assured while on parole.

An increased load of parolees would reduce the prison population and very possibly ultimately affect the need for new prison construction, a critical problem now in the very rapidly-growing State of California. Outpatient clinics would also help to reduce the number of parolees who violate and break their parole, thus requiring their return to prison. This would help to break up a vicious cycle and decrease recidivism and its accompanying cost. The savings would be not only in money required to keep the patients in prison but also in removing their families from public welfare and assistance rolls.

Of particular concern at the moment—because of the rising tide of public interest in sex crimes—is the fact that the inmate population of the Medical Facility contains a significant proportion of sex deviates (other than the feminine type of male homosexual), almost all of whom are participating in the program of group psychotherapy.

It is a corollary of present day penology that most incarcerated individuals are eventually released back into society where their successes or failures will depend in considerable part upon the calibre of their intramural care and treatment and the efficiency of their parole plans and supervision. This is as true of sex deviates as of any other type of case. The general public laity, through its newspapers, radio and periodicals, is concerned and disturbed about parole failures almost in direct proportion to the notoriety and heinousness of the criminal and his offenses. The public is particularly apt to be upset when a sex deviate is released on parole and then violates by committing another sex crime. It is also particularly significant to this situation that there is no known sure-fire treatment method for the great number of known sex deviates, nor is there any criterion upon which to determine when one is ready to be returned to community life. It is significant that the California legislature has recognized these facts and has evinced an intelligent readiness to assist in their solution by passing a sex psychopath research bill and funds to enable it (which, however, are not sufficient in amount nor otherwise available to support the outpatient clinics herein discussed). Lastly, it is equally significant that phases of intramural group psychotherapy are new and experimental and cannot be evaluated until and unless put to trial by actual test after the release of the patient. Nor can this kind of trial be evaluated if the patient is dumped from his carefully regulated intramural classes into a wildly confused environment where he will be denied the professional aids he has come to have faith and dependence in.

Each such man, as he leaves Terminal Island, finds himself once again in the maelstrom of the free world, snatched as it were from a secure and regimented environment and, in particular, from the professional and sympathetic guidance he has been receiving in understanding and overcoming the personal problem which led to his arrest, conviction, and commitment. He is on his own again, with temptations and hostility facing him wherever he turns. Only his parole officer, who is probably carrying a case load of 90 or more other parolees, and perhaps members of the parolee's own family, if he has one, can be counted on to help him over the rough spots. In any event, all the help he has been receiving at the Medical Facility is suddenly cut off. Parole violation is the not infrequent outcome of such a situation. *This* is what outpatient group psychotherapy would hope to help correct.

SUMMARY

As experience accumulated with the practical side of the problem of trying to reduce the incidence of conduct disorder, it became increasingly apparent that intramural effort, no matter how well conceived and executed or how abundant, could not, of itself, regulate the conduct pattern of released offenders; nor, for that matter, any other *potential* offender or *actual* offender. In other words, penology cannot stand alone, nor can psychiatry, or any other isolated discipline. There must be a close working relationship between intramural and extramural effort, between the organized staff of an institution and organized society out side of the institution, between the prison psychiatric staff and those in the community who are directly or indirectly concerned with the prob lem, such as law enforcement officers, courts, civic bodies, women's clubs, service organizations, and so on.

Offenders need psychiatric help quite as much after release from incarceration as they do during incarceration. During incarceration their lives are sharply regimented and relatively simple in comparison with the complexities and vicissitudes that inevitably beset them after release. Two of the factors of vital concern are that the majority of con victed criminals are mentally abnormal in one way or another and that release is a sudden—and often shocking—change in the inmate's en vironment. The parolee may very well become confused by the impact of situations not foreseen or problems not anticipated and so forget or discount much if not all of what he has carefully learned and once con fidently believed in. A much better psychiatric service is available for the incarcerated individual than for the parolee. Therefore, the proposal for an outpatient psychotherapeutic service for parolees is offered to en hance the treatment and parole program of this state and to provide cer tain types of parolees with additional scientific help and guidance, hitherto unavailable, in their efforts to make good.

Since parole itself is a method of treatment as well as continuation of the sentence outside the prison wall, it is anticipated that the closest cooperation and team work would exist between the clinic staff and the staff of the Bureau of Paroles.

Monthly meetings would be held with the parole officers in the area, orienting them to the problems of the parolees and the staff. The clinic staff would be under obligation to report to the parole officer if the parolee appeared to be retrogressing and again becoming a menace in his community. It is further planned to give special training in the objec tives and techniques of psychotherapy to parole officers assigned to supervise parolees undergoing treatment at the clinic.

Careful attention is being given to balancing the potentials for im proving correctional practice offered by the above plan against the dif ficulties, complexities, and dangers that obviously are inherent in it. Some of the professional and technical bugs anticipated in the program are mentioned above; some are suggested only by inference. A certain degree of permissiveness is integral to the healing arts, and permissive ness is thought to be especially necessary in psychotherapy; this obvi ously poses a problem when the therapist becomes a critical factor in granting paroles—and in cancelling paroles and declaring parolees vio lators who should be returned to incarceration. More than ever, in the plan discussed here, the professional activities of the healer will have to be tempered with the responsibilities of the administrator.

79 · Be It Ever So Humble

by SANFORD BATES

Sanford Bates, Commissioner of the New York State Board of Parole, discusses in the following article the significant part that the home, no matter how poor in an economic sense, plays in the life of an individual and, hence, how important it is for parole workers, in planning for parole, to take this into consideration and to make every effort to provide the parolee with a desirable home. [From *Federal Probation*, Vol. VIII, July-Sept. 1944, pp. 21-24. Reprinted by permission.]

ANTONIO BURNS was born in 1920. At the ripe age of 7 he came before the Children's Court as a neglected child; this happened again when he was 8. At the age of 11 he was committed to a parental school, paroled, and later returned for violation. He finally came out at the age of 13. A few years after this, charged with Forcible Entry, he appeared in another children's court and was placed on probation. Two months later, in still a third children's court, he was again charged with Forcible Entry and, although placed on probation, was brought back as a delinquent child in little more than a month. He was placed on probation a third time but finally was sentenced to a vocational school at the age of 16. Released after a year, he was returned in 8 months for further violations. At the age of 19 he was convicted of Robbery, 2nd Degree, and sentenced to State Prison for 7½ to 15 years.

Burns had been in prison 5 years when I first saw him. The Board felt that the amount of time he had served was sufficient punishment, and rightly concentrated their interest on what lay ahead for him in the community. The preparole investigation contained the following: "It should be noted that this man was apparently conditioned by the bad home situation where the mother was addicted to excessive use of liquor and failed to exercise proper supervision." Burns' father was described as a hard-working man and a good husband and provider. He was said to be a well-intentioned individual but unable to cope with the family problems. He was inclined to sit back and say, "What can I do?"

The mother had a definite history of alcoholism. There were long intervals, according to the report of the social agency, when she was constantly intoxicated for extended periods, and the children were neglected and truant from school because she could give them no proper attention. The oldest child in the family had given birth to an illegitimate youngster, whose father was a legless beggar. This man at one time had been arrested in the subway and found to be in possession of narcotic drugs. Antonio's oldest brother, although regularly employed, was described as a rather poor sort; the second brother had been committed to a juvenile institution for stealing; the third was missing and no report could be obtained about him. Brother No. 4 had twice been sentenced to a reformatory and also cited for possession of a so-called dangerous weapon; and Brother No. 5, recently released from State Prison on a sentence of 2 to 4 years, was said to be in the Army. The sixth brother had been known to juvenile authorities for some time and later sent to an adult reformatory for Burglary. Antonio was next in sequence, and the youngest brother, a serious-minded young man now serving in the armed forces, expressed fondness for him.

The investigator described the apartment which housed the family as being in a very poor neighborhood—the house, old and dilapidated; and the hall, in a very untidy condition.

Is it any wonder that the Board suggested to Antonio that it would be better for him to move into a new neighborhood and attempt to make an entirely fresh start? He rather doubtfully acquiesced in the suggestion, saying that he would do whatever the Board felt was best in the circumstances. However, he left no doubt in the mind of the institution parole officer that, whatever the situation might be as to his mother and where she lived, he preferred to go to his home.

What should be done in this case? Who were we to be dogmatic about a situation of this kind? Could we honestly say that the worst of homes was better than no home at all? Was it a wholesome and worthy thing to attempt to cultivate in Antonio's mind a sense of responsibility for his own family? Undoubtedly in this case the decision as to what to recommend for Antonio depended on the character of the family members and particularly his own capabilities of rising above the deleterious influences of his own home. It requires good social-work technique, imbued with a sympathetic understanding of the people with whom we deal, to decide such questions correctly.

You remember how "a tree grew in Brooklyn." Whether or not Miss Betty Smith was talking about an ordinary herbaceous tree or a family tree, we are not quite sure. One of the high lights in that remarkable book is the resentment which little Francie O'Neill showed toward her teacher when the teacher rebuked her for writing about her own home, and said that such things were sordid. After all, some of us have to live in sordid neighborhoods, and the tree of "family solidarity and mutual affection" can sometimes flourish even in the soil of social disintegration.

A significant study into the causes of juvenile delinquency was made in the State of New Jersey a few years ago. A considerable group of inmates in the State Prison and State Reformatory were asked some leading questions. One of them was, "Did your family try to dissuade you from committing crime?" The answers were almost unanimous that they did. Not more than four prisoners, as I recollect it, made the admission that their mothers complacently stood by and made no protest when they were tempted to commit a crime. A correspondingly small number blamed their plight upon other members of their immediate family.

I think we should have to search far and wide to find a mother who really urged her son to commit depredations on society. Fortunately the spectacle of a Ma Barker with a shotgun across her lap, is very rare on our American scene. Homes are broken not so much by the willful acts of those who live in them as by the pressure of community influences and deteriorating factors against which the home has a feeble defense.

THE IMPORTANCE OF THE HOME IN PAROLE PLANNING

The importance of providing a real home for parolees became more acute a year or two ago. At that time in New York, there were approximately a thousand men whom it was necessary to retain in prison because of lack of jobs, even though they were otherwise eligible for parole release. Our law specifically required that they must have self-sustaining work as a condition to release from an institution. We were obliged not only to hold them back but to keep some of them for a considerable time rather than send them out to an unfavorable environment so far as work was concerned. It soon became apparent, however, that even those men who were getting jobs more easily were homeless, or at least had no relatives or friends to call upon and could hardly be expected to find a place that could be called a home.

It has been the practice of our Board in the cases of eligible parolees whose program in the community was not ready, to vote them an open date and release them as soon as the arrangements were made for home, work, and placement in the community. Two years ago, just at the time of the employment boom, I made a study of 100 of these open-date cases and found that in practically 50 per cent the only provision that could be made for suitable home surroundings was the inevitable furnished room. We have not had much success in rehabilitating parolees in "furnished rooms" in New York. Such a status not only gives more liberty and less restraint to the ill-intentioned parolees, but surrounds even the best-intentioned men with an atmosphere of desolation and abandonment, and a lack of wholesome companionship. Furthermore, it greatly complicates the question of supervision. Today manpower is too valuable for our parole officers to waste time on repeated futile visits to a furnished room, waiting on the doorstep for hours at a time, leaving messages that are never received, and returning from such expeditions with a feeling of defeat and ineffectuality.

Realizing that after all it is during a man's leisure time that he is more apt to get into difficulty, the Board quickly came to the conclusion, therefore, that we should give more attention to the home program. We became concerned not only with the plight of the younger men who need family guidance and restraint, but also with the cases of older persons for whom we had erroneously assumed that the furnished room was the best "home" we could provide.

I am aware that many parolees would prefer a furnished room to the family home. I came across a case last week that clearly illustrates this. We had a young parolee who we thought was satisfactorily ensconced in the home of his parents. We were obliged to pick him up for frequenting bars and grills and for an assault on his sister. We strongly suspected that he slugged his sister so that his father would kick him out of the house, and the Parole Board then would have to let him live in a furnished room free from constant family supervision.

We are equally concerned with the parolee who is assailed by loneliness and who cannot be expected to complete his parole period successfully without some kind of sponsorship and companionship. Unless we arrange to secure suitable companions for him, he will find his associates among those who are not respectable nor particularly interested in keeping him from a relapse. It seems to us to be a cardinal principle of good parole supervision that, when released, a man shall have the feeling that he is not only welcome in the community but also a part of some home or family establishment, willing to befriend him and take an interest in his welfare.

THE POLICY OF THE NEW YORK STATE PAROLE BOARD

The Board undertook to carry out this renewed emphasis on home surroundings in several ways:

1. We urged the institutional parole officers to impress on all appli-

cants for parole the need for suitable family or home arrangements, in view of the Board's interest in this phase of the release plan.

2. The Board of Parole itself has exercised more careful scrutiny over programs, especially with respect to the home situation, and has deferred action on many cases until either the inmate could induce some relative or friend to harbor him, or our own investigator could develop a suitable situation. A few denials of parole for this reason have convinced applicants of the importance of this feature.

3. We have instructed the parole staff on the importance not only of interviewing relatives and friends to see if they will give a home to a parolee, but also of attempting an affirmative interpretation to the family of the need for offering a home and guidance to the parolee. In other words, neither the parole officer nor the Board should be satisfied to accept a statement that the family are "fed up" with the inmate and will not under any condition take him back, but we should make every effort to induce the family to give him another chance. Certainly it would seem that if a man's own flesh and blood are not willing to do this, we should not expect it of strangers. Of course one must admit that there are occasional cases where the man's crime in itself grew out of abuse of the family relationship. In these cases it may be, and undoubtedly is, preferable to complete the family break and perhaps set the man up with some more distant group of relatives.

4. If the family remains adamant or return to the home circle seems inadvisable, or if there are absolutely no relatives in this State or any other State who will accept the parolee, efforts should still be made to secure a real home for the inmate in some well-intentioned acceptable group. There must be a great many families with an absent son who are anxious to rent a room and who will actively cooperate with the parole officials in the development of a good sponsorship program. The juvenile courts and children's societies in some localities have had remarkable success in inducing childless parents to extend foster care to the wards of the court. With the help of the clergy and social workers, we may find many who have become childless who will be willing to undertake this responsibility for the older offender. It is notorious, in New York at least, what little interest there is among social agencies in providing homes for homeless men. I am satisfied that the mere threat of return to prison for violations of parole is not sufficient to keep many of our men on the straight and narrow path and that a positive effort in the direction of placing the inmate in a wholesome environment will be much more productive of good results.

5. In the case of homeless men there are, of course, occasional opportunities of obtaining employment which includes room and board. We

should certainly give preference on jobs of this kind (hospital, Merchant Marine, and other so-called sleep-in jobs) to those who may thus be given some approximation of normal family existence and not to men who are thereby going to be separated from their families.

RESOURCEFULNESS IN PAROLE PLANNING

The case of Antonio Burns, with which we started this article, brings us back to the fundamental conviction that there are wholesome, healthful, and reliable elements within the family, no matter how poorly it may be placed in the economic scale. One of the greatest challenges of parole administration, is to get what good there is out of the home situation.

Effective social work along this line can be done and will bring results. I have in mind the case of a Scandinavian immigrant who got into trouble and, as his parole period approached, had absolutely nobody to whom he could turn. A resourceful member of our staff, however, contacted a city missionary in Brooklyn who was of the same racial extraction as the parolee. He hunted through his parish until he found an elderly, respectable, middle-class couple, likewise of Scandinavian origin. When the situation was explained to them, they gladly agreed not only to give a room and a key to the parolee, but to welcome him into their home and take an interest in him. The social worker stated, ". . . this couple appear to be greatly interested in the rehabilitation of the inmate through the method of pleasant surroundings and companionship," and have agreed to "make every effort to render inmate comfortable and provide him with some friendship to alleviate his loneliness."

Parole is, of course, and must be a law-enforcement activity. We should keep in touch with all our men who are serving the rest of their sentences in the community. Parole also is and must be a regenerative process. As such, it needs the assistance of all the wholesome community influences. To supervise 100 parolees is too great a task for one man. It becomes enormously difficult to accomplish good parole supervision by automatic means. When we can elicit and obtain the interest of social agencies, the sympathetic approach from church organizations, and the sustaining help of well-intentioned people of good will in our community, it will be a much more simple and wholesome procedure. One of the great objectives of parole is to cultivate and stimulate the beneficent influence of the family relations. Especially in the case of a man who recently has been released from a penal institution, "there is no place like home."

80 · Prison Opinions About Parole

by DONALD RASMUSSEN

What does the convict think of the methods employed in granting parole, of the way in which parole boards are constituted and function? Is he justified in his usually negative attitude toward the parole system? Professor Donald Rasmussen, of Talladega College, Ala., sought to discover this through a study of inmates of an Illinois penitentiary. The following article summarizes his findings. [From *American Sociological Review*, Vol. 5, Aug. 1940, pp. 592-594. Abridged. Reprinted by permission.]

A STUDY OF prisoner attitudes shows the significant general fact that prisoners, like the public generally, lack a scientific point of view. They are not determinists with respect to the explanation of crime. To the prison inmate, as to the typical judge or lawyer, a criminal chooses his behavior; he might have acted differently had he so desired; he is a free moral agent; he is not a product. Hence, of 103 inmates answering a short answer question, 100 approved the statement that "If a man wants to go good, he will do it with or without a parole system." Yet, like most judges and lawyers, prisoners are inconsistent in their indeterminism. They blame politicians for preventing parole from aiding the convict; they blame and hate the warden, rather than the system which produced him, for the unendurable hardships of the prison community or for his political subservience; they blame the individual guards, rather than the public attitudes which tolerate them, for the unnecessary and stupid discipline which makes automatic puppets of human beings. Hence, the scientific penology of the future must not only sell its philosophy to prison administrators and the general public, but also to the criminal population of the prison community which must cooperate if that penology is to be a success.

But what is the significance of more specific prisoner attitudes? None of these is perhaps more important than the almost universal view that every man has a racket—a fact which permits incompetent or even dishonest men to perform important tasks. This view gives the inmate a basis for rationalizing his own crimes. The convict accuses the warden of being a political appointee; the Parole Board of accepting graft, of incompetence even in the use of its two-minute interviews with convicts, of subservience to newspaper publicity, and of inconsistent changes of policy for no reason explained to the convict. The convict accuses the parole agent of clumsy ignorance in handling the most delicate human relationships such as marriage, obtaining a job, and reinstating himself in the good graces of a society which despises him. Some convicts accuse the chaplain of insincerity, or classify his activities as "the witchcraft racket." Closest to the prisoner is the guard who therefore personifies for him both the incompetence and the hostility of the whole prison regime. The inmate accuses the guard not infrequently of having committed actual crimes on the outside and of sadistic acts on the inside which, to the inmate, are worse than crime. Finally, the more intelligent prisoner sees through the whole silly penal system. He, perhaps, accuses prison officials less for the failings of the penal system than do the rank and file, but he blames society in general for a punishment experience which might, he argues, be justified, were it effective, but which increases and complicates the very problem it is designed to solve.

The discovery of such attitudes was a bit disquieting to the unsophisticated student interne. He may perhaps have once assumed that wardens are honest and effective; parole boards, wise and non-political; parole agents a combination of protectors of society and skilled moral physicians; chaplains, exponents of the Christian ideal; guards, model patterns of integrity, and the whole penal system—imperfect perhaps—but still, the last word in the application of science to reform; but it did not take two summers in Joliet to discover that, on the contrary, there are elements of truth in the exaggerated picture which prisoners have painted of the modern penal system. At any rate, the challenge of prisoner attitude studies is that they demand demonstration of how far there is a factual basis for such critical attitudes. Indeed, he happened to *know* a politically appointed warden, the graduate of a county sheriff's office. He had been told by a guard that the same political "fix" which got him his prison job had kept him from serving a prison term for a crime more serious than those of some of the men he guarded. He had heard the chairman of a Parole Board say that the Board did not desire any more time than the few minutes normally spent in interviewing a parole candidate. He knew of inmates craving good literature who were excluded by a stupid censorship from access to some of our best periodicals. He had heard from a chaplain himself expressions of disgust for, rather than of interest in, the "soul-saving" task which was ostensibly his.

Not until we can truthfully say to convicts that their views of prison and extraprison personnel are false, can we deprive them of the rationalizations for their own crimes. The attitudes of prisoners demand a convincing answer to the question, to what extent has every man, or to what extent has every administrator, a racket?

If prisoners generally have not much to offer in the way of constructive suggestions for penal reform the reverse is true of a few of them. People generally do not appreciate the following facts:

1. That a prisoner does have a perspective of the penal and parole systems that no one else can get, and, therefore, his expressions are necessary in order to have a complete description of the entire penal and parole systems;

2. That there are prisoners who, even though they are in a position to better themselves at the expense of others by giving false information, do look at penal treatment quite objectively;

3. That oftentimes treatment has a greater effect if those being treated are given an opportunity to participate in the organization and the direction of the treatment;

4. Though opinions of prisoners may be expressions of a minority group, convicts and ex-convicts are a part of society deserving of some special consideration; and

5. That one of the requisites to good citizenship for people generally is also required if one is to make a convict a good citizen—the encouragement of truthful, thoughtful criticism of our existing institutions.

There are men in prison who have constructive suggestions and oftentimes they are inmates. The writer managed to find several such people. Their constructive suggestions ranged from getting fly-proof lids for garbage cans to demands for a complete change in our whole culture. They suggested dozens of details to make school training more effective, to make the enforcement of discipline more reasonable, to better the quality of food, to make the participation in recreation broader, to improve the effectiveness of parole supervision. The methods they suggested for bringing about an end to their imprisonment varied from a return to Republicanism to violent revolts, in prison and out. . . .

81 · The Pardoning Power

by AUSTIN W. SCOTT, JR.

A professor of law at the University of Colorado, Austin W. Scott, Jr., describes in the following article the practice of granting pardon. He explains who can grant it and the conditions under which it is granted. After a discussion of the factors influencing pardon officials in their decisions, and of the extent to which pardon is resorted to in cases of capital crimes, he presents his conclusion as to the usefulness of the practice. [From *The Annals*, Vol. 284, Nov. 1952, pp. 95-100. Reprinted by permission. Footnotes omitted.]

THE SUBSTANTIVE criminal law—concerning itself with the technical problem of what act combined with what mental state is necessary to constitute any of the various crimes in our criminal jurisprudence—has been aptly described as "an island of technicality in a sea of discretion." Thus, before trial, the police have broad discretion as to whether to arrest, and the prosecutor as to whether to prosecute, and if so, for what crime. After conviction, the trial judge (or, less frequently, the trial jury) has discretion as to what sentence, within limits, to impose or whether to suspend sentence and place on probation; the parole board has discretion as to the duration of penal treatment; and the pardoning authorities have discretion as to the use of the pardon power.

The technical and inflexible nature of the problem of guilt or innocence of crime (inherited largely from the historical fact that in England, when the criminal law was being developed, so many crimes were punishable by death) makes desirable the placing of a good deal of discretion in the groups concerned with criminal law enforcement—police, prosecutors, judges, juries, parole boards, and pardon authorities. If this discretion is taken away from any one of these groups, the burden becomes correspondingly greater on the others to make wise use of their discretionary powers.

Thus in capital cases it has in the past been not uncommon to deprive judges or juries of their normal discretion as to sentence, by making the death sentence mandatory. The trend in recent years has been, if not to abolish capital punishment, at least to abolish the mandatory death sentence. Accompanying this movement has been something of a decline in the importance of the pardon power in capital cases. But as long as capital punishment continues, power to pardon in capital cases is bound to remain an important element in the administration of criminal justice.

The broad power vested in pardon officials to pardon, to commute sentences, and to grant reprieves, applies, of course, to many crimes other than capital crimes. In this article, however, we shall limit ourselves to a consideration of these powers in relation to capital cases where the death penalty has been imposed.

WHO MAY EXERCISE PARDON POWERS

All civilized countries make use of some form of the pardon power to give flexibility to the administration of justice in criminal cases. In England this power historically is vested in the Crown. But in the United States it is vested in the People, who can delegate the power to whomever they please. As a matter of practice, the People have found it most convenient to give the power to the executive branch of the government. Thus, under the United States Constitution the pardon power in federal cases has been delegated to the President; and practically all the state constitutions have delegated this power in state criminal cases to the governor, either alone or in conjunction with advisers.

A large majority of state constitutions originally gave the power to pardon to the governor alone. The more recent trend has been toward putting more power in the hands of a board. Simplifying matters somewhat, we find that today there are in general three different arrangements among the states. First, in about one-quarter of the states, the executive pardon power is vested in the governor alone; some of these states, however, furnish a pardon attorney to aid the governor in these cases. Second, about half the states have provided for advisory boards whose function is to hold hearings on pardon applications and make recommendations to the governor, who alone may make the final decision; in practice, the governor usually adopts the recommendations of the board. Third, in about a quarter of the states there are boards which, instead of acting simply in an advisory capacity, have the final decision about pardons; in all these states, however, the governor is a member of the board.

TYPES OF PARDON IN CAPITAL CASES

In discussing the power to pardon in cases where the death penalty has been imposed, it will be well to consider separately three different types of executive clemency: (1) full pardon; (2) commutation of sentence to imprisonment for life or a term of years; and (3) reprieve, or stay of execution.

FULL PARDON

In only a rare case does one sentenced to death for crime receive a full pardon. Usually the best he can hope for is a commutation of his sentence to life imprisonment. But there is one type of case, fortunately quite rare in capital cases, where justice demands a full pardon—namely, where subsequent events prove that the convicted person is innocent.

There is some dispute as to how often innocent persons are convicted of serious crimes. Some enthusiasts assert that the many procedural safeguards which are afforded criminal defendants in this country—the right to a jury trial, to counsel, to be informed of the charge, to call witnesses, the privilege against self-incrimination, for instance—make it impossible to convict an innocent person. The District Attorney for New York County reports that only 3 out of 27,288 persons convicted in that county of felony during the years 1938-49 were later shown to be innocent.

On the other hand, Professor Edwin M. Borchard, in his book, *Convicting the Innocent,* has collected and discussed at length 65 cases of innocent persons convicted of crime, mostly in this country, of which 29 are murder cases. He says that these 65 were chosen from a much larger number.

Borchard's cases show that innocent persons are sometimes convicted of crime on mistaken identification by the victim, who is often emotionally disturbed by his experience; sometimes on erroneous inferences drawn from circumstantial evidence; sometimes on the basis of perjured testimony of hostile witnesses. Prosecutors, expected by the public to produce convictions, are seldom as impartial as they are ideally supposed to be, although they do not often stoop so low as intentionally to use perjured testimony against the defendant or to suppress evidence favorable to him. Public pressure for revenge sometimes leads juries to convict innocent persons. If the jury learns that an accused person has previously been convicted of an earlier crime, his chances of being convicted of this later crime are considerably enhanced, so much so that he often refuses to testify in his own behalf for fear the jury will learn of his former conviction.

Thus it is clear that for one reason or another an innocent defendant is sometimes convicted and sentenced to death, a fact which obviously constitutes one of the strongest reasons for abolishing capital punishment. In such a case it is only right that the defendant should be given a full pardon. It seems odd, but in most cases of innocence established some time after conviction, a pardon is the only effective way to rectify the wrong, since courts generally have no power to grant new trials because of newly discovered evidence after a relatively short period of time following conviction.

COMMUTATION OF SENTENCE

Commutation is the substitution of a lighter for a heavier punishment. Unlike pardon, it does not mean forgiveness, and does not effect a restoration of civil rights. Most state constitutions specifically include in the pardoning power the power to grant commutations. In those states whose constitutions do not specifically so provide, it is held that such a power is included in the grant of the pardoning power, for the reason that the greater power (to pardon) necessarily includes the lesser power (to commute).

The power to commute sentences is exercised in a great many cases other than death cases, usually to make eligible for parole a prisoner whose term has not expired. Here we shall consider the power only as used to avoid the death sentence, an important but far less common use of commutation. In practice, the power is generally exercised by commuting death sentences to life imprisonment, although occasionally the sentence is reduced to imprisonment for a term of years.

To prevent the arbitrary or dishonest exercise of the pardoning power by pardon authorities, most of the states require regular annual or biennial reports to the legislature by pardon authorities concerning the granting of pardons, commutations, and reprieves. A study of these reports gives us some indication as to the reasons why commutations are granted in practice. Often the recommendation of the judge who tried the case, the district attorney who prosecuted it, or the state supreme court which reviewed it, is emphasized. Frequently the fact that, of several joint participants in the crime, only one received the death sentence (particularly if this one was not the moving spirit behind the commission of the crime) is given as a reason for commuting the sentence to life imprisonment.

Sometimes the evidence against the defendant, although sufficient to sustain a conviction, is conflicting or is based on circumstantial evidence alone, in which cases the pardon authorities may decide to commute the death sentence. Commutations (or even occasionally full pardons) are sometimes granted because of prior promises made by prosecutors, which the state feels bound to honor, of lighter punishment or immunity in return for turning state's evidence. Sometimes there are extenuating circumstances which do not affect the technical legal question of guilt or innocence of a capital crime but which do call for the exercise of mercy, as for instance in the famous lifeboat cases which are so well known to law students.

A variety of other reasons have been given as well, including such matters as the youth of the condemned person, the evil influence exercised over him by his stronger or older companions, his good prison record, or the fact that this was his first offense. At times the reasons are suggested very vaguely: "because of the peculiar circumstances of the crime" or "because it is considered that justice will be satisfied without the taking of this man's life."

Factors Influencing Pardon Officials. Without doubt there are motivating forces which lead pardon officials to grant pardons or commutations but which are not given as reasons for acting. At times the condemned man is a member of a group which exercises great pressure on pardon officials to grant clemency; conversely, the victim of the crime may be a member of a group which just as vigorously opposes clemency.

Politics is an important factor, too, especially where the governor alone exercises the pardoning power without being insulated by a board of pardons. As an elected official, he is not impervious to the display of public opinion for or against a condemned prisoner.

An interesting question arises as to how the governor's private views on capital punishment affect his commutation of death sentences. We may expect, for instance, that one who strongly disapproves of such punishment would be more prone to commute death sentences than would others. A number of years ago, the Governor of Oklahoma announced his view that the death penalty was legalized murder and stated that he would commute all death sentences to life imprisonment. The Oklahoma Criminal Court of Appeals thereupon denounced the Governor's position in angry tones, stating that the law forbade him to "allow his scruples to influence him in the least." But since it is uniformly held that the exercise of discretion by pardon officials is a matter not to be reviewed or interfered with by the courts, it is difficult to see how, as a practical matter, there can be any effective way of preventing pardon authorities from letting their views on capital punishment influence their decisions on commutations of death sentences.

Extent of Commutation. One last problem is the extent to which pardoning officials have in fact exercised their power to commute death sentences. Figures are not directly available on a national basis as to the number of cases where the death penalty was imposed but sentence was commuted. However, we can learn something by comparing the number of prisoners received by the federal and state prisons each year under sentence of death with the number of prisoners executed at these same prisons during the same period. Those not executed must have either received commutation, died (either naturally or by suicide), escaped, or had their cases reversed by a higher court. The latter three possibilities are not very common, however.

For the seven years 1940-46 inclusive, 771 condemned prisoners were received, of which number 587 were executed. Most of the 184 unaccounted for undoubtedly received commutations. It would seem, then, that, taking the country as a whole, commutations are granted in about 20 to 25 per cent of the cases where the death penalty is imposed. This statement is somewhat confirmed by the earlier assertion of the Select Committee on Capital Punishment that "over a given period, the percentage of death sentences carried out to execution is 71.9 in the United States."

Statistics are available in some of the individual states as to the numerical relationship between those executed and those whose sentences were commuted. Thus in New York from 1920 to 1936 there were 252 executions and 83 commutations. In New Jersey from 1907 to 1937 there were 119 persons electrocuted and 27 granted commutation. Texas granted 7 commutations out of 64 cases in the four years 1947-51.

It seems safe to say that of the many persons who are convicted of crimes whose maximum punishment is death, comparatively few receive a death sentence. Of those who are sentenced to die, most are executed, but about one in four or five obtains a commutation to life imprisonment.

REPRIEVE

A reprieve in the case of one sentenced to death is merely a postponement of execution. In general, the power to pardon carries with it the power to reprieve, whether or not the reprieve is expressly mentioned in the constitution among the other forms of clemency. While reprieves are sometimes granted in noncapital cases, they are most important in capital cases, to stay execution of death.

The reports of pardon authorities indicate a variety of different reasons for granting reprieves in capital cases. They are often granted—as of course they should be if the law does not provide for an automatic stay of execution—pending the appeal of the case to a higher court or to allow the condemned man to apply to the United States Supreme Court for certiorari or to allow him to pursue other procedural remedies in the courts. If newly discovered evidence bearing on the case is found, reprieve should be granted pending an investigation into the matter. A reprieve may be granted a woman prisoner who is pregnant. It is a well-settled rule of law that an insane person cannot be executed, so reprieves are often granted to determine the question of insanity; and, if insanity is found, to postpone execution until sanity is regained. Reprieves are sometimes granted for less important reasons, such as the fact that the date of execution is a holiday or a Sunday or the prisoner's birthday.

CONCLUSION

Pardon authorities are given broad and almost unrestricted discretion over pardons, commutations, and reprieves. This fact is one of the elements of strength in the proper administration of criminal justice. But it has sometimes led to abuse, especially in those states where one man has the final determination over clemency. Unscrupulous governors may build up their political careers by using the pardoning power to please people with political influence. Others, more honest, are influenced by the effect of their decisions on the electorate, rather than by the merits of the particular case.

While the discretion of pardon authorities is so broad that there exists no definite standard by which to determine whether the discretion is being abused or not, yet some situations have arisen which clearly show an abuse of discretion. The most notorious of these cases is that of a former Governor of Oklahoma, who was impeached because he frequently exercised his power to pardon, not on the merits of the case, but rather as an accommodation for friends or for financial rewards for himself.

In spite of occasional abuse, however, it seems obvious that the power to pardon is a necessary part of American criminal jurisprudence, in capital as well as noncapital cases. As long as a conviction cannot be reversed after a period of time for newly discovered evidence proving the defendant's innocence, we need the power to pardon for innocence. There will always be cases of technical guilt but, because of extenuating circumstances, comparatively little moral fault. The pardon power, in other words, is necessary in cases where the strict legal rules of guilt and innocence have produced harsh or unjust results. Doubtless the administration of the pardoning power can be improved, as the Attorney General's Survey of Release Procedures, including Pardon, has concluded. But the power to pardon will continue to play an important part in the ultimate disposition of capital cases as long as capital punishment remains with us.

82 · The Employment of Released Offenders

by CLEMENT J. WYLE

Perhaps the greatest and most urgent problem faced by the freed prisoner is the almost total unwillingness of society to readmit him and, more specifically, to offer him a job, without which reformation becomes practically impossible. Clement J. Wyle conducted a modest survey among employers in various branches of business and industry with the purpose of finding out why the former inmate of a penal institution is almost universally refused employment and under what conditions, if any, he would be offered a job. The results of this survey are presented in the article that follows. [National Probation Association Pamphlet (Reprinted from *Probation*, Oct. 1946), 7 pp. Used by permission.]

Most offenders released from prison or reformatory cannot obtain employment unless they have "connections," lie about their past, or say nothing about it. Seldom will they find an employer willing to give them jobs for which they are qualified, except perhaps during a war when there is a shortage of labor. These are truths which few people will dare deny.

What can be done about all this? And just how can the public be made to realize that released offenders *must* be given every opportunity to engage in legitimate endeavors if they are to be law-abiding?

In an attempt to answer these questions, we *personally* interviewed 475 men who operate successful businesses in the City of New York. We chose this method because it was felt that were they to receive a questionnaire, they might be reluctant to answer truthfully the all-important question: "Would you employ a released offender provided he was qualified for the job?" Verbal assurances that those interviewed would remain anonymous, also enabled us to obtain information which casts much light on the problems involved.

The 475 interviewed, none of whom refused to talk, can be broken down, roughly, into the following groups:

Advertising Executives	30
Bankers	12
Attorneys (Engaged in enterprises where they could hire people not connected with the legal profession)	16
Real estate operators	9
Brokers	7
Chemists	4
Manufacturers	176
Writers	6
Storekeepers	41
Wholesalers	60
Other groups	114

This is not a scientific sample, yet it includes almost all the types of individuals who might consider, at some time or other, the employment of men who have at some time been convicted of a crime.

Of the 475 interviewed, 312 stated unequivocally that they would never hire a released offender. (Some, however, changed their minds during the course of the interview.) Sixty-two hedged and said they were not certain. The balance, 101, stated that they would hire released offenders, provided they were qualified for a job and gave every indication that they would be law-abiding citizens. Curiously, though, only 46 in this group had *knowingly* employed released offenders. The balance thought that they might.

Of the 312 who would have nothing to do with any individual with a "record," 311 stated that they would fire him if they learned about his past. The lone exception was a storekeeper who had once hired a delinquent because "he was desperately in need of an errand boy." That boy grew up with the firm and made good. His past was discovered when he was fingerprinted during the war. The employer, when asked why he would not give other men similar opportunities in view of that favorable experience, merely shrugged his shoulders.

The replies of those who would not employ former offenders have been heard by most of us time and time again:

"Why should I take a chance?" some asked—

"A leopard never changes his spots," said others—

"Those characters can't be trusted," remarked still others—

Oddly enough, only a few opposed hiring ex-inmates on the ground that their business might suffer if the news leaked out. Their chief objection was that these people couldn't be trusted.

After receiving such unfavorable replies, we spent some time with the interviewees explaining why it was essential that released offenders be given employment. Unless they earned a livelihood, wouldn't it necessarily follow that they would revert to lawlessness? Wasn't it possible that even the worst type of offender would be rehabilitated during his term of imprisonment and emerge determined to go straight?

We also pointed out that wardens insist that the majority of their charges change for the better and have no desire to come in conflict with the law again. Wasn't it ludicrous therefore for society to spend millions of dollars rehabilitating men and then place obstacles in their paths?

Of the 312 businessmen who stated that they would never hire released offenders, 68 per cent admitted that these arguments were plausible. But, they argued, after all, we are practical businessmen. What assurances do we have that such employees will not betray us?

After further discussion, most of those interviewed agreed they might hire a released offender—qualified for a specific job—provided someone gave them reasonable assurance that he would not revert to lawlessness. By "assurance" most meant letters of recommendation from respected citizens who had either employed the applicant or knew him well. But how more than a handful of offenders can obtain such references, is a mystery to us.

Let us now consider the 101 businessmen who said that they would hire released offenders. It is doubtful whether all of them actually would, for as we pointed out, only 46 in that group had ever employed such men. Experiences of some of the 46 should be noted.

One man complained that he hired a former burglar as a dress packer.

The packer did not steal, but he quit the job without notice and left the employer during a busy day. We were amazed to find that the employer was not angry. He insisted that the former burglar was a bit "punch-drunk" and should have been sent to a rest home after his release from prison. "That man just wasn't ready to hold a job," he remarked. "But I'll put anyone who is on my payroll."

Another employer said that he now has about twenty former offenders in some of his factories. This employer is an exception. He understands the problems of released men thoroughly. He told us that when one of them applies for a job, he will invariably have a long talk with him, then assign him to a task which does not require much cooperation with others. "If he is compelled to work closely with other employees," we were told, "he may slow them down during fits of restlessness. Consequently I prefer to give him a job that is somewhat interesting yet what I call individualistic. If he day-dreams he cannot do any harm. As he progresses and becomes adjusted I'll advance him, and believe me, many former offenders fill good jobs at good wages in my factories."

We were particularly anxious to publicize the name of this employer. In fact, we told him that his point of view would encourage other businessmen to be as socially minded as he. But the man refused, claiming publicity would do all concerned considerable harm.

Other employers also pointed to their successful dealings with former offenders. Some claimed, however, that such men could hold nothing but menial jobs. But—and this is important—there were a number of employers who insisted that the loyalty of former offenders was so profound that they never regretted hiring them. Unfortunately, such experiences rarely, if ever, are publicized. What are publicized are the occasional failures, with the result that public opinion is invariably directed against all released offenders as a group.

How can we counteract such prejudice?

Employers, with few exceptions, do not realize that so many former offenders revert to lawlessness because they are faced with an alternative —steal or starve. Obviously, the public must be made cognizant of the fact that a considerable number of crimes are committed because of a rather glaring inconsistency. We want offenders to go straight, yet we refuse to give them an opportunity to do so. A broad public relations program therefore must be invoked to hammer this point home.

In this connection the various states could help considerably. Many states spend millions of dollars teaching inmates trades but then refuse to grant them the licenses necessary to practice those trades. If the states are so shortsighted, is it any wonder that private industry also is?

But even were industry to take a more liberal attitude, we cannot deny employers some protection. We cannot expect them to hand out jobs without having reasonable assurance that those they employ are really on the level.

One of the solutions suggested proposes that the state grant "certificates of rehabilitation," [1] restoring the full rights of citizenship to released offenders who have mended their ways. These certificates are to be issued by a competent non-political board, consisting of practical penologists who know how to check up on men who have spent time behind bars without subjecting them to embarrassment and anguish.

We asked the 312 employers who had stated unequivocally that they would never hire a released offender, and the 62 employers who were uncertain, if they would give employment to former offenders who had been granted certificates of rehabilitation by a responsible state board.

Surprisingly, of the 312 who had said they would not hire former offenders, 71 per cent declared that they would, *if the former offenders had certificates of rehabilitation*. So did 83 per cent of the employers who originally said they were not certain.

A number from both groups were enthusiastic about the certificate of rehabilitation plan and felt that it would solve a vexing problem. One said, "Since most released offenders cannot possibly obtain satisfactory references, the certificate would fill a crying need." Another said, "A sort of guarantee from the state would counteract the deep-rooted fears in many employers and lead to the employment of a great number of former offenders."

The bulk of employers are unable to do their own "screening," either because of disinclination or lack of time. Men having certificates of rehabilitation would already have been screened. And when the certificate is issued, it should also wipe out effectively a man's past so that his former conviction would no longer count against him. Nothing contributes more to a person's desire to go straight than a feeling that he has paid his debt to society and has the same privileges as his fellow citizens. Certainly one of the most sacred of these is the right to work.

[1] Certificates are issued by some states, but these are usually difficult to obtain or are of very limited value. In New York, for example, a "certificate of good conduct" may be issued by a unanimous vote of the parole board. Such a certificate however only restores specific rights lost by conviction, such as the right to vote, or the right to obtain certain licenses. It does not remove the stigma and disabilities of conviction, and even this limited certificate cannot be issued until five years after an offender's release from an institution. Certificates of somewhat broader scope may be issued on release in Ohio, Minnesota, Idaho, Nebraska, after six months in North Dakota; after one year in Oregon; and, after three years in Tennessee and North Carolina.

CHAPTER TWENTY-ONE

Crime Prevention

---

83 · Facts and Fancies in Crime Prevention

by VIRGIL W. PETERSON

Crime being a universal problem, people throughout the ages have sought means not only of dealing with it effectively but of preventing it. However, most of the means proposed to prevent crime—even those of the present—belong more in the realm of folk remedies or of speculation than in that of facts. The following article presents a short account by Virgil W. Peterson, the author also of a previous selection, of the erroneous theories held and of the consequently mistaken remedies that have been suggested. He points out how the goal of crime prevention may be reached. [From *Journal of Criminal Law and Criminology*, Vol. 38, Jan.-Feb. 1948, pp. 466-474. Reprinted by permission.]

WITH THE CLOSE of the great war, the prevention of crime has once more assumed a foremost place in our thinking on national affairs. The problem of crime prevention is not a new one nor is it peculiar to modern America. Almost two thousand years ago, during the trial of Caius Silanus by the Roman senate on charges of extortion, it was declared, "Laws punish crimes committed; but how much more merciful would it be . . . to provide against their commission." But man's total inability to cope with the problem is perhaps best attested to by the fact that after more than seventeen hundred years had elapsed, an Italian, Cesare Beccaria, expressed the identical thought in his famous "Essay on Crimes and Punishments." He said, "It is better to prevent crimes than to punish them . . . But the means hitherto employed . . . are generally inadequate or contrary to the end proposed." And this observation of Beccaria is as true today as it was when written in 1764.

Man may boast of splitting the atom. His inventive genius has enabled him to travel around the world within a few hours. Distance, time, and space have been largely conquered. Through his scientific knowledge he has been able to artificially cause rain and snow. But with all of these accomplishments, man still does not understand man. The causes of his behavior and the relations of one human toward another, which lie at the heart of crime and its prevention, still remain an enigma.

Arnold J. Toynbee has stated that "the most extraordinary characteristic of man . . . is the extreme contrast between our ill success in dealing with ourselves and the mastery that we have established over physical nature." He refers to man as: "A god in technology; an ape in life." In the field of human behavior and human relations, we have certainly verified the assertion of a famous French scientist, Lecomte du Nouy, that the depth of man's intelligence has increased but very little during the past ten thousand years. And the knowledge we have been able to acquire we have not been able to put into practice.

These words may sound a pessimistic note. But the primary requisites for any substantial progress consist in attempting to understand something of the magnitude of the problem and in viewing it in its true perspective. Criminal human behavior is not an isolated problem of crime. It is a problem which embraces sociology, economics, politics, cultural backgrounds, law enforcement, psychology, psychiatry, penology, biology, physiology and other branches of comparable sciences. Yet, too frequently in the past, the tremendously complex nature of human behavior has been completely ignored. And programs designed to prevent all crime have considered only one of the manifold factors involved. Such efforts have meant little more than high-sounding phrases and slogans. Upon their completion we still have the slogans—and also the crime.

Several years ago, one panacea advanced to eliminate crime was supervised recreation. Independent research, however, established that the delinquent and potential delinquent were less apt to participate in supervised recreation than the non-delinquent. It became obvious that any crime prevention program based on supervised recreation alone was doomed to disappointment and failure.

At one time it was vigorously proclaimed that the solution to the crime problem would be found in education. It was asserted in effect that criminal behavior results from ignorance; knowledge alone would prevent crime. But psychiatrists have rightfully pointed out that in the field of human behavior it is not as important to *know* the distinction between right and wrong as it is to *feel* this difference. It is this emotional quality, a feeling of the difference between right and wrong, that we refer to as conscience and which is a basic substance of character.

In the Sixteenth Century the great French philosopher, Montaigne, spoke of the absurdity of the prevailing educational system. He said: ". . . its aim has been to make us, not good and wise, but learned; and it has succeeded. It has not taught us to follow and embrace virtue or wisdom, but has impressed upon us their derivation and etymology." Perhaps the same criticism could be leveled at our educational system in America today. At any rate, we have certainly placed much more emphasis on developing and perfecting the physical sciences than we have on the science of character building. And to large segments of our population, pure intellectualism has become such a fetish that even the word moral is something to be abhorred as an earmark of ignorance or of religious superstition. Yet some of the world's greatest criminals who have brought untold suffering to mankind were intellectual giants with moral standards of morons.

During the recent war the subject of juvenile delinquency was one of the foremost topics for discussion in America. The emphasis gradually shifted from the juvenile to the adult. And during the past several months it has become popular to fix the responsibility for all crime and delinquency on the home and the parents. No one can deny the vital importance of the home in molding character and in the development of useful law abiding citizens. But to ignore the important social and political influences that frequently counterbalance the influence of the home and to insist that parents alone are responsible for criminal behavior on the part of their children is utter nonsense.

There are many parents of exemplary habits and conduct who devote all of their energies and talents in the rearing of their children. Within their means nothing is left undone which should aid in the building of character and providing adequate educational opportunities. But the parents are average American citizens. They are industrious but of moderate income. They have a comfortable living but luxuries are few. As the son of such parents matures he begins to make independent observations. He too frequently notes that the few individuals in his community who dress well, ride around in big cars, live in spacious homes and who are always plentifully supplied with money, are those engaged in some racket or perhaps are corrupt petty politicians deriving their livelihood through graft. His parents may call these men "crooks" but he is impressed with the deference shown them by many citizens of the neighborhood. He notes that even in schools, churches and community organizations they are treated with honor and respect, many times because of their liberal financial support. Unquestionably, such influences frequently cause a youth to reappraise his parental training and guidance. His immature judgment may result in a decision that the precepts of his parents are outmoded; they are old-fashioned and not applicable to one who wishes to get ahead. Delinquency and even criminal behavior may follow.

It should also be noted that the gradual transformation of America from a population that was once largely rural to its present industrialized urban character has naturally weakened the influence of the home. At one time a sizable percentage of homes in America were almost complete economic, social and cultural units. The influence of such homes on children was stronger than any other. But today in many urban communities conditions are present which result in a complete deterioration of the home influence.

For example, year after year in Chicago, a small district of less than two and one-half square miles out of a total of two hundred and eleven, accounts for approximately one-fourth of the total murder and rape offenses committed in Chicago and a highly disproportionate number of other crimes. Daylight hold-ups are so commonplace they attract but passing attention from people on the streets. Lawlessness generally prevails. Into this small area are crowded almost 200,000 people. It is not uncommon for buildings intended for three families to house twenty-five. Living conditions are so congested that normal home life is an impossibility. Community cooking facilities are commonplace. One bathroom only is available for several families in many buildings. Health conditions are bad. In recent years available schools could not accommodate all of the children. They were required to attend classes in two and in some instances three shifts. Many of the commercial recreation places are regular breeding places for crime and delinquency. Although in ordinary times most of the residents of the area are poverty stricken, politically protected rackets have materially aided in keeping them financially destitute. Nickels, dimes and quarters of these poor people that should have been expended for milk, bread and the necessities of life have been poured into the policy racket. And the principal policy kings, the Jones brothers, have become millionaires with estates in France, Canada, and Mexico. Yet, these men are the heroes to many in the district—the examples of success. The anti-social conduct and attitudes that prevail are natural products of social conditions to which the people are subjected. As the brilliant writer Richard Wright has pointed out, to expect contrary conduct on the part of the people living in this locality "would be like expecting to see Rolls-Royces rolling off the assembly lines at Ford's River Rouge plant." The conditions in this particular community are not peculiar to Chicago. Almost every large city has several districts in which comparable conditions exist. And it is a meaningless absurdity to fix the sole responsibility on the parents and the homes for the high incidence of crime that prevails in such districts.

The home is still the most important institution in the molding of character. But we are falling into the error of over-simplification of one of our most complex problems if we fail to realize that the average child is subjected to many powerful influences other than those found in the home. It has become so commonplace, however, in dealing with the crime problem to over-emphasize the influence of the home at the expense of all others that public officers have sometimes attempted to place the burden for their official shortcomings on the shoulders of parents. For example, the conditions in numerous taverns in Chicago were intolerable for many years. Liquor license laws were disregarded with impunity. Men with long criminal records and those associated with notorious gangsters operated liquor places in which gambling flourished, prostitutes solicited their trade, sanitary conditions were deplorable and minors were served with liquor. Several vicious murders, rapes, and other crimes were committed by intoxicated minors who were permitted to purchase liquor after the legal closing hour. A particularly notorious case involved an eighteen-year-old boy who had committed a murder following a night of drinking in various taverns. The Criminal Court judge who passed sentence on this youth stated that in his Criminal Court experience he found that a large percentage of crime was traceable to the sale of intoxicating liquor in the early morning hours to juveniles. Licenses were rarely revoked and in many instances the most flagrant violators had their licenses restored when their cases were heard by the License Appeal Commission of the City of Chicago. Retail liquor conditions became so intolerable that a mass meeting was held almost two years ago which was attended by representatives of numerous official bodies, civic agencies, and juvenile protection and welfare organizations. After much discussion on methods of coping with the bad situation which had become serious, the chairman of the city License Appeal Commission spoke. In effect he belittled efforts directed at better enforcement of liquor laws. He admonished those present that the solution to the entire problem was to be found in the home; with proper home influence and parental guidance and discipline youth would not frequent undesirable taverns. Needless to say, this was merely an attempt to avoid responsibility for conditions he could have assisted in improving or eliminating. Instead, he found it expedient to shift the blame to the home.

Over-simplification of the complex problem of human behavior has seriously impeded any substantial progress in preventing crime. Instead of inaugurating comprehensive programs embracing many of the causative factors involved, we have too frequently turned from one panacea to another. At various times diverse philosophies have represented our thinking on ways and means of preventing crime. From the untenable position that severity of punishment alone would operate as a deterrent to crime, we have arrived at the place where we believe that no punishment at all is desirable. On the other hand it is advocated that punishing parents and sending them to jail will prevent juvenile delinquency. At different times we have explained criminal behavior in terms of glandular disturbances, mental aberrations, internal conflicts and maladjustments, broken homes, parental neglect, improper law enforcement, under privilege and over privilege. In turn, we have recommended as cure-alls more playgrounds, youth centers and boys' clubs, the sterilization of imbeciles and better street lighting. We learn and blandly accept the principle that: "What's good for the individual is good for society." Although experience and common sense dictates that there are cases in which treatment favorable to one individual may retard the treatment of scores of others and is therefore injurious to society, it is considered rank heresy and a mark of ignorance to say so.

In one breath we demand slum clearance and the elimination of poverty as a means of reducing crime. In the next breath we suggest the legalization of inherently illegitimate rackets which materially aid in reducing poor people to poverty stricken circumstances. We blame the criminal's anti-social behavior on confusion and frustration but at times he appears to be considerably less confused and frustrated than those attempting to cure him.

These remarks are not made in a spirit of criticism and ridicule. They are made solely as a plea for an open mind and the removal of dogmatism from a field in which there is presently no room for dogmatism. On the basis of past experience, and in view of the fact that the sum total of irrefutable knowledge in the field of crime causation is very meager, it is almost a certainty that some of the basic principles accepted today will be considered unsound and unacceptable in the future.

Our total experience in dealing with human behavior should serve as a warning against too much smugness in our opinions and particularly against forcing such opinions on others. It has been less than four hundred years ago that Jean Bodin, French political philosopher, rose to a distinguished position as an economist. His intelligence was such that, of all the writers of the Sixteenth Century, Bodin alone comprehended the fact that Europe was undergoing rapid changes. He became noted for the breadth and liberality of his mind. Yet Bodin definitely established to his satisfaction the existence of witchcraft. And he insisted that the rigours of the law be visited, not only upon those allegedly practicing witchcraft, but upon those who had the temerity to doubt the reality of sorcery. In this modern era there is little likelihood of anyone attempting to compel us to believe that criminal behavior can be explained in terms of witchcraft. But many times our approach to the problem remains much the same. Theories are developed which are only theories and have never been satisfactorily proven. Yet there are those who insist that anyone who questions their soundness is an out-and-out dunderhead or is possessed of ulterior motives. In this regard about fifteen years ago automobile thefts in Chicago became so prevalent that there was established a special branch of the Municipal Court to handle all cases related to this type of offense. At the time this court was founded, automobile thefts in Chicago exceeded thirty thousand a year as compared with about three thousand in recent years. Several factors contributed to the tremendous decrease in this type of crime and it is naturally a matter of conjecture as to the exact contribution made by the Automobile Court. In recent months a proposal was made to transfer all defendants between seventeen and twenty years of age from the Automobile Court to the branch of the Municipal Court called the Boys Court. It was contended that the facilities of the supervising agencies were more readily accessible in the Boys Court than in the Automobile Court. In substance it was claimed that the philosophy of the Boys Court was more compatible with modern thinking in the treatment of delinquents than that which prevailed in the Automobile Court. Those who opposed the change questioned this premise, pointing out that some of the supervising agencies in the Boys Court already had almost double the case load that could properly be handled. It was further objected that much of the vaunted supervision was on paper only. The suggestion was made that, before changing from a system that had greatly improved conditions to one of problematical effectiveness, it would be wise to proceed with caution. With one or two exceptions there was admirable fair-mindedness on the part of those representing both sides of the controversy. However, a very small minority insisted that those opposing the change were doing so because of a complete lack of appreciation and understanding of the problem and, due to the viciousness of their hearts, they were interested only in saving automobiles, not boys.

A few days ago there was completed an independent study of both courts made under the direction of Dr. Ernest W. Burgess, eminent sociologist of the University of Chicago. There were examined the records of about 420 seventeen-year-old boys whose cases were disposed of in almost equal numbers in the Automobile and Boys Courts during 1943. The percentage of recidivism in the theoretically sound Boys Court was nine per cent higher than in the Automobile Court. These findings do not necessarily prove the superiority of one court over the other from the standpoint of saving boys. In fact, there are strong indications that many of the theories and philosophies present in both courts are unsound. The study does forcefully bring out, however, the danger of ignoring facts that do not coincide with theories. It is in this way, said Montaigne, that: "We know the foundations and causes of a thousand things that never were; and the world skirmishes with a thousand questions of which both the pros and the cons are false."

The excellent studies made by Eleanor and Sheldon Glueck forcefully bring out the need for a careful appraisal of present theories and their application in the field of criminal behavior. The independent research of the Gluecks has reflected that even though the recommendations of the clinic were followed in the post-treatment of delinquents in such matters as place of residence, improvement of family and living conditions, health, schooling, vocational and recreational activities and disciplinary practices, the percentage of recidivism was only slightly less than in those cases where the recommendations were not carried out. In other words, they determined that the putting into effect or the failure to carry out the clinic's recommendations did not have as marked a significance as might have been supposed. In his foreword to the Gluecks' book, "After-Conduct Of Discharged Offenders," Mr. Justice Felix Frankfurter said: "Like so many of the conquests of science, the results of the enquiries reported by the Gluecks have merely pushed back the boundaries of darkness. We still do not know what is chargeable to nature and irremediable by man." This certainly does not imply that scientific research in combatting crime has been futile nor does it mean that we should adopt a defeatist attitude. The fact that the boundaries of darkness have been pushed back is a strong indication they can be pushed back still farther and eventually sound, constructive programs that will materially reduce delinquent and criminal behavior on a nation-wide basis will become a reality.

To attain this goal it will be necessary that independent intensive research be conducted on a much more comprehensive basis than has heretofore been possible. This research should take two directions: first, the collection of irrefutable facts relating to the causes and precipitants of human behavior as well as other aspects of the crime problem, and, second, the development of ways and means of transforming the knowledge acquired into effective action.

Perhaps considerable progress could be made through the establishment of a National Institute for Crime Research functioning under the direction of outstanding administrators in the field of scientific inquiry. An institute of this nature should be privately endowed to remove any tinge of partisan politics. There should be obtained the collaboration and cooperation of leading universities and outstanding authorities in every branch of science dealing with human behavior. During the late war, the forces of science were marshalled. The collaboration of research efforts on the part of leading scientists throughout the nation was secured and man developed furies of destruction which, ironically, may destroy him. Should it not be possible to exert comparable efforts toward the constructive end that human behavior and the relations of one individual toward another may be appreciably improved? Is it not a satire on this so-called enlightened age that we must still say with the ancients that "there is no beast in the world so much to be feared by man, as man?"

84 · The Prison's Role in Crime Prevention

by AUSTIN MacCORMICK

What should be the aims and objectives of the prison? Should prison be a place where the law-breaker is made to pay his debt to society, where he is punished, or where he is rehabilitated so that he may be returned as a useful member of his community? If the latter is the true objective— and the majority of present-day American penologists would agree that it is—how should our prisons be operated in order to achieve it? A distinguished penologist and former Commissioner of Correction of New York City, Austin MacCormick reviews here some of the aspects of this problem and expounds his philosophy regarding the function and objectives of the modern prison. [From *Journal of Criminal Law and Criminology*, Vol. 41, May-June 1950, pp. 36-48. Reprinted by permission. Footnotes omitted.]

A DEFINITION of the term "prison" is necessary in any discussion of th prison's role, for during the past eighty years our correctional institu tions have been adapted to a changing role in a changing society.

While the word "prison" is a convenient over-all designation for in stitutions for convicted male offenders above the level of the county jai and city workhouse, it is no longer an accurate term as commonly usec in the United States. State institutions for persons convicted of felonie and serving sentences, generally speaking, of more than a year are o various types nowadays: prisons (called penitentiaries in some states, al though in others this term is applied only to the larger county jails), re formatories for men and for women, road and forestry camps, farms, anc such special institutions as those for insane and mentally defectivε criminals. The type of prisoner who would have been confined fifty years ago in a maximum security walled prison may be found now in any one of several kinds of minimum or medium security institutions o units. We speak today of *correctional* rather than *penal* institutions, but still use the general term "prison" for convenience.

It is misleading to give an exact figure for the total number of state correctional institutions, for some states have prison systems that would more properly be termed constellations. Texas, for example, has one walled prison and eleven widely scattered farm units to which prisoners of the type usually found in prisons or adult reformatories are sent. Virginia has a walled industrial penitentiary, an industrial farm for women, three farm institutions for men and a series of road camps in which nearly 2,000 men are working. North Carolina has a central prison, but 80 per cent of the state's prisoners are in eighty-eight road camps or farm units. California, in addition to two maximum and four minimum or medium security institutions for adults, operates a dozen road and forestry camps.

In the forty-eight states and the District of Columbia, not counting small farm or road camp units but counting such large prison farms as those in Texas and Virginia, there are 152 correctional institutions for adults: sixty-eight prisons or penitentiaries; twenty-six reformatories for men in twenty-two states and the District of Columbia; twenty-five reformatories or similar institutions for women; twenty-two farm institutions or large farm units, including state farms designed primarily for misdemeanants; eleven special institutions, including three hospitals for insane criminals and four institutions for defective delinquents.

The federal prison system consists of six penitentiaries, three reformatories for men and one for women, nine so-called correctional institutions, three prison camps, a medical center, and a detention institution or jail in New York City. The United States Bureau of Prisons, which administers this system, also operates a training school and a forestry camp for boys.

The diversification of institutions is only one of the manifestations of the progress that our prisons have been making quite steadily for the past thirty-five years, in spite of the fact that there have been four periods during that span which affected prisons greatly: the prohibition era, the depression and the two world wars. This progress has not consisted merely of the improvement of conditions and practices that militated against the rehabilitation of prisoners but has also included the development of programs that affirmatively promote rehabilitation, utilizing scientific techniques and personnel with professional and technical training.

It is this progress and the philosophy that activates it that makes it appropriate to discuss the prison's role as part of a program on *Crime in Today's Society*. Moreover, it is appropriate that persons representing a wide variety of interests should participate in this discussion, as a commissioner of mental hygiene, the head of the country's largest prison system, law school professors, a university professor distinguished for his research work on sex offenders, psychiatrists who have specialized in criminology, an outstanding layman, a university dean, and a former judge who is now dean of the country's leading school of social work. The prison is thus by inference placed in its proper setting as one of the wide variety of instruments that Society uses to prevent and control crime, and penology in its proper setting as a sector of the general field of criminology and the broader field of the social sciences.

It is high time it were more generally recognized that the prison is more than an instrument of society's retributive vengeance, that its basic philosophy is a correctional rather than a punitive philosophy, that we penologists are not zoo-keepers but men and women engaged in a delicate and difficult salvage operation. The prison is not merely a scrap-heap where we dump the slag that is left after science has extracted everything possible from even the lowest-grade ore. It is an important step in the total process of extracting, converting and refining the potentially valuable material that passes on a never empty belt-line through our clinics and our courts.

There is special significance in the title of this paper: *The Prison's Role in Crime Prevention;* not repression, but *prevention*. It is true that crime is prevented not alone by the varied agencies and programs that seek to keep boys and girls from becoming delinquent, not alone by the police forces that try to stop the criminal before he commits his crime, but also by the three services that together constitute what we call the correctional process: probation, institutions and parole.

The public ordinarily does not think of these functions as preventive, for all three services deal with convicted offenders. If it thinks of the prison as a preventive agency, the public means that it is expected to deter potential offenders through fear of punishment. But, as a matter of fact, the primary function of the prison, as of probation and parole, is to reduce crime by preventing its repetition. The more than 60,000 men and women convicted of felonies who enter our prisons every year present possibilities of a very substantial saving in future crime, with all its calculable and incalculable costs. Repeated crime—crime committed by people who have been caught, convicted, sent to prison, and turned out later no better or even worse than when they went in—is one of the most foolish and expensive American luxuries.

How can the prison best prevent the repetition of crime by its charges? By locking them up and throwing away the keys? By subjecting them to such deprivation and cruelty that they will tremble with fear at the thought of ever coming back to prison again? I do not need to say that the answer to both these questions is an emphatic "No."

About a year ago, as a member of a committee set up by a division of the United Nations, I had to write a paper on *The Function of the Prison*. Since the paper would go to European countries where our American correctional philosophy is far from being generally accepted, I could not avoid spelling out again the old arguments on whether or not the prison can best protect society by serving as an instrument of custodial segregation, or of punishment, or of rehabilitation. While writing much of that article I had a feeling I should have been sitting in some medieval cubicle scratching out my ideas by the light of a flickering taper. The inclusion of some of those ideas here is occasioned by the knowledge that even in this country there are many people dealing with crime and criminals, or formulating and administering the criminal laws, who are still reading their penology by the taper's light.

It is obvious that the prison provides society some protection from crime by merely keeping offenders in custodial segregation for varying periods up to life imprisonment. It is equally obvious that this may solve the problem caused by specific criminals without solving the problem of crime in general, just as the segregation of lepers may or may not promote the prevention and cure of leprosy. Even with specific offenders, imprisonment has limited value as a protective device unless they are confined for life.

If, on the other hand, modern society sought to protect itself against those who are a menace to the persons or the purses of their fellow-citizens by life imprisonment or other inordinately long sentences for all sorts of crimes, it would find itself eventually with an ever-increasing burden of crime. It would deserve to, moreover, as a penalty for its abandonment of a defensible social philosophy with respect to crime. The history of Elizabethan England, of Colonial America and, indeed, all history sounds a clear warning that society does not reduce crime but increases it by imposing penalties that those who make up society cannot accept as necessary and just.

In the United States penologists have been working in the opposite direction for the past eighty years, at least. They have sought by indeterminate sentence and parole laws to make it possible for an offender to be released when it is in the best interest of society and to help paroling authorities to determine when the time is ripe for release. They attempt to accomplish this by means of classification, and by medical, psychiatric, psychological and other services in correctional institutions. Progress toward the day when offenders will be imprisoned only as long as is clearly necessary has been retarded by existing legal provisions prescribing heavy mandatory penalties for certain types of crime and for repeated crimes. The trend since the turn of the 20th century, however, in spite of the retrogressive wave of legislation during the "crime wave" of the 1920's, has been increasingly toward greater flexibility in dealing with convicted offenders. The Youth Correction Authority Plan, sponsored by the American Law Institute, and the Federal Corrections Act introduced in Congress with the backing of a committee of federal judges, are examples of current proposals providing for a high degree of flexibility.

Under our present procedures, fully 95 percent of all those now in state and federal prisons and adult reformatories will eventually be released. While many offenders in the United States are held in prison for long terms, the median time served by those released in any given year is less than two years. It is possible that many prisoners are released before they should be; it is not and cannot be claimed that we have achieved a scientifically sound system of sentencing and release procedures. Generally speaking, American penologists would prefer to err in the direction of too short rather than too long sentences. It is contrary to progressive correctional philosophy and is becoming increasingly repugnant to the social conscience of our people to imprison an offender for a long period, without regard for his personal characteristics, merely because his custodial segregation affords society protection for the time being. There is a growing awareness among thoughtful people that society can never be truly protected by any procedure that does not deal justly and wisely with its individual members.

The theory that the prison can most effectively reduce crime and thus promote the protection of society by serving as an instrument of punish-

ment cannot be discussed without reference to the theory of rehabilitation, for in practice the two theories run counter to each other at s
many points. The debate on the punitive versus the rehabilitative theor
has filled the pages of penological literature for generations. It is
debate that has not been conclusively ended on the world stage. So fa
as the United States is concerned, however, it is ended. It woul
be virtually impossible in America today to find a penologist of recog
nized standing who is willing to write or speak on the relative validit
of the two theories except as a literary or oratorical exercise or as
task of restating what he considers self-evident truths.

The position he and his colleagues would take is that whatever validit
the punitive philosophy may have in this country and century is so fa
out-weighed by the merits of the philosophy of rehabilitation that th
latter should take unquestioned precedence in current penal thought
They would insist, moreover, that if punishment is to be considered a
aim of imprisonment, it must be what the Germans termed *Zweckstrafe*
or punishment for a purpose, rather than *Vergeltungsstrafe*, or punish
ment as retribution.

Punishment as retribution belongs to a penal philosophy that i
archaic and discredited by history. Our leading penologists, if prison
were to be operated as instruments of retributive punishment, woulc
refuse to accept appointments to administer them. They recognize tha
even if the idea of retribution by legal penalties is entirely sound today
from the ethical standpoint, which they question in view of the known
inaccuracies and inequities of our legal processes, it is not sound from
the practical standpoint. It is impossible to determine what penaltie
provide the varying but exact amounts of retribution called for by a list
of crimes ranging, for example, from theft of a handkerchief to murder.
When it abandoned the use of the death penalty for the former and a
great variety of other minor and major offenses, society posed for itself
the impossible task of setting up a graded scale of crime values with
commensurate penalties.

The task of producing a legal slide rule on which one can compute
the exact degree of retribution called for by a crime committed by a
person at a given time under specific conditions is still more impossible.
The wide divergence in sentences for the same crimes imposed not only
by courts in the 48 United States but also by those of a single state and
by the courts of the federal judicial system bear indisputable witness
to our failure to develop exact scales of punishment or to use those we
have even-handedly.

Retribution, moreover, implies the payment of a debt to society and
expiation of one's offense. The very crimes that we are most anxious

) prevent—murder, rape, and other crimes involving cruelty and vio-
ence—are those for which society can never exact adequate compensa-
ion by retribution, or the perpetrators make adequate payment by ex-
iation. For these and other crimes it is impossible to pay one's debt to
ociety and it is not good for the offender to believe that it is possible.
'ayment of a debt carries the implication that one is free to start run-
ing up a new account. This is all too often the view of prisoners who
ave served out the full length of a heavy retributive sentence to im-
risonment.

Finally, if it were possible to use the prison as an instrument of retrib-
tive punishment with exactitude and justice, its use for such a purpose
would defeat the achievement of so many more worthy purposes that
he net result to society would not be gain but loss, not benefit but in-
ury. The prison operated on the basis of a purely punitive philosophy
would produce more criminals than it would prevent.

If we are to dismiss the idea of punishment as retribution, what of
unishment for a purpose? What purpose could give validity to the
use of the prison as an instrument of punishment? It is difficult to think
of anything that can be admitted to consideration except deterrence.
It is conceivable that, under a system of law enforcement in which the
apprehension and conviction of offenders are swift and certain, punishment by imprisonment could be so imposed and carried out that it would
deter the ex-prisoner and other potential offenders from the commission
of crime. Only the most unrealistic optimist, however, would claim that
under the present system of law enforcement in the United States deterrence can be effectively accomplished by punitive imprisonment.

In the United States so small a percentage of all offenders are caught
and convicted that what happens to them can have little effect on the
great body of potential and actual violators of the law. Reports of the
Federal Bureau of Investigation for 1939, the last pre-war year, from
78 cities with populations over 25,000 and a total population of about
13,000,000 show that for every 100 major offenses known to the police
there were 27 arrests, 19 prosecutions, and 14 convictions. In some cities
the ratios are even lower than these figures; in one large American city,
for example, the ratio of convictions to known offenses in 1945 was 5 to
100. The odds clearly favor the criminal in such conditions.

Many offenders, moreover, are the type that would not be deterred
even if the odds were heavily against them. Included in this group are
many insane, mentally defective, neurotic, or psychopathic persons, some
with uncontrollable compulsive urges, especially in the sexual field.
There are others who act impulsively, without weighing the costs, perhaps under the stress of anger or passion; others who plan their crimes,

such as insurance murders, but whose cupidity or predatory desires ou
weigh their caution; still others whose recklessness makes unfavorabl
odds more rather than less attractive, and many besides who do n
know whether the odds are in their favor or not and do not care. In thes
groups fall the great majority of the types of offenders we would lik
most of all to deter from crime, because of the nature and frequenc
of the crimes they characteristically commit.

In spite of these facts, strengthening the processes of law enforce
ment so that more offenders are imprisoned would undoubtedly resul
in some degree of deterrence, but what degree is by no means certair
There can be little doubt, moreover, that emphasis on the use of th
prison as an instrument of deterrence would result in a net loss rathe
than a net gain. To achieve the maximum deterrent effect it would b
necessary either to impose excessively long sentences or to inflict harsl
treatment and impose rigid restrictions and deprivations on the pris
oners. The experience of centuries in Europe and America indicate
that these methods not only defeat rehabilitation and increase recidivisn
but encourage in free society a brutalized viewpoint that fosters crime

Experienced penologists do not dismiss the idea of punishment. The
recognize the fact that being sent to a prison, however humanely it i
operated, is punishment in itself. They know that it is impossible t
make a prison so pleasant that the prisoners will not consider their im
prisonment punishment. They believe it is neither necessary nor justifi
able to add to the punishment inherent in loss of liberty, separation
from one's friends and family, and the stigma of a prison sentence. Ex
perience has convinced them that efforts to do so tend to reduce the
number of offenders who become law-abiding citizens on release and to
increase the number who continue in crime. They are certain that em
phasis on the punitive theory of imprisonment works against rather than
for the protection of society.

Penologists in the United States today are generally agreed that the
prison serves most effectively for the protection of society against crime
when its major emphasis is on rehabilitation. They accept this as a
fact that no longer needs to be debated. The best thought in what was
once called the penal field, and is now significantly called the correc
tional field, is directed toward developing plants, personnel and pro
grams that will accomplish the rehabilitation of as many offenders as
possible and will enable those who cannot be released to adjust as well
as possible to the restricted life of the prison. Although prison admin
istrators know that a substantial percentage of adult offenders are not
likely to be salvaged by any methods we have thus far developed, they
direct their programs of rehabilitation to the presumably incorrigible

as well as the probably reclaimable group, and consider only a small minority of prisoners as completely hopeless cases. This may seem to be an impractical and visionary viewpoint, but it is wholly realistic and is based on a clear-cut idea of what rehabilitation is and what it can accomplish.

Rehabilitation is not a vague, haphazard and loosely defined process. The essential elements of a well rounded correctional program of individualized training and treatment in an institution for adult offenders are well known. They include the following: scientific classification and program-planning on the basis of complete case histories, examinations, tests and studies of the individual prisoners; adequate medical services, having corrective as well as curative treatment as their aim, and making full use of psychiatry; psychological services, properly related to the problems of education, work assignment, discipline and preparation for parole; individual and group therapy under the direction of psychiatrists, psychologists, or trained social therapists; employment at tasks comparable in variety, type and pace to the work of the world outside, and especially tasks with vocational training value; education planned in accordance with the individual's needs and interests, with heavy emphasis on vocational training; library services, designed to provide wholesome recreation and indirect education; directed recreation, both indoors and outdoors, so organized as to promote good morale and sound mental and physical health; a religious program so conducted as to affect the spiritual life of the individual as well as that of the whole group; discipline that aims at the development of self-control and preparation for free life, not merely conformity to institutional rules; adequate buildings and equipment for the varied program and activities of the institution; and, above all, adequate and competent personnel, carefully selected, well trained, and serving under such conditions as to promote a high degree of morale and efficiency.

That a high percentage of successes can be achieved by prisons with programs of this type, coupled with a sound parole program, is not problematical; it has been demonstrated. Perhaps the best available statistics in support of this statement are those compiled by the New York State Division of Parole. The State of New York is generally acknowledged to have a superior parole system, in which parolees receive thorough supervision. The programs of its penal and correctional institutions, however, do not include all the essential elements cited above and are not so clearly superior to those of other states as to make New York's figures on rehabilitation successes non-typical.

Each year the New York Division of Parole publishes statistics on parolees who were released from the prisons and adult reformatories of the state five years previously. The pre-war reports showed that about 65 percent of those paroled five years before had maintained clear records, that about half the remainder had been returned to institutions for technical violations of their parole conditions, and that the remainder, about 17 percent, had been convicted of new offenses, of which only half were felonies. During the non-typical war years the percentage of successes rose even higher. The report at the end of 1946 on the "Class of 1942" showed that, five years after release on parole, 73.2 percent had maintained clear records, 14.8 percent had been returned to institutions for technical violations, and 12 percent had been convicted of new offenses: 6.2 percent of felonies and 5.8 percent of misdemeanors.

It is probable that deterrence has also played a part in the success record achieved by the "graduates" of New York institutions and those of the federal prison system and a number of progressive state systems, which also show a high percentage of successes. But the fact remains that the administrators of these institutions stress rehabilitation and place their major emphasis on efforts to achieve it. They consider deterrence as only a by-product of institutional operation.

The position taken by the proponents of the theory of rehabilitation may be summed up as follows: They do not rule out the necessity of custodial segregation, but consider custody a means to an end in the vast majority of cases, and an end in very few cases. They do not deny the desirability of achieving a deterrent effect if it can be done without impairing the effectiveness of rehabilitative programs that offer more assurance of good results than deterrence does. In short, they believe, all things considered, that rehabilitation is not the only aim of the prison but should be its primary aim.

They are certain that operating prisons so as to accomplish the maximum deterrent effect would cause more crime in the long run than it prevented. Being convinced by experience that a large percentage of all adult offenders committed to prison can be rehabilitated, they prefer in the operation of penal and correctional institutions to place their reliance on rehabilitative principles and methods that they consider ethically sound and practically effective rather than on principles and procedures that they cannot accept philosophically or practically.

While this is the viewpoint of most workers in the United States in the correctional services—probation, institutions, and parole—it is not the viewpoint of the great majority of those engaged in what is termed law enforcement: the police, prosecutors, and judges. It is a curious and most revealing fact that a sharp distinction is made between the processes of law enforcement and correction, and that the latter is not considered a part of the former by those who "enforce the laws" but ll too often as antithetical to their aims and a hindrance to their efforts.

There is in this country a distinct break in the philosophy and methodology of what should be a continuous process of law enforcement. It occurs at about the point of conviction. The basis of much of our criminal law and of the processes of apprehension and conviction is the theory of retributive punishment. When the offender has been convicted, a second set of agencies and officials with an entirely different philosophy—that of rehabilitation—takes charge of him. The methods used on both sides of the dividing line reflect the widely divergent underlying philosophies.

Judges stand at the dividing line and may play two roles. As they preside over trials and impose the penalties prescribed by law, they are part of society's ancient machinery of vengeance and retribution. As they utilize the clinical and probation services of their courts or, in imposing a sentence of imprisonment, take into account the possibility that the offender may be salvaged in prison and on parole, they are a part of society's modern machinery of correction. Because of their training, the traditions of their profession, and the punitive purpose of most criminal law, judges, with notable and increasingly numerous exceptions, are still found most frequently in the role of interpreters and administrators of vengeful and retributive justice. In view of their position at the end of the process of apprehension, prosecution and conviction and at the beginning of the process of correction, and in view also of their great influence on the thinking of legislators and the general public, society may well ask the judiciary to take leadership in an effort to develop a single basic philosophy to which all those engaged in dealing with crime and criminals can subscribe.

The lack of such a basic philosophy and of approved methods and procedures derived from it is perhaps the most significant feature of the crime situation in the United States today. It is the chief reason for our failure as a nation to develop a continuous and fully integrated program of crime prevention and control. We are, instead, standing with one foot in the past and the other in the present, with one hand tilting the scales of justice toward retribution and the other tilting them toward rehabilitation. We are dealing with *crime* ineffectively because we have not come to an agreement on how to deal with *criminals*.

It is high time that we resolved our differences and the difficulties arising from them. To do so we must first relegate the idea of retribution to the scrap-heap of outworn ideas where it belongs. We must then strengthen law enforcement to the point where a large percentage of offenders are brought under legal control, and at the same time develop a wide variety of agencies, institutions and programs to deal with convicted offenders on an individualized basis, as we would deal with sic persons in a well organized public health program. Under such a syste of dealing with offenders, the process of diagnosis, prescription an treatment in a given case may call for confinement in a prison for long period, even life. But the prison will be expected to accomplish th restoration to free society as law-abiding citizens of as many of its charg as possible.

There is another contribution the prison can make to crime prever tion that has been almost completely disregarded thus far. Prisons coul play a role of great significance if they were organized and staffed n only to provide training and treatment with a view to rehabilitation bu also to serve as research centers. It is true that the addition of profes sionally trained personnel to the staff of many institutions has resulte in the assembling of considerable information of scientific value an that some noteworthy research work has been done by institution sta members, frequently as part of their daily work, and by university pr fessors and graduate students.

If the prison is to be an effective research center, however, there mus be more than a spotty and sporadic research program. There must b intensive research—carefully planned, adequately financed, and we staffed—into a variety of specific problems and there must be sustaine and comprehensive research covering as much as possible of the entir field of crime causation and treatment. Research in prisons can thro more and more light on the causes of crime but it must have as its pri mary aim the determination of how we can prevent crime and can mos effectively treat offenders whose crime we do not succeed in preventing

One of the most promising research projects ever undertaken in correctional institution, for example, was the study of psychopaths car ried on in 1940-42 at the Federal Reformatory in Chillicothe, Ohio. A special building was constructed for the group under study, a carefull selected staff of Bureau of Prisons and Public Health Service personne was assigned, and the project was pointed at trying to determine wha makes psychopaths act as they do and what training and treatment ar most effective in modifying their behaviour. It is most unfortunate tha it was necessary to terminate this project, because of the loss of key personnel during the war, before any clear conclusions had been reached.

Similarly, the study of sex offenders carried on at Sing Sing Prison under the auspices of the New York State Department of Mental Hy giene, supervised by the State Psychiatric Institute and directed by Dr. David Abrahamsen, is of particular importance because it is concerned with developing effective treatment procedures as well as learning more about the causation of sex offenses of the type generally considered abnormal, aberrant, psychopathic, etc.

It is an interesting fact that some of our oldest and, in many ways, our least productive prisons could become highly useful institutions if they were organized and staffed to serve as research centers. To cite only a few very old prisons that are located in or near large cities, Sing Sing, the Massachusetts State Prison at Charlestown, and the Eastern Penitentiary in Philadelphia could make a greater contribution in their old age than they have ever made in their history of nearly a century and a half if they became centers of research. Almost at their doors are limitless resources for personnel to conduct research in the universities, medical schools, hospitals, clinics, schools of social work, and all the other agencies of Boston, New York and Philadelphia.

Research in prisons must not be concerned exclusively with an attempt to develop new modes of training and treatment. It must concern itself also with appraising methods that have been in vogue for many years and have been carried on without challenge, although their validity has never been proved. This has been well put by James V. Bennett, Director of the United States Bureau of Prisons, in these words:

We have established programs of treatment that are thought of as progressive. But now the time has come to analyze scientifically our methods. Is so-called "modern penology" an effective penology? Are classification, education, occupational training, case work, psychotherapy, and other elements of the modern correctional program producing results? If not, why not, and what is to be substituted? If so, how can they be made more effective? These are questions which the thoughtful prison administrator who is spending hundreds of thousands or millions of dollars from public funds must ask himself. The answer can be given only by research.

In conclusion, when the prison is no longer expected to perform the ignoble task of serving as an instrument of retribution, when it holds offenders in custodial segregation only as a measure of safety, not as punishment, when its primary aim is the rehabilitation, reclamation, reform—call it what you will—of those committed to it, and when it makes through research its full contribution to scientific knowledge of crime causation and treatment, then and then only will the prison fulfill its true function, the protection of society.

85 · What Can We Do to Prevent Crime?

by EDWIN J. LUKAS

In the article that follows, Edwin J. Lukas, director of the Society for the Prevention of Crime, a jurist, and a close student of the crime problem, shows how baseless the popular notions regarding the causes of crime are and how futile—even preposterous—the usual means proposed for preventing it. After outlining the steps to be taken to educate the public to the true facts, he makes suggestions about the way we should proceed to solve the problem realistically and effectively. ["Crime Prevention: Who Prevents What?" *Federal Probation*, Vol. 12, April-June 1948, pp. 19-23. Reprinted by permission.]

To PUT the matter mildly, the mass of people today are being deceived by a grotesque species of criminological quackery. Ponder a few exhibits, among the many: A well-known magazine, boasting an enormous circulation, commendably enough had a monthly feature devoted to "techniques of crime prevention." But each article dipped into the problem with monstrous indifference to the dynamics of criminal behavior. Each capitalized on the folklore and superstitions of an uninformed public, ranging from platitudinous nonsense about the benefit of balanced diets to the consummate effrontery of suggesting that rigid discipline and supervised recreation supply the final answers to crime prevention. There was not a single criminologist, sociologist, psychiatrist, or psychologist among the authors of these "authoritative" articles!

Here is an example of another kind. Recently a proposal was advanced that we annually celebrate National Crime Prevention Week. (It has long been acknowledged that "National [anything] Week" is a means of increasing the sale of flowers and haberdashery.) This was the brain child of an advertising agency promoting the sale of a product by means of a "cops-and-robbers" radio program. The program's commentator from week to week dinned his quaint notions of crime prevention into the ears of the listening audience. An idea of the nature of the prevalently unromantic preventive techniques to be advocated during this annual crusade against crime may be derived from its principal facets for the first year:

(1) Keep your front doors locked constantly.
(2) Remove your key from the ignition lock in your auto when not in use.
(3) Improve street lighting.
(4) Don't count your money in public.

Examine another impulse to exploit the naiveté of the public. A new business enterprise advertised its ability to furnish a "Police Escort for Every Woman." Attractive window-display material in shops along many avenues depicted some thugs in frantic flight and emblazoned thereon in bright red letters was the following intriguing slogan: "An Alarm in Time Prevents Crime." Attached was a shiny object which could be purchased for 89 cents. It was a whistle!

And we shouldn't overlook those psychoquacks who peddle a cultism, embroidered with pseudo-scientific gibberish, as a cure-all for emotional ills, including those which often result in criminal behavior. They are the unlicensed personal problem counselors. There are now over 25,000 such creatures in this country who advertise themselves as being capable of resolving deep neuroses and, indeed, psychosis itself.

These are but a few samples randomly selected from the melange of proposals which greet our ears incessantly. There are countless others—all seriously advanced as crime preventives: that the sale of cola drinks and of tea or coffee to persons under 18 years of age, be prohibited; that comics be banned from newsstands; that slot-machines and juke-boxes be destroyed; that movies, literature, and radio programs depicting criminal episodes be censored; that the sale of all alcoholic beverages be prohibited; that a fish diet be fed to people with emotional problems; that we dot the landscape with playgrounds, canteens, and boys' clubs; etc.

OUTMODED CONCEPTS ABOUT CRIME

The simplicity of the concepts thus espoused is disarming. It would be a fatal error to dismiss the thinking which yields to these allurements as the vaporing of a lunatic fringe, or to imagine that they are not regarded seriously by the public. Unhappily, that is not the case. They reflect the primitive views of the vast majority of laymen in this country today, each of whom considers himself as possessing the qualifications of expertness.

Nor are the public's artless notions concerning prevention self-limiting; they extend as well to correctional treatment of criminal offenders. Having oversimplified the causes of crime, the public also oversimplifies its remedies. With some notable exceptions, the brutalizing practices of the early penology of ancient people—idleness, perfunctory custody, meaningless discipline, isolation, even flogging—are still among the degrading characteristics of a modern penology that is said to have been "reformed."

To be sure, there has been recognition here and there that the popular "rehabilitative" methods of the past have, in large part, failed utterly to produce little more than remorseless and revengeful recidivists. But any honest appraisal of the futility of the current brand of correction would have to include an acknowledgment of the ugly spectacle of youngsters, men and women—thousands of them—failing to receive any but retributive treatment for warped and distorted personality patterns, the neglect of which results more often than not in rendering irremediable what once, earlier, was readily remediable.

The controlling passion of the public remains scapegoatism. The prevailing sentiment is still anchored to the archaic idea that the most effective means by which crime may be prevented is to obliterate root causes by spraying young people with a watered-down ideological D.D.T. At the same time it adheres tenaciously to the doctrine that, to control crime, we should descend implacably upon the offender with an irresistible force; subdue him by making him insensible.

Winston Churchill once remarked: "The mood and temper of the public with regard to the treatment of crime and criminals is one of the most unfailing tests of the civilization of any country." Public opinion, when aroused by an especially heinous offense, often shapes the course of criminal justice administration in a way that, for some of us, provokes a shiver of eeriness and awe.

HOW CAN WE PREVENT CRIME?

How, then, can we prevent crime in an atmosphere so charged with a mixture of naiveté and an uncontrolled instinct for punishment? Isn't it an almost impossible task to effectuate crime prevention in a community whose collective stability is wrenched forcibly from its foundations every time an extraordinary criminal episode occurs?

In light of the incompleteness of our present knowledge of the specific mechanisms which evoke criminal explosions from human beings, the dilemma of professional crime preventers is at least two-pronged. It resides not alone in eliciting an effective method of destroying the old myths concerning what causes crime, and the taboos concerning what may "cure" it. While that task is formidable enough, something else must be erected to replace what has been displaced. Even if we were able successfully to dispel illusions, siphon from the public's thinking processes the huge reservoir of outmoded concepts, and cope with its emotionally charged posture toward the efficacy of punishment, we still would be under the necessity of substituting a practicable program of prevention.

If, then, a sovereign power granted us the right tomorrow to fashion a serviceable program of crime prevention for a typical American community, in what direction might we move?

Suppose we indulge in the luxurious fantasy of speculation, suggesting the bare outlines of answers to these questions.

1. *Basic Working Philosophy Is Fundamental.* At the outset we would have to be guided by a fairly basic working philosophy—an attitude. Attitude, indeed, is the primary ingredient of any enterprise. If the attitude of the public toward crime itself could be made to conform as nearly as possible to those of behavior scientists, most of the current absurdities on which we lavish time and money would become obsolescent.

We would make no substantial progress in promoting the success of any program until at least two postulates were firmly established.

(a) We must be infinitely more interested in preventing the development of a criminal episode before the *pattern of maladjustment* of the offender becomes fixed, than before the *criminal situation* presents itself. We must concentrate on the prevention of crime at its source, in the home, school, and community, on economic, social, and psychological levels. We must prevent the *criminal.* This is prevention in its purest sense.

(b) Then our prejudiced minds would be ready to embrace the increasingly validated criminological concept to which scant attention had been paid in the fashioning of yesteryear's traditional preventive programs. It is this: that in the commission of nearly every crime two sets of influential factors seem to operate simultaneously: (1) those called *predisposing*, rooted deeply in the past of the offender; and (2) those called *precipitating*, existing in the contemporary life of the offender. Not one, or the other, but *both.* In the degree of their importance, it is the former—not the latter—which is dominant.

Were this attitude vouchsafed, were we to bring people to the threshold of a plan with the idea fixed in their minds that crime is but symptomatic of deeply underlying drives and needs, we probably would avoid the superficialities of most past and many present preventive schemes. To paraphrase Sheridan, we no longer would tolerate a tiny rivulet of sound doctrine meandering through a meadow of hokum.

2. *Importance of Cultural and Ethnic Characteristics of a Community.* We could then plunge into another critical phase of our project. We might, for example, want to examine the recent history of our American community, to ascertain with some particularity the cultural and ethnic characteristics of its inhabitants. We would want to know something more than a mere census tabulation discloses about the people whose antisocial tendencies we were attempting to check. Among

the other things we would want to know are their economic status, their mobility, social pathology, physical and mental health, etc.

This would move us along toward two goals: (a) The broadly-gauged cultural characteristics of the population structure of a community sometimes evoke vastly different reactions to what, ostensibly, are identical environmental conditions. In the planning of an indigenous preventive project this phenomenon would have to be reckoned with. (b) To succeed, even partially, in harnessing the enthusiasm, talents, and energies of the people of differentiated cultures to the delicate task of crime prevention, we must formulate versatile methods, peculiarly suited to communicating our ideas to them. In this respect our past public relations have been conspicuously inept. Not only do languages differ in our heterogeneous population but there are also disparities in the ways in which people have habituated themselves to ingesting information and responding to propaganda. We must know how to overcome anomalies in intellectual resistance, and use the kinds of pressures to which they will yield. Their idiosyncrasies, if known, will guide us in educating them.

3. *Public Should Be Told What We Know about Crime.* The next branch of our task might be geared to informing the people of the community concerning the nearest we have come to the causes of crime.

However, instead of performing this inconclusive chore in the forbiddingly dull manner to which we have accustomed ourselves, we ought to dramatize it. Here we must surrender social-science jargon; and, on the other hand, avoid obscuring the issues in a miasma of craven journalese.

Every community has its roster of famous offenders with whose external behavior it is well familiar, but of whose internal drives and other surrounding circumstances it knows literally nothing. We would want to bring these dynamic factors home to the people of the community. We would examine painstakingly and publicize the personal, social, and family histories of a sizable sampling of the more recent crop of the community's juvenile and adult offenders. The public's awareness of the specific social and psychological circumstances which contributed to the antisocial behavior of locally notorious offenders would be helpful in securing its co-operation for creating some of the basic tools with which to prevent a repetition of that behavior among others.

These histories we would delineate in newspapers, over the radio, in classrooms, and at town meetings. Utilizing the tricks of large-scale advertisers of merchandise, we would pound away at the concept, time and time again, that symptoms do not manifest themselves in a vacuum; that they have setting and background; that they manifest themselves differently in variously constituted personalities.

For these hypothetical purposes, suppose the following catalogue of contributing factors was revealed:

(a) That the majority of adult criminals in the community were persons who had been seriously disturbed, or maladjusted, and delinquent children.

(b) That a small percentage of the children who became delinquent was mentally defective, or borderline.

(c) That an even larger percentage suffered from personality distortion, mental tension or conflicts, and faulty habits.

(d) That an appreciable proportion came from homes in which the parents were incompetent to carry out the duties of parenthood.

(e) That many of the delinquent children truanted from school at an early age, and had achieved neither adequate academic education nor vocational training.

(f) That a high proportion of delinquent children came from areas of the community in which the processes of deterioration were marked, in that the cultural standards of those areas were in conflict with standards adopted by others, in which conditions of poverty, undernourishment, and over-crowding prevailed; in which inadequate provisions for wholesome recreational outlets were made; and, finally, in which centers of antisocial attitude existed.

4. *Inventory Should Be Taken of Existing Crime Prevention Facilities.* With this catalogue compiled and publicized, the community would know—better than ever before—the precise nature of the problem they faced. We now are ready for an inventory of the facilities in the community which already exist, or must yet be created, for handling the dominantly contributive factors in the community's crime and delinquency picture.

At this critical juncture one is drawn irresistibly toward unorthodoxy. It ought to be acknowledged that classic methods for the procurement of essential services have failed. The mischievous assortment of known unfilled needs, which require no listing for the readers of this journal, is appalling. We are not conscious of any groundswell of activity toward filling those needs. A truly accurate inventory of the resources of an even well-endowed community would contain inordinately large gaps.

And it may safely be assumed that in a typical community those gaps fall into three categories: (a) the early *recognition* of significant *danger signals* which children are constantly sending out into their homes, schools, and neighborhoods, such as lying, exhibitionism, sexual irregularities, destructiveness, abusiveness, stammering, stealing, fire-setting, excessive shyness, and the infinite variety of other eloquent tokens of insecurity, anxiety, and emotionally unsatisfying personal relationships; (b) the careful clinical *diagnosis* of those overt or subtle signals, together with an investigation of the intimate circumstances in which they are betrayed; and (c) the co-ordinated provision of therapy and manipulation of social or environmental factors, *promptly* upon the coming-in of diagnostic findings.

If we were now discussing somatic diseases, and the parental or medical neglect of their observable symptoms, we would be properly inelegant in our denunciation of that neglect. Yet, no one will deny seriously that we have so far made but cavalier gestures toward recognizing the symptoms of incipient antisocial tendencies before they blossom into explosive behavior. Space limitations forbid the construction of an index to the incredibly long list of items which are lacking. The shelves of our libraries groan under the weight of printed discussions of how, where, when, and by whom these essential services ought to be but are not being performed. Because the process is no longer a secret, when we fail to implement it we make a mockery of what we know. The matter is put succinctly by Dr. Robert M. Lindner, in his *Stone Walls and Men*:

Not education of parents alone, not the psycho-eugenics of mating alone, not slum clearance alone, not the reorganization of social institutions from courts to prisons alone, not any separate phase or aspect or portion or part of our total social configuration by itself will prevent crime, but all of these together and at once.

This suggests *co-ordination* of the services of public and private agencies.

But we cannot mouth that phrase today without becoming uncomfortably self-conscious. Elaborate variations of the technique of co-ordination have been sprinkled through our literature for a quarter-century or more. Barely a conference fades into the limbo of forgetfulness without a pious resolution to build ordered co-operation out of chaotic decentralization.

Yet, as we all know, there is pitifully little co-ordination in any real or significant sense. A city of 50,000 population may have as many as 30 agencies or departments related to the delinquency and crime problem; a city of 500,000 may boast as many as 200. Here and there, in a curiously sporadic fashion, some agencies have consolidated their activities either organically or administratively. In the vast majority of communities, however, the tendency of most public departments and private organizations is each to behave as though it were the sole facility, or to pursue a policy of selectivity so rigid as to bar large numbers of vulnerable youngsters from becoming beneficiaries of their service. Truncated in their operation, they fragment children's welfare by fragmenting children. The net result of what they do is to entrust one small corner of the child to the city, one to the county, one to the state, another to the federal government, and still another to voluntary agencies, each without reference to or in disregard of what the other is doing.

To remedy this we would be tempted to inaugurate a *single, over-all community co-ordinating bureau*. To be sure, there is nothing revolutionary inherent in that suggestion. But this bureau would be somewhat like a war industries mobilization board which, despite imperfections, wrought such wartime miracles in production largely because of its power to license manufacturers, distribute raw materials, supervise their fabrication, and get them to the battle-fronts speedily. We readily yielded to its necessity in a national emergency.

In substantially the same way this bureau would be charged with the mandatory mission to allocate the activities of police, schools, civic organizations, health and leisure-time organizations, family service agencies, guidance clinics, and all the others whose potentialities are related to the presently known attacks on the behavior problem.

This bureau would be armed with sanctions. It could recommend withdrawal of its accredited status from any private agency which failed to gear itself properly to the consummation of its assigned attack on the behavior problems of the community. It also could allocate to public agencies appropriate duties, the nonfeasance of which would be actionable.

In short, *this* co-ordinating bureau would be a creature of the state, armed with governmental power, rather than ministerial duty, to allocate responsibility and to compel its discharge.

This bureau would mobilize resources to rid us of a stubborn behavioral infection, or at least reduce it to its irreducible minimum. It would shrink from becoming the counterpart of most co-ordinating councils which conceive it to serve their highest purpose to call periodic conferences to "explore conditions," "canvass the situation," or "study the problem." Initiated with all good intention, they have been swallowed by a morass of what Grover Cleveland once colorfully described as "innocuous desuetude." Their deterioration from initial enthusiasm to inactivity was implicit in the strictly voluntary nature of each agency's participation.

When participation in the mechanics of this social problem's solution is *compulsory* (as it is to a certain extent with hospitals in the amelioration of the community's health problems), we may expect a larger measure of success than the abortive efforts of the past have elicited. Certain public and private agencies would be entrusted with the duty of diagnosis, others with the duty of treatment. There would be a constant flow of referral from diagnostic centers to treatment centers, the one integrated with the other. Facilities for intra- and extra-mural care, designed to complement each other, would be instantly at the call of therapists.

The power to insure this flow is the heart of community co-ordination. Anything less is a rank futility, an extravagance; anything less is not the prevention of *criminals*.

5. *Only Persons of Highest Caliber Should Be Responsible for Crime Prevention Programs.* The community will be taught not to regard the entire venture as a luxury. Therefore, instinct in this plan is skilled, sensitive personnel. It seems trite to remark that no plan, however enlightened, can be effectuated unless the people administering it are of the highest caliber obtainable. Enthusiastic amateurs, political hangers-on, and frustrated misfits are to crime prevention what defective shell fuses are to a fighting army.

Everyone identified with the plan—teachers, social workers, psychologists, psychiatrists, recreational directors, and others—will be accorded a status and paid salaries sufficient to attract them, and commensurate with the dignity of competent professionals. If the sensitivity or degree of training of those available are not adequate, others will be given the necessary training in institutes created for that purpose. There will be no compromise with the quality of staff, because that brand of compromise breeds failure.

6. *Need for Prompt Discovery and Treatment of Maladjustments Through the Schools.* The school, being the strategic place through which all educable children must pass, would at intake expose every child routinely to a full battery of psychological tests and a psychiatric examination. A complete social history would be compiled with respect to every child. At periodic intervals all significant symptoms would be recorded and, as a result of systematic evaluative procedures, when necessary be made the occasion for referral to diagnostic, therapeutic, or other appropriate casework agencies. In that way, personality defects and unstable home situations will be uncovered early, and we would insure prompt discovery and treatment of maladjustments. We would want to add new items to the curricula of the community's primary and secondary schools. For example, we would propose a nonelective course of training in parenthood (in advance of parenthood). We would teach the niceties of human relationships as solidly as we teach geography and physical hygiene. We would try to equip prospective parents and teachers with the simple devices for recognizing and checking the faulty habits which ripen into antisocial tendencies in themselves and others with whom they make contact.

CONCLUSION

Finally, we would want to indoctrinate the population of the community with a spiritual quality which automatically rejects religious differences or social and political inequalities. We would strive to cultivate a spirit which would eliminate social prejudices of all kinds.

If the foregoing partakes of a quasi-Utopian scheme, it is only because cynicism has descended to a lower estate than hitherto imagined. We are not encouraged to believe that fruition of such a plan is possible in our time. It will come to pass only at slow pace, and in irritatingly small installments. There are signs of significant beginnings, but because of a host of obstacles the transition period will likely be long and fraught with much strife.

Ultimately the prevention of crime at its source will be possible when we embrace the dimension of individualization, dominated by a spirit of systematic, scientific inquiry and remedy.

86 · Criminology at the Crossroads

by GEORGE B. VOLD

In this final selection, Professor George B. Vold, a sociologist of the University of Minnesota whose chief interest is criminology, surveys the struggles encountered by criminology in its quest for an understanding of the nature of criminal behavior and of the means to prevent it. After evaluating the achievements of criminology at the middle of the twentieth century, he points out what seems to him to be the future task of criminological research. [From *Journal of Criminal Law and Criminology*, Vol. 42, July-Aug. 1951, pp. 155-162. Reprinted by permission.]

I

THE MIDDLE of the century is a natural crossroads as we reckon time. The traveler coming to a crossroads needs to look around and choose his direction of further travel. This is the way, also, with universities on their recurring anniversaries. Neither the traveler nor the institution dare assume uncritically that he will get to his destination merely by continuing to go on as before he came to the intersection.

It is this thought, rather than that of imminent crisis, that lies back of the analysis that will be attempted in this paper. There is need for criminology to take stock of its present position and to consider the direction in which it needs to move in the future.

Criminology has shared the same confusions and uncertainties in trying to find explanations for crime that have beset all related fields in the so-called behavior sciences. In this it shares the common fate of all applied fields and tends to become a "me too" science, applying the concepts of other fields ready made to the perplexing problems of accounting for criminal behavior.

Every idea, notion, or nostrum in medicine, psychiatry, psychology, sociology, economics, or religion that in any way could be pointed to as in some way related to crime has had its followers and advocates insisting that it was important in crime causation. The fact of sin, the loss of religious faith, "bumps on the head" à la the phrenologists, feeble-mindedness, physical types, moral imbecility, emotional disturbance, infantilism, frustration, birth trauma, masochistic death wishes, and so on indefinitely, all are ideas or concepts seriously used in past or present attempts to explain crime, or as justifications for programs alleged to be useful in controlling crime. Were criminologists more generally acquainted with the concepts and theories of nuclear physics, there is little doubt but that we should soon find criminological theories articulated in terms of atomic fission and making some use of the celebrated formula of Einstein on the relationships existing among Energy, Mass, and Motion.

II

Before attempting to describe the new horizons (in the language of the title of a currently popular textbook in criminology) that may be seen from the crossroads where we now are, it is in order to review briefly a few gleanings from the road over which we have come.

Steeped in the general background of Western Europe's cultural heritage, which includes a generous mixture of demonology and intellectualism, modern attempting-to-be scientific criminology has consistently concerned itself with the exploration and elaboration of criminal type theories. The interpretation of the nature of man as grounded in intelligence and reasoning, and therefore subject to his own direct control, is the common background of all the social sciences, as well as of the earlier schools of philosophy and psychology.

In criminology, the formulations that flow from this interpretation of the nature of man are usually called the "classical school." According to its convenient formula, man can control his conduct by taking thought and exercising his power of will and mind. This means that human behavior, including criminal behavior, is conceived of as being basically self-generated, self-directed, and self-controlled. Penology (the treatment of crime), under such ideas of crime causation, becomes a series of efforts to get the criminal, and the potentially criminal, to exercise their power of self-control—that is, to get them to will to do right rather than wrong. The principal external instrument available to bring about a change in will, and thus a change in behavior, is the fear of punishment. The criminal codes of Europe and America have sought to implement this view of criminal behavior in the historic institutions of judicial procedure and sanctions.

The break with the classical view of human behavior comes as a natural consequence of the increasingly general acceptance of the idea of evolution, and the growing practice of identifying man with the rest of biological life in nature. Physiology, anatomy, medicine, psychiatry, and to some extent psychology, have all moved in the direction of this change in emphasis and perspective.

In criminology this view is often called the "positive school." One may quarrel with the use of the word "positive," or otherwise reject various specific connotations of the term, but one must not lose sight of the significance of the shift in emphasis from attention to self-motivated, self-directed behavior to the attempt to find differentiating characteristics that would mark off the criminal from the non-criminal. Any significant combination of traits or characteristics that could be used to differentiate criminals from non-criminals would as a matter of course become the principal element in a "criminal type."

Four basic kinds of criminal types, with a great many specific elaborations, or subtypes, may be distinguished quite readily as the principal object of attention or concern in criminological research. Each is worth a word of comment in passing.

(1). First, as a matter of history, was the quest for a physical criminal type. An extension of the then popular "science" of phrenology to the realm of crime, it had a tremendous vogue for forty or fifty years before Lombroso added the further idea that this type was an evolutionary throw-back to earlier stages of development. Except for Professor Hooton and a few of his followers, no one today takes seriously the proposition that there are demonstrable physical differences between those who commit crime and those who do not. It is important to note, however, in passing, that the physical type idea was abandoned only as systematic measurement and the use of control group comparisons were applied to the problem.

(2). Negative results in the research on physical criminal type led not to the abandonment of the type theories but in change in emphasis from physical type to mental type. Goring himself made that transition, as well as the whole next generation of psychologists who happily asserted that the basic characteristic of the criminal type was inferiority of intelligence, if not outright feeblemindedness. Goddard and many other mental testers were misled by the fact that they had measurements for all kinds of criminals, but, until World War I gave them a Draft Army sample, they had no information on a comparable group of non-criminal adults. As soon as research methodology matured sufficiently so that validated measurements could be taken of criminals and comparable groups of non-criminals, concern with the feebleminded, or with low intelligence as the type, takes on less and less significance in research in criminology.

(3). With decreasing emphasis on low intelligence or feeblemindedness as the mental type characteristic of the criminal, the trend has been to shift to yet another type, that of the emotionally disordered as the focus for theory and research. One of the favorite terms used in this connection is that of "psychopathy," or "psychopathic personality." Instead of "deviant physique," or "deviant intelligence" it is now "deviant," or "disordered," or "psychopathic" personality that holds the center of the stage in the currently popular type theories.

An obvious advantage of this as a type characteristic is the difficulty of measurement and the absence of uniform standards of comparisons as between the criminal and the non-criminal. Until it is possible to measure differences in personality make-up accurately, consistently, and in a meaningful manner, either as to kind or as to degree, it will be possible to assert without successful contradiction that personality deviation constitutes the basic element in the criminal type. Case histories of all kinds, (psychiatric, psychological, sociological) can be quoted to support almost any interpretation of personality characteristics that the investigator happens to prefer.

Results from the comparative studies using standardized tests and scales, such as they are, of groups of criminals with what are assumed to be comparable groups of non-criminals have produced to date no very consistent or impressive substantiation of the type theory. A recent article [1] reports results on 113 instances of such measured comparisons involving the use of 30 different standardized scales. In only 47 instances (42 percent of all instances) was there evidence of differentiation and many of these were so near chance expectancy that the net effect of all efforts points to the general conclusion that so far no consistent or stable

[1] Karl F. Schuessler and Donald R. Cressey, "Personality Characteristics of Criminals." *American Journal of Sociology*, March, 1950, pp. 476-484.

differences have been determined. This latest summary of the results of personality testing in this field suggests the conclusion that under conditions of careful and measured comparisons, the notion of deviant personality type is likely to go the way of the other type theories.

(4). One other kind of type theory needs to be noticed since it has given impetus to many studies and considerable discussion, namely, the proposition that the criminal type is characteristically one of social and economic disadvantage. In other words, criminals are assumed to be essentially like other people except they have never had the same opportunities and advantages as the non-criminal. Expressions of this notion run all the way from sob-sister journalism through the arguments of organized political and ideological "party-line" writers to the conclusions of serious students trying to do serious objective studies.

Present results from serious research are not entirely conclusive but the essential points of critical comparison are clear. When really comparable groups of criminals and non-criminals are compared, are there consistent, differentiating differences between the two in terms of environmental opportunities and advantages? None has so far been well established. Low income people are sometimes criminals, but they are also the principal component of the law-abiding population. It has not been established that their involvement with crime in proportion to numbers is notably larger than that among those of higher income brackets who seem to avoid trouble. The fact must be noted, on the other hand, that there is a significant number of those of high, or moderately high income, and of respectable occupational level who run afoul of the law—bankers, lawyers, doctors, school teachers, preachers, as well as highly skilled laborers.

In this, as in the other type areas, it is true that the more carefully conducted studies have generally demonstrated less likelihood of significant differentiation than some of the earlier ones seemed to indicate.

Perhaps most significant of all for the view that expects a rising standard of living to result in less and less criminality is a brief backward glance at the last 50 to 75 years of American history. In the course of those years, we have experienced a real decrease in illiteracy; child labor has been eliminated to a large extent; levels of income have gone up very considerably; leisure has increased; hours of work are shorter and the machine has taken over much of the backbreaking drudgery of ordinary work. It is probably true that America has gone farther than any other nation in achieving a high standard of living, both material and nonmaterial. But as far as is known, there has been no corresponding drop in crime rates, nor any decrease in the sordidness or comprehensiveness of our crime phenomena.

We have better educated criminals than we used to have, criminals who understand complicated machines and know how to operate them, who enjoy leisure, and who feel defrauded if not surrounded in prison with approximately the same standards of luxury to which they have become accustomed. But there is nothing to indicate a depressing effect of this high standard of living on criminality in our society, nor does the high standard of living maintained in many of our penal institutions offer any particular likelihood of low recidivism rates.

III

So much for the past. What paths lie before us as we face the second half of the century? Some trends seem clear and relatively self-evident. With reference to others one can only hazard a guess. These latter are typically of the kind to which the old adage applies—fools rush in where angels fear to tread.

One of the clear trends that lies before us, now as we stand at the crossroads of the century, is the evident fact that criminological research of the future patterned on that of the past fifty years may be expected to give only somewhat more accurate information in fields where the main outline has already come into view. Such research should not be expected to provide much that is particularly new or surprising by way of uncovering unsuspected relations between factors or elements involved in the causes or in the treatment of crime.

It is clear, for instance, that expanding and extending the best we now have in penal institutions so that the general minimum standards will equal or exceed the best we know today cannot be expected to accomplish any general rehabilitation of prison or reformatory inmates. Expanding vocational and trade training in reformatories, for example, may be an excellent idea for its own sake but it should not be thought of as a device that will accomplish large-scale rehabilitation as a matter of course and thus ultimately reduce or eliminate crime from our society. Some of our reformatories have for years operated vocational training programs that compare very well with such schools in civilian society. Some are probably actually better equipped, and at least as well staffed (notably in New York, New Jersey, and Massachusetts), as their civilian counterparts.

We have had, according to present lights, a number of excellent inmate rehabilitation programs in operation in a number of institutions in the United States for many years. The over-all effects are presumably desirable, yet it must be remembered that recidivism rates for these institutions and for the states supporting them are such that no one may assume that rehabilitation is achieved more or less automatically as a by-product of a good institutional program. The general seriousness of the recidivism is highlighted by the follow-up studies of the Gluecks.[2] Many of the claims to great accomplishment in institutions are based on inferences supported by little genuine follow-up information. In many cases the easiest way to feel sure of success is to have no supply of systematic information about failure.

Another aspect of the future that seems clear from our present perspective is that both criminology and penology have been too preoccupied with the hospital analogy, namely, that the criminal is a sick person who needs to be treated for his individual ailments and that therefore the penal institution should be patterned after the hospital to treat the sick. True and accurate as this analogy may be in some cases, it is still far from an adequate conception of the nature of the problem. Somewhere in our thinking and in our practice, as well as in our research, we must find a way to take account of the fact that a considerable area of criminality is a by-product of political and social conflict and in no sense involves sick or deviant personalities.

During the war years recently past, we incarcerated several thousands of conscientious objectors in our federal prisons. They had been convicted of offenses duly adjudicated under our law and in our regular courts. By now most of these people, if not all of them, have been released. It is improbable that more than a handful of the thousands so confined ever were "rehabilitated" or "reformed" in the sense of abandoning their old "criminal" intellectual and spiritual orientation. The reason is clear enough. They viewed themselves not as criminals but as unfortunate victims of superior force. They were more like prisoners of war than like inmates of a psychiatric ward. The "enemy" held them captive in prison, but they did not therefore take over the way of life of their captors.

There is, unfortunately, every reason to believe that many people committed to prisons for what the law calls crime feel and act in a manner much more nearly analogous to the conscientious objector than to a hospital patient. Thieves, burglars, or sex offenders, to say nothing of the embezzlers or the perpetrators of fraud, are often quite as well satisfied with their manner of life as the conscientious objectors were and are. In that situation, no rehabilitation should be expected to take place. In many cases this would be a much more accurate description of the social relations in a prison or a reformatory than an analogy of hospital and patient.

[2] See Glueck, Sheldon and Eleanor, *After-Conduct of Discharged Offenders*. Macmillan. London, 1945, for latest statement of "follow-up" results.

In thinking about criminological research for the future, it must be recognized that besides studies organized to clarify certain questions or problems suggested by past research on individual types, we must also consider the more difficult problem of how to do research on the often violent social and economic conflicts immediately related to much of our crime and corruption. How does a criminologist do scientifically adequate research on the problem of the relations between the underworld and the upper world like the present situation in Kansas City? Up to the present, so-called scientific and academic criminology has contributed very little to the measurement or analysis of that kind of crime phenomena. Newspaper writers and police reporters have actually done much more than the criminologists in giving the country some impression of how a gambling syndicate works, or why a city vice ring may be more important business than a relatively large local industry. Yet information in this field is still largely a matter of rumor and hear-say. Surely better information is a necessary condition for more effective control.

IV

In conclusion, one or two principal ideas should be restated. The crossroads of criminology at the mid-century indicate clearly that the past fifty years of research and discussion have laid down the principal outlines of conventional research methodology as well as provided a limited type of answer to many problems. Further work along the lines already developed is needed to clarify and make more exact information on many problems where we now have only tentative answers.

We need also to face realistically the problem posed by the organized crime syndicate which sometimes operates as one of the important business and pressure groups of the community. The challenge is not so much that of the need for technical research methods and personnel to investigate individual personality problems—it is rather the challenge of battle, a battle of survival between one way of life and another.

In the coming struggle for power between the upper world of the essentially law abiding and the underworld of syndicates, rackets, and special privilege, let there be no doubt as to which side will have the support of professional criminologists everywhere. As individuals and as groups, let us accept the challenge of that battle!

Index

Abbott, Edith, 456
abduction, 78
Abraham, Karl, 309
Abrahamsen, David, 179, 188–201
accidental criminal, 83
accomplices (*see* association; companionship)
accountability, 519–521 (*see also* responsibility)
adjustment tests, 65–66
adolescent, probation work with, 623 (*see also* juvenile delinquent)
adult behavior, and juvenile delinquency, 447–453 (*see also* parent-child relationship)
affection, need for, 51–52
agencies of moral risk, 36
and juvenile delinquency, 447–448 (*see also* tavern)
aggression, in war, 553, 559
alcoholic
family relations of, 311–314, 316, 318, 326
homosexuality in, 309–310, 314–315
inhibition in, 525–526
personality of, 308–320, 322, 323
probation of, 606
rehabilitation of, 328–334
sex behavior of, 314–316
Alcoholics Anonymous, 328–334
alcoholism
causes of, 309, 324–327
as crime factor, 72–73, 146, 320–327
in juvenile delinquent, 321, 447–448, 667–668
racial background and, 325
responsibility and, 523, 524
(*see also* liquor law violation)
Alexander, Franz, 182–188
alienist (*see* psychiatrist)
amelioration, problem of, 98 (*see also* crime prevention; law enforcement)
American Prison Association, 563
American Sociological Society, 10
amnesia, circumscribed, 510–511
Angell, Norman, 14
antisocial behavior

community treatment of, 689–690
as crime, 40–47
development of, in prison, 567–568
arrest, purpose of, 590–591
arson, 27
Ash, Ellis, 563–564
association
as crime factor, 13–14, 14–16, 17, 33–35, 152–153
differential (*see* differential association)
as embezzlement factor, 428–429
security in, 50
(*see also* companionship)
atavism, 139–145
atrocity, in war, 553, 559
attitude scale, 67–68
attitudes
adult, and juvenile delinquency, 451–452
of criminals, 13–14
of prison community, 564, 565
of prisoner, 567–568, 569–575
of public
toward crime prevention, 684–686
toward punishment, 685–686
values and, as cause of crime, 5, 18
Atwood, B. S., 34
authoritarianism, and rehabilitation, 618–620
auto theft
as juvenile delinquency, 669–670
as rural crime, 253–254
auto thief, views of, 73
autocracy, prison as, 566

Banay, Ralph S., 62, 72
Barnes, Harry Elmer, 10, 90–93, 334, 335, 340, 514
Bates, Sanford, 561, 643–648
Beccaria, Cesare, 512, 664
behavior, normal, crime as, 50–52, 54 (*see also* personality)
behavior clinic (*see* mental hygiene clinic)
behavior pattern, 49–52, 525, 615
as crime causation, 11
fear in, 550
of prisoner, 564, 565